EP Third Reader

EP Reader Series

Volume 3

First Edition

CONTENTS

ACKNOWLEDGEMENTS

Thank you to Abigail Baia for her beautiful cover art.

Welcome to Easy Peasy All-in-One Homeschool's Third Reader

We hope you enjoy curling up with this book of books.

This is Easy Peasy's offline version of its assignments for Reading 3. The novels and poetry included are found in the public domain and have been gathered here along with each day's assignment directions. There are differences between this course and the online version because some online reading assignments are not found in the public domain and had to be replaced. Care was taken to ensure the children don't miss out on any important lessons or activities. Online lessons from Easy Peasy's website have been replaced with offline lessons found in this book.

It is noted when children could use online vocabulary games for review, but options for vocabulary review are included in the book.

Day 1

1. Read this poem by Robert Louis Stevenson.
2. Have you made cities out of blocks?

BLOCK CITY
What are you able to build with your blocks?
Castles and palaces, temples and docks.
Rain may keep raining and others go roam,
But I can be happy and building at home.

Let the sofa be mountains, the carpet be sea,
There I'll establish a city for me:
A kirk and a mill and a palace beside,
And a harbor as well where my vessels may ride.

Great is the palace with pillar and wall,
A sort of a tower on the top of it all,
And steps coming down in an orderly way
To where my toy vessels lay safe in the bay.

This one is sailing and that one is moored:
Hark to the song of the sailors on board!
And see the steps of my palace, the kings
Coming and going with presents and things!

Now I have done with it, down let it go!
All in a moment the town is laid low.
Block upon block lying scattered and free,
What is there left of my town by the sea?

Yet as I saw it, I see it again,
The kirk and the palace, the ships and the men
And as long as I live and where'er I may be,
I'll always remember my town by the sea.

Day 2

1. Read these four poems by William Blake.
2. Poem 1:
   - What is a pipe? (Answers)
   - Why does the child weep when he hears the songs? (Answers)

3. *The Shepherd*:
   - a ewe is a mother sheep
   - Does the author think that shepherds have a good job or a bad job? (Answers)
4. *The Echoing Green*:
   - What are the skylark and thrush? (Answers)
   - What two groups of people are in this poem? (Answers)
5. *The Lamb*:
   - Each section of a poem is called a **stanza**. There is a space between each stanza to show you where each stanza starts and stops.
   - Who is the second stanza about? (Answers)

> Piping down the valleys wild,
> Piping songs of pleasant glee,
> On a cloud I saw a child,
> And he laughing said to me:
>
> 'Pipe a song about a Lamb!'
> So I piped with merry cheer.
> 'Piper, pipe that song again.'
> So I piped: he wept to hear.
>
> 'Drop thy pipe, thy happy pipe;
> Sing thy songs of happy cheer!'
> So I sung the same again,
> While he wept with joy to hear.
>
> 'Piper, sit thee down and write
> In a book, that all may read.'
> So he vanished from my sight;
> And I plucked a hollow reed,
>
> And I made a rural pen,
> And I stained the water clear,
> And I wrote my happy songs
> Every child may joy to hear.

The Shepherd

> How sweet is the shepherd's sweet lot!
> From the morn to the evening he strays;
> He shall follow his sheep all the day,
> And his tongue shall be filled with praise.

For he hears the lambs' innocent call,
And he hears the ewes' tender reply;
He is watchful while they are in peace,
For they know when their shepherd is nigh.

The Echoing Green
The sun does arise,
And make happy the skies;
The merry bells ring
To welcome the Spring;
The skylark and thrush,
The birds of the bush,
Sing louder around
To the bells' cheerful sound;
While our sports shall be seen
On the echoing green.

Old John, with white hair,
Does laugh away care,
Sitting under the oak,
Among the old folk.
They laugh at our play,
And soon they all say,
'Such, such were the joys
When we all -- girls and boys --
In our youth-time were seen
On the echoing green.'

Till the little ones, weary,
No more can be merry:
The sun does descend,
And our sports have an end.
Round the laps of their mothers
Many sisters and brothers,
Like birds in their nest,
Are ready for rest,
And sport no more seen
On the darkening green.

The Lamb
Little lamb, who made thee?
Dost thou know who made thee,
Gave thee life, and bid thee feed
By the stream and o'er the mead;
Gave thee clothing of delight,
Softest clothing, woolly, bright;
Gave thee such a tender voice,
Making all the vales rejoice?
Little lamb, who made thee?
Dost thou know who made thee?

Little lamb, I'll tell thee;
Little lamb, I'll tell thee:
He is called by thy name,
For He calls Himself a Lamb.
He is meek, and He is mild,
He became a little child.
I a child, and thou a lamb,
We are called by His name.
Little lamb, God bless thee!
Little lamb, God bless thee!

Day 3

1. Read the poems.
2. What word is repeated most often in the *Laughing Song*? (Answers)
3. What word is repeated most often in *A Cradle Song*? (Answers)
4. Songs are poetry. These could both be songs. Do you know what type of song we would consider the second poem to be? (Answers)

Laughing Song
When the green woods laugh with the voice of joy,
And the dimpling stream runs laughing by;
When the air does laugh with our merry wit,
And the green hill laughs with the noise of it;

When the meadows laugh with lively green,
And the grasshopper laughs in the merry scene;
When Mary and Susan and Emily
With their sweet round mouths sing 'Ha ha he!'

When the painted birds laugh in the shade,
Where our table with cherries and nuts is spread:
Come live, and be merry, and join with me,
To sing the sweet chorus of 'Ha ha he!'

A Cradle Song
Sweet dreams, form a shade
O'er my lovely infant's head!
Sweet dreams of pleasant streams
By happy, silent, moony beams!

Sweet Sleep, with soft down
Weave thy brows an infant crown!
Sweet Sleep, angel mild,
Hover o'er my happy child!

Sweet smiles, in the night
Hover over my delight!
Sweet smiles, mother's smiles,
All the livelong night beguiles.

Sweet moans, dovelike sighs,
Chase not slumber from thy eyes!
Sweet moans, sweeter smiles,
All the dovelike moans beguiles.

Sleep, sleep, happy child!
All creation slept and smiled.
Sleep, sleep, happy sleep,
While o'er thee thy mother weep.

Sweet babe, in thy face
Holy image I can trace;
Sweet babe, once like thee
Thy Maker lay, and wept for me:

Wept for me, for thee, for all,
When He was an infant small.
Thou His image ever see,
Heavenly face that smiles on thee!

Smiles on thee, on me, on all,
Who became an infant small;
Infant smiles are His own smiles;
Heaven and earth to peace beguiles.

Day 4

1. Read the poems.
2. What is the first poem about? (Answers)
3. The "nurse" in the second poem is not a nurse like in a hospital; it's a woman in charge of watching the children, like a nanny.
4. What is the nurse saying to the kids? (Answers)
5. What are the kids saying to the nurse? (Answers)
6. What does the baby call himself because he is so happy? (Answers)

Spring
Sound the flute!
Now it's mute!
Birds delight,
Day and night,
Nightingale,
In the dale,
Lark in sky, --
Merrily,
Merrily, merrily to welcome in the year.

Little boy,
Full of joy,
Little girl,
Sweet and small;
Cock does crow,
So do you;
Merry voice,
Infant noise;
Merrily, merrily to welcome in the year.

Little lamb,
Here I am;
Come and lick
My white neck;
Let me pull
Your soft wool;

Let me kiss
Your soft face;
Merrily, merrily we welcome in the year.

Nurses' Song
When voices of children are heard on the green,
And laughing is heard on the hill,
My heart is at rest within my breast,
And everything else is still.
'Then come home, my children, the sun is gone down,
And the dews of night arise;
Come, come, leave off play, and let us away,
Till the morning appears in the skies.'

'No, no, let us play, for it is yet day,
And we cannot go to sleep;
Besides, in the sky the little birds fly,
And the hills are all covered with sheep.'
'Well, well, go and play till the light fades away,
And then go home to bed.'
The little ones leaped, and shouted, and laughed,
And all the hills echoed.

Infant Joy
'I have no name;
I am but two days old.'
What shall I call thee?
'I happy am,
Joy is my name.'
Sweet joy befall thee!

Pretty joy!
Sweet joy, but two days old.
Sweet joy I call thee:
Thou dost smile,
I sing the while;
Sweet joy befall thee!

Day 5

1. Read the poem.
2. The clay says that love doesn't seek to please whom? (Answers)
3. The pebble says that love seeks to please whom? (Answers)
4. What does the Bible teach about true love? Does it live for itself or others? (Answers)
5. What part of these verses say that about love? (Answers)
   - 1 Corinthians 13:4-5 (NIrV) Love is patient. Love is kind. It does not want what belongs to others. It does not brag. It is not proud. It is not rude. It does not look out for its own interests. It does not easily become angry. It does not keep track of other people's wrongs.

     'Love seeketh not itself to please,
     Nor for itself hath any care,
     But for another gives its ease,
     And builds a heaven in hell's despair.'

     So sung a little clod of clay,
     Trodden with the cattle's feet,
     But a pebble of the brook
     Warbled out these metres meet:

     'Love seeketh only Self to please,
     To bind another to its delight,
     Joys in another's loss of ease,
     And builds a hell in heaven's despite.'

Day 6

1. Today we're going to learn about some features of poetry: rhyme, rhythm and alliteration.
2. Rhyme you are probably most familiar with. Boat and moat rhyme. Cat and sat rhyme. Friend and bend rhyme. Cents and dense rhyme.
   - You can see that the words don't have to be spelled the same in order to have the same sounds.
   - Poetry doesn't have to rhyme, but it often rhymes.
3. Rhythm is the beat of the poem. The rhythm in a song is what makes you bounce or dance or clap. When you read a Dr. Seuss book, your reading naturally falls into a rhythm. Read these two stanzas from *The Cat and the Hat* by Dr. Seuss. Read them OUT LOUD. A stanza is a section of a poem or song.
   - Too wet to go out
     and too cold to play ball.

So we sat in the house.
we did nothing at all.
- Then we saw him pick up
all the things that were down.
He picked up the cake,
and the rake, and the gown,

4. Did you hear yourself keeping a beat as you read? What gives it the rhythm? One reason is the number of words in each line. Count them up. Are they the same?
- Not exactly, five or six in each line.
- Each word has one syllable, one part to it, except for one longer word.
- Can you find the one longer word in the first stanza? It has two syllables, two parts (as if you chunked the word into parts to help you read it).
  o The word is nothing, no-thing.
- With about the same number of sounds in each line, the poem gets a rhythm.
- We'll practice syllables more soon.

5. The final poem feature is alliteration. A-lit-er-a-tion is when two or more words in a row begin with the same sound.
- Examples: Mickey Mouse, fast food, pig pen, bouncy baby boy
- What word could you add to "happy" to make an alliteration?

Day 7

1. Read *The Fly*.
2. Find examples of rhyme in the poem. (Answers)
3. Read *The Cradle Song*.
4. Find examples of alliteration. (Answers)

The Fly

Little Fly,
Thy summer's play
My thoughtless hand
Has brushed away.

Am not I
A fly like thee?
Or art not thou
A man like me?

For I dance,
And drink, and sing,

14

Till some blind hand
Shall brush my wing.

If thought is life
And strength and breath,
And the want
Of thought is death;

Then am I
A happy fly.
If I live,
Or if I die.

A Cradle Song
Sleep, sleep, beauty bright,
Dreaming in the joys of night;
Sleep, sleep; in thy sleep
Little sorrows sit and weep.
Sweet babe, in thy face
Soft desires I can trace,
Secret joys and secret smiles,
Little pretty infant wiles.
As thy softest limbs I feel,
Smiles as of the morning steal
O'er thy cheek, and o'er thy breast
Where thy little heart doth rest.
O the cunning wiles that creep
In thy little heart asleep!
When thy little heart doth wake,
Then the dreadful light shall break.
From thy cheek and from thy eye
O'er the youthful harvest nigh
Infant wiles and infant smiles
Heaven and Earth of peace beguiles.

Day 8

1. Read *The Fly* again (Day 7). This time read it out loud. Do you hear rhythm?
2. Let's learn again about syllables. Syllables are the parts of words. One part is one syllable.
3. One way to practice syllables is to clap when you read a word.

15

4. Read these words and clap one time for each word.
    - day, two, set, cup, brake, trip, class
    - They each have one part, one clap, one syllable.
5. Now read these words and clap two times with each word. Clap with each part of the word.
    - pic-ture, muf-fin, rain-bow, hap-py, run-ning
    - going, friendly, truthful, funny, cupcake
    - They each have two parts, two claps, two syllables.
6. How many syllables are in these words?
    - wonderful, won-der-ful
    - fantastic, fan-tas-tic
    - magnificent, mag-nif-i-cent
    - Clap them out: three, three and four.
7. Count the syllables in each line of the first and second stanza of poem 23. (Answers)

Day 9

1. Read these poems by Robert Louis Stevenson.
2. What does he think is hard in "Bed in Summer"? (Answers)
3. Do you think his eyes are opened or closed in the second poem?

BED IN SUMMER
In winter I get up at night,
And dress by yellow candle light.
In summer quite the other way,
I have to go to bed by day.

I have to go to bed and see
The birds still hopping on the tree,
Or hear the grown-up people's feet,
Still going past me in the street.

And does it not seem hard to you,
When all the sky is clear and blue,
And I should like so much to play,
To have to go to bed by day?

YOUNG NIGHT THOUGHT
All night long and every night,
When my mamma puts out the light

I see the people marching by,
As plain as day, before my eye.

Armies and emperors and kings,
All carrying different kinds of things,
And marching in so grand a way,
You never saw the like by day.

So fine a show was never seen
At the great circus on the green;
For every kind beast and man
Is marching in that caravan.

At first they move a little slow,
But still the faster on they go,
And still beside them close I keep
Until we reach the Town of Sleep.

Day 10

1. Read these poems by Robert Louis Stevenson.
2. What happens in the first poem? (Answers)
3. What are some of the things out at night? (Answers)
4. Do you hear the rhymes and rhythms in these poems?

A GOOD PLAY
We built a ship upon the stairs
All made of the back-bedroom chairs,
And filled it full of sofa pillows
To go a-sailing on the billows.

We took a saw and several nails,
And water in the nursery pails;
And Tom said, "Let us also take
An apple and a slice of cake;"

—Which was enough for Tom and me
To go a-sailing on, till tea.
We sailed along for days and days,
And had the very best of plays;
But Tom fell out and hurt his knee,
So there was no one left but me.

THE MOON
The moon has a face like the clock in the hall;
She shines on thieves on the garden wall,
On streets and fields and harbor quays,
And birdies asleep in the forks of the trees.

The squalling cat and the squeaking mouse,
The howling dog by the door of the house,
The bat that lies in bed at noon,
All love to be out by the light of the moon.

But all of the things that belong to the day
Cuddle to sleep to be out of her way;
And flowers and children close their eyes
Till up in the morning the sun shall rise.

Day 11

1. You are going to read poems by a different poet now, Sara Teasdale.
2. Read the poem.
3. What does she wish for? (Answers)
4. Does she get what she wishes for? (Answers)
5. Find rhyme, rhythm and alliteration in the poem. (Answers)

Wishes
I wish for such a lot of things
That never will come true--
And yet I want them all so much
I think they might, don't you?

I want a little kitty-cat
That's soft and tame and sweet,
And every day I watch and hope
I'll find one in the street.

But nursie says, "Come, walk along,
"Don't stand and stare like that"--
I'm only looking hard and hard
To try to find my cat.

And then I want a blue balloon
That tries to fly away,

I thought if I wished hard enough
That it would come some day.

One time when I was in the park
I knew that it would be
Beside the big old clock at home
A-waiting there for me--

And soon as we got home again,
I hurried thro' the hall,
And looked beside the big old clock--
It wasn't there at all.

I think I'll never wish again--
But then, what shall I do?
The wishes are a lot of fun
Altho' they don't come true.

Day 12

1. Read the poems.
2. In *Faults* people come to tell the author something. What is it? (Answers)
3. In *Snow Song* what is flying in the air? (Answers)
4. In *November* how does the author describe November? (Answers)

Faults
They came to tell your faults to me,
They named them over one by one,
I laughed aloud when they were done;
I knew them all so well before,--
Oh they were blind, too blind to see
Your faults had made me love you more.

Snow Song
Fairy snow, fairy snow,
Blowing, blowing everywhere,
Would that I
Too, could fly
Lightly, lightly through the air.

November
The world is tired, the year is old,
The little leaves are glad to die,
The wind goes shivering with cold
Among the rushes dry.

Day 13

1. Read the poem. It is about the beginning of a day, dawn.
2. Draw a picture of it. What picture does the poem make you see?

Dawn
The greenish sky glows up in misty reds,
The purple shadows turn to brick and stone,
The dreams wear thin, men turn upon their beds,
And hear the milk-cart jangle by alone.

Day 14

1. Read the poem.
2. What did her grandfather send? (Answers)
3. What couldn't she understand? (Answers)
4. What did she wish he sent? (Answers)
5. What is the rhythm and rhyme pattern of this poem? (Answers)

Grandfather's Love
They said he sent his love to me,
They wouldn't put it in my hand,
And when I asked them where it was
They said I couldn't understand.

I thought they must have hidden it,
I hunted for it all the day,
And when I told them so at night
They smiled and turned their heads away.

They say that love is something kind,
That I can never see or touch.
I wish he'd sent me something else,
I like his cough-drops twice as much.

Day 15

1. Read the poem.
2. Why does she think the moon is kind? (Answers)

The Kind Moon

I think the moon is very kind
To take such trouble just for me.
He came along with me from home
To keep me company.

He went as fast as I could run;
I wonder how he crossed the sky?
I'm sure he hasn't legs and feet
Or any wings to fly.

Yet here he is above their roof;
Perhaps he thinks it isn't right
For me to go so far alone,
Tho' mother said I might.

Day 16

1. Read the poem.
2. How does the author describe April? (Answers)
3. Does it look like spring to her? (Answers)
4. What do you think is the "unchanging tree?" (Answers)

April

The roofs are shining from the rain,
The sparrows twitter as they fly,
And with a windy April grace
The little clouds go by.

Yet the back yards are bare and brown
With only one unchanging tree-
I could not be so sure of Spring
Save that it sings in me.

Day 17

1. Read the poem.
2. What is the feeling of this poem? (happy, sad, excited, scared…) (Answers)
3. What words give the poem that feeling? (Answers)

Dusk in June
Evening, and all the birds
In a chorus of shimmering sound
Are easing their hearts of joy
For miles around.

The air is blue and sweet,
The few first stars are white,
Oh let me like the birds
Sing before night.

Day 18

1. Read the poem.
2. What is the poem about? (Answers)
3. How does a cloud "blind the sun?" (Answers)

The Cloud
I am a cloud in the heaven's height,
The stars are lit for my delight,
Tireless and changeful, swift and free,
I cast my shadow on hill and sea
But why do the pines on the mountain's crest
Call to me always, "Rest, rest"?

I throw my mantle over the moon
And I blind the sun on his throne at noon,
Nothing can tame me, nothing can bind,
I am a child of the heartless wind
But oh the pines on the mountain's crest
Whispering always, "Rest, rest."

Day 19

1. Read the poem.
2. Who is the poem about? (Answers)
3. What is Mary thinking about while the men work in the carpenter's shop? (Answers)

> *In the Carpenter's Shop*
> Mary sat in the corner dreaming,
> Dim was the room and low,
> While in the dusk, the saw went screaming
> To and fro.
>
> Jesus and Joseph toiled together,
> Mary was watching them,
> Thinking of kings in the wintry weather
> At Bethlehem.
>
> Mary sat in the corner thinking,
> Jesus had grown a man;
> One by one her hopes were sinking
> As the years ran.
>
> Jesus and Joseph toiled together,
> Mary's thoughts were far
> Angels sang in the wintry weather
> Under a star.
>
> Mary sat in the corner weeping,
> Bitter and hot her tears
> Little faith were the angels keeping
> All the years.

Day 20

1. Read the chickadee poem, which is written by a girl about 11 years old.
2. What does the author think about the chickadee song? (Answers)
3. The last line is the song of the chickadee.

> *Chickadee*
> The chickadee in the apple tree
> Talks all the time very gently.
> He makes me sleepy.

I rock away to the sea-lights.
Far off I hear him talking
The way smooth bright pebbles
Drop into water . . .
Chick-a-dee-dee-dee . . .

Day 21

1. Read these fables by Aesop.
2. After some of the stories, the moral of the story is written. The moral of the story is the lesson of the story. One of the lessons is that if someone has proven dangerous in the past, don't believe them when they act like they aren't any more. Which story is that the lesson of? (Answers)
3. Draw a picture of one of the other fables. Show your picture to someone and explain what happened in the story.

THE FOX AND THE GRAPES

A hungry Fox saw some fine bunches of Grapes hanging from a vine that was trained along a high trellis, and did his best to reach them by jumping as high as he could into the air. But it was all in vain, for they were just out of reach: so he gave up trying, and walked away with an air of dignity and unconcern, remarking, "I thought those Grapes were ripe, but I see now they are quite sour."

THE GOOSE THAT LAID THE GOLDEN EGGS

A Man and his Wife had the good fortune to possess a Goose which laid a Golden Egg every day. Lucky though they were, they soon began to think they were not getting rich fast enough, and, imagining the bird must be made of gold inside, they decided to kill it in order to secure the whole store of precious metal at once. But when they cut it open they found it was just like any other goose. Thus, they neither got rich all at once, as they had hoped, nor enjoyed any longer the daily addition to their wealth.

Much wants more and loses all.

THE CAT AND THE MICE

There was once a house that was overrun with Mice. A Cat heard of this, and said to herself, "That's the place for me," and off she went and took up her quarters in the house, and caught the Mice one by one and ate them. At last the Mice could stand it no longer, and they determined to take to their holes and stay there. "That's awkward," said the Cat to herself: "the only thing to do is to coax them out by a trick." So she considered a while, and then climbed up the wall and let herself hang down by her hind legs from a peg, and pretended to be dead. By and by a Mouse peeped out and saw the Cat hanging there. "Aha!" it cried, "you're very clever, madam, no doubt: but you may turn yourself into a bag of meal hanging there, if you like, yet you won't catch us coming anywhere near you."

If you are wise you won't be deceived by the innocent airs of those whom you have once found to be dangerous.

THE MISCHIEVOUS DOG

There was once a Dog who used to snap at people and bite them without any provocation, and who was a great nuisance to every one who came to his master's house. So his master fastened a bell round his neck to warn people of his presence. The Dog was very proud of the bell, and strutted about tinkling it with immense satisfaction. But an old dog came up to him and said, "The fewer airs you give yourself the better, my friend. You don't think, do you, that your bell was given you as a reward of merit? On the contrary, it is a badge of disgrace."

Notoriety is often mistaken for fame.

THE CHARCOAL-BURNER AND THE FULLER

There was once a Charcoal-burner who lived and worked by himself. A Fuller, however, happened to come and settle in the same neighbourhood; and the Charcoal-burner, having made his acquaintance and finding he was an agreeable sort of fellow, asked him if he would come and share his house: "We shall get to know one another better that way," he said, "and, beside, our household expenses will be diminished." The Fuller thanked him, but replied, "I couldn't think of it, sir: why, everything I take such pains to whiten would be blackened in no time by your charcoal."

THE MICE IN COUNCIL

Once upon a time all the Mice met together in Council, and discussed the best means of securing themselves against the attacks of the cat. After several suggestions had been debated, a Mouse of some standing and experience got up and said, "I think I have hit upon a plan which will ensure our safety in the future, provided you approve and carry it out. It is that we should fasten a bell round the neck of our enemy the cat, which will by its tinkling warn us of her approach." This proposal was warmly applauded, and it had been already decided to adopt it, when an old Mouse got upon his feet and said, "I agree with you all that the plan before us is an admirable one: but may I ask who is going to bell the cat?"

THE BAT AND THE WEASELS

A Bat fell to the ground and was caught by a Weasel, and was just going to be killed and eaten when it begged to be let go. The Weasel said he couldn't do that because he was an enemy of all birds on principle. "Oh, but," said the Bat, "I'm not a bird at all: I'm a mouse." "So you are," said the Weasel, "now I come to look at you"; and he let it go. Some time after this the Bat was caught in just the same way by another Weasel, and, as before, begged for its life. "No," said the Weasel, "I never let a mouse go by any chance." "But I'm not a mouse," said the Bat; "I'm a bird." "Why, so you are," said the Weasel; and he too let the Bat go.

Look and see which way the wind blows before you commit yourself.

THE DOG AND THE SOW

A Dog and a Sow were arguing and each claimed that its own young ones were finer than those of any other animal. "Well," said the Sow at last, "mine can see, at any rate, when they come into the world: but yours are born blind."

THE FOX AND THE CROW

A Crow was sitting on a branch of a tree with a piece of cheese in her beak when a Fox observed her and set his wits to work to discover some way of getting the cheese. Coming and standing under the tree he looked up and said, "What a noble bird I see above me! Her beauty is without equal, the hue of her plumage exquisite. If only her voice is as sweet as her looks are fair, she ought without doubt to be Queen of the Birds." The Crow was hugely flattered by this, and just to show the Fox that she could sing she gave a loud caw. Down came the cheese, of course, and the Fox, snatching it up, said, "You have a voice, madam, I see: what you want is wits."

THE HORSE AND THE GROOM

There was once a Groom who used to spend long hours clipping and combing the Horse of which he had charge, but who daily stole a portion of his allowance of oats, and sold it for his own profit. The Horse gradually got into worse and worse condition, and at last cried to the Groom, "If you really want me to look sleek and well, you must comb me less and feed me more."

Day 22

1.   Read this next set of Aesop's fables.
2.   There are several stories about an ass. That is a donkey. This is an old book and that is a word that has changed in meaning over time. It is not a nice word to say or to call someone. When you read, you can switch it and say donkey.
3.   What is a spendthrift? (hint: the first line of the story about the spendthrift) (Answers)
4.   What do you think is the moral of *The Lion and The Mouse*? (Answers)

THE WOLF AND THE LAMB

A Wolf came upon a Lamb straying from the flock, and felt some compunction about taking the life of so helpless a creature without some plausible excuse; so he cast about for a grievance and said at last, "Last year, sirrah, you grossly insulted me." "That is impossible, sir," bleated the Lamb, "for I wasn't born then." "Well," retorted the Wolf, "you feed in my pastures." "That cannot be," replied the Lamb, "for I have never yet tasted grass." "You drink from my spring, then," continued the Wolf. "Indeed, sir," said the poor Lamb, "I have never yet drunk anything but my mother's milk." "Well, anyhow," said the Wolf, "I'm not going without my dinner": and he sprang upon the Lamb and devoured it without more ado.

THE PEACOCK AND THE CRANE

A Peacock taunted a Crane with the dullness of her plumage. "Look at my brilliant colours," said she, "and see how much finer they are than your poor feathers." "I am not denying," replied the Crane, that yours are far gayer than mine; but when it comes to flying I can soar into the clouds, whereas you are confined to the earth like any dunghill cock."

THE CAT AND THE BIRDS

A Cat heard that the Birds in an aviary were ailing. So he got himself up as a doctor, and, taking with him a set of the instruments proper to his profession, presented himself at the door, and inquired after the health of the Birds. "We shall do very well," they replied, without letting him in, "when we've seen the last of you."

A villain may disguise himself, but he will not deceive the wise.

THE SPENDTHRIFT AND THE SWALLOW

A Spendthrift, who had wasted his fortune, and had nothing left but the clothes in which he stood, saw a Swallow one fine day in early spring. Thinking that summer had come, and that he could now do without his coat, he went and sold it for what it would fetch. A change, however, took place in the weather, and there came a sharp frost which killed the unfortunate

Swallow. When the spendthrift saw its dead body he cried, "Miserable bird! Thanks to you I am perishing of cold myself."

One swallow does not make summer.

THE OLD WOMAN AND THE DOCTOR
An Old Woman became almost totally blind from a disease of the eyes, and, after consulting a Doctor, made an agreement with him in the presence of witnesses that she should pay him a high fee if he cured her, while if he failed he was to receive nothing. The Doctor accordingly prescribed a course of treatment, and every time he paid her a visit he took away with him some article out of the house, until at last, when he visited her for the last time, and the cure was complete, there was nothing left. When the Old Woman saw that the house was empty she refused to pay him his fee; and, after repeated refusals on her part, he sued her before the magistrates for payment of her debt. On being brought into court she was ready with her defence. "The claimant," said she, "has stated the facts about our agreement correctly. I undertook to pay him a fee if he cured me, and he, on his part, promised to charge nothing if he failed. Now, he says I am cured; but I say that I am blinder than ever, and I can prove what I say. When my eyes were bad I could at any rate see well enough to be aware that my house contained a certain amount of furniture and other things; but now, when according to him I am cured, I am entirely unable to see anything there at all."

THE MOON AND HER MOTHER
The Moon once begged her Mother to make her a gown. "How can I?" replied she; "there's no fitting your figure. At one time you're a New Moon, and at another you're a Full Moon; and between whiles you're neither one nor the other."

MERCURY AND THE WOODMAN
A Woodman was felling a tree on the bank of a river, when his axe, glancing off the trunk, flew out of his hands and fell into the water. As he stood by the water's edge lamenting his loss, Mercury appeared and asked him the reason for his grief; and on learning what had happened, out of pity for his distress he dived into the river and, bringing up a golden axe, asked him if that was the one he had lost. The Woodman replied that it was not, and Mercury then dived a second time, and, bringing up a silver axe, asked if that was his. "No, that is not mine either," said the Woodman. Once more Mercury dived into the river, and brought up the missing axe. The Woodman was overjoyed at recovering his property, and thanked his benefactor warmly; and the latter was so pleased with his honesty that he made him a present of the other two axes. When the Woodman told the story to his companions, one of these was filled with envy of his good fortune and determined to try his luck for himself. So he went

and began to fell a tree at the edge of the river, and presently contrived to let his axe drop into the water. Mercury appeared as before, and, on learning that his axe had fallen in, he dived and brought up a golden axe, as he had done on the previous occasion. Without waiting to be asked whether it was his or not the fellow cried, "That's mine, that's mine," and stretched out his hand eagerly for the prize: but Mercury was so disgusted at his dishonesty that he not only declined to give him the golden axe, but also refused to recover for him the one he had let fall into the stream.

Honesty is the best policy.

a mamal horse have long ears tipe! tipe of a donky family!

THE ASS, THE FOX, AND THE LION

An Ass and a Fox went into partnership and sallied out to forage for food together. They hadn't gone far before they saw a Lion coming their way, at which they were both dreadfully frightened. But the Fox thought he saw a way of saving his own skin, and went boldly up to the Lion and whispered in his ear, "I'll manage that you shall get hold of the Ass without the trouble of stalking him, if you'll promise to let me go free." The Lion agreed to this, and the Fox then rejoined his companion and contrived before long to lead him by a hidden pit, which some hunter had dug as a trap for wild animals, and into which he fell. When the Lion saw that the Ass was safely caught and couldn't get away, it was to the Fox that he first turned his attention, and he soon finished him off, and then at his leisure proceeded to feast upon the Ass.

Betray a friend, and you'll often find you have ruined yourself.

THE LION AND THE MOUSE

A Lion asleep in his lair was waked up by a Mouse running over his face. Losing his temper he seized it with his paw and was about to kill it. The Mouse, terrified, piteously entreated him to spare its life. "Please let me go," it cried, "and one day I will repay you for your kindness." The idea of so insignificant a creature ever being able to do anything for him amused the Lion so much that he laughed aloud, and good-humouredly let it go. But the Mouse's chance came, after all. One day the Lion got entangled in a net which had been spread for game by some hunters, and the Mouse heard and recognized his roars of anger and ran to the spot. Without more ado it set to work to gnaw the ropes with its teeth, and succeeded before long in setting the Lion free. "There!" said the Mouse, "you laughed at me when I promised I would repay you: but now you see, even a Mouse can help a Lion."

Day 23

1. Read this next set of fables.
2. The moral of the last story is "Don't count your chickens before they hatch." This is a very famous expression. What does it mean? What is the lesson of the story? (Answers)
3. "Necessity is the mother of invention." This is another famous expression. **Necessity** means something that is needed. What does the expression mean? (Answers)
4. A stag is a male deer.
5. Write down one of the morals I wrote above.

THE CROW AND THE PITCHER

A thirsty Crow found a Pitcher with some water in it, but so little was there that, try as she might, she could not reach it with her beak, and it seemed as though she would die of thirst within sight of the remedy. At last she hit upon a clever plan. She began dropping pebbles into the Pitcher, and with each pebble the water rose a little higher until at last it reached the brim, and the knowing bird was enabled to quench her thirst.

Necessity is the mother of invention.

THE BOYS AND THE FROGS

Some mischievous Boys were playing on the edge of a pond, and, catching sight of some Frogs swimming about in the shallow water, they began to amuse themselves by pelting them with stones, and they killed several of them. At last one of the Frogs put his head out of the water and said, "Oh, stop! stop! I beg of you: what is sport to you is death to us."

THE NORTH WIND AND THE SUN

A dispute arose between the North Wind and the Sun, each claiming that he was stronger than the other. At last they agreed to try their powers upon a traveller, to see which could soonest strip him of his cloak. The North Wind had the first try; and, gathering up all his force for the attack, he came whirling furiously down upon the man, and caught up his cloak as though he would wrest it from him by one single effort: but the harder he blew, the more closely the man wrapped it round himself. Then came the turn of the Sun. At first he beamed gently upon the traveller, who soon unclasped his cloak and walked on with it hanging loosely about his shoulders: then he shone forth in his full strength, and the man, before he had gone many steps, was glad to throw his cloak right off and complete his journey more lightly clad.

Persuasion is better than force

THE MISTRESS AND HER SERVANTS

A Widow, thrifty and industrious, had two servants, whom she kept pretty hard at work. They were not allowed to lie long abed in the mornings, but the old lady had them up and doing as soon as the cock crew. They disliked intensely having to get up at such an hour, especially in winter-time: and they thought that if it were not for the cock waking up their Mistress so horribly early, they could sleep longer. So they caught it and wrung its neck. But they weren't prepared for the consequences. For what happened was that their Mistress, not hearing the cock crow as usual, waked them up earlier than ever, and set them to work in the middle of the night.

THE HARES AND THE FROGS

The Hares once gathered together and lamented the unhappiness of their lot, exposed as they were to dangers on all sides and lacking the strength and the courage to hold their own. Men, dogs, birds and beasts of prey were all their enemies, and killed and devoured them daily: and sooner than endure such persecution any longer, they one and all determined to end their miserable lives. Thus resolved and desperate, they rushed in a body towards a neighbouring pool, intending to drown themselves. On the bank were sitting a number of Frogs, who, when they heard the noise of the Hares as they ran, with one accord leaped into the water and hid themselves in the depths. Then one of the older Hares who was wiser than the rest cried out to his companions, "Stop, my friends, take heart; don't let us destroy ourselves after all: see, here are creatures who are afraid of us, and who must, therefore, be still more timid than ourselves."

THE FOX AND THE STORK

A Fox invited a Stork to dinner, at which the only fare provided was a large flat dish of soup. The Fox lapped it up with great relish, but the Stork with her long bill tried in vain to partake of the savoury broth. Her evident distress caused the sly Fox much amusement. But not long after the Stork invited him in turn, and set before him a pitcher with a long and narrow neck, into which she could get her bill with ease. Thus, while she enjoyed her dinner, the Fox sat by hungry and helpless, for it was impossible for him to reach the tempting contents of the vessel.

THE WOLF IN SHEEP'S CLOTHING

A Wolf resolved to disguise himself in order that he might prey upon a flock of sheep without fear of detection. So he clothed himself in a sheepskin, and slipped among the sheep when they were out at pasture. He completely deceived the shepherd, and when the flock was penned for the night he was shut in with the rest. But that very night as it happened, the shepherd, requiring a supply of mutton for the table, laid hands on the Wolf in mistake for a Sheep, and killed him with his knife on the spot.

THE STAG IN THE OX-STALL

A Stag, chased from his lair by the hounds, took refuge in a farmyard, and, entering a stable where a number of oxen were stalled, thrust himself under a pile of hay in a vacant stall, where he lay concealed, all but the tips of his horns. Presently one of the Oxen said to him, "What has induced you to come in here? Aren't you aware of the risk you are running of being captured by the herdsmen?" To which he replied, "Pray let me stay for the present. When night comes I shall easily escape under cover of the dark." In the course of the afternoon more than one of the farm-hands came in, to attend to the wants of the cattle, but not one of them noticed the presence of the Stag, who accordingly began to congratulate himself on his escape and to express his gratitude to the Oxen. "We wish you well," said the one who had spoken before, "but you are not out of danger yet. If the master comes, you will certainly be found out, for nothing ever escapes his keen eyes." Presently, sure enough, in he came, and made a great to-do about the way the Oxen were kept. "The beasts are starving," he cried; "here, give them more hay, and put plenty of litter under them." As he
spoke, he seized an armful himself from the pile where the Stag lay concealed, and at once detected him. Calling his men, he had him seized at once and killed for the table.

THE MILKMAID AND HER PAIL

A farmer's daughter had been out to milk the cows, and was returning to the dairy carrying her pail of milk upon her head. As she walked along, she started thinking: "The milk in this pail will provide me with cream, which I will make into butter and take to market to sell. With the money I will buy a number of eggs, and these, when hatched, will produce chickens, and by and by I shall have quite a large poultry-yard. Then I shall sell some of my fowls, and with the money which they will bring in I will buy myself a new gown, which I shall wear when I go to the fair; and all the young fellows will admire it, but I shall toss my head and have nothing to say to them." Forgetting all about the pail, and suiting the action to the word, she tossed her head. Down went the pail, all the milk was spilled, and all her fine castles in the air vanished in a moment!

Do not count your chickens before they are hatched.

Day 24

1. Read the set of fables.
2. Do you know what the listed words mean? Read the words and the definitions. Look for them in the first story. I'll test you on them soon.

    quarrel - to have an argument

    fierce - ferocious, wild and violent

persuade - to use words to convince someone of something
contemptuous - acting like someone else is beneath you, that they are no good and you don't want them around
reconcile - become friends again

3. One of the stories has this lesson: You can know if someone is a real friend if they stick with you when bad things happen. Which story has that for its moral? (Answers)

THE DOLPHINS, THE WHALES, AND THE SPRAT

The Dolphins quarrelled with the Whales, and before very long they began fighting with one another. The battle was very fierce, and had lasted some time without any sign of coming to an end, when a Sprat thought that perhaps he could stop it; so he stepped in and tried to persuade them to give up fighting and make friends. But one of the Dolphins said to him contemptuously, "We would rather go on fighting till we're all killed than be reconciled by a Sprat like you!"

THE FOX AND THE MONKEY

A Fox and a Monkey were on the road together, and fell into a dispute as to which of the two was the better born. They kept it up for some time, till they came to a place where the road passed through a cemetery full of monuments, when the Monkey stopped and looked about him and gave a great sigh. "Why do you sigh?" said the Fox. The Monkey pointed to the tombs and replied, "All the monuments that you see here were put up in honour of my forefathers, who in their day were eminent men." The Fox was speechless for a moment, but quickly recovering he said, "Oh! don't stop at any lie, sir; you're quite safe: I'm sure none of your ancestors will rise up and expose you."

Boasters brag most when they cannot be detected.

THE ASS AND THE LAP-DOG

There was once a man who had an Ass and a Lap-dog. The Ass was housed in the stable with plenty of oats and hay to eat and was as well off as an ass could be. The little Dog was made a great pet of by his master, who fondled him and often let him lie in his lap; and if he went out to dinner, he would bring back a tit-bit or two to give him when he ran to meet him on his return. The Ass had, it is true, a good deal of work to do, carting or grinding the corn, or carrying the burdens of the farm: and ere long he became very jealous, contrasting his own life of labour with the ease and idleness of the Lap-dog. At last one day he broke his halter, and frisking into the house just as his master sat down to dinner, he pranced and capered about, mimicking the frolics of the little favourite, upsetting the table and smashing the crockery with his clumsy efforts. Not content with that, he even tried to jump on his master's lap, as he had so often seen the dog allowed to do. At that the servants, seeing the danger their master was in, belaboured the silly Ass with sticks and cudgels, and drove him back to his stable half dead with his beating. "Alas!" he cried, "all this I have brought on myself. Why could I not be satisfied with my natural and honourable position, without wishing to imitate the ridiculous antics of that useless little Lap-dog?"

THE FIR-TREE AND THE BRAMBLE

A Fir-tree was boasting to a Bramble, and said, somewhat contemptuously, "You poor creature, you are of no use whatever. Now, look at me: I am useful for all sorts of things, particularly when men build houses; they can't do without me then." But the Bramble replied, "Ah, that's all very well: but you wait till they come with axes and saws to cut you down, and then you'll wish you were a   Bramble and not a Fir."

Better poverty without a care than wealth with its many obligations.

THE FROGS' COMPLAINT AGAINST THE SUN

Once upon a time the Sun was about to take to himself a wife. The Frogs in terror all raised their voices to the skies, and Jupiter, disturbed by the noise, asked them what they were croaking about. They replied, "The Sun is bad enough even while he is single, drying up our marshes with his heat as he does. But what will become of us if he marries and begets other Suns?"

THE DOG, THE COCK, AND THE FOX

A Dog and a Cock became great friends, and agreed to travel together. At nightfall the Cock flew up into the branches of a tree to roost, while the Dog curled himself up inside the trunk, which was hollow. At break of day the Cock woke up and crew, as usual. A Fox heard, and, wishing to make a breakfast of him, came and stood under the tree and begged him to come down. "I should so like," said he, "to make the acquaintance of one who has such a beautiful voice." The Cock replied, "Would you just wake my porter who sleeps at the foot of the tree? He'll open the door and let you in." The Fox accordingly rapped on the trunk, when out rushed the Dog and tore him in pieces.

THE GNAT AND THE BULL

A Gnat alighted on one of the horns of a Bull, and remained sitting there for a considerable time. When it had rested sufficiently and was about to fly away, it said to the Bull, "Do you mind if I go now?" The Bull merely raised his eyes and remarked, without interest, "It's all one to me; I didn't notice when you came, and I shan't know when you go away."

We may often be of more consequence in our own eyes than in the eyes of our neighbours.

THE BEAR AND THE TRAVELLERS

Two Travellers were on the road together, when a Bear suddenly appeared on the scene. Before he observed them, one made for a tree at the side of the road, and climbed up into the branches and hid there. The other was not so nimble as his companion; and, as he could not escape, he threw himself on the ground and pretended to be dead. The Bear came up and sniffed all round him, but he kept perfectly still and held his breath: for they say that a bear will not touch a dead body. The Bear took him for a corpse, and went away. When the coast was clear, the Traveller in the tree came down, and asked the other what it was the Bear had whispered to him when he put his mouth to his ear. The other replied, "He told me never again to travel with a friend who deserts you at the first sign of danger."

Misfortune tests the sincerity of friendship.

THE SLAVE AND THE LION

A Slave ran away from his master, by whom he had been most cruelly treated, and, in order to avoid capture, betook himself into the desert. As he wandered about in search of food and shelter, he came to a cave, which he entered and found to be unoccupied. Really, however, it was a Lion's den, and almost immediately, to the horror of the wretched fugitive, the Lion himself appeared. The man gave himself up for lost: but, to his utter astonishment, the Lion, instead of springing upon him and devouring him, came and fawned upon him, at the same time whining and lifting up his paw. Observing it to be much swollen and inflamed, he examined it and found a large thorn embedded in the ball of the foot. He accordingly removed it and dressed the wound as well as he could: and in course of time it healed up completely. The Lion's gratitude was unbounded; he looked upon the man as his friend, and they shared the cave for some time together. A day came, however, when the Slave began to long for the society of his fellow-men, and he bade farewell to the Lion and returned to the town. Here he was presently recognised and carried off in chains to his former master, who resolved to make an example of him, and ordered that he should be thrown to the beasts at the next public spectacle in the theatre. On the fatal day the beasts were loosed into the arena, and among the rest a Lion of huge bulk and ferocious aspect; and then the wretched Slave was cast in among them. What was the amazement of the spectators, when the Lion after one glance bounded up to him and lay down at his feet with every expression of affection and delight! It was his old friend of the cave! The audience clamoured that the Slave's life should be spared: and the governor of the town, marvelling at such gratitude and fidelity in a beast, decreed that both should receive their liberty.

THE FLEA AND THE MAN

A Flea bit a Man, and bit him again, and again, till he could stand it no longer, but made a thorough search for it, and at last succeeded in catching it. Holding it between his finger and thumb, he said—or rather shouted, so angry was he--"Who are you, pray, you wretched little creature, that you make so free with my person?" The Flea, terrified, whimpered in a weak little voice, "Oh, sir! pray let me go; don't kill me! I am such a little thing that I can't do you much harm." But the Man laughed and said, "I am going to kill you now, at once: whatever is bad has got to be destroyed, no matter how slight the harm it does."

Do not waste your pity on a scamp.

Day 25

1. Read the next set of stories.
2. What story do you recognize?
3. Draw a picture to illustrate one of the stories.
4. Show your picture to someone and explain it and the story.

Vocabulary

1. Try this vocabulary matching activity. Write the matching letters and numbers together on a separate sheet of paper. (Answers)

1.	contemptuous	A.	become friends again
2.	reconcile	B.	to use words to convince someone of something
3.	quarrel	C.	ferocious, wild and violent
4.	persuade	D.	to have an argument
5.	fierce	E.	acting like someone else is beneath you

THE BOY AND THE SNAILS

A Farmer's Boy went looking for Snails, and, when he had picked up both his hands full, he set about making a fire at which to roast them; for he meant to eat them. When it got well alight and the Snails began to feel the heat, they gradually withdrew more and more into their shells with the hissing noise they always make when they do so. When the Boy heard it, he said, "You abandoned creatures, how can you find heart to whistle when your houses are burning?"

Monkeys

THE APES AND THE TWO TRAVELLERS

Two men were travelling together, one of whom never spoke the truth, whereas the other never told a lie: and they came in the course of their travels to the land of Apes. The King of the Apes, hearing of their arrival, ordered them to be brought before him; and by way of impressing them with his magnificence, he received them sitting on a throne, while the Apes, his subjects, were ranged in long rows on either side of him. When the Travellers came into his presence he asked them what they thought of him as a King. The lying Traveller said, "Sire, every one must see that you are a most noble and mighty monarch." "And what do you think of my subjects?" continued the King. "They," said the Traveller, "are in every way worthy of their royal master." The Ape was so delighted with his answer that he gave him a very handsome present. The other Traveller thought that if his companion was rewarded so splendidly for telling a lie, he himself would certainly receive a still greater reward for telling the truth; so, when the Ape turned to him and said, "And what, sir, is your opinion?" he replied, "I think you are a very fine Ape, and all your subjects are fine Apes too." The King of the Apes was so enraged at his reply that he ordered him to be taken away and clawed to death.

THE ASS AND HIS BURDENS

A Pedlar who owned an Ass one day bought a quantity of salt, and loaded up his beast with as much as he could bear. On the way home the Ass stumbled as he was crossing a stream and fell into the water. The salt got thoroughly wetted and much of it melted and drained away, so that, when he got on his legs again, the Ass found his load had become much less heavy. His master, however, drove him back to town and bought more salt, which he added to what remained in the panniers, and started out again. No sooner had they reached a stream than the Ass lay down in it, and rose, as before, with a much lighter load. But his master detected the trick, and turning back once more, bought a large number of sponges, and piled them on the back of the Ass. When they came to the stream the Ass again lay down: but this time, as the sponges soaked up large quantities of water, he found, when he got up on his legs, that he had a bigger burden to carry than ever.

You may play a good card once too often.

THE SHEPHERD'S BOY AND THE WOLF

A Shepherd's Boy was tending his flock near a village, and thought it would be great fun to hoax the villagers by pretending that a Wolf was attacking the sheep: so he shouted out, "Wolf! wolf!" and when the people came running up he laughed at them for their pains. He did this more than once, and every time the villagers found they had been hoaxed, for there was no Wolf at all. At last a Wolf really did come, and the Boy cried, "Wolf! wolf!" as loud as he could: but the people were so used to hearing him call that they took no notice of his cries for help. And so the Wolf had it all his own way, and killed off sheep after sheep at his leisure.

You cannot believe a liar even when he tells the truth.

THE FOX AND THE GOAT
A Fox fell into a well and was unable to get out again. By and by a thirsty Goat came by, and seeing the Fox in the well asked him if the water was good. "Good?" said the Fox, "it's the best water I ever tasted in all my life. Come down and try it yourself." The Goat thought of nothing but the prospect of quenching his thirst, and jumped in at once. When he had had enough to drink, he looked about, like the Fox, for some way of getting out, but could find none. Presently the Fox said, "I have an idea. You stand on your hind legs, and plant your forelegs firmly against the side of the well, and then I'll climb on to your back, and, from there, by stepping on your horns, I can get out. And when I'm out, I'll help you out too." The Goat did as he was requested, and the Fox climbed on to his back and so out of the well; and then he coolly walked away. The Goat called loudly after him and reminded him of his promise to help him out: but the Fox merely turned and said, "If you had as much sense in your head as you have hair in your beard you wouldn't have got into the well without making certain that you could get out again."

Look before your leap.

THE FISHERMAN AND THE SPRAT
A Fisherman cast his net into the sea, and when he drew it up again it contained nothing but a single Sprat that begged to be put back into the water. "I'm only a little fish now," it said, "but I shall grow big one day, and then if you come and catch me again I shall be of some use to you." But the Fisherman replied, "Oh, no, I shall keep you now I've got you: if I put you back, should I ever see you again? Not likely!"

THE BOASTING TRAVELLER
A Man once went abroad on his travels, and when he came home he had wonderful tales to tell of the things he had done in foreign countries. Among other things, he said he had taken part in a jumping-match at Rhodes, and had done a wonderful jump which no one could beat. "Just go to Rhodes and ask them," he said; "every one will tell you it's true." But one of those who were listening said, "If you can jump as well as all that, we needn't go to Rhodes to prove it. Let's just imagine this is Rhodes for a minute: and now--jump!"

Deeds, not words.

THE CRAB AND HIS MOTHER
An Old Crab said to her son, "Why do you walk sideways like that, my son? You ought to walk straight." The Young Crab replied, "Show me how, dear mother, and I'll follow your example." The Old Crab tried, but tried in vain, and then saw how foolish she had been to find fault with her child.

Example is better than precept.

THE ASS AND HIS SHADOW

A certain man hired an Ass for a journey in summertime, and started out with the owner following behind to drive the beast. By and by, in the heat of the day, they stopped to rest, and the traveller wanted to lie down in the Ass's Shadow; but the owner, who himself wished to be out of the sun, wouldn't let him do that; for he said he had hired the Ass only, and not his Shadow: the other maintained that his bargain secured him complete control of the Ass for the time being. From words they came to blows; and while they were belabouring each other the Ass took to his heels and was soon out of sight.

Day 26

1. Read the next set of stories.
2. What should you do when someone needs help (according to one of the stories)? (Answers)
3. Which story's moral is related to the lesson from Matthew 7:3-5? (Answers)

THE BOY BATHING

A Boy was bathing in a river and got out of his depth, and was in great danger of being drowned. A man who was passing along a road heard his cries for help, and went to the riverside and began to scold him for being so careless as to get into deep water, but made no attempt to help him. "Oh, sir," cried the Boy, "please help me first and scold me afterwards."

Give assistance, not advice, in a crisis.

THE QUACK FROG

Once upon a time a Frog came forth from his home in the marshes and proclaimed to all the world that he was a learned physician, skilled in drugs and able to cure all diseases. Among the crowd was a Fox, who called out, "You a doctor! Why, how can you set up to heal others when you cannot even cure your own lame legs and blotched and wrinkled skin?"

Physician, heal thyself.

THE SWOLLEN FOX

A hungry Fox found in a hollow tree a quantity of bread and meat, which some shepherds had placed there against their return. Delighted with his find he slipped in through the narrow aperture and greedily devoured it all. But when he tried to get out again he found himself so swollen after his big meal that he could not squeeze through the hole, and fell to whining and groaning over his misfortune. Another Fox, happening to pass that way, came and asked him what the matter was; and, on learning the state of the case, said, "Well, my friend, I see nothing for it but for you to stay where you are till you shrink to your former size; you'll get out then easily enough."

THE MOUSE, THE FROG, AND THE HAWK

A Mouse and a Frog struck up a friendship; they were not well mated, for the Mouse lived entirely on land, while the Frog was equally at home on land or in the water. In order that they might never be separated, the Frog tied himself and the Mouse together by the leg with a piece of thread. As long as they kept on dry land all went fairly well; but, coming to the edge of a pool, the Frog jumped in, taking the Mouse with him, and began swimming about and croaking with pleasure. The unhappy Mouse, however, was soon drowned, and floated about on the surface in the wake of the Frog. There he was spied by a Hawk, who pounced down on him and seized him in his talons. The Frog was unable to loose the knot which bound him to the Mouse, and thus was carried off along with him and eaten by the Hawk.

THE BOY AND THE NETTLES

A Boy was gathering berries from a hedge when his hand was stung by a Nettle. Smarting with the pain, he ran to tell his mother, and said to her between his sobs, "I only touched it ever so lightly, mother." "That's just why you got stung, my son," she said; "if you had grasped it firmly, it wouldn't have hurt you in the least."

THE PEASANT AND THE APPLE-TREE

A Peasant had an Apple-tree growing in his garden, which bore no fruit, but merely served to provide a shelter from the heat for the sparrows and grasshoppers which sat and chirped in its branches. Disappointed at its barrenness he determined to cut it down, and went and fetched his axe for the purpose. But when the sparrows and the grasshoppers saw what he was about to do, they begged him to spare it, and said to him, "If you destroy the tree we shall have to seek shelter elsewhere, and you will no longer have our merry chirping to enliven your work in the garden." He, however, refused to listen to them, and set to work with a will to cut through the trunk. A few strokes showed that it was hollow inside and contained a swarm of bees and a large store of honey. Delighted with his find he threw down his axe, saying, "The old tree is worth keeping after all."

Utility is most men's test of worth. (Note: Utility here means usefulness.)

THE JACKDAW AND THE PIGEONS

A Jackdaw, watching some Pigeons in a farmyard, was filled with envy when he saw how well they were fed, and determined to disguise himself as one of them, in order to secure a share of the good things they enjoyed. So he painted himself white from head to foot and joined the flock; and, so long as he was silent, they never suspected that he was not a pigeon like themselves. But one day he was unwise enough to start chattering, when they at once saw through his disguise and pecked him so unmercifully that he was glad to escape and join his own kind again. But the other jackdaws did not recognise him in his white dress, and would not let him feed with them, but drove him away: and so he became a homeless wanderer for his pains.

THE DOG IN THE MANGER

A Dog was lying in a Manger on the hay which had been put there for the cattle, and when they came and tried to eat, he growled and snapped at them and wouldn't let them get at their food. "What a selfish beast," said one of them to his companions; "he can't eat himself and yet he won't let those eat who can."

THE TWO BAGS

Every man carries Two Bags about with him, one in front and one behind, and both are packed full of faults. The Bag in front contains his neighbours' faults, the one behind his own. Hence it is that men do not see their own faults, but never fail to see those of others.

Day 27

1. Read these poems by Robert Louis Stevenson.

> THE COW
> The friendly cow all red and white,
> I love with all my heart:
> She gives me cream with all her might,
> To eat with apple-tart.
>
> She wanders lowing here and there,
> And yet she cannot stray,
> All in the pleasant open air,
> The pleasant light of day.
>
> And blown by all the winds that pass
> And wet with all the showers,
> She walks among the meadow grass
> And eats the meadow flowers.

AT THE SEASIDE
When I was down beside the sea,
A wooden spade they gave to me
To dig the sandy shore.
My holes were hollow like a cup,
In every hole the sea came up,
Till it could hold no more.

HAPPY THOUGHT
The world is so full of a number of things,
I'm sure we should all be as happy as kings.

Day 28

1. I'm going to tell you a story today. When you finish reading it, tell someone what the joke of the story is. (Answers)

There's a famous story called *Stone Soup*. It's an old French tale about three tired and hungry soldiers who had traveled far and went into a village to find a place to sleep and to have their stomachs filled.

But when the villagers saw them coming, they hid all of their food. It had been a poor harvest, and they wanted to keep all they had for themselves. They covered the stores of food, hiding everything they could.

When the soldiers came, they asked for a place to spend the night. The villagers insisted that all of their beds were full, and there certainly was no room for the strangers.

The soldiers asked for a meal, but every last villager insisted there was no food to spare. Each made an excuse and none offered hospitality.

The soldiers looked at each other. Then one said, "Well then, we'll have to make stone soup."

The villagers were surprised at this. They had made many different kinds of soups but never one from stones. Could it be possible? There were many stones around. What if they each could be made into soup?

One of the soldiers chose three smooth stones for the soup and asked for a large iron pot to cook it in. The villagers were so curious at how to make stone soup that someone offered a pot.

The stones were placed inside it, water was poured into it, and a fire was lit under it. The soldiers looked satisfied, but said, "Any soup needs salt and pepper." The villagers agreed and one ran to get them. The soldiers added them to the pot and the villagers were wondering what kind of soup was coming to a boil.

The soldiers began to talk amongst themselves. "Stone soup is wonderful, but carrots make it even better." The villagers looked at one another and one ran to get carrots out from under the blanket where she had hidden them.

The soldiers then began to say how if there were potatoes and a bit of beef it would be good enough for any rich man's table. The sound of that was tempting to the poor villagers, and two ran off to provide potatoes and beef for the stone soup.

One more time the soldiers spoke among themselves about the soup. "When the king dined with us, he loved this very soup with just a bit of barley and milk." This was a king's meal, all from stones! The villagers were so excited that they had the soup of kings in their village, and villagers brought to the pot barley and milk.

The soldiers announced that the soup would soon be ready and that the soldiers would give a taste to them all. Now the villagers began to talk among themselves and say that such a soup should have bread and a roast and cider. It wasn't long before the tables were set and a feast was spread before them all.

Everyone was sure it was the best soup they had ever tasted. And to think, it was made from stones!

Day 29

1. Read these poems by Robert Louis Stevenson.
2. Where is the land of Nod? (Answers)

THE LAND OF NOD
From breakfast on through all the day
At home among my friends I stay,
But every night I go abroad
Afar into the Land of Nod.

All by myself I have to go,
With none to tell me what to do—
All alone beside the streams
And up the mountain-sides of dreams.

The strangest things are there for me,
Both things to eat and things to see,
And many frightening sights abroad
Till morning in the Land of Nod.

Try as I like to find the way,
I never can get back by day,
Nor can remember plain and clear
The curious music that I hear.

MY SHADOW
I have a little shadow that goes in and out with me,
And what can be the use of him is more than I can see.
He is very, very like me, from the heels up to the head;
And I see him jump before me, when I jump into my bed.

The funniest thing about him is the way he likes to grow—
Not at all like proper children, which is always very slow;
For he sometimes shoots up taller, like an india-rubber ball,
And he sometimes gets so little that there's none of him at all.

He hasn't got a notion of how children ought to play,
And can only make a fool of me in every sort of way.
He stays so close beside me, he's a coward you can see;
I'd think shame to stick to nursie as that shadow sticks to me!

One morning, very early, before the sun was up,
I 'rose and found the shining dew on every buttercup;
But my lazy little shadow, like an arrant sleepy head,
Had stayed at home behind me and was fast asleep in bed.

Day 30

1. Read these poems by Robert Louis Stevenson.
2. Practice your vocabulary by going to Day 25 or to Level 3 on the Review Games page on the Easy Peasy website.

SINGING
Of speckled eggs the birdie sings
And nests among the trees;
The sailor sings of ropes and things
In ships upon the seas.

44

The children sing in far Japan,
The children sing in Spain;
The organ with the organ man
Is singing in the rain.

MY BED IS A BOAT

My bed is like a little boat;
Nurse helps me in when I embark;
She girds me in my sailor's coat
And starts me in the dark.

At night, I go on board and say
Good night to all my friends on shore;
I shut my eyes and sail away
And see and hear no more.

And sometimes things to bed I take,
As prudent sailors have to do;
Perhaps a slice of wedding-cake,
Perhaps a toy or two.

All night across the dark we steer:
But when the day returns at last
Safe in my room, beside the pier,
I find my vessel fast.

RAIN

The rain is raining all around.
It falls on field and tree,
It rains on the umbrellas here,
And on the ships at sea.

Day 31

1. You are going to start reading *Heidi.*
2. Today, read this summary of the book.
   - "When Heidi, a little Swiss orphan girl, is five years old, she is taken by her Aunt [Deta] to live with her grandfather. His home is high up on the mountain slopes; he has quarrelled with those who live down below in the village of Dörfli, where he is known as 'Uncle Alp'. Grandfather and Heidi get on very well together, and she settles happily into her new home. She spends many enjoyable hours up on the high

pastures with Peter, who looks after the villagers' goats. She also very much enjoys visiting Peter's blind grandmother, whom she calls Grannie.

When Heidi is eight years old, her Aunt [Deta], who is working in Frankfurt, Germany, comes to see her. She takes Heidi to live in Frankfurt as a companion to a twelve-year-old girl called Clara Sesemann who is an invalid and is unable to walk.... The story ends with Heidi and Grannie talking together, and thanking God for all the good things He has brought into their lives."
(http://www.bookdrum.com/books/heidi/9780140366792/summary.html)

3.   The author's name is Johanna Spyri. She was born in Switzerland. She wrote *Heidi* in German.
4.   The setting of the book is in the Alps, the huge mountain range of Switzerland.

Day 32

1.   Here are some words that may be new to you.
   - The book mentions old-fashioned hob-nailed boots. This book was written a long time ago. Short, fat nails were put into the shoes to help you not slip, like cleats or like treads on your sneakers. The heads of the nails were on the outside of the shoe. The points were hammered into the shoe, but they stayed in the shoe! They didn't go into your foot.
      - **vigorous** – strong and active (vig–or–us)
      - **imposing** – grand and impressive in appearance (im–pose–ing)
      - **loiter** – to dawdle over work or to hang around without purpose (loy–ter)
      - **acquaintance** – a person you know but not very well (a–quain-tens)
2.   You'll read part of a chapter each day. Start reading chapter 1.
3.   How old is the little girl? (Answers)
4.   The hamlet, or small town, is called "The Little Village." What is the name of the mountain they are climbing? (Answers)
5.   What's the name of the young woman escorting Heidi up the mountain? (Answers)
6.   Is the man on the mountain Heidi's uncle? (Answers)
7.   Who has been taking care of Heidi? (Answers)
8.   What does Barbara think of Heidi living with her grandfather? (Answers)
9.   What is Alm-Uncle like? (Answers)
10.   What does Barbara want to know? (Answers)

Chapter 1 GOING UP TO THE ALM UNCLE

The little old town of Mayenfeld is charmingly situated. From it a footpath leads through green, well-wooded stretches to the foot of the heights which look down imposingly upon the valley.

Where the footpath begins to go steeply and abruptly up the Alps, the heath, with its short grass and pungent herbage, at once sends out its soft perfume to meet the wayfarer.

One bright sunny morning in June, a tall, vigorous maiden of the mountain region climbed up the narrow path, leading a little girl by the hand. The youngster's cheeks were in such a glow that it showed even through her sun-browned skin. Small wonder though! for in spite of the heat, the little one, who was scarcely five years old, was bundled up as if she had to brave a bitter frost. Her shape was difficult to distinguish, for she wore two dresses, if not three, and around her shoulders a large red cotton shawl. With her feet encased in heavy hob-nailed boots, this hot and shapeless little person toiled up the mountain.

The pair had been climbing for about an hour when they reached a hamlet half-way up the great mountain named the Alm. This hamlet was called "Im Dörfli" or "The Little Village." It was the elder girl's home town, and therefore she was greeted from nearly every house; people called to her from windows and doors, and very often from the road. But, answering questions and calls as she went by, the girl did not loiter on her way and only stood still when she reached the end of the hamlet. There a few cottages lay scattered about, from the furthest of which a voice called out to her through an open door: "Deta, please wait one moment! I am coming with you, if you are going further up."

When the girl stood still to wait, the child instantly let go her hand and promptly sat down on the ground.

"Are you tired, Heidi?" Deta asked the child.

"No, but hot," she replied

"We shall be up in an hour, if you take big steps and climb with all your little might!" Thus the elder girl tried to encourage her small companion.

A stout, pleasant-looking woman stepped out of the house and joined the two. The child had risen and wandered behind the old acquaintances, who immediately started gossiping about their friends in the neighborhood and the people of the hamlet generally.

"Where are you taking the child, Deta?" asked the newcomer. "Is she the child your sister left?"

"Yes," Deta assured her; "I am taking her up to the Alm-Uncle and there I want her to remain."

"You can't really mean to take her there Deta. You must have lost your senses, to go to him. I am sure the old man will show you the door and won't even listen to what you say."

"Why not? As he's her grandfather, it is high time he should do something for the child. I have taken care of her until this summer and now a good place has been offered to me. The child shall not hinder me from accepting it, I tell you that!"

"It would not be so hard, if he were like other mortals. But you know him yourself. How could he *look* after a child, especially such a little one? She'll never get along with him, I am sure of that!—But tell me of your prospects."

"I am going to a splendid house in Frankfurt. Last summer some people went off to the baths and I took care of their rooms. As they got to like me, they wanted to take me along, but I could not leave. They have come back now and have persuaded me to go with them."

"I am glad I am not the child!" exclaimed Barbara with a shudder. "Nobody knows anything about the old man's life up there. He doesn't speak to a living soul, and from one year's end to the other he keeps away from church. People get out of his way when he appears once in a twelve-month down here among us. We all fear him and he is really just like a heathen or an old Indian, with those thick grey eyebrows and that huge uncanny beard. When he wanders along the road with his twisted stick we are all afraid to meet him alone."

"That is not my fault," said Deta stubbornly. "He won't do her any harm; and if he should, he is responsible, not I."

"I wish I knew what weighs on the old man's conscience. Why are his eyes so fierce and why does he live up there all alone? Nobody ever sees him and we hear many strange things about him. Didn't your sister tell you anything, Deta?"

"Of course she did, but I shall hold my tongue. He would make me pay for it if I didn't."

Barbara had long been anxious to know something about the old uncle and why he lived apart from everybody. Nobody had a good word for him, and when people talked about him, they did not speak openly but as if they were afraid. She could not even explain to herself why he was called the Alm-Uncle. He could not possibly be the uncle of all the people in the village, but since everybody spoke of him so, she did the same. Barbara, who had only lived in the village since her marriage, was glad to get some information from her friend. Deta had been bred there, but since her mother's death had gone away to earn her livelihood.

She confidentially seized Deta's arm and said: "I wish you would tell me the truth about him, Deta; you know it all—people only gossip. Tell me, what has happened to the old man to turn everybody against him so? Did he always hate his fellow-creatures?"

Day 33

1. What is a shepherd? If a shepherd, herds (or watches and keeps together) sheep, then what do you think a goatherd does?
2. Here are some new words you will come across.
3. I put in parenthesis how to say them.
   - **enmity** – hatred, feeling of being against someone (en – mi- tee)
   - **luscious** – highly pleasing to the senses (lush – issss)
4. Read more of chapter 1.
5. What is the goatherd's name? (Answers)
6. Why was Heidi hot? (Answers)
7. Heidi's mother and father died when she was about a year old. Her aunt, Deta, has been taking care of her since. Heidi's mother was Deta's sister. Heidi's father was Alm-Uncle's son, so Heidi is his grandchild.

Chapter 1 continued

"I cannot tell you whether he always did, and that for a very good reason. He being sixty years old, and I only twenty-six, you can't expect me to give you an account of his early youth. But if you'll promise to keep it to yourself and not set all the people in Prätiggan talking, I can tell you a good deal. My mother and he both came from Domleschg."

"How can you talk like that, Deta?" replied Barbara in an offended tone. "People do not gossip much in Prätiggan, and I always can keep things to myself, if I have to. You won't repent of having told me, I assure you!"

"All right, but keep your word!" said Deta warningly. Then she looked around to see that the child was not so close to them as to overhear what might be said; but the little girl was nowhere to be seen. While the two young women had talked at such a rate, they had not noticed her absence; quite a while must have elapsed since the little girl had given up following her companions. Deta, standing still, looked about her everywhere, but no one was on the path, which—except for a few curves—was visible as far down as the village.

"There she is! Can't you see her there?" exclaimed Barbara, pointing to a spot a good distance from the path. "She is climbing up with the goatherd Peter and his goats. I wonder why he is so late to-day. I must say, it suits us well enough; he can look after the child while you tell me everything without being interrupted."

"It will be very easy for Peter to watch her," remarked Deta; "she is bright for her five years and keeps her eyes wide open. I have often noticed that and I am glad for her, for it will be useful with the uncle. He has nothing left in the whole wide world, but his cottage and two goats!"

"Did he once have more?" asked Barbara.

"I should say so. He was heir to a large farm in Domleschg. But setting up to play the fine gentleman, he soon lost everything with drink and play. His parents died with grief and he himself disappeared from these parts. After many years he came back with a half-grown boy, his son, Tobias, that was his name, became a carpenter and turned out to be a quiet, steady fellow. Many strange rumors went round about the uncle and I think that was why he left Domleschg for Dörfli. We acknowledged relationship, my mother's grandmother being a cousin of his. We called him uncle, and because we are related on my father's side to nearly all the people in the hamlet they too all called him uncle. He was named 'Alm-Uncle' when he moved up to the Alm."

"But what happened to Tobias?" asked Barbara eagerly.

"Just wait. How can I tell you everything at once?" exclaimed Deta. "Tobias was an apprentice in Mels, and when he was made master, he came home to the village and married my sister Adelheid. They always had been fond of each other and they lived very happily as man and wife. But their joy was short. Two years afterwards, when Tobias was helping to build a house, a beam fell on him and killed him. Adelheid was thrown into a violent fever with grief and fright, and never recovered from it. She had never been strong and had often suffered from queer spells, when we did not know whether she was awake or asleep. Only a few weeks after Tobias's death they buried poor Adelheid.

"People said that heaven had punished the uncle for his misdeeds. After the death of his son he never spoke to a living soul. Suddenly he moved up to the Alp, to live there at enmity with God and man.

"My mother and I took Adelheid's little year-old baby, Heidi, to live with us. When I went to Ragatz I took her with me; but in the spring the family whose work I had done last year came from Frankfurt and resolved to take me to their town-house. I am very glad to get such a good position."

"And now you want to hand over the child to this terrible old man. I really wonder how you can do it, Deta!" said Barbara with reproach in her voice.

"It seems to me I have really done enough for the child. I do not know where else to take her, as she is too young to come with me to Frankfurt. By the way, Barbara, where are you going? We are half-way up the Alm already."

Deta shook hands with her companion and stood still while Barbara approached the tiny, dark-brown mountain hut, which lay in a hollow a few steps away from the path.

Situated half-way up the Alm, the cottage was luckily protected from the mighty winds. Had it been exposed to the tempests, it would have been a doubtful habitation in the state of decay it was in. Even as it was, the doors and windows rattled and the old rafters shook when the south wind swept the mountain side. If the hut had stood on the Alm top, the wind would have blown it down the valley without much ado when the storm season came.

Here lived Peter the goatherd, a boy eleven years old, who daily fetched the goats from the village and drove them up the mountain to the short and luscious grasses of the pastures. Peter raced down in the evening with the light-footed little goats. When he whistled sharply through his fingers, every owner would come and get his or her goat. These owners were mostly small boys and girls and, as the goats were friendly, they did not fear them. That was the only time Peter spent with other children, the rest of the day the animals were his sole companions. At home lived his mother and an old blind grandmother, but he only spent enough time in the hut to swallow his bread and milk for breakfast and the same repast for supper. After that he sought his bed to sleep. He always left early in the morning and at night he came home late, so that he could be with his friends as long as possible. His father had met with an accident some years ago; he also had been called Peter the goatherd. His mother, whose name was Brigida, was called "Goatherd Peter's wife" and his blind grandmother was called by young and old from many miles about just "grandmother."

Deta waited about ten minutes to see if the children were coming up behind with the goats. As she could not find them anywhere, she climbed up a little higher to get a better view down the valley from there, and peered from side to side with marks of great impatience on her countenance.

The children in the meantime were ascending slowly in a zigzag way, Peter always knowing where to find all sorts of good grazing places for his goats where they could nibble. Thus they strayed from side to side. The poor little girl had followed the boy only with the greatest effort and she was panting in her heavy clothes. She was so hot and uncomfortable that she only climbed by exerting all her strength. She did not say anything but looked enviously at Peter, who jumped about so easily in his light trousers and bare feet. She envied even more the goats that climbed over bushes, stones, and steep inclines with their slender legs. Suddenly sitting down on the ground the child swiftly took off her shoes and stockings. Getting up she undid the heavy shawl and the two little dresses. Out she slipped without more ado and stood up in only a light petticoat. In sheer delight at the relief, she threw up her dimpled arms, that were bare up to her short sleeves. To save the trouble of carrying them, her aunt had dressed her in her Sunday clothes over her workday garments. Heidi arranged her dresses neatly in a heap and joined Peter and the goats. She was now as light-footed as any of them. When Peter, who had not paid much attention, saw her suddenly in her light attire, he grinned. Looking back, he saw the little heap of dresses on the ground and then he grinned yet more, till his mouth seemed to reach from ear to ear; but he said never a word.

Day 34

1. Here is a sentence from the chapter. "How could you be so stupid, Heidi? Have you lost your senses?" the aunt went on, with a tone mingled with vexation and reproach.
2. You probably don't know what vexation and reproach are. That's okay to not know some words. Her "tone" is how her voice sounded. From what she said to Heidi, can you imagine what her voice sounded like? I bet you can. You don't always have to know the words to understand them. You know she sounds upset. If someone is vexed, they are frustrated and annoyed. They are upset. To reproach someone is to scold them. Basically she's angry with Heidi, but you knew that, even if you didn't know those two words. When you don't know a word, don't get stuck. Keep reading and the sentence will probably help explain what the word means.
3. Finish chapter 1.
4. What is Alm-Uncle's reaction to Deta's news that she's leaving Heidi with him? (Answers)

Chapter 1 continued

The child, feeling free and comfortable, started to converse with Peter, and he had to answer many questions. She asked him how many goats he had, and where he led them, what he did with them when he got there, and so forth.

At last the children reached the summit in front of the hut. When Deta saw the little party of climbers she cried out shrilly: "Heidi, what have you done? What a sight you are! Where are your dresses and your shawl? Are the new shoes gone that I just bought for you, and the new stockings that I made myself? Where are they all, Heidi?"

The child quietly pointed down and said "There."

The aunt followed the direction of her finger and descried a little heap with a small red dot in the middle, which she recognized as the shawl.

"Unlucky child!" Deta said excitedly. "What does all this mean? Why have you taken your things all off?"

"Because I do not need them," said the child, not seeming in the least repentant of her deed.

"How can you be so stupid, Heidi? Have you lost your senses?" the aunt went on, in a tone of mingled vexation and reproach. "Who do you think will go way down there to fetch those things up again? It is half-an-hour's walk. Please, Peter, run down and get them. Do not stand and stare at me as if you were glued to the spot."

"I am late already," replied Peter, and stood without moving from the place where, with his hands in his trousers' pockets, he had witnessed the violent outbreak of Heidi's aunt.

"There you are, standing and staring, but that won't get you further," said Deta. "I'll give you this if you go down." With that she held a five-penny-piece under his eyes. That made Peter start and in a great hurry he ran down the straightest path. He arrived again in so short a time that Deta had to praise him and gave him her little coin without delay. He did not often get such a treasure, and therefore his face was beaming and he laughingly dropped the money deep into his pocket.

"If you are going up to the uncle, as we are, you can carry the pack till we get there," said Deta. They still had to climb a steep ascent that lay behind Peter's hut. The boy readily took the things and followed Deta, his left arm holding the bundle and his right swinging the stick. Heidi jumped along gaily by his side with the goats.

After three quarters of an hour they reached the height where the hut of the old man stood on a prominent rock, exposed to every wind, but bathed in the full sunlight. From there you could gaze far down into the valley. Behind the hut stood three old fir-trees with great shaggy branches. Further back the old grey rocks rose high and sheer. Above them you could see green and fertile pastures, till at last the stony boulders reached the bare, steep cliffs.

Overlooking the valley the uncle had made himself a bench, by the side of the hut. Here he sat, with his pipe between his teeth and both hands resting on his knees. He quietly watched the children climbing up with the goats and Aunt Deta behind them, for the children had caught up to her long ago. Heidi reached the top first, and approaching the old man she held out her hand to him and said: "Good evening, grandfather!"

"Well, well, what does that mean?" replied the old man in a rough voice. Giving her his hand for only a moment, he watched her with a long and penetrating look from under his bushy brows. Heidi gazed back at him with an unwinking glance and examined him with much curiosity, for he was strange to look at, with his thick, grey beard and shaggy eyebrows, that met in the middle like a thicket.

Heidi's aunt had arrived in the meantime with Peter, who was eager to see what was going to happen.

"Good-day to you, uncle," said Deta as she approached. "This is Tobias's and Adelheid's child. You won't be able to remember her, because last time you saw her she was scarcely a year old."

"Why do you bring her here?" asked the uncle, and turning to Peter he said: "Get away and bring my goats. How late you are already!"

Peter obeyed and disappeared on the spot; the uncle had looked at him in such a manner that he was glad to go.

"Uncle, I have brought the little girl for you to keep," said Deta. "I have done my share these last four years and now it is your turn to provide for her."

The old man's eyes flamed with anger. "Indeed!" he said. "What on earth shall I do, when she begins to whine and cry for you? Small children always do, and then I'll be helpless."

"You'll have to look out for that!" Deta retorted. "When the little baby was left in my hands a few years ago, I had to find out how to care for the little innocent myself and nobody told me anything. I already had mother on my hands and there was plenty for me to do. You can't blame me if I want to earn some money now. If you can't keep the child, you can do with her whatever you please. If she comes to harm you are responsible and I am sure you do not want to burden your conscience any further."

Deta had said more in her excitement than she had intended, just because her conscience was not quite clear. The uncle had risen during her last words and now he gave her such a look that she retreated a few steps. Stretching out his arm in a commanding gesture, he said to her: "Away with you! Begone! Stay wherever you came from and don't venture soon again into my sight!"

Deta did not have to be told twice. She said "Good-bye" to Heidi and "Farewell" to the uncle, and started down the mountain. Like steam her excitement seemed to drive her forward, and she ran down at a tremendous rate. The people in the village called to her now more than they had on her way up, because they all were wondering where she had left the child. They were well acquainted with both and knew their history. When she heard from door and windows: "Where is the child?" "Where have you left her, Deta?" and so forth, she answered more and more reluctantly: "Up with the Alm-Uncle,—with the Alm-Uncle!" She became much provoked because the women called to her from every side: "How could you do it?" "The poor little creature!" "The idea of leaving such a helpless child up there!" and, over and over again: "The poor little dear!" Deta ran as quickly as she could and was glad when she heard no more calls, because, to tell the

truth, she herself was uneasy. Her mother had asked her on her deathbed to care for Heidi. But she consoled herself with the thought that she would be able to do more for the child if she could earn some money. She was very glad to go away from people who interfered in her affairs, and looked forward with great delight to her new place.

Day 35

1. It keeps talking about the grandfather's penetrating glance or look or eyes. To penetrate something means to break through it. When grandfather looks at you, it's like he can see right inside of you.
2. Start reading chapter 2.
3. How is grandfather treating Heidi? What makes you say that? (Answers)
4. Draw a picture of something from the setting of this chapter. Here are some examples: the outside of the hut and trees, the inside of the hut, the hayloft.

Vocabulary

1. Match the definitions with words from *Heidi*. Write the matching letters and numbers together on a separate sheet of paper. (Answers)

    | 1. | grand and impressive in appearance | A. | luscious |
    | 2. | strong and active | B. | enmity |
    | 3. | hatred | C. | vigorous |
    | 4. | to dawdle over your work | D. | imposing |
    | 5. | highly pleasing to the senses | E. | loiter |
    | 6. | a person you know but not very well | F. | acquaintance |

Chapter 2 WITH GRANDFATHER

After Deta had disappeared, the Uncle sat down again on the bench, blowing big clouds of smoke out of his pipe. He did not speak, but kept his eyes fastened on the ground. In the meantime Heidi looked about her, and discovering the goat-shed, peeped in. Nothing could be seen inside. Searching for some more interesting thing, she saw the three old fir-trees behind the hut. Here the wind was roaring through the branches and the tree-tops were swaying to and fro. Heidi stood still to listen. After the wind had ceased somewhat, she walked round the hut back to her grandfather. She found him in exactly the same position, and planting herself in front of the old man, with arms folded behind her back, she gazed at him. The grandfather, looking up, saw the child standing motionless before him. "What do you want to do now?" he asked her.

"I want to see what's in the hut," replied Heidi.

"Come then," and with that the grandfather got up and entered the cottage.

"Take your things along," he commanded.

"I do not want them any more," answered Heidi.

The old man, turning about, threw a penetrating glance at her. The child's black eyes were sparkling in expectation of all the things to come. "She is not lacking in intelligence," he muttered to himself. Aloud he added: "Why don't you need them any more?"

"I want to go about like the light-footed goats!"

"All right, you can; but fetch the things and we'll put them in the cupboard." The child obeyed the command. The old man now opened the door, and Heidi followed him into a fairly spacious room, which took in the entire expanse of the hut. In one corner stood a table and a chair, and in another the grandfather's bed. Across the room a large kettle was suspended over the hearth, and opposite to it a large door was sunk into the wall. This the grandfather opened. It was the cupboard, in which all his clothes were kept. In one shelf were a few shirts, socks and towels; on another a few plates, cups and glasses; and on the top shelf Heidi could see a round loaf of bread, some bacon and cheese. In this cupboard the grandfather kept everything that he needed for his subsistence. When he opened it, Heidi pushed her things as far behind the grandfather's clothes as she could reach. She did not want them found again in a hurry. After looking around attentively in the room, she asked, "Where am I going to sleep, grandfather?"

"Wherever you want to," he replied. That suited Heidi exactly. She peeped into all the corners of the room and looked at every little nook to find a cosy place to sleep. Beside the old man's bed she saw a ladder. Climbing up, she arrived at a hayloft, which was filled with fresh and fragrant hay. Through a tiny round window she could look far down into the valley.

"I want to sleep up here," Heidi called down. "Oh, it is lovely here. Please come up, grandfather, and see it for yourself."

"I know it," sounded from below.

"I am making the bed now," the little girl called out again, while she ran busily to and fro. "Oh, do come up and bring a sheet, grandfather, for every bed must have a sheet."

"Is that so?" said the old man. After a while he opened the cupboard and rummaged around in it. At last he pulled out a long coarse cloth from under the shirts. It somewhat resembled a sheet, and with this he climbed up to the loft. Here a neat little bed was already prepared. On top the hay was heaped up high so that the head of the occupant would lie exactly opposite the window.

The grandfather was well pleased with the arrangement. To prevent the hard floor from being felt, he made the couch twice as thick. Then he and Heidi together put the heavy sheet on, tucking the ends in well. Heidi looked thoughtfully at her fresh, new bed and said, "Grandfather, we have forgotten something."

"What?" he asked.

"I have no cover. When I go to bed I always creep in between the sheet and the cover."

"What shall we do if I haven't any?" asked the grandfather.

"Never mind, I'll just take some more hay to cover me," Heidi reassured him, and was just going to the heap of hay when the old man stopped her.

"Just wait one minute," he said, and went down to his own bed. From it he took a large, heavy linen bag and brought it to the child.

"Isn't this better than hay?" he asked.

Heidi pulled the sack to and fro with all her might, but she could not unfold it, for it was too heavy for her little arms. The grandfather put the thick cover on the bed while Heidi watched him. After it was all done, she said: "What a nice bed I have now, and what a splendid cover! I only wish the evening was here, that I might go to sleep in it."

"I think we might eat something first," said the grandfather. "Don't you think so?"

Heidi had forgotten everything else in her interest for the bed; but when she was reminded of her dinner, she noticed how terribly hungry she really was. She had had only a piece of bread and a cup of thin coffee very early in the morning, before her long journey. Heidi said approvingly: "I think we might, grandfather!"

Day 36

1. Finish reading chapter 2.
2. How did Heidi show initiative? Initiative is seeing what needs to be done and doing it without being asked. (Answers)
3. Is Heidi happy in her new home? (Answers)
4. Is Heidi's grandfather happy with her? (Answers)

Chapter 2 continued

"Let's go down then, if we agree," said the old man, and followed close behind her. Going up to the fireplace, he pushed the big kettle aside and reached for a smaller one that was suspended on a chain. Then sitting down on a three-legged stool, he kindled a bright fire. When the kettle was boiling, the old man put a large piece of cheese on a long iron fork, and held it over the fire, turning it to and fro, till it was golden-brown on all sides. Heidi had watched him eagerly. Suddenly she ran to the cupboard. When her grandfather brought a pot and the toasted cheese to the table, he found it already nicely set with two plates and two knives and the bread in the middle. Heidi had seen the things in the cupboard and knew that they would be needed for the meal.

"I am glad to see that you can think for yourself," said the grandfather, while he put the cheese on top of the bread, "but something is missing yet."

Heidi saw the steaming pot and ran back to the cupboard in all haste. A single little bowl was on the shelf. That did not perplex Heidi though, for she saw two glasses standing behind. With those three things she returned to the table.

"You certainly can help yourself! Where shall you sit, though?" asked the grandfather, who occupied the only chair himself, Heidi flew to the hearth, and bringing back the little stool, sat down on it.

"Now you have a seat, but it is much too low. In fact, you are too little to reach the table from my chair. Now you shall have something to eat at last!" and with that the grandfather filled the little bowl with milk. Putting it on his chair, he pushed it as near to the stool as was possible, and in that way Heidi had a table before her. He commanded her to eat the large piece of bread and the slice of golden cheese. He sat down himself on a corner of the table and started his own dinner. Heidi drank without stopping, for she felt exceedingly thirsty after her long journey. Taking a long breath, she put down her little bowl.

"How do you like the milk?" the grandfather asked her.

"I never tasted better," answered Heidi.

"Then you shall have more," and with that the grandfather filled the little bowl again. The little girl ate and drank with the greatest enjoyment. After she was through, both went out into the goat-shed. Here the old man busied himself, and Heidi watched him attentively while he was sweeping and putting down fresh straw for the goats to sleep on. Then he went to the little shop alongside and fashioned a high chair for Heidi, to the little girl's greatest amazement.

"What is this?" asked the grandfather.

"This is a chair for me. I am sure of it because it is so high. How quickly it was made!" said the child, full of admiration and wonder.

"She knows what is what and has her eyes on the right place," the grandfather said to himself, while he walked around the hut, fastening a nail or a loose board here and there. He wandered about with his hammer and nails, repairing whatever was in need of fixing. Heidi followed him at every step and watched the performance with great enjoyment and attention.

At last the evening came. The old fir-trees were rustling and a mighty wind was roaring and howling through the tree-tops. Those sounds thrilled Heidi's heart and filled it with happiness and joy. She danced and jumped about under the trees, for those sounds made her feel as if a wonderful thing had happened to her. The grandfather stood under the door, watching her, when suddenly a shrill whistle was heard. Heidi stood still and the grandfather joined her outside. Down from the heights came one goat after another, with Peter in their midst. Uttering a cry of joy, Heidi ran into the middle of the flock, greeting her old friends. When they had all reached the hut, they stopped on their way and two beautiful slender goats came out of the herd, one of them white and the other brown. They came up to the grandfather, who held out some salt in his hands to them, as he did every night. Heidi tenderly caressed first one and then the other, seeming beside herself with joy.

"Are they ours, grandfather? Do they both belong to us? Are they going to the stable? Are they going to stay with us?" Heidi kept on asking in her excitement. The grandfather hardly could put in a "yes, yes, surely" between her numerous questions. When the goats had licked up all the salt, the old man said, "Go in, Heidi, and fetch your bowl and the bread."

Heidi obeyed and returned instantly. The grandfather milked a full bowl from the white goat, cut a piece of bread for the child, and told her to eat. "Afterwards you can go to bed. If you need some shirts and other linen, you will find them in the bottom of the cupboard. Aunt Deta has left a bundle for you. Now good-night, I have to look after the goats and lock them up for the night."

"Good-night, grandfather! Oh, please tell me what their names are," called Heidi after him.

"The white one's name is Schwänli and the brown one I call Bärli," was his answer.

"Good-night, Schwänli! Good-night, Bärli," the little girl called loudly, for they were just disappearing in the shed. Heidi now sat down on the bench and took her supper. The strong wind nearly blew her from her seat, so she hurried with her meal, to be able to go inside and up to her bed. She slept in it as well as a prince on his royal couch.

Very soon after Heidi had gone up, before it was quite dark, the old man also sought his bed. He was always up in the morning with the sun, which rose early over the mountain-side in those summer days. It was a wild, stormy night; the hut was shaking in the gusts and all the boards were creaking. The wind howled through the chimney and the old fir-trees shook so strongly that many a dry branch came crashing down. In the middle of the night the grandfather got up, saying to himself: "I am sure she is afraid." Climbing up the ladder, he went up to Heidi's bed. The first moment everything lay in darkness, when all of a sudden the moon came out behind the clouds and sent his brilliant light across Heidi's bed. Her cheeks were burning red and she lay peacefully on her round and chubby arms. She must have had a happy dream, for she was smiling in her sleep. The grandfather stood and watched her till a cloud flew over the moon and left everything in total darkness. Then he went down to seek his bed again.

Day 37

1. The title of the next chapter is "On the Pasture." Do you know what a pasture is? It's land where animals graze on grass and other short plants. What do you think this chapter is going to be about? Answer before you read the chapter. You don't have to be right about what's going to happen, but you do have to think.
2. Here is a vocabulary word from today's reading:
   - **pungent** — something with a really strong taste or smell
3. Start reading chapter 3.
4. Who is Heidi spending the day with? (Answers)
5. What large bird made the sharp scream? (Answers)

Chapter 3 ON THE PASTURE

Heidi was awakened early next morning by a loud whistle. Opening her eyes, she saw her little bed and the hay beside her bathed in golden sunlight. For a short while she did not know where she was, but when she heard her grandfather's deep voice outside, she recollected everything. She remembered how she had come up the mountain the day before and left old Ursula, who was always shivering with cold and sat near the stove all day. While Heidi lived with Ursula, she had always been obliged to keep in the house, where the old woman could see her. Being deaf, Ursula was afraid to let Heidi go outdoors, and the child had often fretted in the narrow room and had longed to run outside. She was therefore delighted to find herself in her new home and hardly could wait to see the goats again. Jumping out of bed, she put on her few things and in a short time went down the ladder and ran outside. Peter was already there with his flock, waiting for Schwänli and Bärli, whom the grandfather was just bringing to join the other goats.

"Do you want to go with him to the pasture?" asked the grandfather.

"Yes," cried Heidi, clapping her hands.

"Go now, and wash yourself first, for the sun will laugh at you if he sees how dirty you are. Everything is ready there for you," he added, pointing to a large tub of water that stood in the sun. Heidi did as she was told, and washed and rubbed herself till her cheeks were glowing. In the meanwhile the grandfather called to Peter to come into the hut and bring his bag along. The boy followed the old man, who commanded him to open the bag in which he carried his scanty dinner. The grandfather put into the bag a piece of bread and a slice of cheese, that were easily twice as large as those the boy had in the bag himself.

"The little bowl goes in, too," said the Uncle, "for the child does not know how to drink straight from the goat, the way you do. She is going to stay with you all day, therefore milk two bowls full for her dinner. Look out that she does not fall over the rocks! Do you hear?"

Just then Heidi came running in. "Grandfather, can the sun still laugh at me?" she asked. The child had rubbed herself so violently with the coarse towel which the grandfather had put beside the tub that her face, neck and arms were as red as a lobster. With a smile the grandfather said: "No, he can't laugh any more now; but when you come home to-night you must go into the tub like a fish. When one goes about like the goats, one gets dirty feet. Be off!"

They started merrily up the Alp. A cloudless, deep-blue sky looked down on them, for the wind had driven away every little cloud in the night. The fresh green mountain-side was bathed in brilliant sunlight, and many blue and yellow flowers had opened. Heidi was wild with joy and ran from side to side. In one place she saw big patches of fine red primroses, on another spot blue gentians sparkled in the grass, and everywhere the golden rock-roses were nodding to her. In her transport at finding such treasures, Heidi even forgot Peter and his goats. She ran far ahead of him and then strayed away off to one side, for the sparkling flowers tempted her here and there. Picking whole bunches of them to take home with her, she put them all into her little apron.

Peter, whose round eyes could only move about slowly, had a hard time looking out for her. The goats were even worse, and only by shouting and whistling, especially by swinging his rod, could he drive them together.

"Heidi, where are you now?" he called quite angrily.

"Here," it sounded from somewhere. Peter could not see her, for she was sitting on the ground behind a little mound, which was covered with fragrant flowers. The whole air was filled with their perfume, and the child drew it in, in long breaths.

"Follow me now!" Peter called out. "The grandfather has told me to look out for you, and you must not fall over the rocks."

"Where are they?" asked Heidi without even stirring.

"Way up there, and we have still far to go. If you come quickly, we may see the eagle there and hear him shriek."

That tempted Heidi, and she came running to Peter, with her apron full of flowers.

"You have enough now," he declared. "If you pick them all to-day, there won't be any left to-morrow." Heidi admitted that, besides which she had her apron already full. From now on she stayed at Peter's side. The goats, scenting the pungent herbs, also hurried up without delay.

61

Peter generally took his quarters for the day at the foot of a high cliff, which seemed to reach far up into the sky. Overhanging rocks on one side made it dangerous, so that the grandfather was wise to warn Peter.

After they had reached their destination, the boy took off his bag, putting it in a little hollow in the ground. The wind often blew in violent gusts up there, and Peter did not want to lose his precious load. Then he lay down in the sunny grass, for he was very tired.

Heidi, taking off her apron, rolled it tightly together and put it beside Peter's bag. Then, sitting down beside the boy, she looked about her. Far down she saw the glistening valley; a large field of snow rose high in front of her. Heidi sat a long time without stirring, with Peter asleep by her side and the goats climbing about between the bushes. A light breeze fanned her cheek and those big mountains about her made her feel happy as never before. She looked up at the mountain-tops till they all seemed to have faces, and soon they were familiar to her, like old friends. Suddenly she heard a loud, sharp scream, and looking up she beheld the largest bird she had ever seen, flying above her. With outspread wings he flew in large circles over Heidi's head.

Day 38

1. Here are some words from today's reading that maybe you don't know.
   - **earnest** – serious about what you mean or what you are doing
   - **piteous** – used to describe something that you feel sorry for
   - **console** – to comfort
   - **evade** – to avoid
   - **obtrusive** – butting in, intruding on another's space
   - **contempt** – a feeling of despising toward people who are dishonorable or beneath you
   - **indignation** – righteous anger, feeling upset by something that is unjust or not right
2. Read the next part of chapter 3.
3. Why was Peter so excited over getting Heidi's cheese and some of her bread? (Answers)
4. What were some of the goats' names? (Answers)
5. What wouldn't Heidi let Peter do? (Answers)

Chapter 3 continued

"Wake up, Peter!" Heidi called. "Look up, Peter, and see the eagle there!"

Peter got wide wake, and then they both watched the bird breathlessly. It rose higher and higher into the azure, till it disappeared at last behind the mountain-peak.

"Where has it gone?" Heidi asked.

"Home to its nest," was Peter's answer.

"Oh, does it really live way up there? How wonderful that must be! But tell me why it screams so loud?" Heidi inquired.

"Because it has to," Peter replied.

"Oh, let's climb up there and see its nest!" implored Heidi, but Peter, expressing decided disapproval in his voice, answered: "Oh dear, Oh dear, not even goats could climb up there! Grandfather has told me not to let you fall down the rocks, so we can't go!"

Peter now began to call loudly and to whistle, and soon all the goats were assembled on the green field. Heidi ran into their midst, for she loved to see them leaping and playing about.

Peter in the meantime was preparing dinner for Heidi and himself, by putting her large pieces on one side and his own small ones on the other. Then he milked Bärli and put the full bowl in the middle. When he was ready, he called to the little girl. But it took some time before she obeyed his call.

"Stop jumping, now," said Peter, "and sit down; your dinner is ready."

"Is this milk for me?" she inquired.

"Yes it is; those large pieces also belong to you. When you are through with the milk, I'll get you some more. After that I'll get mine."

"What milk do you get?" Heidi inquired.

"I get it from my own goat, that speckled one over there. But go ahead and eat!" Peter commanded again. Heidi obeyed, and when the bowl was empty, he filled it again. Breaking off a piece of bread for herself, she gave Peter the rest, which was still bigger than his own portion had been. She handed him also the whole slice of cheese, saying: "You can eat that, I have had enough!"

Peter was speechless with surprise, for it would have been impossible for him ever to give up any of his share. Not taking Heidi in earnest, he hesitated till she put the things on his knees. Then he saw she really meant it, and he seized his prize. Nodding his thanks to her, he ate the most luxurious meal he had ever had in all his life. Heidi was watching the goats in the meantime, and asked Peter for their names.

The boy could tell them all to her, for their names were about the only thing he had to carry in his head. She soon knew them, too, for she had listened attentively. One of them was the Big Turk, who tried to stick his big horns into all the others. Most of the goats ran away from their rough comrade. The bold Thistlefinch alone was not afraid, and running his horns three or four times into the other, so astonished the Turk with his great daring that he stood still and gave up fighting, for the Thistlefinch had sharp horns and met him in the most warlike attitude. A small, white goat, called Snowhopper, kept up bleating in the most piteous way, which induced Heidi to console it several times. Heidi at last went to the little thing again, and throwing her arms around its head, she asked, "What is the matter with you, Snowhopper? Why do you always cry for help?" The little goat pressed close to Heidi's side and became perfectly quiet. Peter was still eating, but between the swallows he called to Heidi: "She is so unhappy, because the old goat has left us. She was sold to somebody in Mayenfeld two days ago."

"Who was the old goat?"

"Her mother, of course."

"Where is her grandmother?"

"She hasn't any."

"And her grandfather?"

"Hasn't any either."

"Poor little Snowhopper!" said Heidi, drawing the little creature tenderly to her. "Don't grieve any more; see, I am coming up with you every day now, and if there is anything the matter, you can come to me."

Snowhopper rubbed her head against Heidi's shoulder and stopped bleating. When Peter had finally finished his dinner, he joined Heidi.

The little girl had just been observing that Schwänli and Bärli were by far the cleanest and prettiest of the goats. They evaded the obtrusive Turk with a sort of contempt and always managed to find the greenest bushes for themselves. She mentioned it to Peter, who replied: "I know! Of course they are the prettiest, because the uncle washes them and gives them salt. He has the best stable by far."

All of a sudden Peter, who had been lying on the ground, jumped up and bounded after the goats. Heidi, knowing that something must have happened, followed him. She saw him running to a dangerous abyss on the side. Peter had noticed how the rash Thistlefinch had gone nearer and nearer to the dangerous spot. Peter only just came in time to prevent the goat from falling down over the very edge. Unfortunately Peter had stumbled over a stone in his hurry and was only able to catch the goat by one leg. The Thistlefinch, being enraged to find himself stopped in his charming ramble, bleated furiously. Not being able to get up, Peter loudly called for help. Heidi immediately saw that Peter was nearly pulling off the animal's leg. She quickly picked some fragrant herbs and holding them under the animal's nose, she said soothingly: "Come, come,

Thistlefinch, and be sensible. You might fall down there and break your leg. That would hurt you horribly."

The goat turned about and devoured the herbs Heidi held in her hand. When Peter got to his feet, he led back the runaway with Heidi's help. When he had the goat in safety, he raised his rod to beat it for punishment. The goat retreated shyly, for it knew what was coming. Heidi screamed loudly: "Peter, no, do not beat him! look how scared he is."

"He well deserves it," snarled Peter, ready to strike. But Heidi, seizing his arm, shouted, full of indignation: "You mustn't hurt him! Let him go!"

Day 39

1. New words:
   - **compensation** – a payment for something
   - **despondent** – feeling gloomy or discouraged
2. Finish reading chapter 3.
3. Why does Heidi say she won't pick any more flowers? (Answers)
4. Was there really a fire on the mountain? (Answers)

Chapter 3 continued

Heidi's eyes were sparkling, and when he saw her with her commanding mien, he desisted and dropped his rope. "I'll let him go, if you give me a piece of your cheese again to-morrow," he said, for he wanted a compensation for his fright.

"You may have it all to-morrow and every day, because I don't need it," Heidi assured him. "I shall also give you a big piece of bread, if you promise never to beat any of the goats."

"I don't care," growled Peter, and in that way he gave his promise.

Thus the day had passed, and the sun was already sinking down behind the mountains. Sitting on the grass, Heidi looked at the bluebells and the wild roses that were shining in the last rays of the sun. The peaks also started to glow, and Heidi suddenly called to the boy: "Oh, Peter, look! everything is on fire. The mountains are burning and the sky, too. Oh, look! the moon over there is on fire, too. Do you see the mountains all in a glow? Oh, how beautiful the snow looks! Peter, the eagle's nest is surely on fire, too. Oh, look at the fir-trees over there!"

Peter was quietly peeling his rod, and looking up, said to Heidi: "This is no fire; it always looks like that."

"But what is it then?" asked Heidi eagerly, gazing about her everywhere.

"It gets that way of itself," explained Peter.

"Oh look! Everything is all rosy now! Oh, look at this mountain over there with the snow and the sharp peaks. What is its name?"

"Mountains have no names," he answered.

"Oh, see, how beautiful! It looks as if many, many roses were growing on those cliffs. Oh, now they are getting grey. Oh dear! the fire has gone out and it is all over. What a terrible shame!" said Heidi quite despondently.

"It will be the same again tomorrow," Peter reassured her. "Come now, we have to go home."

When Peter had called the goats together, they started downwards.

"Will it be like that every day when we are up?" asked Heidi, eagerly.

"It usually is," was the reply.

"What about tomorrow?" she inquired.

"Tomorrow it will be like that, I am sure," Peter affirmed.

That made Heidi feel happy again. She walked quietly by Peter's side, thinking over all the new things she had seen. At last, reaching the hut, they found the grandfather waiting for them on a bench under the fir-trees. Heidi ran up to him and the two goats followed, for they knew their master. Peter called to her: "Come again tomorrow! Good-night!"

Heidi gave him her hand, assuring him that she would come, and finding herself surrounded by the goats, she hugged Snowhopper a last time.

When Peter had disappeared, Heidi returned to her grandfather. "Oh grandfather! it was so beautiful! I saw the fire and the roses on the rocks! And see the many, many flowers I am bringing you!" With that Heidi shook them out of her apron. But oh, how miserable they looked! Heidi did not even know them any more.

"What is the matter with them, grandfather? They looked so different!" Heidi exclaimed in her fright.

"They are made to bloom in the sun and not to be shut up in an apron," said the grandfather.

"Then I shall never pick them any more! Please, grandfather, tell me why the eagle screeches so loudly," asked Heidi.

,"First go and take a bath, while I go into the shed to get your milk. Afterwards we'll go inside together and I'll tell you all about it during supper-time."

They did as was proposed, and when Heidi sat on her high chair before her milk, she asked the same question as before.

"Because he is sneering at the people down below, who sit in the villages and make each other angry. He calls down to them:—'If you would go apart to live up on the heights like me, you would feel much better!'" The grandfather said these last words with such a wild voice, that it reminded Heidi of the eagle's screech.

"Why do the mountains have no names, grandfather?" asked Heidi.

"They all have names, and if you tell me their shape I can name them for you."

Heidi described several and the old man could name them all. The child told him now about all the happenings of the day, and especially about the wonderful fire. She asked how it came about.

"The sun does it," he exclaimed. "Saying good-night to the mountains, he throws his most beautiful rays to them, that they may not forget him till the morning."

Heidi was so much pleased with this explanation, that she could hardly wait to see the sun's good-night greetings repeated. It was time now to go to bed, and Heidi slept soundly all night. She dreamt that the little Snowhopper was bounding happily about on the glowing mountains with many glistening roses blooming round her.

Day 40

1. The next chapter is called "In Grandmother's Hut." What do you think is going to happen? Answer before you read! It's okay to not be right about what's going to happen, but it's not okay to not think.
2. Read the first part of chapter 4.
3. Grandfather invites Peter to stay for dinner. The book says: With that he prepared a meal which amply satisfied Peter's appetite.
   - It's okay if you don't know what amply means. I bet you can guess. Did grandfather prepare a meal that barely satisfied Peter's stomach or one that really, really satisfied him? What do you think? (Answers)
4. What is wrong with grandmother? (Answers)
5. What is wrong with Peter's hut? (Answers)

Vocabulary

1. Practice this week's vocabulary words.

2. Choose the word that matches the definition. Write your answers in order on a separate piece of paper. (Answers)

1. something with a really strong taste or smell
a) compensation b) pungent c) contempt d) earnest

2. serious about what you mean or what you are doing
a) contempt b) obtrusive c) earnest d) piteous

3. used to describe something that you feel sorry for
a) compensation b) indignation c) piteous d) despondent

4. to comfort
a) contempt b) reproach c) evade d) console

5. to avoid
a) evade   b) obtrusive c) reconcile d) loiter

6. butting in, intruding on another's space
a) contempt b) fierce   c) obtrusive d) vigorous

7. a feeling of despising toward people who are dishonorable or beneath you
a) despondent b) indignation c) quarrel d) contempt

8. righteous anger, feeling upset by something that is unjust or not right
a) indignation b) compensation c) despondent d) luscious

9. a payment for something
a) necessity b) imposing c) compensation d) acquaintance

10. feeling gloomy or discouraged
a) pungent b) contemptuous c) enmity d) despondent

Chapter 4 IN GRANDMOTHER'S HUT

Next morning Peter came again with his goats, and Heidi went up to the pasture with them. This happened day after day, and in this healthy life Heidi grew stronger, and more sunburnt every day. Soon the autumn came and when the wind was blowing across the mountainside, the grandfather would say: "You must stay home to-day, Heidi; for the wind can blow such a little thing as you down into the valley with a single gust."

It always made Peter unhappy when Heidi did not come along, for he saw nothing but misfortunes ahead of him; he hardly knew how to pass his time, and besides, he was deprived of his abundant dinner. The goats were so accustomed to Heidi by this time, that they did not follow Peter when she was not with him.

Heidi herself did not mind staying at home, for she loved nothing better than to watch her grandfather with his saw and hammer. Sometimes the grandfather would make small round cheeses on those days, and there was no greater pleasure for Heidi than to see him stir the butter with his bare arms. When the wind would howl through the fir-trees on those stormy days, Heidi would run out to the grove, thrilled and happy by the wondrous roaring in the branches. The sun had lost its vigor, and the child had to put on her shoes and stockings and her little dress.

The weather got colder and colder, and when Peter came up in the morning, he would blow into his hands, he was so frozen. At last even Peter could not come any more, for a deep snow had fallen over night. Heidi stood at the window, watching the snow falling down. It kept on snowing till it reached the windows; still it did not stop, and soon the windows could not be opened, and they were all shut in. When it had lasted for several days, Heidi thought that it would soon cover up the cottage. It finally stopped, and the grandfather went out to shovel the snow away from the door and windows, piling it up high here and there. In the afternoon the two were sitting near the fire when noisy steps were heard outside and the door was pushed open. It was Peter, who had come up to see Heidi. Muttering, "Good-evening," he went up to the fire. His face was beaming, and Heidi had to laugh when she saw little waterfalls trickling down from his person, for all the ice and snow had melted in the great heat.

The grandfather now asked Peter how he got along in school. Heidi was so interested that she asked him a hundred questions. Poor Peter, who was not an easy talker, found himself in great difficulty answering the little girl's inquiries, but at least it gave him leisure to dry his clothes.

During this conversation the grandfather's eyes had been twinkling, and at last he said to the boy: "Now that you have been under fire, general, you need some strengthening. Come and join us at supper."

With that the old man prepared a meal which amply satisfied Peter's appetite. It had begun to get dark, and Peter knew that it was time to go. He had said good-bye and thank you, when turning to Heidi he remarked:

"I'll come next Sunday, if I may. By the way, Heidi, grandmother asked me to tell you that she would love to see you."

Heidi immediately approved of this idea, and her first word next morning was: "Grandfather, I must go down to grandmother. She is expecting me."

Four days later the sun was shining and the tight-packed frozen snow was crackling under every step. Heidi was sitting at the dinner-table, imploring the old man to let her make the visit then, when he got up, and fetching down her heavy cover, told her to follow him. They went out into the glistening snow; no sound was heard and the snow-laden fir-trees shone and glittered in the sun. Heidi in her transport was running to and fro: "Grandfather, come out! Oh, look at the trees! They are all covered with silver and gold," she called to the grandfather, who had just come out of his workshop with a wide sled. Wrapping the child up in her cover, he put her on the sled, holding her fast. Off they started at such a pace that Heidi shouted for joy, for she seemed to be flying like a bird. The sled had stopped in front of Peter's hut, and grandfather said: "Go in. When it gets dark, start on your way home." When he had unwrapped her, he turned homewards with his sled.

Opening the door, Heidi found herself in a tiny, dark kitchen, and going through another door, she entered a narrow chamber. Near a table a woman was seated, busy with mending Peter's coat, which Heidi had recognized immediately. A bent old woman was sitting in a corner, and Heidi, approaching her at once, said: "How do you do, grandmother? I have come now, and I hope I haven't kept you waiting too long!"

Lifting her head, the grandmother sought for Heidi's hand. Feeling it thoughtfully, she said: "Are you the little girl who lives up with the uncle? Is your name Heidi?"

"Yes," Heidi replied. "The grandfather just brought me down in the sled."

"How is it possible? Your hands are as warm as toast! Brigida, did the uncle really come down with the child?"

Brigida, Peter's mother, had gotten up to look at the child. She said: "I don't know if he did, but I don't think so. She probably doesn't know."

Heidi, looking up, said quite decidedly: "I know that grandfather wrapped me up in a cover when we coasted down together."

"Peter was right after all," said the grandmother. "We never thought the child would live more than three weeks with him. Brigida, tell me what she looks like."

"She has Adelheid's fine limbs and black eyes, and curly hair like Tobias and the old man. I think she looks like both of them."

While the women were talking, Heidi had been taking in everything. Then she said: "Grandmother, look at the shutter over there. It is hanging loose. If grandfather were here, he would fasten it. It will break the window-pane! Just look at it."

"What a sweet child you are," said the grandmother tenderly. "I can hear it, but I cannot see it, child. This cottage rattles and creaks, and when the wind blows, it comes in through every chink.

70

Some day the whole house will break to pieces and fall on top of us. If only Peter knew how to mend it! We have no one else."

"Why, grandmother, can't you see the shutter?" asked Heidi.

"Child, I cannot see anything," lamented the old woman.

"Can you see it when I open the shutter to let in the light?"

"No, no, not even then. Nobody can ever show me the light again."

"But you can see when you go out into the snow, where everything is bright. Come with me, grandmother, I'll show you!" and Heidi, taking the old woman by the hand, tried to lead her out. Heidi was frightened and got more anxious all the time.

"Just let me stay here, child. Everything is dark for me, and my poor eyes can neither see the snow nor the light."

"But grandmother, does it not get light in the summer, when the sun shines down on the mountains to say good-night, setting them all aflame?"

"No, child, I can never see the fiery mountains any more. I have to live in darkness, always."

Day 41

1. New words:
   - **vivacity** — liveliness
   - **fret** — to worry
   - We can figure out how she sounded (and what fret meant) because it describes grandmother as "anxious."
2. Finish chapter 4. I started with a couple of sentences from last time.
3. How does Heidi help grandmother? (Answers)
4. How does Heidi's grandfather help Peter's grandmother? (Answers)

Chapter 4 continued

"But grandmother, does it not get light in the summer, when the sun shines down on the mountains to say good-night, setting them all aflame?"

"No, child, I can never see the fiery mountains any more. I have to live in darkness, always."

Heidi burst out crying now and sobbed aloud. "Can nobody make it light for you? Is there nobody who can do it, grandmother? Nobody?"

The grandmother tried all possible means to comfort the child; it wrung her heart to see her terrible distress. It was awfully hard for Heidi to stop crying when she had once begun, for she cried so seldom. The grandmother said: "Heidi, let me tell you something. People who cannot see love to listen to friendly words. Sit down beside me and tell me all about yourself. Talk to me about your grandfather, for it has been long since I have heard anything about him. I used to know him very well."

Heidi suddenly wiped away her tears, for she had had a cheering thought. "Grandmother, I shall tell grandfather about it, and I am sure he can make it light for you. He can mend your little house and stop the rattling."

The old woman remained silent, and Heidi, with the greatest vivacity, began to describe her life with the grandfather. Listening attentively, the two women would say to each other sometimes: "Do you hear what she says about the uncle? Did you listen?"

Heidi's tale was interrupted suddenly by a great thumping on the door; and who should come in but Peter. No sooner had he seen Heidi, than he smiled, opening his round eyes as wide as possible. Heidi called, "Good-evening, Peter!"

"Is it really time for him to come home!" exclaimed Peter's grandmother. "How quickly the time has flown. Good-evening, little Peter; how is your reading going?"

"Just the same," the boy replied.

"Oh, dear, I was hoping for a change at last. You are nearly twelve years old, my boy."

"Why should there be a change?" inquired Heidi with greatest interest.

"I am afraid he'll never learn it after all. On the shelf over there is an old prayer-book with beautiful songs. I have forgotten them all, for I do not hear them any more. I longed that Peter should read them to me some day, but he will never be able to!"

Peter's mother got up from her work now, saying, "I must make a light. The afternoon has passed and now it's getting dark."

When Heidi heard those words, she started, and holding out her hand to all, she said: "Good-night. I have to go, for it is getting dark." But the anxious grandmother called out: "Wait, child, don't go up alone! Go with her, Peter, and take care that she does not fall. Don't let her get cold, do you hear? Has Heidi a shawl?"

"I haven't, but I won't be cold," Heidi called back, for she had already escaped through the door. She ran so fast that Peter could hardly follow her. The old woman frettingly called out: "Brigida, run after her. Get a warm shawl, she'll freeze in this cold night. Hurry up!" Brigida obeyed. The children had hardly climbed any distance, when they saw the old man coming and with a few vigorous steps he stood beside them.

"I am glad you kept you word, Heidi," he said; and packing her into her cover, he started up the hill, carrying the child in his arms. Brigida had come in time to see it, and told the grandmother what she had witnessed.

"Thank God, thank God!" the old woman said. "I hope she'll come again; she has done me so much good! What a soft heart she has, the darling, and how nicely she can talk." All evening the grandmother said to herself, "If only he lets her come again! I have something to look forward to in this world now, thank God!"

Heidi could hardly wait before they reached the cottage. She had tried to talk on the way, but no sound could be heard through the heavy cover. As soon as they were inside the hut she began: "Grandfather, we must take some nails and a hammer down tomorrow; a shutter is loose in grandmother's house and many other places shake. Everything rattles in her house."

"Is that so? Who says we must?"

"Nobody told me, but I know," Heidi replied. "Everything is loose in the house, and poor grandmother told me she was afraid that the house might tumble down. And grandfather, she cannot see the light. Can you help her and make it light for her? How terrible it must be to be afraid in the dark and nobody there to help you! Oh, please, grandfather, do something to help her! I know you can."

Heidi had been clinging to her grandfather and looking up to him with trusting eyes. At last he said, glancing down: "All right, child, we'll see that it won't rattle any more. We can do it tomorrow."

Heidi was so overjoyed at these words that she danced around the room shouting: "We'll do it tomorrow! We can do it tomorrow!"

The grandfather, keeping his word, took Heidi down the following day with the same instructions as before. After Heidi had disappeared, he went around the house inspecting it.

The grandmother, in her joy at seeing the child again, had stopped the wheel and called: "Here is the child again! She has come again!" Heidi, grasping her outstretched hands, sat herself on a low stool at the old woman's feet and began to chat. Suddenly violent blows were heard outside; the grandmother in her fright nearly upset the spinning-wheel and screamed: "Oh, God, it has come at last. The hut is tumbling down!"

"Grandmother, don't be frightened," said the child, while she put her arms around her. "Grandfather is just fastening the shutter and fixing everything for you."

"Is it possible? Has God not forgotten us after all? Brigida, have you heard it? Surely that is a hammer. Ask him to come in a moment, if it is he, for I must thank him."

When Brigida went out, she found the old man busy with putting a new beam along the wall. Approaching him, she said: "Mother and I wish you a good-afternoon. We are very much obliged to you for doing us such a service, and mother would like to see you. There are few that would have done it, uncle, and how can we thank you?"

"That will do," he interrupted. "I know what your opinion about me is. Go in, for I can find what needs mending myself."

Brigida obeyed, for the uncle had a way that nobody could oppose. All afternoon the uncle hammered around; he even climbed up on the roof, where much was missing. At last he had to stop, for the last nail was gone from his pocket. The darkness had come in the meantime, and Heidi was ready to go up with him, packed warmly in his arms.

Thus the winter passed. Sunshine had come again into the blind woman's life, and made her days less dark and dreary. Early every morning she would begin to listen for Heidi's footsteps, and when the door was opened and the child ran in, the grandmother exclaimed every time more joyfully: "Thank God, she has come again!"

Heidi would talk about her life, and make the grandmother smile and laugh, and in that way the hours flew by. In former times the old woman had always sighed: "Brigida, is the day not over yet?" but now she always exclaimed after Heidi's departure: "How quickly the afternoon has gone by. Don't you think so, too, Brigida?" Her daughter had to assent, for Heidi had long ago won her heart. "If only God will spare us the child!" the grandmother would often say. "I hope the uncle will always be kind, as he is now."—"Does Heidi look well, Brigida?" was a frequent question, which always got a reassuring answer.

Heidi also became very fond of the old grandmother, and when the weather was fair, she visited her every day that winter. Whenever the child remembered that the grandmother was blind, she would get very sad; her only comfort was that her coming brought such happiness. The grandfather soon had mended the cottage; often he would take down big loads of timber, which he used to good purpose. The grandmother vowed that no rattling could be heard any more, and that, thanks to the uncle's kindness, she slept better that winter than she had done for many a year.

Day 42

1. This chapter is called "Two Visitors." Who do you think will come and visit them? (Answer before you read. You don't have to be right, but you do have to think.)
2. Read the beginning of chapter 5.
3. Who were the two visitors? (Answers)
4. What is Deta's "good news"? (Answers)
5. The lame girl cannot walk. She is in a rolling-chair. What do you think that is?

Chapter 5 TWO VISTIORS

Two winters had nearly passed. Heidi was happy, for the spring was coming again, with the soft delicious wind that made the fir-trees roar. Soon she would be able to go up to the pasture, where blue and yellow flowers greeted her at every step. She was nearly eight years old, and had learned to take care of the goats, who ran after her like little dogs. Several times the village teacher had sent word by Peter that the child was wanted in school, but the old man had not paid any attention to the message and had kept her with him as before. It was a beautiful morning in March. The snow had melted on the slopes, and was going fast. Snowdrops were peeping through the ground, which seemed to be getting ready for spring. Heidi was running to and fro before the door, when she suddenly saw an old gentleman, dressed in black, standing beside her. As she appeared frightened, he said kindly: "You must not be afraid of me, for I love children. Give me your hand, Heidi, and tell me where your grandfather is."

"He is inside, making round wooden spoons," the child replied, opening the door while she spoke.

It was the old pastor of the village, who had known the grandfather years ago. After entering, he approached the old man, saying: "Good-morning, neighbor."

The old man got up, surprised, and offering a seat to the visitor, said: "Good-morning, Mr. Parson. Here is a wooden chair, if it is good enough."

Sitting down, the parson said: "It is long since I have seen you, neighbor. I have come to-day to talk over a matter with you. I am sure you can guess what it is about."

The clergyman here looked at Heidi, who was standing near the door.

"Heidi, run out to see the goats," said the grandfather, "and bring them some salt; you can stay till I come."

Heidi disappeared on the spot. "The child should have come to school a year ago," the parson went on to say. "Didn't you get the teacher's warning? What do you intend to do with the child?"

"I do not want her to go to school," said the old man, unrelentingly.

75

"What do you want the child to be?"

"I want her to be free and happy as a bird!"

"But she is human, and it is high time for her to learn something. I have come now to tell you about it, so that you can make your plans. She must come to school next winter; remember that."

"I shan't do it, pastor!" was the reply.

"Do you think there is no way?" the clergyman replied, a little hotly. "You know the world, for you have travelled far. What little sense you show!"

"You think I am going to send this delicate child to school in every storm and weather!" the old man said excitedly. "It is a two hours' walk, and I shall not let her go; for the wind often howls so that it chokes me if I venture out. Did you know Adelheid, her mother? She was a sleep-walker, and had fainting-fits. Nobody shall compel me to let her go; I will gladly fight it out in court."

"You are perfectly right," said the clergyman kindly. "You could not send her to school from here. Why don't you come down to live among us again? You are leading a strange life here; I wonder how you can keep the child warm in winter."

"She has young blood and a good cover. I know where to find good wood, and all winter I keep a fire going. I couldn't live in the village, for the people there and I despise each other; we had better keep apart."

"You are mistaken, I assure you! Make your peace with God, and then you'll see how happy you will be."

The clergyman had risen, and holding out his hand, he said cordially: "I shall count on you next winter, neighbor. We shall receive you gladly, reconciled with God and man."

But the uncle replied firmly, while he shook his visitor by the hand: "Thank you for your kindness, but you will have to wait in vain."

"God be with you," said the parson, and left him sadly.

The old man was out of humor that day, and when Heidi begged to go to the grandmother, he only growled: "Not to-day." Next day they had hardly finished their dinner, when another visitor arrived. It was Heidi's aunt Deta; she wore a hat with feathers and a dress with such a train that it swept up everything that lay on the cottage floor. While the uncle looked at her silently, Deta began to praise him and the child's red cheeks. She told him that it had not been her intention to leave Heidi with him long, for she knew she must be in his way. She had tried to provide for the child elsewhere, and at last she had found a splendid chance for her. Very rich relations of her lady, who owned the largest house in Frankfurt, had a lame daughter. This poor little girl was confined to her rolling-chair and needed a companion at her lessons. Deta had heard from her lady that a sweet, quaint child was wanted as playmate and schoolmate for the invalid. She had gone to the housekeeper and told her all about Heidi. The lady, delighted with the idea, had told her to fetch the child at once. She had come now, and it was a lucky chance for Heidi, "for one never knew what might happen in such a case, and who could tell—"

Day 43

1. Finish reading chapter 5.
2. Vocabulary: Answer the questions below and then look up the definitions. (Answers)
   - **obstinate** — Deta called Heidi obstinate when she refused to come with her. What do you think obstinate might mean?
   - **infirm** — It says the grandmother was old and infirm. What do you think infirm might mean?
3. Why do you think that grandfather let Deta take Heidi? (Answers)
4. Heidi thinks she can come back the next day. Do you think Deta will bring her back whenever she wants? (Answers)

Chapter 5 continued

"Have you finished?" the old man interrupted her at last.

"Why, one might think I was telling you the silliest things. There is not a man in Prätiggan who would not thank God for such news."

"Bring them to somebody else, but not to me," said the uncle, coldly.

Deta, flaming up, replied: "Do you want to hear what I think? Don't I know how old she is; eight years old and ignorant of everything. They have told me that you refuse to send her to church and to school. She is my only sister's child, and I shall not bear it, for I am responsible. You do not care for her, how else could you be indifferent to such luck. You had better give way or I shall get the people to back me. If I were you, I would not have it brought to court; some things might be warmed up that you would not care to hear about."

"Be quiet!" the uncle thundered with flaming eyes. "Take her and ruin her, but do not bring her before my sight again. I do not want to see her with feathers in her hat and wicked words like yours."

With long strides he went out.

"You have made him angry!" said Heidi with a furious look.

"He won't be cross long. But come now, where are your things?" asked Deta.

"I won't come," Heidi replied.

"What?" Deta said passionately. But changing her tone, she continued in a more friendly manner: "Come now; you don't understand me. I am taking you to the most beautiful place you have ever seen." After packing up Heidi's clothes she said again, "Come, child, and take your hat. It is not very nice, but we can't help it."

"I shall not come," was the reply.

"Don't be stupid and obstinate, like a goat. Listen to me. Grandfather is sending us away and we must do what he commands, or he will get more angry still. You'll see how fine it is in Frankfurt. If you do not like it, you can come home again and by that time grandfather will have forgiven us."

"Can I come home again to-night?" asked Heidi.

"Come now, I told you you could come back. If we get to Mayenfeld today, we can take the train to-morrow. That will make you fly home again in the shortest time!"

Holding the bundle, Deta led the child down the mountain. On their way they met Peter, who had not gone to school that day. The boy thought it was a more useful occupation to look for hazel-rods than to learn to read, for he always needed the rods. He had had a most successful day, for he carried an enormous bundle on his shoulder. When he caught sight of Heidi and Deta, he asked them where they were going.

"I am going to Frankfurt with Aunt Deta," Heidi replied; "but first I must see grandmother, for she is waiting."

"Oh no, it is too late. You can see her when you come back, but not now," said Deta, pulling Heidi along with her, for she was afraid that the old woman might detain the child.

Peter ran into the cottage and hit the table with his rods. The grandmother jumped up in her fright and asked him what that meant.

"They have taken Heidi away," Peter said with a groan.

"Who has, Peter? Where has she gone?" the unhappy grandmother asked. Brigida had seen Deta walking up the footpath a short while ago and soon they guessed what had happened. With a trembling hand the old woman opened a window and called out as loudly as she could: "Deta, Deta, don't take the child away. Don't take her from us."

When Heidi heard that she struggled to get free, and said: "I must go to grandmother; she is calling me."

But Deta would not let her go. She urged her on by saying that she might return soon again. She also suggested that Heidi might bring a lovely present to the grandmother when she came back.

Heidi liked this prospect and followed Deta without more ado. After a while she asked: "What shall I bring to the grandmother?"

"You might bring her some soft white rolls, Heidi. I think the black bread is too hard for poor grandmother to eat."

"Yes, I know, aunt, she always gives it to Peter," Heidi confirmed her. "We must go quickly now; we might get to Frankfurt today and then I can be back tomorrow with the rolls."

Heidi was running now, and Deta had to follow. She was glad enough to escape the questions that people might ask her in the village. People could see that Heidi was pulling her along, so she said: "I can't stop. Don't you see how the child is hurrying? We have still far to go," whenever she heard from all sides: "Are you taking her with you?" "Is she running away from the uncle?" "What a wonder she is still alive!" "What red cheeks she has," and so on. Soon they had escaped and had left the village far behind them.

From that time on the uncle looked more angry than ever when he came to the village. Everybody was afraid of him, and the women would warn their children to keep out of his sight.

He came down but seldom, and then only to sell his cheese and buy his provisions. Often people remarked how lucky it was that Heidi had left him. They had seen her hurrying away, so they thought that she had been glad to go.

The old grandmother alone stuck to him faithfully. Whenever anybody came up to her, she would tell them what good care the old man had taken of Heidi. She also told them that he had mended her little house. These reports reached the village, of course, but people only half believed them, for the grandmother was infirm and old. She began her days with sighing again. "All happiness has left us with the child. The days are so long and dreary, and I have no joy left. If only I could hear Heidi's voice before I die," the poor old woman would exclaim, day after day.

Day 44

1. Peek ahead at the chapter title for today. What new things do you think might happen?
2. Read over the vocabulary and then read the chapter. Always be on the lookout for your vocabulary words as you read. You can look back to the vocabulary list here to help you remember what a word means.

- **indignant** – feeling upset over something that's not right
- **retort** – to answer back in an angry way
- **intimidate** – to fill someone with fear (It says that Deta is not easily intimidated. What does that mean?)
- **accost** – to confront boldly (This is how Heidi is told to speak to the servants. How do you think she was to talk to them?)
- **atrocious** – shockingly bad
3. Who is Clara? (Answers)
4. Who is Sebastian? (Answers)
5. Who is Miss Rottenmeier? (Answers)

Chapter 6 A NEW CHAPTER WITH NEW THINGS

In a beautiful house in Frankfurt lived a sick child by the name of Clara Sesemann. She was sitting in a comfortable rolling-chair, which could be pushed from room to room. Clara spent most of her time in the study, where long rows of bookcases lined the walls. This room was used as a living-room, and here she was also given her lessons.

Clara had a pale, thin face with soft blue eyes, which at that moment were watching the clock impatiently. At last she said: "Oh Miss Rottenmeier, isn't it time yet?"

The lady so addressed was the housekeeper, who had lived with Clara since Mrs. Sesemann's death. Miss Rottenmeier wore a peculiar uniform with a long cape, and a high cap on her head. Clara's father, who was away from home a great deal, left the entire management of the house to this lady, on the condition that his daughter's wishes should always be considered.

While Clara was waiting, Deta had arrived at the front door with Heidi. She was asking the coachman who had brought her if she could go upstairs.

"That's not my business," grumbled the coachman; "you must ring for the butler."

Sebastian, the butler, a man with large brass buttons on his coat, soon stood before her.

"May I see Miss Rottenmeier?" Deta asked.

"That's not my business," the butler announced. "Ring for Tinette, the maid." With that, he disappeared.

Deta, ringing again, saw a girl with a brilliant white cap on her head, coming down the stairway. The maid stopped half-way down and asked scornfully: "What do you want?"

Deta repeated her wish again. Tinette told her to wait while she went upstairs, but it did not take long before the two were asked to come up.

Following the maid, they found themselves in the study. Deta held on to Heidi's hand and stayed near the door.

Miss Rottenmeier, slowly getting up, approached the newcomers. She did not seem pleased with Heidi, who wore her hat and shawl and was looking up at the lady's headdress with innocent wonder.

"What is your name?" the lady asked.

"Heidi," was the child's clear answer.

"What? Is that a Christian name? What name did you receive in baptism?" inquired the lady again.

"I don't remember that any more," the child replied.

"What an answer! What does that mean?" said the housekeeper, shaking her head. "Is the child ignorant or pert, Miss Deta?"

"I shall speak for the child, if I may, madam," Deta said, after giving Heidi a little blow for her unbecoming answer. "The child has never been in such a fine house and does not know how to behave. I hope the lady will forgive her manners. She is called Adelheid after her mother, who was my sister."

"Oh well, that is better. But Miss Deta, the child seems peculiar for her age. I thought I told you that Miss Clara's companion would have to be twelve years old like her, to be able to share her studies. How old is Adelheid?"

"I am sorry, but I am afraid she is somewhat younger than I thought. I think she is about ten years old."

"Grandfather said that I was eight years old," said Heidi now. Deta gave her another blow, but as the child had no idea why, she did not get embarrassed.

"What, only eight years old!" Miss Rottenmeier exclaimed indignantly. "How can we get along? What have you learned? What books have you studied?"

"None," said Heidi.

"But how did you learn to read?"

"I can't read and Peter can't do it either," Heidi retorted.

"For mercy's sake! you cannot read?" cried the lady in her surprise. "How is it possible? What else have you studied?"

"Nothing," replied Heidi, truthfully.

"Miss Deta, how could you bring this child?" said the housekeeper, when she was more composed.

Deta, however, was not easily intimidated, and said: "I am sorry, but I thought this child would suit you. She *is* small, but older children are often spoilt and not like her. I must go now, for my mistress is waiting. As soon as I can, I'll come to see how the child is getting along." With a bow she was outside and with a few quick steps hurried down-stairs.

Miss Rottenmeier followed her and tried to call her back, for she wanted to ask Deta a number of questions.

Heidi was still standing on the same spot. Clara had watched the scene, and called to the child now to come to her.

Heidi approached the rolling-chair.

"Do you want to be called Heidi or Adelheid?" asked Clara.

"My name is Heidi and nothing else," was the child's answer.

"I'll call you Heidi then, for I like it very much," said Clara. "I have never heard the name before. What curly hair you have! Was it always like that?"

"I think so."

"Did you like to come to Frankfurt?" asked Clara again.

"Oh, no, but then I am going home again to-morrow, and shall bring grandmother some soft white rolls," Heidi explained.

"What a curious child you are," said Clara. "You have come to Frankfurt to stay with me, don't you know that? We shall have our lessons together, and I think it will be great fun when you learn to read. Generally the morning seems to have no end, for Mr. Candidate comes at ten and stays till two. That is a long time, and he has to yawn himself, he gets so tired. Miss Rottenmeier and he both yawn together behind their books, but when I do it, Miss Rottenmeier makes me take cod-liver oil and says that I am ill. So I must swallow my yawns, for I hate the oil. What fun it will be now, when you learn to read!"

Heidi shook her head doubtfully at these prospects.

"Everybody must learn to read, Heidi. Mr. Candidate is very patient and will explain it all to you. You won't know what he means at first, for it is difficult to understand him. It won't take long to learn, though, and then you will know what he means."

When Miss Rottenmeier found that she was unable to recall Deta, she came back to the children. She was in a very excited mood, for she felt responsible for Heidi's coming and did not know how to cancel this unfortunate step. She soon got up again to go to the dining-room, criticising the butler and giving orders to the maid. Sebastian, not daring to show his rage otherwise, noisily opened the folding doors. When he went up to Clara's chair, he saw Heidi watching him intently. At last she said: "You look like Peter."

Miss Rottenmeier was horrified with this remark, and sent them all into the dining-room. After Clara was lifted on to her chair, the housekeeper sat down beside her. Heidi was motioned to sit opposite the lady. In that way they were placed at the enormous table. When Heidi saw a roll on her plate, she turned to Sebastian, and pointing at it, asked, "Can I have this?" Heidi had already great confidence in the butler, especially on account of the resemblance she had discovered. The butler nodded, and when he saw Heidi put the bread in her pocket, could hardly keep from laughing. He came to Heidi now with a dish of small baked fishes. For a long time the child did not move; then turning her eyes to the butler, she said: "Must I eat that?" Sebastian nodded, but another pause ensued. "Why don't you give it to me?" the child quietly asked, looking at her plate. The butler, hardly able to keep his countenance, was told to place the dish on the table and leave the room.

When he was gone, Miss Rottenmeier explained to Heidi with many signs how to help herself at table. She also told her never to speak to Sebastian unless it was important. After that the child was told how to accost the servants and the governess. When the question came up of how to call Clara, the older girl said, "Of course you shall call me Clara."

A great many rules followed now about behavior at all times, about the shutting of doors and about going to bed, and a hundred other things. Poor Heidi's eyes were closing, for she had risen at five that morning, and leaning against her chair she fell asleep. When Miss Rottenmeier had finished instructions, she said: "I hope you will remember everything, Adelheid. Did you understand me?"

"Heidi went to sleep a long time ago," said Clara, highly amused.

"It is atrocious what I have to bear with this child," exclaimed Miss Rottenmeier, ringing the bell with all her might. When the two servants arrived, they were hardly able to rouse Heidi enough to show her to her bed-room.

Day 45

1. Vocabulary:
   - **perplexity** — confusion
2. Begin reading chapter 7.
3. What do you think Heidi is going to do? (Answers)
4. What was Heidi perplexed about? (Answers)

Vocabulary

1. Match the words to their definitions. Write the matching letters and numbers on a separate piece of paper. (Answers)

1.	perplexity	A.	to answer back in an angry way
2.	indignant	B.	to confront boldly
3.	vivacity	C.	upset over something that's not right
4.	atrocious	D.	to fill someone with fear
5.	obstinate	E.	confusion
6.	retort	F.	liveliness
7.	accost	G.	weak, sickly, frail
8.	intimidate	H.	shockingly bad
9.	fret	I.	stubborn
10.	infirm	J.	to worry

Chapter 7 MISS ROTTENMEIER HAS AN UNCOMFORTABLE DAY

When Heidi opened her eyes next morning, she did not know where she was. She found herself on a high white bed in a spacious room. Looking around she observed long white curtains before the windows, several chairs, and a sofa covered with cretonne; in a corner she saw a wash-stand with many curious things standing on it.

Suddenly Heidi remembered all the happenings of the previous day. Jumping out of bed, she dressed in a great hurry. She was eager to look at the sky and the ground below, as she had always done at home. What was her disappointment when she found that the windows were too high for her to see anything except the walls and windows opposite. Trying to open them, she turned from one to the other, but in vain. The poor child felt like a little bird that is placed in a glittering cage for the first time. At last she had to resign herself, and sat down on a low stool, thinking of the melting snow on the slopes and the first flowers of spring that she had hailed with such delight.

Suddenly Tinette opened the door and said curtly: "Breakfast's ready."

Heidi did not take this for a summons, for the maid's face was scornful and forbidding. She was waiting patiently for what would happen next, when Miss Rottenmeier burst into the room, saying: "What is the matter, Adelheid? Didn't you understand? Come to breakfast!"

Heidi immediately followed the lady into the dining-room, where Clara greeted her with a smile. She looked much happier than usual, for she expected new things to happen that day. When breakfast had passed without disturbance, the two children were allowed to go into the library together and were soon left alone.

"How can I see down to the ground?" Heidi asked.

"Open a window and peep out," replied Clara, amused at the question.

"But it is impossible to open them," Heidi said, sadly.

"Oh no. You can't do it and I can't help you, either, but if you ask Sebastian he'll do it for you."

Heidi was relieved. The poor child had felt like a prisoner in her room. Clara now asked Heidi what her home had been like, and Heidi told her gladly about her life in the hut.

The tutor had arrived in the meantime, but he was not asked to go to the study as usual. Miss Rottenmeier was very much excited about Heidi's coming and all the complications that arose therefrom. She was really responsible for it, having arranged everything herself. She presented the unfortunate case before the teacher, for she wanted him to help her to get rid of the child. Mr. Candidate, however, was always careful of his judgments, and not afraid of teaching beginners.

When the lady saw that he would not side with her, she let him enter the study alone, for the A,B,C held great horrors for her. While she considered many problems, a frightful noise as of something falling was heard in the adjoining room, followed by a cry to Sebastian for help. Running in, she beheld a pile of books and papers on the floor, with the table-cover on top. A black stream of ink flowed across the length of the room. Heidi had disappeared.

"There," Miss Rottenmeier exclaimed, wringing her hands. "Everything drenched with ink. Did such a thing ever happen before? This child brings nothing but misfortunes on us."

The teacher was standing up, looking at the devastation, but Clara was highly entertained by these events, and said: "Heidi has not done it on purpose and must not be punished. In her hurry to get away she caught on the table-cover and pulled it down. I think she must never have seen a coach in all her life, for when she heard a carriage rumbling by, she rushed out like mad."

"Didn't I tell you, Mr. Candidate, that she has no idea whatever about behavior? She does not even know that she has to sit quiet at her lessons. But where has she gone? What would Mr. Sesemann say if she should run away?"

When Miss Rottenmeier went down-stairs to look for the child, she saw her standing at the open door, looking down the street.

"What are you doing here? How can you run away like that?" scolded Miss Rottenmeier.

"I heard the fir-trees rustle, but I can't see them and do not hear them any more," replied Heidi, looking in great perplexity down the street. The noise of the passing carriage had reminded her of the roaring of the south-wind on the Alp.

"Fir-trees? What nonsense! We are not in a wood. Come with me now to see what you have done." When Heidi saw the devastation that she had caused, she was greatly surprised, for she had not noticed it in her hurry.

"This must never happen again," said the lady sternly. "You must sit quiet at your lessons; if you get up again I shall tie you to your chair. Do you hear me?"

Heidi understood, and gave a promise to sit quietly during her lessons from that time on. After the servants had straightened the room, it was late, and there was no more time for studies. Nobody had time to yawn that morning.

In the afternoon, while Clara was resting, Heidi was left to herself. She planted herself in the hall and waited for the butler to come up-stairs with the silver things. When he reached the head of the stairs, she said to him: "I want to ask you something." She saw that the butler seemed angry, so she reassured him by saying that she did not mean any harm.

"All right, Miss, what is it?"

"My name is not Miss, why don't you call me Heidi?"

"Miss Rottenmeier told me to call you Miss."

"Did she? Well then, it must be so. I have three names already," sighed the child.

"What can I do for you?" asked Sebastian now.

"Can you open a window for me?"

"Certainly," he replied.

Sebastian got a stool for Heidi, for the window-sill was too high for her to see over. In great disappointment, Heidi turned her head away.

"I don't see anything but a street of stone. Is it the same way on the other side of the house?"

"Yes."

"Where do you go to look far down on everything?"

"On a church-tower. Do you see that one over there with the golden dome? From there you can overlook everything."

Day 46

1. Vocabulary:
    - **loath** (low – the)
    - Loath means unwilling or reluctant.
2. Finish reading chapter 7. I started with a little from the day before. I may do that from time to time without announcing it.
3. What was Heidi loath to give up? (Answers)
4. What did Heidi see from the tower? (Answers)
5. What did Heidi bring home with her? (Answers)

Chapter 7 continued

"Where do you go to look far down on everything?"

"On a church-tower. Do you see that one over there with the golden dome? From there you can overlook everything."

Heidi immediately stepped down from the stool and ran down-stairs. Opening the door, she found herself in the street, but she could not see the tower any more. She wandered on from street to street, not daring to accost any of the busy people. Passing a corner, she saw a boy who had a barrel-organ on his back and a curious animal on his arm. Heidi ran to him and asked: "Where is the tower with the golden dome?"

"Don't know," was the reply.

"Who can tell me?"

"Don't know."

"Can you show me another church with a tower?"

"Of course I can."

"Then come and show me."

"What are you going to give me for it?" said the boy, holding out his hand. Heidi had nothing in her pocket but a little flower-picture. Clara had only given it to her this morning, so she was loath to part with it. The temptation to look far down into the valley was too great for her, though, and she offered him the gift. The boy shook his head, to Heidi's satisfaction.

"What else do you want?"

"Money."

"I have none, but Clara has some. How much must I give you?"

"Twenty pennies."

"All right, but come."

While they were wandering down the street, Heidi found out what a barrel-organ was, for she had never seen one. When they arrived before an old church with a tower, Heidi was puzzled what to do next, but having discovered a bell, she pulled it with all her might. The boy agreed to wait for Heidi and show her the way home if she gave him a double fee.

The lock creaked now from inside, and an old man opened the door. In an angry voice, he said: "How do you dare to ring for me? Can't you see that it is only for those who want to see the tower?"

"But I do," said Heidi.

"What do you want to see? Did anybody send you?" asked the man.

"No; but I want to look down from up there."

"Get home and don't try it again." With that the tower-keeper was going to shut the door, but Heidi held his coat-tails and pleaded with him to let her come. The tower-keeper looked at the child's eyes, which were nearly full of tears.

"All right, come along, if you care so much," he said, taking her by the hand. The two climbed up now many, many steps, which got narrower all the time. When they had arrived on top, the old man lifted Heidi up to the open window.

Heidi saw nothing but a sea of chimneys, roofs and towers, and her heart sank. "Oh, dear, it's different from the way I thought it would be," she said.

"There! what could such a little girl know about a view? We'll go down now and you must promise never to ring at my tower any more."

On their way they passed an attic, where a large grey cat guarded her new family in a basket. This cat caught half-a-dozen mice every day for herself, for the old tower was full of rats and mice. Heidi gazed at her in surprise, and was delighted when the old man opened the basket.

"What charming kittens, what cunning little creatures!" she exclaimed in her delight, when she saw them crawling about, jumping and tumbling.

"Would you like to have one?" the old man asked.

"For me? to keep?" Heidi asked, for she could not believe her ears.

"Yes, of course. You can have several if you have room for them," the old man said, glad to find a good home for the kittens.

How happy Heidi was! Of course there was enough room in the huge house, and Clara would be delighted when she saw the cunning things.

"How can I take them with me?" the child asked, after she had tried in vain to catch one.

"I can bring them to your house, if you tell me where you live," said Heidi's new friend, while he caressed the old cat, who had lived with him many years.

"Bring them to Mr. Sesemann's house; there is a golden dog on the door, with a ring in his mouth."

The old man had lived in the tower a long time and knew everybody; Sebastian also was a special friend of his.

"I know," he said. "But to whom shall I send them? Do you belong to Mr. Sesemann?"

"No. Please send them to Clara; she will like them, I am sure."

Heidi could hardly tear herself away from the pretty things, so the old man put one kitten in each of her pockets to console her. After that she went away.

The boy was waiting patiently for her, and when she had taken leave of the tower-keeper, she asked the boy: "Do you know where Mr. Sesemann's house is?"

"No," was the reply.

She described it as well as she could, till the boy remembered it. Off they started, and soon Heidi found herself pulling the door-bell. When Sebastian arrived he said: "Hurry up." Heidi went in, and the boy was left outside, for Sebastian had not even seen him.

"Come up quickly, little Miss," he urged. "They are all waiting for you in the dining-room. Miss Rottenmeier looks like a loaded cannon. How could you run away like that?"

Heidi sat down quietly on her chair. Nobody said a word, and there was an uncomfortable silence. At last Miss Rottenmeier began with a severe and solemn voice: "I shall speak with you later, Adelheid. How can you leave the house without a word? Your behavior was very remiss. The idea of walking about till so late!"

"Meow!" was the reply.

"I didn't," Heidi began—"Meow!"

Sebastian nearly flung the dish on the table, and disappeared.

"This is enough," Miss Rottenmeier tried to say, but her voice was hoarse with fury. "Get up and leave the room."

Heidi got up. She began again. "I made—" "Meow! meow! meow!—"

"Heidi," said Clara now, "why do you always say 'meow' again, if you see that Miss Rottenmeier is angry?"

"I am not doing it, it's the kittens," she explained.

"What? Cats? Kittens?" screamed the housekeeper. "Sebastian, Tinette, take the horrible things away!" With that she ran into the study, locking herself in, for she feared kittens beyond anything on earth. When Sebastian had finished his laugh, he came into the room. He had foreseen the excitement, having caught sight of the kittens when Heidi came in. The scene was a very peaceful one now; Clara held the little kittens in her lap, and Heidi was kneeling beside her. They both played happily with the two graceful creatures. The butler promised to look after the new-comers and prepared a bed for them in a basket.

A long time afterwards, when it was time to go to bed, Miss Rottenmeier cautiously opened the door. "Are they away?" she asked. "Yes," replied the butler, quickly seizing the kittens and taking them away.

The lecture that Miss Rottenmeier was going to give Heidi was postponed to the following day, for the lady was too much exhausted after her fright. They all went quietly to bed, and the children were happy in the thought that their kittens had a comfortable bed.

Day 47

1. Read chapter 8.
2. Why is Heidi's heart so sad? (Answers)
3. What does Sebastian save for her? (Answers)

Chapter 8 THERE ARE GREAT DISTURBANCES IN THE SESEMANN HOUSE

A short time after the tutor had arrived next morning, the door-bell rang so violently that Sebastian thought it must be Mr. Sesemann himself. What was his surprise when a dirty street-boy, with a barrel-organ on his back, stood before him!

"What do you mean by pulling the bell like that?" the butler said.

"I want to see Clara."

"Can't you at least say 'Miss Clara', you ragged urchin?" said Sebastian harshly.

"She owes me forty pennies," said the boy.

"You are crazy! How do you know Miss Clara lives here?"

"I showed her the way yesterday and she promised to give me forty pennies."

"What nonsense! Miss Clara never goes out. You had better take yourself off, before I send you!"

The boy, however, did not even budge, and said: "I saw her. She has curly hair, black eyes and talks in a funny way."

"Oh," Sebastian chuckled to himself, "that was the little Miss."

Pulling the boy into the house, he said: "All right, you can follow me. Wait at the door till I call you, and then you can play something for Miss Clara."

Knocking at the study-door, Sebastian said, when he had entered: "A boy is here who wants to see Miss Clara."

Clara, delighted at his interruption, said: "Can't he come right up, Mr. Candidate?"

But the boy was already inside, and started to play. Miss Rottenmeier was in the adjoining room when she heard the sounds. Where did they come from? Hurrying into the study, she saw the street-boy playing to the eager children.

"Stop! stop!" she called, but in vain, for the music drowned her voice. Suddenly she made a big jump, for there, between her feet, crawled a black turtle. Only when she shrieked for Sebastian could her voice be heard. The butler came straight in, for he had seen everything behind the door, and a great scene it had been! Glued to a chair in her fright, Miss Rottenmeier called: "Send the boy away! Take them away!"

Sebastian obediently pulled the boy after him; then he said: "Here are forty pennies from Miss Clara and forty more for playing. It was well done, my boy."

With that he closed the door behind him. Miss Rottenmeier found it wiser now to stay in the study to prevent further disturbances. Suddenly there was another knock at the door. Sebastian appeared with a large basket, which had been brought for Clara.

"We had better have our lesson before we inspect it," said Miss Rottenmeier. But Clara, turning to the tutor, asked: "Oh, please, Mr. Candidate, can't we just peep in, to see what it is?"

"I am afraid that you will think of nothing else," the teacher began. Just then something in the basket, which had been only lightly fastened, moved, and one, two, three and still more little kittens jumped out, scampering around the room with the utmost speed. They bounded over the tutor's boots and bit his trousers; they climbed up on Miss Rottenmeier's dress and crawled around her feet. Mewing and running, they caused a frightful confusion. Clara called out in delight: "Oh, look at the cunning creatures; look how they jump! Heidi, look at that one, and oh, see the one over there?"

Heidi followed them about, while the teacher shook them off. When the housekeeper had collected her wits after the great fright, she called for the servants. They soon arrived and stored the little kittens safely in the new bed.

No time had been found for yawning that day, either!

When Miss Rottenmeier, who had found out the culprit, was alone with the children in the evening, she began severely:

"Adelheid, there is only one punishment for you. I am going to send you to the cellar, to think over your dreadful misdeeds, in company with the rats."

A cellar held no terrors for Heidi, for in her grandfather's cellar fresh milk and the good cheese had been kept, and no rats had lodged there.

But Clara shrieked: "Oh, Miss Rottenmeier, you must wait till Papa comes home, and then he can punish Heidi."

The lady unwillingly replied: "All right, Clara, but I shall also speak a few words to Mr. Sesemann." With those words she left the room. Since the child's arrival everything had been upset, and the lady often felt discouraged, though nothing remarkable happened for a few days.

Clara, on the contrary, enjoyed her companion's society, for she always did funny things. In her lesson she could never get her letters straight. They meant absolutely nothing to her, except that they would remind her of goats and eagles. The girls always spent their evenings together, and Heidi would entertain her friend with tales of her former life, till her longing grew so great that she added: "I have to go home now. I must go tomorrow."

Clara's soothing words and the prospect of more rolls for the grandmother kept the child. Every day after dinner she was left alone in her room for some hours. Thinking of the green fields at home, of the sparkling flowers on the mountains, she would sit in a corner till her desire for all those things became too great to bear. Her aunt had clearly told her that she might return, if she wished to do so, so one day she resolved to leave for the Alm-hut. In a great hurry she packed the bread in the red shawl, and putting on her old straw hat, started off. The poor child did not get very far. At the door she encountered Miss Rottenmeier, who stared at Heidi in mute surprise.

"What are you up to?" she exploded. "Haven't I forbidden you to run away? You look like a vagabond!"

"I was only going home," whispered the frightened child.

"What, you want to run away from this house? What would Mr. Sesemann say? What is it that does not suit you here? Don't you get better treatment than you deserve? Have you ever before had such food, service and such a room? Answer!"

"No," was the reply.

"Don't I know that?" the furious lady proceeded. "What a thankless child you are, just idle and good-for-nothing!"

But Heidi could not bear it any longer. She loudly wailed: "Oh, I want to go home. What will poor Snowhopper do without me? Grandmother is waiting for me every day. Poor Thistlefinch gets blows if Peter gets no cheese, and I must see the sun again when he says good-night to the mountains. How the eagle would screech if he saw all the people here in Frankfurt!"

"For mercy's sake, the child is crazy!" exclaimed Miss Rottenmeier, running up the stairs. In her hurry she had bumped into Sebastian, who was just then coming down.

"Bring the unlucky child up!" she called to him, rubbing her head.

"All right, many thanks," answered the butler, rubbing his head, too, for he had encountered something far harder than she had.

When the butler came down, he saw Heidi standing near the door with flaming eyes, trembling all over. Cheerfully he asked: "What has happened, little one? Do not take it to heart, and cheer up. She nearly made a hole in my head just now, but we must not get discouraged. Oh, no!— Come, up with you; she said so!"

Heidi walked up-stairs very slowly. Seeing her so changed, Sebastian said: "Don't give in! Don't be so sad! You have been so courageous till now; I have never heard you cry yet. Come up now, and when the lady's away we'll go and look at the kittens. They are running round like wild!"

Nodding cheerlessly, the child disappeared in her room.

That night at supper Miss Rottenmeier watched Heidi constantly, but nothing happened. The child sat as quiet as a mouse, hardly touching her food, except the little roll.

Talking with the tutor next morning, Miss Rottenmeier told him her fears about Heidi's mind. But the teacher had more serious troubles still, for Heidi had not even learned her A,B,C in all this time.

Heidi was sorely in need of some clothes, so Clara had given her some. Miss Rottenmeier was just busy arranging the child's wardrobe, when she suddenly returned.

"Adelheid," she said contemptuously, "what do I find? A big pile of bread in your wardrobe! I never heard the like. Yes, Clara, it is true." Then, calling Tinette, she ordered her to take away the bread and the old straw hat she had found.

"No, don't! I must keep my hat! The bread is for grandmother," cried Heidi in despair.

"You stay here, while we take the rubbish away," said the lady sternly.

Heidi threw herself down now on Clara's chair and sobbed as if her heart would break.

"Now I can't bring grandmother any rolls! Oh, they were for grandmother!" she lamented.

"Heidi, don't cry any more," Clara begged. "Listen! When you go home some day, I am going to give you as many rolls as you had, and more. They will be much softer and better than those stale ones you have kept. Those were not fit to eat, Heidi. Stop now, please, and don't cry any more!"

Only after a long, long time did Heidi become quiet. When she had heard Clara's promise, she cried: "Are you really going to give me as many as I had?"

At supper, Heidi's eyes were swollen and it was still hard for her to keep from crying. Sebastian made strange signs to her that she did not understand. What did he mean?

Later, though, when she climbed into her high bed, she found her old beloved straw hat hidden under her cover. So Sebastian had saved it for her and had tried to tell her! She crushed it for joy, and wrapping it in a handkerchief, she hid it in the furthest corner of her wardrobe.

Day 48

1. Read chapter 9.
2. Who came home? (Answers)
3. Who is coming to live at the house? (Answers)

Chapter 9 THE MASTER OF THE HOUSE HEARS OF STRANGE DOINGS

A few days afterwards there was great excitement in the Sesemann residence, for the master of the house had just arrived. The servants were taking upstairs one load after another, for Mr. Sesemann always brought many lovely things home with him.

When he entered his daughter's room, Heidi shyly retreated into a corner. He greeted Clara affectionately, and she was equally delighted to see him, for she loved her father dearly. Then he called to Heidi: "Oh, there is our little Swiss girl. Come and give me your hand! That's right. Are you good friends, my girls, tell me now? You don't fight together, what?"

"Oh, no, Clara is always kind to me," Heidi replied.

"Heidi has never even tried to fight, Papa," Clara quickly remarked.

"That's good, I like to hear that," said the father rising. "I must get my dinner now, for I am hungry. I shall come back soon and show you what I have brought home with me."

In the dining-room he found Miss Rottenmeier surveying the table with a most tragic face. "You do not look very happy at my arrival, Miss Rottenmeier. What is the matter? Clara seems well enough," he said to her.

"Oh, Mr. Sesemann, we have been terribly disappointed," said the lady.

"How do you mean?" asked Mr. Sesemann, calmly sipping his wine.

"We had decided, as you know, to have a companion for Clara. Knowing as I did that you would wish me to get a noble, pure child, I thought of this Swiss child, hoping she would go through life like a breath of pure air, hardly touching the earth."

"I think that even Swiss children are made to touch the earth, otherwise they would have to have wings."

"I think you understand what I mean. I have been terribly disappointed, for this child has brought the most frightful animals into the house. Mr. Candidate can tell you!"

"The child does not look very terrible. But what do you mean?"

"I cannot explain it, because she does not seem in her right mind at times."

Mr. Sesemann was getting worried at last, when the tutor entered.

"Oh, Mr. Candidate, I hope you will explain. Please take a cup of coffee with me and tell me about my daughter's companion. Make it short, if you please!"

But this was impossible for Mr. Candidate, who had to greet Mr. Sesemann first. Then he began to reassure his host about the child, pointing out to him that her education had been neglected till then, and so on. But poor Mr. Sesemann, unfortunately, did not get his answer, and had to listen to very long-winded explanations of the child's character. At last Mr. Sesemann got up, saying: "Excuse me, Mr. Candidate, but I must go over to Clara now."

He found the children in the study. Turning to Heidi, who had risen at his approach, he said: "Come, little one, get me—get me a glass of water."

"Fresh water?"

"Of course, fresh water," he replied. When Heidi had gone, he sat down near Clara, holding her hand. "Tell me, little Clara," he asked, "please tell me clearly what animals Heidi has brought into the house; is she really not right in her mind?"

Clara now began to relate to her father all the incidents with the kittens and the turtle, and explained Heidi's speeches that had so frightened the lady. Mr. Sesemann laughed heartily and asked Clara if she wished Heidi to remain.

"Of course, Papa. Since she is here, something amusing happens every day; it used to be so dull, but now Heidi keeps me company."

"Very good, very good, Clara; Oh! Here is your friend back again. Did you get nice fresh water?" asked Mr. Sesemann.

Heidi handed him the glass and said: "Yes, fresh from the fountain."

"You did not go to the fountain yourself, Heidi?" said Clara.

"Certainly, but I had to get it from far, there were so many people at the first and at the second fountain. I had to go down another street and there I got it. A gentleman with white hair sends his regards to you, Mr. Sesemann."

Clara's father laughed and asked: "Who was the gentleman?"

"When he passed by the fountain and saw me there with a glass, he stood still and said: 'Please give me to drink, for you have a glass; to whom are you bringing the water?' Then I said: 'I am bringing it to Mr. Sesemann.' When he heard that he laughed very loud and gave me his regards for you, with the wish that you would enjoy your drink."

"I wonder who it was? What did the gentleman look like?"

"He has a friendly laugh and wears a gold pendant with a red stone on his thick gold chain; there is a horsehead on his cane."

"Oh, that was the doctor—" "That was my old doctor," exclaimed father and daughter at the same time.

In the evening, Mr. Sesemann told Miss Rottenmeier that Heidi was going to remain, for the children were very fond of each other and he found Heidi normal and very sweet. "I want the child to be treated kindly," Mr. Sesemann added decidedly. "Her peculiarities must not be punished. My mother is coming very soon to stay here, and she will help you to manage the child, for there is nobody in this world that my mother could not get along with, as you know, Miss Rottenmeier."

"Of course, I know that, Mr. Sesemann," replied the lady, but she was not very much pleased at the prospect.

Mr. Sesemann only stayed two weeks, for his business called him back to Paris. He consoled his daughter by telling her that his mother was coming in a very few days. Mr. Sesemann had hardly left, when the grandmother's visit was announced for the following day.

Clara was looking forward to this visit, and told Heidi so much about her dear grandmama that Heidi also began to call her by that name, to Miss Rottenmeier's disapproval, who thought that the child was not entitled to this intimacy.

Day 49

1. Read chapter 10.
2. Tell someone about this chapter. What is Heidi's big accomplishment? (Answers)

Chapter 10 A GRANDMAMA

The following evening great expectation reigned in the house. Tinette had put on a new cap, Sebastian was placing footstools in front of nearly every armchair, and Miss Rottenmeier walked with great dignity about the house, inspecting everything.

When the carriage at last drove up, the servants flew downstairs, followed by Miss Rottenmeier in more measured step. Heidi had been sent to her room to await further orders, but it was not long before Tinette opened the door and said brusquely: "Go into the study!"

The grandmama, with her kind and loving way, immediately befriended the child and made her feel as if she had known her always. To the housekeeper's great mortification, she called the child Heidi, remarking to Miss Rottenmeier: "If somebody's name is Heidi, I call her so."

The housekeeper soon found that she had to respect the grandmother's ways and opinions. Mrs. Sesemann always knew what was going on in the house the minute she entered it. On the following afternoon Clara was resting and the old lady had shut her eyes for five minutes, when she got up again and went into the dining-room. With a suspicion that the housekeeper was probably asleep, she went to this lady's room, knocking loudly on the door. After a while somebody stirred inside, and with a bewildered face Miss Rottenmeier appeared, staring at the unexpected visitor.

"Rottenmeier, where is the child? How does she pass her time? I want to know," said Mrs. Sesemann.

"She just sits in her room, not moving a finger; she has not the slightest desire to do something useful, and that is why she thinks of such absurd things that one can hardly mention them in polite society."

"I should do exactly the same thing, if I were left alone like that. Please bring her to my room now, I want to show her some pretty books I have brought with me."

"That is just the trouble. What should she do with books? In all this time she has not even learned the A,B,C for it is impossible to instil any knowledge into this being. If Mr. Candidate was not as patient as an angel, he would have given up teaching her long ago."

"How strange! The child does not look to me like one who cannot learn the A,B,C," said Mrs. Sesemann. "Please fetch her now; we can look at the pictures anyway."

The housekeeper was going to say more, but the old lady had turned already and gone to her room. She was thinking over what she had heard about Heidi, making up her mind to look into the matter.

Heidi had come and was looking with wondering eyes at the splendid pictures in the large books, that Grandmama was showing her. Suddenly she screamed aloud, for there on the picture she saw a peaceful flock grazing on a green pasture. In the middle a shepherd was standing, leaning on his crook. The setting sun was shedding a golden light over everything. With glowing eyes Heidi devoured the scene; but suddenly she began to sob violently.

The grandmama took her little hand in hers and said in the most soothing voice: "Come, child, you must not cry. Did this remind you of something? Now stop, and I'll tell you the story to-night. There are lovely stories in this book, that people can read and tell. Dry your tears now, darling, I must ask you something. Stand up now and look at me! Now we are merry again!"

Heidi did not stop at once, but the kind lady gave her ample time to compose herself, saying from time to time: "Now it's all over. Now we'll be merry again."

When the child was quiet at last, she said: "Tell me now how your lessons are going. What have you learnt, child, tell me?"

"Nothing," Heidi sighed; "but I knew that I never could learn it."

"What is it that you can't learn?"

"I can't learn to read; it is too hard."

"What next? Who gave you this information?"

"Peter told me, and he tried over and over again, but he could not do it, for it is too hard."

"Well, what kind of boy is he? Heidi, you must not believe what Peter tells you, but try for yourself. I am sure you had your thoughts elsewhere when Mr. Candidate showed you the letters."

"It's no use," Heidi said with such a tone as if she was resigned to her fate.

"I am going to tell you something, Heidi," said the kind lady now. "You have not learnt to read because you have believed what Peter said. You shall believe me now, and I prophesy that you will learn it in a very short time, as a great many other children do that are like you and not like Peter. When you can read, I am going to give you this book. You have seen the shepherd on the green pasture, and then you'll be able to find out all the strange things that happen to him. Yes, you can hear the whole story, and what he does with his sheep and his goats. You would like to know, wouldn't you, Heidi?"

Heidi had listened attentively, and said now with sparkling eyes: "If I could only read already!"

"It won't be long, I can see that. Come now and let us go to Clara." With that they both went over to the study.

Since the day of Heidi's attempted flight a great change had come over the child. She had realized that it would hurt her kind friends if she tried to go home again. She knew now that she could not leave, as her Aunt Deta had promised, for they all, especially Clara and her father and the old lady, would think her ungrateful. But the burden grew heavier in her heart and she lost her appetite, and got paler and paler. She could not get to sleep at night from longing to see the mountains with the flowers and the sunshine, and only in her dreams she would be happy. When she woke up in the morning, she always found herself on her high white bed, far away from home. Burying her head in her pillow, she would often weep a long, long time.

Mrs. Sesemann had noticed the child's unhappiness, but let a few days pass by, hoping for a change. But the change never came, and often Heidi's eyes were red even in the early morning. So she called the child to her room one day and said, with great sympathy in her voice: "Tell me, Heidi, what is the matter with you? What is making you so sad?"

But as Heidi did not want to appear thankless, she replied sadly: "I can't tell you."

"No? Can't you tell Clara perhaps?"

"Oh, no, I can't tell anyone," Heidi said, looking so unhappy that the old lady's heart was filled with pity.

"I tell you something, little girl," she continued. "If you have a sorrow that you cannot tell to anyone, you can go to Our Father in Heaven. You can tell Him everything that troubles you, and if we ask Him He can help us and take our suffering away. Do you understand me, child? Don't you pray every night? Don't you thank Him for all His gifts and ask Him to protect you from evil?"

"Oh no, I never do that," replied the child.

"Have you never prayed, Heidi? Do you know what I mean?"

"I only prayed with my first grandmother, but it is so long ago, that I have forgotten."

"See, Heidi, I understand now why you are so unhappy. We all need somebody to help us, and just think how wonderful it is, to be able to go to the Lord, when something distresses us and causes us pain. We can tell Him everything and ask Him to comfort us, when nobody else can do it. He can give us happiness and joy."

Heidi was gladdened by these tidings, and asked: "Can we tell Him everything, everything?"

"Yes, Heidi, everything."

The child, withdrawing her hand from the grandmama, said hurriedly, "Can I go now?"

"Yes, of course," was the reply, and with this Heidi ran to her room. Sitting down on a stool she folded her hands and poured out her heart to God, imploring Him to help her and let her go home to her grandfather.

About a week later, Mr. Candidate asked to see Mrs. Sesemann, to tell her of something unusual that had occurred. Being called to the lady's room, he began: "Mrs. Sesemann, something has happened that I never expected," and with many more words the happy grandmama was told that Heidi had suddenly learned to read with the utmost correctness, most rare with beginners.

"Many strange things happen in this world," Mrs. Sesemann remarked, while they went over to the study to witness Heidi's new accomplishment. Heidi was sitting close to Clara, reading her a story; she seemed amazed at the strange, new world that had opened up before her. At supper Heidi found the large book with the beautiful pictures on her plate, and looking doubtfully at grandmama, she saw the old lady nod. "Now it belongs to you, Heidi," she said.

"Forever? Also when I am going home?" Heidi inquired, confused with joy.

"Certainly, forever!" the grandmama assured her. "Tomorrow we shall begin to read it."

"But Heidi, you must not go home; no, not for many years," Clara exclaimed, "especially when grandmama goes away. You must stay with me."

Heidi still looked at her book before going to bed that night, and this book became her dearest treasure. She would look at the beautiful pictures and read all the stories aloud to Clara. Grandmama would quietly listen and explain something here and there, making it more beautiful than before. Heidi loved the pictures with the shepherd best of all; they told the story of the prodigal son, and the child would read and re-read it till she nearly knew it all by heart. Since Heidi had learned to read and possessed the book, the days seemed to fly, and the time had come near that the grandmama had fixed for her departure.

Day 50

1. Read chapter 11.
2. Grandmother says that Heidi stopped hoping in God and turned away from Him. She said that God would forget her and let her go. Do you think it's possible for God to forget one of His children? I don't think so! What does Isaiah 49:15 say? God is responding to His people saying that He's not forgotten them.
   - Isaiah 49:15 "The LORD answers, "Can a mother forget the baby who is nursing at her breast? Can she stop showing her tender love to the child who was born to her? She might forget her child. But I will not forget you.""
3. Tell someone about this chapter.
4. Copy the first sentence from the chapter.

Chapter 11 HEIDI GAINS IN SOME RESPECTS AND LOSES IN OTHERS

The grandmama sent for Heidi every day after dinner, while Clara was resting and Miss Rottenmeier disappeared into her room. She talked to Heidi and amused her in various ways, showing her how to make clothes for pretty little dolls that she had brought. Unconsciously Heidi had learned to sew, and made now the sweetest dresses and coats for the little people out of lovely materials the grandmama would give her. Often Heidi would read to the old lady, for the oftener she read over the stories the dearer they became to her. The child lived everything through with the people in the tales and was always happy to be with them again. But she never looked really cheerful and her eyes never sparkled merrily as before.

In the last week of Mrs. Sesemann's stay, Heidi was called again to the old lady's room. The child entered with her beloved book under her arm. Mrs. Sesemann drew Heidi close to her, and laying the book aside, she said: "Come, child, and tell me why you are so sad. Do you still have the same sorrow?"

"Yes," Heidi replied.

"Did you confide it to Our Lord?"

"Yes."

"Do you pray to Him every day that He may make you happy again and take your affliction away?"

"Oh no, I don't pray any more."

"What do I hear, Heidi? Why don't you pray?"

"It does not help, for God has not listened. I don't wonder," she added, "for if all the people in Frankfurt pray every night, He cannot listen to them all. I am sure He has not heard me.".

"Really? Why are you so sure?"

"Because I have prayed for the same thing many, many weeks and God has not done what I have asked Him to."

"That is not the way, Heidi. You see, God in heaven is a good Father to all of us, who knows what we need better than we do. When something we ask for is not very good for us, He gives us something much better, if we confide in Him and do not lose confidence in His love. I am sure what you asked for was not very good for you just now; He has heard you, for He can hear the prayers of all the people in the world at the same time, because He is God Almighty and not a mortal like us. He heard your prayers and said to Himself: 'Yes, Heidi shall get what she is praying for in time.' Now, while God was looking down on you to hear your prayers, you lost confidence and went away from Him. If God does not hear your prayers any more, He will forget you also and let you go. Don't you want to go back to Him, Heidi, and ask His forgiveness? Pray to Him every day, and hope in Him, that He may bring cheer and happiness to you."

Heidi had listened attentively; she had unbounded confidence in the old lady, whose words had made a deep impression on her. Full of repentance, she said: "I shall go at once and ask Our Father to pardon me. I shall never forget Him any more!"

"That's right, Heidi; I am sure He will help you in time, if you only trust in Him," the grandmother consoled her. Heidi went to her room now and prayed earnestly to God that He would forgive her and fulfill her wish.

The day of departure had come, but Mrs. Sesemann arranged everything in such a way that the children hardly realized she was actually going. Still everything was empty and quiet when she had gone, and the children hardly knew how to pass their time.

Next day, Heidi came to Clara in the afternoon and said: "Can I always, always read to you now, Clara?"

Clara assented, and Heidi began. But she did not get very far, for the story she was reading told of a grandmother's death. Suddenly she cried aloud: "Oh, now grandmother is dead!" and wept in the most pitiful fashion. Whatever Heidi read always seemed real to her, and now she thought it was her own grandmother at home. Louder and louder she sobbed: "Now poor grandmother is dead and I can never see her any more; and she never got one single roll!"

Clara attempted to explain the mistake, but Heidi was too much upset. She pictured to herself how terrible it would be if her dear old grandfather would die too while she was far away. How quiet and empty it would be in the hut, and how lonely she would be!

Miss Rottenmeier had overheard the scene, and approaching the sobbing child she said impatiently: "Adelheid, now you have screamed enough. If I hear you again giving way to yourself in such a noisy fashion, I shall take your book away forever!"

Heidi turned pale at that, for the book was her greatest treasure. Quickly drying her tears, she choked down her sobs. After that Heidi never cried again; often she could hardly repress her sobs and was obliged to make the strangest faces to keep herself from crying out. Clara often looked at her, full of surprise, but Miss Rottenmeier did not notice them and found no occasion to carry out her threat. However, the poor child got more cheerless every day, and looked so thin and pale that Sebastian became worried. He tried to encourage her at table to help herself to all the good dishes, but listlessly she would let them pass and hardly touch them. In the evening she would cry quietly, her heart bursting with longing to go home.

Thus the time passed by. Heidi never knew if it was summer or winter, for the walls opposite never changed. They drove out very seldom, for Clara was only able to go a short distance. They never saw anything else than streets, houses and busy people; no grass, no fir-trees and no mountains. Heidi struggled constantly against her sorrow, but in vain. Autumn and winter had passed, and Heidi knew that the time was coming when Peter would go up the Alp with his goats, where the flowers were glistening in the sunshine and the mountains were all afire. She would sit down in a corner of her room and put both hands before her eyes, not to see the glaring sunshine on the opposite wall. There she would remain, eating her heart away with longing, till Clara would call for her to come.

Day 51

1. Read the first half of chapter 12.
2. Why do they think there is a ghost in the house? (Answers)
3. Who do you think is the "ghost"?

Chapter 12 THE HOUSE IS HAUNTED

For several days Miss Rottenmeier had been wandering silently about the house. When she went from room to room or along the corridors, she would often glance back as if she were afraid that somebody was following her. If she had to go to the upper floor, where the gorgeous guest-rooms were, or to the lower story, where the big ball-room was situated, she always told Tinette to come with her. The strange thing was, that none of the servants dared to go anywhere alone and always found an excuse to ask each other's company, which requests were always granted. The cook, who had been in the house for many years, would often shake her head and mutter: "That I should live to see this!"

Something strange and weird was happening in the house. Every morning, when the servants came down-stairs, they found the front door wide open. At first everybody had thought that the house must have been robbed, but nothing was missing. Every morning it was the same, despite the double locks that were put on the door. At last John and Sebastian, taking courage, prepared themselves to watch through a night to see who was the ghost. Armed and provided with some strengthening liquor, they repaired to a room down-stairs. First they talked, but soon, getting sleepy, they leaned silently back in their chairs. When the clock from the old church tower struck one, Sebastian awoke and roused his comrade, which was no easy matter. At last, however, John was wide awake, and together they went out into the hall. The same moment a strong wind put out the light that John held in his hand. Rushing back, he nearly upset Sebastian, who stood behind him, and pulling the butler back into the room, he locked the door in furious haste. When the light was lit again, Sebastian noticed that John was deadly pale and trembling like an aspen leaf. Sebastian, not having seen anything, asked anxiously: "What is the matter? What did you see?"

"The door was open and a white form was on the stairs; it went up and was gone in a moment," gasped John. Cold shivers ran down the butler's back. They sat without moving till the morning came, and then, shutting the door, they went upstairs to report to the housekeeper what they had seen. The lady, who was waiting eagerly, heard the tale and immediately sat down to write to Mr. Sesemann. She told him that fright had paralyzed her fingers and that terrible things were happening in the house. Then followed a tale of the appearance of the ghost. Mr. Sesemann replied that he could not leave his business, and advised Miss Rottenmeier to ask his mother to come to stay with them, for Mrs. Sesemann would easily despatch the ghost. Miss Rottenmeier was offended with the tone of the letter, which did not seem to take her account seriously. Mrs. Sesemann also replied that she could not come, so the housekeeper decided to tell the children all about it. Clara, at the uncanny tale, immediately exclaimed that she would not stay alone another moment and that she wished her father to come home. The housekeeper arranged to sleep with the frightened child, while Heidi, who did not know what ghosts were, was perfectly unmoved. Another letter was despatched to Mr. Sesemann, telling him that the excitement might have serious effects on his daughter's delicate constitution, and mentioning several misfortunes that might probably happen if he did not relieve the household from this terror.

This brought Mr. Sesemann. Going to his daughter's room after his arrival, he was overjoyed to see her as well as ever. Clara was also delighted to see her father.

"What new tricks has the ghost played on you, Miss Rottenmeier?" asked Mr. Sesemann with a twinkle in his eye.

"It is no joke, Mr. Sesemann," replied the lady seriously. "I am sure you will not laugh tomorrow. Those strange events indicate that something secret and horrible has happened in this house in days gone by."

"Is that so? this is new to me," remarked Mr. Sesemann. "But will you please not suspect my venerable ancestors? Please call Sebastian; I want to speak to him alone."

Mr. Sesemann knew that the two were not on good terms, so he said to the butler:

"Come here, Sebastian, and tell me honestly, if you have played the ghost for Miss Rottenmeier's pastime?"

"No, upon my word, master; you must not think that," replied Sebastian frankly. "I do not like it quite myself."

"Well, I'll show you and John what ghosts look like by day. You ought to be ashamed of yourselves, strong young men like you! Now go at once to my old friend, Dr. Classen, and tell him to come to me at nine o'clock to-night. Tell him that I came from Paris especially to consult him, and that I want him to sit up all night with me. Do you understand me, Sebastian?"

"Yes indeed! I shall do as you say, Mr. Sesemann." Mr. Sesemann then went up to Clara's room to quiet and comfort her.

Punctually at nine o'clock the doctor arrived. Though his hair was grey, his face was still fresh, and his eyes were lively and kind. When he saw his friend, he laughed aloud and said: "Well, well, you look pretty healthy for one who needs to be watched all night."

"Have patience, my old friend," replied Mr. Sesemann. "I am afraid the person we have to sit up for will look worse, but first we must catch him."

"What? Then somebody *is* sick in this house? What do you mean?"

"Far worse, doctor, far worse. A ghost is in the house. My house is haunted."

When the doctor laughed, Mr. Sesemann continued: "I call that sympathy; I wish my friend Miss Rottenmeier could hear you. She is convinced that an old Sesemann is wandering about, expiating some dreadful deed."

Day 52

1. A candelabrum is a fancy candle holder that holds lots of candles at once.
2. Finish reading chapter 12.
3. Who was the "ghost"? (Answers)
4. What was Heidi doing in the middle of the night? (Answers)

Chapter 12 continued

When the doctor laughed, Mr. Sesemann continued: "I call that sympathy; I wish my friend Miss Rottenmeier could hear you. She is convinced that an old Sesemann is wandering about, expiating some dreadful deed."

"How did she make his acquaintance?" asked the doctor, much amused.

Mr. Sesemann then explained the circumstances. He said that the matter was either a bad joke which an acquaintance of the servants was playing in his absence, or it was a gang of thieves, who, after intimidating the people, would surely rob his house by and by.

With these explanations they entered the room where the two servants had watched before. A few bottles of wine stood on the table and two bright candelabra shed a brilliant light. Two revolvers were ready for emergencies.

They left the door only partly open, for too much light might drive the ghost away. Then, sitting down comfortably, the two men passed their time by chatting, taking a sip now and then.

"The ghost seems to have spied us and probably won't come to-day," said the doctor.

"We must have patience. It is supposed to come at one," replied his friend.

So they talked till one o'clock. Everything was quiet, and not a sound came from the street. Suddenly the doctor raised his finger.

"Sh! Sesemann, don't you hear something?"

While they both listened, the bar was unfastened, the key was turned, and the door flew open. Mr. Sesemann seized his revolver.

"You are not afraid, I hope?" said the doctor, getting up.

"Better be cautious!" whispered Mr. Sesemann, seizing the candelabrum in the other hand. The doctor followed with his revolver and the light, and so they went out into the hall.

On the threshhold stood a motionless white form, lighted up by the moon.

"Who is there?" thundered the doctor, approaching the figure. It turned and uttered a low shriek. There stood Heidi, with bare feet and in her white night-gown, looking bewildered at the bright light and the weapons. She was shaking with fear, while the two men were looking at her in amazement.

"Sesemann, this seems to be your little water carrier," said the doctor.

"Child, what does this mean?" asked Mr. Sesemann. "What did you want to do? Why have you come down here?"

Pale from fright, Heidi said: "I do not know."

The doctor came forward now. "Sesemann, this case belongs to my field. Please go and sit down while I take her to bed."

Putting his revolver aside, he led the trembling child up-stairs.

"Don't be afraid; just be quiet! Everything is all right; don't be frightened."

When they had arrived in Heidi's room, the doctor put the little girl to bed, covering her up carefully. Drawing a chair near the couch, he waited till Heidi had calmed down and had stopped trembling. Then taking her hand in his, he said kindly: "Now everything is all right again. Tell me where you wanted to go?"

"I did not want to go anywhere," Heidi assured him; "I did not go myself, only I was there all of a sudden."

"Really! Tell me, what did you dream?"

"Oh, I have the same dream every night. I always think I am with my grandfather again and can hear the fir-trees roar. I always think how beautiful the stars must be, and then I open the door of the hut, and oh, it is so wonderful! But when I wake up I am always in Frankfurt." Heidi had to fight the sobs that were rising in her throat.

"Does your back or your head hurt you, child?"

"No, but I feel as if a big stone was pressing me here."

"As if you had eaten something that disagreed with you?"

"Oh no, but as if I wanted to cry hard."

"So, and then you cry out, don't you?"

"Oh no, I must never do that, for Miss Rottenmeier has forbidden it."

"Then you swallow it down? Yes? Do you like to be here?"

"Oh yes," was the faint, uncertain reply.

"Where did you live with your grandfather?"

"Up on the Alp."

"But wasn't it a little lonely there?"

"Oh no, it was so beautiful!"—But Heidi could say no more. The recollection, the excitement of the night and all the restrained sorrow overpowered the child. The tears rushed violently from her eyes and she broke out into loud sobs.

The doctor rose, and soothing her, said: "It won't hurt to cry; you'll go to sleep afterward, and when you wake up everything will come right." Then he left the room.

Joining his anxious friend down-stairs, he said: "Sesemann, the little girl is a sleep-walker, and has unconsciously scared your whole household. Besides, she is so home-sick that her little body has wasted away. We shall have to act quickly. The only remedy for her is to be restored to her native mountain air. This is my prescription, and she must go tomorrow."

"What, sick, a sleep-walker, and wasted away in my house! Nobody even suspected it! You think I should send this child back in this condition, when she has come in good health? No, doctor, ask everything but that. Take her in hand and prescribe for her, but let her get well before I send her back."

"Sesemann," the doctor replied seriously, "just think what you are doing. We cannot cure her with powders and pills. The child has not a strong constitution, and if you keep her here, she might never get well again. If you restore her to the bracing mountain air to which she is accustomed, she probably will get perfectly well again."

When Mr. Sesemann heard this he said, "If that is your advice, we must act at once; this is the only way then." With these words Mr. Sesemann took his friend's arm and walked about with him to talk the matter over. When everything was settled, the doctor took his leave, for the morning had already come and the sun was shining in through the door.

Day 53

1. Read the beginning of chapter 13.
2. What is happening in this chapter?
3. What do you think it is going to be like when Heidi gets home? Do you think everything will be the same? Do you think something will have changed? What? What do you think will be grandfather's reaction?

Chapter 13 ON A SUMMER EVENING

Mr. Sesemann, going upstairs in great agitation, knocked at the housekeeper's door. He asked her to hurry, for preparations for a journey had to be made. Miss Rottenmeier obeyed the summons with the greatest indignation, for it was only half-past four in the morning. She dressed in haste, though with great difficulty, being nervous and excited. All the other servants were summoned likewise, and one and all thought that the master of the house had been seized by the ghost and that he was ringing for help. When they had all come down with terrified looks, they were most surprised to see Mr. Sesemann fresh and cheerful, giving orders. John was sent to get the horses ready and Tinette was told to prepare Heidi for her departure while Sebastian was commissioned to fetch Heidi's aunt. Mr. Sesemann instructed the housekeeper to pack a trunk in all haste for Heidi.

Miss Rottenmeier experienced an extreme disappointment, for she had hoped for an explanation of the great mystery. But Mr. Sesemann, evidently not in the mood to converse further, went to his daughter's room. Clara had been wakened by the unusual noises and was listening eagerly. Her father told her of what had happened and how the doctor had ordered Heidi back to her home, because her condition was serious and might get worse. She might even climb the roof, or be exposed to similar dangers, if she was not cured at once.

Clara was painfully surprised and tried to prevent her father from carrying out his plan. He remained firm, however, promising to take her to Switzerland himself the following summer, if she was good and sensible now. So the child, resigning herself, begged to have Heidi's trunk packed in her room. Mr. Sesemann encouraged her to get together a good outfit for her little friend.

Heidi's aunt had arrived in the meantime. Being told to take her niece home with her, she found no end of excuses, which plainly showed that she did not want to do it; for Deta well remembered the uncle's parting words. Mr. Sesemann dismissed her and summoned Sebastian. The butler was told to get ready for travelling with the child. He was to go to Basle that day and spend the night at a good hotel which his master named. The next day the child was to be brought to her home.

"Listen, Sebastian," Mr. Sesemann said, "and do exactly as I tell you. I know the Hotel in Basle, and if you show my card they will give you good accommodations. Go to the child's room and barricade the windows, so that they can only be opened by the greatest force. When Heidi has gone to bed, lock the door from outside, for the child walks in her sleep and might come to harm in the strange hotel. She might get up and open the door; do you understand?"

"Oh!—Oh!—So it was she?" exclaimed the butler.

"Yes, it was! You are a coward, and you can tell John he is the same. Such foolish men, to be afraid!" With that Mr. Sesemann went to his room to write a letter to Heidi's grandfather.

Sebastian, feeling ashamed, said to himself that he ought to have resisted John and found out alone.

Heidi was dressed in her Sunday frock and stood waiting for further commands.

Mr. Sesemann called her now. "Good-morning, Mr. Sesemann," Heidi said when she entered.

"What do you think about it, little one?" he asked her. Heidi looked up to him in amazement.

"You don't seem to know anything about it," laughed Mr. Sesemann. Tinette had not even told the child, for she thought it beneath her dignity to speak to the vulgar Heidi.

"You are going home to-day."

"Home?" Heidi repeated in a low voice. She had to gasp, so great was her surprise.

"Wouldn't you like to hear something about it?" asked Mr. Sesemann smiling.

"Oh yes, I should like to," said the blushing child.

"Good, good," said the kind gentleman. "Sit down and eat a big breakfast now, for you are going away right afterwards."

The child could not even swallow a morsel, though she tried to eat out of obedience. It seemed to her as if it was only a dream.

"Go to Clara, Heidi, till the carriage comes," Mr. Sesemann said kindly.

Heidi had been wishing to go, and now she ran to Clara's room, where a huge trunk was standing.

"Heidi, look at the things I had packed for you. Do you like them?" Clara asked.

There were a great many lovely things in it, but Heidi jumped for joy when she discovered a little basket with twelve round white rolls for the grandmother. The children had forgotten that the moment for parting had come, when the carriage was announced. Heidi had to get all her own treasures from her room yet. The grandmama's book was carefully packed, and the red shawl that Miss Rottenmeier had purposely left behind. Then putting on her pretty hat, she left her room to say good-bye to Clara. There was not much time left to do so, for Mr. Sesemann was waiting to put Heidi in the carriage. When Miss Rottenmeier, who was standing on the stairs to bid farewell to her pupil, saw the red bundle in Heidi's hand, she seized it and threw it on the ground. Heidi looked imploringly at her kind protector, and Mr. Sesemann, seeing how much she treasured it, gave it back to her. The happy child at parting thanked him for all his goodness. She also sent a message of thanks to the good old doctor, whom she suspected to be the real cause of her going.

While Heidi was being lifted into the carriage, Mr. Sesemann assured her that Clara and he would never forget her. Sebastian followed with Heidi's basket and a large bag with provisions. Mr. Sesemann called out: "Happy journey!" and the carriage rolled away.

Only when Heidi was sitting in the train did she become conscious of where she was going. She knew now that she would really see her grandfather and the grandmother again, also Peter and the goats. Her only fear was that the poor blind grandmother might have died while she was away.

The thing she looked forward to most was giving the soft white rolls to the grandmother. While she was musing over all these things, she fell asleep. In Basle she was roused by Sebastian, for there they were to spend the night.

The next morning they started off again, and it took them many hours before they reached Mayenfeld. When Sebastian stood on the platform of the station, he wished he could have travelled further in the train rather than have to climb a mountain. The last part of the trip might be dangerous, for everything seemed half-wild in this country. Looking round, he discovered a small wagon with a lean horse. A broad-shouldered man was just loading up large bags, which had come by the train. Sebastian, approaching the man, asked some information concerning the least dangerous ascent to the Alp. After a while it was settled that the man should take Heidi and her trunk to the village and see to it that somebody would go up with her from there.

Not a word had escaped Heidi, until she now said, "I can go up alone from the village. I know the road." Sebastian felt relieved, and calling Heidi to him, presented her with a heavy roll of bills and a letter for the grandfather. These precious things were put at the bottom of the basket, under the rolls, so that they could not possibly get lost.

Heidi promised to be careful of them, and was lifted up to the cart. The two old friends shook hands and parted, and Sebastian, with a slightly bad conscience for having deserted the child so soon, sat down on the station to wait for a returning train.

The driver was no other than the village baker, who had never seen Heidi but had heard a great deal about her. He had known her parents and immediately guessed she was the child who had lived with the Alm-Uncle. Curious to know why she came home again, he began a conversation.

"Are you Heidi, the child who lived with the Alm-Uncle?"

"Yes."

"Why are you coming home again? Did you get on badly?"

"Oh no; nobody could have got on better than I did in Frankfurt."

"Then why are you coming back?"

"Because Mr. Sesemann let me come."

"Pooh! why didn't you stay?"

"Because I would rather be with my grandfather on the Alp than anywhere on earth."

"You may think differently when you get there," muttered the baker. "It is strange though, for she must know," he said to himself.

Day 54

1. Finish reading chapter 13.
2. Had grandfather changed? Has what people think about him changed? (Answers)
3. Do you remember what problem grandfather had about Heidi before she left? (Answers)

Chapter 13 continued

They conversed no more, and Heidi began to tremble with excitement when she recognized all the trees on the road and the lofty peaks of the mountains. Sometimes she felt as if she could not sit still any longer, but had to jump down and run with all her might. They arrived at the village at the stroke of five. Immediately a large group of women and children surrounded the cart, for the trunk and the little passenger had attracted everybody's notice. When Heidi had been lifted down, she found herself held and questioned on all sides. But when they saw how frightened she was, they let her go at last. The baker had to tell of Heidi's arrival with the strange gentleman, and assured all the people that Heidi loved her grandfather with all her heart, let the people say what they would about him.

Heidi, in the meantime, was running up the path; from time to time she was obliged to stop, for her basket was heavy and she lost her breath. Her one idea was: "If only grandmother still sits in her corner by her spinning wheel!—Oh, if she should have died!" When the child caught sight of the hut at last, her heart began to beat. The quicker she ran, the more it beat, but at last she tremblingly opened the door. She ran into the middle of the room, unable to utter one tone, she was so out of breath.

"Oh God," it sounded from one corner, "our Heidi used to come in like that. Oh, if I just could have her again with me before I die. Who has come?"

"Here I am! grandmother, here I am!" shouted the child, throwing herself on her knees before the old woman. She seized her hands and arms and snuggling up to her did not for joy utter one more word. The grandmother had been so surprised that she could only silently caress the child's curly hair over and over again. "Yes, yes," she said at last, "this is Heidi's hair, and her beloved voice. Oh my God, I thank Thee for this happiness." Out of her blind eyes big tears of joy fell down on Heidi's hand. "Is it really you, Heidi? Have you really come again?"

"Yes, yes, grandmother," the child replied. "You must not cry, for I have come and will never leave you any more. Now you won't have to eat hard black bread any more for a little while. Look what I have brought you."

Heidi put one roll after another into the grandmother's lap.

"Ah, child, what a blessing you bring to me!" the old woman cried. "But you are my greatest blessing yourself, Heidi!" Then, caressing the child's hair and flushed cheeks, she entreated: "Just say one more word, that I may hear your voice."

113

While Heidi was talking, Peter's mother arrived, and exclaimed in her amazement: "Surely, this is Heidi. But how can that be?"

The child rose to shake hands with Brigida, who could not get over Heidi's splendid frock and hat.

"You can have my hat, I don't want it any more; I have my old one still," Heidi said, pulling out her old crushed straw hat. Heidi had remembered her grandfather's words to Deta about her feather hat; that was why she had kept her old hat so carefully. Brigida at last accepted the gift after a great many remonstrances. Suddenly Heidi took off her pretty dress and tied her old shawl about her. Taking the grandmother's hand, she said: "Good-bye, I must go home to grandfather now, but I shall come again tomorrow. Good-night, grandmother."

"Oh, please come again to-morrow, Heidi," implored the old woman, while she held her fast.

"Why did you take your pretty dress off?" asked Brigida.

"I'd rather go to grandfather that way, or else he might not know me any more, the way you did."

Brigida accompanied the child outside and said mysteriously: "He would have known you in your frock; you ought to have kept it on. Please be careful, child, for Peter tells us that the uncle never says a word to anyone and always seems so angry." But Heidi was unconcerned, and saying good-night, climbed up the path with the basket on her arm. The evening sun was shining down on the grass before her. Every few minutes Heidi stood still to look at the mountains behind her. Suddenly she looked back and beheld such glory as she had not even seen in her most vivid dream. The rocky peaks were flaming in the brilliant light, the snow-fields glowed and rosy clouds were floating overhead. The grass was like an expanse of gold, and below her the valley swam in golden mist. The child stood still, and in her joy and transport tears ran down her cheeks. She folded her hands, and looking up to heaven, thanked the Lord that He had brought her home again. She thanked Him for restoring her to her beloved mountains,—in her happiness she could hardly find words to pray. Only when the glow had subsided, was Heidi able to follow the path again.

She climbed so fast that she could soon discover, first the tree-tops, then the roof, finally the hut. Now she could see her grandfather sitting on his bench, smoking a pipe. Above the cottage the fir-trees gently swayed and rustled in the evening breeze. At last she had reached the hut, and throwing herself in her grandfather's arms, she hugged him and held him tight. She could say nothing but "Grandfather! grandfather! grandfather!" in her agitation.

The old man said nothing either, but his eyes were moist, and loosening Heidi's arms at last, he sat her on his knee. When he had looked at her a while, he said: "So you have come home again, Heidi? Why? You certainly do not look very cityfied! Did they send you away?"

"Oh no, you must not think that, grandfather. They all were so good to me; Clara, Mr. Sesemann and grandmama. But grandfather, sometimes I felt as if I could not bear it any longer to be away from you! I thought I should choke; I could not tell any one, for that would have been ungrateful. Suddenly, one morning Mr. Sesemann called me very early, I think it was the doctor's fault and—but I think it is probably written in this letter;" with that Heidi brought the letter and the bank-roll from her basket, putting them on her grandfather's lap.

"This belongs to you," he said, laying the roll beside him. Having read the letter, he put it in his pocket.

"Do you think you can still drink milk with me, Heidi?" he asked, while he stepped into the cottage. "Take your money with you, you can buy a bed for it and clothes for many years."

"I don't need it at all, grandfather," Heidi assured him; "I have a bed and Clara has given me so many dresses that I shan't need any more all my life."

"Take it and put it in the cupboard, for you will need it some day."

Heidi obeyed, and danced around the hut in her delight to see all the beloved things again. Running up to the loft, she exclaimed in great disappointment: "Oh grandfather, my bed is gone."

"It will come again," the grandfather called up from below; "how could I know that you were coming back? Get your milk now!"

Heidi, coming down, took her old seat. She seized her bowl and emptied it eagerly, as if it was the most wonderful thing she had ever tasted. "Grandfather, our milk is the best in all the world."

Suddenly Heidi, hearing a shrill whistle, rushed outside, as Peter and all his goats came racing down. Heidi greeted the boy, who stopped, rooted to the spot, staring at her. Then she ran into the midst of her beloved friends, who had not forgotten her either. Schwänli and Bärli bleated for joy, and all her other favorites pressed near to her. Heidi was beside herself with joy, and caressed little Snowhopper and patted Thistlefinch, till she felt herself pushed to and fro among them.

"Peter, why don't you come down and say good-night to me?" Heidi called to the boy.

"Have you come again?" he exclaimed at last. Then he took Heidi's proffered hand and asked her, as if she had been always there: "Are you coming up with me tomorrow?"

"No, tomorrow I must go to grandmother, but perhaps the day after."

Peter had a hard time with his goats that day, for they would not follow him. Over and over again they came back to Heidi, till she entered the shed with Bärli and Schwänli and shut the door.

When Heidi went up to her loft to sleep, she found a fresh, fragrant bed waiting for her; and she slept better that night than she had for many, many months, for her great and burning longing had been satisfied. About ten times that night the grandfather rose from his couch to listen to Heidi's quiet breathing. The window was filled up with hay, for from now on the moon was not allowed to shine on Heidi any more. But Heidi slept quietly, for she had seen the flaming mountains and had heard the fir-trees roar.

Day 55

1. Read the beginning of chapter 14.
2. What Bible story does Heidi read to her grandfather? (Answers)
3. What happens at the end of the story?
4. There is a reason the author chose the story of the prodigal son. Which of the characters in *Heidi* do you think might be like the prodigal son?

Vocabulary

1. Review your vocabulary from Aesop's fables. Either go to Day 25 or go to Level 3 on the review game page on the Easy Peasy website.

Chapter 14 ON SUNDAY WHEN THE CHURCH BELLS RING

Heidi was standing under the swaying fir-trees, waiting for her grandfather to join her. He had promised to bring up her trunk from the village while she went in to visit the grandmother. The child was longing to see the blind woman again and to hear how she had liked the rolls. It was Saturday, and the grandfather had been cleaning the cottage. Soon he was ready to start. When they had descended and Heidi entered Peter's hut, the grandmother called lovingly to her: "Have you come again, child?"

She took hold of Heidi's hand and held it tight. Grandmother then told the little visitor how good the rolls had tasted, and how much stronger she felt already. Brigida related further that the grandmother had only eaten a single roll, being so afraid to finish them too soon. Heidi had listened attentively, and said now: "Grandmother, I know what I shall do. I am going to write to Clara and she'll surely send me a whole lot more."

But Brigida remarked: "That is meant well, but they get hard so soon. If I only had a few extra pennies, I could buy some from our baker. He makes them too, but I am hardly able to pay for the black bread."

Heidi's face suddenly shone. "Oh, grandmother, I have an awful lot of money," she cried. "Now I know what I'll do with it. Every day you must have a fresh roll and two on Sundays. Peter can bring them up from the village."

"No, no, child," the grandmother implored. "That must not be. You must give it to grandfather and he'll tell you what to do with it."

But Heidi did not listen but jumped gaily about the little room, calling over and over again: "Now grandmother can have a roll every day. She'll get well and strong, and," she called with fresh delight, "maybe your eyes will see again, too, when you are strong and well."

The grandmother remained silent, not to mar the happiness of the child. Seeing the old hymn-book on the shelf, Heidi said:

"Grandmother, shall I read you a song from your book now? I can read quite nicely!" she added after a pause.

"Oh yes, I wish you would, child. Can you really read?"

Heidi, climbing on a chair, took down the dusty book from a shelf. After she had carefully wiped it off, she sat down on a stool.

"What shall I read, grandmother?"

"Whatever you want to," was the reply. Turning the pages, Heidi found a song about the sun, and decided to read that aloud. More and more eagerly she read, while the grandmother, with folded arms, sat in her chair. An expression of indescribable happiness shone in her countenance, though tears were rolling down her cheeks. When Heidi had repeated the end of the song a number of times, the old woman exclaimed: "Oh, Heidi, everything seems bright to me again and my heart is light. Thank you, child, you have done me so much good."

Heidi looked enraptured at the grandmother's face, which had changed from an old, sorrowful expression to a joyous one.

She seemed to look up gratefully, as if she could already behold the lovely, celestial gardens told of in the hymn.

Soon the grandfather knocked on the window, for it was time to go. Heidi followed quickly, assuring the grandmother that she would visit her every day now; on the days she went up to the pasture with Peter, she would return in the early afternoon, for she did not want to miss the chance to make the grandmother's heart joyful and light. Brigida urged Heidi to take her dress along, and with it on her arm the child joined the old man and immediately told him what had happened.

On hearing of her plan to purchase rolls for the grandmother every day, the grandfather reluctantly consented.

At this the child gave a bound, shouting: "Oh grandfather, now grandmother won't ever have to eat hard, black bread any more. Oh, everything is so wonderful now! If God Our Father had done immediately what I prayed for, I should have come home at once and could not have brought half as many rolls to grandmother. I should not have been able to read either. Grandmama told me that God would make everything much better than I could ever dream. I shall always pray from now on, the way grandmama taught me. When God does not give me something I pray for, I shall always remember how everything has worked out for the best this time. We'll pray every day, grandfather, won't we, for otherwise God might forget us."

"And if somebody should forget to do it?" murmured the old man.

"Oh, he'll get on badly, for God will forget him, too. If he is unhappy and wretched, people don't pity him, for they will say: 'he went away from God, and now the Lord, who alone can help him, has no pity on him'."

"Is that true, Heidi? Who told you so?"

"Grandmama explained it all to me."

After a pause the grandfather said: "Yes, but if it has happened, then there is no help; nobody can come back to the Lord, when God has once forgotten him."

"But grandfather, everybody can come back to Him; grandmama told me that, and besides there is the beautiful story in my book. Oh, grandfather, you don't know it yet, and I shall read it to you as soon as we get home."

The grandfather had brought a big basket with him, in which he carried half the contents of Heidi's trunk; it had been too large to be conveyed up the steep ascent. Arriving at the hut and setting down his load, he had to sit beside Heidi, who was ready to begin the tale. With great animation Heidi read the story of the prodigal son, who was happy at home with his father's cows and sheep. The picture showed him leaning on his staff, watching the sunset. "Suddenly he wanted to have his own inheritance, and be able to be his own master. Demanding the money from his father, he went away and squandered all. When he had nothing in the world left, he had to go as servant to a peasant, who did not own fine cattle like his father, but only swine; his clothes were rags, and for food he only got the husks on which the pigs were fed. Often he would think what a good home he had left, and when he remembered how good his father had been to him and his own ungratefulness, he would cry from repentance and longing. Then he said to himself: 'I shall go to my father and ask his forgiveness.' When he approached his former home, his father came out to meet him—"

Day 56

1. Finish reading chapter 14.
2. Where did grandfather and Heidi go? (Answers)
3. What has grandfather decided about where to spend the winter? (Answers)
4. Why does grandfather's heart feel light? (Answers)
5. How did grandfather make peace with God? (Answers)

Chapter 14 continued

"What do you think will happen now?" Heidi asked. "You think that the father is angry and will say: 'Didn't I tell you?' But just listen: 'And his father saw him and had compassion and ran and fell on his neck. And the son said: Father, I have sinned against Heaven and in Thy sight, and am no more worthy to be called Thy son. But the father said to his servants: Bring forth the best robe and put it on him; and put a ring on his hand and shoes on his feet; and bring hither the fatted calf and kill it; and let us eat and be merry: For this my son was dead and is alive again; he was lost, and is found.' And they began to be merry."

"Isn't it a beautiful story, grandfather?" asked Heidi, when he sat silently beside her.

"Yes, Heidi, it is," said the grandfather, but so seriously that Heidi quietly looked at the pictures. "Look how happy he is," she said, pointing to it.

A few hours later, when Heidi was sleeping soundly, the old man climbed up the ladder. Placing a little lamp beside the sleeping child, he watched her a long, long time. Her little hands were folded and her rosy face looked confident and peaceful. The old man now folded his hands and said in a low voice, while big tears rolled down his cheeks: "Father, I have sinned against Heaven and Thee, and am no more worthy to be Thy son!"

The next morning found the uncle standing before the door, looking about him over valley and mountain. A few early bells sounded from below and the birds sang their morning anthems.

Re-entering the house, he called: "Heidi, get up! The sun is shining! Put on a pretty dress, for we are going to church!"

That was a new call, and Heidi obeyed quickly. When the child came downstairs in her smart little frock, she opened her eyes wide. "Oh, grandfather!" she exclaimed, "I have never seen you in your Sunday coat with the silver buttons. Oh, how fine you look!"

The old man, turning to the child, said with a smile: "You look nice, too; come now!" With Heidi's hand in his they wandered down together. The nearer they came to the village, the louder and richer the bells resounded. "Oh grandfather, do you hear it? It seems like a big, high feast," said Heidi.

When they entered the church, all the people were singing. Though they sat down on the last bench behind, the people had noticed their presence and whispered it from ear to ear. When the pastor began to preach, his words were a loud thanksgiving that moved all his hearers. After the service the old man and the child walked to the parsonage. The clergyman had opened the door and received them with friendly words. "I have come to ask your forgiveness for my harsh words," said the uncle. "I want to follow your advice to spend the winter here among you. If the people look at me askance, I can't expect any better. I am sure, Mr. Pastor, you will not do so."

The pastor's friendly eyes sparkled, and with many a kind word he commended the uncle for this change, and putting his hand on Heidi's curly hair, ushered them out. Thus the people, who had been all talking together about this great event, could see that their clergyman shook hands with the old man. The door of the parsonage was hardly shut, when the whole assembly came forward with outstretched hands and friendly greetings. Great seemed to be their joy at the old man's resolution; some of the people even accompanied him on his homeward way. When they had parted at last, the uncle looked after them with his face shining as with an inward light. Heidi looked up to him and said: "Grandfather, you have never looked so beautiful!"

"Do you think so, child?" he said with a smile. "You see, Heidi, I am more happy than I deserve; to be at peace with God and men makes one's heart feel light. God has been good to me, to send you back."

When they arrived at Peter's hut, the grandfather opened the door and entered. "How do you do, grandmother," he called out. "I think we must start to mend again, before the fall wind comes."

"Oh my God, the uncle!" exclaimed the grandmother in joyous surprise. "How happy I am to be able to thank you for what you have done, uncle! Thank you, God bless you for it."

With trembling joy the grandmother shook hands with her old friend. "There is something else I want to say to you, uncle," she continued. "If I have ever hurt you in any way, do not punish me. Do not let Heidi go away again before I die. I cannot tell you what Heidi means to me!" So saying, she held the clinging child to her.

"No danger of that, grandmother, I hope we shall all stay together now for many years to come."

Brigida now showed Heidi's feather hat to the old man and asked him to take it back. But the uncle asked her to keep it, since Heidi had given it to her.

"What blessings this child has brought from Frankfurt," Brigida said. "I often wondered if I should not send our little Peter too. What do you think, uncle?"

The uncle's eyes sparkled with fun, when he replied: "I am sure it would not hurt Peter; nevertheless I should wait for a fitting occasion before I sent him."

The next moment Peter himself arrived in great haste. He had a letter for Heidi, which had been given to him in the village. What an event, a letter for Heidi! They all sat down at the table while the child read it aloud. The letter was from Clara Sesemann, who wrote that everything had got so dull since Heidi left. She said that she could not stand it very long, and therefore her father had promised to take her to Ragatz this coming fall. She announced that Grandmama was coming too, for she wanted to see Heidi and her grandfather. Grandmama, having heard about the rolls, was sending some coffee, too, so that the grandmother would not have to eat them dry. Grandmama also insisted on being taken to the grandmother herself when she came on her visit.

Great was the delight caused by this news, and what with all the questions and plans that followed, the grandfather himself forgot how late it was. This happy day, which had united them all, caused the old woman to say at parting: "The most beautiful thing of all, though, is to be able to shake hands again with an old friend, as in days gone by; it is a great comfort to find again, what we have treasured. I hope you'll come soon again, uncle. I am counting on the child for tomorrow."

This promise was given. While Heidi and her grandfather were on their homeward path, the peaceful sound of evening bells accompanied them. At last they reached the cottage, which seemed to glow in the evening light.

Day 57

1. Read chapter 15. This is the first chapter in part two of the book. This part of the book is entitled, "Heidi Makes Use of Her Experience." What experiences do you think will come in handy?
2. Who is going to visit Heidi? (Answers)
3. Why is the doctor sad and lonely? (Answers)

Chapter 15 PREPARATIONS FOR A JOURNEY

The kind doctor who had sent Heidi home to her beloved mountains was approaching the Sesemann residence on a sunny day in September. Everything about him was bright and cheerful, but the doctor did not even raise his eyes from the pavement to the blue sky above. His face was sad and his hair had turned very gray since spring. A few months ago the doctor had lost his only daughter, who had lived with him since his wife's early death. The blooming girl had been his only joy, and since she had gone from him the ever-cheerful doctor was bowed down with grief.

When Sebastian opened the door to the physician he bowed very low, for the doctor made friends wherever he went.

"I am glad you have come doctor," Mr. Sesemann called to his friend as he entered. "Please let us talk over this trip to Switzerland again. Do you still give the same advice, now that Clara is so much better?"

"What must I think of you, Sesemann?" replied the doctor, sitting down. "I wish your mother was here. Everything is clear to her and things go smoothly then. This is the third time to-day that you have called me, and always for the same thing!"

"It is true, it must make you impatient," said Mr. Sesemann. Laying his hand on his friend's shoulder, he continued: "I cannot say how hard it is for me to refuse Clara this trip. Haven't I promised it to her and hasn't she looked forward to it for months? She has borne all her suffering so patiently, just because she had hoped to be able to visit her little friend on the Alp. I hate to rob her of this pleasure. The poor child has so many trials and so little change."

"But, Sesemann, you must do it," was the doctor's answer. When his friend remained silent, he continued: "Just think what a hard summer Clara has had! She never was more ill and we could not attempt this journey without risking the worst consequences. Remember, we are in September now, and though the weather may still be fine on the Alp, it is sure to be very cool. The days are getting short, and she could only spend a few hours up there, if she had to return for the night. It would take several hours to have her carried up from Ragatz. You see yourself how impossible it is! I shall come in with you, though, to talk to Clara, and you'll find her sensible. I'll tell you of my plan for next May. First she can go to Ragatz to take the baths. When it gets warm on the mountain, she can be carried up from time to time. She'll be stronger then and much more able to enjoy those excursions than she is now. If we hope for an improvement in her condition, we must be extremely cautious and careful, remember that!"

Mr. Sesemann, who had been listening with the utmost submission, now said anxiously: "Doctor, please tell me honestly if you still have hope left for any change?"

With shrugging shoulders the doctor replied: "Not very much. But think of me, Sesemann! Have you not a child, who loves you and always welcomes you? You don't have to come back to a lonely house and sit down alone at your table. Your child is well taken care of, and if she has many privations, she also has many advantages. Sesemann, you do not need to be pitied! Just think of my lonely home!"

Mr. Sesemann had gotten up and was walking round the room, as he always did when something occupied his thoughts. Suddenly he stood before his friend and said: "Doctor, I have an idea. I cannot see you sad any longer. You must get away. You shall undertake this trip and visit Heidi in our stead."

The doctor had been surprised by this proposal, and tried to object. But Mr. Sesemann was so full of his new project that he pulled his friend with him into his daughter's room, not leaving him time for any remonstrances. Clara loved the doctor, who had always tried to cheer her up on his visits by bright and funny tales. She was sorry for the change that had come over him and would have given much to see him happy again. When he had shaken hands with her, both men pulled up their chairs to Clara's bedside. Mr. Sesemann began to speak of their journey and how sorry he was to give it up. Then he quickly began to talk of his new plan.

Clara's eyes had filled with tears. But she knew that her father did not like to see her cry, and besides she was sure that her papa would only forbid her this pleasure because it was absolutely necessary to do so.

So she bravely fought her tears, and caressing the doctor's hand, said:

"Oh please, doctor, do go to Heidi; then you can tell me all about her, and can describe her grandfather to me, and Peter, with his goats,—I seem to know them all so well. Then you can take all the things to her that I had planned to take myself. Oh, please doctor, go, and then I'll be good and take as much cod-liver oil as ever you want me to."

Who can tell if this promise decided the doctor? At any rate he answered with a smile: "Then I surely must go, Clara, for you will get fat and strong, as we both want to see you. Have you settled yet when I must go?"

"Oh, you had better go tomorrow morning, doctor," Clara urged.

"She is right," the father assented; "the sun is shining and you must not lose any more glorious days on the Alp."

The doctor had to laugh. "Why don't you chide me for being here still? I shall go as quickly as I can, Sesemann."

Clara gave many messages to him for Heidi. She also told him to be sure to observe everything closely, so that he would be able to tell her all about it when he came back. The things for Heidi were to be sent to him later, for Miss Rottenmeier, who had to pack them, was out on one of her lengthy wanderings about town.

The doctor promised to comply with all Clara's wishes and to start the following day.

Clara rang for the maid and said to her, when she arrived: "Please, Tinette, pack a lot of fresh, soft coffee-cake in this box." A box had been ready for this purpose many days. When the maid was leaving the room she murmured: "That's a silly bother!"

Sebastian, who had happened to overhear some remarks, asked the physician when he was leaving to take his regards to the little Miss, as he called Heidi.

With a promise to deliver this message the doctor was just hastening out, when he encountered an obstacle. Miss Rottenmeier, who had been obliged to return from her walk on account of the strong wind, was just coming in. She wore a large cape, which the wind was blowing about her like two full sails. Both had retreated politely to give way to each other. Suddenly the wind seemed to carry the housekeeper straight towards the doctor, who had barely time to avoid her. This little incident, which had ruffled Miss Rottenmeier's temper very much, gave the doctor occasion to soothe her, as she liked to be soothed by this man, whom she respected more than anybody in the world. Telling her of his intended visit, he entreated her to pack the things for Heidi as only she knew how.

Clara had expected some resistance from Miss Rottenmeier about the packing of her presents. What was her surprise when this lady showed herself most obliging, and immediately, on being told, brought together all the articles! First came a heavy coat for Heidi, with a hood, which Clara meant her to use on visits to the grandmother in the winter. Then came a thick warm shawl and a large box with coffee-cake for the grandmother. An enormous sausage for Peter's mother followed, and a little sack of tobacco for the grandfather. At last a lot of mysterious little parcels and boxes were packed, things that Clara had gathered together for Heidi. When the tidy pack lay ready on the ground, Clara's heart filled with pleasure at the thought of her little friend's delight.

Sebastian now entered, and putting the pack on his shoulder, carried it to the doctor's house without delay.

Day 58

1. Read the beginning of chapter 16.
2. Why does Heidi thank the doctor? (Answers)
3. What was Heidi's disappointment? (Answers)

Chapter 16 A GUEST ON THE ALP

The early dawn was tinging the mountains and a fresh morning-breeze rocked the old fir-trees to and fro. Heidi opened her eyes, for the rustling of the wind had awakened her. These sounds always thrilled her heart, and now they drew her out of bed. Rising hurriedly, she soon was neatly dressed and combed.

Coming down the little ladder and finding the grandfather's bed empty, she ran outside. The old man was looking up at the sky to see what the weather was going to be like that day. Rosy clouds were passing overhead, but gradually the sky grew more blue and deep, and soon a golden light passed over the heights, for the sun was rising in all his glory.

"Oh, how lovely! Good-morning, grandfather," Heidi exclaimed.

"Are your eyes bright already?" the grandfather retorted, holding out his hand.

Heidi then ran over to her beloved fir-trees and danced about, while the wind was howling in the branches.

After the old man had washed and milked the goats, he brought them out of the shed. When Heidi saw her friends again, she caressed them tenderly, and they in their turn nearly crushed her between them. Sometimes when Bärli got too wild, Heidi would say: "But Bärli, you push me like the Big Turk," and that was enough to quiet the goat.

Soon Peter arrived with the whole herd, the jolly Thistlefinch ahead of all the others. Heidi, being soon in the mist of them, was pushed about among them. Peter was anxious to say a word to the little girl, so he gave a shrill whistle, urging the goats to climb ahead. When he was near her he said reproachfully: "You really might come with me today!"

"No, I can't, Peter," said Heidi. "They might come from Frankfurt any time. I must be home when they come."

"How often you have said that," grumbled the boy.

"But I mean it," replied Heidi. "Do you really think I want to be away when they come from Frankfurt? Do you really think that, Peter?"

"They could come to uncle," Peter growled.

Then the grandfather's strong voice was heard: "Why doesn't the army go forward? Is it the field-marshal's fault, or the fault of the troop?"

Peter immediately turned about and led his goats up the mountain without more ado.

Since Heidi had come home again to her grandfather she did many things that had never occurred to her before. For instance, she would make her bed every morning, and run about the hut, tidying and dusting. With an old rag she would rub the chairs and table till they all shone, and the grandfather would exclaim: "It is always Sunday with us now; Heidi has not been away in vain."

On this day after breakfast, when Heidi began her self-imposed task, it took her longer than usual, for the weather was too glorious to stay within. Over and over again a bright sunbeam would tempt the busy child outside. How could she stay indoors, when the glistening sunshine was pouring down and all the mountains seemed to glow? She had to sit down on the dry, hard ground and look down into the valley and all about her. Then, suddenly remembering her little duties, she would hasten back. It was not long, though, till the roaring fir-trees tempted her again. The grandfather had been busy in his little shop, merely glancing over at the child from time to time. Suddenly he heard her call: "Oh grandfather, come!"

He was frightened and came out quickly He saw her running down the hill crying: "They are coming, they are coming. Oh, the doctor is coming first."

When Heidi at last reached her old friend, he held out his hand, which Heidi immediately seized. In the full joy of her heart, she exclaimed: "How do you do, doctor? And I thank you a thousand times!"

"How are you, Heidi? But what are you thanking me for already?" the doctor asked, with a smile.

"Because you let me come home again," the child explained.

The gentleman's face lit up like sunshine. He had certainly not counted on such a reception on the Alp. On the contrary! Not even noticing all the beauty around him, he had climbed up sadly, for he was sure that Heidi probably would not know him any more. He thought that he would be far from welcome, being obliged to cause her a great disappointment. Instead, he beheld Heidi's bright eyes looking up at him in gratefulness and love. She was still holding his arm, when he said: "Come now, Heidi, and take me to your grandfather, for I want to see where you live."

Like a kind father he had taken her hand, but Heidi stood still and looked down the mountain-side.

"But where are Clara and grandmama?" she asked.

"Child, I must tell you something now which will grieve you as much as it grieves me," replied the doctor. "I had to come alone, for Clara has been very ill and could not travel. Of course grandmama has not come either; but the spring will soon be here, and when the days get long and warm, they will surely visit you."

Day 59

1. Finish reading chapter 16.
2. What did Heidi like more, the presents or the visit by the doctor? (Answers)
3. What was grandmother's favorite gift? (Answers)
4. What do you think was Peter's favorite gift? (Answers)
5. Are you grateful for being warm and fed?

Chapter 16 continued

"Child, I must tell you something now which will grieve you as much as it grieves me," replied the doctor. "I had to come alone, for Clara has been very ill and could not travel. Of course grandmama has not come either; but the spring will soon be here, and when the days get long and warm, they will surely visit you."

Heidi was perfectly amazed; she could not understand how all those things that she had pictured to herself so clearly would not happen after all. She was standing perfectly motionless, confused by the blow.

It was some time before Heidi remembered that, after all, she had come down to meet the doctor. Looking up at her friend, she was struck by his sad and cheerless face. How changed he was since she had seen him! She did not like to see people unhappy, least of all the good, kind doctor. He must be sad because Clara and grandmama had not come, and to console him she said: "Oh, it won't last long till spring comes again; then they will come for sure; they'll be able to stay much longer then, and that will please Clara. Now we'll go to grandfather."

Hand in hand she climbed up with her old friend. All the way she tried to cheer him up by telling him again and again of the coming summer days. After they had reached the cottage, she called out to her grandfather quite happily:

"They are not here yet, but it won't be very long before they are coming!"

The grandfather warmly welcomed his guest, who did not seem at all a stranger, for had not Heidi told him many things about the doctor? They all three sat down on the bench before the door, and the doctor told of the object of his visit. He whispered to the child that something was coming up the mountain very soon which would bring her more pleasure than his visit. What could it be?

The uncle advised the doctor to spend the splendid days of autumn on the Alp, if possible, and to take a little room in the village instead of in Ragatz; then he could easily walk up every day to the hut, and from there the uncle could take him all around the mountains. This plan was accepted.

The sun was in its zenith and the wind had ceased. Only a soft delicious breeze fanned the cheeks of all.

The uncle now got up and went into the hut, returning soon with a table and their dinner.

"Go in, Heidi, and set the table here. I hope you will excuse our simple meal," he said, turning to his guest.

"I shall gladly accept this delightful invitation; I am sure that dinner will taste good up here," said the guest, looking down over the sun-bathed valley.

Heidi was running to and fro, for it gave her great joy to be able to wait on her kind protector. Soon the uncle appeared with the steaming milk, the toasted cheese, and the finely-sliced, rosy meat that had been dried in the pure air. The doctor enjoyed his dinner better than any he had ever tasted.

"Yes, we must send Clara up here. How she could gather strength!" he said; "If she would have an appetite like mine today, she couldn't help getting nice and fat."

At this moment a man could be seen walking up with a large sack on his shoulders. Arriving on top, he threw down his load, breathing in the pure, fresh air.

Opening the cover, the doctor said: "This has come for you from Frankfurt, Heidi. Come and look what is in it."

Heidi timidly watched the heap, and only when the gentleman opened the box with the cakes for the grandmother she said joyfully: "Oh, now grandmother can eat this lovely cake." She was taking the box and the beautiful shawl on her arm and was going to race down to deliver the gifts, when the men persuaded her to stay and unpack the rest. What was her delight at finding the tobacco and all the other things. The men had been talking together, when the child suddenly planted herself in front of them and said: "These things have not given me as much pleasure as the dear doctor's coming." Both men smiled.

When it was near sunset, the doctor rose to start on his way down. The grandfather, carrying the box, the shawl and the sausage, and the guest holding the little girl by the hand, they wandered down the mountain-side. When they reached Peter's hut, Heidi was told to go inside and wait for her grandfather there. At parting she asked: "Would you like to come with me up to the pasture to-morrow, doctor?"

"With pleasure. Good-bye, Heidi," was the reply. The grandfather had deposited all the presents before the door, and it took Heidi long to carry in the huge box and the sausage. The shawl she put on the grandmother's knee.

Brigida had silently watched the proceedings, and could not open her eyes wide enough when she saw the enormous sausage. Never in her life had she seen the like, and now she really possessed it and could cut it herself.

"Oh grandmother, don't the cakes please you awfully? Just look how soft they are!" the child exclaimed. What was her amazement when she saw the grandmother more pleased with the shawl, which would keep her warm in winter.

"Grandmother, Clara has sent you that," Heidi said.

"Oh, what kind good people they are to think of a poor old woman like me! I never thought I should ever own such a splendid wrap."

At this moment Peter came stumbling in.

"The uncle is coming up behind me, and Heidi must—" that was as far as he got, for his eyes had fastened on the sausage. Heidi, however, had already said good-bye, for she knew what he had meant. Though her uncle never went by the hut any more without stepping in, she knew it was too late to-day. "Heidi, come, you must get your sleep," he called through the open door. Bidding them all good-night, he took Heidi by the hand and under the glistening stars they wandered home to their peaceful cottage.

Day 60

1. The next chapter is called **retaliation**. Retaliation means getting back at someone.
2. In the first paragraph you will read the word **monosyllables**. Do you see the word **syllable** in there? Do you remember what a syllable is? (Look again at Day 6 if you forget.) Mono means one. It says that Peter was giving monosyllables for answers. He was answering the doctor with words with only one syllable. Basically he was giving short replies, yes, no…and nothing more. (If you used the "Reading 2" course/book, then you learned that this type of reply can be referred to as a Laconic answer.)
3. In this chapter you will read **luminous** and **radiant**. They are synonyms, words with similar meaning. They mean lit up, shining, bright.
4. Read chapter 17.
5. Why does Peter want to get back at the doctor? (Answers)
6. You read, "The doctor was loath to go." What does that mean? (Answers)
7. You read that the sun was at its "zenith." Guess what that means? (Answers)

Vocabulary

1. Review your Heidi vocabulary by going to Day 35 or to the review game page on the Easy Peasy website and playing the first Heidi game under Level 3.

Chapter 17 RETALIATION

Early the next morning the doctor climbed up the mountain in company with Peter and his goats. The friendly gentleman made several attempts to start a conversation with the boy, but as answer to his questions he got nothing more than monosyllables. When they arrived on top, they found Heidi already waiting, fresh and rosy as the early dawn.

"Are you coming?" asked Peter as usual.

"Of course I shall, if the doctor comes with us," replied the child.

The grandfather, coming out of the hut, greeted the newcomer with great respect. Then he went up to Peter, and hung on his shoulder the sack, which seemed to contain more than usual that day.

When they had started on their way, Heidi kept urging forward the goats, which were crowding about her. When at last she was walking peacefully by the doctor's side, she began to relate to him many things about the goats and all their strange pranks, and about the flowers, rocks and birds they saw. When they arrived at their destination, time seemed to have flown. Peter all the time was sending many an angry glance at the unconscious doctor, who never even noticed it.

Heidi now took the doctor to her favorite spot. From there they could hear the peaceful-sounding bells of the grazing cattle below. The sky was deep blue, and above their heads the eagle was circling with outstretched wings. Everything was luminous and bright about them, but the doctor had been silent. Suddenly looking up, he beheld Heidi's radiant eyes.

"Heidi, it is beautiful up here," he said. "But how can anybody with a heavy heart enjoy the beauty? Tell me!"

"Oh," exclaimed Heidi, "one never has a sad heart here. One only gets unhappy in Frankfurt."

A faint smile passed over the doctor's face. Then he began: "But if somebody has brought his sorrow away with him, how would you comfort him?"

"God in Heaven alone can help him."

"That is true, child," remarked the doctor. "But what can we do when God Himself has sent us the affliction?"

After meditating a moment, Heidi replied: "One must wait patiently, for God knows how to turn the saddest things to something happy in the end. God will show us what He has meant to do for us. But He will only do so if we pray to Him patiently."

"I hope you will always keep this beautiful belief, Heidi," said the doctor. Then looking up at the mighty cliffs above, he continued: "Think how sad it would make us not to be able to see all these beautiful things. Wouldn't that make us doubly sad? Can you understand me, child?"

A great pain shot through Heidi's breast. She had to think of the poor grandmother. Her blindness was always a great sorrow to the child, and she had been struck with it anew. Seriously she replied:

"Oh yes, I can understand it. But then we can read grandmother's songs; they make us happy and bright again."

"Which songs, Heidi?"

"Oh, those of the sun, and of the beautiful garden, and then the last verses of the long one. Grandmother loves them so that I always have to read them over three times," said Heidi.

"I wish you would say them to me, child, for I should like to hear them," said the doctor.

Heidi, folding her hands, began the consoling verses. She stopped suddenly, however, for the doctor did not seem to listen. He was sitting motionless, holding his hand before his eyes. Thinking that he had fallen asleep, she remained silent. But the verses had recalled his childhood days; he seemed to hear his mother and see her loving eyes, for when he was a little boy she had sung this song to him. A long time he sat there, till he discovered that Heidi was watching him.

"Heidi, your song was lovely," he said with a more joyful voice. "We must come here another day and then you can recite it to me again."

During all this time Peter had been boiling with anger. Now that Heidi had come again to the pasture with him, she did nothing but talk to the old gentleman. It made him very cross that he was not even able to get near her. Standing a little distance behind Heidi's friend, he shook his fist at him, and soon afterwards both fists, finally raising them up to the sky, as Heidi and the doctor remained together.

When the sun stood in its zenith and Peter knew that it was noon, he called over to them with all his might: "Time to eat."

When Heidi was getting up to fetch their dinner, the doctor just asked for a glass of milk, which was all he wanted. The child also decided to make the milk her sole repast, running over to Peter and informing him of their resolution.

When the boy found that the whole contents of the bag was his, he hurried with his task as never in his life before. But he felt guilty on account of his former anger at the kind gentleman. To show his repentance he held his hands up flat to the sky, indicating by his action that his fists did not mean anything any more. Only after that did he start with his feast.

Heidi and the doctor had wandered about the pasture till the gentleman had found it time to go. He wanted Heidi to remain where she was, but she insisted on accompanying him. All the way down she showed him many places where the pretty mountain flowers grew, all of whose names she could tell him. When they parted at last, Heidi waved to him. From time to time he turned about, and seeing the child still standing there, he had to think of his own little daughter who used to wave to him like that when he went away from home.

The weather was warm and sunny that month. Every morning the doctor came up to the Alp, spending his day very often with the old man. Many a climb they had together that took them far up, to the bare cliffs near the eagle's haunt. The uncle would show his guest all the herbs that grew on hidden places and were strengthening and healing. He could tell many strange things of the beasts that lived in holes in rock or earth, or in the high tops of trees.

In the evening they would part, and the doctor would exclaim: "My dear friend, I never leave you without having learned something."

But most of his days he spent with Heidi. Then the two would sit together on the child's favorite spot, and Peter, quite subdued, behind them. Heidi had to recite the verses, as she had done the first day, and entertain him with all the things she knew.

At last the beautiful month of September was over. One morning the doctor came up with a sadder face than usual. The time had come for him to go back to Frankfurt, and great was the uncle's sadness at that news. Heidi herself could hardly realize that her loving friend, whom she had been seeing every day, was really leaving. The doctor himself was loath to go, for the Alp had become as a home to him. But it was necessary for him to go, and shaking hands with the grandfather, he said good-bye, Heidi going along with him a little way.

Hand in hand they wandered down, till the doctor stood still. Then caressing Heidi's curly hair, he said: "Now I must go, Heidi! I wish I could take you along with me to Frankfurt; then I could keep you."

At those words, all the rows and rows of houses and streets, Miss Rottenmeier and Tinette rose before Heidi's eyes. Hesitating a little, she said: "I should like it better if you would come to see us again."

"I believe that will be better. Now farewell!" said the friendly gentleman. When they shook hands his eyes filled with tears. Turning quickly he hurried off.

Heidi, standing on the same spot, looked after him. What kind eyes he had! But they had been full of tears. All of a sudden she began to cry bitterly, and ran after her friend, calling with all her might, but interrupted by her sobs:

"Oh doctor, doctor!"

Looking round he stood still and waited till the child had reached him. Her tears came rolling down her cheeks while she sobbed: "I'll come with you to Frankfurt and I'll stay as long as ever you want me to. But first I must see grandfather."

"No, no, dear child," he said affectionately, "not at once. You must remain here, I don't want you to get ill again. But if I should get sick and lonely and ask you to come to me, would you come and stay with me? Can I go away and think that somebody in this world still cares for me and loves me?"

"Yes, I shall come to you the same day, for I really love you as much as grandfather," Heidi assured him, crying all the time.

Shaking hands again, they parted. Heidi stayed on the same spot, waving her hand and looking after her departing friend till he seemed no bigger than a little dot. Then he looked back a last time at Heidi and the sunny Alp, muttering to himself: "It is beautiful up there. Body and soul get strengthened in that place and life seems worth living again."

Day 61

1. Read the beginning of chapter 18.
2. Describe the house Heidi and her grandfather are living in for the winter. (Answers)

Chapter 18 WINTER IN THE VILLAGE

The snow lay so deep around the Alm-hut that the windows seemed to stand level with the ground and the house-door had entirely disappeared. Round Peter's hut it was the same. When the boy went out to shovel the snow, he had to creep through the window; then he would sink deep into the soft snow and kick with arms and legs to get free. Taking a broom, the boy would have to clear away the snow from the door to prevent its falling into the hut.

The uncle had kept his word; when the first snow had fallen, he had moved down to the village with Heidi and his goats. Near the church and the parish house lay an old ruin that once had been a spacious building. A brave soldier had lived there in days gone by; he had fought in the Spanish war, and coming back with many riches, had built himself a splendid house. But having lived too long in the noisy world to be able to stand the monotonous life in the little town, he soon went away, never to come back. After his death, many years later, though the house was already beginning to decay, a distant relation of his took possession of it. The new proprietor did not want to build it up again, so poor people moved in. They had to pay little rent for the house, which was gradually crumbling and falling to pieces. Years ago, when the uncle had come to the village with Tobias, he had lived there. Most of the time it had been empty, for the winter lasted long, and cold winds would blow through the chinks in the walls. When poor people lived there, their candles would be blown out and they would shiver with cold in the dark. But the uncle, had known how to help himself. In the fall, as soon as he had resolved to live in the village, he came down frequently, fitting up the place as best he could.

On approaching the house from the back, one entered an open room, where nearly all the walls lay in ruins. On one side the remains of a chapel could be seen, now covered with the thickest ivy. A large hall came next, with a beautiful stone floor and grass growing in the crevices. Most of the walls were gone and part of the ceiling also. If a few thick pillars had not been left supporting the rest, it would undoubtedly have tumbled down. The uncle had made a wooden partition here for the goats, and covered the floor with straw. Several corridors, most of them half decayed, led finally to a chamber with a heavy iron door. This room was still in good condition and had dark wood panelling on the four firm walls. In one corner was an enormous stove, which nearly reached up to the ceiling. On the white tiles were painted blue pictures of old towers surrounded by high trees, and of hunters with their hounds. There also was a scene with a quiet lake, where, under shady oak-trees, a fisherman was sitting. Around the stove a bench was placed. Heidi loved to sit there, and as soon as she had entered their new abode, she began to examine the pictures. Arriving at the end of the bench, she discovered a bed, which was placed between the wall and the stove. "Oh grandfather, I have found my bed-room," exclaimed the little girl. "Oh, how fine it is! Where are you going to sleep?"

"Your bed must be near the stove, to keep you warm," said the old man. "Now come and look at mine."

With that the grandfather led her into his bed-room. From there a door led into the hugest kitchen Heidi had ever seen. With a great deal of trouble the grandfather had fitted up this place. Many boards were nailed across the walls and the door had been fastened with heavy wires, for beyond, the building lay in ruins. Thick underbrush was growing there, sheltering thousands of insects and lizards. Heidi was delighted with her new home, and when Peter arrived next day, she did not rest till he had seen every nook and corner of the curious dwelling-place.

Heidi slept very well in her chimney corner, but it took her many days to get accustomed to it. When she woke up in the morning and could not hear the fir-trees roar, she would wonder where she was. Was the snow too heavy on the branches? Was she away from home? But as soon as she heard her grandfather's voice outside, she remembered everything and would jump merrily out of bed.

After four days had gone by, Heidi said to her grandfather: "I must go to grandmother now, she has been alone so many days."

But the grandfather shook his head and said: "You can't go yet, child. The snow is fathoms deep up there and is still falling. Peter can hardly get through. A little girl like you would be snowed up and lost in no time. Wait a while till it freezes and then you can walk on top of the crust."

Heidi was very sorry, but she was so busy now that the days flew by. Every morning and afternoon she went to school, eagerly learning whatever was taught her. She hardly ever saw Peter there, for he did not come very often. The mild teacher would only say from time to time: "It seems to me, Peter is not here again! School would do him good, but I guess there is too much snow for him to get through." But when Heidi came home towards evening, Peter generally paid her a visit.

After a few days the sun came out for a short time at noon, and the next morning the whole Alp glistened and shone like crystal. When Peter was jumping as usual into the snow that morning, he fell against something hard, and before he could stop himself he flew a little way down the mountain. When he had gained his feet at last, he stamped upon the ground with all his might. It really was frozen as hard as stone. Peter could hardly believe it, and quickly running up and swallowing his milk, and putting his bread in his pocket, he announced: "I must go to school to-day!"

"Yes, go and learn nicely," answered his mother.

Then, sitting down on his sled, the boy coasted down the mountain like a shot. Not being able to stop his course when he reached the village, he coasted down further and further, till he arrived in the plain, where the sled stopped of itself. It was already late for school, so the boy took his time and only arrived in the village when Heidi came home for dinner.

Day 62

1.   Finish chapter 18.

2. Why does Peter decide to go to school? (Answers)
3. What brings the grandmother joy? (Answers)
4. What do you think is Heidi's idea so that grandmother could hear the words of the songs every day? (Answers)

Chapter 18 continued

"We've got it!" announced the boy, on entering.

"What, general?" asked the uncle.

"The snow," Peter replied.

"Oh, now I can go up to grandmother!" Heidi rejoiced. "But Peter, why didn't you come to school? You could coast down to-day," she continued reproachfully.

"I went too far on my sled and then it was too late," Peter replied.

"I call that deserting!" said the uncle. "People who do that must have their ears pulled; do you hear?"

The boy was frightened, for there was no one in the world whom he respected more than the uncle.

"A general like you ought to be doubly ashamed to do so," the uncle went on. "What would you do with the goats if they did not obey you any more?"

"Beat them," was the reply.

"If you knew of a boy that was behaving like a disobedient goat and had to get spanked, what would you say?"

"Serves him right."

"So now you know it, goat-general: if you miss school again, when you ought to be there, you can come to me and get your due."

Now at last Peter understood what the uncle had meant. More kindly, the old man then turned to Peter and said, "Come to the table now and eat with us. Then you can go up with Heidi, and when you bring her back at night, you can get your supper here."

This unexpected change delighted Peter. Not losing any time, he soon disposed of his full plate. Heidi, who had given the boy most of her dinner, was already putting on Clara's new coat. Then together they climbed up, Heidi chatting all the time. But Peter did not say a single word. He was preoccupied and had not even listened to Heidi's tales. Before they entered the hut, the boy said stubbornly: "I think I had rather go to school than get a beating from the uncle." Heidi promptly confirmed him in his resolution.

When they went into the room, Peter's mother was alone at the table mending. The grandmother was nowhere to be seen. Brigida now told Heidi that the grandmother was obliged to stay in bed on those cold days, as she did not feel very strong. That was something new for Heidi. Quickly running to the old woman's chamber, she found her lying in a narrow bed, wrapped up in her grey shawl and thin blanket.

"Thank Heaven!" the grandmother exclaimed when she heard her darling's step. All autumn and winter long a secret fear had been gnawing at her heart, that Heidi would be sent for by the strange gentleman of whom Peter had told her so much. Heidi had approached the bed, asking anxiously: "Are you very sick, grandmother?"

"No, no, child," the old woman reassured her, "the frost has just gone into my limbs a little."

"Are you going to be well again as soon as the warm weather comes?" inquired Heidi.

"Yes, yes, and if God wills, even sooner. I want to go back to my spinning-wheel and I nearly tried it to-day. I'll get up to-morrow, though," the grandmother said confidently, for she had noticed how frightened Heidi was.

The last speech made the child feel more happy. Then, looking wonderingly at the grandmother, she said: "In Frankfurt people put on a shawl when they go out. Why are you putting it on in bed, grandmother?"

"I put it on to keep me warm, Heidi. I am glad to have it, for my blanket is very thin."

"But, grandmother, your bed is slanting down at your head, where it ought to be high. No bed ought to be like that."

"I know, child, I can feel it well." So saying, the old woman tried to change her position on the pillow that lay under her like a thin board. "My pillow never was very thick, and sleeping on it all these years has made it flat."

"Oh dear, if I had only asked Clara to give me the bed I had in Frankfurt!" Heidi lamented. "It had three big pillows on it; I could hardly sleep because I kept sliding down from them all the time. Could you sleep with them, grandmother?"

"Of course, because that would keep me warm. I could breathe so much easier, too," said the grandmother, trying to find a higher place to lie on. "But I must not talk about it any more, for I have to be thankful for many things. I get the lovely roll every day and have this beautiful warm shawl. I also have you, my child! Heidi, wouldn't you like to read me something to-day?"

Heidi immediately fetched the book and read one song after another. The grandmother in the meantime was lying with folded hands; her face, which had been so sad a short time ago, was lit up with a happy smile.

Suddenly Heidi stopped.

"Are you well again, grandmother?" she asked.

"I feel very much better, Heidi. Please finish the song, will you?"

The child obeyed, and when she came to the last words,

> When mine eyes grow dim and sad,
> Let Thy love more brightly burn,
> That my soul, a wanderer glad,
> Safely homeward may return.

"Safely homeward may return!" she exclaimed: "Oh, grandmother, I know what it is like to come home." After a while she said: "It is getting dark, grandmother, I must go home now. I am glad that you feel better again."

The grandmother, holding the child's hand in hers, said: "Yes, I am happy again, though I have to stay in bed. Nobody knows how hard it is to lie here alone, day after day. I do not hear a word from anybody and cannot see a ray of sunlight. I have very sad thoughts sometimes, and often I feel as if I could not bear it any longer. But when I can hear those blessed songs that you have read to me, it makes me feel as if a light was shining into my heart, giving me the purest joy."

Shaking hands, the child now said good-night, and pulling Peter with her, ran outside. The brilliant moon was shining down on the white snow, light as day. The two children were already flying down the Alp, like birds soaring through the air.

After Heidi had gone to bed that night, she lay awake a little while, thinking over everything the grandmother had said, especially about the joy the songs had given her. If only poor grandmother could hear those comforting words every day! Heidi knew that it might be a week or two again before she could repeat her visit. The child became very sad when she thought how uncomfortable and lonely the old woman would be. Was there no way for help? Suddenly Heidi had an idea, and it thrilled her so that she felt as if she could not wait till morning came to put her plan in execution. But in her excitement she had forgotten her evening prayer, so sitting up in bed, she prayed fervently to God. Then, falling back into the fragrant hay, she soon slept peacefully and soundly still the bright morning came.

Day 63

1. Read chapter 19.
2. What happens in chapter 19? (Answers)

Chapter 19 WINTER STILL CONTINUES

Peter arrived punctually at school next day. He had brought his lunch with him in a bag, for all the children that came from far away ate in school, while the others went home. In the evening Peter as usual paid his visit to Heidi.

The minute he opened the door she ran up to him, saying: "Peter, I have to tell you something."

"Say it," he replied.

"You must learn to read now," said the child.

"I have done it already."

"Yes, yes, Peter, but I don't mean it that way," Heidi eagerly proceeded; "you must learn so that you really know how afterwards."

"I can't," Peter remarked.

"Nobody believes you about that any more, and I won't either," Heidi said resolutely. "When I was in Frankfurt, grandmama told me that it wasn't true and that I shouldn't believe you."

Peter's astonishment was great.

"I'll teach you, for I know how; when you have learnt it, you must read one or two songs to grandmother every day."

"I shan't!" grumbled the boy.

This obstinate refusal made Heidi very angry. With flaming eyes she planted herself before the boy and said: "I'll tell you what will happen, if you don't want to learn. Your mother has often said that she'll send you to Frankfurt. Clara showed me the terrible, large boys' school there, where you'll have to go. You must stay there till you are a man, Peter! You mustn't think that there is only one teacher there, and such a kind one as we have here. No, indeed! There are whole rows of them, and when they are out walking they have high black hats on their heads. I saw them myself, when I was out driving!"

Cold shivers ran down Peter's back.

"Yes, you'll have to go there, and when they find out that you can't read or even spell, they'll laugh at you!"

"I'll do it," said Peter, half angry and half frightened.

"Oh, I am glad. Let us start right away!" said Heidi joyfully, pulling Peter over to the table. Among the things that Clara had sent, Heidi had found a little book with the A,B,C and some rhymes. She had chosen this for the lessons. Peter, having to spell the first rhyme, found great difficulty, so Heidi said, "I'll read it to you, and then you'll be able to do it better. Listen:

> "If A, B, C you do not know,
> Before the school board you must go."

"I won't go," said Peter stubbornly.

"Where?"

"Before the court."

"Hurry up and learn the three letters, then you won't have to!"

Peter, beginning again, repeated the three letters till Heidi said:

"Now you know them."

Having observed the good result of the first rhyme, she began to read again:

> D, E, F you then must read,
> Or of misfortune take good heed!
> Who over L and M doth stumble,
> Must pay a penance and feel humble.
> There's trouble coming; if you knew,
> You'd quickly learn N, O, P, Q.
> If still you halt on R, S, T,
> You'll suffer for it speedily.

Heidi, stopping, looked at Peter, who was so frightened by all these threats and mysterious horrors that he sat as still as a mouse. Heidi's tender heart was touched, and she said comfortingly: "Don't be afraid, Peter; if you come to me every day, you'll soon learn all the letters and then those things won't happen. But come every day, even when it snows. Promise!"

Peter did so, and departed. Obeying Heidi's instructions, he came daily to her for his lesson.

Sometimes the grandfather would sit in the room, smoking his pipe; often the corners of his mouth would twitch as if he could hardly keep from laughing.

He generally invited Peter to stay to supper afterwards, which liberally rewarded the boy for all his great exertions.

Thus the days passed by. In all this time Peter had really made some progress, though the rhymes still gave him difficulty.

When they had come to U, Heidi read:

> Whoever mixes U and V,
> Will go where he won't want to be! and further,
> If W you still ignore,
> Look at the rod beside the door.

Often Peter would growl and object to those measures, but nevertheless he kept on learning, and soon had but three letters left.

The next few days the following rhymes, with their threats, made Peter more eager than ever.

> If you the letter X forget
> For you no supper will be set.
> If you still hesitate with Y,
> For shame you'll run away and cry.

When Heidi read the last,

And he who makes his Z with blots,
Must journey to the Hottentots,

Peter sneered: "Nobody even knows where they are!"

"I am sure grandfather does," Heidi retorted, jumping up. "Just wait one minute and I shall ask him. He is over with the parson," and with that she had opened the door.

"Wait!" shrieked Peter in great alarm, for he saw himself already transported to those dreadful people. "What is the matter with you?" said Heidi, standing still.

"Nothing, but stay here. I'll learn," he blubbered. But Heidi, wanting to know something about the Hottentots herself, could only be kept back by piteous screams from Peter. So at last they settled down again, and before it was time to go, Peter knew the last letter, and had even begun to read syllables. From this day on he progressed more quickly.

It was three weeks since Heidi had paid her last visit to the grandmother, for much snow had fallen since. One evening, Peter, coming home, said triumphantly:

"I can do it!"

"What is it you can do, Peter?" asked his mother, eagerly.

"Read."

"What, is it possible? Did you hear it, grandmother?" exclaimed Brigida.

The grandmother also was curious to learn how this had happened.

"I must read a song now; Heidi told me to," Peter continued. To the women's amazement, Peter began. After every verse his mother would exclaim, "Who would have ever thought it!" while the grandmother remained silent.

One day later, when it happened that it was Peter's turn to read in school, the teacher said:

"Peter, must I pass you by again, as usual? Or do you want to try—I shall not say to read, but to stammer through a line?"

Peter began and read three lines without stopping.

In dumb astonishment, the teacher, putting down his book, looked at the boy.

"What miracle has happened to you?" he exclaimed. "For a long time I tried to teach you with all my patience, and you were not even able to grasp the letters, but now that I had given you up as hopeless, you have not only learnt how to spell, but even to read. How did this happen, Peter?"

"It was Heidi," the boy replied.

In great amazement, the teacher looked at the little girl. Then the kind man continued:

"I have noticed a great change in you, Peter. You used to stay away from school, sometimes more than a week, and lately you have not even missed a day. Who has brought about this change?"

"The uncle."

Every evening now Peter on his return home read one song to his grandmother, but never more. To the frequent praises of Brigida, the old woman once replied: "I am glad he has learnt something, but nevertheless I am longing for the spring to come. Then Heidi can visit me, for when she reads, the verses sound so different. I cannot always follow Peter, and the songs don't thrill me the way they do when Heidi says them!"

And no wonder! For Peter would often leave out long and difficult words,—what did three or four words matter! So it happened sometimes that there were hardly any nouns left in the hymns that Peter read.

Day 64

1. Read the beginning of chapter 20.
2. What does Heidi receive? (Answers)
3. What is grandmother worried about? (Answers)

Chapter 20 NEWS FROM DISTANT FRIENDS

May had come. Warm sunshine was bathing the whole Alp in glorious light, and having melted the last snow, had brought the first spring flowers to the surface. A merry spring wind was blowing, drying up the damp places in the shadow. High above in the azure heaven the eagle floated peacefully.

Heidi and her grandfather were back on the Alp. The child was so happy to be home again that she jumped about among the beloved objects. Here she discovered a new spring bud, and there she watched the gay little gnats and beetles that were swarming in the sun.

The grandfather was busy in his little shop, and a sound of hammering and sawing could be heard. Heidi had to go and see what the grandfather was making. There before the door stood a neat new chair, while the old man was busy making a second.

"Oh, I know what they are for," said Heidi gaily. "You are making them for Clara and grandmama. Oh, but we need a third—or do you think that Miss Rottenmeier won't come, perhaps?"

"I really don't know," said grandfather: "but it is safer to have a chair for her, if she should come."

Heidi, thoughtfully looking at the backless chairs, remarked: "Grandfather, I don't think she would sit down on those."

"Then we must invite her to sit down on the beautiful green lounge of grass," quietly answered the old man.

While Heidi was still wondering what the grandfather had meant, Peter arrived, whistling and calling. As usual, Heidi was soon surrounded by the goats, who also seemed happy to be back on the Alp. Peter, angrily pushing the goats aside, marched up to Heidi, thrusting a letter into her hand.

"Did you get a letter for me on the pasture?" Heidi said, astonished.

"No."

"Where did it come from?"

"From my bag."

The letter had been given to Peter the previous evening; putting it in his lunch-bag, the boy had forgotten it there till he opened the bag for his dinner. Heidi immediately recognized Clara's handwriting, and bounding over to her grandfather, exclaimed: "A letter has come from Clara. Wouldn't you like me to read it to you, grandfather?"

Heidi immediately read to her two listeners, as follows:—

Dear Heidi:—

We are all packed up and shall travel in two or three days. Papa is leaving, too, but not with us, for he has to go to Paris first. The dear doctor visits us now every day, and as soon as he opens the door, he calls, 'Away to the Alp!' for he can hardly wait for us to go. If you only knew how he enjoyed being with you last fall! He came nearly every day this winter to tell us all about you and the grandfather and the mountains and the flowers he saw. He said that it was so quiet in the pure, delicious air, away from towns and streets, that everybody has to get well there. He is much better himself since his visit, and seems younger and happier. Oh, how I look forward to it all! The doctor's advice is, that I shall go to Ragatz first for about six weeks, then I can go to live in the village, and from there I shall come to see you every fine day. Grandmama, who is coming with me, is looking forward to the trip too. But just think, Miss Rottenmeier does not want to go. When grandmama urges her, she always declines politely. I think Sebastian must have given her such a terrible description of the high rocks and fearful abysses, that she is afraid. I think he told her that it was not safe for anybody, and that only goats could climb such dreadful heights. She used to be so eager to go to Switzerland, but now neither Tinette nor she wants to take the risk. I can hardly wait to see you again!

Good-bye, dear Heidi, with much love from grandmama,

I am your true friend,
            Clara.

When Peter heard this, he swung his rod to right and left. Furiously driving the goats before him, he bounded down the hill.

Heidi visited the grandmother next day, for she had to tell her the good news. Sitting up in her corner, the old woman was spinning as usual. Her face looked sad, for Peter had already announced the near visit of Heidi's friends, and she dreaded the result.

After having poured out her full heart, Heidi looked at the old woman. "What is it, grandmother?" said the child. "Are you not glad?"

"Oh yes, Heidi, I am glad, because you are happy."

"But, grandmother, you seem so anxious. Do you still think Miss Rottenmeier is coming?"

"Oh no, it is nothing. Give me your hand, for I want to be sure that you are still here. I suppose it will be for the best, even if I shall not live to see the day!"

"Oh, but then I would not care about this coming," said the child.

The grandmother had hardly slept all night for thinking of Clara's coming. Would they take Heidi away from her, now that she was well and strong? But for the sake of the child she resolved to be brave.

"Heidi," she said, "please read me the song that begins with 'God will see to it.'"

Heidi immediately did as she was told; she knew nearly all the grandmother's favorite hymns by now and always found them quickly.

"That does me good, child," the old woman said. Already the expression of her face seemed happier and less troubled. "Please read it a few times over, child," she entreated.

Thus evening came, and when Heidi wandered homewards, one twinkling star after another appeared in the sky. Heidi stood still every few minutes, looking up to the firmament in wonder. When she arrived home, her grandfather also was looking up to the stars, murmuring to himself: "What a wonderful month!—one day clearer than the other. The herbs will be fine and strong this year."

The blossom month had passed, and June, with the long, long days, had come. Quantities of flowers were blooming everywhere, filling the air with perfume. The month was nearing its end, when one morning Heidi came running out of the hut, where she had already completed her duties. Suddenly she screamed so loud that the grandfather hurriedly came out to see what had happened.

Day 65

1. Finish reading chapter 20.
2. Why is Peter so mad? (Answers)

Vocabulary

1. Review your vocabulary from the third chapter of Heidi by either going to Day 40 or to the Review Games page of the Easy Peasy website.

Chapter 20 continued

"Grandfather! Come here! Look, look!"

A strange procession was winding up the Alm. First marched two men, carrying an open sedan chair with a young girl in it, wrapped up in many shawls. Then came a stately lady on horseback, who, talking with a young guide beside her, looked eagerly right and left. Then an empty rolling-chair, carried by a young fellow, was followed by a porter who had so many covers, shawls and furs piled up on his basket that they towered high above his head.

"They are coming! they are coming!" cried Heidi in her joy, and soon the party had arrived at the top. Great was the happiness of the children at seeing each other again. When grandmama had descended from her horse, she tenderly greeted Heidi first, and then turned to the uncle, who had approached the group. The two met like two old friends, they had heard so much about each other.

After the first words were exchanged, the grandmother exclaimed: "My dear uncle, what a wonderful residence you have. Who would have ever thought it! Kings could envy you here! Oh, how well my Heidi is looking, just like a little rose!" she continued, drawing the child closely to her side and patting her cheeks. "What glory everywhere! Clara, what do you say to it all?"

Clara, looking about her rapturously, cried: "Oh, how wonderful, how glorious! I have never dreamt it could be as beautiful as that. Oh grandmama, I wish I could stay here!"

The uncle had busied himself in the meantime with getting Clara's rolling-chair for her. Then, going up to the girl, he gently lifted her into her seat. Putting some covers over her knees, he tucked her feet in warmly. It seemed as if the grandfather had done nothing else all his life than nurse lame people.

"My dear uncle," said the grandmama, surprised, "please tell me where you learned that, for I shall send all the nurses I know here immediately."

The uncle smiled faintly, while he replied: "It comes more from care than study."

His face became sad. Before his eyes had risen bygone times. For that was the way he used to care for his poor wounded captain, whom he had found in Sicily after a violent battle. He alone had been allowed to nurse him till his death, and now he would take just as good care of poor, lame Clara.

When Clara had looked a long time at the cloudless sky above and all the rocky crags, she said longingly: "I wish I could walk round the hut to the fir-trees. If I only could see all the things you told me so much about!"

Heidi pushed with all her might, and behold! the chair rolled easily over the dry grass. When they had come into the little grove, Clara could not see her fill of those splendid trees that must have stood there so many, many years. Although the people had changed and vanished, they had remained the same, ever looking down into the valley.

When they passed the empty goat-shed, Clara said pitifully: "Oh grandmama, if I could only wait up here for Schwänli and Bärli! I am afraid I shan't see Peter and his goats, if we have to go away so soon again."

"Dear child, enjoy now what you can," said the grandmama, who had followed.

"Oh, what wonderful flowers!" exclaimed Clara again; "whole bushes of exquisite, red blossoms. Oh, if I could only pick some of those bluebells!"

Heidi, immediately gathering a large bunch, put them in Clara's lap.

"Clara, this is really nothing in comparison with the many flowers in the pasture. You must come up once and see them. There are so many that the ground seems golden with them. If you ever sit down among them, you will feel as if you could never get up any more, it is so beautiful."

"Oh, grandmama, do you think I can ever go up there?" Clara asked with a wild longing in her eyes. "If I could only walk with you, Heidi, and climb round everywhere!"

146

"I'll push you!" Heidi said for comfort. To show how easy it was, she pushed the chair at such a rate that it would have tumbled down the mountain, if the grandfather had not stopped it at the last moment.

It was time for dinner now. The table was spread near the bench, and soon everybody sat down. The grandmother was so overcome by the view and the delicious wind that fanned her cheek that she remarked: "What a wondrous place this is! I have never seen its like! But what do I see?" she continued. "I think you are actually eating your second piece of cheese, Clara?"

"Oh grandmama, it tastes better than all the things we get in Ragatz," replied the child, eagerly eating the savory dish.

"Don't stop, our mountain wind helps along where the cooking is faulty!" contentedly said the old man.

During the meal the uncle and the grandmama had soon got into a lively conversation. They seemed to agree on many things, and understood each other like old friends. A little later the grandmama looked over to the west.

"We must soon start, Clara, for the sun is already low; our guides will be here shortly."

Clara's face had become sad, and she entreated: "Oh, please let us stay here another hour or so. We haven't even seen the hut yet. I wish the day were twice as long."

The grandmama assented to Clara's wish to go inside. When the rolling-chair was found too broad for the door, the uncle quietly lifted Clara in his strong arms and carried her in. Grandmama was eagerly looking about her, glad to see everything so neat. Then going up the little ladder to the hay-loft, she discovered Heidi's bed. "Is that your bed, Heidi? What a delicious perfume! It must be a healthy place to sleep," she said, looking out through the window. The grandfather, with Clara, was coming up, too, with Heidi following.

Clara was perfectly entranced. "What a lovely place to sleep! Oh, Heidi, you can look right up to the sky from your bed. What a good smell! You can hear the fir-trees roar here, can't you? Oh, I never saw a more delightful bed-room!"

The uncle, looking at the old lady, said now: "I have an idea that it would give Clara new strength to stay up here with us a little while. Of course, I only mean if you did not object. You have brought so many wraps that we can easily make a soft bed for Clara here. My dear lady, you can easily leave the care to me. I'll undertake it gladly."

The children screamed for joy, and grandmama's face was beaming.

"What a fine man you are!" she burst out. "I was just thinking myself that a stay here would strengthen the child, but then I thought of the care and trouble for you. And now you have offered to do it, as if it was nothing at all. How can I thank you enough, uncle?"

After shaking hands many times, the two prepared Clara's bed, which, thanks to the old lady's precautions, was soon so soft that the hay could not be felt through at all.

The uncle had carried his new patient back to her rolling-chair, and there they found her sitting, with Heidi beside her. They were eagerly talking of their plans for the coming weeks. When they were told that Clara might stay for a month or so, their faces beamed more than ever.

The guide, with the horse, and the carriers of the chair, now appeared, but the last two were not needed any more and could be sent away.

When the grandmother got ready to leave, Clara called gaily to her: "Oh grandmama, it won't be long, for you must often come and see us."

While the uncle was leading the horse down the steep incline, the grandmama told him that she would go back to Ragatz, for the Dörfli was too lonely for her. She also promised to come back from time to time.

Before the grandfather had returned, Peter came racing down to the hut with all his goats. Seeing Heidi, they ran up to her in haste, and so Clara made the acquaintance of Schwänli and Bärli and all the others.

Peter, however, kept away, only sending furious looks at the two girls. When they bade him good-night, he only ran away, beating the air with his stick.

The end of the joyous day had come. The two children were both lying in their beds.

"Oh, Heidi!" Clara exclaimed, "I can see so many glittering stars, and I feel as if we were driving in a high carriage straight into the sky."

"Yes, and do you know why the stars twinkle so merrily?" inquired Heidi.

"No, but tell me."

"Because they know that God in heaven looks after us mortals and we never need to fear. See, they twinkle and show us how to be merry, too. But Clara, we must not forget to pray to God and ask Him to think of us and keep us safe."

Sitting up in bed, they then said their evening prayer. As soon as Heidi lay down, she fell asleep. But Clara could not sleep quite yet, it was too wonderful to see the stars from her bed.

In truth she had never seen them before, because in Frankfurt all the blinds were always down long before the stars came out, and at night she had never been outside the house. She could hardly keep her eyes shut, and had to open them again and again to watch the twinkling, glistening stars, till her eyes closed at last and she saw two big, glittering stars in her dream.

Day 66

1. At the beginning of the chapter Alm-uncle is looking at the "mountain and dale." The dale is the valley, the low parts between the mountains.
2. Read chapter 21.
3. What is grandfather making Clara do? Do you know why he is doing that? (Answers)

Chapter 21 FURTHER EVENTS ON THE ALPS

The sun was just rising, and the Alm-Uncle was watching how mountain and dale awoke to the new day, and the clouds above grew brighter.

Next, the old man turned to go back into the hut, and softly climbed the ladder. Clara, having just a moment ago opened her eyes, looked about her in amazement. Bright sunbeams danced on her bed. Where was she? But soon she discovered her sleeping friend, and heard the grandfather's cheery voice:

"How did you sleep? Not tired?"

Clara, feeling fresh and rested, said that she had never slept better in all her life. Heidi was soon awake, too, and lost no time in coming down to join Clara, who was already sitting in the sun.

A cool morning breeze fanned their cheeks, and the spicy fragrance from the fir-trees filled their lungs with every breath. Clara had never experienced such well-being in all her life. She had never breathed such pure, cool morning air and never felt such warm, delicious sunshine on her feet and hands. It surpassed all her expectations.

"Oh, Heidi, I wish I could always stay up here with you!" she said.

"Now you can see that everything is as beautiful as I told you," Heidi replied triumphantly. "Up on the Alp with grandfather is the loveliest spot in all the world."

The grandfather was just coming out of the shed with two full bowls of steaming, snow-white milk. Handing one to each of the children, he said to Clara: "This will do you good, little girl. It comes from Schwänli and will give you strength. To your health! Just drink it!" he said encouragingly, for Clara had hesitated a little. But when she saw that Heidi's bowl was nearly empty already, she also drank without even stopping. Oh, how good it was! It tasted like cinnamon and sugar.

"We'll take two tomorrow," said the grandfather.

After their breakfast, Peter arrived. While the goats were rushing up to Heidi, bleating loudly, the grandfather took the boy aside.

"Just listen, and do what I tell you," he said. "From now on you must let Schwänli go wherever she likes. She knows where to get the richest herbs, and you must follow her, even if she should go higher up than usual. It won't do you any harm to climb a little more, and will do all the others good. I want the goats to give me splendid milk, remember. What are you looking at so furiously?"

Peter was silent, and without more ado started off, still angrily looking back now and then. As Heidi had followed a little way, Peter called to her: "You must come along, Heidi, Schwänli has to be followed everywhere."

"No, but I can't," Heidi called back: "I won't be able to come as long as Clara is with me. Grandfather has promised, though, to let us come up with you once."

With those words Heidi returned to Clara, while the goatherd was hurrying onward, angrily shaking his fists.

The children had promised to write a letter to grandmama every day, so they immediately started on their task. Heidi brought out her own little three-legged stool, her school-books and her papers, and with these on Clara's lap they began to write. Clara stopped after nearly every sentence, for she had to look around. Oh, how peaceful it was with the little gnats dancing in the sun and the rustling of the trees! From time to time they could hear the shouting of a shepherd re-echoed from many rocks.

The morning had passed, they knew not how, and dinner was ready. They again ate outside, for Clara had to be in the open air all day, if possible. The afternoon was spent in the cool shadow of the fir-trees. Clara had many things to relate of Frankfurt and all the people that Heidi knew. It was not long before Peter arrived with his flock, but without even answering the girls' friendly greeting, he disappeared with a grim scowl.

While Schwänli was being milked in the shed, Clara said:

"Oh, Heidi, I feel as if I could not wait for my milk. Isn't it funny? All my life I have only eaten because I had to. Everything always tasted to me like cod-liver oil, and I have often wished that I should never have to eat. And now I am so hungry!"

"Oh yes, I know," Heidi replied. She had to think of the days in Frankfurt when her food seemed to stick in her throat.

When at last the full bowls were brought by the old man, Clara, seizing hers, eagerly drank the contents in one draught and even finished before Heidi.

"Please, may I have a little more?" she asked, holding out the bowl.

Nodding, much pleased, the grandfather soon refilled it. This time he also brought with him a slice of bread and butter for the children. He had gone to Maiensass that afternoon to get the butter, and his trouble was well rewarded: they enjoyed it as if it had been the rarest dish.

This evening Clara fell asleep the moment she lay down. Two or three days passed in this pleasant way. The next brought a surprise. Two strong porters came up the Alp, each carrying on his back a fresh, white bed. They also brought a letter from grandmama, in which she thanked the children for their faithful writing, and told them that the beds were meant for them. When they went to sleep that night, they found their new beds in exactly the same position as their former ones had been.

Clara's rapture in her new life grew greater every day, and she could not write enough of the grandfather's kindly care and of Heidi's entertaining stories. She told her grandmama that her first thought in the morning always was: "Thank God, I am still in the Alm-hut."

Grandmama was highly pleased at those reports, and put her projected visit off a little while, for she had found the ride pretty tiring.

The grandfather took excellent care of his little patient, and no day passed on which he did not climb around to find the most savory herbs for Schwänli. The little goat thrived so that everybody could see it in the way her eyes were flashing.

It was the third week of Clara's stay. Every morning after the grandfather had carried her down, he said to her: "Would my Clara try to stand a little?" Clara always sighed, "Oh, it hurts me so!" but though she would cling to him, he made her stand a little longer every day.

This summer was the finest that had been for years. Day after day the sun shone on a cloudless sky, and at night it would pour its purple, rosy light down on the rocks and snow-fields till everything seemed to glow like fire.

Heidi had told Clara over and over again of all the flowers on the pasture, of the masses of golden roses and the blue-flowers that covered the ground. She had just been telling it again, when a longing seized her, and jumping up she ran over to her grandfather, who was busy carving in the shop.

"Oh, grandfather," she cried from afar, "won't you come with us to the pasture tomorrow? Oh, it's so beautiful up there now."

"All right, I will," he replied; "but tell Clara that she must do something to please me; she must try to stand longer this evening for me."

Heidi merrily came running with her message. Of course, Clara promised, for was it not her greatest wish to go up with Heidi to the pasture! When Peter returned this evening, he heard of the plan for the morrow. But for answer Peter only growled, nearly hitting poor Thistlefinch in his anger.

The children had just resolved to stay awake all night to talk about the coming day, when their conversation suddenly ceased and they were both peacefully slumbering. In her dreams Clara saw before her a field that was thickly strewn with light-blue flowers, while Heidi heard the eagle scream to her from above, "Come, come, come!"

Day 67

1. In the beginning of the chapter Peter's sin, his anger, is going to get the best of him and cause him to do something bad. Then it says that his "conscience smote him." Your conscience is the thought you have inside of you that something is right or wrong. After he does it, his conscience is telling him that he did something really bad.
2. Read the beginning of chapter 22.
3. How does Clara feel on the mountain? (Answers)

Chapter 22 SOMETHING UNEXPECTED HAPPENS

The next day dawned cloudless and fair. The grandfather was still with the children, when Peter came climbing up; his goats kept at a good distance from him, to evade the rod, which was striking right and left. The truth was that the boy was terribly embittered and angry by the changes that had come. When he passed the hut in the morning, Heidi was always busy with the strange child, and in the evening it was the same. All summer long Heidi had not been up with him a single time; it was too much! And to-day she was coming at last, but again in company with this hateful stranger.

It was then that Peter noticed the rolling-chair standing near the hut. After carefully glancing about him, he rushed at the hated object and pushed it down the incline. The chair fairly flew away and had soon disappeared.

Peter's conscience smote him now, and he raced up the Alp, not daring to pause till he had reached a blackberry bush. There he could hide, when the uncle might appear. Looking down, he watched his fallen enemy tumbling downwards, downwards.

Sometimes it was thrown high up into the air, to crash down again the next moment harder than ever. Pieces were falling from it right and left, and were blown about. Now the stranger would have to travel home and Heidi would be his again! But Peter had forgotten that a bad deed always brings a punishment.

Heidi just now came out of the hut. The grandfather, with Clara, followed. Heidi at first stood still, and then, running right and left, she returned to the old man.

"What does this mean? Have you rolled the chair away Heidi?" he asked.

"I am just looking for it everywhere, grandfather. You said it was beside the shop door," said the child, still hunting for the missing object. A strong wind was blowing, which at this moment violently closed the shop-door.

"Grandfather, the wind has done it," exclaimed Heidi eagerly. "Oh dear! if it has rolled all the way down to the village, it will be too late to go to-day. It will take us a long time to fetch it."

"If it has rolled down there, we shall never get it any more, for it will be smashed to pieces," said the old man, looking down and measuring the distance from the corner of the hut.

"I don't see how it happened," he remarked.

"What a shame! now I'll never be able to go up to the pasture," lamented Clara. "I am afraid I'll have to go home now. What a pity, what a pity!"

"You can find a way for her to stay, grandfather, can't you?"

"We'll go up to the pasture to-day, as we have planned. Then we shall see what further happens."

The children were delighted, and the grandfather lost no time in getting ready. First he fetched a pile of covers, and seating Clara on a sunny spot on the dry ground, he got their breakfast.

"I wonder why Peter is so late to-day," he said, leading his goats out of the shed. Then, lifting Clara up on one strong arm, he carried the covers on the other.

"Now, march!" he cried. "The goats come with us."

That suited Heidi, and with one arm round Schwänli and the other round Bärli, she wandered up. Her little companions were so pleased at having her with them again that they nearly crushed her with affection.

What was their astonishment when, arriving on top, they saw Peter already lying on the ground, with his peaceful flock about him.

"What did you mean by going by us like that? I'll teach you!" called the uncle to him.

153

Peter was frightened, for he knew the voice.

"Nobody was up yet," the boy retorted.

"Have you seen the chair?" asked the uncle again.

"Which?" Peter growled.

The uncle said no more. Unfolding the covers, he put Clara down on the dry grass. Then, when he had been assured of Clara's comfort, he got ready to go home. The three were to stay there till his return in the evening. When dinner time had come, Heidi was to prepare the meal and see that Clara got Schwänli's milk.

The sky was a deep blue, and the snow on the peaks was glistening. The eagle was floating above the rocky crags. The children felt wonderfully happy. Now and then one of the goats would come and lie down near them. Tender little Snowhopper came oftener than any and would rub her head against their shoulders.

They had been sitting quietly for a few hours, drinking in the beauty about them, when Heidi suddenly began to long for the spot where so many flowers grew. In the evening it would be too late to see them, for they always shut their little eyes by then.

"Oh, Clara," she said hesitatingly, "would you be angry if I went away from you a minute and left you alone? I want to see the flowers; But wait!—" Jumping away, she brought Clara some bunches of fragrant herbs and put them in her lap. Soon after she returned with little Snowhopper.

"So, now you don't need to be alone," said Heidi. When Clara had assured her that it would give her pleasure to be left alone with the goats, Heidi started on her walk. Clara slowly handed one leaf after another to the little creature; it became more and more confiding, and cuddling close to the child, ate the herbs out of her hand. It was easy to see how happy it was to be away from the boisterous big goats, which often annoyed it. Clara felt a sensation of contentment such as she had never before experienced. She loved to sit there on the mountain-side with the confiding little goat by her. A great desire rose in her heart that hour. She longed to be her own master and be able to help others instead of being helped by them. Many other thoughts and ideas rushed through her mind. How would it be to live up here in continual sunshine? The world seemed so joyous and wonderful all of a sudden. Premonitions of future undreamt-of happiness made her heart beat. Suddenly she threw both arms about the little goat and said: "Oh, little Snowhopper how beautiful it is up here! If I could always stay with you!"

Heidi in the meantime had reached the spot, where, as she had expected, the whole ground was covered with yellow rock-roses. Near together in patches the bluebells were nodding gently in the breeze. But all the perfume that filled the air came from the modest little brown flowers that hid their heads between the golden flower-cups. Heidi stood enraptured, drawing in the perfumed air.

Suddenly she turned and ran back to Clara, shouting to her from far: "Oh, you must come, Clara, it is so lovely there. In the evening it won't be so fine any more. Don't you think I could carry you?"

"But Heidi," Clara said, "of course you can't; you are much smaller than I am. Oh, I wish I could walk!"

Heidi meditated a little. Peter was still lying on the ground. He had been staring down for hours, unable to believe what he saw before him. He had destroyed the chair to get rid of the stranger, and there she was again, sitting right beside his playmate.

Heidi now called to him to come down, but as reply he only grumbled: "Shan't come."

"But you must; come quickly, for I want you to help me. Quickly!" urged the child.

"Don't want to," sounded the reply.

Day 68

1. Finish reading chapter 22.
2. What do the girls thank God for? (Answers)
3. What does Heidi teach Clara about when God doesn't seem to answer your prayer? (Answers)

Vocabulary

1. Review your vocabulary by going to Day 45 or playing the third Heidi vocabulary game under Level 3 on the Review Games page of the Easy Peasy website.

Chapter 22 continued

Heidi now called to him to come down, but as reply he only grumbled: "Shan't come."

"But you must; come quickly, for I want you to help me. Quickly!" urged the child.

"Don't want to," sounded the reply.

Heidi hurried up the mountain now and shouted angrily to the boy: "Peter, if you don't come this minute, I shall do something that you won't like."

Those words scared Peter, for his conscience was not clear. His deed had rejoiced him till this moment, when Heidi seemed to talk as if she knew it all. What if the grandfather should hear about it! Trembling with fear, Peter obeyed.

"I shall only come if you promise not to do what you said," insisted the boy.

"No, no, I won't. Don't be afraid," said Heidi compassionately: "Just come along; it isn't so hard."

Peter, on approaching Clara, was told to help raise the lame child from the ground on one side, while Heidi helped on the other. This went easily enough, but difficulties soon followed. Clara was not able to stand alone, and how could they get any further?

"You must take me round the neck," said Heidi, who had seen what poor guides they made.

The boy, who had never offered his arm to anybody in his life, had to be shown how first, before further efforts could be made. But it was too hard. Clara tried to set her feet forward, but got discouraged.

"Press your feet on the ground more and I am sure it will hurt you less," suggested Heidi.

"Do you think so?" said Clara, timidly.

But, obeying, she ventured a firmer step and soon another, uttering a little cry as she went.

"Oh, it really has hurt me less," she said joyfully.

"Try it again," Heidi urged her. Clara did, and took another step, and then another, and another still. Suddenly she cried aloud: "Oh, Heidi, I can do it. Oh, I really can. Just look! I can take steps, one after another."

Heidi rapturously exclaimed: "Oh, Clara, can you really? Can you walk? Oh, can you take steps now? Oh, if only grandfather would come! Now you can walk, Clara, now you can walk," she kept on saying joyfully.

Clara held on tight to the children, but with every new step she became more firm.

"Now you can come up here every day," cried Heidi. "Now we can walk wherever we want to and you don't have to be pushed in a chair any more. Now you'll be able to walk all your life. Oh, what joy!"

Clara's greatest wish, to be able to be well like other people, had been fulfilled at last. It was not very far to the flowering field. Soon they reached it and sat down among the wealth of bloom. It was the first time that Clara had ever rested on the dry, warm earth. All about them the flowers nodded and exhaled their perfume. It was a scene of exquisite beauty.

The two children could hardly grasp this happiness that had come to them. It filled their hearts brimming full and made them silent. Peter also lay motionless, for he had gone to sleep.

Thus the hours flew, and the day was long past noon. Suddenly all the goats arrived, for they had been seeking the children. They did not like to graze in the flowers, and were glad when Peter awoke with their loud bleating. The poor boy was mightily bewildered, for he had dreamt that the rolling-chair with the red cushions stood again before his eyes. On awaking, he had still seen the golden nails; but soon he discovered that they were nothing but flowers. Remembering his deed, he obeyed Heidi's instructions willingly.

When they came back to their former place, Heidi lost no time in setting out the dinner. The bag was very full to-day, and Heidi hurried to fulfill her promise to Peter, who with bad conscience had understood her threat differently. She made three heaps of the good things, and when Clara and she were through, there was still a lot left for the boy. It was too bad that all this treat did not give him the usual satisfaction, for something seemed to stick in his throat.

Soon after their belated dinner, the grandfather was seen climbing up the Alp. Heidi ran to meet him, confusedly telling him of the great event. The old man's face shone at this news. Going over to Clara, he said: "So you have risked it? Now we have won."

Then picking her up, he put one arm around her waist, and the other one he stretched out as support, and with his help she marched more firmly than ever. Heidi jumped and bounded gaily by their side. In all this excitement the grandfather did not lose his judgment, and before long lifted Clara on his arm to carry her home. He knew that too much exertion would be dangerous, and rest was needed for the tired girl.

Peter, arriving in the village late that day, saw a large disputing crowd. They were all standing about an interesting object, and everybody pushed and fought for a chance to get nearest. It was no other than the chair.

"I saw it when they carried it up," Peter heard the baker say. "I bet it was worth at least five hundred francs. I should just like to know how it has happened."

"The wind might have blown it down," remarked Barbara, who was staring open-mouthed at the beautiful velvet cushions. "The uncle said so himself."

"It is a good thing if nobody else has done it," continued the baker. "When the gentleman from Frankfurt hears what has happened, he'll surely find out all about it, and I should pity the culprit. I am glad I haven't been up on the Alm for so long, else they might suspect me, as they would anybody who happened to be up there at the time."

Many more opinions were uttered, but Peter had heard enough. He quietly slipped away and went home. What if they should find out he had done it? A policeman might arrive any time now and they might take him away to prison. Peter's hair stood up on end at this alarming thought.

He was so troubled when he came home that he did not answer any questions and even refused his dish of potatoes. Hurriedly creeping into bed, he groaned.

"I am sure Peter has eaten sorrel again, and that makes him groan so," said his mother.

"You must give him a little more bread in the morning, Brigida. Take a piece of mine," said the compassionate grandmother.

When Clara and Heidi were lying in their beds that night, glancing up at the shining stars, Heidi remarked: "Didn't you think to-day, Clara, that it is fortunate God does not always give us what we pray for fervently, because He knows of something better?"

"What do you mean, Heidi?" asked Clara.

"You see, when I was in Frankfurt I prayed and prayed to come home again, and when I couldn't, I thought He had forgotten me. But if I had gone away so soon you would never have come here and would never have got well."

Clara, becoming thoughtful, said: "But, Heidi, then we could not pray for anything any more, because we would feel that He always knows of something better."

"But, Clara, we must pray to God every day to show we don't forget that all gifts come from Him. Grandmama has told me that God forgets us if we forget Him. But if some wish remains unfulfilled we must show our confidence in Him, for he knows best."

"How did you ever think of that?" asked Clara.

"Grandmama told me, but I know that it is so. We must thank God to-day that He has made you able to walk, Clara."

"I am glad that you have reminded me, Heidi, for I have nearly forgotten it in my excitement."

The children both prayed and sent their thanks up to heaven for the restoration of the invalid.

Next morning a letter was written to grandmama, inviting her to come up to the Alp within a week's time, for the children had planned to take her by surprise. Clara hoped then to be able to walk alone, with Heidi for her guide.

The following days were happier still for Clara. Every morning she awoke with her heart singing over and over again, "Now I am well! Now I can walk like other people!"

She progressed, and took longer walks every day. Her appetite grew amazingly, and the grandfather had to make larger slices of the bread and butter that, to his delight, disappeared so rapidly. He had to fill bowl after bowl of the foaming milk for the hungry children. In that way they reached the end of the week that was to bring the grandmama.

Day 69

1. Read the beginning of chapter 23.
2. What is happening in this chapter?

Chapter 23 PARTING TO MEET AGAIN

The day before her visit the grandmama had sent a letter to announce her coming. Peter brought it up with him next morning. The grandfather was already before the hut with the children and his merry goats. His face looked proud, as he contemplated the rosy faces of the girls and the shining hair of his two goats.

Peter, approaching, neared the uncle slowly. As soon as he had delivered the letter, he sprang back shyly, looking about him as if he was afraid. Then with a leap he started off.

"I should like to know why Peter behaves like the Big Turk when he is afraid of the rod," said Heidi, watching his strange behavior.

"Maybe Peter fears a rod that he deserves," said the old man.

All the way Peter was tormented with fear. He could not help thinking of the policeman who was coming from Frankfurt to fetch him to prison.

It was a busy morning for Heidi, who put the hut in order for the expected visitor. The time went by quickly, and soon everything was ready to welcome the good grandmama.

The grandfather also returned from a walk, on which he had gathered a glorious bunch of deep-blue gentians. The children, who were sitting on the bench, exclaimed for joy when they saw the glowing flowers.

Heidi, getting up from time to time to spy down the path, suddenly discovered grandmama, sitting on a white horse and accompanied by two men. One of them carried plenty of wraps, for without those the lady did not dare to pay such a visit.

The party came nearer and nearer, and soon reached the top.

"What do I see? Clara, what is this? Why are you not sitting in your chair? How is this possible?" cried the grandmama in alarm, dismounting hastily. Before she had quite reached the children she threw her arms up in great excitement:

"Clara, is that really you? You have red, round cheeks, my child! I hardly know you any more!" Grandmama was going to rush at her grandchild, when Heidi slipped from the bench, and Clara, taking her arm, they quietly took a little walk. The grandmama was rooted to the spot from fear. What was this? Upright and firm, Clara walked beside her friend. When they came back their rosy faces beamed. Rushing toward the children, the grandmother hugged them over and over again.

Looking over to the bench, she beheld the uncle, who sat there smiling. Taking Clara's arm in hers, she walked over to him, continually venting her delight. When she reached the old man, she took both his hands in hers and said:

"My dear, dear uncle! What have we to thank you for! This is your work, your care and nursing—"

"But our Lord's sunshine and mountain air," interrupted the uncle, smiling.

Then Clara called, "Yes, and also Schwänli's good, delicious milk. Grandmama, you ought to see how much goat-milk I can drink now; oh, it is so good!"

"Indeed I can see that from your cheeks," said the grandmama, smiling. "No, I hardly recognize you any more. You have become broad and round! I never dreamt that you could get so stout and tall! Oh, Clara, is it really true? I cannot look at you enough. But now I must telegraph your father to come. I shan't tell him anything about you, for it will be the greatest joy of all his life. My dear uncle, how are we going to manage it? Have you sent the men away?"

"I have, but I can easily send the goatherd."

So they decided that Peter should take the message. The uncle immediately whistled so loud that it resounded from all sides. Soon Peter arrived, white with fear, for he thought his doom had come. But he only received a paper that was to be carried to the post-office of the village.

Relieved for the moment, Peter set out. Now all the happy friends sat down round the table, and grandmama was told how the miracle had happened. Often the talk was interrupted by exclamations of surprise from grandmama, who still believed it was all a dream. How could this be her pale, weak little Clara? The children were in a constant state of joy, to see how their surprise had worked.

Meanwhile Mr. Sesemann, having finished his business in Paris, was also preparing a surprise. Without writing his mother he traveled to Ragatz on a sunny summer morning. He had arrived on this very day, some hours after his mother's departure, and now, taking a carriage, he drove to Mayenfeld.

The long ascent to the Alp from there seemed very weary and far to the traveller. When would he reach the goat-herd's hut? There were many little roads branching off in several directions, and sometimes Mr. Sesemann doubted if he had taken the right path. But not a soul was near, and no sound could be heard except the rustling of the wind and the hum of little insects. A merry little bird was singing on a larch-tree, but nothing more.

Standing still and cooling his brow, he saw a boy running down the hill at topmost speed. Mr. Sesemann called to him, but with no success, for the boy kept at a shy distance.

"Now, my boy, can't you tell me if I am on the right path to the hut where Heidi lives and the people from Frankfurt are staying?"

A dull sound of terror was the only reply. Peter shot off and rushed head over heels down the mountain-side, turning wild somersaults on his perilous way. His course resembled the course his enemy had taken some days ago.

"What a funny, bashful mountaineer!" Mr. Sesemann remarked to himself, thinking that the appearance of a stranger had upset this simple son of the Alps. After watching the downward course of the boy a little while, he soon proceeded on his way.

In spite of the greatest effort, Peter could not stop himself, and kept rolling on. But his fright and terror were still more terrible than his bumps and blows. This stranger was the policeman, that was a certain fact! At last, being thrown against a bush, he clutched it wildly.

"Good, here's another one!" a voice near Peter said. "I wonder who is going to be pushed down tomorrow, looking like a half-open potato-bag?" The village baker was making fun of him. For a little rest after his weary work, he had quietly watched the boy.

Day 70

1. Read the next part of chapter 23.
2. What is happening?
3. Peter had tried to hide what he had done wrong. Who knew what he had done? (Answers)
4. Have you ever had the "little watchman" in your heart make you feel bad and fearful about what you have done wrong?

Vocabulary

1. Play charades. Use the vocabulary list below for your words. Choose a word and act it out. Everyone else needs to guess which word you are acting out. Everyone who is playing should be able to see this list to choose words and to help them guess.

   vigorous -- strong and active
   imposing -- grand and impressive in appearance
   loiter -- to dawdle or to hang around some place without any purpose
   enmity -- hatred

luscious -- highly pleasing to the senses
(list continues on the next page)
reproach -- scold
indignant -- feeling upset over something that's not right
retort -- to answer back in an angry way
intimidate -- to fill someone with fear
atrocious -- shockingly bad
vivacity -- liveliness
fret -- to worry
pungent -- something with a really strong taste or smell
earnest -- serious about what you mean or what you are doing
piteous -- used to describe something that you feel sorry for
console -- to comfort
evade -- to avoid
obtrusive -- butting in, intruding on another's space
contempt -- a feeling of despising toward people you think are beneath you
indignation -- righteous anger, feeling upset by something that is unjust

Chapter 23 continued

In spite of the greatest effort, Peter could not stop himself, and kept rolling on. But his fright and terror were still more terrible than his bumps and blows. This stranger was the policeman, that was a certain fact! At last, being thrown against a bush, he clutched it wildly.

"Good, here's another one!" a voice near Peter said. "I wonder who is going to be pushed down tomorrow, looking like a half-open potato-bag?" The village baker was making fun of him. For a little rest after his weary work, he had quietly watched the boy.

Peter regained his feet and slunk away. How did the baker know the chair had been pushed? He longed to go home to bed and hide, for there alone he felt safe. But he had to go up to the goats, and the uncle had clearly told him to come back as quickly as he could. Groaning, he limped away up to the Alp. How could he run now, with his fear and all his poor, sore limbs?

Mr. Sesemann had reached the hut soon after meeting Peter, and felt reassured. Climbing further, with renewed courage, he at last saw his goal before him, but not without long and weary exertion. He saw the Alm-hut above him, and the swaying fir-trees. Mr. Sesemann eagerly hurried to encounter his beloved child. They had seen him long ago from the hut, and a treat was prepared for him that he never suspected.

As he made the last steps, he saw two forms coming towards him. A tall girl, with light hair and rosy face, was leaning on Heidi, whose dark eyes sparkled with keen delight. Mr. Sesemann stopped short, staring at this vision. Suddenly big tears rushed from his eyes, for this shape before him recalled sweet memories. Clara's mother had looked exactly like this fair maiden. Mr. Sesemann at this moment did not know if he was awake or dreaming.

"Papa, don't you know me any more?" Clara called with beaming eyes. "Have I changed so much?"

Mr. Sesemann rushed up to her, folding her in his arms. "Yes, you *have* changed. How is it possible? Is it really true? Is it really you, Clara?" asked the over-joyed father, embracing her again and again, and then gazing at her, as she stood tall and firm by his side.

His mother joined them now, for she wanted to see the happiness of her son.

"What do you say to this, my son? Isn't our surprise finer than yours?" she greeted him. "But come over to our benefactor now,—I mean the uncle."

"Yes, indeed, I also must greet our little Heidi," said the gentleman, shaking Heidi's hand. "Well? Always fresh and happy on the mountain? I guess I don't need to ask, for no Alpine rose can look more blooming. Ah, child, what joy this is to me!"

With beaming eyes the child looked at the kind gentleman who had always been so good to her. Her heart throbbed in sympathy with his joy. While the two men, who had at last approached each other, were conversing, grandmama walked over to the grove. There, under the fir-trees, another surprise awaited her. A beautiful bunch of wondrously blue gentians stood as if they had grown there.

"How exquisite, how wonderful! What a sight!" she exclaimed, clapping her hands. "Heidi, come here! Have you brought me those? Oh, they are beautiful!"

The children had joined her, Heidi assuring her that it was another person's deed.

"Oh grandmama, up on the pasture it looks just like that," Clara remarked. "Just guess who brought you the flowers?"

At that moment a rustle was heard, and they saw Peter, who was trying to sneak up behind the trees to avoid the hut. Immediately the old lady called to him, for she thought that Peter himself had picked the flowers for her. He must be creeping away out of sheer modesty, the kind lady thought. To give him his reward, she called:

"Come here, my boy! don't be afraid."

Petrified with fear, Peter stood still. What had gone before had robbed him of his courage. He thought now that all was over with him. With his hair standing up on end and his pale face distorted by anguish, he approached.

"Come straight to me, boy," the old lady encouraged him. "Now tell me, boy, if you have done that."

In his anxiety, Peter did not see the grandmama's finger that pointed to the flowers. He only saw the uncle standing near the hut, looking at him penetratingly, and beside him the policeman, the greatest horror for him in the world. Trembling in every limb, Peter answered, "Yes!"

"Well, but what are you so frightened about?"

"Because—because it is broken and can never be mended again," Peter said, his knees tottering under him.

The grandmama now walked over to the hut: "My dear uncle," she asked kindly, "is this poor lad out of his mind?"

"Not at all," was the reply; "only the boy was the wind which blew away the wheel-chair. He is expecting the punishment he well deserves."

Grandmama was very much surprised, for she vowed that Peter looked far from wicked. Why should he have destroyed the chair? The uncle told her that he had noticed many signs of anger in the boy since Clara's advent on the Alp. He assured her that he had suspected the boy from the beginning.

"My dear uncle," the old lady said with animation, "we must not punish him further. We must be just. It was very hard on him when Clara robbed him of Heidi, who is and was his greatest treasure. When he had to sit alone day after day, it roused him to a passion which drove him to this wicked deed. It was rather foolish, but we all get so when we get angry."

The lady walked over to the boy again, who was still quivering with fear.

Sitting down on the bench, she began:

"Come, Peter, I'll tell you something. Stop trembling and listen. You pushed the chair down, to destroy it. You knew very well that it was wicked and deserved punishment. You tried very hard to conceal it, did you not? But if somebody thinks that nobody knows about a wicked deed, he is wrong; God always knows it. As soon as He finds that a man is trying to conceal an evil he has done, He wakens a little watchman in his heart, who keeps on pricking the person with a thorn till all his rest is gone. He keeps on calling to the evildoer: 'Now you'll be found out! Now your punishment is near!'—His joy has flown, for fear and terror take its place. Have you not just had such an experience, Peter?"

Peter nodded, all contrite. He certainly had experienced this.

"You have made a mistake," the grandmama continued, "by thinking that you would hurt Clara by destroying her chair. It has so happened that what you have done has been the greatest good for her. She would probably never have tried to walk, if her chair had been there. If she should stay here, she might even go up to the pasture every single day. Do you see, Peter? God can turn a misdeed to the good of the injured person and bring trouble on the offender. Have you understood me, Peter? Remember the little watchman when you long to do a wicked deed again. Will you do that?"

"Yes, I shall," Peter replied, still fearing the policeman, who had not left yet.

"So now that matter is all settled," said the old lady in conclusion. "Now tell me if you have a wish, my boy, for I am going to give you something by which to remember your friends from Frankfurt. What is it? What would you like to have?"

Peter, lifting his head, stared at the grandmama with round, astonished eyes. He was confused by this sudden change of prospect.

Being again urged to utter a wish, he saw at last that he was saved from the power of the terrible man. He felt as if the most crushing load had fallen off him. He knew now that it was better to confess at once, when something had gone wrong, so he said: "I have also lost the paper."

Day 71

1. Continue reading.
2. How would you end the story? What would you write as the conclusion after what you read today?

Chapter 23 continued

Being again urged to utter a wish, he saw at last that he was saved from the power of the terrible man. He felt as if the most crushing load had fallen off him. He knew now that it was better to confess at once, when something had gone wrong, so he said: "I have also lost the paper."

Reflecting a while, the grandmama understood and said: "That is right. Always confess what is wrong, then it can be settled. And now, what would you like to have?"

So Peter could choose everything in the world he wished. His brain got dizzy. He saw before him all the wonderful things in the fair in Mayenfeld. He had often stood there for hours, looking at the pretty red whistles and the little knives; unfortunately Peter had never possessed more than half what those objects cost.

He stood thinking, not able to decide, when a bright thought struck him.

"Ten pennies," said Peter with decision.

"That certainly is not too much," the old lady said with a smile, taking out of her pocket a big, round thaler, on top of which she laid twenty pennies. "Now I'll explain this to you. Here you have as many times ten pennies as there are weeks in the year. You'll be able to spend one every Sunday through the year."

"All my life?" Peter asked quite innocently.

The grandmama began to laugh so heartily at this that the two men came over to join her.

Laughingly she said: "You shall have it my boy; I will put it in my will and then you will do the same, my son. Listen! Peter the goatherd shall have a ten-penny piece weekly as long as he lives."

Mr. Sesemann nodded.

Peter, looking at his gift, said solemnly: "God be thanked!" Jumping and bounding, he ran away. His heart was so light that he felt he could fly.

A little later the whole party sat round the table holding a merry feast. After dinner, Clara, who was lively as never before, said to her father:

"Oh, Papa, if you only knew all the things grandfather did for me. It would take many days to tell you; I shall never forget them all my life. Oh, if we could please him only half as much as what he did for me."

"It is my greatest wish, too, dear child," said her father; "I have been trying to think of something all the time. We have to show our gratitude in some way."

Accordingly Mr. Sesemann walked over to the old man, and began: "My dear friend, may I say one word to you. I am sure you believe me when I tell you that I have not known any real joy for years. What was my wealth to me when I could not cure my child and make her happy! With the help of the Lord you have made her well. You have given her a new life. Please tell me how to show my gratitude to you. I know I shall never be able to repay you, but what is in my power I shall do. Have you any request to make? Please let me know."

The uncle had listened quietly and had looked at the happy father.

"Mr. Sesemann, you can be sure that I also am repaid by the great joy I experience at the recovery of Clara," said the uncle firmly. "I thank you for your kind offer, Mr. Sesemann. As long as I live I have enough for me and the child. But I have one wish. If this could be fulfilled, my life would be free of care."

"Speak, my dear friend," urged Clara's father.

"I am old," continued the uncle, "and shall not live many years. When I die I cannot leave Heidi anything. The child has no relations except one, who even might try to take advantage of her if she could. If you would give me the assurance, Mr. Sesemann, that Heidi will never be obliged to go into the world and earn her bread, you would amply repay me for what I was able to do for you and Clara."

"My dear friend, there is no question of that," began Mr. Sesemann; "the child belongs to us! I promise at once that we shall look after her so that there will not be any need of her ever earning her bread. We all know that she is not fashioned for a life among strangers. Nevertheless, she has made, some true friends, and one of them will be here very shortly. Dr. Classen is just now completing his last business in Frankfurt. He intends to take your advice and live here. He has never felt so happy as with you and Heidi. The child will have two protectors near her, and I hope with God's will, that they may be spared a long, long time."

"And may it be God's will!" added the grandmama, who with Heidi had joined them, shaking the uncle tenderly by the hand. Putting her arms around the child, she said: "Heidi, I want to know if you also have a wish?"

"Yes indeed, I have," said Heidi, pleased.

"Tell me what it is, child!"

"I should like to have my bed from Frankfurt with the three high pillows and the thick, warm cover. Then grandmother will be able to keep warm and won't have to wear her shawl in bed. Oh, I'll be so happy when she won't have to lie with her head lower than her heels, hardly able to breathe!"

Heidi had said all this in one breath, she was so eager.

"Oh dear, I had nearly forgotten what I meant to do. I am so glad you have reminded me, Heidi. If God sends us happiness we must think of those who have many privations. I shall telegraph immediately for the bed, and if Miss Rottenmeier sends it off at once, it can be here in two days. I hope the poor blind grandmother will sleep better when it comes."

Heidi, in her happiness, could hardly wait to bring the old woman the good news. Soon it was resolved that everybody should visit the grandmother, who had been left alone so long. Before starting, however, Mr. Sesemann revealed his plans. He proposed to travel through Switzerland with his mother and Clara. He would spend the night in the village, so as to fetch Clara from the Alm next morning for the journey. From there they would go first to Ragatz and then further. The telegram was to be mailed that night.

Clara's feelings were divided, for she was sorry to leave the Alp, but the prospect of the trip delighted her.

When everything was settled, they all went down, the uncle carrying Clara, who could not have risked the lengthy walk. All the way down Heidi told the old lady of her friends in the hut; the cold they had to bear in winter and the little food they had.

Brigida was just hanging up Peter's shirt to dry, when the whole company arrived. Rushing into the house, she called to her mother: "Now they are all going away. Uncle is going, too, carrying the lame child."

"Oh, must it really be?" sighed the grandmother. "Have you seen whether they took Heidi away? Oh, if she only could give me her hand once more! Oh, I long to hear her voice once more!"

The same moment the door was flung open and Heidi held her tight.

"Grandmother, just think. My bed with the three pillows and the thick cover is coming from Frankfurt. Grandmama has said that it will be here in two days."

Heidi thought that grandmother would be beside herself with joy, but the old woman, smiling sadly, said:

"Oh, what a good lady she must be! I know I ought to be glad she is taking you with her, Heidi, but I don't think I shall survive it long."

"But nobody has said so," the grandmama, who had overheard those words, said kindly. Pressing the old woman's hand, she continued: "It is out of the question. Heidi will stay with you and make you happy. To see Heidi again, we will come up every year to the Alm, for we have many reasons to thank the Lord there."

Immediately the face of the grandmother lighted up, and she cried tears of joy.

"Oh, what wonderful things God is doing for me!" said the grandmother, deeply touched. "How good people are to trouble themselves about such a poor old woman as I. Nothing in this world strengthens the belief in a good Father in Heaven more than this mercy and kindness shown to a poor, useless little woman, like me."

"My dear grandmother," said Mrs. Sesemann, "before God in Heaven we are all equally miserable and poor; woe to us, if He should forget us!—But now we must say good-bye; next year we shall come to see you just as soon as we come up the Alp. We shall never forget you!" With that, Mrs. Sesemann shook her hand. It was some time before she was allowed to leave, however, because the grandmother thanked her over and over again, and invoked all Heaven's blessings on her and her house.

Mr. Sesemann and his mother went on down, while Clara was carried up to spend her last night in the hut.

Next morning, Clara shed hot tears at parting from the beloved place, where such gladness had been hers. Heidi consoled her with plans for the coming summer, that was to be even more happy than this one had been. Mr. Sesemann then arrived, and a few last parting words were exchanged.

Clara, half crying, suddenly said: "Please give my love to Peter and the goats, Heidi! Please greet Schwänli especially from me, for she has helped a great deal in making me well. What could I give her?"

"You can send her salt, Clara. You know how fond she is of that," advised little Heidi.

"Oh, I will surely do that," Clara assented. "I'll send her a hundred pounds of salt as a remembrance from me."

It was time to go now, and Clara was able to ride proudly beside her father. Standing on the edge of the slope, Heidi waved her hand, her eyes following Clara till she had disappeared.

Day 72

1. Read the rest of the book!
2. How does the story end?
3. Write a book report. Write the book's name and author. Write what the book was about. Write what you liked and didn't like about the book.
4. You can save this in your portfolio.

Chapter 23 continued

The bed has arrived. Grandmother sleeps so well every night now, that before long she will be stronger than ever. Grandmama has not forgotten the cold winter on the Alp and has sent a great many warm covers and shawls to the goatherd's hut. Grandmother can wrap herself up now and will not have to sit shivering in a corner.

In the village a large building is in progress. The doctor has arrived and is living at present in his old quarters. He has taken the uncle's advice and has bought the old ruins that sheltered Heidi and her grandfather the winter before. He is rebuilding for himself the portion with the fine apartment already mentioned. The other side is being prepared for Heidi and her grandfather. The doctor knows that his friend is an independent man and likes to have his own dwelling. Bärli and Schwänli, of course, are not forgotten; they will spend the winter in a good solid stable that is being built for them.

The doctor and the Alm-Uncle become better friends every day. When they overlook the progress of the building, they generally come to speak of Heidi. They both look forward to the time when they will be able to move into the house with their merry charge. They have agreed to share together the pleasure and responsibility that Heidi brings them. The uncle's heart is filled with gratitude too deep for any words when the doctor tells him that he will make ample provision for the child. Now her grandfather's heart is free of care, for if he is called away, another father will take care of Heidi and love her in his stead.

At the moment when our story closes, Heidi and Peter are sitting in grandmother's hut. The little girl has so many interesting things to relate and Peter is trying so hard not to miss anything, that in their eagerness they are not aware that they are near the happy grandmother's chair. All summer long they have hardly met, and very many wonderful things have happened. They are all glad at being together again, and it is hard to tell who is the happiest of the group. I think Brigida's face is more radiant than any, for Heidi has just told her the story of the perpetual ten-penny piece. Finally the grandmother says: "Heidi, please read me a song of thanksgiving and praise. I feel that I must praise and thank the Lord for the blessings He has brought to us all!" The End.

Day 73

1. Read these poems by Robert Louis Stevenson.

    THE WIND
    I saw you toss the kites on high
    And blow the birds about the sky;
    And all around I heard you pass,
    Like ladies' skirts across the grass—

O wind, a-blowing all day long!
O wind, that sings so loud a song!
I saw the different things you did,
But always you yourself you hid.

I felt you push, I heard you call,
I could not see yourself at all—
O wind, a-blowing all day long,
O wind, that sings so loud a song!

O you that are so strong and cold,
O blower, are you young or old?
Are you a beast of field and tree,
Or just a stronger child than me?

O wind, a-blowing all day long,
O wind, that sings so loud a song!

A GOOD BOY

I woke before the morning, I was happy all the day,
I never said an ugly word, but smiled and stuck to play.
And now at last the sun is going down behind the wood,
And I am very happy, for I know that I've been good.
My bed is waiting cool and fresh, with linen smooth and fair,
And I must off to sleepsin-by, and not forget my prayer.
I know that, till to-morrow I shall see the sun arise,
No ugly dream shall fright my mind, no ugly sight my eyes.
But slumber hold me tightly, till I waken in the dawn,
And hear the thrushes singing in the lilacs round the lawn.

Day 74

1. Read these poems by Robert Louis Stevenson.

THE SWING

How do you like to go up in a swing,
Up in the air so blue?
Oh, I do think it the pleasantest thing
Ever a child can do!

Up in the air and over the wall,
Till I can see so wide,
Rivers and trees and cattle and all
Over the countryside—

Till I look down on the garden green,
Down on the roof so brown—
Up in the air I go flying again,
Up in the air and down!

Vocabulary

1. Find the synonyms or antonyms. Match the vocabulary words to the word that is either its synonym (similar in meaning) or its antonym (opposite in meaning). Write the matching letters and numbers on a separate piece of paper. (Answers)

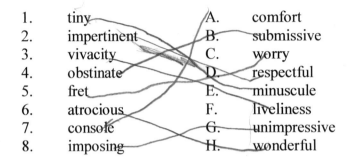

1.	tiny	A.	comfort
2.	impertinent	B.	submissive
3.	vivacity	C.	worry
4.	obstinate	D.	respectful
5.	fret	E.	minuscule
6.	atrocious	F.	liveliness
7.	console	G.	unimpressive
8.	imposing	H.	wonderful

Day 75

1. Read this poem by Robert Louis Stevenson about day dreaming.

THE LITTLE LAND
When at home alone I sit
And am very tired of it,
I have just to shut my eyes
To go sailing through the skies—

To go sailing far away
To the pleasant Land of play;
To the fairy land afar
Where the Little People are;

Where the clover-tops are trees,
And the rain-pools are the seas,
And the leaves like little ships
Sail about on tiny trips;

And above the daisy tree
Through the grasses,
High o'erhead the Bumble Bee
Hums and passes.

172

In that forest to and fro
I can wander, I can go;
See the spider and the fly,
And the ants go marching by

Carrying parcels with their feet
Down the green and grassy street.
I can in the sorrel sit
Where the ladybird alit.

I can climb the jointed grass;
And on high
See the greater swallows pass
In the sky,

And the round sun rolling by
Heeding no such things as I.
Through that forest I can pass
Till, as in a looking-glass,

Humming fly and daisy tree
And my tiny self I see,
Painted very clear and neat
On the rain-pool at my feet.

Should a leaflet come to land
Drifting near to where I stand,
Straight I'll board that tiny boat
Round the rain-pool sea to float.

Little thoughtful creatures sit
On the grassy coasts of it;
Little things with lovely eyes
See me sailing with surprise.

Some are clad in armour green—
(These have sure to battle been!)—
Some are pied with ev'ry hue,
Black and crimson, gold and blue;

Some have wings and swift are gone;
But they all look kindly on.
When my eyes I once again
Open, and see all things plain;

173

High bare walls, great bare floor;
Great big knobs on drawer and door;
Great big people perched on chairs,
Stitching tucks and mending tears,

Each a hill that I could climb,
And talking nonsense all the time—
O dear me, That I could be
A sailor on the rain-pool sea,
A climber in, the clover tree,
And just come back, a sleepy-head,
Late at night to go to bed.

Day 76

1. Your new book is called, *The Bears of Blue River*.
2. Today read the first half of chapter 1.
3. Where does this story take place? (hint: look at the first sentence) (Answers)
4. This story takes place in the 1820s. What clue is there in the book as to when it takes place? (Answers)
5. What's the name of the boy who is the hero of the bear stories in this book? (Answers)

CHAPTER 1 THE BIG BEAR

AWAY back in the "twenties," when Indiana was a baby state, and great forests of tall trees and tangled underbrush darkened what are now her bright plains and sunny hills, there stood upon the east bank of Big Blue River, a mile or two north of the point where that stream crosses the Michigan road, a cozy log cabin of two rooms one front and one back.

The house faced the west, and stretching off toward the river for a distance equal to twice the width of an ordinary street, was a blue-grass lawn, upon which stood a dozen or more elm and sycamore trees, with a few honey-locusts scattered here and there. Immediately at the water's edge was a steep slope of ten or twelve feet. Back of the house, mile upon mile, stretched the deep dark forest, inhabited by deer and bears, wolves and wildcats, squirrels and birds, without number.

In the river the fish were so numerous that they seemed to entreat the boys to catch them, and to take them out of their crowded quarters. There were bass and black suckers, sunfish and catfish, to say nothing of the sweetest of all, the big-mouthed redeye.

South of the house stood a log barn, with room in it for three horses and two cows; and enclosing this barn, together with a piece of ground, five or six acres in extent, was a palisade fence, eight or ten feet high, made by driving poles into the ground close together. In this enclosure the farmer kept his stock, consisting of a few sheep and cattle, and here also the chickens, geese, and ducks were driven at nightfall to save them from "varmints," as all prowling animals were called by the settlers.

The man who had built this log hut, and who lived in it and owned the adjoining land at the time of which I write, bore the name of Balser Brent. "Balser" is probably a corruption of Baltzer, but, however that may be, Balser was his name, and Balser was also the name of his boy, who was the hero of the bear stories which I am about to tell you.

Mr. Brent and his young wife had moved to the Blue River settlement from North Carolina, when young Balser was a little boy five or six years of age. They had purchased the "eighty" upon which they lived, from the United States, at a sale of public land held in the town of Brookville on Whitewater, and had paid for it what was then considered a good round sum one dollar per acre. They had received a deed for their "eighty" from no less a person than James Monroe, then President of the United States. This deed, which is called a patent, was written on sheepskin, signed by the President's own hand, and is still preserved by the descendants of Mr. Brent as one of the title-deeds to the land it conveyed. The house, as I have told you, consisted of two large rooms, or buildings, separated by a passageway six or eight feet broad which was roofed over, but open at both ends on the north and south. The back room was the kitchen, and the front room was parlour, bedroom, sitting room and library all in one.

At the time when my story opens Little Balser, as he was called to distinguish him from his father, was thirteen or fourteen years of age, and was the happy possessor of a younger brother, Jim, aged nine, and a little sister one year old, of whom he was very proud indeed.

On the south side of the front room was a large fireplace. The chimney was built of sticks, thickly covered with clay. The fire place was almost as large as a small room in one of our cramped modern houses, and was broad and deep enough to take in backlogs which were so large and heavy that they could not be lifted, but were drawn in at the door and rolled over the floor to the fireplace.

The prudent father usually kept two extra backlogs, one on each side of the fireplace, ready to be rolled in as the blaze died down; and on these logs the children would sit at night, with a rough slate made from a flat stone and do their "ciphering," as the study of arithmetic was then called. The fire usually furnished all the light they had, for candles and "dips," being expensive luxuries, were used only when company was present.

The fire, however, gave sufficient light, and its blaze upon a cold night extended halfway up the chimney, sending a ruddy, cozy glow to every nook and corner of the room.

The back room was the storehouse and kitchen; and from the beams and along the walls hung rich hams and juicy side-meat, jerked venison, dried apples, onions, and other provisions for the winter. There was a glorious fireplace in this room also, and a crane upon which to hang pots and cooking utensils.

The floor of the front room was made of logs split in halves with the flat, hewn side up ; but the floor of the kitchen was of clay, packed hard and smooth.

The settlers had no stoves, but did their cooking in round pots called Dutch ovens. They roasted their meats on a spit or steel bar like the ramrod of a gun. The spit was kept turning before the fire, presenting first one side of the meat and then the other, until it was thoroughly cooked. Turning the spit was the children's work.

South of the palisade enclosing the barn was the clearing a tract of twenty or thirty acres of land, from which Mr. Brent had cut and burned the trees. On this clearing the stumps stood thick as the hair on an angry dog's back; but the hard-working farmer ploughed between and around them, and each year raised upon the fertile soil enough wheat and corn to supply the wants of his family and his stock, and still had a little grain left to take to Brookville, sixty miles away, where he had bought his land, there to exchange for such necessities of life as could not be grown upon the farm or found in the forests.

The daily food of the family all came from the farm, the forest, or the creek. Their sugar was obtained from the sap of the sugar-trees; their meat was supplied in the greatest abundance by a few hogs, and by the inexhaustible game of which the forests were full. In the woods were found deer just for the shooting; and squirrels, rabbits, wild turkeys, pheasants, and quails, so numerous that a few hours' hunting would supply the table for days. The fish in the river, as I told you, fairly longed to be caught.

One day Mrs. Brent took down the dinner horn and blew upon it two strong blasts. This was a signal that Little Balser, who was helping his father down in the clearing, should come to the house. Balser was glad enough to drop his hoe and to run home. When he reached the house his mother said: "Balser, go up to the drift and catch a mess of fish for dinner. Your father is tired of deer meat three times a day, and I know he would like a nice dish of fried redeyes at noon."

"All right, mother," said Balser. And he immediately took down his fishing-pole and line, and got the spade to dig bait. When he had collected a small gourdful of angle worms, his mother called to him: "You had better take a gun. You may meet a bear; your father loaded the gun this morning, and you must be careful in handling it."

Balser took the gun, which was a heavy rifle considerably longer than himself, and started up the river toward the drift, about a quarter of a mile away.

There had been rain during the night and the ground near the drift was soft. Here, Little Balser noticed fresh bear tracks, and his breath began to come quickly. You may be sure he peered closely into every dark thicket, and looked behind all the large trees and logs, and had his eyes wide open lest perchance "Mr. Bear" should step out and surprise him with an affection ate hug, and thereby put an end to Little Balser forever. So he walked on cautiously, and, if the truth must be told, somewhat tremblingly, until he reached the drift.

Balser was but a little fellow, yet the stern necessities of a settler's life had compelled his father to teach him the use of a gun; and although Balser had never killed a bear, he had shot several deer, and upon one occasion had killed a wildcat," almost as big as a cow," he said.

Day 77

1. Finish reading chapter 1.
2. What did Balser plan to do when he saw a bear? (Answers)
3. What really happened when Balser saw a bear? (Answers)
4. How did Balser escape? (Answers)
5. What happened to the bear? (Answers)

Chapter 1 continued

I have no doubt the wildcat seemed "almost as big as a cow" to Balser when he killed it, for it must have frightened him greatly, as wildcats were sometimes dangerous animals for children to encounter.

Although Balser had never met a bear face to face and alone, yet he felt, and many a time had said, that there wasn't a bear in the world big enough to frighten him, if he but had his gun.

He had often imagined and minutely detailed to his parents and little brother just what he would do if he should meet a bear. He would wait calmly and quietly until his bearship should come within a few yards of him, and then he would slowly lift his gun.

Bang! and Mr. Bear would be dead with a bullet in his heart.

But when he saw the fresh bear tracks, and began to realize that he would probably have an opportunity to put his theories about bear killing into practice, he began to after all, he would frightened and miss Then he thought of bear, in that case, wonder if, after all he would become frightened and miss his aim. Then he thought of how the bear, in that case, would be calm and deliberate, and would put his theories into practice by walking very politely up to him, and making a very satisfactory dinner of a certain boy whom he could name. But as he walked on and no bear appeared, his courage grew stronger as the prospect of meeting the enemy grew less, and he again began saying to himself that no bear could frighten him, because he had his gun and he could and would kill it.

So Balser reached the drift; and having looked carefully about him, leaned his gun against a tree, unwound his fishing-line from the pole, and walked out to the end of a log which extended into the river some twenty or thirty feet.

Here he threw in his line, and soon was so busily engaged drawing out sunfish and redeyes, and now and then a bass, which was hungry enough to bite at a worm, that all thought of the bear went out of his mind.

After he had caught enough fish for a sumptuous dinner he bethought him of going home, and as he turned toward the shore, imagine, if you can, his consternation when he saw upon the bank, quietly watching him, a huge black bear.

If the wildcat had seemed as large as a cow to Balser, of what size do you suppose that bear appeared? A cow! An elephant, surely, was small compared with the huge black fellow standing upon the bank.

It is true Balser had never seen an elephant, but his father had, and so had his friend Tom Fox, who lived down the river; and they all agreed that an elephant was "purt nigh as big as all outdoors."

The bear had a peculiar, determined expression about him that seemed to say: "That boy can't get away; he's out on the log where the water is deep, and if he jumps into the river I can easily jump in after him and catch him before he can swim a dozen strokes. He'll have to come off the log in a short time, and then I'll proceed to devour him."

About the same train of thought had also been rapidly passing through Balser's mind. His gun was on the bank where he had left it, and in order to reach it he would have to pass the bear. He dared not jump into the water, for any attempt to escape on his part would bring the bear upon him instantly. He was very much frightened, but, after all, was a cool-headed little fellow for his age; so he concluded that he would not press matters, as the bear did not seem inclined to do so, but so long as the bear remained watching him on the bank would stay upon the log where he was, and allow the enemy to eye him to his heart's con tent.

There they stood, the boy and the bear, each eying the other as though they were the best of friends, and would like to eat each other, which, in fact, was literally true.

Time sped very slowly for one of them, you may be sure; and it seemed to Balser that he had been standing almost an age in the middle of Blue River on that wretched shaking log, when he heard his mother's dinner horn, reminding him that it was time to go home.

Balser quite agreed with his mother, and gladly would he have gone, I need not tell you; but there stood the bear, patient, determined, and fierce; and Little Balser soon was convinced in his own mind that his time had come to die.

He hoped that when his father should go home to dinner and find him still absent, he would come up the river in search of him, and frighten away the bear. Hardly had this hope sprung up in his mind, when it seemed that the same thought had also occurred to the bear, for he began to move down toward the shore end of the log upon which Balser was standing.

Slowly came the bear until he reached the end of the log, which for a moment he examined suspiciously, and then, to Balser's great alarm, cautiously stepped out upon it and began to walk toward him.

Balser thought of the folks at home, and, above all, of his baby sister; and when he felt that he should never see them again, and that they would in all probability never know of his fate, he began to grow heavy-hearted and was almost paralyzed with fear.

On came the bear, putting one great paw in front of the other, and watching Balser intently with his little black eyes. His tongue hung out, and his great red mouth was open to its widest, showing the sharp, long, glittering teeth that would soon be feasting on a first-class boy dinner.

When the bear got within a few feet of Balser so close he could almost feel the animal's hot breath as it slowly approached the boy grew desperate with fear, and struck at the bear with the only weapon he had his string of fish.

Now, bears love fish and blackberries above all other food; so when Balser's string of fish struck the bear in the mouth, he grabbed at them, and in doing so lost his foothold on the slippery log and fell into the water with a great splash and plunge.

This was Balser's chance for life, so he flung the fish to the bear, and ran for the bank with a speed worthy of the cause.

When he reached the bank his self-confidence returned, and he remembered all the things he had said he would do if he should meet a bear.

The bear had caught the fish, and again had climbed upon the log, where he was deliberately devouring them.

This was Little Balser's chance for death to the bear. Quickly snatching up the gun, he rested it in the fork of a small tree near by, took deliberate aim at the bear, which was not five yards away, and shot him through the heart. The bear dropped into the water dead, and floated downstream a little way, where he lodged at a ripple a short distance below.

Balser, after he had killed the bear, be came more frightened than he had been at any time during the adventure, and ran home screaming. That afternoon his father went to the scene of battle and took the bear out of the water. It was very fat and large, and weighed, so Mr. Brent said, over six hundred pounds. Balser was firmly of the opinion that he himself was also very fat and large, and weighed at least as much as the bear. He was certainly entitled to feel "big"; for he had got himself out of an ugly scrape in a brave, manly, and cool-headed manner, and had achieved a victory of which a man might have been proud.

The news of Balser's adventure soon spread among the neighbours and he became quite a hero; for the bear he had killed was one of the largest that had ever been seen in that neighbourhood, and, besides the gallons of rich bear oil it yielded, there were three or four hundred pounds of bear meat; and no other food is more strengthening for winter diet.

There was also the soft, furry skin, which Balser's mother tanned, and with it made a coverlid for Balser's bed, under which he and his little brother lay many a cold night, cozy and "snug as a bug in a rug."

Day 78

1. In the beginning of the chapter it mentions the phrase "Anno Domini." That's what AD comes from, as in BC and AD. BC is how we count time on the calendar before Christ was born. AD is how we label years on the calendar after Jesus was born. Something happened that divided history. Everything else happened either before or after it. That's what the phrase means in this chapter.
2. Read the beginning of chapter 2.
3. Why did Balser think he could never have a gun before he was twenty-one? (Answers)
4. How does he get a gun? (Answers)

CHAPTER II HOW BALSER GOT A GUN

FOR many years after the killing of the big bear, as told in the preceding chapter, time was reckoned by Balser as beginning with that event. It was, if I may say it, his "Anno Domini." In speaking of occurrences, events, and dates, he always fixed them in a general way by saying, " That happened before I killed the big bear;" or, "That took place after I killed the big bear." The great immeasurable eternity of time was divided into two parts: that large unoccupied portion preceding the death of the big bear, and the part, full to overflowing with satisfaction and pride, after that momentous event.

Balser's adventure had raised him vastly in the estimation of his friends and neighbours, and, what was quite as good, had increased his respect for himself, and had given him confidence, which is one of the most valuable qualities for boy or man. Frequently when Balser met strangers, and the story of the big bear was told, they would pat the boy on the shoulder and call him a little man, and would sometimes ask him if he owned a gun. Much to Balser's sorrow, he was compelled to admit that he did not. The questions as to whether or not he owned a gun had put into his mind the thought of how delightful life would be if he but possessed one ; and his favourite visions by day and his sweetest dreams by night were all about a gun; one not so long nor so heavy as his father's, but of the shorter, lighter pattern known as a smooth-bore carbine. He had heard his father speak of this gun, and of its effectiveness at short range; and although at long distances it was not so true of aim as his father's gun, still he felt confident that, if he but possessed the coveted carbine he could, single-handed and alone, exterminate all the races of bears, wolves and wildcats that inhabited the forests round about, and "pestered" the farmers with their depredations.

But how to get the gun! That was the question. Raiser's father had received a gun as a present from his father when Balser Sr. had reached the advanced age of twenty-one, and it was considered a rich gift. The cost of a gun for Balser would equal half of the sum total that his father could make during an entire year; and although Little Balser looked forward in fond expectation to the time when he should be twenty-one and should receive a gun from his father, yet he did not even hope that he would have one before then, however much he might dream about it. Dreams cost nothing, and guns were expensive; too expensive even to be hoped for. So Balser contented himself with inexpensive dreams, and was willing, though not content, to wait.

But the unexpected usually happens, at an unexpected time, and in an unexpected manner.

About the beginning of the summer after the killing of the big bear, when Balser's father had "laid by" his corn, and the little patch of wheat had just begun to take on a golden brown as due notice that it was nearly ready to be harvested, there came a few days of idleness for the busy farmer. Upon one of those rare idle days Mr. Brent and Balser went down the river on a fishing and hunting expedition. There was but one gun in the family, therefore Balser could not hunt when his father was with him, so he took his fishing-rod, and did great execution among the finny tribe, while his father watched along the river for game, as it came down to drink.

Upon the day mentioned Balser and his father had wandered down the river as far as the Michigan road, and Mr. Brent had left the boy near the road fishing, after telling him to go home in an hour or two, and that he, Mr. Brent, would go by another route and be home in time for supper.

So Balser was left by himself, fishing at a deep hole perhaps a hundred yards north of the road. This was at a time when the river was in flood, and the ford where travellers usually crossed was too deep for passage.

Balser had been fishing for an hour or more, and had concluded to go home, when he saw approaching along the road from the east a man and woman on horseback. They soon reached the ford and stopped, believing it to be impassable. They were mud-stained and travel-worn, and their horses, covered with froth, were panting as if they had been urged to their greatest speed. After a little time the gentleman saw Balser, and called to him. The boy immediately went to the travellers, and the gentleman said: "My little man, can you tell me if it is safe to attempt the ford at this time?"

"It will swim your horses," answered Balser.

"I knew it would," said the lady, in evident distress. She was young and pretty, and seemed to be greatly fatigued and frightened. The gentleman was very attentive, and tried to soothe her, but in a moment or two she began to weep, and said: "They will catch us, I know. They will catch us. They cannot be more than a mile behind us now, and we have no place to turn."

"Is some one trying to catch you?" asked Balser.

The gentleman looked down at the little fellow for a moment, and was struck by his bright, manly air. The thought occurred to him that Balser might suspect them of being fugitives from justice, so he explained: "Yes, my little fellow, a gentleman is trying to catch us. He is this lady's father. He has with him a dozen men, and if they overtake us they will certainly kill me and take this lady home. Do you know of any place where we may hide?"

"Yes, sir," answered Balser, quickly;" help me on behind you, and I'll take you to my father's house. There's no path up the river, and if they attempt to follow they'll get lost in the woods."

Balser climbed on the horse behind the gentleman, and soon they plunged into the deep forest, and rode up the river toward Balser's home. The boy knew the forest well, and in a short time the little party of three was standing at the hospitable cabin door. Matters were soon explained to Balser's mother, and she, with true hospitality, welcomed the travellers to her home. During the conversation Balser learned that the gentleman and lady were running away that they might be married, and, hoping to finish a good job, the boy volunteered the advice that they should be married that same evening under his father's roof. He also offered to go in quest of a preacher who made his home some two miles to the east.

The advice and the offer of services were eagerly accepted, and the lady and gentle man were married that night, and remained a few days at the home of Mr. Brent until the river was low enough to cross.

The strangers felt grateful to the boy who had given them such timely help, and asked him what they could do for him in return.

Balser hesitated a moment, and said, "There's only one thing I want very bad, but that would cost so much there's no use to speak of it."

"What is it, Balser? Speak up, and if it is anything I can buy, you shall have it."

"A gun! A gun! A smooth-bore carbine. I'd rather have it than anything else in the world."

"You shall have it if there's one to be bought in Indianapolis. We are going there, and will return within a week or ten days, and you shall have your carbine if I can find one."

Within two weeks after this conversation Balser was the happiest boy in Indiana, for he owned a carbine, ten pounds of fine powder, and lead enough to kill every living creature within a radius of five miles.

Of course the carbine had to be tested at once. So the day after he received it Balser started out with his father on a hunting expedition, fully determined in his own mind to kill a bear twice as large as his first one. They took with them corn-bread and dried venison for dinner, and started east toward Conn's Creek, where the houses of the settlers were thinly scattered and game plentiful.

They had with them two faithful dogs, "Tige" and "Prince." Balser considered these dogs the most intelligent animals that walked on four feet. They were deer-hounds with a cross of bulldog, and were swift of foot and very strong.

Our hunters had travelled perhaps three or four miles into the forest when they started a deer, in pursuit of which the dogs bounded off with their peculiar bark, and soon deer and dogs were lost to sight. Balser and his father listened carefully for the voices of the dogs, for should the deer turn at bay, the dogs, instead of the quick bark, to which they gave voice in the chase, would utter a long-drawn-out note half howl, half yelp.

The bay of the hounds had died away in the distance, and Balser and his father had heard nothing of them for two or three hours. The hunters had seen other deer as they walked along, but they had been unable to obtain a shot smaller game was plentiful, but Balser and his father did not care to frighten away large game by shooting at squirrels or birds. So they continued their walk until they reached the bank of Conn's Creek, near the hour of noon; by that time Balser's appetite was beginning to call loudly for dinner, and he could not resist the temptation to shoot a squirrel, which he saw upon a limb of a neighbouring tree. The squirrel fell to the ground and was soon skinned and cleaned. Balser then kindled a fire and cutting several green twigs, sharpened the ends and fastened small pieces of the squirrel upon them.

He next stuck the twigs in the ground so that they leaned toward the fire, with the meat hanging directly over the blaze. Soon the squirrel was roasted to a delicious brown, and then Balser served dinner to his father, who was sitting on a rock near by. The squirrel, the corn-bread, and the venison quickly disappeared, and Balser, if permitted to do so, would have found another squirrel and would have cooked it. Just as dinner was finished, there came from a long way up-stream the howling bark of Tige and Prince, telling, plainly as if they had spoken English, that the deer was at bay.

Thereupon Balser quickly loaded his gun, and he and his father looked carefully to their primings. Then Mr. Brent directed Balser to climb down the cliff and move toward the dogs through the thicket in the bottom, while he went by another route, along the bluff. Should the hunters be separated, they were to meet at an agreed place in the forest. Balser climbed cautiously down the cliff and was soon deep in a dark thicket of tangled underbrush near the creek.

Now and then the deep bay of the dogs reached his ears from the direction whence he had first heard it, and he walked as rapidly as the tangled briers and under growth would permit toward his faithful fellow-hunters.

Day 79

1. Finish reading chapter 2.
2. When Balser comes across another bear is he courageous and does he shoot it right away? (Answers)
3. How does he escape? (Answers)
4. What do he and his father take home with them? (Answers)

Chapter 2 continued

He was so intent on the game which he knew the dogs held at bay, that he did not look about him with his accustomed caution, and the result of his unwatchfulness was that he found himself within ten feet of two huge bears before he was at all aware of their presence. They were evidently male and female, and upon seeing him the great he-bear gave forth a growl that frightened Balser to the depths of his soul. Retreat seemed almost impossible; and should he fire at one of the bears, his gun would be empty and he would be at the mercy of the other. To attempt to outrun a bear, even on level ground, would be almost a hopeless undertaking; for the bear, though an awkward-looking creature, is capable of great speed when it comes to a foot-race. But there, where the tangled underbrush was so dense that even walking through it was a matter of great difficulty, running was out of the question, for the thicket which would greatly impede Balser would be but small hindrance to the bears.

After Balser had killed the big bear at the drift, he felt that he never again would suffer from what hunters call "buck ager"; but when he found himself confronted by those black monsters, he began to tremble in every limb, and for the life of him could not at first lift his gun. The he-bear was the first to move. He raised himself on his haunches, and with a deep growl started for poor Balser. Balser should have shot the bear as he came toward him, but acting solely from an instinct of self preservation he started to run. He made better headway than he had thought possible, and soon came to a small open space of ground where the undergrowth was not so thick, and where the bright light of the sun dispelled the darkness. The light restored Balser's confidence, and the few moments of retreat gave him time to think and to pull himself together. So, turning quickly, he lifted his gun to his shoulder and fired at the bear, which was not two yards behind him. Unfortunately, his aim was unsteady, and his shot wounded the bear in the neck, but did not kill him.

Balser saw the disastrous failure he had made, and felt that the bear would be much surer in his attack upon him than he had been in his attack upon the bear. The boy then threw away his gun, and again began a hasty retreat.

He called for his father, and cried, "Tige! Prince! Tige! Tige!" not so much with a hope that either the dogs or his father would hear, but because he knew not what else to do. Balser ran as fast as he could, still the bear was at his heels, and the frightened boy expected every moment to feel a stroke from the brute's huge rough paw. Soon it came, with a stunning force that threw Balser to the ground, upon his back. The bear was over him in an instant, and caught his left arm between his mighty jaws. It seemed then that the light of the world went out for a moment, and he remembered nothing but the huge, blood-red mouth of the bear, his hot breath almost burning his cheeks, and his deep, terrible growls nearly deafening his ears. Balser's whole past life came up before him like a picture, and he remembered every thing that had ever happened to him. He thought of how deeply his dear father and mother would grieve, and for the only time in his life regretted having received the carbine, for it was the gun, after all, that had got him into this trouble. All this happened in less time than it takes you to read ten lines of this page, but it seemed very, very long to Balser, lying there with the huge body of the bear over him.

Suddenly a note of hope struck his ear the sweetest sound he had ever heard. It was the yelp of dear old Tige, who had heard his call and had come to the rescue. If there is any creature on earth that a bear thoroughly hates, it is a dog. Tige wasted not a moment's time, but was soon biting and pulling at the bear's hind legs. The bear immediately turned upon the dog, and gave Balser an opportunity to rise. Of this opportunity he quickly took advantage, you may be sure. Soon Prince came up also, and in these two strong dogs the bear had foemen worthy of his steel.

Balser's great danger and narrow escape had quickened all his faculties, so he at once ran back to the place where he had dropped his gun, and although his left arm had been terribly bitten, he succeeded in loading, and soon came back to the help of the dogs, who had given him such timely assistance.

The fight between the dogs and the bear was going on at a merry rate, when Balser returned to the scene of action. With Prince on one side and Tige on the other, both so strong and savage, and each quick and nimble as a cat, the bear had all he could do to defend himself, and continually turned first one way and then another in his effort to keep their fangs away from his legs or throat. This enabled Balser to approach within a short distance of the bear, which he cautiously did. Taking care not to wound either of his faithful friends, he was more fortunate in his aim than he had been the first time, and gave the bear a mortal wound.

The wounded animal made a hasty retreat back into the thicket, followed closely by the dogs; but Balser had seen more than enough of bear society in the thicket, and prudently concluded not to follow. He then loaded his gun with a heavy charge of powder only, and fired it to attract his father's attention. This he repeated several times, until at last he saw the welcome form of his father hurrying toward him from the bluff. When his father reached him and saw that he had been wounded, Mr. Brent was naturally greatly troubled; but Balser said: "I'll tell you all about it soon. Let's go in after the bears. Two of them are in the thicket up there next to the cliff, and the dogs have followed them. If Tige had not come up just in time, one of the bears would have killed me ; but I think the shot I gave him must have killed him by this time."

So without another word, Balser having loaded his gun, they started into the dark thicket toward the cliff, in the direction whence came the voices of the dogs.

They had not proceeded farther than a hundred yards when they found the bear which Balser had shot, lying dead in the path over which Balser had so recently made his desperate retreat. The dogs were farther in, toward the cliff, where the vines, trees, and brush grew so thick that it was almost dark.

The two hunters, however, did not stop, but hurried on to the help of their dogs. Soon they saw through the gloom of the thicket the she-bear, and about her the dogs were prancing, barking, and snapping most furiously.

Carefully Balser and his father took their position within a few yards of the bear, and Balser, upon a signal from his father, called off the dogs so that a shot might be made at the bear without danger of killing either Tige or Prince.

Soon the report of two guns echoed through the forest, almost at the same instant, and the great she-bear fell over on her side, quivered for a moment, and died. This last battle took place close by the stone cliff, which rose from the bottom-land to a height of fifty or sixty feet.

Balser and his father soon worked their way through the underbrush to where the she-bear lay dead. After having examined the bear, Balser's attention was attracted to a small opening in the cliff, evidently the mouth of a cave which had probably been the home of the bear family that he and his father had just exterminated. The she-bear had taken her stand at the door of her home, and in defending it had lost her life. Balser examined the opening in the cliff, and concluded to enter; but his father said: "You don't know what's in there. Let's first send in one of the dogs."

So Tige was called and told to go into the cave. Immediately after he had entered he gave forth a series of sharp yelps which told plainly enough that he had found something worth barking at. Then Balser called the dog out, and Mr. Brent collected pieces of dry wood, and made a fire in front of the cave, hoping to drive out any animal that might be on the inside.

He more than suspected that he would find a pair of cubs.

As the smoke brought nothing forth, he concluded to enter the cave himself and learn what was there. Dropping upon his knees, he began to crawl in at the narrow opening, and the boy and the two dogs followed closely. Mr. Brent had taken with him a lighted torch, and when he had gone but a short distance into the cave he saw in a remote corner a pair of gray-black, frowzy little cubs, as fat and round as a roll of butter. They were lying upon a soft bed of leaves and grass, which had been collected by their father and mother.

Balser's delight knew no bounds, for, next to his gun, what he wanted above all things was a bear cub, and here were two of them. Quickly he and his father each picked up a cub and made their way out of the cave.

The cubs, not more than one-half larger than a cat, were round and very fat, and wore a coat of fur, soft and sleek as the finest silk. Young bears usually are gray until after they are a year old, but these were an exception to the rule, for they were almost black.

Leaving the old bears dead upon the ground, Balser and his father hurried down to the creek, where Mr. Brent washed and dressed his son's wounded arm. They then marked several trees upon the bank of the creek by breaking twigs, so that they might be able to find the bears when they returned that evening with the horses to take home the meat and skins.

All this, which has taken so long to tell, occurred within the space of a few minutes; but the work while it lasted was hard and tiresome, and, although it was but a short time past noon, Balser and his father were only too glad to turn their faces homeward, each with a saucy little bear cub under his arm.

"As we have killed their mother," said Balser, referring to the cubs, "we must take care of her children and give them plenty of milk, and bring them up to be good, honest bears."

The evening of the same day Mr. Brent and a few of his neighbours brought home the bear meat and skins. Balser did not go with his father because his arm was too sore. He was, however, very proud of his wound, and thought that the glory of the day and the two bear cubs were purchased cheaply enough after all.

Day 80

1. Read the beginning of chapter 3.
2. What did Balser name the bear cubs? (Answers)
3. Balser and Jim had dunked the bears' heads in water and expected the bears wanted to get even with them. What did the bears do to get back at them? (Answers)
4. You read that when they went out in the canoe on their trip to pick blackberries, they didn't know they would return in sadness. What do you think will happen? (Answers)

Vocabulary

1. Review your vocabulary on Day 70 or play Heidi vocabulary activities under level 3 on the review game page of the Easy Peasy website.

CHAPTER III LOST IN THE FOREST

BALSER'S arm mended slowly, for it had been terribly bitten by the bear. The heavy sleeve of his buckskin jacket had saved him from a wound which might have crippled him for life; but the hurt was bad enough as it was, and Balser passed through many days and nights of pain before it was healed. He bore the suffering like a little man, however, and felt very "big" as he walked about with his arm in a buckskin sling.

Balser was impatient that he could not hunt; but he spent his time more or less satisfactorily in cleaning and polishing his gun and playing with the bear cubs, which his little brother Jim had named "Tom" and "Jerry." The cubs soon became wonderfully tame, and drank eagerly from a pan of milk. They were too small to know how to lap, so the boys put their hands in the pan and held up a finger, at which the cubs sucked lustily. It was very laughable to see the little round black fellows nosing in the milk for the finger. And sometimes they would bite, too, until the boys would snatch away their hands and soundly box the cubs on the ears. A large panful of milk would disappear before you could say "Christmas," and the bears' silky sides would stand out as big and round as a pippin.

The boys were always playing pranks upon the cubs, and the cubs soon learned to retaliate. They would climb everywhere about the premises, up the trees, on the roofs of the barn and house, and over the fence. Their great delight was the milk-house and kitchen, where they had their noses into everything, and made life miserable for Mrs. Brent. She would run after them with her broomstick if they but showed their sharp little snouts in the doorway. Then off they would scamper, yelping as though they were nearly killed, and ponder upon new mischief. They made themselves perfectly at home, and would play with each other like a pair of frisky kittens, rolling over and over on the sod, pretending to fight, and whining and growling as if they were angry in real earnest. One day Balser and his little brother Jim were sitting on a log, which answered the purpose of a settee, under the eaves in front of the house. The boys were wondering what had become of Tom and Jerry, as they had not seen them for an hour or more, and their quietness looked suspicious.

"I wonder if those cubs have run away," said Balser.

"No," said Jim, "bet they won't run away; they've got things too comfortable here to run away. Like as not they're off some place plannin' to get even with us because we ducked them in the water trough awhile ago. They looked awful sheepish when they got out, and as they went off together I jus' thought to myself they were goin' away to think up some trick on us."

Balser and Jim were each busily engaged eating the half of a blackberry pie. The eave of the house was not very high, per haps seven or eight feet from the ground, and Balser and Jim were sitting under it, holding the baby and eating their pie.

Hardly had Jim spoken when the boys heard a scraping sound from above, then a couple of sharp little yelps; and down came Tom and Jerry from the roof, striking the boys squarely on the head.

To say that the boys were frightened does not half tell it. They did not know what had happened. They fell over, and the baby dropped to the ground with a cry that brought her mother to the scene of action in a moment. The blackberry pie had in some way managed to spread itself all over the baby's face, and she was a very comical sight when her mother picked her up.

The bears had retaliated upon the boys sooner than even Jim had anticipated, and they all had a great laugh over it; the bears seeming to enjoy it more than any body else. The boys were ready to admit that the joke was on them, so they took the cubs back to the milk-house, and gave them a pan of rich milk as a peace-offering.

The scrapes these cubs got themselves and the boys into would fill a large volume; but I cannot tell you any more about them now, as I want to relate an adventure having no fun in it, which befell Balser and some of his friends soon after his arm was well.

It was blackberry time, and several children had come to Balser's home for the purpose of making a raid upon a large patch of wild blackberries that grew on the other side of the river, a half-hour's walk from Mr. Brent's cabin.

Soon after daybreak one morning, the little party, consisting of Balser and Jim, Tom Fox and his sister Liney (which is "short" for Pauline), and three children from the family of Mr. Neigh, paddled across the river in a canoe which Balser and his father had made from a large gum log, and started westward for the blackberry patch.

Tom and Jerry had noticed the preparations for the journey with considerable curiosity, and felt very much hurt that they were not to be taken along. But they were left behind, imprisoned in a pen which the boys had built for them, and their whines and howls of complaint at such base treatment could be heard until the children were well out of sight of the house.

The party hurried along merrily, little thinking that their journey home would be one of sadness; and soon they were in the midst of the blackberries, picking as rapidly as possible, and filling their gourds with the delicious fruit.

They worked hard all the morning, and the deerskin sacks which they had brought with them were nearly full.

Toward noon the children became hungry, and without a dissenting voice agreed to eat dinner.

They had taken with them for lunch a loaf of bread and a piece of cold venison, but Balser suggested that he should go into the woods and find a squirrel or two to help out their meal. In the meantime Tom Fox had started out upon a voyage of discovery, hoping that he, too, might contribute to the larder.

In a few minutes Balser's gun was heard at a distance, and then again and again, and soon he was back in camp with three fat squirrels.

Almost immediately after him came Tom Fox carrying something in his coonskin cap.

"What have you there, Limpy?" cried Liney.

The children called Tom "Limpy" because he always had a sore toe or a stone bruise on his heel.

"You'll never guess," answered Tom, All the children took a turn at guessing, and then gave it up.

"Turkey eggs," said Tom. "We'll have eggs as well as squirrel for dinner today."

"How will you cook them?" asked one of the Neigh children.

"I'll show you," answered Tom.

So now they were guessing how Limpy would cook the eggs, but he would not tell them, and they had to give it up.

The boys then lighted a fire from the flint-lock on the gun, and Balser, having dressed the squirrel, cut twigs as he had done when he and his father dined on Conn's Creek, and soon pieces of tender squirrel were roasting near the flame, giving forth a most tempting odour.

Day 81

1.   Venison is deer meat.
2.   **Indistinct** means not distinct, not clear, unclear.
3.   Read the next part of chapter 3.
4.   Why was Balser so good at finding Liney? (Answers)
5.   Why weren't Balser and Liney with the other children when they went home? (Answers)
6.   Why did Balser's dad light fire to a pile of grass, leaves and wood? (Answers)
7.   What do you think has happened to Liney? Why isn't she answering? What do you think is going to happen?

Chapter 3 continued

In the meantime Limpy had gone away, and none of the children knew where he was, or what he was doing. Soon, however, he returned bearing a large flat rock eight or ten inches in diameter, and two or three inches thick. This rock he carefully washed and scrubbed in a spring, until it was perfectly clean. He then took coals from the fire which Balser had kindled, and soon had a great fire of his own, in the midst of which was the stone. After the blaze had died down, he made a bed of hot coals on which, by means of a couple of sticks, he placed the rock, and then dusted away the ashes.

Now do you know how I'm going to cook the eggs?" he asked. They, of course, all knew ; and the girls greased the rock with the fat of the squirrel, broke the eggs, and allowed them to fall upon the hot stone, where they were soon thoroughly roasted, and the children had a delicious meal. After dinner they sat in the cool shade of the tree under which they dined, and told stories and asked riddles for an hour or two before they again began berry picking. Then they worked until about six o'clock, and stopped to have another play before returning home.

They played "Ring around a rosey," "Squat where ye be," "Wolf," "Dirty dog," and then wound up with the only never-grow-old, "Hide-and-seek."

The children hid behind logs and trees, and in dense clumps of bushes. The boys would often climb trees, when, if "caught," the one who was "it" was sure to run "home" before the hider could slide half way down his tree. Now and then a hollow tree was found, and that, of course, was the best hiding-place of all.

Beautiful little Liney Fox found one hollow tree too many; and as long as they lived all the children of the party remembered it and the terrible events that followed her discovery. She was seeking a place to hide, and had hurried across a small open space to conceal herself behind a huge sycamore tree. When she reached the tree and went around it to hide upon the opposite side, she found it was hollow at the root.

Balser was "it," and with his eyes "hid" was counting one hundred as rapidly and loudly as he could. He had got to sixty, he afterward said, when a shriek reached his ears. This was when Liney found the hollow tree. Balser at once knew that it was Liney's voice; for, although he was but a little fellow, he was quite old enough to have admired Liney's exquisite beauty, and to have observed that she was as kind and gentle and good as she was pretty.

So what wonder that Balser, whom she openly claimed as her best friend, should share not only in the general praise, but should have a boy's admiration for her all his own?

In persons accustomed to exercise the alertness which is necessary for a good hunter, the sense of locating the direction and position from which a sound proceeds becomes highly developed, and as Balser had been hunting almost ever since he was large enough to walk, he knew instantly where Liney was.

He hurriedly pushed his way through the bushes, and in a moment reached the open space of ground, perhaps one hundred yards across, on the opposite side of which stood the tree that Liney had found. Some twenty or thirty yards beyond the tree stood Liney. She was so frightened that she could not move, and apparently had become powerless to scream.

Balser hastened toward her at his utmost speed, and when he reached a point from which he could see the hollow side of the tree, imagine his horror and fright upon beholding an enormous bear emerging from the opening. The bear started slowly toward the girl, who seemed unable to move.

"Run, Liney! run for your life!" screamed Balser, who fearlessly rushed toward the bear to attract its attention from the girl, and if possible to bring it in pursuit of himself.

"I just felt," said Balser afterward, "that I wanted to lie down and let the bear eat me at once if I could only keep it away from Liney. I shouted and threw clods and sticks at it, but on it went toward her. I reckon it thought she was the nicest and preferred her to me. It was right, too, for she was a heap the nicest, and I didn't blame the bear for wanting her.

"Again I shouted," Run, Liney! run!" My voice seemed to waken her, and she started to run as fast as she could go, with the bear after her, and I after the bear as fast as I could go. I was shouting and doing my best to make the bear run after me instead of Liney; but it kept right on after her, and she kept on running faster and faster into the dark woods. In a short time I caught up with the bear, and kicked it on the side as hard as I could kick. That made it mad, and it turned upon me with a furious growl, as much as to say that it would settle with me pretty quick and then get Liney. After I had kicked it I started to run toward my gun, which was over by the blackberry patch. For a while I could hear the bear growling and puffing right at my heels, and it made me just fly, you may be sure. I never ran so fast in all my life, for I knew that I could not hold out long against the bear, and that if I didn't get my gun quick he would surely get me. I did not care as much as you might think, nor was I very badly frightened, for I was so glad I had saved Liney. But naturally I wanted to save myself too, if possible, so, as I have said, I ran as I never ran before or since, for that matter.

"Soon the growls of the bear began to grow indistinct, and presently they ceased and I thought I had left it behind. So I kept on running toward my gun, and never stopped to look back until I heard another scream from Liney. Then I looked behind me, and saw that the bear had turned and was again after her, although she was quite a distance ahead of it. "I thought at first that I should turn back and kick the bear again, and just lie down and let it eat me if nothing else would satisfy it; but I was so near my gun that I concluded to get it and then hurry back and shoot the bear instead of kicking it.

"I heard Liney scream again and heard her call 'B-a-1-s-e-r,' and that made me run even faster than the bear had made me go. It was but a few seconds until I had my gun and had started back to help Liney.

"Soon I was at the hollow sycamore, but the bushes into which Liney had run were so thick and dark that I could see neither her nor the bear. I quickly ran into the woods where I thought Liney had one, and when I was a little way into the thicket I called to her, but she did not answer. I then went on, following the track of the bear as well as I could. Bears, you know, have long flat feet that do not sink into the ground and leave a distinct track like a deer's foot does, so I soon lost the bear tracks and did not know which way to go.

"I kept going, however, calling loudly for Liney every now and then, and soon I was so deep into the forest that it seemed almost night. I could not see far in any direction on account of the thick under brush, and at a little distance objects appeared indistinct. On I went, knowing not where, calling "Liney! Liney!" at nearly every step; but I heard no answer, and it seemed that I liked Liney Fox better than anybody in all the world, and would have given my life to save her."

After Balser had gone into the woods to help Liney the other children gathered in a frightened group about the tree under which they had eaten dinner. There they waited in the greatest anxiety and fear until the sun had almost sunk below the horizon, but Balser and Liney did not return. Shortly before dark the children started homeward, very heavy-hearted and sorrowful, you may be sure. When they reached the river they paddled across and told Mr. Brent that Balser and Liney were lost in the woods, and that when last seen a huge bear was in pursuit of Liney. Balser's father lost not a moment, but ran to a hill near the house, upon the top of which stood a large stack of dry grass, leaves, and wood, placed there for the purpose of signaling the neighbours in case of distress. He at once put fire to the dry grass, and soon there was a blaze, the light from which could be seen for miles around.

Day 82

1. Finish reading chapter 3.
2. What had happened to Liney? (Answers)
3. Who does Balser vow to kill? (Answers)

Chapter 3 continued

Mr. Brent immediately crossed the river, and leaving Tom Fox behind to guide the neighbours, walked rapidly in the direction of the place where Balser and Liney had last been seen. He took with him the dogs, and a number of torches which he intended to light from a tinder-box if he should need them.

The neighbours soon hurried to the Brent home in response to the fire signal, and several of them started out to rescue the children, if possible. If help were to be given, it must be done at once. A night in the woods meant almost certain death to the boy and girl; for, besides bears and wolves, there had been for several weeks a strolling band of Indians in the neighbourhood.

Although the Indians were not brave enough to attack a settlement, they would be only too ready to steal the children, did they but have the opportunity. These Indians slept all day in dark, secluded spots, and roamed about at night, visiting the houses of the settlers under cover of darkness, for the purpose of carrying off anything of value upon which they could lay their hands. Recently several houses had been burned, and a man while out hunting had been shot by an unseen enemy.

These outrages were all justly attributed to the Indians; and if they should meet Balser and Liney in the lonely forest, Heaven itself only knew what might become of the children, a bear would be a more merciful enemy.

All night Mr. Brent and the neighbours searched the forest far and near.

Afterward Balser told the story of that terrible night, and I will let him speak: "I think it was after six o'clock when I went into the woods in pursuit of Liney and the bear. It was almost dark at that time in the forest, and a little later, when the sun had gone down and a fine drizzle of rain had begun to fall, the forest was so black that once I ran against a small tree because I did not see it.

"I wandered about for what seemed a very long time, calling for Liney; then I grew hopeless and began to realize that I was lost. I could not tell from which direction I had come, nor where I was going. Everything looked alike all about me a deep, black bank of nothing, and a nameless fear stole over me. I had my gun, but of what use was it, when I could not see my hand before me? Now and then I heard wolves howling, and it seemed that their voices came from every direction. Once a black shadow ran by me with a snarl and a snap, and I expected every moment to have the hungry pack upon me, and to be torn into pieces. What if they should attack Liney? The thought almost drove me wild.

"I do not know how long I had wandered through the forest, but it must have been eight or nine hours, when I came to the river. I went to the water's edge and put my hand in the stream to learn which way the current ran, for I was so confused and so entirely lost that I did not know which direction was down-stream. I found that the water was running toward my right, and then I climbed back to the bank and stood in helpless confusion for a few minutes. "Nothing could be gained by standing there watching the water, like a fish-hawk, so I walked slowly down the river. I had been going down-stream for perhaps twenty minutes, when I saw a tall man come out of the woods, a few yards ahead of me, and walk rapidly toward the river bank. He carried something on his shoulder, as a man would carry a sack of wheat, and when he had reached the river bank, where there was more light, I could see from his dress that he was an Indian. I could not tell what it was he carried, but in a moment I thought of Liney and ran toward him. I reached the place where he had gone down the bank just in time to see him place his burden in a canoe. He himself was on the point of stepping in when I called to him to stop, and told him I would shoot him if he did not. My fright was gone in an instant, and I would not have feared all the lions, bears, and Indians that roamed the wilderness. I had but one thought to save Liney, and something told me that she lay at the other end of the canoe.

"The open space of the river made it light enough for me to see the Indian, and I was so close to him that even in the darkness I could not miss my aim. In place of answering my call, he glanced hurriedly at me, in surprise, and quickly lifted his gun to shoot me. But I was quicker than he, and I fired first. The Indian dropped his gun and plunged into the river. I did not know whether he had jumped or fallen in, but he immediately sank. I thought I saw his head a moment afterward above the surface of the water near the opposite bank, and I do not know to this day whether or not I killed him. At the time I did not care, for the one thing on my mind was to rescue Liney.

"I did not take long to climb into the canoe, and sure enough there she was at the other end. I had not taken the precaution to tie the boat to the bank, and I was so overjoyed at finding Liney, and was so eager in my effort to lift her, and to learn if she were dead or alive, that I upset the unsteady thing. I thought we should both drown before we could get out, for Liney was as helpless as if she were dead, which I thought was really the case.

"After a hard struggle I reached shallow water and carried Liney to the top of the bank. I laid her on the ground, and took away the piece of wood which the Indian had tied between her teeth to keep her from crying out. Then I rubbed her hands and face and rolled her over and over until she came to. After a while she raised her head and opened her eyes, and looked about her as if she were in a dream.

"Oh, Balser!" she cried, and then fainted away again. I thought she was dead this time sure, and was in such agony that I could not even feel. Hardly knowing what I was doing, I picked her up to carry her home, dead as I supposed. I had carried her for perhaps half an hour, when, becoming very tired, I stopped to rest. Then Liney wakened up again, and I put her down. But she could not stand, and, of course, could not walk.

"She told me that after she had run into the woods away from the bear, she became frightened and was soon lost. She had wandered aimlessly about for a long time, how long she did not know, but it seemed ages. She had been so terrified by the wolves and by the darkness, that she was almost unconscious, and hardly knew what she was doing. She said that every now and then she had called my name, for she knew that I would try to follow her. Her calling for me had evidently attracted the Indian, whom she had met after she had been in the woods a very long time.

"The Indian seized her, and placed the piece of wood between her teeth to keep her from screaming. He then threw her over his shoulder, and she remembered very little of what happened after that until she was awakened in the canoe by the flash and the report of my gun. She said that she knew at once I had come, and then she knew nothing more until she awakened on the bank. She did not know of the upsetting of the canoe, nor of my struggle in the water, but when I told her about it, she said: "Balser, you've saved my life three times in one night."

"Then I told her that I would carry her home. She did not want me too, though, and tried to walk, but could not; so I picked her up and started homeward.

"Just then I happened to look toward the river and saw the Indian's canoe floating down-stream, bottom upward. I saw at once that here was an opportunity for us to ride home, so I put Liney down, took off my wet jacket and moccasins, and swam out to the canoe. After I had drawn it to the bank and had turned out the water, I laid Liney at the bow, found a pole with which to guide the canoe, climbed in myself, and pushed off. We floated very slowly, but, slow as it was, it was a great deal better than having to walk.

"It was just beginning to be daylight when I heard the barking of dogs. I would have known their voices among ten thousand, for they were as familiar to me as the voice of my mother. It was dear old Tige and Prince, and never in my life was any voice more welcome to my ears than that sweet sound. I whistled shrilly between my fingers, and soon the faithful animals came rushing out of the woods and plunged into the water, swimming about us as if they knew as well as a man could have known what they and their master had been looking for all night." Balser's father had followed closely upon the dogs, and within an hour the children were home amid the wildest rejoicing you ever heard.

When Liney became stronger she told how she had seen the hollow in the sycamore tree, and had hurried toward it to hide; and how, just as she was about to enter the hollow tree, a huge bear raised upon its haunches and thrust its nose almost in her face. She said that the bear had followed her for a short distance, and then for some reason had given up the chase. Her recollection of everything that had happened was confused and indistinct, but one little fact she remembered with a clearness that was very curious: the bear, she said, had but one ear.

When Balser heard this, he arose to his feet, and gave notice to all persons present that there would soon be a bear funeral, and that a one-eared bear would be at the head of the procession. He would have the other ear of that bear if he had to roam the forest until he was an old man to find it.

How he got it, and how it got him, I will tell you in the next chapter.

Day 83

1. Read the beginning of chapter 4.
2. Who can translate bear-cub language? (Answers)
3. What stories did people tell about the one-eared bear? (Answers)
4. It mentions "patron saint." There are branches of Christianity which call certain dead Christians saints and believe that they are particularly watching over certain people, like hunters in this story. The Bible, however, calls all believers saints. It does say that we have a "great cloud of witnesses" formed of those of faith who have gone before us. It's like we have a crowd cheering for us in heaven as we follow Jesus. But the Bible says that God, Himself, is the only One who can help us. He may use angels or other people, but He is the one directing the rescue. From what the Bible teaches, He's the only one who can hear and answer prayers.
5. The author keeps giving hints about what is to come. It's called foreshadowing. He leaves a hint that Tom is going to need (and use) his hatchet. What do you think he will do?

CHAPTER IV THE ONE-EARED BEAR

"You, Tom! You, Jerry! come here!" called Balser one morning, while he and Jim were sitting in the shade near the river in front of the house, overseeing the baby.

"You, Tom! You, Jerry!" called Balser a second time with emphasis. The cubs, snoozing in the sun a couple of paces away, rolled lazily over two or three times in an effort to get upon their feet, and then trotted to their masters with a comical, waddling gait that always set the boys laughing, it was such a swagger.

When they had come, Balser said, "Stop right there!" and the cubs, being always tired, gladly enough sat upon their haunches, and blinked sleepily into Balser's face, with a greedy expression upon their own, as if to say, "Well, where 's the milk?"
"Milk, is it?" asked Balser. "You're always hungry. You're nothing but a pair of gluttons. Eat, eat, from morning until night. Well, this time you'll get nothing. There's no milk for you."

The cubs looked disgusted, so Jim said, and no doubt he was right, for Jim and the cubs were great friends and understood each other thoroughly.

197

"Now, I've been a good father to you," said Balser. "I've always given you as much milk as you could hold, without bursting, and have tried to bring you up to be good respectable bears, and to do my duty by you. I have whipped you whenever you needed it, although it often hurt me worse than it did you."

The bears grunted, as if to say: "But not in the same place."

"Now what I want," continued Balser, regardless of the interruption, "is, that you tell me what you know, if anything, concerning a big one-eared bear that lives hereabouts. Have you ever heard of him?"

Tom gave a grunt, and Jim, who had been studying bear language, said he meant "Yes."

Jerry then put his nose to Tom's ear, and whined something in a low voice.

"What does he say, Jim" asked Balser.

"He says for Tom not to tell you any thing until you promise to give them milk," answered Jim, seriously.

"Jerry, you're the greatest glutton alive, I do believe," said Balser; "but if you'll tell me anything worth knowing about the one-eared bear, I'll give you the biggest pan of milk you ever saw."

Jerry in his glee took two or three fancy steps, awkwardly fell over himself a couple of times, got up, and grunted to Tom to go ahead. Jim was the interpreter, and Tom grunted and whined away, in a mighty effort to earn the milk.

"The one-eared bear," said he, "is my uncle. Used to hear dad and mother talk about him. Dad bit his ear off. That's how he came to have only one. Dad and he fought about mother, and when dad bit uncle's ear off mother went with dad and wouldn't have anything to do with the other fellow. Couldn't abide a one-eared husband, she said."

"That's interesting," answered Balser. "Where does he live?"

Tom pointed his nose toward the northwest, and opened his mouth very wide.

"Up that way in a cave," interpreted Jim, pointing as the cub had indicated.
"How far is it?" asked Balser.

Jerry lay down and rolled over twice.
"Two hours' walk," said Jim.

"How shall I find the place?" asked Balser.

198

Tom stood upon his hind legs, and scratched the bark of a tree with his forepaws as high as he could reach.

"Of course," said Balser, "by the bear scratches on the trees. I understand."

Jerry grunted "milk," so Jim said, and the whole party, boys, bears, and baby moved off to the milk-house, where the cubs had a great feast.

After the milk had disappeared, Jerry grew talkative, and grunted away like the satisfied little pig that he was.

Again Jim, with a serious face, acted as interpreter.

"Mighty bad bear," said Jerry. "Soured on the world since mother threw him over. Won't have anything to do with anybody. He's as big and strong as a horse, fierce as a lion, and meaner than an Injun. He's bewitched, too, with an evil spirit, and nobody can ever kill him."

"That's the name he has among white folks," remarked Balser.

"Better be careful when you hunt him, for he's killed more men and boys than you have fingers and toes," said Tom. Then the cubs, being full of milk and drowsy, stretched themselves out in the sun, and no amount of persuasion could induce them to utter another grunt. The bears had told the truth that is, if they had told anything; for since it had been learned throughout the settlement that it was a one-eared bear which had pursued Liney, many stories had been told of hair breadth escapes and thrilling adventures with that same fierce prowler of the woods.

One hunter said that he had shot at him as many as twenty times, at short range, but for all he knew, had never even wounded him.

The one-eared bear could not be caught by any means whatsoever. He had broken many traps, and had stolen bait so frequently from others, that he was considered altogether too knowing for a natural bear; and it was thought that he was inhabited by an evil spirit which gave him supernatural powers.

He certainly was a very shrewd old fellow, and very strong and fierce ; and even among those of the settlers who were not superstitious enough to believe that he was inhabited by an evil spirit, he was looked upon as a "rogue" bear; that is, a sullen, morose old fellow, who lived by himself, as old bachelors live. The bachelors, though, being men, should know better and act more wisely.

Notwithstanding all these evil reports concerning the one-eared bear, Balser clung to his resolution to hunt the bear, to kill him if possible, and to give Liney the remaining bear as a keepsake.

Balser's father knew that it was a perilous undertaking, and tried to persuade the boy to hunt some less dangerous game ; but he would not listen to any of the warnings, and day by day longed more ardently for the blood of the one-eared bear.

So one morning shortly after the conversation with the cubs, Balser shouldered his gun and set out toward the northwest, accompanied by Limpy Fox and the dogs.

In truth, the expedition had been delayed that Limpy's sore toe might heal. That was one of Liney's jokes.

Limpy had no gun, but he fairly bristled with knives and a hatchet, which for several days he had been grinding and whetting until they were almost as sharp as a razor.

The boys roamed through the forest all day long, but found no trace of the one-eared bear, nor of any other, for that matter. So toward evening they turned their faces home ward, where they arrived soon after sunset, very tired and hungry.

Liney had walked over to Balser's house to learn the fate of the one-eared bear, and fully expected to hear that he had been slaughtered, for she looked upon Balser as a second Saint Hubert, who, as you know, is the patron saint of hunters.

One failure, however, did not shake her faith in Balser, nor did it affect his resolution to kill the one-eared bear.

Next day the boys again went hunting, and again failed to find the bear they sought. They then rested for a few days, and tried again, with still another failure.

After several days of fruitless tramping through the forests, their friends began to laugh at them. "If he ever catches sight of Tom," said Liney, "he'll certainly die, for Tom's knives and hatchet would frighten any bear to death."

Balser also made sport of Tom's armament, but Tom, a little "miffed," said: "You needn't be so smart; it hasn't been long since you had nothing but a hatchet. You think because you've got a gun you're very big and cute. I'll bet the time will come when you'll be glad enough that I have a hatchet."
Tom was a truer prophet than he thought, for the day soon came when the hatchet proved itself true steel.

The boys had started out before sun-up one morning, and were deep into the forest when daylight was fairly abroad. Tige and Prince were with them, and were trotting lazily along at the boys' heels, for the day was very warm, and there was no breeze in the forest. They had been walking for several hours, and had almost lost hope, when suddenly a deep growl seemed to come from the ground almost at their feet. The boys sprang back in a hurry, for right in their path stood an enormous bear, where a moment before there had been nothing.

"Lordy! it's the one-eared bear," cried Tom, and the hairs on his head fairly stood on end.

Day 84

1. Read the next part of chapter 4.
2. It says, "Balser was loath to follow…" Do you remember what loath means? What does the sentence mean? (Answers)
3. Why did Balser and Tom decide to go home? (Answers)
4. What happened on their way home? (Answers)

Chapter 4 continued

My! what a monster of fierceness the bear was. His head, throat, and paws, were covered with blood, evidently from some animal that he had been eating, and his great red mouth, sharp white teeth, and cropped ear gave him a most ferocious and terrifying appearance.

Balser's first impulse, now that he had found the long-sought one-eared bear, I am sorry to say, was to retreat. That was Tom's first impulse also, and, notwithstanding his knives and hatchet, he acted upon it quicker than a circus clown can turn a somersault.

Balser also started to run, but thought better of it, and turned to give battle to the bear, fully determined to act slowly and deliberately, and to make no mistake about his aim.

He knew that a false aim would end his down days, and would add one more victim to the already long list of the one-eared bear.

The dogs barked furiously at the bear, and did not give Balser an opportunity to shoot. The bear and dogs were gradually moving farther away from Balser, and almost before he knew it the three had disappeared in the thicket. Balser was loath to follow until Tom should return, so he called in an under tone: "Tom! Limpy!"

Soon Tom cautiously came back, peering fearfully about him, hatchet in hand, ready to do great execution upon the bear he afterward said.

"You're a pretty hunter, you are. You'd better go home and get an ax. The bear has got away just because I had to wait for you," said Balser, only too glad to have someone to blame for the bear's escape.

The boys still heard the dogs barking, and hurried on after them as rapidly as the tangle of undergrowth would permit. Now and then they caught a glimpse of the bear, only to lose it again as he ran down a ravine or through a dense thicket. The dogs, how ever, kept in close pursuit, and loudly called to their master to notify him of their whereabouts.

The boys and bears played at this exciting game of hide-and-seek for two or three hours, but Balser had no opportunity for a good shot, and Tom found no chance to use his deadly hatchet.

When the bear showed a disposition to run away rather than to fight, Limpy grew brave, and talked himself into a high state of heroism.

It was an hour past noon and the boys were laboriously climbing a steep ascent in pursuit of the bear and dogs, which they could distinctly see a few yards ahead of them, at the top of a hill. The underbrush had become thinner, although the shadow of the trees was deep and dark, and Balser thought that at last the bear was his. He repeated over and over to himself his father's advice: "When you attack a bear, be slow and deliberate. Do nothing in a hurry. Don't shoot until you're sure of your aim."

He remembered vividly his hasty shot when he wounded the bear on Conn's Creek, and his narrow escape from death at that time had so impressed upon him the soundness of his father's advice, that he repeated it night and morning with his prayers.

When he saw the bear at the top of the hill, so close to him, he raised his gun to his shoulder and held it there for a moment, awaiting a chance for a sure shot. But disappointment, instead of the bear, was his, for while he held his gun ready to fire, the bear suddenly disappeared, as if the earth had opened and swallowed him.

It all happened so quickly that even the dogs looked astonished. Surely, this was a demon bear.

The boys hurried to the spot where they had last seen the animal, and, although they carefully searched for the mouth of a cave, or burrow, through which the bear might have escaped, they saw none, but found the earth everywhere solid and firm. They extended their search for a hundred feet or more about them, but still with the same result. They could find no hole or opening into which the bear could possibly have entered. His mysterious disappearance right before their eyes seemed terribly uncanny.

There was certainly something wrong with the one-eared bear. He had sprung from the ground, just at their feet, where a moment before there had been nothing; and now he had as mysteriously disappeared into the solid earth, and had left no trace behind him.

Balser and Tom stood for a moment in the greatest amazement, and all they had heard about the evil spirit which inhabited the one-eared bear quickly flashed through their minds.

"We'd better let him go, Balser," said Tom, "for we'll never kill him, that's sure. He's been leading us a wild-goose chase all the morning only to get us up here to kill us. I never saw such an awful place for darkness. The bushes and trees don't seem natural. They all have thorns and great knots on them, and their limbs and twigs look like huge bony arms and ringers reaching out after us. I tell you this ain't a natural place, and that bear is an evil spirit, as sure as you live. Lordy! let's get out of here, for I never was so scared in my life."

Balser was also afraid, but Tom's words had made him wish to appear brave, and he said: "Shucks! Limpy; I hope you ain't afraid when you have your hatchet."

"For goodness' sake, don't joke in such a place as this, Balser," said Tom, with chattering teeth. "I'm not afraid of any natural bear when I have my hatchet, but a bewitched bear is too much for me, and I'm not ashamed to own it."

"How do you know he's bewitched?" asked Balser, trying to talk himself out of his own fears.

"Bewitched? Didn't he come right out of the ground just at our very feet, and didn't he sink into the solid earth right here before our eyes? What more do you want, I'd like to know? Just you try to sink into the ground and see if you can. Nobody can, unless he's bewitched."

Balser felt in his heart that Tom told the truth, and, as even the dogs seemed anxious to get away from the dark, mysterious place, they all descended the hill on the side opposite to that by which they had ascended. When they reached the bottom of the hill, they unexpectedly found that they were at the river's edge, and after taking a drink they turned their faces toward home. They thought of dinner, but their appetite had been frightened away by the mysterious disappearance of the bear, and they did not care to eat. So they fed the dogs and again started homeward down the river.

After a few minutes' walking they came to a bluff several hundred feet long, and perhaps fifty feet high, which at that time, the water being low, was separated from the river by a narrow strip of rocky, muddy ground. This strip of ground was overgrown with reeds and willows, and the bluff was covered with vines and bushes which clung in green masses to its steep sides and completely hid the rocks and earth. Tom was in front, Balser came next, and the dogs, dead tired, were trailing along some distance behind. Suddenly Tom threw up his hands and jumped frantically backward, exclaiming in terrified tones:

"Oh, Lord! the one-eared bear again." When Tom jumped backward his foot caught in a vine, and he fell violently against Balser, throwing them both to the ground. In falling, Tom dropped his hatchet, which he had snatched from his belt, and Balser dropped his gun, the lock of which struck a stone and caused the charge to explode. Thus the boys were on their backs and weaponless, while the one-eared bear stood almost within arm's length, growling in a voice like distant thunder, and looking so horrid and fierce that he seemed a very demon in a bear's skin.

Tom and Balser were so frightened that for a moment they could not move; but the deep growls which terrified them also brought the dogs, who came quickly to the rescue, barking furiously.

Day 85

1. Finish reading chapter 4.
2. A fortnight is two weeks.
3. How did Tom's hatchet save the day? (Answers)

Vocabulary

1. Review your words from Day 25 by matching the words to their definitions or by going to the review game page and using the Aesop's fables link under Level 3.

Chapter 4 continued

The bear sprang upon the boys just as the dogs came up, and Balser received the full force of a great flat horny paw upon his back, and was almost stunned. The long sharp claws of the bear tore through the buckskin jacket as if it were paper, and cut deep gashes in Balser's flesh. The pain seemed to revive him from the benumbing effect of the stroke, and when the bear's attention was attracted by the dogs, Balser crawled out from beneath the monster and arose to his feet, wounded, bloody, and dizzy.

Tom also felt the force of the bear's great paw, and was lying a few feet from Balser, with his head in a tangle of vines and reeds.

Balser, having escaped from under the bear, the brute turned upon Tom, who was lying prostrate in the bushes.

The dogs were still vigorously fighting the bear, and every second or two a stroke from the powerful paw brought a sharp yelp of pain from either Tige or Prince, and left its mark in deep, red gashes upon their bodies. The pain, however, did not deter the faithful animals from their efforts to rescue the boys; and while the bear was making for Tom it was kept busy in defend ing itself from the dogs.

In an instant the bear reached Tom, who would have been torn in pieces at once, had not Balser quickly unsheathed his long hunting knife and rushed into the fight. He sprang for the bear and landed on his back, clinging to him with one arm about his neck, while with the other he thrust his sharp hunting knife almost to the hilt into the brute's side.

This turned the attack from Tom, and brought it upon Balser, who soon had his hands full again.

The bear rose upon his hind feet, and before Balser could take a step in retreat, caught him in his mighty arms for the purpose of hugging him to death, which is a bear's favourite method of doing battle.

The hunting knife was still sticking in the rough black side of the bear, where Balser had thrust it, and blood flowed from the wound in a great stream.

The dogs were biting at the bear's hind legs, but so intent was the infuriated monster upon killing Balser that he paid no attention to them, but permitted them to work their pleasure upon him, while he was having the satisfaction of squeezing the life out of the boy.

In the meantime Tom recovered and rose to his feet. He at once realized that Balser would be a dead boy if something were not done immediately. Luckily, Tom saw his hatchet, lying a few feet away, and snatching it up he attacked the bear, chopping away at his great back as if it were a tree.

At the third or fourth stroke from Tom's hatchet, the bear loosened his grip upon Balser and fell in a great black heap to the ground, growling and clawing in all directions as if he were frantic with rage and pain. He bit at the rocks and bushes, gnashed his teeth, and dug into the ground with his claws.

Balser, when released from the bear, fell in a half conscious condition, close to the river's edge. Tom ran to him, and, hardly knowing what he did, dashed water in his face to remove the blood-stains and to wash the wounds. The water soon revived Balser, who rose to his feet; and, Tom helping his friend, the boys started to run, or rather to walk away as fast as their wounds and bruises would permit, while the dogs continued to bark and the bear to growl.

As the boys were retreating, Tom, turned his head to see if the bear was following, but as it was still lying on the ground, growling and biting at the rocks and scratching the earth, he thought perhaps that the danger was over, and that the bear was so badly wounded that he could not rise, or he certainly would have been on his feet fighting Tige and Prince, who gave him not one moment's peace. Balser and Tom paused for an instant, and were soon convinced that the bear was helpless.

"I believe he can't get up," said Balser. "Of course he can't," answered Tom, pompously. "I cut his old backbone in two with my hatchet. When he was hugging you I chopped away at him hard enough to cut down a hickory sapling."

The boys limped back to the scene of conflict, and found that they were right. The bear could not rise to his feet, but lay in a huge struggling black heap on the ground. Balser then cautiously went over to where his gun lay, picked it up, and ran back to Tom. He tried to load the gun, but his arms were so bruised and torn that he could not; so he handed it to Tom, who loaded it with a large bullet and a heavy charge of powder.

Balser then called off the dogs, and Tom, as proud as the President of the United States, held the gun within a yard of the bear's head and pulled the trigger. The great brute rolled over on his side, his mighty limbs quivered, he uttered a last despairing growl which was piteous for it was almost a groan and his fierce, turbulent spirit fled forever. Balser then drew his hunting knife from the bear's body, cut off the remaining ear, and put it in the pocket of his buckskin coat.

The boys were sorely wounded, and Balser said that the bear had squeezed his "insides" out of place. This proved to be true to a certain extent, for when he got home it was found that two of his ribs were broken.

The young hunters were only too glad to start homeward, for they had seen quite enough of the one-eared bear for one day.

After walking in silence a short distance down the river, Balser said to Tom: "I'll never again say anything bad about your hatchet. It saved my life to-day, and was worth all the guns in the world in such a fight as we have just gone through."

Tom laughed, but was kind-hearted enough not to say, "I told you so."

You may imagine the fright the boys gave their parents when they arrived home wounded, limping, and blood-stained; but soon all was told, and Balser and Tom were the heroes of the settlement.

They had killed the most dangerous animal that had ever lived on Blue River, and had conquered where old and experienced hunters had failed.

The huge carcass of the bear was brought home that evening, and when the skin was removed, his backbone was found to have been cut almost through by Tom's hatchet.

When they cut the bear open somebody said he had two galls, and that fact, it was claimed, accounted for his fierceness.

Where the bear had sprung from when the boys first saw him in the forest, or how he had managed to disappear into the ground at the top of the hill was never satisfactorily explained. Some settlers insisted that he had not been inhabited by an evil spirit, else the boys could not have killed him, but others clung to the belief with even greater faith and persistency.

Liney went every day to see Balser, who was confined to his bed for a fortnight. One day, while she was sitting by him, and no one else was in the room, he asked her to hand him his buckskin jacket; the one he had worn on the day of the bear fight. The jacket was almost in shreds from the frightful claws of the bear, and tears came to the girl's eyes as she placed it on the bed.

Balser put his hand into one of the deep pockets, and, drawing out the bear's ear, handed it to Liney, saying: "I cut this off for you because I like you."

The girl took the bear's ear, blushed a deep red, thanked him, and murmured: "And I will keep it, ugly as it is, because I because I like you."

Day 86

1. The author compares the bears stretched out and snoring to a "pair of grampuses." Those are orcas, a type of whale.
2. A gander is a male goose.
3. Read the beginning of chapter 5.
4. Describe what the day is like at the beginning of the chapter. (Answers)
5. What story does Tom always tell? (Answers)
6. A wolf's den is underground.

CHAPTER V THE WOLF HUNT

IT was a bright day in August. The whispering rustle of the leaves as they turned their white sides to the soft breath of the southwest wind, the buzzing of the ostentatiously busy bees, the lapping of the river as it gurgled happily along on its everlasting travels, the half-drowsy note of a thrush, and the peevish cry of a catbird seemed only to accentuate the Sabbath hush that was upon all nature.

The day was very warm, but the deep shade of the elms in front of the cabin afforded a delightful retreat, almost as cool as a cellar.

Tom and Liney Fox had walked over to visit Balser and Jim; and Sukey Yates, with her two brothers, had dropped in to stay a moment or two, but finding such good company, had remained for the day.

The children were seated at the top of the slope that descended to the river, and the weather being too warm to play any game more vigorous than "thumbs up," they were occupying the time with drowsy yawns and still more drowsy conversation, the burden of which was borne by Tom.

Balser often said that he didn't mind "talking parties," if he could only keep Tom Fox from telling the story of the time when he went to Cincinnati with his father and saw a live elephant. But that could never be done; and Tom had told it twice upon the afternoon in question, and there is no knowing how often he would have inflicted it upon his small audience, had it not been for an interruption which effectually disposed of "Cincinnati" and the live elephant for that day.

A bustling old hen with her brood of downy chicks was peevishly clucking about, now and then lazily scratching the earth, and calling up her ever-hungry family when ever she was lucky enough to find a delicious worm or racy bug.

The cubs were stretched at full length in the bright blaze of the sun, snoring away like a pair of grampuses, their black silky sides rising and falling with every breath. They looked so pretty and so innocent that you would have supposed a thought of mischief could never have entered their heads. (Mischief! They never thought of anything else. From morning until night, and from night until morning, they studied, planned, and executed deeds of mischief that would have done credit to the most freckle-faced boy in the settlement. Will you tell me why it is that the boy most plentifully supplied with freckles and warts is the most fruitful in schemes of mischief?)

A flock of gray geese and snowy ganders were floating on the placid surface of the river, opposite the children, where a projection of the bank had caused the water to back, making a little pool of listless eddies.

Suddenly from among the noiseless flock of geese came a mighty squawking and a sound of flapping wings, and the flock, half flying, half swimming, came struggling at their utmost speed toward home.

"Look, Balser! Look!" said Liney in a whisper. "A wolf!"

Balser turned in time to see a great, lank, gray wolf emerge from the water, carrying a gander by the neck.

The bird could not squawk, but he flapped his wings violently, thereby retarding some what the speed of Mr. Wolf.

Balser hurried to the house for his gun, and with Tom Fox quickly paddled across the river in pursuit of the wolf. The boys entered the forest at the place the wolf had chosen. White feathers from the gander furnished a distinct spoor, and Balser had no difficulty in keeping on the wolf's track. The boys had been walking rapidly for thirty or forty minutes, when they found that the tracks left by the wolf and the scattered feathers of the gander led toward a thick clump of pawpaw bushes and vines, which grew at the foot of a small rocky hill. Into this thicket the boys cautiously worked their way, and, after careful examination, they found, ingeniously concealed by dense foliage, a small hole or cleft in the rocks at the base of the hill, and they at once knew that the wolf had gone to earth, and that this was his den.

Foxes make for themselves and their families the snuggest, most ingenious home in the ground you can possibly imagine. They seek a place at the base of a hill or bluff, and dig what we would call in our houses a narrow hallway, straight into the hill. They loosen the dirt with their front feet, and throw it back of them; then with their hind feet they keep pushing it farther toward the opening of the hole, until they have cast it all out. When they have removed the loose dirt, they at once scatter it over the ground and carefully cover it with leaves and vines, to avoid attracting unwelcome visitors to their home.

When the hallway is finished, the fox digs upward into the hill, and there he makes his real home. His reason for doing this is to prevent water from flowing through his hall into his living apartment. The latter is often quite a cave in the earth, and furnishes as roomy and cozy a home for Mr. and Mrs. Fox and their children as you could find in the world. It is cool in summer and warm in winter. It is softly carpeted with leaves, grass, and feathers, and the foxes lie there snugly enough when the winter comes on, with its freezing and snowing and blowing.

When the fox gets hungry he slips out of his cozy home, and briskly trots to some well-known chicken roost; or perhaps he finds a covey of quails huddled under a bunch of straw. In either case he carries home with him a dainty dinner, and after he has feasted, he cares not how the wind blows, nor how the river freezes, nor how the snow falls, for he is housed like a king, and is as warm and comfortable and happy as if he owned the earth and lived in a palace.

Wolves also make their dens in the earth, but they usually hunt for a place where the hallway, at least, is already made for them. They seek a hill with a rocky base, and find a cave partially made, the entrance to which is a small opening between the rocks. With this for a commencement, they dig out the interior and make their home, somewhat upon the plan of the fox.

The old wolf which Balser and Tom had chased to earth had found a fine dinner for his youngsters, and while the boys were watching the hole, no doubt the wolf family was having a glorious feast upon the gander.

Day 87

1. A shilling is a coin.
2. Read the next part of chapter 5.
3. Tell someone what is happening in this section.

Chapter 5 continued

The boys, of course, were at their rope's end. The dogs were not with them, and, even had they been, they were too large to enter the hole leading to the wolf's den. So the boys seated themselves upon a rock a short distance from the opening, and after a little time adopted the following plan of action.

Balser was to lie upon his breast on the hillside, a few yards above the opening of the wolf den, while Tom was to conceal himself in the dense foliage, close to the mouth of the cave, and they took their positions accordingly. Both were entirely hidden by vines and bushes, and remained silent as the tomb. They had agreed that they should lie entirely motionless until the shadow of a certain tree should fall across Tom's face, which they thought would occur within an hour. Then Tom, who could mimic the calls and cries of many birds and beasts, was to squawk like a goose, and tempt the wolf from his den so that Balser could shoot him.

It was a harder task than you may imagine to lie on the ground amid the bushes and leaves; for it seemed, at least so Tom said, that all the ants and bugs and worms in the woods had met at that particular place, and at that exact time, for the sole purpose of "drilling" up and down, and over and around, his body, and to bite him at every step. He dared not move to frighten away the torments, nor to scratch. He could not even grumble, which to Tom was the sorest trial of all.

The moment the shadow of the tree fell upon his face Tom squawked like a goose, so naturally, that Balser could hardly believe it was Tom, and not a real goose. Soon he uttered another squawk, and almost at the same instant Mr. Wolf came out of his hall door, doubtless thinking to himself that that was his lucky day, for he would have two ganders, one for dinner and one for supper, and plenty of cold goose for breakfast and dinner the next day. But he was mistaken, for it was the unluckiest day of the poor wolf's life. Bang! went Balser's gun, and the wolf, who had simply done his duty as a father, by providing a dinner for his family, paid for his feast with his life.

"We'll drag the body a short distance away from the den," said Balser, "and you lie down again, and this time whine like a wolf. Then the old she-wolf will come out and we'll get her too."

Tom objected.

"I wouldn't lie there another hour and let them ants and bugs chaw over me as they did, for all the wolves in the state."

"But just think, Tom," answered Balser, "when the wagons go to Brookville this fall we can get a shilling apiece for the wolfskins! Think of it! A shilling! One for you and one for me. I'll furnish the powder and shot if you'll squawk and whine. Squawks and whines don't cost anything, but powder and lead does. Now that's a good fellow, just lie down and whine a little. She'll come out pretty quick."

Tom still refused, and Balser still insisted. Soon Balser grew angry and called Tom a fool. Tom answered in kind, and in a moment the boys clinched for a fight. They scuffled and fought awhile, and soon stumbled over the dead wolf and fell to the ground. Balser was lucky enough to fall on top, and proceeded to pound Tom at a great rate.

"Now will you whine?" demanded Balser.

"No," answered Tom.
"Then take that, and that, and that. Now will you whine?"

"No," cried Tom, determined not to yield.

So Balser went at it again, but there was no give up to stubborn Tom, even if he was on the under side.

At last Balser wiped the perspiration from his face, and, sitting astride of his stubborn foe, said: "Tom, if you'll whine I'll lend you my gun for a whole day."

"And powder and bullets?" asked Tom.

"Well, I guess not," answered Balser. "I'll lick you twenty times first."

"If you'll lend me your gun and give me ten full loads, I'll whine till I fetch every wolf in the woods, if the bugs do eat me up."

"That's a go," said Balser, glad enough to compromise with a boy who didn't know when he was whipped.

Then they got up, and were as good friends as if no trouble had occurred between them.

Balser at once lay down upon the hillside above the wolf den, and Tom took his place to whine.

The boys understood their job thoroughly, and Tom's whines soon brought out the old she-wolf. She looked cautiously about her for a moment, stole softly over to her dead mate, and dropped by his side with a bullet through her heart.

Tom was about to rise, but Balser said: "Whine again; whine again, and the young ones will come out."

Tom whined, and sure enough, out came two scrawny, long-legged wolf whelps.

The boys rushed upon them, and caught them by the back of the neck, to avoid being bitten, for the little teeth of the pups were as sharp as needles and could inflict an ugly wound. Balser handed the whelp he had caught to Tom, and proceeded to cut two forked sticks from a tough bush, which the children called "Indian arrow." These forked branches the boys tied about the necks of the pups, with which to lead them home.

Tom then cut a strong limb from a tree with his pocket-knife. This was quite an undertaking, but in time he cut it through, and trimmed off the smaller branches. The boys tied together the legs of the old wolves and swung them over the pole, which they took upon their shoulders, and started home leading the pups. They arrived home an hour or two before sunset, and found that Liney and Sukey had arranged supper under the elms.

The boys scoured their faces and hands with soft soap, for that was the only soap they had, and sat down to supper with cheeks shining, and hair pasted to their heads slick and tight.

"When a fellow gets washed up this way, and has his hair combed so slick, it makes him feel like it was Sunday," said Tom, who was uneasily clean.

"Tom, I wouldn't let people know how seldom I washed my face if I were you," said Liney, with a slight blush. "They'll think you clean up only on Sunday."

Tom, however, did not allow Liney's remarks to interrupt his supper, but continued to make sad havoc among the good things on the log.

There was white bread made from wheat flour, so snowy and light that it beat cake "all holler!" the boys "allowed." Wheat bread was a luxury to the settler folks in those days, for the mill nearest to the Blue River settlement was over on Whitewater, at Brookville, fifty miles away. Wheat and the skins of wild animals were the only products that the farmers could easily turn into cash, so the small crops were too precious to be used daily, and wheat flour bread was used only for special occasions, such as Christmas, or New Year's, or company dinner.

Day 88

1. They use a gourd as a cup. You'll read about them using gourds other times as well. Some types of gourds are pumpkins and squash. The insides can be eaten and people use the outsides, the shells, for different things like cups, or to hold something, or to make a jack-o-lantern.

2. Finish reading chapter 5.
3. What special new drink did they try? What did they think of it? (Answers)
4. Why did the bear cubs run into the river? (Answers)

Chapter 5 continued

Usually three or four of the farmers joined in a little caravan, and went in their wagons to Brookville twice a year. They would go in the spring with the hides of animals killed during the winter, that being the hunting season, and the hides then taken being of superior quality to those taken at any other time.

Early in the fall they would go again to Brookville, to market their summer crop of wheat.

Mr. Fox and a few neighbours had returned from an early trip to market only a day or two before the children's party at Balser's home, and had brought with them a few packages of a fine new drink called coffee. That is, it was new to the Western settler, at the time of which I write, milk sweetened with "tree sugar" being the usual table drink. Liney had brought over a small gourdful of coffee as a present to Mrs. Brent, and a pot of the brown beverage had been prepared for the supper under the elms.

The Yates children and Tom were frank enough to admit that the coffee was bitter, and not fit to drink; but Liney had made it, and Balser drank it, declaring it was very good indeed. Liney knew he told a story, but she thanked him for it, nevertheless, and said that the Yates children and Tom were so thoroughly "country" and green that she couldn't expect them to like a civilized drink.

This would have made trouble with Tom, but Balser, who saw it coming, said: "Now you shut up, Tom Fox." And Balser had so recently whipped Tom that his word bore the weight of authority.

Besides the coffee and the white bread there was a great gourd full of milk with the cream mixed in, just from the spring house, delicious and cold. There was a cold loin of venison, which had been spitted and roasted over a bed of hot coals in the kitchen fireplace that morning. There was a gourd full of quail eggs, which had been boiled hard and then cooled in the spring house. There were heaping plates of fried chicken, and rolls of glorious yellow butter just from the churn, rich with the genuine butter taste, that makes one long to eat it by the spoonful ; then there was a delicious apple pie, sweet and crusty, floating in cream almost as thick as molasses in winter.

They were backwoods, homely children; but the supper to which they sat down under the elms was fit for a king, and the appetite with which they ate it was too good for any king.

During the supper the bear cubs had been nosing about the log table, begging each one by turns for a bite to eat. They were so troublesome that Jim got a long stick, and whenever they came within each he gave them a sharp rap upon the head, and soon they waddled away in a pet of indignant disgust.

For quite a while after Jim had driven them off there had been a season of suspicious quietude on the part of the cubs.

Suddenly a chorus of yelps, howls, growls, and whines came from the direction of the wolf pups. The attention of all at the table was, of course, at once attracted by the noise, and those who looked beheld probably the most comical battle ever fought. Tom and Jerry, with their everlasting desire to have their noses into everything that did not concern them, had gone to investigate the wolf pups, and in the course of the investigation a fight ensued, whereby the wolves were liberated. The cubs were the stronger, but the wolves were more active, thus the battle was quite even. The bears, being awkward, of course, were in each other's way most of the time, and would fall over themselves and roll upon the ground for a second or two, before they could again get upon their clumsy feet. The consequence was that the wolves soon had the best of the fight, and, being once free from the cubs, scampered off to the woods and were never seen again.

When the wolves had gone the cubs turned round and round, looking for their late antagonists; but, failing to find them, sat down upon their haunches, grinned at each other in a very silly manner, and then began to growl and grumble in the worst bear language any one had ever heard.

Balser scolded the cubs roundly, and told them he had taught them better than to swear, even in bear talk. He then switched them for having liberated the wolves, and went back to supper.

The switching quieted the bears for a short time, but soon their spirit of mischief again asserted itself.

After another period of suspicious silence on the part of the cubs, Jim put a general inquiry to the company: "What do you s'pose they're up to this time?"

"Goodness only knows," responded Balser. "But if I hear another grunt out of them, I'll take a stick to them that'll hurt, and off they'll go to their pen for the night."

The settlers frequently caught swarms of bees in the woods, and Balser's father had several hives near the house. These hives were called "gums," because they were made from sections of a hollow gum tree, that being the best wood for the home of the bees. These hollow gums were placed on end upon small slanting platforms, and were covered with clapboards, which were held tightly in their places by heavy stones. There was a small hole, perhaps as large as the end of your finger, cut in the wood at the base, through which the bees entered, and upon the inside of the hive they constructed their comb and stored their honey.

I told you once before how bears delight to eat fish and blackberries. They are also very fond of honey. In fact, bears seem to have a general appetite and enjoy everything, from boys to blackberries.

Hardly had Balser spoken his threat then another duet of howls and yelps reached his ears.

"Now what on earth is it?" he asked, and immediately started around the house in the direction whence the howls had come.

"Geminy! I believe they've upset the bee-gum," said Jim.

"Don't you know they have?" asked Balser. By that time the boys were in sight of the bears.

"Well, I know now they have, if that suits you any better. Golly! Look at them paw and scratch, and rub their eyes when the bees sting. Good enough for you. Give it to 'em, bees!" And Jim threw back his head and almost split his sides with laughter.

Sure enough, the bears had got to nosing about the bee-gums, and in their ever hungry greediness had upset one. This, of course, made the bees very angry, and they attacked the cubs in a buzzing, stinging swarm that set them yelping, growling, and snapping, in a most desperate and comical manner. All their snapping and growling, however, did no good, for the bees continued to buzz and sting without any indication of being merciful. A little of this sort of thing went a long way with the black mischief-makers, and they soon ran to Balser and Jim for help. The bees, of course, followed, and when the boys and girls saw the bees coming toward them they broke helter-skelter in all directions, and ran as fast as they could go. The bears then ran to the river, and plunged in to escape their tormentors.

When the gum had been placed in position again and the bees had become quiet, the cubs, thinking the field clear, came out of the water dripping wet. Then they waddled up close to the girls, and out of pure mischief shook themselves and sprinkled the dainty clean frocks with a shower from their frowzy hides.

That sealed the fate of the cubs for the day, and when Balser marched them off to their pen they looked so meek and innocent that one would have thought that they had been attending bear Sunday-school all their lives, and were entirely lacking in all unwarrantable and facetious instincts.

They went to bed supperless that evening, but had their revenge, for their yelps and whines kept the whole family awake most of the night.

By the time the bears had been put to bed, darkness was near at hand, so the supper dishes and gourds were washed and carried to the kitchen. Then the visitors said good night and left for home.

Day 89

1. Read the beginning of chapter 6.

2. What did the boys train the bear cubs to do? (Answers)

CHAPTER VI BORROWED FIRE

ONE day Tom Fox was told by his mother to kindle the fire, which had been allowed to grow so dim that only a smouldering bed of embers was left upon the hearth. Hanging from the crane was a large kettle, almost full of water. Now, in addition to his reputation for freckles, Tom was also believed to be the awkwardest boy in the Blue River settlement. Upon the day above referred to, he did all in his power to live up to his reputation, by upsetting the kettle of water upon the fire, thereby extinguishing the last spark of that necessary element in the Fox household.

Of course there was not a lucifer match on all Blue River, from its source to its mouth; and as Mr. Fox had taken the tinderbox with him on a hunting expedition, and would not return till night, Limpy received a sound thrashing, and was sent to the house loft, there to ponder for the rest of the day over his misdeeds.

Mrs. Fox then sent Liney over to Mrs. Brent's to borrow fire. Limpy would have been glad to go, had his mother seen fit to send him, but the task would have been a reward rather than a punishment. Liney was delighted to have an opportunity to visit the Brent cabin, so away she went, very willingly indeed. Before the day was finished she was doubly glad she had gone, and the help she was able to give to a friend in need made her devoutly thankful to the kind fate which, operating through Mrs. Fox, had sent her on her errand. The terrible adventure, which befell her, and the frightful but I am telling my story before I come to it.

When Balser was a boy, each season brought its separate work and recreation on the farm, as it does now. But especially was this true in the time of the early settlers.

The winter was the hunting season. The occupation of hunting, which was looked upon as sport and recreation combined, was also a business with the men who cleared the land and felled the forests of Indiana; for a wagon-load of good pelts, taken during the winter season when the fur is at its best, was no inconsiderable matter, and brought at market more money than the same wagon filled with wheat would have been worth. So the settler of Balser's time worked quite as hard in the winter with his rifle, as he did with his hoe and plough in the fields during the months of summer.
Spring, of course, was the time for breaking up and ploughing. Summer was the wheat harvest. Then, also, the various kinds of wild berries were gathered, and dried or preserved. In the summer casks of rich blackberry wine were made, to warm the cold hunter upon his return from the chase during the cold days to come, or to regale company upon long winter evenings before the blazing fire. Blackberries could be had by the bushel for the mere gathering, and the wine could be made so cheaply that almost every house was well stocked with the delicious beverage.

Then came the corn gathering, and bringing in the fodder. The latter was brought in by wagon-loads, and was stacked against the sides of the barn and of the cow shed. It answered a double purpose: it made the barn and sheds warm and cozy homes for the stock during the cold bleak winter, and furnished food for the cattle and the horses, so that by spring they had eaten part of their houses. The wheat straw was stacked in the barnyard.; and into this the sheep and calves burrowed little caves, wherein they would lie so snug and warm that it made no difference to them how much the wind blew, or the snow and rain fell, or how hard it froze outside; for the bad weather made their cozy shelter seem all the more comfortable by contrast.

The fall also had its duties, part task, and part play. The woods abounded in hickory nuts, walnuts, and hazelnuts, and a supply of all these had to be gathered, for they furnished no small part of the winter food. Preparation was always made for this work by the boys of Mr. Brent's family long before a hickory nut had thought of falling. Shortly after the wolf hunt which I described to you in the last chapter, Balser and Jim began to make ready for the nut campaign. Their first task was to build a small wagon, for the purpose of carrying home the nuts. They found a tree twelve or fourteen inches in diameter, which they felled. They then sawed off four round sections of the tree, each about one inch thick, to serve as wheels. From the outer edge of these wheels they removed the bark, and bound them with tires made from the iron hoops of a barrel. They then cut round holes in the centre in which to insert the axles of the wagon. With their hatchets they split clapboards, which they made smooth, and of the clapboards they made the bottom, sides, and ends.

The boys worked pretty hard for ten or twelve days, and completed as perfect a two-horse wagon, in miniature, as any one ever beheld. There were the tongue, the axletree, the sideboard, the headboard, and the tail-gate and floor, all fitted so tightly together that you would have declared a wagon maker had made them. The wheels, bound with barrel-hoop tires, were marvels of their kind. The wagon bed would hold as much as could be contained in two large flour sacks, and when filled with nuts would prove quite a load to draw, consequently the boys must have a team of some sort. The team which they eventually rigged up was probably the most absurd and curious combination that ever drew a load.

The boys selected strong pieces of deer hide, and made four sets of harness. For what purpose, do you suppose? You never could guess. Two for the dogs, Tige and Prince, and two for the bear cubs, Tom and Jerry, who they proposed should do some thing to earn their bread and milk, for they were growing to be great awkward, big-footed, long-legged fellows, and were very strong. So the four sets of harness were finished, and one day the odd team was hitched up for trial. The little wagon was loaded with rocks, and the boys tried to start the team. The dogs seemed willing enough to obey, but the cubs, which were hitched in front, went every way but the right one, and showed a disposition to rebel against the indignity of work.

The bears were then taken from the lead, the dogs were put in their places, and the bears were put next to the wagon. The team was started again, but the cubs lay down flat upon the ground and refused to move. After trying in vain to induce the cubs to do their duty, Balser spoke to Jim, who was standing at the dogs' heads, and Jim started forward, leading the dogs, and Jim and the dogs dragged after them the cubs and the wagon. At almost every step the heavily loaded wagon would roll upon the hind feet of the cubs, and Balser threw thorns upon the ground, which pricked the bears as they were dragged along, until the black sluggards came to the conclusion that it was easier to work than to be dragged over thorns; so they arose to their feet, and followed the dogs, without, however, drawing an ounce of the load.

The boys kept patiently at this sort of training for three weeks; and at the end of that time, between bribes in the way of milk and honey, and beatings with a thick stick, the cubs little by little submitted to their task, and eventually proved to be real little oxen at drawing a load. The dogs, of course, had been broken in easily.

By the time the cubs were ready for work, the hickory nuts, walnuts, and hazelnuts were ready to be gathered ; and the boys only waited for a heavy black frost to loosen the nuts from their shells, and a strong wind to shake them from the branches.

During the summer of which I told you in the preceding chapters, Mr. Brent had raised the roof of his house, so as to make a room in the loft for the boys. This room was floored with rough boards, between which large cracks were left, so that heat from the room below might arise and warm the boys' room. The upper room was reached by the most primitive of stairways. It was nothing more than a small log, or thick pole, with notches cut on each side for footholds, or steps. In going up this stairway the boys climbed hand over hand, and foot over foot, as a bear climbs a tree; and to come down without falling was a task of no small proportions to one inexperienced in the art.

One morning Jim awakened, and looked out from under the warm bearskin which served for a blanket, comforter, and sheet. He listened for a moment to the wind, which was blowing a gale, and then awakened Balser.

"Balser! Balser!" said Jim. "Wake up! There's frost enough to freeze a brass monkey, and the wind is blowing hard enough to blow down the trees, to say nothing of the nuts. Let's get up and have an early start."

Balser was willing, and soon the boys had climbed out from under the warm bearskin, and were downstairs preparing to kindle the fires.
The fire-kindling was no hard task; for the backlog which had been put in the fire place the evening before was a great roll of red coals, and all that the boys had to do to kindle the fire was to "poke " the backlog, and it fell in chunks of half-charred, burning hickory, that hissed and popped and flamed, and made the room warm before you could say Jack Robinson." Then the boys threw on a large armful of cut wood, and soon the blaze was crackling cozily, and the kettle singing merrily on the flames.

The morning was cold, and the boys sat upon the great hearth, with their palms to the fire, getting "good and warm for the day," while the gray, frosty dawn was slowly frightening the shadows of night away from the forest, to which they seemed to cling.

Then came the mother, who made the breakfast of sweet fried venison, buckwheat-cakes floating in maple syrup and butter, hoe-cake, and eggs. Instead of coffee they drank warm milk, sweetened with maple sugar, and I can tell you it was a breakfast to wax fat on.

Day 90

1. Read the second part of chapter 6.
2. Tell someone what is happening.
3. What do you think is going to happen?

Chapter 6 continued

The sun was hardly above the horizon, when breakfast was finished, and the dogs and cubs were fed. Then they were harnessed to the wagon, and boys, bears, dogs, and wagon, all started on their way to the woods. Hickory trees did not grow plentifully in the bottom-lands, so the boys made for the hills, perhaps a mile away.

Shortly after they had reached the hills, Jim cried out: "Oh, here's a great big shellbark! I'll bet the ground's covered with nuts."

Sure enough, the ground was covered with them, and the boys filled their wagon in a very short time. Then they started home. The trip home was marred by an upset, owing to the perversity of the cubs; but the boys righted the wagon, loaded it with nuts again, and after considerable trouble deposited them safely at home, and went back for another load.

The dog-bear team worked admirably, barring a general tendency to run over logs and stones, and two great loads of hickory nuts were safely brought to the house before dinner.

After the boys, bears, and dogs had eaten a hurried meal, they again went forth in quest of nuts; but they took a different course this time, toward the south that is, in the direction of the house of Mr. Fox for the purpose of visiting a hazel thicket, which was a mile from home. Soon the hazel patch was reached, and about five o'clock the wagon was full of beautiful, brown little nuts, than which there is none sweeter.

When the wagon was loaded the boys hitched up the team, much to the delight of the latter, for by that time the dogs and cubs had come to think it great sport, and the caravan moved homeward.

Soon after leaving the hazel patch, the boys entered a dark strip of woods and undergrowth, through which it was very hard work to draw the wagon. So they attached a long piece of tanned deerskin to the tongue of the wagon, and gave the team a helping hand.

There was but one path through this dark strip of forest over which the wagon could be drawn, and it led through a low piece of ground that was wet and marshy. Upon the soft earth of the path Balser soon noticed the long, broad tracks of a bear, and the dogs at once began to bark and plunge in their harness. The tracks appeared to Balser to be an hour old, so he quieted the dogs, but did not release them from the wagon as he should have done. The boys went forward, regardless of the warning bear tracks, and the dogs and bears, drawing the wagon, followed closely at their heels. As they proceeded the bear tracks became fresher, and Balser began to grow somewhat fearful. Jim had become frightened, and had taken a position at the rear of the wagon to give a helping hand by pushing at the load. He said he could push better than he could pull anyway.

After the little party had got well into the darkest part of the forest, the dogs began to show such evident signs of uneasiness that Balser grasped his gun, and held it in readiness, prepared for a fight, should one become necessary.

The ground had been frozen earlier in the day, but it had thawed, and the path was slippery. Balser, who was walking a short distance ahead of the train, as a sort of advance guard, suddenly stopped and held up his hand warningly to Jim; for right ahead of him in the path stood a huge bear, with its head turned backward, looking inquiringly in the direction of the boys. Jim at once stopped the team. The dogs, of course, were dancing with impatience to be released from the harness, and even the dull-witted bears seemed to realize that something was wrong.

"It's running away," said Balser. "It's not safe to shoot at it from behind. I might wound it, and then we should be the ones to run. What shall we do?"

"Let it run," answered Jim, quickly. "I don't like to run with a bear after me, any way. If you're going to shoot, I'll run now so as to get a good start."

"No, you don't! You stand right where you are, and take care of the team. If you move a foot, I'll lick you," answered Balser, as he moved cautiously ahead in the direction of the retreating bear.

Jim was frozen by fear to the spot upon which he stood, as Balser walked out of sight. In a moment he again heard Balser speak, and then he heard a loud, deep growl.

The dogs barked and plunged; the cubs whined and gave forth savage little baby bear growls, half whines, for they were only learning to growl. Jim began to weep and to scream. Balser, who had disappeared from sight around a curve in the path, cried out:

"Let the dogs loose, for goodness' sake, Jim! It's after me."

The dogs seemed to understand Balser's cry better than Jim did ; for they barked and plunged more violently than ever in their harness. Jim seemed dazed, and could not, or at least did not, unharness the dogs. Then it was that the good dog sense of old Prince showed itself. Instead of waiting for help from Jim, who he saw had lost his wits, the good dog began to gnaw at the leather harness which held him and Tige to the wagon, and in a short time the dogs were freed from the wagon, though still tied to each other.

Tige caught inspiration from Prince, and the dogs backed away from each other and pulled with all their strength, until the harness slipped over the head of Prince and left the dogs free. Then Prince plunged rapidly into the thicket to the rescue of his master, followed closely by Tige, dragging the broken harness.

"Help! help!" cried Balser. "Why don't you send the dogs?" And his voice seemed to be going farther and farther away.

"Where are you?" cried Jim, in despair. His terror was so strong upon him that he could not move, and could not have helped Balser, had he been able to go to him. Jim was a little fellow, you must remember.

"Help! help!" cried Balser again, his voice sounding from a still greater distance. "I've wounded it, and it's about to kill me. Help! help!" but the cries came fainter and fainter.

Jim stood his ground and screamed manfully. Soon after Balser had left Jim and the wagon, the bear turned toward its pursuer and presented to Balser its broadside. This gave the boy a good chance for a shot. For the moment, Balser forgot his father's admonition to be deliberate and to act slowly, and his forgetfulness almost cost him his life. Balser shot, and wounded the bear in the neck, but did not kill it. Then it turned, and Balser, fearing to run back upon the path lest he should bring the bear upon Jim, started into the thicket, toward the river, with the bear in hot pursuit. Balser gained rapidly upon the bear at first, but he knew that his advantage could not last, for the bear was sure to catch him soon. What should he do? He hastily went over in his mind the possibilities in the case, and soon determined to put forth his utmost speed to gain as much upon the bear as possible, and then to climb the first tree, of the proper size, to which he should come. With this intent he flung his carbine over his back, by a strap attached to the gun for that purpose, and ran for dear life.

Soon the boy reached a small beech tree, the branches of which were ten or twelve feet from the ground. Up this tree he climbed with the agility of a squirrel. He afterward said: "I was so badly scared that it seemed as if my hands and feet had claws like a wild cat."

The bear had followed so closely upon his track, that, just as the boy was about to draw himself up among the branches of the tree, the bear rose upon its hind legs and caught the boy's toes between his teeth. Balser screamed with pain, and tried to draw his foot away; but the harder he pulled the harder pulled the bear, and the pain was so great that he thought he could not stand it. While he clung to the limb with one hand, he reached toward the bear with the other, and caught it by the nose. He twisted the bear's nose until the brute let loose of his foot. Then he quickly drew himself into the tree, and seated himself none too soon astride of a limb.

When Balser had fixed himself firmly on the limb he proceeded at once to load his gun. This was no slight matter under the circumstances; for, aside from the fact that his position in the tree was an uneasy one, the branches were in his way when he began to use his ramrod. Balser had hardly poured the powder into his gun, when the bear again rose on its hind legs, and put its front paws upon the body of the tree, with evident intent to climb after the boy who had wounded it and had so insultingly twisted its nose.

Bears like to scratch the bark of trees, and seem to take the same pride in placing their marks high upon the tree trunks that a young man does in making a long jump or a good shot. Vanity, in this case, proved to be the bear's undoing, as it has often been with men and boys. When it was reaching upward to make a high scratch, that it thought would be the envy of every bear that would see it, it should have been climbing; for while it was scratching Balser was loading, Not hurriedly, as he had shot, but slowly and deliberately, counting one, two, three with every movement; for when he had shot so hurriedly a few minutes before and had only wounded the bear, he had again learned the great lesson to make haste slowly.

The lesson was to be impressed upon Balser's mind more firmly than ever before he was through with the wounded bear; for to the day of his death he never forgot the events which befell him after he came down from the tree. Although Balser was deliberate, he had no time to waste, for soon the bear began climbing the tree, aided by a few small branches upon the lower part of the trunk, which had given help to Balser. Up the bear went, slowly and surely. Its great red tongue hang out at one side of its mouth, and its black, woolly coat was red and gory with blood from the wound that Balser had inflicted upon its huge neck. Its sharp little eyes were fixed upon Balser, and seemed to blaze with fury and rage, and its long bright teeth gleamed as its lips were drawn back in anger when it growled. Still the bear climbed, and still Balser was loading his gun. Would he have it loaded before the bear reached him?

Now the powder was all in a double charge. Now the first patch was in, and Balser was trying to ram it home. The branches of the trees were in his way, and the ramrod would not go into the gun. Inanimate things are often stubborn just when docility is most needed. Ah! At last the ramrod is in, and the first patch goes home, hard and fast upon the powder. On comes the bear, paw over paw, foot over foot, taking its time…

Day 91

1. To cast a bullet means to make a bullet. Lead is melted down and poured into a mold where it cools and hardens into a bullet. (The book spells molds, moulds. The author spells a lot of things with a "u" in it that we don't use in America anymore.)
2. Finish reading chapter 6.
3. Who saved the day in this chapter? How? (Answers)

Chapter 6 continued

On comes the bear, paw over paw, foot over foot, taking its time with painful deliberation, and, bearlike, carefully choosing its way; for it thinks full sure the boy cannot escape. Hurriedly Balser reaches into his pouch for a bullet. He finds one and puts it to the muzzle of his gun. Ah! worse luck! The bullet will not go in. It is too large. Balser feels with his finger a little ridge extending around the bullet, left there because he had not held the bullet moulds tightly together when he had cast the bullet. The boy impatiently throws the worthless bullet at the bear and puts his hand into the pouch for another. This time the bullet goes in, and the ramrod drives it home. Still there is the last patch to drive down, the one which holds the bullet, and still the bear climbs toward its intended victim. Its growls seem to shake the tree and its eyes look like burning embers.

The patches and the bullets Balser kept in the same pouch, so, when the bullet has been driven home, the boy's hand again goes into the pouch for the last patch. He can find nothing but bullets. Down goes his hand to each corner of the pouch in search of a patch; but alas! the patch, like a false friend, is wanting when most needed. On comes the bear. Not a moment is to be lost. A patch must be found; so the boy snatches off his cap of squirrel skin, and with his teeth bites out a piece of the skin which will answer his purpose. Then he dashes the mutilated cap in the bear's face, only a foot or two below him. Quickly is the squirrel-skin patch driven home, but none too quickly, for the bear is at Balser's feet, reaching for him with his great, rough, horny paw, as a cat reaches for a mouse. Balser quickly lifts himself to the limb above him, and hurriedly turning the muzzle of his gun right into the great red mouth, pulls the trigger.

Bang! And the bear falls to the ground, where it lies apparently dead. It was only apparently dead, though, as you will presently see. Balser breathed a sigh of relief as the bear fell backward, for he was sure that he had killed it. No bear, thought he, could survive a bullet driven by the heavy charge of powder behind the one which had sped so truly into the bear's mouth.

Again Balser failed to make haste slowly. He should have remained in his secure position until he was sure that the bear was really dead; for a badly wounded bear, although at the point of death, is more dangerous than one without a scar. With out looking at the bear Balser called Jim to come to him, and began climbing down the tree, with his carbine slung over his shoulder, and his back to the bear. All this happened in a very short space of time. In fact, the time during which Balser was load ing his gun, and while the bear was climbing the tree, was the same time in which the dogs were freeing themselves from the wagon; and Balser's second shot was heard by Jim just as the dogs went bounding off to Balser's relief. When the boy jumped to the ground, lo! the bear was alive again, and was on its feet, more ferocious than ever, and more eager for fight. Like our American soldiers, the bear did not know when it was whipped.

At the time the dogs bounded away from Jim, there came down the path toward him a young girl. Who do you think it was? Liney Fox. She was carrying in her hand a lighted torch, and was swinging it gently from side to side that she might keep it ablaze. This was the fire which Liney had been sent to borrow. She had heard Balser's cry and had heard both the shots that Balser had fired. She ran quickly to Jim, and with some difficulty drew from him an explanation of the situation. Then, as the dogs bounded away, she followed them, feeling sure that their instinct would lead them to Balser. The girl's strength seemed to be increased a thousand fold, and she ran after the dogs in the hope that she might help the boy who had saved her life upon the night when she was lost in the forest. How could she help him? She did not know; but she would at least go to him and do her best.

Just as Balser reached the ground, the bear raised itself upon its hind feet and struck at the boy, but missed him. Then Balser ran to the side of the tree opposite the bear, and bear and boy for a few moments played at a desperate game of hide-and-seek around the tree. It seemed a very long time to Balser. He soon learned that the bear could easily beat him at the game, and in desperation he started to run toward the river, perhaps two hundred yards away. He cried for help as he ran, and at that moment the dogs came up, and Liney followed in frantic, eager haste after them. Balser had thrown away his gun, and was leading the bear in the race perhaps six or eight feet. Close upon the heels of the bear were the dogs, and closer than you would think upon the heels of the dogs came Liney. Her bonnet had fallen back and her hair was flying behind her, and the torch was all ablaze by reason of its rapid movement through the air.

At the point upon the river's bank toward which Balser ran was a little stone cliff, almost perpendicular, the top of which was eight or ten feet from the water. Balser had made up his mind that if he could reach this cliff he would jump into the river, and perhaps save himself in that manner. Just as the boy reached the edge of the cliff Liney unfortunately called out "Balser!"

Her voice stopped him for a moment, and he looked back toward her. In that moment the bear overtook him and felled him to the ground with a stroke of its paw. Balser felt benumbed and was almost senseless. Instantly the bear was standing over him, and the boy was blinded by the stream of blood which flowed into his eyes and over his face from the wound in the bear's great mouth. He felt the bear shake him, as a cat shakes a mouse, and then for a moment the sun seemed to go out, and all was dark. He could see nothing. He heard the dogs bark, as they clung to the bear's ears and neck close to his face, and he heard Liney scream; but it all seemed like a far-away dream. Then he felt some thing burn his face, and sparks and hot ashes fell upon his skin and blistered him.

He could not see what was happening, but the pain of the burns seemed to revive him, and he was conscious that he was relieved from the terrible weight of the bear upon his breast. This is what happened: after Balser had fallen, the dogs had held the bear's attention for a brief moment or two, and had given Liney time to reach the scene of conflict. The bear had caught Balser's leather coat between its jaws, and was shaking him just as Liney came up. It is said that the shake which a cat gives a mouse produces unconsciousness; and so it is true that the shake which the larger animals give to their prey before killing it has a benumbing effect, such as Balser felt. When Liney reached Balser and the bear, she had no weapon but her torch, but with true feminine intuition she did, without stopping to think, the only thing she could do, and for that matter the best thing that anyone could have done. She thrust the burn ing torch into the bear's face and held it there, despite its rage and growls.

Then it was that Balser felt the heat and sparks, and then it was that the bear, blinded by the fire, left Balser. The bear was frantic with pain, and began to rub its eyes and face with its paws, just as a man would do under the same circumstances. It staggered about in rage and blindness, making the forest echo with its frightful growls, until it was upon the edge of the little precipice of which I have spoken. Then Liney struck it again with her burning torch, and gave it a push, which, although her strength was slight, sent the bear rolling over the cliff into the river. After that she ran back to Balser, who was still lying upon the ground, covered with blood. She thought he was terribly wounded, so she tore off her muslin petticoat, and wiped the blood from Balser's face and hands. Her joy was great when she learned that it was the bear's blood and not Balser's that she saw. The boy soon rose to his feet, dazed and half blinded.

"Where's the bear?" he asked.

"We pushed him into the river," said Jim, who had come in at the last moment.

"Yes, 'we pushed him in,'" said Balser, in derision. "Liney, did you?"

"Yes," answered Liney. "I don't know how I did it; but after I had put my torch in the bear's face, when he was over you, I pushed him into the river." And she cast down her sweet, modest eyes, as if ashamed of what she had done.

"Liney, Liney" began Balser; but his voice was choked by a great lump of sobs in his throat. "Liney, Liney" he began again; but his gratitude was so great he could not speak. He tried again, and the tears came in a flood.

"Cry-baby!" said Jim.

"Jim, you're a little fool," said Liney, turning upon the youngster with a blaze of anger in her eyes.

"Jim's right," sobbed Balser. "I am a c-c-cry-baby."
"No, no! Balser," said Liney, soothingly, as she took his hand. "I know. I understand without you telling me."

"Yes," sobbed Balser, "I c-c-cry because I thank you so much."

"Don't say that, Balser," answered Liney. "Think of the night in the forest, and think of what you did for me."

"Oh! But I'm a boy."

Balser was badly bruised, but was not wounded, except in the foot where the bear had caught him as he climbed the tree. That wound, however, was slight, and would heal quickly. The cubs had broken away from the loaded wagon, and Jim, Liney, Balser, dogs, and cubs all marched back to Mr. Brent's in a slow and silent procession, leaving the load of nuts upon the path, and the bear dead upon a ripple in the river.

Day 92

1. Read the beginning of chapter 7.
2. A boy, whose nickname was Polly, called for help. What was Polly running away from? (Answers)
3. People have come up with lots of stories about the fire bear and had superstitions about him. They were just stories though.
4. Polly's nickname comes from "Polly want a cracker?" It's a famous phrase about a parrot named Polly. The boy's surname, meaning his last name, is Parrot and that's how they started calling him Polly.

CHAPTER VII THE FIRE BEAR

ONE evening in December, a few weeks after Liney had saved Balser's life by means of the borrowed fire, Balser's father and mother and Mr. and Mrs. Fox, went to Marion, a town of two houses and a church, three miles away, to attend "Protracted Meeting." Liney and Tom and the Fox baby remained with Balser and Jim and the Brent baby, at the Brent cabin.

When the children were alone Liney proceeded to put the babies to sleep, and when those small heads of their respective house holds were dead to the world in slumber, rocked to that happy condition in a cradle made from the half of a round, smooth log, hollowed out with an adze, the other children huddled together in the fireplace to talk and to play games. Chief among the games was that never failing source of delight, "Simon says thumbs up."

Outside the house the wind, blowing through the trees of the forest, rose and sank in piteous wails and moans, by turns, and the snow fell in angry, fitful blasts, and whirled and turned, eddied and drifted, as if it were a thing of life. The weather was bitter cold; but the fire on the great hearth in front of the children seemed to feel that while the grown folks were away it was its duty to be careful of the children, and to be gentle, tender, and comforting to them; so it spluttered, popped, and cracked like the sociable, amiable, and tender-hearted fire that it was. It invited the children to go near it and to take its warmth, and told, as plainly as a fire could, and a fire can talk, not English perhaps, but a very understandable language of its own, that it would not burn them for worlds. So, as I said, the children sat inside the huge fireplace, and cared little whether or not the cold north wind blew.

After "Simon" had grown tiresome, Liney told riddles, all of which Tom, who had heard them before, spoiled by giving the answer before the others had a chance to guess. Then Limpy propounded a few riddles, but Liney, who had often heard them, would not disappoint her brother by telling the answers. Balser noticed this, and said, "Limpy, you ought to take a few lessons in good manners from your sister."

"Why ought I?" asked Tom, somewhat indignantly.

"Because she doesn't tell your riddles as you told hers," answered Balser.

"He wants to show off," said Jim.

"No, he doesn't," said Liney. But she cast a grateful glance at Balser, which said, "Thank you" as plainly as if she had spoken the words. Tom hung his head, and said he didn't like riddles anyway.

"Let's crack some nuts," proposed Jim, who was always hungry.

This proposition seemed agreeable to all, so Balser brought in a large gourd filled with nuts, and soon they were all busy cracking and picking.

Then Liney told stories from "The Pilgrim's Progress" and the Bible. She was at the most thrilling part of the story of Daniel in the lions' den, and her listeners were eager, nervous, and somewhat fearful, when the faint cry of "Help!" seemed to come right down through the mouth of the chimney.

"Listen!" whispered Balser, holding up his hands for silence. In a moment came again the cry, "Help!" The second cry was still faint, but louder than the first; and the children sprang together with a common impulse, and clung to Balser in unspoken fear.
"Help! help!" came the cry, still nearer and louder.

"Some one wants help," whispered Balser. "I must go to him." The latter clause was spoken rather hesitatingly.

"No, no!" cried Liney. "You must not go. It may be Indians trying to get you out there to kill you, or it may be a ghost. You'll surely be killed if you go."

Liney's remark somewhat frightened Balser, and completely frightened the other children; but it made Balser feel all the more that he must not be a coward before her. However much he feared to go in response to the cry for help, he must not let Liney see that he was afraid. Besides, the boy knew that it was his duty to go; and although with Balser the sense of duty moved more slowly than the sense of fear, yet it moved more surely. So he quickly grasped his gun, and carefully examined the load and priming. Then he took a torch, lighted it at the fire, and out he rushed into the blinding, freezing storm.

"Who's there?" cried Balser, holding his torch on high.

"Help! help!" came the cry from a short distance down the river, evidently in the forest back of the barn. Balser hurried in the direction whence the cry had come, and when he had proceeded one hundred yards or so, he met a man running toward him, almost out of breath from fright and exhaustion. Balser's torch had been extinguished by the wind, snow, and sleet, and he could not see the man's face.

"Who are you, and what's the matter with you?" asked brave little Balser, mean while keeping his gun ready to shoot, if need be.

"Don't you know me, Balser?" gasped the other.

"Is it you, Polly?" asked Balser. "What on earth's the matter?"

"The Fire Bear! The Fire Bear!" cried Poll." He's been chasin' me fur Lord knows how long. There he goes! There! Don't you see him? He's movin' down to the river. He's crossin' the river on the ice now. There! There!" And he pointed in the direction he wished Balser to look. Sure enough, crossing on the ice below the barn, was the sharply defined form of a large bear, glowing in the darkness of the night as if it were on fire.

This was more than even Balser's courage could withstand; so he started for the house as fast as his legs could carry him, and Polly came panting and screaming at his heels.

Polly's name, I may say, was Samuel Parrott. He was a harmless, simple fellow, a sort of hanger-on of the settlement, and his surname, which few persons remembered, had suggested the nickname of Poll, or Polly, by which he was known far and wide.
By the time Balser had reached the house he was ashamed of his precipitate retreat, and proposed that he and Polly should go out and further investigate the Fire Bear.

This proposition met with such a decided negative from Polly, and such a vehement chorus of protests from Liney and the other children, that Balser, with reluctance in his manner, but gladness in his heart, consented to remain indoors, and to let the Fire Bear take his way unmolested.

"When did you first see him?" asked Balser of Polly Parrot.

"'Bout a mile down the river, by Fox's Bluff," responded Polly. "I've been runnin' every step of the way, jist as hard as I could run, and that there Fire Bear not more'n ten feet behind me, growlin' like thunder, and blazin' and smokin' away like a bonfire."

"Nonsense," said Balser. "He wasn't blazing when I saw him."

"Of course he wasn't," responded Poll. "He'd about burned out. D'ye think a bear could blaze away forever like a volcano?" Poll's logical statement seemed to be convincing to the children.

"And he blazed up, did he?" asked Liney, her bright eyes large with wonder and fear.

"Blazed up!" ejaculated Polly. "Bless your soul, Liney, don't you see how hot I am? Would a man be sweatin' like I am on such a night as this, unless he's been powerful nigh to a mighty hot fire?"

Poll's corroborative evidence was too strong for doubt to contend against, and a depressing conviction fell upon the entire company, including Balser, that it was really the Fire Bear which Polly and Balser had seen. Although Balser, in common with most of the settlers, had laughed at the stories of the Fire Bear which had been told in the settlement, yet now he was convinced, because he had seen it with his own eyes. It was true that the bear was not ablaze when he saw him, but certainly he looked like a great glowing ember, and, with Polly's testimony, Balser was ready to believe all he had heard concerning this most frightful spectre of Blue River, the Fire Bear.

One of the stories concerning the Fire Bear was to the effect that when he was angry he blazed forth into a great flame, and that when he was not angry he was simply aglow. At times, when the forests were burned, or when barns or straw-stacks were destroyed by fire, many persons, especially of the ignorant class, attributed the incendiarism to the Fire Bear. Others, who pretended to more wisdom, charged the Indians with the crimes. Of the latter class had been Balser.

But to see is to believe.

Day 93

1. A shoat is a young pig.
2. A spoor is the scent or track of an animal, it's what you follow on a hunt.
3. The rest of chapter 7 is about Balser wanting a good luck charm. We know there is no such thing as luck. God is in control.
4. Read the first part of chapter 8.
5. Copy the sentence, "There is nothing like a counter-fear to keep a coward's courage up."
6. Who is the coward? What is he afraid of? Do you understand what is his fear and what is his counter-fear, or opposite fear? (Answers)
7. You'll read how Liney held an object and prayed over it for days that God would use it to protect Balser. Now she feels guilty that it wasn't the right thing to do. An object of course can't help him. God can help him and prayers can help him. But it did make Balser feel more confident to hold it because he trusted so much in Liney's prayers.
8. The author writes a note at the beginning of this chapter. He wants you to believe that this story really happened. Do you believe him?

CHAPTER VIII THE BLACK GULLY

NOTE. The author, fearing that the account of fire springing from the earth, given in the following story, may be considered by the reader too improbable for any book but one of Arabian fables, wishes to say that the fire and the explosion occurred in the place and manner described.

THE Fire Bear had never before been seen in the Blue River neighbourhood. His former appearances had been at or near the mouth of Conn's Creek, where that stream flows into Flatrock, five or six miles south east of Balser's home.

Flatrock River takes its name from the fact that it flows over layers of broad flat rocks. The soil in its vicinity is underlaid at a depth of a few feet by a formation of stratified limestone, which crops out on the hillsides and precipices, and in many places forms deep, canon-like crevasses, through which the river flows. In these cliffs and miniature canons are many caves, and branching off from the river's course are many small side-canons, or gullies, which at night are black and repellent, and in many instances are quite difficult to explore.

One of these side-canons was so dark and forbidding that it was called by the settlers "The Black Gully." The conformation of the rocks composing its precipitous sides was grotesque in the extreme; and the overhanging trees, thickly covered with vines, cast so deep a shadow upon the ravine that even at midday its dark recesses bore a cast of gloom like that of night untimely fallen. How Balser happened to visit the Black Gully, and the circumstances under which he saw it sufficiently terrible and awe-inspiring to cause the bravest man to tremble I shall soon tell you.

The country in the vicinity of Flatrock was full of hiding-places, and that was supposed to be the home of the Fire Bear.

The morning after Polly and Balser had seen the Fire Bear, they went forth bright and early to follow the tracks of their fiery enemy, and if possible to learn where he had gone after his unwelcome visit.

They took up the spoor at the point where the bear had crossed the river the night before, and easily followed his path three or four miles down the stream. There they found the place where he had crossed the river to the east bank. The tracks, which were plainly visible in the new-fallen snow, there turned southeast toward his reputed home among the caves and gullies of Flatrock and Conn's Creek.

The trackers hurried forward so eagerly in their pursuit that they felt no fatigue. They found several deer, and at one time they saw at a great distance a bear; but they did not pursue either, for their minds were too full of the hope that they might discover the haunts of the monster upon whose death depended, as they believed, their lives and that of Liney Fox. When Balser and Polly reached the stony ground of Flatrock the bear tracks began to grow indistinct, and soon they were lost entirely among the smooth rocks from which the snow had been blown away.

The boys had, however, accomplished their purpose, for they were convinced that they had discovered the haunts of the bear. They carefully noticed the surrounding country, and spoke to each other of the peculiar cliffs and trees in the neighbourhood, so that they might remember the place when they should return. Then they found a dry little cave wherein they kindled a fire and roasted a piece of venison which they had taken with them. When their roast was cooked, they ate their dinner of cold hoe-cake and venison, and then sat by the fire for an hour to warm and rest before beginning their long, hard journey home through the snow. Polly smoked his after-dinner pipe, the pipe was a hollow corn-cob with the tip of a buck's horn for a stem, and the two bear hunters talked over the events of the day and discussed the coming campaign against the Fire Bear.

"I s'pose we'll have to hunt him by night," said Polly. "He's never seen at any other time, they say."

"Yes, we'll have to hunt him by night," said Balser; "but darkness will help us in the hunt, for we can see him better at night than any other time, and he can't see us as well as he could in daylight."

"Balser, you surprise me," answered Polly. "Have you hunted bears all this time and don't know that a bear can see as well after night as in the daytime better, maybe?"

"Maybe that's so," responded Balser. "I know that cats and owls can see better by night, but I didn't know about bears. How do you know it's true?"
"How do I know? Why, didn't that there bear make a bee-line for this place last night, and wasn't last night as dark as the inside of a whale, and don't they go about at night more than in the daytime? Tell me that. When do they steal sheep and shoats? In daytime? Tell me that. Ain't it always at

night? Did you ever hear of a bear stealing a shoat in the daytime? No, sirree; but they can see the littlest shoat that ever grunted, on the darkest night, see him and snatch him out of the pen and get away with him quicker than you or I could, a durned sight."

"I never tried; did you, Polly?" asked Balser.

Polly wasn't above suspicion among those who knew him, and Balser's question slightly disconcerted him.

"Well, I durned if that ain't the worst fool question I ever heerd a boy ask," answered Polly. Then, somewhat anxious to change the conversation, he continued: "What night do you propose to come down here? Tomorrow night?"

"No, not for a week. Not till seven nights after to-night," answered Balser, mindful of the charm which he hoped Liney's prayers would make for him.

"Seven nights? Geminy! I'm afraid I'll get scared of this place by that time. I'll bet this is an awful place at night; nothing but great chunks of blackness in these here gullies, so thick you could cut it with a knife. I'm not afraid now because I'm desperate. I'm so afraid of dyin' because I saw the Fire Bear that I don't seem to be afraid of nothin' else."

Polly was right. There is nothing like a counter-fear to keep a coward's courage up.

After they were warm and had rested, Balser and Polly went out of the cave and took another survey of the surrounding country from the top of the hill. They started homeward, and reached the cozy cabin on Blue River soon after sunset, tired, hungry, and cold. A good warm supper soon revived them, and as it had been agreed that Polly should remain at Mr. Brent's until after the Fire Bear hunt, they went to bed in the loft and slept soundly till morning.

After Balser announced his determination to hunt the Fire Bear, many persons asked him when he intended to undertake the perilous task, but the invariable answer he gave was, that he would begin after the seventh night from the one upon which the Fire Bear had visited Blue River. "Why after the seventh night?" was frequently asked; but the boy would give no other answer.

Balser had invited Tom Fox to go with him; and Tom, in addition to his redoubt able hatchet, intended to carry his father's gun. Polly would take Mr. Brent's rifle, and of course Balser would carry the greatest of all armaments, his smooth-bore carbine. Great were the preparations made in selecting bullets and in drying powder. Knives and hatchets were sharpened until they were almost as keen as a razor. Many of the men and boys of the neighbour hood volunteered to accompany Balser, but he would take with him no one but Tom and Polly.
"Too many hunters spoil the chase," said Balser, borrowing his thought from the cooks and the broth maxim.

Upon the morning of the eighth day Balser went over to see Liney, and to receive from her the precious charm redolent with forty-nine prayers from her pure heart. When she gave it to him he said: "It's a charm; I know it is." And he held it in his hand and looked at it affectionately. "It looks like a charm, and it feels like a charm. Liney, I seem to feel your prayers upon it."

"Ah! Balser, don't say that. It sounds almost wicked. It has seemed wicked all the time for me to try to make a charm."

"Don't feel that way, Liney. You didn't try to make it. You only prayed to God to make it, and God is good and loves to hear you pray. If He don't love to hear you pray, Liney, He don't love to hear any one."

"No, no, Balser, I'm so wicked. The night we saw the Fire Bear father read in the Bible where it says, 'The prayers of the wicked availeth not.' Oh, Balser, do you think it's wicked to try to make a charm that is, to pray to God to make one?"

"No, indeed, Liney. God makes them of His own accord. He made you." But Liney only half understood.

Day 94

1. Read the next part of chapter 8.
2. What's worse than missing a bear when you shoot at him? (Answers)
3. What does the bear have stuck in his teeth? (Answers)

Chapter 8 continued

The charm worked at least one spell. It made the boy braver and gave him self-confidence.

Balser, Tom, and Polly had determined to ride down to Flatrock on horseback, and for that purpose one of Mr. Fox's horses and two of Mr. Brent's were brought into service. At three o'clock upon the famous eighth day the three hunters started for Flatrock, and spent the night in the vicinity of the mouth of Conn's Creek; but they did not see the Fire Bear. Four other expeditions were made, for Balser had no notion of giving up the hunt, and each expedition was a failure. But the fifth well, I will tell you about it.

Upon the fifth expedition the boys reached Flatrock River just after sunset. A cold drizzling rain had begun to fall, and as it fell it froze upon the surface of the rocks. The wind blew and moaned through the tree-tops, and the darkness was so dense it seemed heavy. The boys had tied their horses in a cave, which they had used for the same purpose upon former visits, and were discussing the advisability of giving up the hunt for that night and returning home. Tom had suggested that the rain might extinguish the Fire Bear's fire so he could not be seen. The theory seemed plausible. Polly thought that a bear with any sense at all would remain at home in his cave upon such a night as that, and all these arguments, together with the slippery condition of the earth, which made walking among the rocks and cliffs very dangerous, induced Balser to conclude that it was best to return to Blue River without pursuing the hunt that night. He announced his decision, and had given up all hope of seeing the Fire Bear upon that expedition. But they were not to be disappointed after all, for, just as the boys were untying their horses to return home, a terrific growl greeted their ears, coming, it seemed, right from the mouth of the cave in which they stood.

"That's him," cried Polly. "I know his voice. I heerd it for one mortal hour that night when he was a chasin' me, and I'll never furgit it. I'd know it among a thousand bears. It's him. Oh, Balser, let's go home! For the Lord's sake, Balser, let's go home! I'd rather die three months from now than now. Three months is a long time to live, after all."

"Polly, what on earth are you talking about? Are you crazy? Tie up your horse at once," said Balser. "If the bear gets away from us this time, we'll never have another chance at him. Quick! Quick!"

Polly's courage was soon restored, and the horses were quickly tied again.

Upon entering the cave a torch had been lighted, and by the light of the torch, which Polly held, the primings of the guns were examined, knives and hatchets were made ready for immediate use, and out the hunters sallied in pursuit of the Fire Bear.

On account of the ice upon the rocks it was determined that Polly should carry the torch with him. Aside from the dangers of the slippery path, there was another reason for carrying the torch. Fire attracts the attention of wild animals, and often prevents them from running away from the hunter. This is especially true of deer. So Polly carried the torch, and a fatal burden it proved to be for him. After the hunters had emerged from the cave, they at once started toward the river, and upon passing a little spur of the hill they beheld at a distance of two or three hundred yards the Fire Bear, glowing like a fiery heap against the black bank of night. He was running rapidly up the stream toward Black Gully, which came down to the river's edge between high cliffs. This was the place I described to you a few pages back. Balser and Polly had seen Black Gully before, and had noticed how dark, deep, and forbidding it was. It had seemed to them to be a fitting place for the revels of witches, demons, snakes, and monsters of all sorts, and they thought surely it was haunted, if any place ever was. They feared the spot even in the daytime.

Polly, who was ingenious with a pocket knife, had carved out three whistles, and in the bowl of each was a pea. These whistles produced a shrill noise when blown upon, which could be heard at a great distance, and each hunter carried one fastened to a string about his neck. In case the boys should be separated, one long whistle was to be sounded for the purpose of bringing them together; three whistles should mean that the bear had been seen, and one short one was to be the cry for help. When Balser saw the bear he blew a shrill blast upon his whistle to attract the brute's attention. The ruse produced the desired effect, for the bear stopped. His curiosity evidently was aroused by the noise and by the sight of the fire, and he remained standing for a moment or two while the boys ran forward as rapidly as the slippery rocks would permit. Soon they were within a hundred yards of the bear; then fifty, forty, thirty, twenty. Still the Fire Bear did not move. His glowing form stood before them like a pillar of fire, the only object that could be seen in the darkness that surrounded him. He seemed to be the incarnation of all that was brave and demoniac. When within twenty yards of the bear Balser said hurriedly to his companions: "Halt! I'll shoot first, and you fellows hold your fire and shoot one at a time, after me. Don't shoot till I tell you, and take good aim. Polly, I'll hold your torch when I want you to shoot." Polly held the torch in one hand and his gun in the other, and fear was working great havoc with his usefulness. Balser continued: "It's so dark we can't see the sights of our guns, and if we're not careful we may all miss the bear, or still worse, we may only wound him. Hold up the torch, Polly, so I can see the sights of my gun."

Balser's voice seemed to attract the bear's attention more even than did the torch, and he pricked up his short fiery ears as if to ask, "What are you talking about?" When Balser spoke next it was with a tongue of fire, and the words came from his gun. The bear seemed to understand the gun's language better than that of Balser, for he gave forth in answer a terrific growl of rage, and bit savagely at the wound which Balser had inflicted. Alas! It was only a wound; for Balser's bullet, instead of piercing the bear's heart, had hit him upon the hind quarters.

"I've only wounded him," cried Balser, and the note of terror in his voice seemed to create a panic in the breasts of Tom and Polly, who at once raised their guns and fired. Of course they both missed the bear, and before they could lower their guns the monster was upon them.

Balser was in front, and received the full force of the brute's ferocious charge. The 'boy went down under the bear's mighty rush, and before he had time to draw his knife, or to disengage his hatchet from his belt, the infuriated animal was standing over him. As Balser fell his hand caught a rough piece of soft wood which was lying upon the ground, and with this he tried to beat the bear upon the head. The bear, of course, hardly felt the blows which Balser dealt with the piece of wood, and it seemed that another terrible proof was about to be given of the fatal consequences of looking upon the Fire Bear. Tom and Polly had both run when the bear charged, but Tom quickly came to Balser's relief, while Polly remained at a safe distance. The bear was reaching for Balser's throat, but by some fortunate chance he caught between his jaws the piece of wood with which Balser had been vainly striking him; and doubtless thinking that the wood was a part of Balser, the bear bit it and shook it ferociously.

When Tom came up to the scene of conflict he struck the bear upon the head with the sharp edge of his hatchet, and chopped out one of his eyes. The pain of the wound seemed to double the bear's fury, and he sprang over Balser's prostrate form toward Tom. The bear rose upon his haunches and faced Tom, who manfully struck at him with his hatchet, and never thought of running.

Ah! Tom was a brave one when the necessity for bravery arose. But Tom's courage was better than his judgment, for in a moment he was felled to the ground by a stroke from the bear's paw, and the bear was standing over him, growling and bleeding terribly. Polly had come nearer and his torch threw a ghastly glamour over the terrible scene. As in the fight with Balser, the bear tried to catch Tom's throat between his jaws; but here the soft piece of wood which Balser had grasped when he fell proved a friend indeed, for the bear had bitten it so savagely that his teeth had been embedded in its soft fibre, and it acted as a gag in his mouth. He could neither open nor close his jaws. After a few frantic efforts to bite Tom, the bear seemed to discover where the trouble was, and tried to push the wood out of his mouth with his paws. This gave Tom a longed-for opportunity, of which he was not slow to take advantage, and he quickly drew himself from under the bear, rose to his feet, and ran away.

In the meantime Balser rose from the ground and reached the bear just as Tom started to run. Balser knew by that time that he had no chance of success in a hand-to-hand conflict with the brute. So he struck the bear a blow upon the head with his hatchet as he passed, and followed Tom at a very rapid speed. Balser at once determined that he and Tom and Polly should reach a place of safety, quickly load their guns, and return to the attack. In a moment he looked back, and saw the bear still struggling to free his mouth from the piece of wood which had saved two lives that night.

As the bear was not pursuing them, Balser concluded to halt; and he and Tom loaded their guns, while Polly held the torch on high to furnish light. Polly's feeble wits had almost fled, and he seemed unconscious of what was going on about him. He did mechanically whatever Balser told him to do, but his eyes had a far away look, and it was evident that the events of the night had paralyzed his poor, weak brain. When the guns were loaded Balser and Tom hurried forward toward the bear, and poor Polly followed, bearing his torch.

Bang! went Balser's gun, and the bear rose upon his hind feet, making the cliffs and ravines echo with his terrible growls.

"Take good aim, Tom; hold up the torch, Polly," said Balser. "Fire!" and the bear fell over on his back and seemed to be dead. Polly and Tom started toward the bear, but Balser cried out: "Stop! He may not be dead yet. We'll give him another volley. We've got him now, sure, if we're careful."

Tom and Polly stopped, and it was fortunate for them that they did so; for in an instant the bear was on his feet, apparently none the worse for the ill-usage the boys had given him. The Fire Bear stood for a little time undetermined whether to attack the boys again or to run. After halting for a moment between two opinions, he concluded to retreat, and with the piece of wood still in his mouth, he started at a rapid gait toward Black Gully, a hundred yards away.
"Load, Tom; load quick. Hold the torch, Polly," cried Balser. And again the guns were loaded, while poor demented Polly held the torch.

The bear moved away rapidly, and in a moment the boys were following him with loaded guns. When the brute reached the mouth of Black Gully he entered it. Evidently his home was in that uncanny place.

"Quick, quick, Polly!" cried Balser; and within a moment after the bear had entered Black Gully his pursuers were at the mouth of the ravine, making ready for another attack. Balser gave a shrill blast upon his whistle, and the bear turned for a moment, and deliberately sat down upon his haunches not fifty yards away. The place looked so black and dismal that the boys at first feared to enter, but soon their courage came to their rescue, and they marched in, with Polly in the lead. The bear moved farther up the gully toward an overhanging cliff, whose dark, rugged outlines were faintly illumined by the light of Polly's torch. The jutting rocks seemed like monster faces, and the bare roots of the trees were like the horny ringers and the bony arms of fiends.

The boys followed the bear, and when he came to a halt near the cliff and again sat upon his haunches, it was evident that the Fire Bear's end was near at hand. How frightful it all appeared! There sat the Fire Bear, like a burning demon, sullen and motionless, giving forth, every few seconds, deep guttural growls that reverberated through the dark cavernous place. Not a star was seen, nor a gleam of light did the overcast sky afford. There stood poor, piteous Polly, all his senses fled and gone, unconsciously holding his torch above his head. The light of the torch seemed to give life to the shadows of the place, and a sense of fear stole over Balser that he could not resist.

Day 95

1. Boreas is what the author is calling the wind. Boreas is the name of the ancient Greek's god of the North wind.
2. Read the first part of chapter 9.
3. Who was Balser and his mother waiting for? (Answers)
4. What had happened to him? How did Balser know? (Answers)

CHAPTER IX ON THE STROKE OF NINE

LATE one afternoon it was the day before Christmas Balser and Jim were seated upon the extra backlog in the fire place, ciphering. Mrs. Brent was sitting in front of the fire in a rude home-made rocking-chair, busily knitting, while she rocked the baby's cradle with her foot and softly sang the refrain of "Annie Laurie" for a lullaby. Snow had begun to fall at noon, and as the sun sank westward the north wind came in fitful gusts at first, and then in stronger blasts, till near the hour of four, when Boreas burst forth in the biting breath of the storm. How he howled and screamed down the chimney at his enemy, the fire! And how the fire crackled and spluttered and laughed in the face of his wrath, and burned all the brighter because of his raging! Don't tell me that a fire can't talk ! A fire upon a happy hearth is the sweetest conversationalist on earth, and Boreas might blow his lungs out ere he could stop the words of cheer and health and love and happiness which the fire spoke to Jim and Balser and their mother in the gloaming of that cold and stormy day.

"Put on more wood," said the mother, in a whisper, wishing not to awaken the baby. "Your father will soon be home from Brookville, and we must make the house good and warm for him. I hope he will come early. It would be dreadful for him to be caught far away from home in such a storm as we shall have tonight."

Mr. Brent had gone to Brookville several days before with wheat and pelts for market, and was expected home that evening. Balser had wanted to go with his father, but the manly little fellow had given up his wish and had remained at home that he might take care of his mother, Jim, and the baby.

Balser quietly placed a few large hickory sticks upon the fire, and then whispered to Jim: "Let's go out and feed the stock and fix them for the night."

So the boys went to the barnyard and fed the horses and cows, and drove the sheep into the shed, and carried fodder from the huge stack and placed it against the north sides of the barn and shed to keep the wind from blowing through the cracks and to exclude the snow. When the stock was comfortable, cozy, and warm, the boys milked the cows, and brought to the house four bucketfuls of steaming milk, which they strained and left in the kitchen, rather than in the milk-house, that it might not freeze over night.

Darkness came on rapidly, and Mrs. Brent grew more and more anxious for her husband's return. Fearing that he might be late, she postponed supper until Jim's ever ready appetite began to cry aloud for satisfaction, and Balser intimated that he, too, might be induced to eat. So their mother leisurely went to work to get supper, while the baby was left sleeping before the cheery, talkative fire in the front room.

A fat wild turkey roasted to a delicious brown upon the spit, eggs fried in the sweetest of lard, milk warm from the cows, corn-cakes floating in maple syrup and yellow butter, sweet potatoes roasted in hot ashes, and a great slice of mince pie furnished a supper that makes one hungry but to think about it. The boys, however, were hungry without thinking, and it would have done your heart good to see that supper disappear.

As they sat at supper they would pause in their eating and listen attentively to every noise made by the creaking of the trees or the falling of a broken twig, hoping that it was the step of the father. But the supper was finished all too soon, and the storm continued to increase in its fury; the snow fell thicker and the cold grew fiercer, still Mr. Brent did not come.
Mrs. Brent said nothing, but as the hours flew by her anxious heart imparted its trouble to Balser, and he began to fear for his father's safety. The little clock upon the rude shelf above the fireplace hoarsely and slowly drawled out the hour of seven, then eight, and then nine. That was very late for the Brent family to be out of bed, and nothing short of the anxiety they felt could have kept

them awake. Jim, of course, had long since fallen asleep, and he lay upon a soft bear skin in front of the fire, wholly unconscious of storms or troubles of any sort.

Mrs. Brent sat watching and waiting while Jim and the baby slept,, and to her anxious heart it seemed that the seconds lengthened into minutes, and the minutes into hours, by reason of her loneliness. While she rocked beside the baby's cradle, Balser was sitting in his favourite place upon the backlog next to the fire. He had been reading, or trying to read, "The Pilgrim's Progress," but visions of his father and of the team lost in the trackless forest, facing death by freezing, to say nothing of wolves that prowled the woods in packs of hundreds upon such a night as that, continually came between his eyes and the page, and blurred the words until they held no meaning. Gradually drowsiness stole over him, too, and just as the slow-going clock began deliberately to strike the hour of nine his head fell back into a little corner made by projecting logs in the wall of the fireplace, and, like Jim, he forgot his troubles as he slept.

Balser did not know how long he had been sleeping when the neighing of a horse was heard. Mrs. Brent hastened to the door, but when she opened it, instead of her husband she found one of the horses, an intelligent, raw-boned animal named Buck, standing near the house. Balser had heard her call, and he quickly ran out of doors and went to the horse. The harness was broken, and dragging upon the ground behind the horse were small portions of the wreck of the wagon. Poor Buck's flank was red with blood, and his legs showed all too plainly the marks of deadly conflict with a savage, hungry foe. The wreck of the wagon, the broken harness, and the wounds upon the horse told eloquently, as if spoken in words, the story of the night. Wolves had attacked Balser's father, and Buck had come home to give the alarm.

Balser ran quickly to the fire pile upon the hill and kindled it for the purpose of calling help from the neighbours. Then he went back to the house and took down his gun. He tied a bundle of torches over his shoulder, lighted one, and started out in the blinding, freezing storm to help his father, if possible.

He followed the tracks of the horse, which with the aid of his torch were easily discernible in the deep snow, and soon he was far into the forest, intent upon his mission of rescue.

After the boy had travelled for an hour he heard the howling of wolves, and hastened in the direction whence the sound came, feeling in his heart that he would find his father surrounded by a ferocious pack. He hurried forward as rapidly as he could run, and his worst fears were realized.

Soon he reached the top of a hill over looking a narrow ravine which lay to the eastward. The moon had risen and the snow had ceased to fall. The wind was blowing a fiercer gale than ever, and had broken rifts in the black bank of snowcloud, so that gleams of the moon now and then enabled Balser's vision to penetrate the darkness. Upon looking down into the ravine he beheld his father standing in the wagon, holding in his hand a singletree which he used as a weapon of defence. The wolves jumped upon the wagon in twos and threes, and when beaten off by Mr. Brent would crowd around the wheels and howl to get their courage up, and renew the attack.

Day 96

1. Before you read the rest of the chapter, I want to tell you something. No one dies in this chapter. Everyone is okay at the end of the chapter. Finish chapter 9.
2. What do you realize at the end of the chapter? (Answers)

Chapter 9 continued

Mr. Brent saw the boy starting down the hill toward the wagon and motioned to him to go back. Balser quickly perceived that it would be worse than madness to go to his father. The wolves would at once turn their attack upon him, and his father would be compelled to abandon his advantageous position in the wagon and go to his relief, in which case both father and son would be lost. Should Balser fire into the pack of wolves from where he stood, he would bring upon himself and his father the same disaster.

He felt his helplessness grievously, but his quick wit came to his assistance. He looked about him for a tree which he could climb, and soon found one. At first he hesitated to make use of the tree, for it was dead and apparently rotten; but there was none other at hand, so he hastily climbed up and seated himself firmly upon a limb which seemed strong enough to sustain his weight Balser was now safe from the wolves, and at a distance of not more than twenty yards from his father. There he waited until the clouds for a moment permitted the full light of the moon to rest upon the scene, and then he took deliberate aim and fired into the pack of howling wolves.

A sharp yelp answered his shot, and then a black, seething mass of growling, fighting, snapping beasts fell upon the carcass of the wolf that Balser's shot had killed, and almost instantly they devoured their unfortunate companion.

Balser felt that if he could kill enough wolves to satisfy the hunger of the living ones they would abandon their attack upon his father, for wolves, like cowardly men, are brave only in desperation. They will attack neither man nor animal except when driven to do so by hunger.

After Balser had killed the wolf, clouds obscured the moon before he could make another shot. He feared to fire in the dark lest he might kill his father, so he waited impatiently for the light which did not come.

Meanwhile, the dead wolf having been devoured, the pack again turned upon Mr. Brent, and Balser could hear his father's voice and the clanking of the iron upon the singletree as he struck at the wolves to ward them off.

It seemed to Balser that the moon had gone under the clouds never to appear again. Mr. Brent continually called loudly to the wolves, for the human voice is an awesome sound even to the fiercest animals. To Balser the tone of his father's voice, mingled with the howling of wolves, was a note of desperation that almost drove him frantic.

The wind increased in fury every moment, and Balser felt the cold piercing to the marrow of his bones. He had waited it seemed to him hours for the light of the moon again to shine, but the clouds appeared to grow deeper and the darkness more dense.

While Balser was vainly endeavouring to watch the conflict at the wagon, he heard a noise at the root of the tree in which he had taken refuge, and, looking down, he discovered a black monster standing quietly beneath him. It was a bear that had been attracted to the scene of battle by the noise. Balser at once thought, "Could I kill this huge bear, his great carcass certainly would satisfy the hunger of the wolves that surround my father." Accordingly he lowered the point of his gun, and, taking as good aim as the darkness would permit, he fired upon the bear. The bear gave forth a frightful growl of rage and pain, and as it did so its companion, a beast of enormous size, came running up, apparently for the purpose of rendering assistance.

Balser hastily reloaded his gun and prepared to shoot the other bear. This he soon did, and while the wolves howled about his father the two wounded bears at the foot of the tree made night hideous with their ravings.

Such a frightful bedlam of noises had never before been heard.

Balser was again loading his gun, hoping to finish the bears, when he saw two lighted torches approaching along the path over which he had just come, and as they came into view imagine his consternation when he recognized the forms of Liney Fox and her brother Tom. Tom carried his father's gun, for Mr. Fox had gone to Brookville, and Liney, in addition to her torch, carried Tom's hatchet. Liney and Tom were approaching rapidly, and Balser called out to them to stop. They did not hear him, or did not heed him, but continued to go forward to their death. The bears at the foot of the tree were wounded, and would be more dangerous than even the pack of wolves howling at the wagon.

"Go back! Go back!" cried Balser desperately, "or you'll be killed. Two wounded bears are at the root of the tree I'm in, and a hundred wolves are howling in the hollow just below me. Run for your lives! Run! You'll be torn in pieces if you come here."

The boy and girl did not stop, but continued to walk rapidly toward the spot from which they had heard Balser call. The clouds had drifted away from the moon, and now that the light was of little use to Balser for he was intent upon saving Liney and Tom there was plenty of it.

The sound of his voice and the growling of the bears had attracted the attention of the wolves. They were wavering in their attack upon Mr. Brent, and evidently had half a notion to fall upon the bears that Balser had wounded. Meantime Liney and Tom continued to approach, and their torches, which under ordinary circumstances would have frightened the animals away, attracted the attention of the bears and the wolves, and drew the beasts upon them. They were now within a few yards of certain death, and again Balser in agony cried out : "Go back, Liney! Go back! Run for your lives!" In his eagerness he rose to his feet, and took a step or two out upon the rotten limb on which he had been seated.

As he called to Liney and Tom, and motioned to them frantically to go back, the limb upon which he was standing broke, and he fell a distance of ten or twelve feet to the ground, and lay half stunned between the two wounded bears. Just as Balser fell, Liney and Tom came up to the rotten tree, and at the same time the pack of wolves abandoned their attack upon Mr. Brent and rushed like a herd of howling demons upon the three helpless children.

One of the bears immediately seized Balser, and the other one struck Liney to the ground. By the light of the torches Mr. Brent saw all that had happened, and when the wolves abandoned their attack upon him he hurried forward to rescue Balser, Liney, and Tom, although in so doing he was going to meet his death. In a few seconds Mr. Brent was in the midst of the terrible fight, and a dozen wolves sprang upon him. Tom's gun was useless, so he snatched the hatchet from Liney, who was lying prostrate under one of the bears, and tried to rescue her from its jaws. Had he done so, however, it would have been only to save her for the wolves. But his attempt to rescue Liney was quickly brought to an end. The wolves sprang upon Tom, and soon he, too, was upon the ground. The resinous torches which had fallen from the hands of Tom and Liney continued to burn, and cast a lurid light upon the terrible scene.

Consciousness soon returned to Balser, and he saw with horror the fate that was in store for his father, his friends, and himself. Despair took possession of his soul, and he knew that the lamp of life would soon be black in all of them forever. While his father and Tom lay upon the ground at the mercy of the wolves, and while Liney was lying within arm's reach of him in the jaws of the wounded bear, and he utterly helpless to save the girl of whom he was so fond, Balser's mother shook him by the shoulder and said, "Balser, your father is coming." Balser sprang to his feet, looked dazed for a moment, and then ran, half weeping, half laughing, into his father's arms . . . just as the sleepy little clock had finished striking nine.

Day 97

1. Read the first part of chapter 9.
2. What was Liney's Christmas present from Balser? (Answers)
3. What was the castle? (Answers)
4. Here is an old picture of a hollow sycamore tree.

CHAPTER IX A CASTLE ON THE BRANDYWINE

CHRISTMAS morning the boys awakened early and crept from beneath their warm bearskins in eager anticipation of gifts from Santa Claus. Of course they had long before learned who Santa Claus was, but they loved the story, and in the wisdom of their innocence clung to an illusion which brought them happiness.

The sun had risen upon a scene such as winter only can produce. Surely Aladdin had come to Blue River upon the wings of the Christmas storm, had rubbed his lamp, and lo! the humble cabin was in the heart of a fairyland such as was never conceived by the mind of a genie. Snow lay upon the ground like a soft carpet of white velvet ten inches thick. The boughs of the trees were festooned with a foliage that spring cannot rival. Even the locust trees, which in their pride of blossom cry out in June time for our admiration, seemed to say, "See what we can do in winter," and the sycamore and beech drooped their branches, as if to call attention to their winter flowers given by that rarest of artists, Jack Frost.

The boys quickly donned their heavy buck skin clothing and moccasins, and climbed down the pole to the room where their father and mother were sleeping. Jim awakened his parents with a cry of "Christmas Gift," but Balser's attention was attracted to a barrel standing by the fireplace, which his father had brought from Brookville, and into which the boys had not been permitted to look the night before. Balser had a shrewd suspicion of what the barrel contained, and his delight knew no bounds when he found, as he had hoped, that it was filled with steel traps of the size used to catch beavers, coons, and foxes.

Since he had owned a gun, Balser's great desire had been to possess a number of traps. As I have already told you, the pelts of animals taken in winter are of great value, and our little hero longed to begin life on his own account as a hunter and trapper.

I might tell you of the joyous Christmas morning in the humble cabin when the gifts which Mr. Brent had brought from Brookville were distributed. I might tell you of the new gown for mother, of the bright, red mufflers, of the shoes for Sunday wear and the "store" caps for the boys, to be used upon holiday occasions. I might tell you of the candies and nuts, and of the rarest of all the gifts, an orange for each member of the family, for that fruit had never before been seen upon Blue River. But I must take you to the castle on Brandywine.

You may wonder how there came to be a castle in the wilderness on Brandywine, but I am sure, when you learn about it, you will declare that it was fairer than any castle ever built of mortar and stone, and that the adventures which befell our little heroes were as glorious as ever fell to the lot of spurred and belted knight. Immediately after breakfast, when the chores had all been finished, Balser and Jim started down the river to visit Liney and Tom. Balser carried with him two Christmas presents for his friends a steel trap for Tom, and the orange which his father had brought him from Brookville for Liney.

I might also tell you of Tom's delight when he received the trap, and of Liney's smile of pleasure, worth all the oranges in the world, when she received her present; and I might tell you how she divided the orange into pieces, and gave one to each of the family; and how, after it had all been eaten, tears came to her bright eyes when she learned that Balser had not tasted the fruit. I might tell you much more that would be interesting, and show you how good and true and gentle were these honest, simple folk, but I must drop it all and begin my story.

Balser told Tom about the traps, and a trapping expedition was quickly agreed upon between the boys.

The next day Tom went to visit Balser, and for three or four days the boys were busily engaged in making two sleds upon which to carry provisions for their campaign. The sleds when finished were each about two feet broad and six feet long. They were made of elm, and were very strong, and were so light that when loaded the boys could easily draw them over the snow. By the time the sleds were finished the snow was hard, and everything was ready for the moving of the expedition.

First, the traps were packed. Then provisions, consisting of sweet potatoes, a great lump of maple sugar, a dozen loaves of white bread, two or three gourds full of butter, a side of bacon, a bag of meal, a large piece of bear meat for the dogs, and a number of other articles and simple utensils such as the boys would need in cooking, were loaded upon the sleds. They took with them no meat other than bacon and the bear meat for the dogs, for they knew they could make traps from the boughs of trees in which they could catch quail and pheasants, and were sure to be able, in an hour's hunting, to provide enough venison to supply their wants for a much longer time than they would remain in camp. There were also wild turkeys to be killed, and fish to be caught through openings which the boys would make in the ice of the creek.

Over the loaded sleds they spread woolly bearskins to be used for beds and covering during the cold nights, and they also took with them a number of tanned deerskins, with which to carpet the floor of their castle and to close its doors and windows. Tom took with him his wonderful hatchet, an axe, and his father's rifle. Axe, hatchets, and knives had been sharpened, and bullets had been moulded in such vast numbers that one would have thought the boys were going to war. Powder horns were filled, and a can of that precious article was placed carefully upon each of the sleds.

Bright and early one morning Balser, Tom, and Jim, and last, but by no means least, Tige and Prince, crossed Blue River, and started in a northwestern direction toward a point on Brandywine where a number of beaver dams were known to exist, ten miles distant from the Brent cabin.

Tom and Tige drew one of the sleds, and Balser and Prince drew the other. During the first part of the trip, Jim would now and then lend a helping hand, but toward the latter end of the journey he said he thought it would be better for him to ride upon one of the sleds to keep the load from falling off. Balser and Tom, however, did not agree with him, nor did the dogs; so Jim walked behind and grumbled, and had his grumbling for his pains, as usually is the case with grumblers.

Two or three hours before sunset the boys reached Brandywine, a babbling little creek in springtime, winding its crooked rippling way through overhanging boughs of water elm, sycamore, and willows, but, at the time of our heroes' expedition, frozen over with the mail of winter. It is in small creeks, such as Brandywine, that beavers love to make their dams.

Our little caravan, upon reaching Brandywine, at once took to the ice and started up stream along its winding course.

Jim had grown tired. "I don't believe you fellows know where you're going," said he. "I don't see any place to camp."

"You'll see it pretty quickly," said Balser; and when they turned a bend in the creek they beheld a huge sycamore springing from a little valley that led down to the water's edge.

"There's our home," said Balser.

The sycamore was hollow, and at its roots was an opening for a doorway.

Upon beholding the tree Jim gave a cry of delight, and was for entering their new home at once, but Balser held him back and sent in the dogs as an exploring advance guard. Soon the dogs came out and informed the boys that everything within the tree was all right, and Balser and Tom and Jim stooped low and entered upon the possession of their castle on Brandywine.

The first task was to sweep out the dust and dry leaves. This the boys did with bundles of twigs rudely fashioned into brooms. The dry leaves and small tufts of black hair gave evidence all too strongly that the castle which the boys had captured was the home of some baron bear who had incautiously left his stronghold unguarded. Jim spoke of this fact with unpleasant emphasis, and was ready to "bet" that the bear would come back when they were all asleep, and would take possession of his castle and devour the intruders.

"What will you bet?" said Tom.

"I didn't say I would bet anything. I just said I'd bet, and you'll see I'm right," returned Jim.

Day 98

1. Read the next part of chapter 9.
2. A quote from the chapter: "The dogs were not fastidious and a sleeping-place was soon made for them entirely to their satisfaction." What does it mean that their sleeping-place was to their satisfaction? If they were able to quickly make a sleeping-place that they were happy with, what do you think it means that they "were not fastidious?" (hint: It didn't take much to make them happy.) (Answers)
3. Why is the author calling the boys to wake up? "Awaken!" (Answers)

Chapter 9 continued

Balser and Tom well knew that Jim's prophecy might easily come true, but they had faith in the watchfulness of their sentinels, Tige and Prince, and the moon being at its full, they hoped rather than feared that his bearship might return, and were confident that, in case he did, his danger would be greater than theirs.

After the castle floor had been carefully swept, the boys carried in the deerskins and spread them on the ground for a carpet. The bearskins were then taken in, and the beds were made; traps, guns, and provisions were stored away, and the sleds were drawn around to one side of the door, and placed leaning against the tree.

The boys were hungry, and Jim insisted that supper should be prepared at once; but Tom, having made several trips around the tree, remarked mysteriously that he had a plan of his own. He said there was a great deal of work to be done before sundown, and that supper could be eaten after dark when they could not work. Tom was right, for the night gave promise of bitter cold.

Limpy did not tell his plans at once, but soon they were developed.

The hollow in the tree in which the boys had made their home was almost circular in form. It was at least ten or eleven feet in diameter, and extended up into the tree twenty or thirty feet. Springing from the same root, and a part of the parent tree, grew two large sprouts or branches, which at a little distance looked like separate trees. They were, however, each connected with the larger tree, and the three formed one.

"What on earth are you pounding at that tree for?" asked Jim, while Tom was striking one of the smaller trees with the butt end of the hatchet, and listening intently as if he expected to hear a response. Tom did not reply to Jim, but in a moment entered the main tree with axe in hand, and soon Balser and Jim heard him chopping.

The two boys at once followed Tom, to learn what their eccentric companion was doing. Tom did not respond to their questions, but after he had chopped vigorously for a few minutes the result of his work gave them an answer, for he soon cut an opening into the smaller tree, which was also hollow. Tom had discovered the hollow by striking the tree with his hatchet. In fact, Tom was a genius after his own peculiar pattern.

The newly discovered hollow proved to be three or four feet in diameter, and, like that in the larger tree, extended to a considerable height. After Tom had made the opening between the trees, he sat upon the ground, and with his hatchet hewed it to an oval shape, two feet high and two feet broad.

Jim could not imagine why Tom had taken so much trouble to add another room to their house, which was already large enough. But when Tom, having finished the opening upon the inside, went out and began to climb the smaller tree with the help of a few low-growing branches, the youngest member of the expedition became fully convinced in his own mind that the second in command was out of his head entirely. When Tom, having climbed to a height of twelve or fifteen feet, began to chop with his hatchet, Jim remarked, in most emphatic language, that he thought "a fellow who would chop at a sycamore tree just for the sake of making chips, when he might be eating his supper, was too big a fool to live."

Tom did not respond to Jim's sarcasm, but persevered in his chopping until he had made an opening at the point to which he had climbed. Balser had quickly guessed the object of Tom's mighty labors, but he did not enlighten Jim. He had gone to other work, and by the time Tom had made the opening from the outside of the smaller tree, had collected a pile of firewood, and had carried several loads of it into the castle. Then Tom came down, and Jim quickly followed him into the large tree, for by that time his mysterious movements were full of interest to the little fellow.

Now what do you suppose was Tom's object in wasting so much time and energy with his axe and hatchet?

A fireplace.

You will at once understand that the opening which Tom had cut in the tree at the height of twelve or fifteen feet was for the purpose of making a chimney through which the smoke might escape.

The boys kindled a fire, and in a few minutes there was a cheery blaze in their fire place that lighted up the room and made "everything look just like home," Jim said.

Then Jim went outside and gave a great hurrah of delight when he saw the smoke issuing from the chimney that ingenious Tom had made with his hatchet.

Jim watched the smoke for a few moments, and then walked around the tree to survey the premises. The result of his survey was the discovery of a hollow in the third tree of their castle, and when he informed Balser and Tom of the important fact, it was agreed that the room which Jim had found should be prepared for Tige and Prince. The dogs were not fastidious, and a sleeping-place was soon made for them entirely to their satisfaction.

Meantime the fire was blazing and crackling in the fireplace, and the boys began to prepare supper. They had not had time to kill game, so they fried a few pieces of bacon and a dozen eggs, of which they had brought a good supply, and roasted a few sweet potatoes in the ashes. Then they made an opening in the ice, from which they drew a bucketful of sparkling ice water, and when all was ready they sat down to supper, served with the rarest of all dressings, appetite sauce, and at least one of the party, Jim, was happy as a boy could be.

The dogs then received their supper of bear meat.

The members of the expedition, from the commanding officer Balser to the high privates Tige and Prince, were very tired after their hard day's work, and when Tom and Balser showed the dogs their sleeping-place, they curled up close to each other and soon were in the land of dog dreams.

By the time supper was finished night had fallen, and while Tom and Balser were engaged in stretching a deerskin across the door to exclude the cold air, Jim crept between the bearskins and soon was sound asleep, dreaming no doubt of suppers and dinners and breakfasts, and scolding in his dreams like the veritable little grumbler that he was. A great bed of embers had accumulated in the fireplace, and upon them Balser placed a hickory knot for the purpose of retaining fire till morning, and then he covered the fire with ashes.

After all was ready Balser and Tom crept in between the bearskins, and lying spoon fashion, one on each side of Jim, lost no time in making a rapid, happy journey to the land of Nod.

Tom slept next to the wall, next to Tom lay Jim, and next to Jim was Balser. The boys were lying with their feet to the fire, and upon the opposite side of room was the doorway closed by the deerskin, of which I have already told you.

Of course they went to bed "all standing," as sailors say when they lie down to sleep with their clothing on, for the weather was cold, and the buckskin clothing and moccasins were soft and pleasant to sleep in, and would materially assist the bear skins in keeping the boys warm.

It must have been a pretty sight in the last flickering light of the smouldering fire to see the three boys huddled closely together, covered by the bearskins. I have no doubt had you seen them upon that night they would have appeared to you like a sleeping bear. In fact, before the night was over they did appear to but I must not go ahead of my story.

The swift-winged hours of darkness sped like moments to the sleeping boys. The smouldering coals in the fireplace were black and lustreless. The night wind softly moaned through the branches of the sycamore, and sighed as it swept the bare limbs of the willows and the rustling tops of the underbrush. Jack Frost was silently at work, and the cold, clear air seemed to glitter in the moonlight. It was an hour past midnight. Had the boys been awake and listening, or had Tige and Prince been attending to their duties as sentinels, they would have heard a crisp noise of footsteps, as the icy surface of the snow cracked, and as dead twigs broke beneath a heavy weight. Ah, could the boys but awaken! Could the dogs be aroused but for one instant from their deep lethargy of slumber!

Balser! Tom! Jim! Tige! Prince! Awaken! Awaken!

On comes the heavy footfall, cautiously. As it approaches the castle a few hurried steps are taken, and the black, awkward form lifts his head and sniffs the air for signs of danger.

Day 99

1. Read the next part of chapter 9.
2. How did each of the boys show courage? (Answers)

Chapter 9 continued

Balser! Tom! Jim! Tige! Prince! Awaken! Awaken!
On comes the heavy footfall, cautiously. As it approaches the castle a few hurried steps are taken, and the black, awkward form lifts his head and sniffs the air for signs of danger.

The baron has returned to claim his own, and Jim's prophecy, at least in part, has come true. The tracks upon the snow left by the boys and dogs, and the sleds leaning against the tree, excite the bear's suspicion, and he stands like a statue for five minutes, trying to make up his mind whether or not he shall enter his old domain. The memory of his cozy home tempts him, and he cautiously walks to the doorway of his house. The deerskin stretched across the opening surprises him, and he carefully examines it with the aid of his chief counsellor, his nose. Then he thrusts it aside with his head and enters.

He sees the boys on the opposite side of the tree, and doubtless fancies that his mate has gotten home before him, so he complacently lies down beside the bearskins, and soon, he, too, is in the land of bear dreams.

When a bear sleeps he snores, and the first loud snort from the baron's nostrils aroused Balser. At first Balser's mind was in confusion, and he thought that he was at home. In a moment, however, he remembered where he was, and waited in the dark ness for a repetition of the sound that had awakened him. Soon it came again, and Balser in his drowsiness fancied that Tom had changed his place and was lying beside him, though never in all his life had he heard such sounds proceed from Limpy's nose. So he reached out his hand, and at once was undeceived, for he touched the bear, and at last Balser was awake. The boy's hair seemed to stand erect upon his head, and his blood grew cold in his veins, has he realized the terrible situation. All was darkness. The guns, hatchets, and knives were upon the opposite side of the tree, and to reach them or to reach the doorway Balser would have to climb over the bear. Cold as the night was, perspiration sprang from every pore of his skin, and terror took possession of him such as he had never before known. It seemed a long time that he lay there, but it could not have been more than a few seconds until the bear gave forth another snort, and Tom raised up from his side of the bed, and said: "Balser, for goodness' sake stop snoring. The noise you make would bring a dead man to life."

Tom's voice aroused the bear, and it immediately rose upon its haunches with a deep growl that seemed to shake the tree. Then Jim awakened and began to scream. At the same instant Tige and Prince entered the tree, and a fight at once ensued between the bear and dogs. The bear was as badly frightened as the boys, and when it and the dogs ran about the room the boys were thrown to the ground and trampled upon.

The beast, in his desperate effort to escape, ran into the fireplace and scattered the coals and ashes. As he could not escape through the fireplace, he backed into the room, and again made the rounds of the tree with the dogs at his heels. Again the boys were knocked about as if they were ninepins. They made an effort to reach the door, but all I have told you about took place so quickly, and the darkness was so intense, that they failed to escape. Mean time the fight between the dogs and the bear went on furiously, and the barking, yelping, growling, and snarling made a noise that was deafening. Balser lifted Jim to his arms and tried to save him from injury, but his efforts were of small avail, for with each plunge of the bear the boys were thrown to the ground or dashed against the tree, until it seemed that there was not a spot upon their bodies that was not bruised and scratched. At last, after a minute or two of awful struggle and turmoil a minute or two that seemed hours to the boys the bear made his exit through the door followed closely by Tige and Prince, who clung to him with a persistency not to be shaken off.

You may be sure that the boys lost no time in making their exit also. Their first thoughts, of course, were of each other, and when Balser learned that Jim and Tom had received no serious injury, he quickly turned his head in the direction whence the bear and dogs had gone, and saw them at a point in the bend of the creek not fifty yards away.

The bear had come to bay, and the dogs were in front of him, at a safe distance, barking furiously, Then Balser's courage returned, and he hastily went into the tree, brought out his carbine, and hurried toward the scene of conflict. The moon was at its full, and the snow upon the trees and upon the ground helped to make the night almost as light as day. The bear was sitting erect upon his haunches, hurling defiant growls at the dogs, and when Balser approached him, the brute presented his breast as a fair mark.

Tom also fetched his gun and followed closely at Balser's heels. The attention of the bear was so occupied with the dogs that he gave no heed to the boys, and they easily approached him to within a distance of five or six yards. Tom and Balser stood for a moment or two with their guns ready to fire, and Balser said: "Tom, you shoot first. I'll watch carefully, and hold my fire until the bear makes a rush, should you fail to kill him."

Much to Balser's surprise, Tom quickly and fearlessly took three or four steps toward the bear, and when he lifted his father's long gun to fire, the end of it was within three yards of the bear's breast.

Balser held his ground, much frightened at Tom's reckless bravery, but did not dare to speak. When Tom fired, the bear gave forth a fearful growl, and sprang like a wildcat right upon the boy. Tom fell to the ground upon his back, and the bear stood over him. The dogs quickly made an attack, and Balser hesitated to fire, fearing that he might kill Tom or one of the dogs. Then came Jim, who rushed past Balser toward Tom and the bear, and if Jim's courage had ever before been doubted, all such doubts were upon that night removed for ever. The little fellow carried in his hand Tom's hatchet, and without fear or hesitancy he ran to the bear and began to strike him with all his little might.

Meantime poor, prostrate Tom was crying piteously for help, and, now that Jim was added to the group, it seemed impossible for Balser to fire at the bear. But no time was to be lost. If Balser did not shoot, Tom certainly would be killed in less than ten seconds. So, without stopping to take thought, and upon the impulse of one of those rare intuitions under the influence of which persons move so accurately, Balser lifted his gun to his shoulder. He could see the bear's head plainly as it swayed from side to side, just over Tom's throat, and it seemed that he could not miss his aim. Almost without looking, he pulled the trigger. He felt the rebound of the gun and heard the report breaking the heavy silence of the night. Then he dropped the gun upon the snow and covered his face with his hands, fearing to see the result of his shot. He stood for a moment trembling. The dogs had stopped barking; the bear had stopped growling; Jim had ceased to cry out; Tom had ceased his call for help, and the deep silence rested upon Balser's heart like a load of lead. He could not take his hands from his face.

After a moment he felt Jim's little hand upon his arm, and Tom said, as he drew himself from beneath the bear, "Balser, there's no man or boy living but you that could have made that shot in the moonlight."

Then Balser knew that he had killed the bear, and he sank upon the snow and wept as if his heart would break.

Notwithstanding the intense cold, the excitement of battle had made the boys unconscious of it, and Tom and Jim stood by Balser's side as he sat upon the snow, and they did not feel the sting of the night.

Poor little Jim, who was so given to grumbling, much to the surprise of his companions fell upon his knees, and said, "Don't cry, Balser, don't cry," although the tears were falling over the little fellow's own cheeks. "Don't cry any more, Balser, the bear is dead all over. I heard the bullet whiz past my ears, and I heard it strike the bear's head just as plain as you can hear that owl hoot; and then I knew that you had saved Tom and me, because nobody can shoot as well as you can." The little fellow's tenderness and his pride in Balser seemed all the sweeter, because it sprang from his childish gruffness.

Tom and Jim helped Balser to his feet, and they went over to the spot where the bear was lying stone dead with Balser's bullet in his brain. The dogs were sniffing at the dead bear, and the monster brute lay upon the snow in the moonlight, and looked like a huge incarnate fiend.

After examining him for a moment the boys slowly walked back to the tree. When they had entered they raked the coals together, put on an armful of wood, called in the dogs to share their comfort, hung up the deerskin at the door, drew the bearskins in front of the fire, and sat down to talk and think, since there was no sleep left in their eyes for the rest of that night.

After a long silence Jim said, "I told you he'd come back."

"But he didn't eat us," replied Tom, determined that Jim should not be right in everything.

Day 100

1. Finish the book.
2. How does the book end? (Answers)
3. Write a short book report. Write about the book. Include the title, main character, setting, plot (short description of what happens), and what you liked and didn't like about the book. You could save this in your portfolio.

Chapter 9 continued

"He'd have eaten you, Limpy Fox, if Balser hadn't been the best shot in the world."

"That's what he would," answered Tom, half inclined to cry.

"Nonsense," said Balser, "anybody could have done it"

"Well, I reckon not," said Jim. "Me and Tom and the dogs and the bear was as thick as six in a bed; and honest, Balser, I think you had to shoot around a curve to miss us all but the bear."

After a few minutes Jim said : "Golly! wasn't that an awful fight we had in here before the bear got out?"

"Yes, it was," returned Balser, seriously.

"Well, I rather think it was," continued Jim. "Honestly, fellows, I ran around this here room so fast for a while, that that I could see my own back most of the time."

Balser and Tom laughed, and Tom said: "Jim, if you keep on improving, you'll be a bigger liar than that fellow in the Bible before you're half his age."

Then the boys lapsed into silence, and the dogs lay stretched before the fire till the welcome sun began to climb the hill of the sky and spread his blessed tints of gray and blue and pink and red, followed by the glorious flood of day.

After breakfast the boys skinned the bear and cut his carcass into small pieces that is, such portions of it as they cared to keep. They hung the bearskin and meat upon the branches of their castle beyond the reach of wolves and foxes, and they gave to Tige and Prince each a piece of meat that made their sides stand out with fulness.

The saving of the bear meat and skin consumed most of the morning, and at noon the boys took a loin steak from the bear and broiled it upon the coals for dinner. After dinner they began the real work of the expedition by preparing to set the traps.

When all was ready they started up the creek, each boy carrying a load of traps over his shoulder. At a distance of a little more than half a mile from the castle they found a beaver dam stretching across the creek, and at the water's edge near each end of the dam they saw numberless tracks made by the little animals whose precious pelts they were so anxious to obtain.

I should like to tell you of the marvellous home of that wonderful little animal the beaver, and of his curious habits and instincts; how he chops wood and digs into the ground and plasters his home, under the water, with mud, using his tail for shovel and trowel. But all that you may learn from any book on natural history, and I assure you it will be found interesting reading.

The boys placed five or six traps upon the beaver paths on each side of the creek, and then continued their journey up stream until they found a little opening in the ice down to which, from the bank above, ran a well-beaten path, telling plainly of the many kinds of animals that had been going there to drink. There they set a few traps and baited them with small pieces of bear meat, and then they returned home, intending to visit the traps next morning at an early hour, and hoping to reap a rich harvest of pelts.

When the boys reached home it lacked little more than an hour of sunset, but the young fellows had recovered from the excitement of the night before, which had somewhat destroyed their appetites for breakfast and dinner, and by the time they had returned from setting their traps those same appetites were asserting themselves with a vigour that showed plainly enough a fixed determination to make up for lost time.

"How would a wild turkey or a venison steak taste for supper?" asked Balser.

Jim simply looked up at him with a greedy, hungry expression, and exclaimed the one word "Taste?"

"Well, I'll go down the creek a little way and see what I can find. You fellows stay here and build a fire, so that we can have a fine bed of coals when I return."

Balser shouldered his gun and went down the creek to find his supper. He did not take the dogs, for he hoped to kill a wild turkey, and dogs are apt to bark in the pursuit of squirrels and rabbits, thereby frightening the turkey, which is a shy and wary bird.

When the boy had travelled quite a long distance down stream, he began to fear that, after all, he should be compelled to content himself with a rabbit or two for supper. So he turned homeward and scanned the woods carefully for the humble game, that he might not go home entirely empty handed.

Upon his journey down the creek rabbits had sprung up on every side of him, but now that he wanted a pair for supper they all had mysteriously disappeared, and he feared that he and the boys and the dogs would be compelled to content themselves with bear meat.

When the boy was within a few hundred yards of home, and had almost despaired of obtaining even a rabbit, he spied a doe and a fawn, standing upon the opposite side of the creek at a distance of sixty or seventy yards, watching him intently with their great brown eyes, so full of fatal curiosity.

Balser imitated the cry of the fawn, and held the attention of the doe until he was enabled to lessen the distance by fifteen or twenty yards. Then he shot the fawn, knowing that if he did so, its mother, the doe, would run for a short distance and would return to the fawn. In the meantime Balser would load his gun and would kill the doe when she returned. And so it happened that the doe and the fawn each fell a victim to our hunter's skill. Balser threw the fawn over his shoulder and carried it to the castle; then the boys took one of the sleds and fetched home the doe.

They hung the doe high upon the branches of the sycamore, and cut the fawn into small pieces, which they put upon the ice of the creek and covered with snow, that the meat might quickly cool. The bed of coals was ready, and the boys were ready too, you may be sure.

Soon the fawn meat cooled, and soon each boy was devouring a savoury piece that had been broiled upon the coals.

After supper the boys again built a fine fire, and sat before it talking of the events of the day, and wondering how many beavers, foxes, coons, and muskrats they would find in their traps next morning.

As the fire died down drowsiness stole over our trappers, who were in the habit of going to bed soon after sunset, and they again crept in between the bearskins with Jim in the middle. They, however, took the precaution to keep Tige and Prince in the same room with them, and the boys slept that night without fear of an intrusion such as had disturbed them the night before.

Next morning, bright and early, the boys hurried up the creek to examine their traps, and greatly to their joy found five beavers and several minks, coons, and muskrats safely captured. Near one of the traps was the foot of a fox, which its possessor had bitten off in the night when he learned that he could not free it from the cruel steel.

The boys killed the animals they had caught by striking them on the head with a heavy club, which method of inflicting death did not damage the pelts as a sharp instrument or bullet would have done. After resetting the traps, our hunters placed the game upon the sled and hurried home to their castle, where the pelts were carefully removed, stretched upon forked sticks, and hung up to dry.

Our heroes remained in camp for ten or twelve days, and each morning brought them a fine supply of fur. They met with no other adventure worthy to be related, and one day was like another. They awakened each morning with the sun, and ate their breakfast of broiled venison, fish, or quail, with now and then a rabbit. Upon one occasion they had the breast of a wild turkey. They sought the traps, took the game, prepared the pelts, ate their dinners and suppers of broiled meats and baked sweet potatoes, and slumbered cozily beneath their warm bearskins till morning.

One day Balser noticed that the snow was melting and was falling from the trees. He and his companions had taken enough pelts to make a heavy load upon each of the sleds. They feared that the weather might suddenly grow warm and that the snow might disappear. So they leisurely packed the pelts and their belongings, and next morning started for home on Blue River, the richest, happiest boys in the settlement. They were glad to go home, but it was with a touch of sadness, when they passed around the bend in the creek, that they said "Good-by" to their "Castle on Brandywine."

Day 101

1.   Read this story, called, *The Lesson*.

Benny liked to be first. He rushed into the cloakroom to hang up his coat. He didn't notice that on the way to the hook he stomped on Richard's lunch. Benny dashed to the front of the math line, sending Sally's pencils flying to the floor. Benny zipped to the front of the line for dismissal. He didn't notice that on the way he trounced on Sara's toes. Then he barreled outside, letting the door close behind him, right in Sara's face.

The next morning Benny's teacher spoke to him very seriously.

"Benny, do you realize that you are always pushing to get to the front of the line?"

"Yes," Benny replied proudly. "I like to be first."

"Everyone likes to be first, Benny. Do you realize that you are hurting other people and their things on your way to being first?"

"Like what?"

"Well, you trounced on Sara's toes and you stomped on Richard's lunch and you knocked Sally's pencils onto the floor."

"I did? I guess I didn't notice."

"Benny, this isn't the first time you and I have talked about your pushing yourself in front of other people. Do you remember that I told you I would have to call your parents if your behavior did not change?
"Yes, ma'am."

"I think I need their cooperation so we can all work together to help you understand how what you do affects your classmates. I will call them sometime today.

"Yes, ma'am."

All evening long Bennie waited nervously for his parents to say something about school. Nothing happened. "Maybe my teacher forgot to call," he thought hopefully.

Benny was still hopeful the next morning as he sloshed milk onto his cereal, spilling some drops on the table and sending a few flakes flying. Then his father walked into the kitchen and Benny noticed the look on his face. His father looked even more serious than his teacher had looked.

"Benny, your teacher called late last night, after you went to bed. Your mother and I were embarrassed to hear what she had to say. Do you know why she called?"

"Yes, sir. She thinks I shouldn't try to be first all the time. But I LIKE to be first!"

"Benny, haven't your mother and I always taught you to take turns? Haven't we taught you to think about other people's rights?"

"I guess so."

"Tonight we'll have to do a little more teaching – instead of going to the basketball game.'"

"DAD!"

"No arguing. Now get your things together. I want to get you to school on time."

Benny zipped up his jacket. He picked up his book bag and lunch box. He and his father walked silently to the car. Benny wondered if his dad would start his teaching on the way to school.

Benny's dad swung his car out of the driveway, just as the trash truck turned the corner. Benny noticed the squeal of brakes.

Soon they were on the highway. Benny's dad sped up when he saw the yellow stoplight. Benny noticed the light turn red just before they crossed the intersection.

The rush hour traffic was heavy. Benny's father pulled into the right lane. Benny noticed the sign that said, "Right lane must turn right."

"Dad, we're not going to turn right are we? The school is in the other direction."

Benny's father was concentrating too hard to reply. He zipped down the right lane, then beeped his horn and butted back into the left lane. Benny noticed that several drivers behind them also beeped their horns.

As they approached the school, Benny saw a lot of cars waiting to turn into the driveway. Suddenly, Benny's father swerved into the private lane that ran by the school parking lot. Benny barely had time to notice the big Not for School Use sign, when his dad broke into line of parents waiting to deliver their children and then lurched to a stop at the sidewalk. Benny noticed that other parents had been waiting longer.

"I guess Dad likes to be first, too," he thought.

"So long, son. Have a good day. Remember to take turns."

"Okay, Dad"

As he climbed out of the car, Benny noticed his friends Richard and Sara walking toward the building. He caught up with them just as they reached the school, and he held the door to let Sara and Richard go in first.

Day 102

1. Think about the story you read on Day 101 and answer these questions. You can look back at the story if you need to.
2. What is the title of the story? (Answers)
3. Who is the main character? (Answers)
4. What are three settings in the story? (Answers)
5. What is the conflict, the problem of the story? (Answers)
6. What are a couple of the things that happened to try to solve the problem? (This is the plot.) (Answers)
7. Was the problem solved? How? (Answers)
8. What do you think is the main idea, or the most important idea of this story? (Answers)

Day 103

1. Read these poems.
2. What's the main idea of the "Little Things" poem? (Answers)

The Arrow and the Song by Longfellow
I shot an arrow into the air,
It fell to earth, I knew not where;
For, so swiftly it flew, the sight
Could not follow it in its flight.
I breathed a song into the air,
It fell to earth, I knew not where;

For who has sight so keen and strong
That it can follow the flight of song?
Long, long afterward, in an oak
I found the arrow, still unbroke;
And the song, from beginning to end,
I found again in the heart of a friend.

Let Dogs Delight to Bark and Bite by Isaac Watts
Let dogs delight to bark and bite,
For God hath made them so;
Let bears and lions growl and fight,
For 'tis their nature too.
But, children, you should never let
Such angry passions rise;
Your little hands were never made
To tear each other's eyes.

Little Things by Ebenezer Brewer
Little drops of water,
Little grains of sand,
Make the mighty ocean
And the pleasant land.
Thus the little minutes,
Humble though they be,
Make the mighty ages
Of eternity.

Day 104

1. Read this poem by George MacDonald.

Rebecca Giles

Little White Lily
Sat by a stone,
Drooping and waiting
Till the sun shone.

Little White Lily
Sunshine has fed;
Little White Lily
Is lifting her head.

Little White Lily
Said: "It is good
Little White Lily's
Clothing and food."

Little White Lily
Dressed like a bride!
Shining with whiteness,
And crownèd beside!

Little White Lily
Drooping with pain,
Waiting and waiting

For the wet rain.
Little White Lily
Holdeth her cup;
Rain is fast falling
And filling it up.

Little White Lily
Said: "Good again,
When I am thirsty
To have the nice rain.

Now I am stronger,
Now I am cool;
Heat cannot burn me,
My veins are so full."

Little White Lily
Smells very sweet;
On her head sunshine,
Rain at her feet.

Thanks to the sunshine,
Thanks to the rain,
Little White Lily
Is happy again.

Day 105

1. Read this poem.
2. What's the poem about? (Answers)

"I'll tell you how the leaves came down,"
The great Tree to his children said:
"You're getting sleepy, Yellow and Brown,
Yes, very sleepy, little Red.
It is quite time to go to bed."

"Ah!" begged each silly, pouting leaf,
"Let us a little longer stay;
Dear Father Tree, behold our grief!
Tis such a very pleasant day,
We do not want to go away."

So, for just one more merry day

261

To the great Tree the leaflets clung,
Frolicked and danced, and had their way,
Upon the autumn breezes swung,
Whispering all their sports among—

"Perhaps the great Tree will forget,
And let us stay until the spring,
If we all beg, and coax, and fret.
"But the great Tree did no such thing;
He smiled to hear their whispering.

"Come, children, all to bed," he cried;
And ere the leaves could urge their prayer,
He shook his head, and far and wide,
Fluttering and rustling everywhere,
Down sped the leaflets through the air.

I saw them; on the ground they lay,
Golden and red, a huddled swarm,
Waiting till one from far away,
White bedclothes heaped upon her arm,
Should come to wrap them safe and warm.

The great bare Tree looked down and smiled.
"Good-night, dear little leaves," he said.
And from below each sleepy child
Replied, "Good-night," and murmured,
"It is *so* nice to go to bed!"

Day 106

1. Learn how to find the main idea of what you are reading.
2. Often when we talk about main ideas, we are referring to non-fiction paragraphs, paragraphs that are teaching us about something.
3. We usually will find the main idea in the first sentence of the paragraph.
4. The main idea is followed by the details that tell us more about the main idea.
5. In the following paragraph what's the main idea? (hint: Where is the main idea usually found?) (Answers)
6. What are the details of this paragraph? (Answers)

A solar system is made up of a star and the rocks that orbit it. The sun is the star in the center of our solar system. The rocks are eight planets that orbit the sun. Earth is one of them; Jupiter is the biggest. In our solar system there are also many moons which orbit individual planets. Together they all make our system.

Day 107

1. Practice finding the main idea. Choose the main idea for each of the following paragraphs from the given options. Write your answers on a separate sheet of paper. (Answers)

Ballet is a form of art. It's a type of dance that requires a lot of discipline. Ballerinas spend years practicing and training their bodies to bend and stretch and turn and leap. They can dance alone or with others telling stories on a stage with just their movements. They make their bodies into living art.

   a) Ballet requires a lot of hard work.
   b) Ballerinas dance on stages.
   c) Ballet is an art form.
   d) Ballerinas are flexible.

Soccer is the most popular sport in the world. Its most common name is football, which makes sense since it is played with your feet. Players are not allowed to touch the ball with their hands except in a few cases. Children can be seen playing soccer in city streets and in empty lots. They just need a ball and some friends. That makes it accessible to many people, making it a sport common to the whole world.

   a) Soccer is called football in a lot of places around the world.
   b) Soccer is popular around the world.
   c) Soccer is played with a ball.
   d) Soccer is played with your feet.

Day 108

1. Practice finding the main idea. Find the main idea for each of the following paragraphs. (Answers)

Macedonia is a small country in the Balkans. The Balkans are in Eastern Europe. Macedonia was part of a larger communist country and then became its own country. It is in a fight with Greece over its name. Greece thinks the real Macedonia is in Greece. Macedonia can claim for itself the birthplace of Mother Theresa. She was born in its capital city. Macedonia is a beautiful country, a small country tucked in the corner of Europe.

Turkey is a country that spans two continents. Most of the country lies in Asia. One of its major cities, Istanbul, lies partly in Europe. Just the most western edge of the country is in Europe, though it often considers itself a European country. It's not uncommon to see signs in Asia advertising the "largest _____ in Europe!" Turkey has two personalities rolled into one country.

Day 109

1. Practice finding the main idea. Find the main idea for each of the following paragraphs. (Answers)

    Homeschooling is the best way to learn. Children can learn where they are most comfortable, home. They can learn from someone who cares the most about them, a parent. They never have to get behind because they don't have to move on until they get it. School goes at just their pace. Homeschooling is ideal for learning.

    Airplanes are a fast way to travel but not always so convenient. Sometimes a flight is less than an hour long, but you can spend up to two hours waiting at the airport before hand. You have to check you luggage and go through security multiple times. You have to walk to your gate which can be far away and then sometimes even take a bus to get to your airplane, all just to take a flight forty minutes away. Flying can be a hassle, but it's still faster than driving.

Day 110

1. Read this poem.
2. What is happening in this poem? (Answers)

    Wynken, Blynken, and Nod one night
    Sailed off in a wooden shoe,—
    Sailed on a river of crystal light
    Into a sea of dew.

    "Where are you going, and what do you wish?
    "The old moon asked the three."
    We have come to fish for the herring-fish
    That live in this beautiful sea;
    Nets of silver and gold have we,"
    Said Wynken, Blynken, And Nod.

    The old moon laughed and sang a song,
    As they rocked in the wooden shoe;
    And the wind that sped them all night long
    Ruffled the waves of dew;

    The little stars were the herring-fish
    That lived in the beautiful sea.
    "Now cast your nets wherever you wish,—
    Never afeard are we!"

So cried the stars to the fishermen three,
Wynken, Blynken, And Nod.

All night long their nets they threw
To the stars in the twinkling foam,—
Then down from the skies came the wooden shoe,
Bringing the fishermen home:

Twas all so pretty a sail, it seemed
As if it could not be;
And some folk thought 'twas a dream they'd dreamed
Of sailing that beautiful sea;
But I shall name you the fishermen three:
Wynken,Blynken,And Nod.

Wynken and Blynken are two little eyes,
And Nod is a little head,
And the wooden shoe that sailed the skies
Is a wee one's trundle-bed;

So shut your eyes while Mother sings
Of wonderful sights that be,
And you shall see the beautiful things
As you rock on the misty sea
Where the old shoe rocked the fishermen three,
Wynken,Blynken,And Nod.

Day 111

1. Read these poems.

If I Had But Two Little Wings by Samuel Taylor Coleridge
If I had but two little wings
And were a little feathery bird,
To you I'd fly, my dear!
But thoughts like these are idle things
And I stay here.
But in my sleep to you I fly:
I'm always with you in my sleep!
The world is all one's own.
And then one wakes, and where am I?
All, all alone.

Sweet and Low by Alfred Tennyson
Sweet and low, sweet and low,
Wind of the western sea,
Low, low, breathe and blow,
Wind of the western sea!
Over the rolling waters go,
Come from the dropping moon and blow,
Blow him again to me;
While my little one, while my pretty one sleeps.
Sleep and rest, sleep and rest,
Father will come to thee soon;
Rest, rest, on mother's breast,
Father will come to thee soon;
Father will come to his babe in the nest,
Silver sails all out of the west
Under the silver moon:
Sleep, my little one, sleep, my pretty one, sleep.

Day 112

1. Read this poem.
2. Humility is the opposite of pride.
3. What's the main idea? (Answers)

The Violet by Jane Taylor
Down in a green and shady bed
A modest violet grew;
Its stalk was bent, it hung its head,
As if to hide from view.

And yet it was a lovely flower,
No colours bright and fair;
It might have graced a rosy bower,
Instead of hiding there.

Yet there it was content to bloom,
In modest tints arrayed;
And there diffused its sweet perfume,
Within the silent shade.

Then let me to the valley go,
This pretty flower to see;
That I may also learn to grow
In sweet humility.

Day 113

1. Read this poem. This is a famous story read at Christmas time.

    A Visit From St. Nicholas by Clement Clarke Moore

    'Twas the night before Christmas, when all through the house
    Not a creature was stirring, not even a mouse;

    The stockings were hung by the chimney with care,
    In hopes that St. Nicholas soon would be there;

    The children were nestled all snug in their beds,
    While visions of sugar-plums danced in their heads;

    And mamma in her 'kerchief, and I in my cap,
    Had just settled our brains for a long winter's nap,

    When out on the lawn there arose such a clatter,
    I sprang from the bed to see what was the matter.

    Away to the window I flew like a flash,
    Tore open the shutters and threw up the sash.

    The moon on the breast of the new-fallen snow
    Gave the luster of mid-day to objects below,

    When, what to my wondering eyes should appear,
    But a miniature sleigh, and eight tiny reindeer.

    With a little old driver, so lively and quick,
    I knew in a moment it must be St. Nick.

    More rapid than eagles his coursers they came,
    And he whistled, and shouted, and called them by name:

    "Now, *Dasher*! now, *Dancer*! now, *Prancer* and *Vixen*!
    On, *Comet*! on, *Cupid*! on, *Donder* and *Blitzen*!

    To the top of the porch! to the top of the wall!
    Now dash away! dash away! dash away all!"

    As dry leaves that before the wild hurricane fly,
    When they meet with an obstacle, mount to the sky;

267

So up to the house-top the coursers they flew,
With the sleigh full of toys, and St. Nicholas, too.

And then, in a twinkling, I heard on the roof
The prancing and pawing of each little hoof.

As I drew in my head, and was turning around,
Down the chimney St. Nicholas came with a bound.

He was dressed all in fur, from his head to his foot,
And his clothes were all tarnished with ashes and soot;

A bundle of toys he had flung on his back,
And he looked like a peddler just opening his pack.

His eyes—how they twinkled! his dimples how merry!
His cheeks were like roses, his nose like a cherry!

His droll little mouth was drawn up like a bow,
And the beard of his chin was as white as the snow;

The stump of a pipe he held tight in his teeth,
And the smoke it encircled his head like a wreath;

He had a broad face and a little round belly,
That shook when he laughed, like a bowlful of jelly.

He was chubby and plump, a right jolly old elf,
And I laughed when I saw him, in spite of myself;

A wink of his eye and a twist of his head,
Soon gave me to know I had nothing to dread;

He spoke not a word, but went straight to his work,
And filled all the stockings; then turned with a jerk,

And laying his finger aside of his nose,
And giving a nod, up the chimney he rose;

He sprang to his sleigh, to his team gave a whistle,
And away they all flew like the down on a thistle.

But I heard him exclaim, ere he drove out of sight,"
Happy Christmas to all, and to all a good-night."

Day 114

1. Read this poem.
2. Why does the old man say it's okay for him to stand on his head? (Answers)

Father William by Lewis Carroll
"You are old, Father William," the young man said,
"And your hair has become very white;
And yet you incessantly stand on your head—
Do you think, at your age, it is right?"

"In my youth," Father William replied to his son,
"I feared it might injure the brain;
But now that I'm perfectly sure I have none,
Why, I do it again and again."

"You are old," said the youth, "as I mentioned before,
And have grown most uncommonly fat;
Yet you turned a back-somersault in at the door—
Pray, what is the reason of that?"

"In my youth," said the sage, as he shook his gray locks,
"I kept all my limbs very supple
By the use of this ointment—one shilling the box—
Allow me to sell you a couple."

"You are old," said the youth, "and your jaws are too weak
For anything tougher than suet;
Yet you finished the goose, with the bones and the beak:
Pray, how did you manage to do it?"

"In my youth," said his father, "I took to the law,
And argued each case with my wife;
And the muscular strength which it gave to my jaw
Has lasted the rest of my life."

"You are old," said the youth; "one would hardly suppose
That your eye was as steady as ever;
Yet you balanced an eel on the end of your nose—
What made you so awfully clever?"

"I have answered three questions, and that is enough,
"Said his father, "don't give yourself airs!
Do you think I can listen all day to such stuff?
Be off, or I'll kick you down-stairs!"

Day 115

1. Read the poem.
2. Does the nightingale eat the worm? (Answers)

The Nightingale by William Cowper
A nightingale, that all day long
Had cheered the village with his song,
Nor yet at eve his note suspended,
Nor yet when eventide was ended,

Began to feel, as well he might,
The keen demands of appetite;
When, looking eagerly around,
He spied far off, upon the ground,

A something shining in the dark,
And knew the glow-worm by his spark;
So, stooping down from hawthorn top,
He thought to put him in his crop.

The worm, aware of his intent,
Harangued him thus, right eloquent:
"Did you admire my lamp," quoth he,
"As much as I your minstrelsy,

You would abhor to do me wrong,
As much as I to spoil your song;
For 'twas the self-same power divine,
Taught you to sing and me to shine;

That you with music, I with light,
Might beautify and cheer the night.
"The songster heard his short oration,
And warbling out his approbation,

Released him, as my story tells,
And found a supper somewhere else.

Day 116

1. You are going to start reading a new book today, *Five Little Peppers and How They Grew.*
2. Pepper is the last name of the family. The five little Peppers are the five children of the Pepper family. They call their mother Mamsie. Their father has died. They are very poor. Their mother works very hard to provide for them and has taught her children to be hard workers and to value being together. When the mother says that she is rich, it's because she has her children with her.
3. Vocabulary:
   - **eminent** – prominent, noteworthy, important
   - **incredulously** – with unbelief
   - **anxiety** – worry
   - **oblige** – required
   - **disdainfully** – with contempt, scornfully, to look down on others
4. Today read the first chapter of the book.
5. What are the names of the five little Peppers? (Answers)
6. How old is Ben? (Answers)

Chapter 1 A Home View

The little old kitchen had quieted down from the bustle and confusion of mid-day; and now, with its afternoon manners on, presented a holiday aspect, that as the principal room in the brown house, it was eminently proper it should have. It was just on the edge of the twilight; and the little Peppers, all except Ben, the oldest of the flock, were enjoying a "breathing spell," as their mother called it, which meant some quiet work suitable for the hour. All the "breathing spell" they could remember however, poor things; for times were always hard with them nowadays; and since the father died, when Phronsie was a baby, Mrs. Pepper had had hard work to scrape together money enough to put bread into her children's mouths, and to pay the rent of the little brown house.

But she had met life too bravely to be beaten down now. So with a stout heart and a cheery face, she had worked away day after day at making coats, and tailoring and mending of all descriptions; and she had seen with pride that couldn't be concealed, her noisy, happy brood growing up around her, and filling her heart with comfort, and making the little brown house fairly ring with jollity and fun.

"Poor things!" she would say to herself, "they haven't had any bringing up; they've just scrambled up!" And then she would set her lips together tightly, and fly at her work faster than ever. "I must get schooling for them some way, but I don't see how!"

Once or twice she had thought, "Now the time is coming!" but it never did: for winter shut in very cold, and it took so much more to feed and warm them, that the money went faster than ever. And then, when the way seemed clear again, the store changed hands, so that for a long time she failed to get her usual supply of sacks and coats to make; and that made sad havoc in the quarters and half-dollars laid up as her nest egg. But---- "Well, it'll come some time," she would say to herself; "because it must!" And so at it again she would fly, brisker than ever.

"To help mother," was the great ambition of all the children, older and younger; but in Polly's and Ben's souls, the desire grew so overwhelmingly great as to absorb all lesser thoughts. Many and vast were their secret plans, by which they were to astonish her at some future day, which they would only confide--as they did everything else--to one another. For this brother and sister were everything to each other, and stood loyally together through "thick and thin."

Polly was ten, and Ben one year older; and the younger three of the "Five Little Peppers," as they were always called, looked up to them with the intensest admiration and love. What they failed to do, couldn't very well be done by anyone!

"Oh dear!" exclaimed Polly as she sat over in the corner by the window helping her mother pull out basting threads from a coat she had just finished, and giving an impatient twitch to the sleeve, "I do wish we could ever have any light--just as much as we want!"

"You don't need any light to see these threads," said Mrs. Pepper, winding up hers carefully, as she spoke, on an old spool. "Take care, Polly, you broke that; thread's dear now."

"I couldn't help it," said Polly, vexedly; "it snapped; everything's dear now, it seems to me! I wish we could have--oh! ever an' ever so many candles; as many as we wanted. I'd light 'em all, so there! and have it light here one night, anyway!"

"Yes, and go dark all the rest of the year, like as anyway," observed Mrs. Pepper, stopping to untie a knot. "Folks who do so never have any candles," she added, sententiously.

"How many'd you have, Polly?" asked Joel, curiously, laying down his hammer, and regarding her with the utmost anxiety.

"Oh, two hundred!" said Polly, decidedly. "I'd have two hundred, all in a row!"

"Two hundred candles!" echoed Joel, in amazement. "My whockety! what a lot!"

"Don't say such dreadful words, Joel," put in Polly, nervously, stopping to pick up her spool of basting thread that was racing away all by itself; "tisn't nice."

"Tisn't worse than to wish you'd got things you haven't," retorted Joel. "I don't believe you'd light 'em all at once," he added, incredulously.

"Yes, I would too!" replied Polly, recklessly; "two hundred of 'em, if I had a chance; all at once, so there, Joey Pepper!"

"Oh," said little Davie, drawing a long sigh. "Why, 'twould be just like heaven, Polly! but wouldn't it cost money, though!"

"I don't care," said Polly, giving a flounce in her chair, which snapped another thread; "oh dear me! I didn't mean to, mammy; well, I wouldn't care how much money it cost, we'd have as much light as we wanted, for once; so!"

"Mercy!" said Mrs. Pepper, "you'd have the house afire! Two hundred candles! who ever heard of such a thing!"

"Would they burn?" asked Phronsie, anxiously, getting up from the floor where she was crouching with David, overseeing Joel nail on the cover of an old box; and going to Polly's side she awaited her answer patiently.

"Burn?" said Polly. "There, that's done now, mamsie dear!" And she put the coat, with a last little pat, into her mother's lap. "I guess they would, Phronsie pet." And Polly caught up the little girl, and spun round and round the old kitchen till they were both glad to stop.

"Then," said Phronsie, as Polly put her down, and stood breathless after her last glorious spin, "I do so wish we might, Polly; oh, just this very one minute!"

And Phronsie clasped her fat little hands in rapture at the thought.

"Well," said Polly, giving a look up at the old clock in the corner; "deary me! it's half-past five; and most time for Ben to come home!"

Away she flew to get supper. So for the next few moments nothing was heard but the pulling out of the old table into the middle of the floor, the laying the cloth, and all the other bustle attendant upon the being ready for Ben. Polly went skipping around, cutting the bread, and bringing dishes; only stopping long enough to fling some scraps of reassuring nonsense to the two boys, who were thoroughly dismayed at being obliged to remove their traps into a corner.

Phronsie still stood just where Polly left her. Two hundred candles! oh! what could it mean! She gazed up to the old beams overhead, and around the dingy walls, and to the old black stove, with the fire nearly out, and then over everything the kitchen contained, trying to think how it would seem. To have it bright and winsome and warm! to suit Polly--"oh!" she screamed.

"Goodness!" said Polly, taking her head out of the old cupboard in the corner, "how you scared me, Phronsie!"

"Would they ever go out?" asked the child gravely, still standing where Polly left her.

"What?" asked Polly, stopping with a dish of cold potatoes in her hand. "What, Phronsie?"

"Why, the candles," said the child, "the ever-an'-ever so many pretty lights!"

"Oh, my senses!" cried Polly, with a little laugh, "haven't you forgotten that! Yes--no, that is, Phronsie, if we could have 'em at all, we wouldn't ever let 'em go out!"

"Not once?" asked Phronsie, coming up to Polly with a little skip, and nearly upsetting her, potatoes and all--"not once, Polly, truly?"

"No, not forever-an'-ever," said Polly; "take care, Phronsie! there goes a potato; no, we'd keep 'em always!"

"No, you don't want to," said Mrs. Pepper, coming out of the bedroom in time to catch the last words; "they won't be good to-morrow; better have them to-night, Polly."

"Ma'am!" said Polly, setting down her potato-dish on the table, and staring at her mother with all her might--"have what, mother?"

"Why, the potatoes, to be sure," replied Mrs. Pepper; "didn't you say you better keep them, child?"

"Twasn't potatoes--at all," said Polly, with a little gasp; "twas--dear me! here's Ben!" For the door opened, and Phronsie, with a scream of delight, bounded into Ben's arms.

"It's just jolly," said Ben, coming in, his chubby face all aglow, and his big blue eyes shining so honest and true; "it's just jolly to get home! supper ready, Polly?"

"Yes," said Polly; "that is--all but--" and she dashed off for Phronsie's eating apron.

"Sometime," said Phronsie, with her mouth half full, when the meal was nearly over, "we're going to be awful rich; we are, Ben, truly!"

"No?" said Ben, affecting the most hearty astonishment; "you don't say so, Chick!"

"Yes," said Phronsie, shaking her yellow head very wisely at him, and diving down into her cup of very weak milk and water to see if Polly had put any sugar in by mistake--a proceeding always expectantly observed. "Yes, we are really, Bensie, very dreadful rich!"

"I wish we could be rich now, then," said Ben, taking another generous slice of the brown bread; "in time for mamsie's birthday," and he cast a sorrowful glance at Polly.

"I know," said Polly; "oh dear! if we only could celebrate it!"

"I don't want any other celebration," said Mrs. Pepper, beaming on them so that a little flash of sunshine seemed to hop right down on the table, "than to look round on you all; I'm rich now, and that's a fact!"

"Mamsie don't mind her five bothers," cried Polly, jumping up and running to hug her mother; thereby producing a like desire in all the others, who immediately left their seats and followed her example.

"Mother's rich enough," ejaculated Mrs. Pepper; her bright, black eyes glistening with delight, as the noisy troop filed back to their bread and potatoes; "if we can only keep together, dears, and grow up good, so that the little brown house won't be ashamed of us, that's all I ask."

"Well," said Polly, in a burst of confidence to Ben, after the table had been pushed back against the wall, the dishes nicely washed, wiped, and set up neatly in the cupboard, and all traces of the meal cleared away; "I don't care; let's try and get a celebration, somehow, for mamsie!"

"How are you going to do it?" asked Ben, who was of a decidedly practical turn of mind, and thus couldn't always follow Polly in her flights of imagination.

"I don't know," said Polly; "but we must some way."

"That's no good," said Ben, disdainfully; then seeing Polly's face, he added kindly: "let's think, though; and perhaps there'll be some way."

"Oh, I know," cried Polly, in delight; "I know the very thing, Ben! let's make her a cake; a big one, you know, and"-- "She'll see you bake it," said Ben; "or else she'll smell it, and that'd be just as bad."

"No, she won't either," replied Polly. "Don't you know she's going to help Mrs. Henderson to-morrow; so there!"

"So she is," said Ben; "good for you, Polly, you always think of everything!"

"And then," said Polly, with a comfortable little feeling at her heart at Ben's praise, "why, we can have it all out of the way splendidly, you know, when she comes home--and besides, Grandma Bascom'll tell me how. You know we've only got brown flour, Ben; I mean to go right over and ask her now."

"Oh, no, you mustn't," cried Ben, catching hold of her arm as she was preparing to fly off. "Mammy'll find it out; better wait till tomorrow; and besides Polly--" And Ben stopped, unwilling to dampen this propitious beginning. "The stove'll act like everything, to-morrow! I know 'twill; then what'll you do!"

"It shan't!" said Polly, running up to look it in the face; "if it does, I'll shake it; the mean old thing!"

The idea of Polly's shaking the lumbering old black affair, sent Ben into such a peal of laughter that it brought all the other children running to the spot; and nothing would do but they must one and all, be told the reason. So Polly and Ben took them into confidence, which so elated them that half an hour after, when long past her bedtime, Phronsie declared, "I'm not going to bed! I want to sit up like Polly!"

"Don't tease her," whispered Polly to Ben, who thought she ought to go; so she sat straight up on her little stool, winking like everything to keep awake.

At last, as Polly was in the midst of one of her liveliest sallies, over tumbled Phronsie, a sleepy little heap, upon the floor.

"I want--to go--to bed!" she said; "take me--Polly!"

"I thought so," laughed Polly, and bundled her off into the bedroom.

Day 117

1. Vocabulary:
   - **ample** – full, enough, plentiful
   - **deliberation** – carefully thinking over a decision
   - **dismally** – with gloom and dreariness, pitifully
2. The grandmother in this chapter sounds funny when she talks, so the words she says are spelled funny. "Maybe 'tis there." That is maybe it is there. The apostrophe (') lets you know something is missing. Here's another. "So's to have 'em safe" means "so is to have them safe." The word "ain't" means isn't, but it's not a proper word.
3. Read the first half of chapter 2.
4. Is Grandma Bascom their grandmother? Who is she? (Answers)
5. What do the children go to get from grandmother? (Answers)

Chapter 2 Making Happiness for Mamsie

And so, the minute her mother had departed for the minister's house next morning, and Ben had gone to his day's work, chopping wood for Deacon Blodgett, Polly assembled her force around the old stove, and proceeded to business. She and the children had been up betimes that morning to get through with the work; and now, as they glanced around with a look of pride on the neatly swept floor, the dishes all done, and everything in order, the moment their mother's back was turned they began to implore Polly to hurry and begin.

"It's most 'leven o'clock," said Joel, who, having no work to do outside, that day, was prancing around, wild to help along the festivities; "it's most 'leven o'clock, Polly Pepper! you won't have it done."

"Oh, no; 'tisn't either, Joe;" said Polly, with a very flushed face, and her arms full of kindlings, glancing up at the old clock as she spoke; "tisn't but quarter of nine; there, take care, Phronsie! you can't lift off the cover; do help her, Davie."

"No; let me!" cried Joel, springing forward; "it's my turn; Dave got the shingles; it's my turn, Polly."

"So 'tis," said Polly; "I forgot; there," as she flung in the wood, and poked it all up in a nice little heap coaxingly. "It can't help but burn; what a cake we'll have for mamsie!"

"It'll be so big," cried Phronsie, hopping around on one set of toes, "that mamsie won't know what to do, will she, Polly?"

"No, I don't believe she will," said Polly, gayly, stuffing in more wood; "Oh, dear! there goes Ben's putty; it's all come out!"

"So it has," said Joel, going around back of the stove to explore; and then he added cheerfully, "it's bigger'n ever; oh! it's an awful big hole, Polly!"

"Now, whatever shall we do!" said Polly, in great distress; "that hateful old crack! and Ben's clear off to Deacon Blodgett's!"

"I'll run and get him," cried Joel, briskly; "I'll bring him right home in ten minutes."

"Oh, no, you must not, Joe," cried Polly in alarm; "it wouldn't ever be right to take him off from his work; mamsie wouldn't like it."

"What will you do, then?" asked Joel, pausing on his way to the door.

"I'm sure I don't know," said Polly, getting down on her knees to examine the crack; "I shall have to stuff it with paper, I s'pose."

"'Twon't stay in," said Joel, scornfully; "don't you know you stuffed it before, last week?"

"I know," said Polly, with a small sigh; and sitting down on the floor, she remained quite still for a minute, with her two black hands thrust out straight before her.

"Can't you fix it?" asked Davie, soberly, coming up; "then we can't have the cake."

"Dear me!" exclaimed Polly, springing up quickly; "don't be afraid; we're going to have that cake! There, you ugly old thing, you!" (this to the stove) "see what you've done!" as two big tears flew out of Phronsie's brown eyes at the direful prospect; and the sorrowful faces of the two boys looked up into Polly's own, for comfort. "I can fix it, I most know; do get some paper, Joe, as quick as you can."

"Don't know where there is any," said Joel, rummaging around; "it's all tore up; 'xcept the almanac; can't I take that?"

"Oh dear, no!" cried Polly; "put it right back, Joe; I guess there's some in the wood-shed."

"There isn't either," said little Davie, quickly; "Joel and I took it to make kites with."

"Oh dear," groaned Polly; "I don't know what we shall do; unless," as a bright thought struck her, "you let me have the kites, boys."

"Can't," said Joel; "they're all flew away; and torn up."

"Well, now, children," said Polly, turning round impressively upon them, the effect of which was heightened by the extremely crocky appearance she had gained in her explorations, "we must have some paper, or something to stop up that old hole with--some way, there!"

"I know," said little Davie, "where we'll get it; it's upstairs;" and without another word he flew out of the room, and in another minute he put into Polly's hand an old leather boottop, one of his most treasured possessions. "You can chip it," he said, "real fine, and then 'twill go in."

"So we can," said Polly; "and you're a real good boy, Davie, to give it; that's a splendid present to help celebrate for mamsie!"

"I'd a-given a boot-top," said Joel, looking grimly at the precious bit of leather which Polly was rapidly stripping into little bits, "if I'd a-had it; I don't have anything!"

"I know you would, Joey," said Polly, kindly; "there now, you'll stay, I guess!" as with the united efforts of the two boys, cheered on by Phronsie's enthusiastic little crow of delight, the leather was crowded into place, and the fire began to burn.

"Now, boys," said Polly, getting up, and drawing a long breath, "I'm going over to Grandma Bascom's to get her to tell me how to make the cake; and you must stay and keep house."

"I'm going to nail," said Joel; "I've got lots to do."

"All right," said Polly, tying on her hood; "Phronsie'll love to watch you; I won't be gone long," and she was off.

"Grandma Bascom," wasn't really the children's grandmother; only everybody in the village called her so by courtesy. Her cottage was over across the lane, and just a bit around the corner; and Polly flew along and up to the door, fully knowing that now she would be helped out of her difficulty. She didn't stop to knock, as the old lady was so deaf she knew she wouldn't hear her, but opened the door and walked in. Grandma was sweeping up the floor, already as neat as a pin; when she saw Polly coming, she stopped, and leaned on her broom.

"How's your ma?" she asked, when Polly had said "good morning," and then hesitated.

"Oh, mammy's pretty well," shouted Polly into the old lady's ear; "and to-morrow's her birthday!"

"Tomorrow'll be a bad day!" said grandma. "Oh, don't never say that. You mustn't borrow trouble, child."

"I didn't," said Polly; "I mean--it's her birthday, grandma!" this last so loud that grandma's cap-border vibrated perceptibly.

"The land's sakes 'tis!" cried Mrs. Bascom, delightedly; "you don't say so!"

"Yes," said Polly, skipping around the old lady, and giving her a small hug; "and we're going to give her a surprise."

"What is the matter with her eyes?" asked grandma, sharply, turning around and facing her; "she's been a-sewin' too stiddy, hain't she?"

"A surprise!" shouted Polly, standing upon tiptoe, to bring her mouth on a level with the old lady's ear; "a cake, grandma, a big one!"

"A cake!" exclaimed grandma, dropping the broom to settle her cap, which Polly in her extreme endeavors to carry on the conversation, had knocked slightly awry; "well, that'll be fine."

"Yes," said Polly, picking up the broom, and flinging off her hood at the same time; "and, oh! won't you please tell me how to make it, grandma!"

"To be sure; to be sure;" cried the old lady, delighted beyond measure to give advice; "I've got splendid receets; I'll go get 'em right off," and she ambled to the door of the pantry.

"And I'll finish sweeping up," said Polly, which grandma didn't hear; so she took up the broom, and sent it energetically, and merrily flying away to the tune of her own happy thoughts.

"Yes, they're right in here," said grandma, waddling back with an old tin teapot in her hand;-- "goodness, child! what a dust you've kicked up! that ain't the way to sweep." And she took the broom out of Polly's hand, who stood quite still in mortification.

"There," she said, drawing it mildly over the few bits she could scrape together, and gently coaxing them into a little heap; "that's the way; and then they don't go all over the room.

"I'm sorry," began poor Polly.

"'Tain't any matter," said Mrs. Bascom kindly, catching sight of Polly's discomfited face; "tain't a mite of matter; you'll sweep better next time; now let's go to the cake;" and putting the broom into the corner, she waddled back again to the table, followed by Polly, and proceeded to turn out the contents of the teapot, in search of just the right "receet."

But the right one didn't seem to appear; not even after the teapot was turned upside down and shaken by both grandma's and Polly's anxious hands. Every other "receet" seemed to tumble out gladly, and stare them in the face--little dingy rolls of yellow paper, with an ancient odor of spice still clinging to them; but all efforts to find this particular one failed utterly.

"Won't some other one do?" asked Polly, in the interval of fruitless searching, when grandma bewailed and lamented, and wondered, "where I could a put it!"

"No, no, child," answered the old lady; "now, where do you s'pose 'tis!" and she clapped both hands to her head, to see if she could possibly remember; "no, no, child," she repeated. "Why, they had it down to my niece Mirandy's weddin'--'twas just elegant! light as a feather; and 'twan't rich either," she added; "no eggs, nor"-- "Oh, I couldn't have eggs;" cried Polly, in amazement at the thought of such luxury; "and we've only brown flour, grandma, you know."

"Well, you can make it of brown," said Mrs. Bascom, kindly; "when the raisins is in 'twill look quite nice."

"Oh, we haven't any raisins," answered Polly.

"Haven't any raisins!" echoed grandma, looking at her over her spectacles; "what are you goin' to put in?"

"Oh--cinnamon," said Polly, briskly; "we've got plenty of that, and--it'll be good, I guess, grandma!" she finished, anxiously; "anyway, we must have a cake; there isn't any other way to celebrate mamsie's birthday."

"Well, now," said grandma, bustling around; "I shouldn't be surprised if you had real good luck, Polly. And your ma'll set ever so much by it; now, if we only could find that receet!" and returning to the charge she commenced to fumble among her bits of paper again; "I never shall forget how they eat on it; why, there wasn't a crumb left, Polly!"

"Oh, dear," said Polly, to whom "Mirandy's wedding cake" now became the height of her desires; "if you only can find it! can't I climb up and look on the pantry shelves?"

Day 118

1. Read the rest of chapter 2.
2. Why does Phronsie ask if she'll ever wear shoes again? (Answers)
3. Tell someone a summary of the chapter.

Chapter 2 continued

"Maybe 'tis there," said Mrs. Bascom, slowly; "you might try; sometimes I do put things away, so's to have 'em safe."

So Polly got an old wooden chair, according to direction, and then mounted up on it, with grandma below to direct, she handed down bowl after bowl, interspersed at the right intervals with cracked teacups and handleless pitchers. But at the end of these explorations, "Mirandy's wedding cake" was further off than ever.

"Tain't a mite o' use," at last said the old lady, sinking down in despair, while Polly perched on the top of the chair and looked at her; "I must a-give it away."

"Can't I have the next best one, then?" asked Polly, despairingly, feeling sure that "Mirandy's wedding cake" would have celebrated the day just right; "and I must hurry right home, please," she added, getting down from the chair, and tying on her hood; "or Phronsie won't know what to do."

So another "receet" was looked over, and selected; and with many charges, and bits of advice not to let the oven get too hot, etc., etc., Polly took the precious bit in her hand, and flew over home.

"Now, we've got to--" she began, bounding in merrily, with dancing eyes; but her delight had a sudden stop, as she brought up so suddenly at the sight within, that she couldn't utter another word. Phronsie was crouching, a miserable little heap of woe, in one corner of the mother's big calico-covered rocking-chair, and crying bitterly, while Joel hung over her in the utmost concern.

"What's the matter?" gasped Polly. Flinging the "receet" on the table, she rushed up to the old chair and was down on her knees before it, her arms around the little figure. Phronsie turned, and threw herself into Polly's protecting arms, who gathered her up, and sitting down in the depths of the chair, comforted her as only she could.

"What is it?" she asked of Joel, who was nervously begging Phronsie not to cry; "now, tell me all that's happened."

"I was a-nailing," began Joel; "oh dear! don't cry, Phronsie! do stop her, Polly."

"Go on," said Polly, hoarsely.

"I was a-nailing," began Joel, slowly; "and--and--Davie's gone to get the peppermint," he added, brightening up.

"Tell me, Joe," said Polly, "all that's been going on," and she looked sternly into his face; "or I'll get Davie to," as little Davie came running back, with a bottle of castor oil, which in his flurry he had mistaken for peppermint. This he presented with a flourish to Polly, who was too excited to see it.

"Oh, no!" cried Joel, in intense alarm; "Davie isn't going to! I'll tell, Polly; I will truly."

"Go on, then," said Polly; "tell at once;" (feeling as if somebody didn't tell pretty quick, she should tumble over.)

"Well," said Joel, gathering himself up with a fresh effort, "the old hammer was a-shaking and Phronsie stuck her foot in the way--and--I couldn't help it, Polly--no, I just couldn't, Polly."

Quick as a flash, Polly tore off the little old shoe, and well-worn stocking, and brought to light Phronsie's fat little foot. Tenderly taking hold of the white toes, the boys clustering around in the greatest anxiety, she worked them back and forth, and up and down. "Nothing's broken," she said at last, and drew a long breath.

"It's there," said Phronsie, through a rain of tears; "and it hurts, Polly;" and she began to wiggle the big toe, where around the nail was settling a small black spot.

"Poor little toe," began Polly, cuddling up the suffering foot. Just then, a small and peculiar noise struck her ear; and looking up she saw Joel, with a very distorted face, making violent efforts to keep from bursting out into a loud cry. All his attempts, however, failed; and he flung himself into Polly's lap in a perfect torrent of tears. "I didn't--mean to--Polly," he cried; "'twas the--ugly, old hammer! oh dear!"

"There, there, Joey, dear," said Polly, gathering him up in the other corner of the old chair, close to her side; "don't feel bad; I know you didn't mean to," and she dropped a kiss on his stubby black hair.

When Phronsie saw that anybody else could cry, she stopped immediately, and leaning over Polly, put one little fat hand on Joel's neck. "Don't cry," she said; "does your toe ache?"

At this, Joel screamed louder than ever; and Polly was at her wit's end to know what to do; for the boy's heart was almost broken. That he should have hurt Phronsie! the baby, the pet of the whole house, upon whom all their hearts centered--it was too much. So for the next few moments, Polly had all she could do by way of comforting and consoling him. Just as she had succeeded, the door opened, and Grandma Bascom walked in.

"Settin' down?" said she; "I hope your cake ain't in, Polly," looking anxiously at the stove, "for I've found it;" and she waved a small piece of paper triumphantly towards the rocking-chair as she spoke.

"Do tell her," said Polly to little David, "what's happened; for I can't get up."

So little Davie went up to the old lady, and standing on tiptoe, screamed into her ear all the particulars he could think of, concerning the accident that had just happened.

"Hey?" said grandma, in a perfect bewilderment; "what's he a-sayin', Polly--I can't make it out."

"You'll have to go all over it again, David," said Polly, despairingly; "she didn't hear one word, I don't believe."

So David tried again; this time with better success. And then he got down from his tiptoes, and escorted grandma to Phronsie, in flushed triumph.

"Land alive!" said the old lady, sitting down in the chair which he brought her; "you got pounded, did you?" looking at Phronsie, as she took the little foot in her ample hand.

"Yes'm," said Polly, quickly; "twasn't any one's fault; what'll we do for it, grandma?"

"Wormwood," said the old lady, adjusting her spectacles in extreme deliberation, and then examining the little black and blue spot, which was spreading rapidly, "is the very best thing; and I've got some to home--you run right over," she said, turning round on David, quickly, "an' get it; it's a-hang-in' by the chimbley."

"Let me; let me!" cried Joel, springing out of the old chair, so suddenly that grandma's spectacles nearly dropped off in fright; "oh! I want to do it for Phronsie!"

"Yes, let Joel, please," put in Polly; "he'll find it, grandma." So Joel departed with great speed; and presently returned, with a bunch of dry herbs, which dangled comfortingly by his side, as he came in.

"Now I'll fix it," said Mrs. Bascom, getting up and taking off her shawl; "there's a few raisins for you, Polly; I don't want 'em, and they'll make your cake go better," and she placed a little parcel on the table as she spoke. "Yes, I'll put it to steep; an' after it's put on real strong, and tied up in an old cloth, Phronsie won't know as she's got any toes!" and grandma broke up a generous supply of the herb, and put it into an old tin cup, which she covered up with a saucer, and placed on the stove.

"Oh!" said Polly; "I can't thank you! for the raisins and all--you're so good!"

"They're awful hard," said Joel, investigating into the bundle with Davie, which, however, luckily the old lady didn't hear.

"There, don't try," she said cheerily; "an' I found cousin Mirandy's weddin' cake receet, for--"

"Did you?" cried Polly; "oh! I'm so glad!" feeling as if that were comfort enough for a good deal.

"Yes, 'twas in my Bible," said Mrs. Bascom; "I remember now; I put it there to be ready to give John's folks when they come in; they wanted it; so you'll go all straight now; and I must get home, for I left some meat a-boilin'." So grandma put on her shawl, and waddled off, leaving a great deal of comfort behind her.

"Now, says I," said Polly to Phronsie, when the little foot was snugly tied up in the wet wormwood, "you've got to have one of mamsie's old slippers."

"Oh, ho," laughed Phronsie; "won't that be funny, Polly!"

"I should think it would," laughed Polly, back again, pulling on the big cloth slipper, which Joel produced from the bedroom, the two boys joining uproariously, as the old black thing flapped dismally up and down, and showed strong symptoms of flying off. "We shall have to tie it on."

"It looks like a pudding bag," said Joel, as Polly tied it securely through the middle with a bit of twine; "an old black pudding bag!" he finished.

"Old black pudding bag!" echoed Phronsie, with a merry little crow; and then all of a sudden she grew very sober, and looked intently at the foot thrust out straight before her, as she still sat in the chair.

"What is it, Phronsie?" asked Polly, who was bustling around, making preparations for the cake-making.

"Can I ever wear my new shoes again?" asked the child, gravely, looking dismally at the black bundle before her.

"Oh, yes; my goodness, yes!" cried Polly; "as quick again as ever; you'll be around again as smart as a cricket in a week --see if you aren't!"

"Will it go on?" asked Phronsie, still looking incredulously at the bundle, "and button up?"

"Yes, indeed!" cried Polly, again; "button into every one of the little holes, Phronsie Pepper; just as elegant as ever!"

"Oh!" said Phronsie; and then she gave a sigh of relief, and thought no more of it, because Polly had said that all would be right.

Day 119

1. Read chapter 3.
2. Tell someone about the chapter.

Chapter 3 Mamsie's Birthday

"Run down and get the cinnamon, will you, Joey?" said Polly; "it's in the 'Provision Room."

The "Provision Room" was a little shed that was tacked on to the main house, and reached by a short flight of rickety steps; so called, because as Polly said, "'twas a good place to keep provisions in, even if we haven't any; and besides," she always finished, "it sounds nice!"

"Come on, Dave! then we'll get something to eat!"

So the cinnamon was handed up, and then Joel flew back to Davie.

And now, Polly's cake was done, and ready for the oven. With many admiring glances from herself, and Phronsie, who with Seraphina, an extremely old but greatly revered doll, tightly hugged in her arms was watching everything with the biggest of eyes from the depths of the old chair, it was placed in the oven, the door shut to with a happy little bang, then Polly gathered Phronsie up in her arms, and sat down in the chair to have a good time with her and to watch the process of cooking.

There was a bumping noise that came from the "Provision Room" that sounded ominous, and then a smothered sound of words, followed by a scuffling over the old floor.

"Boys!" called Polly. No answer; everything was just as still as a mouse. "Joel and David!" called Polly again, in her loudest tones.

"Yes," came up the crooked stairs, in Davie's voice.

"Come up here, right away!" went back again from Polly. So up the stairs trudged the two boys, and presented themselves rather sheepishly before the big chair.

"What was that noise?" she asked; "what have you been doing?"

"Twasn't anything but the pail," answered Joel, not looking at her.

"We had something to eat," said Davie, by way of explanation; "you always let us."

"I know," said Polly; "that's right, you can have as much bread as you want to; but what you been doing with the pail?"

"Nothing," said Joel; "'twouldn't hangup, that's all."

"And you've been bumping it," said Polly; "oh! Joel, how could you! You might have broken it; then what would mamsie say?"

"I didn't," said Joel, stoutly, with his hands in his pockets, "bump it worse'n Davie, so there!"

"Why, Davie," said Polly, turning to him sorrowfully, "I shouldn't have thought you would!"

"Well, I'm tired of hanging it up," said little Davie, vehemently; "and I said I wasn't a-goin' to; Joel always makes me; I've done it for two million times, I guess!"

"Oh, dear," said Polly, sinking back into the chair, "I don't know what I ever shall do; here's Phronsie hurt; and we want to celebrate to-morrow; and you two boys are bumping and banging out the bread pail, and"-- "Oh! we won't!" cried both of the children, perfectly overwhelmed with remorse; "we'll hang it right up."

"I'll hang it," said Davie, clattering off down the stairs with a will.

"No, I will!" shouted Joel, going after him at double pace; and presently both came up with shining faces, and reported it nicely done.

"And now," said Polly, after they had all sat around the stove another half-hour, watching and sniffing expectantly, "the cake's done!--dear me! it's turning black!"

And quickly as possible Polly twitched it out with energy, and set it on the table.

Oh, dear; of all things in the world! The beautiful cake over which so many hopes had been formed, that was to have given so much happiness on the morrow to the dear mother, presented a forlorn appearance as it stood there in anything but holiday attire. It was quite black on the top, in the center of which was a depressing little dump, as if to say, "My feelings wouldn't allow me to rise to the occasion."

"Now," said Polly, turning away with a little fling, and looking at the stove, "I hope you're satisfied, you old thing; you've spoiled our mamsie's birthday!" and without a bit of warning, she sat right down in the middle of the floor and began to cry as hard as she could.

"Well, I never!" said a cheery voice, that made the children skip.

"It's Mrs. Beebe; oh, it's Mrs. Beebe!" cried Davie; "see, Polly."

Polly scrambled up to her feet, ashamed to be caught thus, and whisked away the tears; the others explaining to their new visitor the sad disappointment that had befallen them; and she was soon oh-ing, and ah-ing enough to suit even their distressed little souls.

"You poor creeters, you!" she exclaimed at last, for about the fiftieth time. "Here, Polly, here's some posies for you, and"-- "Oh, thank you!" cried Polly, with a radiant face, "why, Mrs. Beebe, we can put them in here, can't we? the very thing!"

And she set the little knot of flowers in the hollow of the cake, and there they stood and nodded away to the delighted children, like brave little comforters, as they were.

"The very thing!" echoed Mrs. Beebe, tickled to death to see their delight; "it looks beautiful, I declare! and now, I must run right along, or pa'll be worrying;" and so the good woman trotted out to her waiting husband, who was impatient to be off. Mr. Beebe kept a little shoe shop in town; and always being of the impression if he left it for ten minutes that crowds of customers would visit it. He was the most restless of companions on any pleasure excursion.

"And Phronsie's got hurt," said Mrs. Beebe, telling him the news, as he finished tucking her up, and started the old horse.

"Ho? you don't say so!" he cried; "whoa!"

"Dear me!" said Mrs. Beebe; "how you scat me, pal what's the matter?"

"What?--the little girl that bought the shoes?" asked her husband.

"Yes," replied his wife, "she's hurt her foot."

"Now," said the old gentleman; "that's too bad," and he began to feel in all his pockets industriously; "there, can you get out again, and take her that?" and he laid a small piece of peppermint candy, thick and white, in his wife's lap.

"Oh, yes," cried Mrs. Beebe, good-naturedly, beginning to clamber over the wheel.

So the candy was handed in to Phronsie, who insisted that Polly should hold her up to the window to thank Mr. Beebe. So amid nods, and shakings of hands, the Beebes drove off, and quiet settled down over the little brown house again.

"Now, children," said Polly, after Phronsie had made them take a bite of her candy all around, "let's get the cake put away safe, for mamsie may come home early."

"Where'll you put it?" asked Joel, wishing the world was all peppermint candy.

"Oh--in the cupboard," said Polly, taking it up; "there, Joe, you can climb up, and put it clear back in the corner, oh! wait; I must take the posies off, and keep them fresh in water;" so the cake was finally deposited in a place of safety, followed by the eyes of all the children.

"Now," said Polly, as they shut the door tight, "don't you go to looking at the cupboard, Joey, or mammy'll guess something."

"Can't I just open it a little crack, and take one smell when she isn't looking?" asked Joel; "I should think you might, Polly; just one."

"No," said Polly, firmly; "not one, Joe; she'll guess if you do." But Mrs. Pepper was so utterly engrossed with her baby when she came home and heard the account of the accident, that she wouldn't have guessed if there'd been a dozen cakes in the cupboard. Joel was consoled, as his mother assured him in a satisfactory way that she never should think of blaming him; and Phronsie was comforted and coddled to her heart's content. And so the evening passed rapidly and happily away; Ben smuggling Phronsie off into a corner, where she told him all the doings of the day-- the disappointment of the cake, and how it was finally crowned with flowers; all of which Phronsie, with no small pride in being the narrator, related gravely to her absorbed listener. "And don't you think, Bensie," she said, clasping her little hand in a convincing way over his two bigger, stronger ones, "that Polly's stove was very naughty to make poor Polly cry?"

"Yes, I do," said Ben, and he shut his lips tightly together.

To have Polly cry, hurt him more than he cared to have Phronsie see.

"What are you staring at, Joe?" asked Polly, a few minutes later, as her eyes fell upon Joel, who sat with his back to the cupboard, persistently gazing at the opposite wall.

"Why, you told me yourself not to look at the cupboard," said Joel, in the loudest of stage whispers.

"Dear me; that'll make mammy suspect worse'n anything else if you look like that," said Polly.

"What did you say about the cupboard?" asked Mrs. Pepper, who caught Joe's last word.

"We can't tell," said Phronsie, shaking her head at her mother; "cause there's a ca"-- "Ugh!" and Polly clapped her hand on the child's mouth; "don't you want Ben to tell us a story?"

"Oh, yes!" cried little Phronsie, in which all the others joined with a whoop of delight; so a most wonderful story, drawn up in Ben's best style, followed till bedtime.

The first thing Polly did in the morning, was to run to the old cupboard, followed by all the others, to see if the cake was safe; and then it had to be drawn out, and dressed anew with the flowers, for they had decided to have it on the breakfast table.

"It looks better," whispered Polly to Ben, "than it did yesterday; and aren't the flowers pretty?"

"It looks good enough to eat, anyway," said Ben, smacking his lips.

"Well, we tried," said Polly, stilling a sigh; "now, boys, call mamsie; everything's ready."

Oh! how surprised their mother appeared when she was ushered out to the feast, and the full glory of the table burst upon her. Her delight in the cake was fully enough to satisfy the most exacting mind. She admired and admired it on every side, protesting that she shouldn't have supposed Polly could possibly have baked it as good in the old stove; and then she cut it, and gave a piece to every child, with a little posy on top. Wasn't it good, though! for like many other things, the cake proved better on trial than it looked, and so turned out to be really quite a good surprise all around.

"Why can't I ever have a birthday?" asked Joel, finishing the last crumb of his piece; "I should think I might," he added, reflectively.

"Why, you have, Joe," said Ben; "eight of 'em."

"What a story!" ejaculated Joel; "when did I have 'em? I never had a cake; did I, Polly?"

"Not a cake-birthday, Joel," said his mother; "you haven't got to that yet."

"When's it coming?" asked Joel, who was decidedly of a matter-of-fact turn of mind.

"I don't know," said Mrs. Pepper, laughing; "but there's plenty of time ahead."

Day 120

1. Read the first part of chapter 4.
2. "When our ship comes in" is an expression that means when we are rich.
3. What are the children daydreaming about in the beginning of the chapter? (Answers)
4. How did Phronsie get all wet? (Answers)

Vocabulary

1. Match the words from your book with their definitions. Write the matching words and definitions on a separate piece of paper. (Answers)

1.	ample	A.	with gloom and dreariness, pitifully
2.	anxiety	B.	prominent, noteworthy, important
3.	deliberation	C.	with unbelief
4.	disdainfully	D.	required
5.	dismally	E.	carefully thinking over a decision
6.	eminent	F.	full, enough, plentiful
7.	incredulously	G.	worry
8.	oblige	H.	with contempt, to look down on others or something

Chapter 4 Trouble for the Little Brown House

"Oh, I do wish," said Joel, a few mornings after, pushing back his chair and looking discontentedly at his bowl of mush and molasses, "that we could ever have something new besides this everlasting old breakfast! Why can't we, mammy?"

"Better be glad you've got that, Joe," said Mrs. Pepper, taking another cold potato, and sprinkling on a little salt; "folks shouldn't complain so long as they've anything to eat."

"But I'm so tired of it--same old thing!" growled Joel; "seems as if I she'd turn into a meal-bag or a molasses jug!"

"Well, hand it over, then," proposed Ben, who was unusually hungry, and had a hard day's work before him.

"No," said Joel, alarmed at the prospect, and putting in an enormous mouthful; "it's better than nothing."

"Oh, dear," said little Phronsie, catching Joel's tone, "it isn't nice; no, it isn't." And she put down her spoon so suddenly that the molasses spun off in a big drop, that trailed off the corner of the table, and made Polly jump up and run for the floor-cloth.

"Oh, Phronsie," she said, reprovingly; "you ought not to. Never mind, pet," as she caught sight of two big tears trying to make a path in the little molasses-streaked face, "Polly'll wipe it up."

"Shan't we ever have anything else to eat, Polly?" asked the child, gravely, getting down from her high chair to watch the operation of cleaning the floor.

"Oh, yes," said Polly, cheerfully, "lots and lots--when our ship comes in."

"What'll they be?" asked Phronsie, in the greatest delight, prepared for anything.

"Oh, I don't know," said Polly; "ice cream for one thing, Phronsie, and maybe, little cakes."

"With pink on top?" interrupted Phronsie, getting down by Polly's side.

"Oh, yes," said Polly, warming with her subject; "ever and ever so much pink, Phronsie Pepper; more than you could eat!"

Phronsie just clasped her hands and sighed. More than she could eat was beyond her!

"Ho!" said Joel, who caught the imaginary bill of fare, "that's nothing, Polly. I'd speak for a plum-puddin'."

"Like the one mother made us for Thanksgiving?" asked Polly, getting up and waiting a minute, cloth in hand, for the answer.

"Yes, sir," said Joel, shutting one eye and looking up at the ceiling, musingly, while he smacked his lips in remembrance; "wasn't that prime, though!"

"Yes," said Polly, thoughtfully; "would you have 'em all like that, Joe?"

"Every one," replied Joe, promptly; "I'd have seventy-five of 'em."

"Seventy-five what?" asked Mrs. Pepper, who had gone into the bedroom, and now came out, a coat in hand, to sit down in the west window, where she began to sew rapidly. "Better clear up the dishes, Polly, and set the table back--seventy-five what, Joel?"

"Plum-puddings," said Joel, kissing Phronsie.

"Dear me!" ejaculated Mrs. Pepper; "you don't know what you're saying, Joel Pepper; the house couldn't hold 'em!"

"Wouldn't long," responded Joel; "we'd eat 'em."

"That would be foolish," interposed Ben; "I'd have roast beef and fixings--and oysters--and huckleberry pie."

"Oh, dear," cried Polly; "how nice, Ben! you always do think of the very best things."

But Joel declared he wouldn't waste his time "over old beef; he'd have something like!" And then he cried:

"Come on, Dave, what'd you choose?"

Little Davie had been quietly eating his breakfast amid all this chatter, and somehow thinking it might make the mother feel badly, he had refrained from saying just how tiresome he had really found this "everlasting breakfast" as Joel called it. But now he looked up eagerly, his answer all ready. "Oh, I know," he cried, "what would be most beautiful! toasted bread--white bread--and candy."

"What's candy?" asked Phronsie.

"Oh, don't you know, Phronsie," cried Polly, "what Mrs. Beebe gave you the day you got your shoes--the pink sticks; and"-- "And the peppermint stick Mr. Beebe gave you, Phronsie," finished Joel, his mouth watering at the remembrance.

"That day, when you got your toe pounded," added Davie, looking at Joel.

"Oh!" cried Phronsie; "I want some now, I do!"

"Well, Davie," said Polly, "you shall have that for breakfast when our ship comes in then."

"Your ships aren't ever coming," broke in Mrs. Pepper, wisely, "if you sit there talking--folks don't ever make any fortunes by wishing."

"True enough," laughed Ben, jumping up and setting back his chair. "Come on, Joe; you've got to pile to-day."

"Oh, dear," said Joel, dismally; "I wish Mr. Blodgett's wood was all a-fire."

"Never say that, Joel," said Mrs. Pepper, looking up sternly; "it's biting your own nose off to wish that wood was a-fire-- and besides it's dreadfully wicked."

Joel hung his head, for his mother never spoke in that way unless she was strongly moved; but he soon recovered, and hastened off for his jacket.

"I'm sorry I can't help you do the dishes, Polly," said David, running after Joel.

"I'm going to help her," said Phronsie; "I am."

So Polly got the little wooden tub that she always used, gave Phronsie the well-worn cup-napkin, and allowed her to wipe the handleless cups and cracked saucers, which afforded the little one intense delight.

"Don't you wish, Polly," said little Phronsie, bustling around with a very important air, nearly smothered in the depths of a big brown apron that Polly had carefully tied under her chin, "that you didn't ever-an'-ever have so many dishes to do?"

"Um--maybe," said Polly, thoughtlessly. She was thinking of something else besides cups and saucers just then; of how nice it would be to go off for just one day, and do exactly as she had a mind to in everything. She even envied Ben and the boys who were going to work hard at Deacon Blodgett's woodpile.

"Well, I tell you," said Phronsie, confidentially, setting down a cup that she had polished with great care, "I'm going to do 'em all to-morrow, for you, Polly--I can truly; let me now, Polly, do."

"Nonsense!" said Polly, giving a great splash with her mop in the tub, ashamed of her inward repinings. "Phronsie, you're no bigger than a mouse!"

"Yes, I am," retorted Phronsie, very indignantly. Her face began to get very red, and she straightened up so suddenly to show Polly just how very big she was that her little head came up against the edge of the tub--over it went! a pile of saucers followed.

"There now," cried Polly, "see what you've done!"

"Ow!" whimpered Phronsie, breaking into a subdued roar; "oh, Polly! it's all running down my back."

"Is it?" said Polly, bursting out into a laugh; "never mind, Phronsie, I'll dry you."

"Dear me, Polly!" said Mrs. Pepper, who had looked up in time to see the tub racing along by itself towards the "Provision Room" door, a stream of dish-water following in its wake, "she will be wet clear through; do get off her things, quick."

"Yes'm," cried Polly, picking up the tub, and giving two or three quick sops to the floor. "Here you are, Pussy," grasping Phronsie, crying as she was, and carrying her into the bedroom.

"Oh, dear," wailed the child, still holding the wet dish towel; "I won't ever do it again, if you'll only let me do 'em all to-morrow."

"When you're big and strong," said Polly, giving her a hug, "you shall do 'em every day."

"May I really?" said little Phronsie, blinking through the tears, and looking radiant.

"Yes, truly--every day."

"Then I'll grow right away, I will," said Phronsie, bursting out merrily; and she sat down and pulled off the well-worn shoes, into which a big pool of dish-water had run, while Polly went for dry stockings.

"So you shall," said Polly, coming back, a big piece of gingerbread in her hand; "and this'll make you grow, Phronsie."

"O-o-h!" and Phronsie's little white teeth shut down quickly on the comforting morsel. Gingerbread didn't come often enough into the Pepper household to be lightly esteemed.

"Now," said Mrs. Pepper, when order was restored, the floor washed up brightly, and every cup and platter in place, hobnobbing away to themselves on the shelves of the old corner cupboard, and Polly had come as usual with needle and thread to help mother-- Polly was getting so that she could do the plain parts on the coats and jackets, which filled her with pride at the very thought--"now," said Mrs. Pepper, "you needn't help me this morning, Polly: I'm getting on pretty smart; but you may just run down to the parson's, and see how he is."

"Is he sick?" asked Polly, in awe.

To have the parson sick, was something quite different from an ordinary person's illness.

"He's taken with a chill," said Mrs. Pepper, biting off a thread, "so Miss Huldy Folsom told me last night, and I'm afraid he's going to have a fever."

"Oh, dear," said Polly, in dire distress; "whatever'd we do, mammy!"

"Don't know, I'm sure," replied Mrs. Pepper, setting her stitches firmly; "the Lord'll provide. So you run along, child, and see how he is."

"Can't Phronsie go?" asked Polly, pausing half-way to the bedroom door.

"Well, yes, I suppose she might," said Mrs. Pepper, assentingly.

"No, she can't either," said Polly, coming back with her sun-bonnet in her hand, and shutting the door carefully after her, "cause she's fast asleep on the floor."

"Is she?" said Mrs. Pepper; "well, she's been running so this morning, she's tired out, I s'pose."

"And her face is dreadfully red," continued Polly, tying on her bonnet; "now, what'll I say, mammy?"

"Well, I should think 'twould be," said Mrs. Pepper, replying to the first half of Polly's speech; "she cried so. Well, you just tell Mrs. Henderson your ma wants to know how Mr. Henderson is this morning, and if 'twas a chill he had yesterday, and how he slept last night, and"-- "Oh, ma," said Polly, "I can't ever remember all that."

"Oh, yes, you can," said Mrs. Pepper, encouragingly; "just put your mind on it, Polly; 'tisn't anything to what I used to have to remember--when I was a little girl, no bigger than you are.

Day 121

1. Measles are a skin disease that makes red spots all over your body.
2. Finish chapter 4.
3. Who has the measles? (Answers)

Chapter 4 continued

"…Well, you just tell Mrs. Henderson your ma wants to know how Mr. Henderson is this morning, and if 'twas a chill he had yesterday, and how he slept last night, and"-- "Oh, ma," said Polly, "I can't ever remember all that."

"Oh, yes, you can," said Mrs. Pepper, encouragingly; "just put your mind on it, Polly; 'tisn't anything to what I used to have to remember--when I was a little girl, no bigger than you are."

Polly sighed, and feeling sure that something must be the matter with her mind, gave her whole attention to the errand; till at last after a multiplicity of messages and charges not to forget any one of them, Mrs. Pepper let her depart.

Up to the old-fashioned green door, with its brass knocker, Polly went, running over in her mind just which of the messages she ought to give first. She couldn't for her life think whether "if 'twas a chill he had yesterday?" ought to come before "how he slept?" She knocked timidly, hoping Mrs. Henderson would help her out of her difficulty by telling her without the asking. All other front doors in Badgertown were ornaments, only opened on grand occasions, like a wedding or a funeral. But the minister's was accessible alike to all. So Polly let fall the knocker, and awaited the answer.

A scuffling noise sounded along the passage; and then Polly's soul sank down in dire dismay. It was the minister's sister, and not gentle little Mrs. Henderson. She never could get on with Miss Jerusha in the least. She made her feel as she told her mother once--"as if I don't know what my name is." And now here she was; and all those messages.

Miss Jerusha unbolted the door, slid back the great bar, opened the upper half, and stood there. She was a big woman, with sharp black eyes, and spectacles--over which she looked--which to Polly was much worse, for that gave her four eyes.

"Well, and what do you want?" she asked.

"I came to see--I mean my ma sent me," stammered poor Polly.

"And who is your ma?" demanded Miss Jerusha, as much like a policeman as anything; "and where do you live?"

"I live in Primrose Lane," replied Polly, wishing very much that she was back there.

"I don't want to know where you live, before I know who you are," said Miss Jerusha; "you should answer the question I asked first; always remember that."

"My ma's Mrs. Pepper," said Polly.

"Mrs. who?" repeated Miss Jerusha.

By this time Polly was so worn that she came very near turning and fleeing, but she thought of her mother's disappointment in her, and the loss of the news, and stood quite still.

"What is it, Jerusha?" a gentle voice here broke upon Polly's ear.

"I don't know," responded Miss Jerusha, tartly, still holding the door much as if Polly were a robber; "it's a little girl, and I can't make out what she wants."

"Why, it's Polly Pepper!" exclaimed Mrs. Henderson, pleasantly. "Come in, child." She opened the other half of the big door, and led the way through the wide hail into a big, old-fashioned room, with painted floor, and high, old side-board, and some stiff-backed rocking-chairs.

Miss Jerusha stalked in also and seated herself by the window, and began to knit. Polly had just opened her mouth to tell her errand, when the door also opened suddenly and Mr. Henderson walked in.

"Oh!" said Polly, and then she stopped, and the color flushed up into her face.

"What is it, my dear?" and the minister took her hand kindly, and looked down into her flushed face.

"You are not going to have a fever, and be sick and die!" she cried.

"I hope not, my little girl," he smiled back, encouragingly; and then Polly gave her messages, which now she managed easily enough.

"There," broke in Miss Jerusha, "a cat can't sneeze in this town but everybody'll know it in quarter of an hour."

And then Mrs. Henderson took Polly out to see a brood of new little chicks, that had just popped their heads out into the world; and to Polly, down on her knees, admiring, the time passed very swiftly indeed.

"Now I must go, ma'am," she said at last, looking up into the lady's face, regretfully, "for mammy didn't say I was to stay."

"Very well, dear; do you think you could carry a little pat of butter? I have some very nice my sister sent me, and I want your mother to share it."

"Oh, thank you, ma'am!" cried Polly, thinking, "how glad David'll be, for he does so love butter! only"-- "Wait a bit, then," said Mrs. Henderson, who didn't seem to notice the objection. So she went into the house, and Polly went down again in admiration before the fascinating little puff-balls.

But she was soon on the way, with a little pat of butter in a blue bowl, tied over with a clean cloth; happy in her gift for mammy, and in the knowledge of the minister being all well.

"I wonder if Phronsie's awake," she thought to herself, turning in at the little brown gate; "if she is, she shall have a piece of bread with lots of butter."

"Hush!" said Mrs. Pepper, from the rocking-chair in the middle of the floor. She had something in her arms. Polly stopped suddenly, almost letting the bowl fall.

"It's Phronsie," said the mother, "and I don't know what the matter is with her; you'll have to go for the doctor, Polly, and just as fast as you can."

Polly still stood, holding the bowl, and staring with all her might. Phronsie sick!

"Don't wake her," said Mrs. Pepper.

Poor Polly couldn't have stirred to save her life, for a minute; then she said--"Where shall I go?"

"Oh, run to Dr. Fisher's; and don't be gone long."

Polly set down the bowl of butter, and sped on the wings of the wind for the doctor. Something dreadful was the matter, she felt, for never had a physician been summoned to the hearty Pepper family since she could remember, only when the father died. Fear lent speed to her feet; and soon the doctor came, and bent over poor little Phronsie, who still lay in her mother's arms, in a burning fever.

"It's measles," he pronounced, "that's all; no cause for alarm; you ever had it?" he asked, turning suddenly around on Polly, who was watching with wide-open eyes for the verdict.

"No, sir," answered Polly, not knowing in the least what "measles" was.

"What shall we do!" said Mrs. Pepper; "there haven't any of them had it."

The doctor was over by the little old table under the window, mixing up some black-looking stuff in a tumbler, and he didn't hear her.

"There," he said, putting a spoonful into Phronsie's mouth, "she'll get along well enough; only keep her out of the cold." Then he pulled out a big silver watch. He was a little thin man, and the watch was immense. Polly for her life couldn't keep her eyes off from it; if Ben could only have one so fine!

"Polly," whispered Mrs. Pepper, "run and get my purse; it's in the top bureau drawer."

"Yes'm," said Polly, taking her eyes off, by a violent wrench, from the fascinating watch; and she ran quickly and got the little old stocking-leg, where the hard earnings that staid long enough to be put anywhere, always found refuge. She put it into her mother's lap, and watched while Mrs. Pepper counted out slowly one dollar in small pieces.

"Here sir," said Mrs. Pepper, holding them out towards the doctor; "and thank you for coming."

"Hey!" said the little man, spinning round; "that dollar's the Lord's!"

Mrs. Pepper looked bewildered, and still sat holding it out. "And the Lord has given it to you to take care of these children with; see that you do it." And without another word he was gone.

"Wasn't he good, mammy?" asked Polly, after the first surprise was over.

"I'm sure he was," said Mrs. Pepper. "Well, tie it up again, Polly, tie it up tight; we shall want it, I'm sure," sighing at her little sick girl.

"Mayn't I take Phronsie, ma?" asked Polly.

"No, no," said Phronsie. She had got mammy, and she meant to improve the privilege.

"What is 'measles' anyway, mammy?" asked Polly, sitting down on the floor at their feet.

"Oh, 'tis something children always have," replied Mrs. Pepper; "but I'm sure I hoped it wouldn't come just yet."

"I shan't have it," said Polly, decisively; "I know I shan't! nor Ben--nor Joe--nor--nor Davie--I guess," she added, hesitatingly, for Davie was the delicate one of the family; at least not nearly so strong as the others.

Mrs. Pepper looked at her anxiously; but Polly seemed as bright and healthy as ever, as she jumped up and ran to put the kettle on the stove.

"What'll the boys say, I wonder!" she thought to herself, feeling quite important that they really had sickness in the house. As long as Phronsie wasn't dangerous, it seemed quite like rich folks; and she forgot the toil, and the grind of poverty. She looked out from time to time as she passed the window, but no boys came.

"I'll put her in bed, Polly," said Mrs. Pepper, in a whisper, as Phronsie closed her eyes and breathed regularly.

"And then will you have your dinner, ma?"

"Yes," said Mrs. Pepper, "I don't care--if the boys come."

"The boys'll never come," said Polly, impatiently; "I don't believe--why! here they are now!"

"Oh, dear," said Joel, coming in crossly, "I'm so hungry--oh-- butter! where'd you get it? I thought we never should get here!"

"I thought so too," said Polly. "Hush! why, where's Ben?"

"He's just back," began Joel, commencing to eat, "and Davie; something is the matter with Ben-- he says he feels funny."

"Something the matter with Ben!" repeated Polly. She dropped the cup she held, which broke in a dozen pieces.

"Oh, whocky!" cried Joel; "see what you've done, Polly Pepper!"

But Polly didn't hear; over the big, flat door-stone she sped, and met Ben with little David, coming in the gate. His face was just like Phronsie's! And with a cold, heavy feeling at her heart, Polly realized that this was no play.

"Oh, Ben!" she cried, flinging her arms around his neck, and bursting into tears; "don't! please--I wish you wouldn't; Phronsie's got 'em, and that's enough!"

"Got what?" asked Ben, while Davie's eyes grew to their widest proportions.

"Oh, measles!" cried Polly, bursting out afresh; "the hate-fullest, horridest measles! and now you're taken!"

"Oh no, I'm not," responded Ben, cheerfully, who knew what measles were; "wipe up, Polly; I'm all right; only my head aches, and my eyes feel funny."

But Polly, only half-reassured, controlled her sobs; and the sorrowful trio repaired to mother.

"Oh, dear!" ejaculated Mrs. Pepper, sinking in a chair in dismay, at sight of Ben's red face; "whatever'll we do now!"

The prop and stay of her life would be taken away if Ben should be laid aside. No more stray half or quarter dollars would come to help her out when she didn't know where to turn.

Polly cleared off the deserted table--for once Joel had all the bread and butter he wanted. Ben took some of Phronsie's medicine, and crawled up into the loft, to bed; and quiet settled down on the little household.

"Polly," whispered Ben, as she tucked him in, "it'll be hard buckling-to now, for you, but I guess you'll do it."

Day 122

1. "necessary draught" — drinking the medicine she needed — draught is pronounced *draft* — the act of drinking or a portion of liquid to be drunk, especially medicine
2. Read the first half of chapter 5 and tell someone what is happening in the story.

Chapter 5 More Trouble

"Oh, dear," said Polly to herself, the next morning, trying to get a breakfast for the sick ones out of the inevitable mush; "everything's just as bad as it can be! they can't ever eat this; I wish I had an ocean of toast!"

"Toast some of the bread in the pail, Polly," said Mrs. Pepper.

She looked worn and worried; she had been up nearly all night, back and forth from Ben's bed in the loft to restless, fretful little Phronsie in the big four-poster in the bedroom; for Phronsie wouldn't get into the crib. Polly had tried her best to help her, and had rubbed her eyes diligently to keep awake, but she was wholly unaccustomed to it, and her healthy, tired little body succumbed-- and then when she awoke, shame and remorse filled her very heart.

"That isn't nice, ma," she said, glancing at the poor old pail, which she had brought out of the "Provision Room." "Old brown bread! I want to fix 'em something nice."

"Well, you can't, you know," said Mrs. Pepper, with a sigh; "but you've got butter now; that'll be splendid!"

"I know it," said Polly, running to the corner cupboard where the precious morsel in the blue bowl remained; "whatever should we do without it, mummy?"

"Do without it!" said Mrs. Pepper; "same's we have done."

"Well, 'twas splendid in Mrs. Henderson to give it to us, anyway," said Polly, longing for just one taste; "seems as if 'twas a year since I was there--oh, ma!" and here Polly took up the thread that had been so rudely snapped; "don't you think, she's got ten of the prettiest--yes, the sweetest little chickens you ever saw! Why can't we have some, mammy?"

"Costs money," replied Mrs. Pepper. "We've got too many in the house to have any outside."

"Oh, dear," said Polly, with a red face that was toasting about as much as the bread she was holding on the point of an old fork; "we never have had anything. There," she added at last; "that's the best I can do; now I'll put the butter on this little blue plate; ain't that cunning, ma?"

"Yes," said Mrs. Pepper, approvingly; "it takes you, Polly." So Polly trotted first to Ben, up the crooked, low stairs to the loft; and while she regaled him with the brown toast and butter, she kept her tongue flying on the subject of the little chicks, and all that she saw on the famous Henderson visit. Poor Ben pretended hard to eat, but ate nothing really; and Polly saw it all, and it cut her to the heart--so she talked faster than ever.

"Now," she said, starting to go back to Phronsie; "Ben Pepper, just as soon as you get well, we'll have some chickens--so there!"

"Guess we shan't get 'em very soon," said Ben, despondently, "if I've got to lie here; and, besides, Polly, you know every bit we can save has got to go for the new stove."

"Oh, dear," said Polly, "I forgot that; so it has; seems to me everything's giving out!"

"You can't bake any longer in the old thing," said Ben, turning over and looking at her; "poor girl, I don't see how you've stood it so long."

"And we've been stuffing it," cried Polly merrily, "till 'twon't stuff any more."

"No," said Ben, turning back again, "that's all worn out."

"Well, you must go to sleep," said Polly, "or mammy'll be up here; and Phronsie hasn't had her breakfast either."

Phronsie was wailing away dismally, sitting up in the middle of the old bed. Her face pricked, she said, and she was rubbing it vigorously with both fat little hands, and then crying worse than ever.

"Oh me! oh my!" cried Polly; "how you look, Phronsie!"

"I want my mammy!" cried poor Phronsie.

"Mammy can't come now, Phronsie dear; she's sewing. See what Polly's got for you--butter: isn't that splendid!"

Phronsie stopped for just one moment, and took a mouthful; but the toast was hard and dry, and she cried harder than before.

"Now," said Polly, curling up on the bed beside her, "if you'll stop crying, Phronsie Pepper, I'll tell you about the cunningest, yes, the very cunningest little chickens you ever saw. One was white, and he looked just like this," said Polly, tumbling over on the bed in a heap; "he couldn't stand up straight, he was so fat."

"Did he bite?" asked Phronsie, full of interest.

"No, he didn't bite me," said Polly; "but his mother put a bug in his mouth--just as I'm doing you know," and she broke off a small piece of the toast, put on a generous bit of butter, and held it over Phronsie's mouth.

"Did he swallow it?" asked the child, obediently opening her little red lips.

"Oh, snapped it," answered Polly, "quick as ever he could, I tell you; but 'twasn't good like this, Phronsie."

"Did he have two bugs?" asked Phronsie, eying suspiciously the second morsel of dry toast that Polly was conveying to her mouth.

"Well, he would have had," replied Polly, "if there'd been bugs enough; but there were nine other chicks, Phronsie."

"Poor chickies," said Phronsie, and looked lovingly at the rest of the toast and butter on the plate; and while Polly fed it to her, listened with absorbed interest to all the particulars concerning each and every chick in the Henderson hen-coop.

"Mother," said Polly, towards evening, "I'm going to sit up with Ben tonight; say I may, do, mother."

"Oh no, you can't," replied Mrs. Pepper; "you'll get worn out; and then what shall I do? Joel can hand him his medicine."

"Oh, Joe would tumble to sleep, mammy," said Polly, "the first thing--let me."

"Perhaps Phronsie'll let me go to-night," said Mrs. Pepper, reflectively.

"Oh, no she won't, I know," replied Polly, decisively; "she wants you all the time."

"I will, Polly," said Davie, coming in with an armful of wood, in time to hear the conversation. "I'll give him his medicine, mayn't I, mammy?" and David let down his load, and came over where his mother and Polly sat sewing, to urge his rights.

"I don't know," said his mother, smiling on him. "Can you, do you think?"

"Yes, ma'am!" said Davie, straightening himself up.

When they told Ben, he said he knew a better way than for Davie to watch; he'd have a string tied to Davie's arm, and the end he'd hold in bed, and when 'twas time for medicine, he'd pull the string, and that would wake Davie up!

Polly didn't sleep much more on her shake-down on the floor than if she had watched with Ben; for Phronsie cried and moaned, and wanted a drink of water every two minutes, it seemed to her. As she went back into her nest after one of these travels, Polly thought: "Well, I don't care, if nobody else gets sick; if Ben'll only get well. To-morrow I'm goin' to do mammy's sack she's begun for Mr. Jackson; it's all plain sew-in', just like a bag; and I can do it, I know----" and so she fell into a troubled sleep, only to be awakened by Phronsie's fretful little voice: "I want a drink of water, Polly, I do."

"Don't she drink awfully, mammy?" asked Polly, after one of these excursions out to the kitchen after the necessary draught.

"Yes," said Mrs. Pepper; "and she mustn't have any more; 'twill hurt her." But Phronsie fell into a delicious sleep after that, and didn't want any more, luckily.

Day 123

1. Finish reading chapter 5.
2. Write a summary of this chapter. What's the main idea, the main topic? If you can, write your summaries in one sentence. You'll have to use words like AND or BUT. If you write your summary in one sentence, get a high five and/or hug. (Answers)

Chapter 5 continued

"Here, Joe," said Mrs. Pepper, the next morning, "take this coat up to Mr. Peterses; and be sure you get the money for it."

"How'll I get it?" asked Joe, who didn't relish the long, hot walk.

"Why, tell 'em we're sick--Ben's sick," added Mrs. Pepper, as the most decisive thing; "and we must have it; and then wait for it."

"Tisn't pleasant up at the Peterses," grumbled Joel, taking the parcel and moving slowly off.

"No, no, Polly," said Mrs. Pepper, "you needn't do that," seeing Polly take up some sewing after doing up the room and finishing the semi-weekly bake; "you're all beat out with that tussle over the stove; that sack'll have to go till next week."

"It can't, mammy," said Polly, snipping off a basting thread; "we've got to have the money; how much'll he give you for it?"

"Thirty cents," replied Mrs. Pepper.

"Well," said Polly, "we've got to get all the thirty centses we can, mammy dear; and I know I can do it, truly--try me once," she implored.

"Well." Mrs. Pepper relented, slowly.

"Don't feel bad, mammy dear," comforted Polly, sewing away briskly; "Ben'll get well pretty soon, and then we'll be all right."

"Maybe," said Mrs. Pepper; and went back to Phronsie, who could scarcely let her out of her sight.

Polly stitched away bravely. "Now if I do this good, mammy'll let me do it other times," she said to herself.

Davie, too, worked patiently out of doors, trying to do Ben's chores. The little fellow blundered over things that Ben would have accomplished in half the time, and he had to sit down often on the steps of the little old shed where the tools were kept, to wipe his hot face and rest.

"Polly," said Mrs. Pepper, "hadn't you better stop a little? Dear me! how fast you sew, child!"

Polly gave a delighted little hum at her mother's evident approval.

"I'm going to do 'em all next week, mammy," she said; "then Mr. Atkins won't take 'em away from us, I guess."

Mr. Atkins kept the store, and gave out coats and sacks of coarse linen and homespun to Mrs. Pepper to make; and it was the fear of losing the work that had made the mother's heart sink.

"I don't believe anybody's got such children as I have," she said; and she gave Polly a motherly little pat that the little daughter felt clear to the tips of her toes with a thrill of delight.

About half-past two, long after dinner, Joe came walking in, hungry as a beaver, but flushed and triumphant.

"Why, where have you been all this time?" asked his mother.

"Oh, Joe, you didn't stop to play?" asked Polly, from her perch where she sat sewing, giving him a reproachful glance.

"Stop to play!" retorted Joe, indignantly; "no, I guess I didn't! I've been to Old Peterses."

"Not all this time!" exclaimed Mrs. Pepper.

"Yes, I have too," replied Joel, sturdily marching up to her. "And there's your money, mother;" and he counted out a quarter of a dollar in silver pieces and pennies, which he took from a dingy wad of paper, stowed away in the depths of his pocket.

"Oh, Joe," said Mrs. Pepper, sinking back in her chair and looking at him; "what do you mean?"

Polly put her work in her lap, and waited to hear.

"Where's my dinner, Polly?" asked Joel; "I hope it's a big one.

"Yes, 'tis," said Polly; "you've got lots to-day, it's in the corner of the cupboard, covered up with the plate--so tell on, Joe."

"That's elegant!" said Joel, coming back with the well-filled plate, Ben's and his own share.

"Do tell us, Joey," implored Polly; "mother's waiting."

"Well," said Joel, his mouth half full, "I waited--and he said the coat was all right;--and---and--Mrs. Peters said 'twas all right;--and Mirandy Peters said 'twas all right; but they didn't any of 'em say anythin' about payin', so I didn't think 'twas all right--and--and-- can't I have some more butter, Polly?"

"No," said Polly, sorry to refuse him, he'd been so good about the money; "the butter's got to be saved for Ben and Phronsie."

"Oh," said Joe, "I wish Miss Henderson would send us some more, I do! I think she might!"

"For shame, Joe," said Mrs. Pepper; "she was very good to send this, I think; now what else did you say?" she asked.

"Well," said Joel, taking another mouthful of bread, "so I waited; you told me to, mother, you know--and they all went to work; and they didn't mind me at all, and--there wasn't anything to look at, so I sat--and sat--Polly, can't I have some gingerbread?"

"No," said Polly, "it's all gone; I gave the last piece to Phronsie the day she was taken sick."

"Oh, dear," said Joel, "everything's gone."

"Well, do go on, Joe, do."

"And--then they had dinner; and Mr. Peters said, 'Hasn't that boy gone home yet?' and Mrs. Peters said, 'no'--and he called me in, and asked me why I didn't run along home; and I said, Phronsie was sick, and Ben had the squeezles----"

"The what?" said Polly.

"The squeezles," repeated Joel, irritably; "that's what you said."

"It's measles, Joey," corrected Mrs. Pepper; "never mind, I wouldn't feel bad."

"Well, they all laughed, and laughed, and then I said you told me to wait till I did get the money."

"Oh, Joe," began Mrs. Pepper, "you shouldn't have told 'em so--what did he say?"

"Well, he laughed, and said I was a smart boy, and he'd see; and Mirandy said, 'do pay him, pa, he must be tired to death'--and don't you think, he went to a big desk in the corner, and took out a box, and 'twas full most of money-- lots! oh! and he gave me mine--and--that's all; and I'm tired to death." And Joel flung himself down on the floor, expanded his legs as only Joel could, and took a comfortable roll.

"So you must be," said Polly, pityingly, "waiting at those Peterses."

"Don't ever want to see any more Peterses," said Joel; never, never, never!

"Oh, dear," thought Polly, as she sewed on into the afternoon, "I wonder what does all my eyes! feels just like sand in 'em;" and she rubbed and rubbed to thread her needle. But she was afraid her mother would see, so she kept at her sewing. Once in awhile the bad feeling would go away, and then she would forget all about it. "There now, who says I can't do it! that's most done," she cried, jumping up, and spinning across the room, to stretch herself a bit, "and to-morrow I'll finish it."

"Well," said Mrs. Pepper, "if you can do that, Polly, you'll be the greatest help I've had yet."

So Polly tucked herself into the old shake-down with a thankful heart that night, hoping for morning.

Alas! when morning did come, Polly could hardly move. The measles! what should she do! A faint hope of driving them off made her tumble out of bed, and stagger across the room to look in the old cracked looking-glass. All hope was gone as the red reflection met her gaze. Polly was on the sick list now!

"I won't be sick," she said; "at any rate, I'll keep around." An awful feeling made her clutch the back of a chair, but she managed somehow to get into her clothes, and go groping blindly into the kitchen. Somehow, Polly couldn't see very well. She tried to set the table, but 'twas no use. "Oh, dear," she thought, "whatever'll mammy do?"

"Hullo!" said Joel, coming in, "what's the matter, Polly?" Polly started at his sudden entrance, and, wavering a minute, fell over in a heap.

"Oh ma! ma!" screamed Joel, running to the foot of the stairs leading to the loft, where Mrs. Pepper was with Ben; "something's taken Polly! and she fell; and I guess she's in the wood-box!"

Day 124

1. Read the first half of chapter 6.
2. Tell someone about what is happening in this chapter so far.

Chapter 6 Hard Days for Polly

"Ma," said David, coming softly into the bedroom, where poor Polly lay on the bed with Phronsie, her eyes bandaged with a soft old handkerchief, "I'll set the table."

"There isn't any table to set," said Mrs. Pepper, sadly; "there isn't anybody to eat anything, Davie; you and Joel can get something out of the cupboard."

"Can we get whatever we've a mind to, ma?" cried Joel, who followed Davie, rubbing his face with a towel after his morning ablutions.

"Yes," replied his mother, absently.

"Come on, Dave!" cried Joel; "we'll have a breakfast!"

"We mustn't," said little Davie, doubtfully, "eat the whole, Joey."

But that individual already had his head in the cupboard, which soon engrossed them both.

Dr. Fisher was called in the middle of the morning to see what was the matter with Polly's eyes. The little man looked at her keenly over his spectacles; then he said, "When were you taken?"

"This morning," answered Polly, her eyes smarting.

"Didn't you feel badly before?" questioned the doctor. Polly thought back; and then she remembered that she had felt very badly; that when she was baking over the old stove the day before her back had ached dreadfully; and that, somehow, when she sat down to sew, it didn't stop; only her eyes had bothered her so; she didn't mind her back so much.

"I thought so," said the doctor, when Polly answered. "And those eyes of yours have been used too much; what has she been doing, ma'am?" He turned around sharply on Mrs. Pepper as he asked this.

"Sewing," said Mrs. Pepper, "and everything; Polly does everything, sir."

"Humph!" said the doctor; "well, she won't again in one spell; her eyes are very bad."

At this a whoop, small but terrible to hear, came from the middle of the bed; and Phronsie sat bolt upright. Everybody started; while Phronsie broke out, "Don't make my Polly sick! oh! please don't!"

"Hey!" said the doctor; and he looked kindly at the small object with a very red face in the middle of the bed. Then he added, gently, "We're going to make Polly well, little girl; so that she can see splendidly."

"Will you, really?" asked the child, doubtfully.

"Yes," said the doctor; "we'll try hard; and you mustn't cry; 'cause then Polly'll cry, and that will make her eyes very bad; very bad indeed," he repeated, impressively.

"I won't cry," said Phronsie; "no, not one bit." And she wiped off the last tear with her fat little hand, and watched to see what next was to be done.

And Polly was left, very rebellious indeed, in the big bed, with a cooling lotion on the poor eyes, that somehow didn't cool them one bit.

"If 'twas anythin' but my eyes, mammy, I could stand it," she bewailed, flouncing over and over in her impatience; "and who'll do all the work now?"

"Don't think of the work, Polly," said Mrs. Pepper.

"I can't do anything but think," said poor Polly.

Just at that moment a queer noise out in the kitchen was heard.

"Do go out, mother, and see what 'tis," said Polly.

"I've come," said a cracked voice, close up by the bedroom door, followed by a big black cap, which could belong to no other than Grandma Bascom, "to set by you a spell; what's the matter?" she asked, and stopped, amazed to see Polly in bed.

"Oh, Polly's taken," screamed Mrs. Pepper in her ear.

"Taken!" repeated the old lady, "what is it--a fit?"

"No," said Mrs. Pepper; "the same as Ben's got; and Phronsie; the measles."

"The measles, has she?" said grandma; "well, that's bad; and Ben's away, you say."

"No, he isn't either," screamed Mrs. Pepper, "he's got them, too!"

"Got two what?" asked grandma.

"Measles! he's got the measles too," repeated Mrs. Pepper, loud as she could; so loud that the old lady's cap trembled at the noise.

"Oh! the dreadful!" said grandma; "and this girl too?" laying her hand on Phronsie's head.

"Yes," said Mrs. Pepper, feeling it a little relief to tell over her miseries; "all three of them!"

"I haven't," said Joel, coming in in hopes that grandma had a stray peppermint or two in her pocket, as she sometimes did; "and I'm not going to, either."

"Oh, dear," groaned his mother; "that's what Polly said; and she's got 'em bad. It's her eyes," she screamed to grandma, who looked inquiringly.

"Her eyes, is it?" asked Mrs. Bascom; "well, I've got a receet that cousin Samanthy's folks had when John's children had 'em; and I'll run right along home and get it," and she started to go.

"No, you needn't," screamed Mrs. Pepper; "thank you, Mrs. Bascom; but Dr. Fisher's been here; and he put something on Polly's eyes; and he said it mustn't be touched."

"Hey?" said the old lady; so Mrs. Pepper had to go all over it again, till at last she made her understand that Polly's eyes were taken care of, and they must wait for time to do the rest.

"You come along of me," whispered grandma, when at last her call was done, to Joel who stood by the door. "I've got some peppermints to home; I forgot to bring 'em."

"Yes'm," said Joel, brightening up.

"Where you going, Joe?" asked Mrs. Pepper, seeing him move off with Mrs. Bascom; "I may want you."

"Oh, I've got to go over to grandma's," said Joel briskly; "she wants me."

"Well, don't be gone long then," replied his mother.

"There," said grandma, going into her "keeping-room" to an old-fashioned chest of drawers; opening one, she took therefrom a paper, from which she shook out before Joe's delighted eyes some red and white peppermint drops. "There now, you take these home; you may have some, but be sure you give the most to the sick ones; and Polly--let Polly have the biggest."

"She won't take 'em," said Joel, wishing he had the measles. "Well, you try her," said grandma; "run along now." But it was useless to tell Joel that, for he was half-way home already. He carried out grandma's wishes, and distributed conscientiously the precious drops. But when he came to Polly, she didn't answer; and looking at her in surprise he saw two big tears rolling out under the bandage and wetting the pillow.

"I don't want 'em, Joe," said Polly, when he made her understand that "twas peppermints, real peppermints;" "you may have 'em."

"Try one, Polly; they're real good," said Joel, who had an undefined wish to comfort; "there, open your mouth."

So Polly opened her mouth, and Joel put one in with satisfaction.

"Isn't it good?" he asked, watching her crunch it.

"Yes," said Polly, "real good; where'd you get 'em?"

"Over to Grandma Bascom's," said Joel; "she gave me lots for all of us; have another, Polly?"

"No," said Polly, "not yet; you put two on my pillow where I can reach 'em; and then you keep the rest, Joel."

"I'll put three," said Joel, counting out one red and two white ones, and laying them on the pillow; "there!"

"And I want another, Joey, I do," said Phronsie from the other side of the bed.

"Well, you may have one," said Joel; "a red one, Phronsie; yes, you may have two. Now come on, Dave; we'll have the rest out by the wood-pile."

How they ever got through that day, I don't know. But late in the afternoon carriage wheels were heard; and then they stopped right at the Peppers' little brown gate.

"Polly," said Mrs. Pepper, running to the bedroom door, "it's Mrs. Henderson!"

"Is it?" said Polly, from the darkened room, "oh! I'm so glad! is Miss Jerushy with her?" she asked, fearfully.

"No," said Mrs. Pepper, going back to ascertain; "why, it's the parson himself! Deary! how we look!"

"Never mind, mammy," called back Polly, longing to spring out of bed and fix up a bit.

"I'm sorry to hear the children are sick," said Mrs. Henderson, coming in, in her sweet, gentle way.

"We didn't know it," said the minister, "until this morning--can we see them?"

"Oh yes, sir," said Mrs. Pepper; "Ben's upstairs; and Polly and Phronsie are in here."

"Poor little things!" said Mrs. Henderson, compassionately; "hadn't you better," turning to the minister, "go up and see Ben first, while I will visit the little girls?"

So the minister mounted the crooked stairs; and Mrs. Henderson went straight up to Polly's side; and the first thing Polly knew, a cool, gentle hand was laid on her hot head, and a voice said, "I've come to see my little chicken now!"

"Oh, ma'am," said Polly, bursting into a sob, "I don't care about my eyes--only mammy--" and she broke right down.

310

"I know," said the minister's wife, soothingly; "but it's for you to bear patiently, Polly--what do you suppose the chicks were doing when I came away?" And Mrs. Henderson, while she held Polly's hand, smiled and nodded encouragingly to Phronsie, who was staring at her from the other side of the bed.

"I don't know, ma'am," said Polly; "please tell us."

Day 125

1. Finish reading chapter 6.
2. Tell someone about the chapter.

Vocabulary

1. Start a dictionary. In your reading find three words you don't know and write them in this dictionary. Write the word and what it means.

Chapter 6 continued

"Well, they were all fighting over a grasshopper--yes, ten of them."

"Which one got it?" asked Polly in intense interest; "oh! I hope the white one did!"

"Well, he looked as much like winning as any of them," said the lady, laughing.

"Bless her!" thought Mrs. Pepper to herself out in the kitchen, finishing the sack Polly had left; "she's a parson's wife, I say!"

And then the minister came down from Ben's room, and went into the bedroom; and Mrs. Henderson went up-stairs into the loft.

"So," he said kindly, as after patting Phronsie's head he came over and sat down by Polly, "this is the little girl who came to see me when I was sick."

"Oh, sir," said Polly, "I'm so glad you wasn't!"

"Well, when I come again," said Mr. Henderson, rising after a merry chat, "I see I shall have to slip a book into my pocket, and read for those poor eyes."

"Oh, thank you!" cried Polly; and then she stopped and blushed.

"Well, what is it?" asked the minister, encouragingly.

"Ben loves to hear reading," said Polly.

"Does he? well, by that time, my little girl, I guess Ben will be down-stairs; he's all right, Polly; don't you worry about him--and I'll sit in the kitchen, by the bedroom door, and you can hear nicely."

So the Hendersons went away. But somehow, before they went, a good many things found their way out of the old-fashioned chaise into the Peppers' little kitchen.

But Polly's eyes didn't get any better, with all the care; and the lines of worry on Mrs. Pepper's face grew deeper and deeper. At last, she just confronted Dr. Fisher in the kitchen, one day after his visit to Polly, and boldly asked him if they ever could be cured. "I know she's--and there isn't any use keeping it from me," said the poor woman--"she's going to be stone-blind!"

"My good woman"--Dr. Fisher's voice was very gentle; and he took the hard, brown hand in his own--"your little girl will not be blind; I tell you the truth; but it will take some time to make her eyes quite strong--time, and rest. She has strained them in some way, but she will come out of it."

"Praise the Lord!" cried Mrs. Pepper, throwing her apron over her head; and then she sobbed on, "and thank you, sir--I can't ever thank you--for--for--if Polly was blind, we might as well give up!"

The next day, Phronsie, who had the doctor's permission to sit up, only she was to be kept from taking cold, scampered around in stocking-feet in search of her shoes, which she hadn't seen since she was first taken sick.

"Oh, I want on my very best shoes," she cried; "can't I, mammy?"

"Oh, no, Phronsie; you must keep them nice," remonstrated her mother; "you can't wear 'em every-day, you know."

"'Tisn't every-day," said Phronsie, slowly; it's only one day."

"Well, and then you'll want 'em on again tomorrow," said her mother.

"Oh, no, I won't!" cried Phronsie; "never, no more to-morrow, if I can have 'em to-day; please, mammy dear!"

Mrs. Pepper went to the lowest drawer in the high bureau, and took there from a small parcel done up in white tissue paper. Slowly unrolling this before the delighted eyes of the child, who stood patiently waiting, she disclosed the precious red-topped shoes which Phronsie immediately clasped to her bosom.

"My own, very own shoes! whole mine!" she cried, and trudged out into the kitchen to put them on herself.

"Hulloa!" cried Dr. Fisher, coming in about a quarter of an hour later to find her tugging laboriously at the buttons-- "new shoes! I declare!"

"My own!" cried Phronsie, sticking out one foot for inspection, where every button was in the wrong button-hole, "and they've got red tops, too!"

"So they have," said the doctor, getting down on the floor beside her; "beautiful red tops, aren't they?"

"Be-yew-ti-ful," sang the child delightedly.

"Does Polly have new shoes every day?" asked the doctor in a low voice, pretending to examine the other foot.

Phronsie opened her eyes very wide at this.

"Oh, no, she don't have anything, Polly don't."

"And what does Polly want most of all--do you know? see if you can tell me." And the doctor put on the most alluring expression that he could muster.

"Oh, I know!" cried Phronsie, with a very wise look. "There now," cried the doctor, "you're the girl for me! to think you know! so, what is it?"

Phronsie got up very gravely, and with one shoe half on, she leaned over and whispered in the doctor's ear:

"A stove!"

"A what?" said the doctor, looking at her, and then at the old, black thing in the corner, that looked as if it were ashamed of itself; "why, she's got one."

"Oh," said the child, "it won't burn; and sometimes Polly cries, she does, when she's all alone-- and I see her."

"Now," said the doctor, very sympathetically, "that's too bad; that is! and then what does she do?"

"Oh, Ben stuffs it up," said the child, laughing; "and so does Polly too, with paper; and then it all tumbles out quick; oh! just as quick!" And Phronsie shook her yellow head at the dismal remembrance.

"Do you suppose," said the doctor, getting up, "that you know of any smart little girl around here, about four years old and that knows how to button on her own red-topped shoes, that would like to go to ride to-morrow morning in my carriage with me?

"Oh, I do!" cried Phronsie, hopping on one toe; "it's me!"

"Very well, then," said Dr. Fisher, going to the bedroom door, "we'll lookout for to-morrow, then."

To poor Polly, lying in the darkened room, or sitting up in the big rocking-chair--for Polly wasn't really very sick in other respects, the disease having all gone into the merry brown eyes--the time seemed interminable. Not to do anything! The very idea at any time would have filled her active, wide-awake little body with horror; and now, here she was!

"Oh, dear, I can't bear it!" she said, when she knew by the noise in the kitchen that everybody was out there; so nobody heard, except a fat, old black spider in the corner, and he didn't tell anyone!

"I know it's a week," she said, "since dinnertime! If Ben were only well, to talk to me."

"Oh, I say, Polly," screamed Joel at that moment running in, "Ben's a-comin' down the stairs!"

"Stop, Joe," said Mrs. Pepper; "you shouldn't have told; he wanted to surprise Polly."

"Oh, is he!" cried Polly, clasping her hands in rapture; "mammy, can't! take off this horrid bandage, and see him?"

"Dear me, no!" said Mrs. Pepper, springing forward; "not for the world, Polly! Dr. Fisher'd have our ears off!"

"Well, I can hear, any way," said Polly, resigning herself to the remaining comfort; "here he is! oh, Ben!"

"There," said Ben, grasping Polly, bandage and all; "now we're all right; and! say, Polly, you're a brick!"

"Mammy told me not to say that the other day," said Joel, with a very virtuous air.

"Can't help it," said Ben, who was a little wild over Polly, and besides, he had been sick himself, and had borne a good deal too.

"Now," said Mrs. Pepper, after the first excitement was over, "you're so comfortable together, and Phronsie don't want me now, I'll go to the store; I must get some more work if Mr. Atkins'll give it to me."

"I'll be all right now, mammy, that Ben's here," cried Polly, settling back into her chair, with Phronsie on the stool at her feet.

"I'm goin' to tell her stories, ma," cried Ben, "so you needn't worry about us."

314

"Isn't it funny, Ben," said Polly, as the gate clicked after the mother, "to be sitting still, and telling stories in the daytime?"

"Rather funny!" replied Ben.

"Well, do go on," said Joel, as usual, rolling on the floor, in a dreadful hurry for the story to begin. Little David looked up quietly, as he sat on Ben's other side, his hands clasped tight together, just as eager, though he said nothing.

"Well; once upon a time," began Ben delightfully, and launched into one of the stories that the children thought perfectly lovely.

"Oh, Bensie," cried Polly, entranced, as they listened with bated breath, "however do you think of such nice things!"

"I've had time enough to think, the last week," said Ben, laughing, "to last a life-time!"

"Do go on," put in Joel, impatient at the delay.

"Don't hurry him so," said Polly, reprovingly; "he isn't strong."

"Ben," said David, drawing a long breath, his eyes very big--."did he really see a bear?"

"No," said Ben; "oh! where was I?"

"Why, you said Tommy heard a noise," said Polly, "and he thought it was a bear."

"Oh, yes," said Ben; "I remember; 'twasn't a--"

"Oh, make it a bear, Ben!" cried Joel, terribly disappointed; "don't let it be not a bear."

"Why, I can't," said Ben; "twouldn't sound true."

"Never mind, make it sound true," insisted Joel; "you can make anything true."

"Very well," said Ben, laughing; "I suppose I must."

"Make it two bears, Ben," begged little Phronsie.

"Oh, no, Phronsie, that's too much," cried Joel; "that'll spoil it; but make it a big bear, do Ben, and have him bite him somewhere, and most kill him."

"Oh, Joel!" cried Polly, while David's eyes got bigger than ever.

So Ben drew upon his powers as story-teller, to suit his exacting audience, and was making his bear work havoc upon poor Tommy in a way captivating to all, even Joel, when---- "Well, I declare," sounded Mrs. Pepper's cheery voice coming in upon them, "if this isn't comfortable!"

"Oh, mammy!" cried Phronsie, jumping out of Polly's arms, whither she had taken refuge during the thrilling tale, and running to her mother who gathered her baby up, "we've had a bear! a real, live bear, we have! Ben made him!"

"Have you!" said Mrs. Pepper, taking off her shawl, and laying her parcel of work down on the table, "now, that's nice!"

"Oh, mammy!" cried Polly, "it does seem so good to be all together again!"

"And I thank the Lord!" said Mrs. Pepper, looking down on her happy little group; and the tears were in her eyes-- "and children, we ought to be very good and please Him, for He's been so good to us."

Day 126

1. Read chapter 7.
2. Write a summary of the chapter. If you can, write your summaries in one sentence. You'll have to use words like AND or BUT. If you write your summary in one sentence, get a high five and/or hug.

Chapter 7 The Cloud Over the Little Brown House

When Phronsie, with many crows of delight, and much chattering, had gotten fairly started the following morning on her much-anticipated drive with the doctor, the whole family excepting Polly drawn up around the door to see them off, Mrs. Pepper resolved to snatch the time and run down for an hour or two to one of her customers who had long been waiting for a little "tailoring" to be done for her boys.

"Now, Joel," she said, putting on her bonnet before the cracked looking-glass, "you stay along of Polly; Ben must go up to bed, the doctor said; and Davie's going to the store for some molasses; so you and Polly must keep house."

"Yes'm," said Joel; "may I have somethin' to eat, ma?"

"Yes," said Mrs. Pepper; "but don't you eat the new bread; you may have as much as you want of the old."

"Isn't there any molasses, mammy?" asked Joel, as she bade Polly good-bye! and gave her numberless charges "to be careful of your eyes," and "not to let a crack of light in through the curtain," as the old green paper shade was called.

"No; if you're very hungry, you can eat bread," said Mrs. Pepper, sensibly.

"Joel," said Polly, after the mother had gone, "I do wish you could read to me."

"Well, I can't," said Joel, glad he didn't know how; "I thought the minister was comin'."

"Well, he was," said Polly, "but mammy said he had to go out of town to a consequence."

"A what!" asked Joel, very much impressed.

"A con--" repeated Polly. "Well, it began with a con--and I am sure--yes, very sure it was consequence."

"That must be splendid," said Joel, coming up to her chair, and slowly drawing a string he held in his hand back and forth, "to go to consequences, and everything! When I'm a man, Polly Pepper, I'm going to be a minister, and have a nice time, and go--just everywhere!"

"Oh, Joel!" exclaimed Polly, quite shocked; "you couldn't be one; you aren't good enough."

"I don't care," said Joel, not at all dashed by her plainness, "I'll be good then--when I'm a big man; don't you suppose, Polly," as a new idea struck him, "that Mr. Henderson ever is naughty?"

"No," said Polly, very decidedly; "never, never, never!"

"Then, I don't want to be one," said Joel, veering round with a sigh of relief, "and besides I'd rather have a pair of horses like Mr. Slocum's, and then I could go everywheres, I guess!"

"And sell tin?" asked Polly, "just like Mr. Slocum?"

"Yes," said Joel; "this is the way I'd go--Gee-whop! gee-whoa!" and Joel pranced with his imaginary steeds all around the room, making about as much noise as any other four boys, as he brought up occasionally against the four-poster or the high old bureau.

"Well!" said a voice close up by Polly's chair, that made her skip with apprehension, it was so like Miss Jerusha Henderson's--Joel was whooping away behind the bedstead to his horses that had become seriously entangled, so he didn't hear anything. But when Polly said, bashfully, "I can't see anything, ma'am," he came up red and shining to the surface, and stared with all his might.

"I came to see you, little girl," said Miss Jerusha severely, seating herself stiffly by Polly's side.

"Thank you, ma'am," said Polly, faintly.

"Who's this boy?" asked the lady, turning around squarely on Joel, and eying him from head to foot.

"He's my brother Joel," said Polly.

Joel still stared.

"Which brother?" pursued Miss Jerusha, like a census-taker.

"He is next to me," said Polly, wishing her mother was home; "he's nine, Joel is."

"He's big enough to do something to help his mother," said Miss Jerusha, looking him through and through. "Don't you think you might do something, when the others are sick, and your poor mother is working so hard?" she continued, in a cold voice.

"I do something," blurted out Joel, sturdily, "lots and lots!"

"You shouldn't say 'lots,'" reproved Miss Jerusha, with a sharp look over her spectacles, "tisn't proper for boys to talk so; what do you do all day long?" she asked, turning back to Polly, after a withering glance at Joel, who still stared.

"I can't do anything, ma'am," replied Polly, sadly, "I can't see to do anything."

"Well, you might knit, I should think," said her visitor, "it's dreadful for a girl as big as you are to sit all day idle; I had sore eyes once when I was a little girl--how old are you?" she asked, abruptly.

"Eleven last month," said Polly.

"Well, I wasn't only nine when I knit a stocking; and I had sore eyes, too; you see I was a very little girl, and--"

"Was you ever little?" interrupted Joel, in extreme incredulity, drawing near, and looking over the big square figure.

"Hey?" said Miss Jerusha; so Joel repeated his question before Polly could stop him.

"Of course," answered Miss Jerusha; and then she added, tartly, "little boys shouldn't speak unless they're spoken to. Now," and she turned back to Polly again, "didn't you ever knit a stocking?"

"No, ma'am," said Polly, "not a whole one."

"Dear me!" exclaimed Miss Jerusha; "did I ever!" And she raised her black mitts in intense disdain. "A big girl like you never to knit a stocking! to think your mother should bring you up so! and--"

"She didn't bring us up," screamed Joel, in indignation, facing her with blazing eyes.

"Joel," said Polly, "be still."

"And you're very impertinent, too," said Miss Jerusha; "a good child never is impertinent."

Polly sat quite still; and Miss Jerusha continued:

"Now, I hope you will learn to be industrious; and when I come again, I will see what you have done."

"You aren't ever coming again," said Joel, defiantly; "no, never!"

"Joel!" implored Polly, and in her distress she pulled up her bandage as she looked at him; "you know mammy'll be so sorry at you! Oh, ma'am, and" she turned to Miss Jerusha, who was now thoroughly aroused to the duty she saw before her of doing these children good, "I don't know what is the reason, ma'am; Joel never talks so; he's real good; and--"

"It only shows," said the lady, seeing her way quite clear for a little exhortation, "that you've all had your own way from infancy; and that you don't do what you might to make your mother's life a happy one."

"Oh, ma'am," cried Polly, and she burst into a flood of tears, "please, please don't say that!"

"And I say," screamed Joel, stamping his small foot, "if you make Polly cry you'll kill her! Don't Polly, don't!" and the boy put both arms around her neck, and soothed and comforted her in every way he could think of. And Miss Jerusha, seeing no way to make herself heard, disappeared feeling pity for children who would turn away from good advice.

But still Polly cried on; all the pent-up feelings that had been so long controlled had free vent now. She really couldn't stop! Joel, frightened to death, at last said, "I'm going to wake up Ben."

That brought Polly to; and she sobbed out, "Oh, no, Jo--ey--I'll stop."

"I will," said Joel, seeing his advantage; "I'm going, Polly," and he started to the foot of the stairs.

"No, I'm done now, Joe," said Polly, wiping her eyes, and choking back her thoughts--"oh, Joe! I must scream! my eyes aches so!" and poor Polly fairly writhed all over the chair.

"What'll I do?" said Joel, at his wits' end, running back, "do you want some water?"

"Oh, no," gasped Polly; "doctor wouldn't let me; oh! I wish mammy'd come!"

"I'll go and look for her," suggested Joel, feeling as if he must do something; and he'd rather be out at the gate, than to see Polly suffer.

"That won't bring her," said Polly; trying to keep still; "I'll try to wait."

"Here she is now!" cried Joel, peeping out of the window; "oh! goody!"

Day 127

1. Read chapter 8.
2. Write a summary of the chapter. If you write your summary in one sentence, get a high five and/or hug.

Chapter 8 Joel's Turn

"Well"--Mrs. Pepper's tone was unusually blithe as she stepped into the kitchen--"you've had a nice time, I suppose--what in the world!" and she stopped at the bedroom door.

"Oh, mammy, if you'd been here!" said Joel, while Polly sat still, only holding on to her eyes as if they were going to fly out; "there's been a big woman here; she came right in--and she talked awfully! and Polly's been a-cryin', and her eyes ache dreadfully--and"-- "Been crying!" repeated Mrs. Pepper, coming up to poor

Polly. "Polly been crying!" she still repeated.

"Oh, mammy, I couldn't help it," said Polly; "she said"-- and in spite of all she could do, the rain of tears began again, which bade fair to be as uncontrolled as before. But Mrs. Pepper took her up firmly in her arms, as if she were Phronsie, and sat down in the old rocking-chair and just patted her back.

"There, there," she whispered, soothingly, "don't think of it, Polly; mother's got home."

"Oh, mammy," said Polly, crawling up to the comfortable neck for protection, "I ought not to mind; but 'twas Miss Jerusha Henderson; and she said--"

"What did she say?" asked Mrs. Pepper, thinking perhaps it to be the wiser thing to let Polly free her mind.

"Oh, she said that we ought to be doing something; and I ought to knit, and"-- "Go on," said her mother.

"And then Joel got naughty; oh, mammy, he never did so before; and I couldn't stop him," cried Polly, in great distress; "I really couldn't, mammy--and he talked to her; and he told her she wasn't ever coming here again."

"Joel shouldn't have said that," said Mrs. Pepper, and under her breath something was added that Polly even failed to hear--"but no more she isn't!"

"And, mammy," cried Polly--and she flung her arms around her mother's neck and gave her a grasp that nearly choked Mrs. Pepper, "ain't I helpin' you some, mammy? Oh! I wish I could do something big for you? Ain't you happy, mammy?"

"For the land's sakes!" cried Mrs. Pepper, straining Polly to her heart, "whatever has that woman--whatever could she have said to you? Such a girl as you are, too!" cried Mrs. Pepper, hugging Polly, and covering her with kisses so tender, that Polly, warmed and cuddled up to her heart's content, was comforted to the full.

"Well," said Mrs. Pepper, when at last she thought she had formed between Polly and Joel about the right idea of the visit, "well, now we won't think of it, ever any more; 'tisn't worth it, Polly, you know."

But poor Polly! and poor mother! They both were obliged to think of it. Nothing could avert the suffering of the next few days, caused by that long flow of burning tears.

"Nothing feels good on 'em, mammy," said Polly, at last, twisting her hands in the vain attempt to keep from rubbing the aching, inflamed eyes that drove her nearly wild with their itching, "there isn't any use in trying anything."

"There will be use," energetically protested Mrs. Pepper, bringing another cool bandage, "as long as you've got an eye in your head, Polly Pepper!"

Dr. Fisher's face, when he first saw the change that the fateful visit had wrought, and heard the accounts, was very grave indeed. Everything had been so encouraging on his last visit, that he had come very near promising Polly speedy freedom from the hateful bandage.

But the little Pepper household soon had something else to think of more important even than Polly's eyes, for now the heartiest, the jolliest of all the little group was down-- Joel. How he fell sick, they scarcely knew, it all came so suddenly. The poor, bewildered family had hardly time to think, before delirium and, perhaps, death stared them in the face.

When Polly first heard it, by Phronsie's pattering downstairs and screaming: "Oh, Polly, Joey's dreadful sick, he is!" she jumped right up, and tore off the bandage.

"Now, I will help mother! I will, so there!" and in another minute she would have been up in the sick room. But the first thing she knew, a gentle but firm hand was laid upon hers; and she found herself back again in the old rocking-chair, and listening to the Doctor's words which were quite stern and decisive.

"Now, I tell you," he said, "you must not take off that bandage again; do you know the consequences? You will be blind! and then you will be a care to your mother all your life!"

"I shall be blind, anyway," said Polly, despairingly; "so 'twon't make any difference."

"No; your eyes will come out of it all right, only I did hope"--and the good doctor's face fell-- "that the other two boys would escape; but"--and he brightened up at sight of Polly's forlorn visage--"see you do your part by keeping still."

But there came a day soon when everything was still around the once happy little brown house-- when only whispers were heard from white lips; and thoughts were fearfully left unuttered.

On the morning of one of these days, when Mrs. Pepper felt she could not exist an hour longer without sleep, kind Mrs. Beebe came to stay until things were either better or worse.

Still the cloud hovered, dark and forbidding. At last, one afternoon, when Polly was all alone, she could endure it no longer. She flung herself down by the side of the old bed, and buried her face in the gay patched bed-quilt.

"Dear God," she said, "make me willing to have anything"--she hesitated--"yes, anything happen; to be blind forever, and to have Joey sick, only make me good."

How long she stayed there she never knew; for she fell asleep--the first sleep she had had since Joey was taken sick. And little Mrs. Beebe coming in found her thus.

"Polly," the good woman said, leaning over her, "you poor, pretty creeter, you; I'm goin' to tell you somethin'--there, there, just to think! Joel's goin' to get well!"

"Oh, Mrs. Beebe!" cried Polly, tumbling over in a heap on the floor, her face, as much as could be seen under the bandage, in a perfect glow, "Is he, really?"

"Yes, to be sure; the danger's all over now," said the little old lady, inwardly thinking--"If I hadn't a-come!"

"Well, then, the Lord wants him to," cried Polly, in rapture; "don't he, Mrs. Beebe?"

"To be sure--to be sure," repeated the kind friend, only half understanding.

"Well, I don't care about my eyes, then," cried Polly; and to Mrs. Beebe's intense astonishment and dismay, she spun round and round in the middle of the floor.

"Oh, Polly, Polly!" the little old lady cried, running up to her, "do stop! the doctor wouldn't let you! he wouldn't really, you know! it'll all go to your eyes."

"I don't care," repeated Polly, in the middle of a spin; but she stopped obediently; "seems as if I just as soon be blind as not; it's so beautiful Joey's going to get well!"

Day 128

1. Read the first part of chapter 9.
2. Tell someone what is happening the chapter. Why do you think the chapter is called, "Sunshine Again?"

Chapter 9 Sunshine Again

But as Joel was smitten down suddenly, so he came up quickly, and his hearty nature asserted itself by rapid strides toward returning health; and one morning he astonished them all by turning over suddenly and exclaiming:

"I want something to eat!"

"Bless the Lord!" cried Mrs. Pepper, "now he's going to live!"

"But he mustn't eat," protested Mrs. Beebe, in great alarm, trotting for the cup of gruel. "Here, you pretty creeter you, here's something nice." And she temptingly held the spoon over Joel's mouth; but with a grimace he turned away.

"Oh, I want something to eat! some gingerbread or some bread and butter."

"Dear me!" ejaculated Mrs. Beebe. "Gingerbread!" Poor Mrs. Pepper saw the hardest part of her trouble now before her, as she realized that the returning appetite must be fed only on strengthening food; for where it was to come from she couldn't tell.

"The Lord only knows where we'll get it," she groaned within herself.

Yes, He knew. A rap at the door, and little David ran down to find the cause.

"Oh, mammy," he said, "Mrs. Henderson sent it--see! see!" And in the greatest excitement he placed in her lap a basket that smelt savory and nice even before it was opened. When it was opened, there lay a little bird delicately roasted, and folded in a clean napkin; also a glass of jelly, crimson and clear.

"Oh, Joey," cried Mrs. Pepper, almost overwhelmed with joy, "see what Mrs. Henderson sent you! now you can eat fit for a king!"

That little bird certainly performed its mission in life; for as Mrs. Beebe said, "It just touched the spot!" and from that very moment Joel improved so rapidly they could hardly believe their eyes.

"Hoh! I haven't been sick!" he cried on the third day, true to his nature. "Mammy, I want to get up."

"Oh, dear, no! you mustn't, Joel," cried Mrs. Pepper in a fright, running up to him as he was preparing to give the bedclothes a lusty kick; "you'll send 'em in."

"Send what in?" asked Joel, looking up at his mother in terror, as the dreadful thought made him pause.

"Why, the measles, Joey; they'll all go in if you get out."

"How they goin' to get in again, I'd like to know?" asked Joel, looking at the little red spots on his hands in incredulity; say, ma!

"Well, they will," said his mother, "as you'll find to your sorrow if you get out of bed."

"Oh, dear," said Joel, beginning to whimper, as he drew into bed again, "when can I get up, mammy!"

"Oh, in a day or two," responded Mrs. Pepper, cheerfully; "you're getting on so finely you'll be as smart as a cricket! Shouldn't you say he might get up in a day or two, Mrs. Beebe?" she appealed to that individual who was knitting away cheerily in the corner.

"Well, if he keeps on as he's begun, I shouldn't know what to think," replied Mrs. Beebe. "It beats all how quick he's picked up. I never see anything like it, I'm sure!"

And as Mrs. Beebe was a great authority in sickness, the old, sunny cheeriness began to creep into the brown house once more, and to bubble over as of yore.

"Seems as if 'twas just good to live," said Mrs. Pepper, thankfully once, when her thoughts were too much for her. "I don't believe I shall ever care how poor we are," she continued, "as long as we're together."

"And that's just what the Lord meant, maybe," replied good Mrs. Beebe, who was preparing to go home.

Joel kept the house in a perfect uproar all through his getting well. Mrs. Pepper observed one day, when he had been more turbulent than usual, that she was "almost worn to a thread."

"Twasn't anything to take care of you, Joe," she added, "when you were real sick, because then I knew where you were; but--well, you won't ever have the measles again, I s'pose, and that's some comfort!"

Little David, who had been nearly stunned by the sickness that had laid aside his almost constant companion, could express his satisfaction and joy in no other way than by running every third minute and begging to do something for him. And Joel, who loved dearly to be waited on, improved every opportunity that offered; which Mrs. Pepper observing, soon put a stop to.

"You'll run his legs off, Joel," at last she said, when he sent David the third time down to the wood-pile for a stick of just the exact thickness, and which the little messenger declared wasn't to be found. "Haven't you any mercy? You've kept him going all day, too," she added, glancing at David's pale face.

"Oh, mammy," panted David, "don't; I love to go. Here Joe, is the best I could find," handing him a nice smooth stick.

"I know you do," said his mother; "but Joe's getting better now, and he must learn to spare you."

"I don't want to spare folks," grumbled Joel, whittling away with energy; "I've been sick--real sick," he added, lifting his chubby face to his mother to impress the fact.

"I know you have," she cried, running to kiss her boy; "but now, Joe, you're most well. To-morrow I'm going to let you go down-stairs; what do you think of that!"

"Hooray!" screamed Joel, throwing away the stick and clapping his hands, forgetting all about his serious illness, "that'll be prime!"

"Aren't you too sick to go, Joey?" asked Mrs. Pepper, mischievously.

"No, I'm not sick," cried Joel, in the greatest alarm, fearful his mother meant to take back the promise; "I've never been sick. Oh, mammy! you know you'll let me go, won't your?"

"I guess so," laughed his mother.

"Come on, Phron," cried Joel, giving her a whirl.

David, who was too tired for active sport, sat on the floor and watched them frolic in great delight.

"Mammy," said he, edging up to her side as the sport went on, "do you know, I think it's just good--it's--oh, it's so frisky since Joe got well, isn't it, mammy?"

"Yes, indeed," said Mrs. Pepper, giving him a radiant look in return for his; "and when Polly's around again with her two eyes all right--well, I don't know what we shall do, I declare!"

"Boo!" cried a voice, next morning, close to Polly's elbow, unmistakably Joel's.

"Oh, Joel Pepper!" she cried, whirling around, "is that really you!"

"Yes," cried that individual, confidently, "it's I; oh, I say, Polly, I've had fun up-stairs, I tell you what!"

"Poor boy!" said Polly, compassionately.

"I wasn't a poor boy," cried Joel, indignantly; "I had splendid things to eat; oh, my!" and he closed one eye and smacked his lips in the delightful memory.

"I know it," said Polly, "and I'm so glad, Joel."

"I don't suppose I'll ever get so many again," observed Joel, reflectively, after a minute's pause, as one and another of the wondrous delicacies rose before his mind's eye; "not unless I have the measles again--say, Polly, can't I have 'em again?"

"Mercy, no!" cried Polly, in intense alarm, "I hope not."

"Well, I don't," said Joel, "I wish I could have 'em sixty--no--two hundred times, so there!"

"Well, mammy couldn't take care of you," said Ben; "you don't know what you're sayin', Joe."

"Well, then, I wish I could have the things without the measles," said Joel, willing to accommodate; "only folks won't send 'em," he added, in an injured tone.

Day 129

1. Finish reading chapter 9.
2. Write a summary of the chapter. If you write your summary in one sentence, get a high five and/or hug.

Chapter 9 continued

"Polly's had the hardest time of all," said her mother, affectionately patting the bandage.

"I think so too," put in Ben; "if my eyes were hurt I'd give up."

"So would I," said David; and Joel, to be in the fashion, cried also, "I know I would;" while little Phronsie squeezed up to Polly's side, "And I, too."

"Would what, Puss?" asked Ben, tossing her up high. "Have good things," cried the child, in delight at understanding the others, "I would really, Ben," she cried, gravely, when they all screamed.

"Well, I hope so," said Ben, tossing her higher yet. "Don't laugh at her, boys," put in Polly; "we're all going to have good times now, Phronsie, now we've got well."

"Yes," laughed the child from her high perch; "we aren't ever goin' to be sick again, ever--any more," she added impressively.

The good times were coming for Polly--coming pretty near, and she didn't know it! All the children were in the secret; for as Mrs. Pepper declared, "They'd have to know it; and if they were let into the secret they'd keep it better."

So they had individually and collectively been entrusted with the precious secret, and charged with the extreme importance of "never letting any one know," and they had been nearly bursting ever since with the wild desire to impart their knowledge.

'I'm afraid I shall tell," said David, running to his mother at last; "oh, mammy, I don't dare stay near Polly, I do want to tell so bad."

"Oh, no, you won't, David," said his mother encouragingly, "when you know mother don't want you to; and besides, think how Polly'll look when she sees it."

"I know," cried David in the greatest rapture, "I wouldn't tell for all the world! I guess she'll look nice, don't you mother?" and he laughed in glee at the thought.

"Poor child! I guess she will!" and then Mrs. Pepper laughed too, till the little old kitchen rang with delight at the accustomed sound,

The children all had to play "clap in and clap out" in the bedroom while it came; and "stage coach," too--"anything to make a noise," Ben said. And then after they got nicely started in the game, he would be missing to help about the mysterious thing in the kitchen, which was safe since Polly couldn't see him go on account of her bandage. So she didn't suspect in the least. And although the rest were almost dying to be out in the kitchen, they conscientiously stuck to their bargain to keep Polly occupied. Only Joel would open the door and peep once; and then Phronsie behind him began-- "Oh, I see the sto--" but David swooped down on her in a twinkling, and smothered the rest by tickling her.

Once they came very near having the whole thing pop out. "Whatever is that noise in the kitchen?" asked Polly, as they all stopped to take breath after the scuffle of "stage coach." "It sounds just like grating."

"I'll go and see," cried Joel, promptly; and then he flew out where his mother and Ben and two men were at work on a big, black thing in the corner. The old stove, strange to say, was nowhere to be seen! Something else stood in its place, a shiny, black affair, with a generous supply of oven doors, and altogether such a comfortable, home-like look about it, as if it would say--"I'm going to make sunshine in this house!"

"Oh, Joel," cried his mother, turning around on him with very black hands, "you haven't told!"

"No," said Joel, "but she's hearin' the noise, Polly is."

"Hush!" said Ben, to one of the men.

"We can't put it up without some noise," the man replied, "but we'll be as still as we can."

"Isn't it a big one, ma?" asked Joel, in the loudest of stage whispers, that Polly on the other side of the door couldn't have failed to hear if Phronsie hadn't laughed just then.

"Go back, Joe, do," said Ben, "play tag--anything," he implored, "we'll be through in a few minutes."

"It takes forever!" said Joel, disappearing within the bedroom door. Luckily for the secret, Phronsie just then ran a pin sticking up on the arm of the old chair, into her finger; and Polly, while comforting her, forgot to question Joel. And then the mother came in, and though she had ill-concealed hilarity in her voice, she kept chattering and bustling around with Polly's supper to such an extent that there was no chance for a word to be got in.

Next morning it seemed as if the "little brown house," would turn inside out with joy.

"Oh, mammy!" cried Polly, jumping into her arms the first thing, as Dr. Fisher untied the bandage, "my eyes are new! just the same as if I'd just got 'em! Don't they look different?" she asked, earnestly, running to the cracked glass to see for herself.

"No," said Ben, "I hope not; the same brown ones, Polly."

"Well," said Polly, hugging first one and then another, "everybody looks different through them, anyway."

"Oh," cried Joel, "come out into the kitchen, Polly; it's a great deal better out there."

"May I?" asked Polly, who was in such a twitter looking at everything that she didn't know which way to turn.

"Yes," said the doctor, smiling at her.

"Well, then," sang Polly, "come mammy, we'll go first; isn't it just lovely--oh, *Mammy*!"--and Polly turned so very pale, and looked as if she were going to tumble right over, that Mrs. Pepper grasped her arm in dismay.

"What is it?" she asked, pointing to the corner, while all the children stood round in the greatest excitement.

"Why," cried Phronsie, "it's a stove--don't you know, Polly?" But Polly gave one plunge across the room, and before anybody could think, she was down on her knees with her arms flung right around the big, black thing, and laughing and crying over it, all in the same breath!

And then they all took hold of hands and danced around it like wild little things; while Dr. Fisher stole out silently-- and Mrs. Pepper laughed till she wiped her eyes to see them ' go.

"We aren't ever goin' to have any more burnt bread," sang Polly, all out of breath.

"Nor your back isn't goin' to break any more," panted Ben, with a very red face.

"Hooray!" screamed Joel and David, to fill any pause that might occur, while Phronsie gurgled and laughed at everything just as it came along. And then they all danced and capered again; all but Polly, who was down before the precious stove examining and exploring into ovens and everything that belonged to it.

"Oh, ma," she announced, coming up to Mrs. Pepper, who had been obliged to fly to her sewing again, and exhibiting a very crocky face and a pair of extremely smutty hands, "it's most all ovens, and it's just splendid!"

"I know it," answered her mother, delighted in the joy of her child. "My! how black you are, Polly!"

"Oh, I wish," cried Polly, as the thought struck her, "that Dr. Fisher could see it! Where did he go to, ma?"

"I guess Dr. Fisher has seen it before," said Mrs. Pepper, and then she began to laugh. "You haven't ever asked where the stove came from, Polly."

And to be sure, Polly had been so overwhelmed that if the stove had really dropped from the clouds it would have been small matter of astonishment to her, as long as it had come; that was the main thing!

"Mammy," said Polly, turning around slowly, with the stove-lifter in her hand, "did Dr. Fisher bring that stove?"

"He didn't exactly bring it," answered her mother, "but I guess he knew something about it."

"Oh, he's the splendidest, goodest man!" cried Polly, "that ever breathed! Did he really get us that stove?"

"Yes," said Mrs. Pepper, "he would; I couldn't stop him. I don't know how he found out you wanted one so bad; but he said it must be kept as a surprise when your eyes got well."

"And he saved my eyes!" cried Polly, full of gratitude. "I've got a stove and two new eyes, mammy, just to think!"

"We ought to be good after all our mercies," said Mrs. Pepper thankfully, looking around on her little group. Joel was engaged in the pleasing occupation of seeing how far he could run his head into the biggest oven, and then pulling it out to exhibit its blackness, thus engrossing the others in a perfect hubbub.

"I'm going to bake my doctor some little cakes," declared Polly, when there was comparative quiet.

"Do, Polly," cried Joel, "and then leave one or two over."

"No," said Polly; "we can't have any, because these must be very nice. Mammy, can't I have some white on top, just once?" she pleaded.

"I don't know," dubiously replied Mrs. Pepper; ~eggs are dreadful dear, and--"

"I don't care," said Polly, recklessly; "I must just once for Dr. Fisher."

"I tell you, Polly," said Mrs. Pepper, "what you might do; you might make him some little apple tarts--most every one likes them, you know."

"Well," said Polly, with a sigh, "I s'pose they'll have to do; but some time, mammy, I'm going to bake him a big cake, so there!"

Day 130

1. Read chapter 10.
2. Write a summary of the chapter. If you write your summary in one sentence, get a high five and/or hug.

Vocabulary

1. Add to your dictionary. In your reading find three words you don't know and write them in this dictionary. Write the word and what it means.

Chapter 10 A Threatened Blow

One day, a few weeks after, Mrs. Pepper and Polly were busy in the kitchen. Phronsie was out in the "orchard," as the one scraggy apple-tree was called by courtesy, singing her rag doll to sleep under its sheltering branches. But "Baby" was cross and wouldn't go to sleep, and Phronsie was on the point of giving up, and returning to the house, when a strain of music made her pause with dolly in her apron. There she stood with her finger in her mouth, in utter astonishment, wondering where the sweet sounds came from.

"Oh, Phronsie!" screamed Polly, from the back door, "where are--oh, here, come quick! it's the beau-ti-fullest!"

"What is it?" eagerly asked the little one, hopping over the stubby grass, leaving poor, discarded "Baby" on its snubby nose where it dropped in her hurry.

"Oh, a monkey!" cried Polly; "do hurry! the sweetest little monkey you ever saw!"

"What is a monkey?" asked Phronsie, skurrying after Polly to the gate where her mother was waiting for them.

"Why, a monkey's--a--monkey," explained Polly, "I don't know any better'n that. Here he is! Isn't he splendid!" and she lifted Phronsie up to the big post where she could see finely.

"O-oh! ow!" screamed little Phronsie, "see him, Polly! just see him!"

A man with an organ was standing in the middle of the road playing away with all his might, and at the end of a long rope was a lively little monkey in a bright red coat and a smart cocked hat. The little creature pulled off his hat, and with one long jump coming on the fence, he made Phronsie a most magnificent bow. Strange to say, the child wasn't in the least frightened, but put out her little fat hand, speaking in gentle tones, "Poor little monkey! come here, poor little monkey!"

Turning up his little wrinkled face, and glancing fearfully at his master, Jocko began to grimace and beg for something to eat. The man pulled the string and struck up a merry tune, and in a minute the monkey spun around and around at such a lively pace, and put in so many queer antics that the little audience were fairly convulsed with laughter.

"I can't pay you," said Mrs. Pepper, wiping her eyes, when at last the man pulled up the strap whistling to Jocko to jump up, "but I'll give you something to eat; and the monkey, too, he shall have something for his pains in amusing my children."

The man looked very cross when she brought him out only brown bread and two cold potatoes.

"Haven't you got nothin' better'n that?"

"It's as good as we have," answered Mrs. Pepper.

The man threw down the bread in the road. But Jocko thankfully ate his share, Polly and Phronsie busily feeding him; and then he turned and snapped up the portion his master had left in the dusty road.

Then they moved on, Mrs. Pepper and Polly going back to their work in the kitchen. A little down the road the man struck up another tune. Phronsie who had started merrily to tell "Baby" all about it, stopped a minute to hear, and--she didn't go back to the orchard!

About two hours after, Polly said merrily:

"I'm going to call Phronsie in, mammy; she must be awfully tired and hungry by this time."

She sang gayly on the way, "I'm coming, Phronsie, coming--why, where!--" peeping under the tree.

"Baby" lay on its face disconsolately on the ground--and the orchard was empty! Phronsie was gone!

"It's no use," said Ben, to the distracted household and such of the neighbors as the news had brought hurriedly to the scene, "to look any more around here--but somebody must go toward Hingham; he'd be likely to go that way."

"No one could tell where he would go," cried Polly, wringing her hands.

"But he'd change, Ben, if he thought folks would think he'd gone there," said Mrs. Pepper.

"We must go all roads," said Ben, firmly; "one must take the stage to Boxville, and I'll take Deacon Brown's wagon on the Hingham road, and somebody else must go to Toad Hollow."

"I'll go in the stage," screamed Joel, who could scarcely see out of his eyes, he had cried so; "I'll find--find her--I know.

"Be spry, then, Joe, and catch it at the corner!"

Everybody soon knew that little Phronsie Pepper had gone off with "a cross organ man and an awful monkey!" and in the course of an hour dozens of people were out on the hot, dusty roads in search.

"What's the matter?" asked a testy old gentleman in the stage, of Joel who, in his anxiety to see both sides of the road at once, bobbed the old gentleman in the face so often as the stage lurched, that at last he knocked his hat over his eyes.

"My sister's gone off with a monkey," explained Joel, bobbing over to the other side, as he thought he caught sight of something pink that he felt sure must be Phronsie's apron. "Stop! stop! there she is!" he roared, and the driver, who had his instructions and was fully in sympathy, pulled up so suddenly that the old gentleman flew over into the opposite seat.

"Where?"

But when they got up to it Joel saw that it was only a bit of pink calico flapping on a clothes-line; so he climbed back and away they rumbled again.

The others were having the same luck. No trace could be found of the child. To Ben, who took the Hingham road, the minutes seemed like hours.

"I won't go back," he muttered, "until I take her. I can't see mother's face!"

But the ten miles were nearly traversed; almost the last hope was gone. Into every thicket and lurking place by the road-side had he peered--but no Phronsie! Deacon Brown's horse began to lag.

"Go on!" said Ben hoarsely; "oh, dear Lord, make me find her!"

The hot sun poured down on the boy's face, and he had no cap. What cared he for that? On and on he went. Suddenly the horse stopped. Ben doubled up the reins to give him a cut, when "*Whoa*!" he roared so loud that the horse in very astonishment gave a lurch that nearly flung him headlong. But he was over the wheel in a twinkling, and up with a bound to a small thicket of scrubby bushes on a high hill by the road-side. Here lay a little bundle on the ground, and close by it a big, black dog; and over the whole, standing guard, was a boy a little bigger than Ben, with honest gray eyes. And the bundle was Phronsie!

"Don't wake her up," said the boy, warningly, as Ben, with a hungry look in his eyes, leaped up the hill, "she's tired to death!"

"She's my sister!" cried Ben, "our Phronsie!"

"I know it," said the boy kindly; "but I wouldn't wake her up yet if I were you. I'll tell you all about it," and he took Ben's hand which was as cold as ice.

Day 131

1. Read chapter 11.
2. Tell someone about the chapter.

Chapter 11 Safe

"It's all right, Prince," the boy added, encouragingly to the big dog who, lifting his noble head, had turned two big eyes steadily on Ben. "He's all right! lie down again!"

Then, flinging himself down on the grass, he told Ben how he came to rescue Phronsie.

"Prince and I were out for a stroll," said he. "I live over in Hingham," pointing to the pretty little town just a short distance before them in the hollow; "that is," laughing, "I do this summer. Well, we were out strolling along about a mile below here on the cross-road; and all of a sudden, just as if they sprung right up out of the ground, I saw a man with an organ, and a monkey, and a little girl, coming along the road. She was crying, and as soon as Prince saw that, he gave a growl, and then the man saw us, and he looked so mean and cringing I knew there must be something wrong, and I inquired of him what he was doing with that little girl, and then she looked up and begged so with her eyes, and all of a sudden broke away from him and ran towards me screaming--'I want Polly!' Well, the man sprang after her; then I tell you"--here the boy forgot his caution about waking Phronsie--"we went for him, Prince and I! Prince is a noble fellow," (here the dog's ears twitched very perceptibly) "and he kept at that man; oh! how he bit him! till he had to run for fear the monkey would get killed."

"Was Phronsie frightened?" asked Ben; "she's never seen strangers."

"Not a bit," said the boy, cheerily; "she just clung to me like everything--I only wish she was my sister," he added impulsively.

"What were you going to do with her if I hadn't come along?" asked Ben.

"Well, I got out on the main road," said the boy, "because I thought anybody who had lost her, would probably come through this way; but if somebody hadn't come, I was going to carry her in to Hingham; and the father and I'd had to contrive some way to do."

"Well," said Ben, as the boy finished and fastened his bright eyes on him, "somebody did come along; and now I must get her home about as fast as I can for poor mammy-- and Polly!"

"Yes," said the boy, "I'll help you lift her; perhaps she won't wake up."

The big dog moved away a step or two, but still kept his eye on Phronsie.

"There," said the boy, brightly, as they laid the child on the wagon seat; "now when you get in you can hold her head; that's it," he added, seeing them both fixed to his satisfaction. But still Ben lingered.

"Thank you," he tried to say.

"I know," laughed the boy; "only it's Prince instead of me," and he pulled forward the big black creature, who had followed faithfully down the hill to see the last of it. "To the front, sir, there! We're coming to see you," he continued, "if you will let us--where do you live?"

"Do come," said Ben, lighting up, for he was just feeling he couldn't bear to look his last on the merry, honest face; "anybody'll tell you where Mrs. Pepper lives."

"Is she a Pepper?" asked the boy, laughing, and pointing to the unconscious little heap in the wagon; "and are you a Pepper?"

"Yes," said Ben, laughing too. "There are five of us besides mother.

"Jolly! that's something like! Good-bye! Come on, Prince!" Then away home to mother! Phronsie never woke up or turned over once till she was put, a little pink sleepy heap, into her mother's arms. Joel was there, crying bitterly at his forlorn search. The testy old gentleman in the seat opposite had relented and ordered the coach about and brought him home in an outburst of grief when all hope was gone. And one after another they all had come back, disheartened, to the distracted mother. Polly alone, clung to hope!

"Ben will bring her, mammy; I know God will let him," she whispered.

But when Ben did bring her, Polly, for the second time in her life, tumbled over with a gasp, into old Mrs. Bascom's lap.

Home and mother! Little Phronsie slept all that night straight through. The neighbors came in softly, and with awestruck visages stole into the bedroom to look at the child; and as they crept out again, thoughts of their own little ones tugging at their hearts, the tears would drop unheeded.

Day 132

1. Read the beginning of chapter 12.
2. Tell someone what is happening in the chapter so far.

Chapter 12 New Friends

Up the stairs of the hotel, two steps at a time, ran a boy with a big, black dog at his heels. "Come on, Prince; soft, now," as they neared a door at the end of the corridors

It opened into a corner room overlooking "the Park," as the small open space in front of the hotel was called. Within the room there was sunshine and comfort, it being the most luxurious one in the house, which the proprietor bad placed at the disposal of thi5 most exacting guest. He didn't look very happy, however--the gentleman who sat in an easy chair by the window; a large, handsome old gentleman, whose whole bearing showed plainly that personal comfort had always been his, and was, therefore, neither a matter of surprise nor thankfulness.

"Where have you been?" he asked, turning around to greet the boy who came in, followed by Prince.

"Oh, such a long story, father!" he cried, flushed; his eyes sparkling as he flung back the dark hair from his forehead. "You can't even guess!"

"Never mind now," said the old gentleman, testily; "your stories are always long; the paper hasn't come--strange, indeed, that one must needs be so annoyed! do ring that bell again.

So the bell was pulled; and a porter popped in his head.

"What is it, sir?"

"The paper," said the old gentleman, irritably; "hasn't it come yet?"

336

"No, sir," said the man; and then he repeated, "taint in yet, please, sir."

"Very well--you said so once; that's all," waving his hand; then as the door closed, he said to his son, "That pays one for coming to such an out-of-the-way country place as this, away from papers--I never will do it again."

As the old gentleman, against the advice of many friends who knew his dependence on externals, had determined to come to this very place, the boy was not much startled at the decisive words. He stood very quietly, however, until his father finished. Then he said:

"It's too bad, father! supposing I tell you my story? Perhaps you'll enjoy hearing it while you wait--it's really quite newspaperish."

"Well, you might as well tell it now, I suppose," said the old gentleman; "but it is a great shame about that paper! to advertise that morning papers are to be obtained--it's a swindle, Jasper! a complete swindle!" and the old gentleman looked so very irate that the boy exerted himself to soothe him.

"I know," he said; "but they can't help the trains being late."

"They shouldn't have the trains late," said his father, unreasonably. "There's no necessity for all this prating about 'trains late.' I'm convinced it's because they forgot to send down for the papers till they were all sold."

"I don't believe that's it, father," said the boy, trying to change the subject; "but you don't know how splendid Prince has been, nor"-- "And then such a breakfast!" continued the old gentleman.

"My liver certainly will be in a dreadful state if these things continue!" And he got up, and going to the corner of the room, opened his medicine chest, and taking a box of pills, he swallowed two, which done, he came back with a somewhat easier expression to his favorite chair.

"He was just splendid, father," began the boy; "he went for him, I tell you!"

"I hope, Jasper, your dog has not been doing anything violent," said the old gentleman. "I must caution you; he'll get you into trouble some day; and then there'll be a heavy bill to pay; he grows more irritable every day."

"Irritable!" cried the boy, flinging his arms around the dog's neck, who was looking up at the old gentleman in high disdain. "He's done the most splendid thing you ever saw! Why, he saved a little girl, father, from a cross old organ-man, and he drove that man--oh! you ought to have seen him run!"

And now that it was over, Jasper put back his head and laughed long and loud as he remembered the rapid transit of the musical pair.

"Well, how do you know she wasn't the man's daughter?" asked his father, determined to find fault someway. "You haven't any business to go around the country setting your dog on people. I shall have an awful bill to pay some day, Jasper--an awful bill!" he continued, getting up and commencing to pace up and down the floor in extreme irritation.

"Father," cried the boy, half laughing, half vexed, springing to his side, and keeping step with him, "we found her brother; he came along when we were by the side of the road. We couldn't go any further, for the poor little thing was all tired out. And don't you think they live over in Badgertown, and"-- "Well," said the old gentleman, pausing in his walk, and taking out his watch to wonder if that paper would ever come, "she had probably followed the organ-man; so it served her right after all."

"Well, but father," and the boy's dark eyes glowed, "she was such a cunning little thing! she wasn't more than four years old; and she had such a pretty little yellow head; and she said so funny--'I want Polly.'"

"Did she?" said the old gentleman, getting interested in spite of himself; "what then?"

"Why, then, sir," said Jasper, delighted at his success in diverting his thoughts, "Prince and I waited--and waited; and I was just going to bring her here to ask you what we should do, when"-- "Dear me!" said the old gentleman, instinctively starting back as if he actually saw the forlorn little damsel, "you needn't ever bring such people here, Jasper! I don't know what to do with them, I'm sure!"

"Well," said the boy, laughing, "we didn't have to, did we, Prince?" stroking the big head of the dog who was slowly following the two as they paced up and down, but keeping carefully on the side of his master; "for just as we really didn't know what to do, don't you think there was a big wagon came along, drawn by the ricketiest old horse, and a boy in the wagon looking both sides of the road, and into every bush, just as wild as he could be, and before I could think, hardly, he spied us, and if he didn't jump! I thought he'd broken his leg"--

"And I suppose he just abused you for what you had done," observed the old gentleman, petulantly; "that's about all the gratitude there is in this world."

"He didn't seem to see me at all," said the boy. "I thought he'd eat the little girl up."

"Ought to have looked out for her better then," grumbled the old gentleman, determined to find fault with somebody.

"And he's a splendid fellow, I just know," cried Jasper, waxing enthusiastic; "and his name is Pepper."

"Pepper!" repeated his father; "no nice family ever had the name of Pepper!"

"Well, I don't care," and Jasper's laugh was loud and merry; "he's nice anyway,--I know; and the little thing's nice; and I'm going to see them--can't I, father?"

"Dear me!" said his father; "how can you, Jasper? You do have the strangest tastes I ever saw!"

"It's dreadful dull here," pleaded the boy, touching the right string; "you know that yourself, father, and I don't know any boys around here; and Prince and I are so lonely on our walks--do permit me, father!"

The old gentleman, who really cared very little about it, turned away, muttering, "Well, I'm sure I don't care; go where you like," when a knock was heard at the door, and the paper was handed in, which broke up the conversation, and restored good humor.

The next day but one, Ben was out by the wood-pile, trying to break up some kindlings for Polly who was washing up the dishes, and otherwise preparing for the delights of baking day.

"Hullo!" said a voice he thought he knew.

He turned around to see the merry-faced boy, and the big, black dog who immediately began to wag his tail as if willing to recognize him.

"You see I thought you'd never look round," said the boy with a laugh. "How's the little girl?"

"Oh! you have come, really," cried Ben, springing over the wood-pile with a beaming face. "Polly!"

But Polly was already by the door, with dish-cloth in hand.

Day 133

1. Read the next part of chapter 12.
2. Tell someone what is happening.

Chapter 12 continued

"This is my sister, Polly," began Ben--and then stopped, not knowing the boy's name.

"I'm Jasper King," said the boy, stepping upon the flat stone by Polly's side; and taking off his cap, he put out his hand. "And this is Prince," he added.

Polly put her hand in his, and received a hearty shake; and then she sprang over the big stove, dish-cloth and all, and just flung her arms around the dog's neck.

"Oh, you splendid fellow, you!" said she. "Don't you know we all think you're as good as gold?"

The dog submitted to the astonishing proceeding as if he liked it, while Jasper, delighted with Polly's appreciation, beamed down on them, and struck up friendship with her on the instant.

"Now, I must call Phronsie," said Polly, getting up, her face as red as a rose.

"Is her name Phronsie?" asked the boy with interest.

"No, it's Sophronia," said Polly, "but we call her Phronsie."

"What a very funny name," said Jasper, "Sophronia is, for such a little thing--and yours is Polly, is it not?" he asked, turning around suddenly on her.

"Yes," said Polly; "no, not truly Polly; it's Mary, my real name is--but I've always been Polly."

"I like Polly best, too," declared Jasper, "it sounds so nice."

"And his name is Ben," said Polly.

"Ebenezer, you mean," said Ben, correcting her.

"Well, we call him Ben," said Polly; "it don't ever seem as if there was any Ebenezer about it."

"I should think not," laughed Jasper.

"Well, I must get Phronsie," again said Polly, running back into the bedroom, where that small damsel was busily engaged in washing "Baby" in the basin of water that she had with extreme difficulty succeeded in getting down on the floor. She had then, by means of a handful of soft soap, taken from Polly's soap-bowl during the dish-washing, and a bit of old cotton, plastered both herself and "Baby" to a comfortable degree of stickiness.

"Phronsie," said Polly--"dear me! what you doing? the big dog's out there, you know, that scared the naughty organ-man; and the boy"--but before the words were half out, Phronsie had slipped from under her hands, and to Polly's extreme dismay, clattered out into the kitchen.

"Here she is!" cried Jasper, meeting her at the door. The little soapy hands were grasped, and kissing her--"Ugh!" he said, as the soft soap plentifully spread on her face met his mouth.

"Oh, Phronsie! you shouldn't," cried Polly, and then they all burst out into a peal of laughter at Jasper's funny grimaces.

"She's been washing 'Baby,'" explained Polly, wiping her eyes, and looking at Phronsie who was hanging over Prince in extreme affection. Evidently Prince still regarded her as his especial property.

"Have you got a baby?" asked Jasper. "I thought she was the baby," pointing to Phronsie.

"Oh, I mean her littlest dolly; she always calls her 'Baby,'" said Polly. "Come, Phronsie, and have your face washed, and a clean apron on."

When Phronsie could be fairly persuaded that Prince would not run away during her absence, she allowed herself to be taken off; and soon re-appeared, her own, dainty little self. Ben, in the meantime, had been initiating Jasper into the mysteries of cutting the wood, the tool-house, and all the surroundings of the "little brown house." They had received a reinforcement in the advent of Joel and David, who stared delightedly at Phronsie's protector, made friends with the dog, and altogether had had such a thoroughly good time, that Phronsie, coming back, clapped her hands in glee to hear them.

"I wish mammy was home," said Polly, polishing up the last cup carefully.

"Let me put it up," said Jasper, taking it from her, "it goes up here, don't it, with the rest?" reaching up to the upper-shelf of the old cupboard.

"Yes," said Polly.

"Oh, I should think you'd have real good times!" said the boy, enviously. "I haven't a single sister or brother."

"Haven't you?" said Polly, looking at him in extreme pity. "Yes, we do have real fun," she added, answering his questioning look; "the house is just brimful sometimes, even if we are poor."

"We aren't poor," said Joel, who never could bear to be pitied. Then, with a very proud air, he said in a grand way-- "At any rate, we aren't going to be, long, for something's coming!"

"What do you mean, Joey?" asked Ben, while the rest looked equally amazed.

"Our ships," said Joel confidently, as if they were right before their eyes; at which they all screamed!

"See Polly's stove!" cried Phronsie, wishing to entertain in her turn. "Here 'tis," running up to it, and pointing with her fat little finger.

"Yes, I see," cried Jasper, pretending to be greatly surprised; "it's new, isn't it?"

"Yes," said the child; "it's very all new; four yesterdays ago!"

And then Polly stopped in sweeping up and related, with many additions and explanations from the others, the history of the stove, and good Dr. Fisher (upon whom they all dilated at great length), and the dreadful measles, and everything. And Jasper sympathized, and rejoiced with them to their hearts content, and altogether got so very home-like, that they all felt as if they had known him for a year. Ben neglected his work a little, but then visitors didn't come every day to the Peppers; so while Polly worked away at her bread, which she was "going to make like biscuits," she said, the audience gathered in the little old kitchen was in the merriest mood, and enjoyed everything to the fullest extent.

"Do put in another stick, Bensie dear," said Polly; "this bread won't be fit for anything!"

"Isn't this fun, though!" cried Jasper, running up to try the oven; "I wish I could ever bake," and he looked longingly at the little brown biscuits waiting their turn out on the table.

"You come out some day," said Polly, sociably, "and we'll all try baking--mammy'd like to have you, I know," feeling sure that nothing would be too much for Mrs. Pepper to do for the protector of little Phronsie.

"I will!" cried Jasper, perfectly delighted. "You can't think how awfully dull it is out in Hingham!"

"Don't you live there?" asked Polly, with a gasp, almost dropping a tin full of little brown lumps of dough she was carrying to the oven.

"Live there!" cried Jasper; and then he burst out into a merry laugh. "No, indeed! I hope not! Why, we're only spending the summer there, father and I, in the hotel."

"Where's your mother?" asked Joel, squeezing in between Jasper and his audience. And then they all felt instinctively that a very wrong question had been asked.

"I haven't any mother," said the boy, in a low voice.

They all stood quite still for a moment; then Polly said, "I wish you'd come out sometime; and you may bake--or anything else," she added; and there was a kinder ring to her voice than ever.

No mother! Polly for her life, couldn't imagine how anybody could feel without a mother, but the very words alone smote her heart; and there was nothing she wouldn't have done to give pleasure to one who had done so much for them.

"I wish you could see our mother," she said, gently. "Why, here she comes now! oh, mamsie, dear," she cried. "Do, Joe, run and take her bundle."

Mrs. Pepper stopped a minute to kiss Phronsie--her baby was dearer than ever to her now. Then her eye fell on Jasper, who stood respectfully waiting and watching her with great interest.

"Is this," she asked, taking it all in at the first glance--the boy with the honest eyes as Ben had described him--and the big, black dog--"is this the boy who saved my little girl?"

"Oh, ma'am," cried Jasper, "I didn't do much; 'twas Prince."

"I guess you never'll know how much you did do," said Mrs. Pepper. Then looking with a long, keen gaze into the boy's eyes that met her own so frankly and kindly: "I'll trust him," she said to herself; "a boy with those eyes can't help but be good."

"Her eyes are just the same as Polly's," thought Jasper, "just such laughing ones, only Polly's are brown," and he liked her on the spot.

And then, somehow, the hubbub ceased. Polly went on with her work, and the others separated, and Mrs. Pepper and Jasper had a long talk. When the mother's eyes fell on Phronsie playing around on the floor, she gave the boy a grateful smile that he thought was beautiful.

Day 134

1. Finish reading chapter 12.
2. Can you summarize the chapter for someone?

Chapter 12 continued

And then, somehow, the hubbub ceased. Polly went on with her work, and the others separated, and Mrs. Pepper and Jasper had a long talk. When the mother's eyes fell on Phronsie playing around on the floor, she gave the boy a grateful smile that he thought was beautiful.

"Well, I declare," said Jasper, at last, looking up at the old clock in the corner by the side of the cupboard, "I'm afraid I'll miss the stage, and then father never'll let me come again. Come, Prince."

"Oh, don't go," cried Phronsie, wailing. "Let doggie stay! Oh, make him stay, mammy!"

"I can't, Phronsie," said Mrs. Pepper, smiling, "if he thinks he ought to go."

"I'll come again," said Jasper, eagerly, "if I may, ma'am."

He looked up at Mrs. Pepper as he stood cap in hand, waiting for the answer.

"I'm sure we should be glad if your father'll be willing," she added; thinking, proudly, "My children are an honor to anybody, I'm sure," as she glanced around on the bright little group she could call her own. "But be sure, Jasper," and she laid her hand on his arm as she looked down into his eyes, "that you father is willing, that's all."

"Oh, yes, ma'am," said the boy; "but he will be, I guess, if he feels well."

"Then come on Thursday," said Polly; "and can't we bake something then, mammy?"

"I'm sure I don't care," laughed Mrs. Pepper; "but you won't find much but brown flour and meal to bake with."

"Well, we can pretend," said Polly; "and we can cut the cakes with the heart-shape, and they'll do for anything.

"Oh, I'll come," laughed Jasper, ready for such lovely fun in the old kitchen; "look out for me on Thursday, Ben!"

So Jasper and Prince took their leave, all the children accompanying them to the gate; and then after seeing him fairly started on a smart run to catch the stage, Prince scampering at his heels, they all began to sing his praises and to wish for Thursday to come.

But Jasper didn't come! Thursday came and went; a beautiful, bright, sunny day, but with no signs of the merry boy whom all had begun to love, nor of the big black dog. The children had made all the needful preparations with much ostentation and bustle, and were in a state of excited happiness, ready for any gale. But the last hope had to be given up, as the old clock ticked away hour after hour. And at last Polly had to put Phronsie to bed, who wouldn't stop crying enough to eat her supper at the dreadful disappointment.

"He couldn't come, I know," said both Ben and Polly, standing staunchly up for their new friend; but Joel and David felt that he had broken his word.

"He promised," said Joel, vindictively.

"I don't believe his father'd let him," said Polly, wiping away a sly tear; "I know Jasper'd come, if he could."

Mrs. Pepper wisely kept her own counsel, simply giving them a kindly caution:

"Don't you go to judging him, children, till you know."

"Well, he promised," said Joel, as a settler.

"Aren't you ashamed, Joel," said his mother, "to talk about any one whose back is turned? Wait till he tells you the reason himself."

Joel hung his head, and then began to tease David in the corner, to make up for his disappointment.

The next morning Ben had to go to the store after some more meal. As he was going out rather dismally, the storekeeper, who was also postmaster, called out, "Oh, halloa, there!"

"What is it?" asked Ben, turning back, thinking perhaps Mr. Atkins hadn't given him the right change.

"Here," said Mr. Atkins, stepping up to the Post-office department, quite smart with its array of boxes and official notices, where Ben had always lingered, wishing there might be sometime a letter for him--or some of them. "You've got a sister Polly, haven't you?"

"Yes," said Ben, wondering what was coming next.

"Well, she's got a letter," said the postmaster, holding up a nice big envelope, looking just like those that Ben had so many times wished for. That magic piece of white paper danced before the boy's eyes for a minute; then he said-- "It can't be for her, Mr. Atkins; why, she's never had one." "Well, she's got one now, sure enough," said Mr. Atkins; "here 'tis, plain enough," and he read what he had no need to study much as it had already passed examination by his own and his wife's faithful eyes: "Miss Polly Pepper, near the Turnpike, Badgertown'--that's her, isn't it?" he added, laying it down before Ben's eyes. "Must be a first time for everything, you know, my boy!" and he laughed long over his own joke; "so take it and run along home." For Ben still stood looking at it, and not offering to stir.

"If you say so," said the boy, as if Mr. Atkins had given him something out of his own pocket; "but I'm afraid 'tisn't for Polly." Then buttoning up the precious letter in his jacket, he spun along home as never before.

"Polly! Polly!" he screamed. "Where is she, mother?"

"I don't know," said Mrs. Pepper, coming out of the bedroom. "Dear me! is anybody hurt, Ben?"

"I don't know," said Ben, in a state to believe anything, "but Polly's got a letter."

"Polly got a letter!" cried Mrs. Pepper; "what do you mean, Ben?"

"I don't know," repeated the boy, still holding out the precious letter; "but Mr. Atkins gave it to me; where is Polly?"

"I know where she is," said Joel; "she's up-stairs." And he flew out in a twinkling, and just as soon reappeared with Polly scampering after him in the wildest excitement.

And then the kitchen was in an uproar as the precious missive was put into Polly's hand; and they all gathered around her, wondering and examining, till Ben thought he would go wild with the delay.

"I wonder where it did come from," said Polly, in the greatest anxiety, examining again the address.

"Where does the postmark say?" asked Mrs. Pepper, looking over her shoulder.

"It's all rubbed out," said Polly, peering at it "you can't see anything."

"Do open it," said Ben, "and then you'll find out."

"But p'raps 'tisn't for me," said Polly, timidly.

"Well, Mr. Atkins says 'tis," said Ben, impatiently; "here, I'll open it for you, Polly."

"No, let her open it for herself, Ben," protested his mother.

"But she won't," said Ben; "do tear it open, Polly."

"No, I'm goin' to get a knife," she said.

"I'll get one," cried Joel, running up to the table drawer; "here's one, Polly."

"Oh, dear," groaned Ben; "you never'll get it open at this rate!"

But at last it was cut; and they all holding their breath, gazed awe-struck, while Polly drew out the mysterious missive.

"What does it say?" gasped Mrs. Pepper.

"Dear Miss Polly," began both Ben and Polly in a breath. "Let Polly read," said Joel, who couldn't hear in the confusion.

"Well, go on Polly," said Ben; "hurry!"

"Dear Miss Polly, I was so sorry I couldn't come on Thursday' "--

"Oh, it's Jasper! it's Jasper!" cried all the children in a breath.

"I told you so!" cried Ben and Polly, perfectly delighted to find their friend vindicated fully-- "there! Joey Pepper!"

"Well, I don't care," cried Joe, nothing daunted, "he didn't come, anyway--do go on, Polly."

"I was so sorry I couldn't come' "--began Polly.

"You read that," said Joel.

"I know it," said Polly, "but it's just lovely; 'on Thursday; but my father was sick, and I couldn't leave him. If you don't mind I'll come again--I mean I'll come some other day, if it's just as convenient for you, for I do so want the baking, and the nice time. I forgot to say that I had a cold, to,' (here Jasper had evidently had a struggle in his mind whether there should be two O's or one, and he had at last decided it, by crossing out one) but my father is willing I should come when I get well. Give my love to all, and especially remember me respectfully to your mother. Your friend,

Jasper Elyot King."

"Oh, lovely! lovely!" cried Polly, flying around with the letter in her hand; "so he is coming!"

Ben was just as wild as she was, for no one knew but Polly just how the new friend had stepped into his heart. Phronsie went to sleep happy, hugging "Baby."

"And don't you think, Baby, dear," she whispered sleepily, and Polly heard her say as she was tucking her in, "that Japser is really comin'; really--and the big, be-you-ti-ful doggie, too!"

Day 135

1. Read chapter 13.
2. Tell someone about the chapter.

Vocabulary

1. Add to your dictionary. In your reading find three words you don't know and write them in your dictionary. Write the word and what it means.

Chapter 13 Phronsie Pays a Debt of Gratitude

"And now I tell you," said Polly, the next day, "let's make Jasper something; can't we, ma?"

"Oh, do! do!" cried all the other children, "let's; but what'll it be, Polly?"

"I don't know about this," interrupted Mrs. Pepper; "I don't see how you could get anything to him if you could make it."

"Oh, we could, mamsie," said Polly, eagerly, running up to her; "for Ben knows; and he says we can do it."

"Oh, well, if Ben and you have had your heads together, I suppose it's all right," laughed Mrs. Pepper, "but I don't see how you can do it."

"Well, we can, mother, truly," put in Ben. "I'll tell you how, and you'll say it'll be splendid. You see Deacon Blodgett's goin' over to Hingham, to-morrow; I heard him tell Miss Blodgett so; and he goes right past the hotel; and we can do it up real nice--and it'll please Jasper so--do, mammy!"

"And it's real dull there, Jasper says," put in Polly, persuasively; "and just think, mammy, no brothers and sisters!" And Polly looked around on the others.

After that there was no need to say anything more; her mother would have consented to almost any plan then.

"Well, go on, children," she said; "you may do it; I don't see but what you can get 'em there well enough; but I'm sure I don't know what you can make."

"Can't we," said Polly--and she knelt down by her mother's side and put her face in between the sewing in Mrs. Pepper's lap, and the eyes bent kindly down on her--"make some little cakes, real cakes I mean? now don't say no, mammy!" she said, alarmed, for she saw a "no" slowly coming in the eyes above her, as Mrs. Pepper began to shake her head.

"But we haven't any white flour, Polly," began her mother. "I know," said Polly; "but we'll make 'em of brown, it'll do, if you'll give us some raisins--you know there's some in the bowl, mammy."

"I was saving them for a nest egg," said Mrs. Pepper; meaning at some future time to indulge in another plum-pudding that the children so loved.

"Well, do give 'em to us," cried Polly; "do, ma!"

"I want 'em for a plum-pudding sometime," said Mrs. Pepper.

"Ow!"--and Joel with a howl sprung up from the floor where he had been trying to make a cart for "Baby" out of an old box, and joined Mrs. Pepper and Polly. "No, don't give 'em away, ma!" he screamed; "let's have our plum-pudding-- now, Polly Pepper, you're a-goin' to bake up all our raisins in nasty little cakes--and"--

"Joey!" commanded Mrs. Pepper, "hush! what word did you say!"

"Well," blubbered Joel, wiping his tears away with his grimy little hand, "Polly's --a-goin'--to give"-- "I should rather you'd never have a plum-pudding than to say such words," said Mrs. Pepper, sternly, taking up her work again. "And besides, do you think what Jasper has done for you?" and her face grew very white around the lips.

"Well, he can have plum-puddings," said Joel, whimpering, "forever an' ever, if he wants them-- and--and"-- "Well, Joey," said Polly, "there, don't feel bad," and she put her arms around him, and tried to wipe away the tears that still rolled down his cheeks. "We won't give 'em if you don't want us to; but Jasper's sick, and there isn't anything for him to do, and"--here she whispered slyly up into his ear --"don't you remember how you liked folks to send you things when you had the measles?"

"Yes, I know," said Joel, beginning to smile through his tears; "wasn't it fun, Polly?"

"I guess 'twas," laughed Polly back again, pleased at the return of sunshine. "Well, Jasper'll be just as pleased as you were, 'cause we love him and want to do somethin' for him, he was so good to Phronsie."

"I will, Polly, I will," cried Joel, completely won over; "do let's make 'em for him; and put 'em in thick; oh! thick as you can;" and determined to do nothing by halves, Joel ran generously for the precious howl of raisins, and after setting it on the table, began to help Polly in all needful preparations.

Mrs. Pepper smiled away to herself to see happiness restored to the little group. And soon a pleasant hum and bustle went on around the baking table, the centre of attraction.

"Now," said Phronsie, coming up to the table and standing on tip-toe to see Polly measure out the flour, "I'm a-goin' to bake something for my sick man, I am."

"Oh, no, Phronsie, you can't," began Polly.

"Hey?" asked Joel, with a daub of flour on the tip of his chubby nose, gained by too much peering into Polly's flour-bag. "What did she say, Polly?" watching her shake the clouds of flour in the sieve.

"She said she was goin' to bake something for Jasper," said Polly. "There," as she whisked in the flour, "now that's done."

"No, I didn't say Japser," said Phronsie; "I didn't say Japser," she repeated, emphatically.

"Why, what did you say, Pet?" asked Polly, astonished, while little Davie repeated, "What did you say, Phronsie?"

"I said my sick man," said Phronsie, shaking her yellow head; "poor sick man."

"Who does she mean?" said Polly in despair, stopping a moment her violent stirring that threatened to overturn the whole cake-bowl.

"I guess she means Prince," said Joel. "Can't I stir, Polly?"

"Oh, no," said Polly; "only one person must stir cake."

"Why?" asked Joel; "why, Polly?"

"Oh, I don't know," said Polly, "cause 'tis so; never mind now, Joel. Do you mean Prince, Phronsie?"

"No, I don't mean Princey," said the child decisively; "I mean my sick man."

"It's Jasper's father, I guess she means," said Mrs. Pepper over in the corner; "but what in the world!"

"Yes, yes," cried Phronsie, perfectly delighted at being at last understood, and hopping on one toe; "my sick man."

"I shall give up!" said Polly, tumbling over in a chair, with the cake spoon in her hand, from which a small sticky lump fell on her apron, which Joel immediately pounced upon and devoured. "What do you want to bake, Phronsie?" she gasped, holding the spoon sticking up straight, and staring at the child.

"A gingerbread boy," said the child, promptly; "he'd like that best; poor, sick man!" and she commenced to climb up to active preparations.

Day 136

1. Read the first half of chapter 14.
2. Tell someone what is happening in this chapter.

Chapter 14 A Letter to Jasper

"Mamsie, what shall we do?" implored Polly of her mother.

"I don't know," said her mother; "however did that get into her head, do you suppose?"

"I am sure I can't tell," said Polly, jumping up and beginning to stir briskly to make up for lost time. "P'r'aps she heard us talking about Jasper's having to take care of his sick father, and how hard it must be to he sick away from home."

"Yes," said Phronsie, "but he'll be glad to see my gingerbread boy, I guess; poor, sick man."

"Oh, Phronsie," cried Polly, in great distress, "you aren't ever going to make a 'gingerbread boy' to-day! see, we'll put in a cunning little cake for Mr. King--full of raisins, Phronsie; won't that be lovely!" and Polly began to fill a little scalloped tin with some of the cake mixture.

"N-no," said the child, eying it suspiciously; "that isn't like a 'gingerbread boy,' Polly; he'll like that best."

"Mamsie," said Polly, "we can't let her make a dreadful, horrid 'gingerbread boy' to send Mr. King! he never'll let Jasper come here again."

"Oh, let her," cried Joel; "she can bake it, and Dave an' I'll eat it," and he picked up a raisin that had fallen under the table and began crunching it with great gusto.

"That wouldn't be fair," said Polly, gloomily. "Do get her off from it, mammy."

"Phronsie," said Mrs. Pepper, going up back of the child, who sat patiently in her high chair waiting for Polly to let her begin, "hadn't you rather wait and give your 'gingerbread boy' to Jasper for his father, when he comes?"

"Oh, no, no," cried Phronsie, twisting in her chair in great apprehension, "I want to send it now, I do."

"Well, Polly," said her mother, laughing, "after all it's best, I think, to let her; it can't do any harm anyway--and instead of Mr. King's not letting Jasper come, if he's a sensible man that won't make any difference; and if he isn't, why, then there'd be sure to something come up sometime to make trouble."

"Well," said Polly, "I suppose she's got to; and perhaps," as a consoling idea struck her, "perhaps she'll want to eat it up herself when it's done. Here, Phronsie," giving her a handful of the cake mixture, which she stiffened with flour to the right thickness, "there, you can call that a 'gingerbread boy;' see, won't it make a beautiful one!"

"You needn't think," said Mrs. Pepper, seeing Phronsie's delighted face, and laughing as she went back to her work, "but what that gingerbread boy'll go."

When the little cakes were done, eight of them, and set upon the table for exhibition, they one and all protested that they never saw so fine a lot. Polly was delighted with the praise they received, and her mother's commendation that she was "growing a better cook every day." "How glad Jasper'll be, won't he, mamsie?" said she.

The children walked around and around the table, admiring and pointing out the chief points of attraction, as they appeared before their discriminating eyes.

"I should choose that one," said Joel, pointing at one which was particularly plummy, with a raisin standing up on one end with a festive air, as if to say, "there's lots of us inside, you better believe!"

"I wouldn't," said Davie, "I'd have that--that's cracked so pretty."

"So 'tis," said Mrs. Pepper; "they're all as light as a feather, Polly."

"But my 'gingerbread boy,'" cried Phronsie, running eagerly along with a particularly ugly looking specimen of a cake figure in her hand, "is the be-yew-tifullest, isn't it, Polly?"

"Oh, dear," groaned Polly, "it looks just awfully, don't it, Ben!"

"Hoh, hoh!" laughed Joel in derision; "his leg is crooked, see Phronsie--you better let Davie an' me have it."

"No, no," screamed the child in terror; "that's my sick man's 'gingerbread boy,' it is!"

"Joe, put it down," said Ben. "Yes, Phronsie, you shall have it; there, it's all safe;" and he put it carefully into Phronsie's apron, when she breathed easier.

"And he hasn't but one eye," still laughed Joel, while little Davie giggled too.

"He did have two," said Polly, "but she punched the other in with her thumb; don't, boys," she said, aside, "you'll make her feel bad; do stop laughing. Now, how'll we send the things?"

"Put 'em in a basket," said Ben; "that's nicest."

"But we haven't got any basket," said Polly, "except the potato basket, and they'd be lost in that."

"Can't we take your work-basket, mamsie?" asked Ben; "they'd look so nice in that."

"Oh," said Mrs. Pepper, "that wouldn't do; I couldn't spare it, and besides, it's all broken at the side, Ben; that don't look nice."

"Oh, dear," said Polly, sitting down on one of the hard wooden chairs to think, "I do wish we had things nice to send to sick people." And her forehead puckered up in a little hard knot.

"We'll have to do 'em up in a paper, Polly," said Ben; "there isn't any other way; they'll look nice in anything, 'cause they are nice," he added, comfortingly.

"If we only had some flowers," said Polly, "that would set 'em off."

"You're always a-thinkin' of flowers, Polly," said Ben. "I guess the cakes'll have to go without 'em."

"I suppose they will," said Polly, stifling a little sigh. "Where's the paper?"

"I've got a nice piece up-stairs," said Ben, "just right; I'll get it."

"Put my 'gingerbread boy' on top," cried Phronsie, handing him up.

So Polly packed the little cakes neatly in two rows, and laid the 'gingerbread boy' in a fascinating attitude across the top.

"He looks as if he'd been struck by lightning!" said Ben, viewing him critically as he came in the door with the paper.

"Be still," said Polly, trying not to laugh; "that's because he baked so funny; it made his feet stick out."

"Children," said Mrs. Pepper, "how'll Jasper know where the cakes come from?"

"Why, he'll know it's us," said Polly, "of course; 'cause it'll make him think of the baking we're going to have when he gets well."

"Well, but you don't say so," said Mrs. Pepper, smiling; "tisn't polite to send it this way."

"Whatever'll we do, mammy!" said all four children in dismay, while Phronsie simply stared. "Can't we send 'em at all?"

"Why yes," said their mother; "I hope so, I'm sure, after you've got 'em baked; but you might answer Jasper's letter I should think, and tell him about 'em, and the 'gingerbread boy'."

"Oh dear," said Polly, ready to fly, "I couldn't mamsie; I never wrote a letter."

"Well, you never had one before," said her mother, composedly biting her thread. "Never say you can't, Polly, cause you don't know what you can do till you've tried."

"You write, Ben," said Polly, imploringly.

"No," said Ben, "I think the nicest way is for all to say somethin', then 'twon't be hard for any of us."

"Where's the paper," queried Polly, "coming from, I wonder!"

"Joel," said Mrs. Pepper, "run to the bureau in the bedroom, and open the top drawer, and get a green box there."

So Joel, quite important at the errand, departed, and presently put the designated box into his mother's hand.

"There, now I'm going to give you this," and she took out a small sheet of paper slightly yellowed by age; but being gilt-edged, it looked very magnificent to the five pairs of eyes directed to it.

"Now Ben, you get the ink bottle and the pen, and then go to work."

So Ben reached down from the upper shelf in the cupboard the ink bottle, and a pen in a black wooden penholder.

"Oh, mamsie," cried Polly, "that's where Phronsie bit it off when she was a baby, isn't it?" holding up the stubby end where the little ball had disappeared.

"Yes," said Mrs. Pepper, "and now you're going to write about her 'gingerbread boy' with it--well, time goes, to be sure." And she bent over her work again, harder than ever. Poor woman! if she could only scrape together enough money to get her children into school--that was the earnest wish of her heart. She must do it soon, for Ben was twelve years old; but with all her strivings and scrimpings she could only manage to put bread into their mouths, and live from day to day. "I know I ought to be thankful for that," she said to herself, not taking time even to cry over her troubles. "But oh, the learning! they must have that!"

"Now," said Polly, "how'll we do it Ben?" as they ranged themselves around the table, on which reposed the cakes; "you begin."

"How do folks begin a letter?" asked Ben in despair, of his mother.

"How did Jasper begin his?" asked Mrs. Pepper back again. "Oh," cried Polly, running into the bedroom to get the precious missive. "Dear Miss Polly'--that's what it says."

"Well," said Mrs. Pepper, "then you'd better say, 'Dear Mister Jasper'--or you might say, 'Dear Mr. King.'"

"Oh, dear!" cried Polly, "that would be the father then-- s'pose he should think we wrote to him!" and Polly looked horror-stricken to the last degree.

"There, there 'tis," said Ben: 'Dear Mister Jasper'--now what'll we say?"

"Why, say about the cakes," replied Polly.

"And the 'gingerbread boy,'" cried Phronsie. "Oh, tell about him, Polly, do."

"Yes, yes, Phronsie," said Polly, "we will--why, tell him how we wish he could have come, and that we baked him some cakes, and that we do so want him to come just as soon as he can."

"All right!" said Ben; so he went to work laboriously; only his hard breathing showing what a hard task it was, as the stiff old pen scratched up and down the paper.

"There, that's done," he cried at length in great satisfaction, holding it up for inspection.

"Oh, I do wish," cried Polly in intense admiration, "I could write so nice and so fast as you can, Ben."

"Read it, Polly," said Mrs. Pepper, in pride.

Day 137

1. Finish reading chapter 14.

Chapter 14 continued

"Read it, Polly," said Mrs. Pepper, in pride.

So Polly began: "Dear Mister Jasper we were all dreadfully sorry that you didn't come and so we baked you some cakes.'--You didn't say anything about his being sick, Ben."

"I forgot it," said Ben, "but I put it in farther down--you'll see if you read on."

"Baked you some cakes--that is, Polly did, for this is Ben that's writing."

"You needn't said that, Ben," said Polly, dissatisfied; "we all baked 'em, I'm sure. And just as soon as you get well we do want you to come over and have the baking. We're real sorry you're sick-- boneset's good for colds."

"Oh, Ben!" said Mrs. Pepper, "I guess his father knows what to give him."

"And oh! the bitter stuff!" cried Polly, with a wry face. "Well, it's hard work to write," said Ben, yawning. "I'd rather chop wood."

"I wish I knew how," exclaimed Joel, longingly.

"Just you try every day; Ben'll teach you, Joe," said his mother, eagerly, "and then I'll let you write."

"I will!" cried Joe; "then, Dave, you'll see how I'll write-- I tell you!"

"And I'm goin' to--ma, can't I?" said Davie, unwilling to be outdone.

"Yes, you may, be sure," said Mrs. Pepper, delighted; "that'll make a man of you fast."

"Oh, boys," said Polly, lifting a very red face, "you joggle the table so I can't do anything."

"I wasn't jogglin'," said Joel; "the old thing tipped. Look!" he whispered to Davie, "see Polly, she's writing crooked."

So while the others hung around her and looked over her shoulder while they made their various comments, Polly finished her part, and also held it up for inspection.

"Let us see," said Ben, taking it up.

"It's after, 'boneset's good for colds,'" said Polly, puckering up her face again at the thought.

"We most of us knew you were sick--I'm Polly now--because you didn't come; and we liked your letter telling us so, -- "Oh, Polly! we weren't glad to hear he was sick!" cried Ben, in horror.

"I didn't say so!" cried Polly, starting up. "Why, Ben Pepper, I never said so!" and she looked ready to cry.

"It sounds something like it, don't it, mammy?" said Ben, unwilling to give her pain, but appealing to Mrs. Pepper.

"Polly didn't mean it," said her mother consolingly; "but if I were you, I'd say something to explain it."

"I can't put anything in now," said poor Polly; "there isn't any room nor any more paper either-- what shall I do! I told you, Ben, I couldn't write." And Polly looked helplessly from one to the other for comfort.

"Yes, you can," said Ben; "there, now I'll show you: write it fine, Polly--you write so big--little bits of letters, like these."

So Polly took the pen again with a sigh. "Now he won't think so, I guess," she said, much relieved, as Ben began to read again.

"I'll begin yours again," Ben said: "We most of us knew you were sick because you didn't come, and we liked your letter telling us so because we'd all felt so badly, and Phronsie cried herself to sleep'-- (that's good, I'm sure.) 'The "gingerbread boy" is for your father--please excuse it, but Phronsie would make it for him because he is sick. There isn't any more to write, and besides I can't write good, and Ben's tired. From all of us.'"

"Why, how's he to know?" cried Ben. "That won't do to sign it."

"Well, let's say from Ben and Polly then," said Polly; "only all the others want to be in the letter."

"Well, they can't write," said Ben.

"We might sign their names for 'em," suggested Polly.

"Here's mine," said Ben, putting under the "From all of us" a big, bold "Ben."

"And here's mine," echoed Polly, setting a slightly crooked "Polly" by its side.

"Now Joe, you better let Ben hold your hand," said Polly, warningly. But Joel declaring he could write had already begun, so there was no hope for it; and a big drop of ink falling from the pen, he spattered the "J" so that no one could tell what it was. The children looked at each other in despair.

"Can we ever get it out, mammy?" said Polly, running to Mrs. Pepper with it.

"I don't know," said her mother. "How could you try it, Joe?"

"I didn't mean to," said Joel, looking very downcast and ashamed. "The ugly old pen did it!"

"Well," said Polly, "it's got to go; we can't help it." But she looked so sorrowful over it that half the pleasure was gone for Ben; for Polly wanted everything just right, and was very particular about things.

"Now, Dave." Ben held his hand, and "David" went down next to Joel.

But when it was Phronsie's turn, she protested that Polly, and no one else, must hold her hand.

"It's a dreadful hard name to write--Phronsie is," said Polly, as she guided Phronsie's fat little hand that clung faithfully to the stubby old pen. "There, it's over now," she cried; "and I'm thankful! I wouldn't write another for anything!"

"Read it all over now, Ben," cried Mrs. Pepper, "and don't speak, children, till he gets through."

"Don't it sound elegant!" said Polly, clasping her hands, when he had finished. "I didn't think we ever could do it so nice, did you, Ben?"

"No, indeed, I didn't," replied Ben, in a highly ecstatic frame of mind. "Now--oh! what'll we do for an envelope?" he asked in dismay.

"You'll have to do without that," said Mrs. Pepper, "for there isn't any in the house--but see here, children," she added, as she saw the sorry faces before her--"you just fold up the letter, and put it inside the parcel; that'll be just as good."

"Oh dear," said Polly; "but it would have been splendid the other way, mammy--just like other folks!"

"You must make believe this is like other folks," said Mrs. Pepper, cheerily, "when you can't do any other way."

"Yes," said Ben, "that's so, Polly; tie 'em up quick's you can, and I'll take 'em over to Deacon Blodgett's, for he's goin' to start early in the morning."

So after another last look all around, Polly put the cakes in the paper, and tied it with four or five strong knots, to avoid all danger of its undoing.

"He never'll untie it, Polly," said Ben; "that's just like a girl's knots!"

"Why didn't you tie it then?" said Polly; "I'm sure it's as good as a boy's knots, and they always muss up a parcel so." And she gave a loving, approving little pat to the top of the package, which, despite its multitude of knots, was certainly very neat indeed.

Ben, grasping the pen again, "here goes for the direction."

"Deary, yes!" said Polly. "I forgot all about that; I thought 'twas done."

"How'd you s'pose he'd get it?" asked Ben, coolly beginning the "M."

"I don't know," replied Polly, looking over his shoulder; "s'pose anybody else had eaten 'em up, Ben!" And she turned pale at the very thought.

"There," said Ben, at last, after a good many flourishes, "now 'tis done! you can't think of another thing to do to it, Polly!"

"Mamsie, see!" cried Polly, running with it to Mrs. Pepper, "isn't that fine! 'Mr. Jasper E. King, at the Hotel Hingham."

"Yes," said Mrs. Pepper, admiringly, to the content of all the children, "I should think it was!"

"Let me take it in my hand," screamed Joel, reaching eagerly up for the tempting brown parcel.

"Be careful then, Joe," said Polly, with an important air. So Joel took a comfortable feel, and then Davie must have the same privilege. At last it was off, and with intense satisfaction the children watched Ben disappear with it down the long hill to Deacon Blodgett's.

The next day Ben came running in from his work at the deacon's.

"Oh, Polly, you had 'em!" he screamed, all out of breath. "You had 'em!"

"Had what?" asked Polly in astonishment. "Oh, Bensie, what do you mean?"

"Your flowers," he panted. "You sent some flowers to Jasper."

"Flowers to Jasper!" repeated Polly, afraid Ben had gone out of his wits.

"Yes," said Ben; "I'll begin at the beginning. You see, Polly, when I went down this morning, Betsey was to set me to work. Deacon Blodgett and Mrs. Blodgett had started early, you know; and while I was a-cleanin' up the woodshed, as she told me, all of a sudden she said, as she stood in the door looking on, 'Oh, Ben, Mis' Blodgett took some posies along with your parcel.' 'What?' said I; I didn't know as I'd heard straight. 'Posies, I said,' says Betsey; 'beautiful ones they were, too, the best in the garden. I heard her tell Mr. Blodgett it would be a pity if that sick boy couldn't have some flowers, and she knew the Pepper children were crazy about 'em, so she twisted 'em in the string around the parcel, and there they stood up and looked fine, I tell you, as they drove away.' So, Polly!"

"Bensie Pepper!" cried Polly, taking hold of his jacket, and spinning him round, "I told you so! I told you so!"

"I know you did," said Ben, as she gave him a parting whirl, "an' I wish you'd say so about other things, Polly, if you can get 'em so easy."

Day 138

1. Read the first part of chapter 15.
2. Tell someone what is happening in the book. Why do you think the chapter is called "Jolly Days?"

Chapter 15 Jolly Days

"Oh Ben," cried Jasper, overtaking him by a smart run as he was turning in at the little brown gate one morning three days after, "do wait."

"Halloa!" cried Ben, turning around, and setting down his load--a bag of salt and a basket of potatoes--and viewing Jasper and Prince with great satisfaction.

"Yes, here I am," said Jasper. "And how I've run; that fellow on the stage was awful slow in getting here--oh, you're so good," he said and his eyes, brimful of gladness, beamed on Ben. "The cakes were just prime, and 'twas great fun to get your letter."

"Did you like it?" asked Ben, the color up all over his brown face-- "Like it!" cried Jasper. "Why 'twas just splendid; and the cakes were royal! Isn't Polly smart though, to bake like that!" he added admiringly.

"I guess she is," said Ben, drawing himself up to his very tallest dimensions. "She knows how to do everything, Jasper King!"

"I should think she did," responded the boy quickly. "I wish she was my sister," he finished longingly.

"Well, I don't," quickly replied Ben, "for then she wouldn't be mine; and I couldn't think of being without Polly! Was your father angry about--about--'the gingerbread boy'?" he asked timidly, trembling for an answer.

"Oh dear," cried Jasper, tumbling over on the grass, "don't, don't! I shan't be good for anything if you make me laugh! oh! wasn't it funny;" and he rolled over and over, shaking with glee.

"Yes," said Ben, immensely relieved to find that no offence had been taken. "But she would send it; Polly tried not to have her, and she most cried when Phronsie was so determined, cause she said your father never'd let you come again"-- "Twas just lovely in Phronsie," said the boy, sitting up and wiping his eyes, "but oh it was so funny! you ought to have seen my father, Ben Pepper."

"Oh, then he was angry," cried Ben.

"No indeed he wasn't!" said Jasper; "don't you think it! do you know it did him lots of good, for he'd been feeling real badly that morning, he hadn't eaten any breakfast, and when he saw that gingerbread boy"--here Jasper rolled over again with a peal of laughter--"and heard the message, he just put back his head, and he laughed--why, I never heard him laugh as he did then! the room shook all over; and he ate a big dinner, and all that afternoon he felt as good as could be. But he says he's coming to see the little girl that baked it for him before we go home."

Ben nearly tumbled over by the side of Jasper at these words-- "Coming to see us!" he gasped,

"Yes," said Jasper, who had scarcely got over his own astonishment about it, for if the roof had suddenly whisked off on to the church steeple, he couldn't have been more amazed than when he heard his father say cheerily: "Well, Jasper my boy, I guess I shall have to drive over and see your little girl, since she's been polite enough to bake me this," pointing to the wild-looking "gingerbread boy."

"Come in and tell 'em about it," cried Ben, radiantly, picking up his potatoes and salt. "It's all right, Polly!" he said in a jubilant voice, "for here's Jasper, and he'll tell you so himself."

"Hush!" said Jasper warningly, "don't let Phronsie hear; well, here's my pet now," and after bobbing lovingly to the others, with eyes beaming over with fun, he caught up the little girl who was screaming--"Oh, here's Japser! and my beyew-ti-ful doggie!"

"Now Phronsie," he cried, "give me a kiss; you haven't any soft soap to-day, have you? no; that's a good, nice one, now; your 'gingerbread boy' was just splendid!"

"Did he eat it?" asked the child in grave delight.

"Well--no--he hasn't eaten it yet," said Jasper, smiling on the others; "he's keeping it to look at, Phronsie."

"I should think so!" groaned Polly.

"Never mind, Polly," Ben whispered; "Jasper's been a-tellin' me about it; his father liked it--he did truly."

"Oh!" said Polly, "I'm so glad!"

"He had eyes," said Phronsie, going back to the charms of the "gingerbread boy."

"I know it," said Jasper admiringly; "so lie did."

"Rather deep sunk, one of 'em was," muttered Ben.

"And I'll bake you one, Japser," said the child as he put her down; "I will very truly--some day."

"Will you," smiled Jasper; "well then," and there was a whispered conference with Phronsie that somehow sent that damsel into a blissful state of delight. And then while Phronsie monopolized Prince, Jasper told them all about the reception of the parcel--how very dull and forlorn he was feeling that morning, Prince and he shut up in-doors--and how his father had had a miserable night, and had eaten scarcely no breakfast, and just at this juncture there came a knock at the door, "and" said Jasper, "your parcel walked in, all dressed up in flowers!"

"They weren't our flowers," said Polly, honestly. "Mrs. Blodgett put 'em on."

"Well she couldn't have, if you hadn't sent the parcel," said Jasper in a tone of conviction.

Then he launched out into a description of how they opened the package--Prince looking on, and begging for one of the cakes.

"Oh, didn't you give him one?" cried Polly at this. "Good old Prince!"

"Yes I did," said Jasper, "the biggest one of all."

"The one I guess," interrupted Joel, "with the big raisin on top."

Polly spoke up quickly to save any more remarks on Joel's part. "Now tell us about your father--and the 'gingerbread boy."

So Jasper broke out with a merry laugh, into this part of the story, and soon had them all in such a gale of merriment, that Phronsie stopped playing out on the door-step with Prince, and came in to see what the matter was.

"Never mind," said Polly, trying to get her breath, just as Jasper was relating how Mr. King set up the "gingerbread boy" on his writing table before him, while he leaned back in his chair for a hearty laugh.

"And to make it funnier still," said Jasper "don't you think, a little pen-wiper he has, made like a cap, hanging on the pen-rack above him, tumbled off just at this very identical minute right on the head of the 'gingerbread boy,' and there it stuck!"

"Oh!" they all screamed, "if we could only have seen it."

"What was it?" asked Phronsie, pulling Polly's sleeve to make her hear.

So Jasper took her in his lap, and told how funny the "gingerbread boy" looked with a cap on, and Phronsie clapped her hands, and laughed with the rest, till the little old kitchen rang and rang again.

And then they had the baking! and Polly tied one of her mother's ample aprons on Jasper, as Mrs. Pepper had left directions if he should come while she was away; and he developed such a taste for cookery, and had so many splendid improvements on the Peppers' simple ideas, that the children thought it the most fortunate thing in the world that he came; and one and all voted him a most charming companion.

"You could cook a Thanksgiving dinner in this stove, just as easy as not," said Jasper, putting into the oven something on a little cracked plate that would have been a pie if there were any centre; but lacking that necessary accompaniment, probably was a short-cake. "Just as easy as not," be repeated with emphasis, slamming the door, to give point to his remarks.

"No, you couldn't either," said Ben at the table with equal decision; "not a bit of it, Jasper King!"

"Why, Ben Pepper?" asked Jasper, "that oven's big enough! I should like to know why not?"

"'Cause there isn't anything to cook," said Ben coolly, cutting out a piece of dough for a jumble; "we don't keep Thanksgiving."

"Not keep Thanksgiving!" said Jasper, standing quite still; "never had a Thanksgiving! well, I declare," and then he stopped again.

"Yes," answered Ben; "we had one once; 'twas last year-- but that wasn't much."

"Well then," said Jasper, leaning over the table, "I'll tell you what I should think you'd do--try Christmas."

"Oh, that's always worse," said Polly, setting down her rolling-pin to think--which immediately rolled away by itself off from the table.

"We never had a Christmas," said little Davie reflectively; "what are they like, Jasper?"

Jasper sat quite still, and didn't reply to this question for a moment or two.

To be among children who didn't like Thanksgiving, and who "never had seen a Christmas," and "didn't know what it was like," was a new revelation to him.

"They hang up stockings," said Polly softly.

How many, many times she had begged her mother to try it for the younger ones; but there was never anything to put in them, and the winters were cold and hard, and the strictest economy only carried them through.

"Oh!" said little Phronsie in horror, "are their feet in 'em, Polly?"

Day 139

1. Finish chapter 15.

Chapter 15 continued

"No dear," said Polly; while Jasper instead of laughing, only stared. Something requiring a deal of thought was passing through the boy's mind just then. "They shall have a Christmas!" he muttered, "I know father'll let me." But he kept his thoughts to himself; and becoming his own gay, kindly self, he explained and told to Phronsie and the others, so many stories of past Christmases he had enjoyed, that the interest over the baking soon dwindled away, until a horrible smell of something burning brought them all to their senses.

"Oh! the house is burning?" cried Polly. "Oh get a pail of water!"

"Tisn't either," said Jasper, snuffing wisely; "oh! I know-- I forgot all about it--I do beg your pardon." And running to the stove, he knelt down and drew out of the oven, a black, odorous mass, which with a crest-fallen air he brought to Polly.

"I'm no end sorry I made such a mess of it," he said, "I meant it for you."

"Tisn't any matter," said Polly kindly.

"And now do you go on," cried Joel and David both in the same breath, "all about the Tree, you know."

"Yes, yes," said the others; "if you're not tired, Jasper."

"Oh, no," cried their accommodating friend, "I love to tell about it; only wait--let's help Polly clear up first."

So after all traces of the frolic had been tidied up, and made nice for the mother's return, they took seats in a circle and Jasper regaled them with story and reminiscence, till they felt as if fairy land were nothing to it!

"How did you ever live through it, Jasper King," said Polly, drawing the first long breath she had dared to indulge in. "Such an elegant time!"

Jasper laughed. "I hope I'll live through plenty more of them," he said merrily. "We're going to sister Marian's again, father and I; we always spend our Christmas there, you know, and she's to have all the cousins, and I don't know how many more; and a tree--but the best of all, there's going to be a German carol sung by choir boys--I shall like that best of all."

"What are choir boys?" asked Polly who was intensely fond of music.

"In some of the churches," explained Jasper, "the choir is all boys; and they do chant, and sing anthems perfectly beautifully, Polly!"

"Do you play on the piano, and sing?" asked Polly, looking at him in awe.

"Yes," said the boy simply; "I've played ever since I was a little fellow, no bigger'n Phronsie."

"Oh, Jasper!" cried Polly, clasping her hands, her cheeks all aflame--"do you mean to say you do really and truly play on the piano?"

"Why yes," said the boy, looking into her flashing eyes. "Polly's always crazy about music," explained Ben; "she'll drum on the table, and anywhere, to make believe it's a piano."

"There's Dr. Fisher going by," said Joel, who, now that they had gotten on the subject of music, began to find prickles running up and down his legs from sitting so still. "I wish he'd stop."

"Is he the one that cured your measles--and Polly's eyes?" asked Jasper running to the window. "I want to see him."

"Well there he is," cried Ben, as the doctor put his head out of the gig and bowed and smiled to the little group in the window.

"He's just lovely," cried Polly, "oh! I wish you knew him."

"If father's sick again," said Jasper, "we'll have him--he looks nice, anyway--for father don't like the doctor over in Hingham--do you know perhaps we'll come again next summer; wouldn't that be nice!"

"Oh!" cried the children rapturously; "do come, Jasper, do!"

"Well, maybe," said Jasper, "if father likes it and sister Marian and her family will come with us; they do some summers. You'd like little Dick, I know," turning to Phronsie. "And I guess all of you'd like all of them," he added, looking at the group of interested listeners. "They wanted to come this year awfully; they said--'Oh grandpapa, do let us go with you and Jappy, and"----

"What!" said the children.

"Oh," said Jasper with a laugh, "they call me Jappy--its easier to say than Jasper; ever so many people do for short. You may if you want to," he said looking around on them all.

"How funny!" laughed Polly, "But I don't know as it is any worse than Polly or Ben."

"Or Phronsie," said Jappy. "Don't you like Jappy?" he said, bringing his head down to her level, as she sat on the little stool at his feet, content in listening to the merry chat.

"Is that the same as Japser?" she asked gravely.

"Yes, the very same," he said.

When they parted--Jappy and the little Peppers were sworn friends; and the boy, happy in his good times in the cheery little home, felt the hours long between the visits that his father, when he saw the change that they wrought in his son, willingly allowed him to make.

"Oh dear!" said Mrs. Pepper one day in the last of September--as a carriage drawn by a pair of very handsome horses, stopped at their door, "here comes Mr. King I do believe; we never looked worse'n we do to-day!"

"I don't care," said Polly, flying out of the bedroom. "Jappy's with him, mamma, and it'll be nice I guess. At any rate, Phronsie's clean as a pink," she thought to herself looking at the little maiden, busy with "baby" to whom she was teaching deportment in the corner. But there was no time to "fix up;" for a tall, portly gentleman, leaning on his heavy gold cane, was walking up from the little brown gate to the big flat-stone that served as a step. Jasper and Prince followed decorously.

"Is this little Miss Pepper?" he asked pompously of Polly, who answered his rap on the door. Now whether she was little "Miss Pepper" she never had stopped to consider.

"I don't know sir; I'm Polly." And then she blushed bright as a rose, and the laughing brown eyes looked beyond to Jasper, who stood on the walk, and smiled encouragingly.

"Is your mother in?" asked the old gentleman, who was so tall he could scarcely enter the low door. And then Mrs. Pepper came forward, and Jasper introduced her, and the old gentleman bowed, and sat down in the seat Polly placed for him. And Mrs. Pepper thanked him with a heart overflowing with gratitude, through lips that would tremble even then, for all that Jasper had done for them. And the old gentleman said--"Humph!" but he looked at his son, and something shone in his eye just for a moment.

Phronsie had retreated with "baby" in her arms behind the door on the new arrival. But seeing everything progressing finely, and overcome by her extreme desire to see Jappy and Prince, she began by peeping out with big eyes to observe how things were going on. Just then the old gentleman happened to say, "Well, where is my little girl that baked me a cake so kindly?"

Then Phronsie, forgetting all else but her "poor sick man," who also was "Jasper's father," rushed out from behind the door, and coming up to the stately old gentleman in the chair, she looked up pityingly, and said, shaking her yellow head, "Poor, sick man, was my boy good?"

After that there was no more gravity and ceremony. In a moment, Phronsie was perched upon old Mr. King's knee, and playing with his watch; while the others, freed from all restraint, were chatting and laughing happily, till some of the cheeriness overflowed and warmed the heart of the old gentleman.

"We go to-morrow," he said, rising, and looking at his watch. "Why, is it possible that we have been here an hour! there, my little girl, will you give me a kiss?" and he bent his handsome old head down to the childish face upturned to his confidingly.

"Don't go," said the child, as she put up her little lips in grave confidence. "I do like you--I do!"

"Oh, Phronsie," began Mrs. Pepper.

"Don't reprove her, madam," said the old gentleman, who liked it immensely. "Yes, we go to-morrow," he said, looking around on the group to whom this was a blow they little expected. They had surely thought Jasper was to stay a week longer.

"I received a telegram this morning, that I must be in the city on Thursday. And besides, madam," he said, addressing Mrs. Pepper, "I think the climate is bad for me now, as it induces rheumatism. The hotel is also getting unpleasant; there are many annoyances that I cannot put up with; so that altogether, I do not regret it."

Mrs. Pepper, not knowing exactly what to say to this, wisely said nothing. Meantime, Jappy and the little Peppers were having a sorry time over in the corner by themselves.

"Well, I'll write," cried Jasper, not liking to look at Polly just then, as he was sure he shouldn't want anyone to look at him, if he felt like crying. "And you must answer 'em all."

"Oh, we will! we will!" they cried. "And Jappy, do come next summer," said Joel.

"If father'll only say yes, we will, I tell you!" he responded eagerly.

"Come, my boy," said his father the third time; and Jasper knew by the tone that there must be no delay.

Mr. King had been nervously putting his hand in his pocket during the last few moments that the children were together; but when he glanced at Mrs. Pepper's eyes, something made him draw it out again hastily, as empty as he put it in. "No, 'twouldn't do," he said to himself; "she isn't the kind of woman to whom one could offer money."

The children crowded back their tears, and hastily said their last good-bye, some of them hanging on to Prince till the last moment.

And then the carriage door shut with a bang, Jasper giving them a bright parting smile, and they were gone.

And the Peppers went into their little brown house, and shut the door.

Day 140

1. Read the first part of chapter 16.
2. Tell someone about what you read.

Vocabulary

1. Add to your dictionary. In your reading find three words you don't know and write them in your dictionary. Write the word and what it means.
2. You should save your dictionary in your portfolio.

Chapter 16 Getting a Christmas for the Little Ones

And so October came and went. The little Peppers were very lonely after Jasper had gone; even Mrs. Pepper caught herself looking up one day when the wind blew the door open suddenly, half expecting to see the merry whole-souled boy, and the faithful dog come scampering in.

But the letters came--and that was a comfort; and it was fun to answer them. The first one spoke of Jasper's being under a private tutor, with his cousins; then they were less frequent, and they knew he was studying hard. Full of anticipations of Christmas himself, he urged the little Peppers to try for one. And the life and spirit of the letter was so catching, that Polly and Ben found their souls fired within them to try at least to get for the little ones a taste of Christmastide.

"Now, mammy," they said at last, one day in the latter part of October, when the crisp, fresh air filled their little healthy bodies with springing vitality that must bubble over and rush into something, "we don't want a Thanksgiving--truly we don't. But may we try for a Christmas--just a little one," they added, timidly, "for the children?" Ben and Polly always called the three younger ones of the flock "the children."

To their utter surprise, Mrs. Pepper looked mildly assenting, and presently she said-- "Well, I don't see why you can't try; 'twon't do any harm, I'm sure."

You see Mrs. Pepper had received a letter from Jasper, which at present she didn't feel called upon to say anything about.

"Now," said Polly, drawing a long breath, as she and Ben stole away into a corner to "talk over" and lay plans, "what does it mean?"

"Never mind," said Ben; "as long as she's given us leave I don't care what it is."

"I neither," said Polly, with the delicious feeling as if the whole world were before them where to choose; "it'll be just gorgeous, Ben!"

"What's that?" asked Ben, who was not as much given to long words as Polly, who dearly loved to be fine in language as well as other things.

"Oh, it's something Jappy said one day; and I asked him, and he says it's fine, and lovely, and all that," answered Polly, delighted that she knew something she could really tell Ben.

"Then why not say fine?" commented Ben, practically, with a little upward lift of his nose.

"Oh, I'd know, I'm sure," laughed Polly. "Let's think what'll we do for Christmas--how many weeks are there, anyway, Ben?" And she began to count on her fingers.

"That's no way," said Ben, "I'm going to get the Almanac." So he went to the old clock where hanging up by its side, was a "Farmer's Almanac."

"Now, we'll know," he said, coming back to their corner. So with heads together they consulted and counted up till they found that eight weeks and three days remained in which to get ready.

"Dear me!" said Polly. "It's most a year, isn't it, Ben?"

"'Twon't be much time for us," said Ben, who thought of the many hours to be devoted to hard work that would run away with the time. "We'd better begin right away, Polly."

"Well, all right," said Polly, who could scarcely keep her fingers still, as she thought of the many things she should so love to do if she could. "But first, Ben, what let's do?"

"Would you rather hang up their stockings?" asked Ben, as if he had unlimited means at his disposal; "or have a tree?"

"Why," said Polly, with wide open eyes at the two magnificent ideas, "we haven't got anything to put in the stockings when we hang 'em, Ben."

"That's just it," said Ben. "Now, wouldn't it be better to have a tree, Polly? I can get that easy in the woods, you know."

"Well," interrupted Polly, eagerly, "we haven't got anything to hang on that, either, Ben. You know Jappy said folks hang all sorts of presents on the branches. So I don't see," she continued, impatiently, "as that's any good. We can't do anything, Ben Pepper, so there! there isn't anything to do anything with," and with a flounce Polly sat down on the old wooden stool, and folding her hands looked at Ben in a most despairing way.

"I know," said Ben, "we haven't got much."

"We haven't got anything," said Polly, still looking at him. "Why, we've got a tree," replied Ben, hopefully. "Well, what's a tree," retorted Polly, scornfully. "Anybody can go out and look at a tree outdoors."

"Well, now, I tell you, Polly," said Ben, sitting down on the floor beside her, and speaking very slowly and decisively, "we've got to do something 'cause we've begun; and we might make a tree real pretty."

"How?" asked Polly, ashamed of her ill-humor, but not in the least seeing how anything could be made of a tree. "How, Ben Pepper?"

"Well," said Ben, pleasantly, "we'd set it up in the corner--"

"Oh, no, not in the corner," cried Polly, whose spirits began to rise a little as she saw Ben so hopeful. "Put it in the middle of the room, do!"

"I don't care where you put it," said Ben, smiling, happy that Polly's usual cheerful energy had returned, "but I thought.--'twill be a little one, you know, and I thought 'twould look better in the corner."

"What else?" asked Polly, eager to see how Ben would dress the tree.

"Well," said Ben, "you know the Henderson boys gave me a lot of corn last week."

"I don't see as that helps much," said Polly, still incredulous. "Do you mean hang the cobs on the branches, Ben? That would be just dreadful!"

"I should think likely," laughed Ben. "No, indeed, Polly Pepper! but if we should pop a lot, oh! a bushel, and then we should string 'em, we could wind it all in and out among the branches, and--"

"Why, wouldn't that be pretty?" cried Polly, "real pretty-- and we can do that, I'm sure."

"Yes," continued Ben; "and then, don't you know, there's some little candle ends in that box in the Provision Room, maybe mammy'd give us them."

"I don't believe but she would," cried Polly; "twould be just like Jappy's if she would! Let's ask her now--this very same minute!"

And they scampered hurriedly to Mrs. Pepper, who to their extreme astonishment, after all, said "yes," and smiled encouragingly on the plan.

"Isn't mammy good?" said Polly, with loving gratitude, as they seated themselves again.

"Now we're all right," exclaimed Ben, "and I tell you we can make the tree look perfectly splendid, Polly Pepper!"

"And I'll tell you another thing, Ben," Polly said, "oh! something elegant! You must get ever so many hickory nuts; and you know those bits of bright paper I've got in the bureau drawer? Well, we can paste them on to the nuts and hang 'em on for the balls Jappy tells of."

"Polly," cried Ben, "it'll be such a tree as never was, won't it?"

"Yes; but dear me," cried Polly, springing up, "the children are coming! Wasn't it good, grandma wanted 'em to come over this afternoon, so's we could talk! Now hush!" as the door opened to admit the noisy little troop.

"If you think of any new plan," whispered Ben, behind his hand, while Mrs. Pepper engaged their attention, "you'll have to come out into the wood-shed to talk after this."

"I know it," whispered Polly back again; "oh! we've got just heaps of things to think of, Bensie!"

Such a contriving and racking of brains as Polly and Ben set up after this! They would bob over at each other, and smile with significant gesture as a new idea would strike one of them, in the most mysterious way that, if observed, would drive the others almost wild. And then, frightened lest in some hilarious moment the secret should pop out, the two conspirators would betake themselves to the wood-shed as before agreed on. But Joel, finding this out, followed them one day--or, as Polly said, tagged--so that was no good.

"Let's go behind the wood-pile," she said to Ben, in desperation; "he can't hear there, if we whisper real soft."

"Yes, he will," said Ben, who knew Joers hearing faculties much better. "We'll have to wait till they're a-bed."

Day 141

1. Finish chapter 16.
2. Write or tell a summary of the chapter. If you can do it in one sentence, get a high five and/or hug.

Chapter 16 continued

So after that, when nightfall first began to make its appearance, Polly would hint mildly about bedtime.

"You hustle us so!" said Joel, after he had been sent off to bed for two or three nights unusually early.

"Oh, Joey, it's good for you to get to bed," said Polly, coaxingly; "it'll make you grow, you know, real fast,"

"Well, I don't grow a-bed," grumbled Joel, who thought something was in the wind. "You and Ben are going to talk, I know, and wink your eyes, as soon as we're gone."

"Well, go along, Joe, that's a good boy," said Polly, laughing, "and you'll know some day."

"What'll you give me?" asked Joel, seeing a bargain, his foot on the lowest stair leading to the loft, "say, Polly?"

"Oh, I haven't got much to give," she said, cheerily; "but I'll tell you what, Joey--I'll tell you a story every day that you go to bed,"

"Will you?" cried Joe, hopping back into the room. "Begin now, Polly, begin now!"

"Why, you haven't been to bed yet," said Polly, "so I can't till to-morrow."

"Yes, I have--you've made us go for three--no, I guess fourteen nights," said Joel, indignantly.

"Well, you were made to go," laughed Polly. "I said if you'd go good, you know; so run along, Joe, and I'll tell you a nice one to-morrow."

"It's got to be long," shouted Joel, when he saw he could get no more, making good time up to the loft,

To say that Polly, in the following days, was Master Joel's slave, was stating the case lightly. However, she thought by her story-telling she got off easily, as each evening saw the boys drag their unwilling feet to-bedward, and leave Ben and herself in peace to plan and work undisturbed. There they would sit by the little old table, around the one tallow candle, while Mrs. Pepper sewed away busily, looking up to smile or to give some bits of advice; keeping her own secret meanwhile, which made her blood leap fast, as the happy thoughts nestled in her heart of her little ones and their coming glee. And Polly made the loveliest of paper dolls for Phronsie out of the rest of the bits of bright paper; and Ben made windmills and whistles for the boys; and a funny little carved basket with a handle, for Phronsie, out of a hickory nut shell; and a new pink calico dress for Seraphina peered out from the top drawer of the old bureau in the bedroom, whenever anyone opened it--for Mrs. Pepper kindly let the children lock up their treasures there as fast as completed.

"I'll make Seraphina a bonnet," said Mrs. Pepper, "for there's that old bonnet-string in the bag, you know, Polly, that'll make it beautiful."

"Oh, do, mother," cried Polly, "she's been wanting a new one awfully."

"And I'm going to knit some mittens for Joel and David," continued Mrs. Pepper; "cause I can get the yarn cheap now. I saw some down at the store yesterday I could have at half price."

"I don't believe anybody'll have as good a Christmas as we shall," cried Polly, pasting on a bit of trimming to the gayest doll's dress; "no, not even Jappy."

An odd little smile played around Mrs. Pepper's mouth, but she said not a word, and so the fun and the work went on.

The tree was to be set up in the Provision Room; that was finally decided, as Mrs. Pepper showed the children how utterly useless it would be to try having it in the kitchen.

"I'll find the key, children," she said, "I think I know where 'tis, and then we can keep them out."

"Well, but it looks so," said Polly, demurring at the prospect.

"Oh, no, Polly," said her mother; "at any rate it's clean."

"Polly," said Ben, "we can put evergreen around, you know,

"So we can," said Polly, brightly; "oh, Ben, you do think of the best things; we couldn't have had them in the kitchen."

"And don't let's hang the presents on the tree," continued Ben; "let's have the children hang up their stockings; they want to, awfully--for I heard David tell Joel this morning before we got up--they thought I was asleep, but I wasn't--that he did so wish they could, but, says he, 'Don't tell mammy, 'cause that'll make her feel bad."

"The little dears!" said Mrs. Pepper, impulsively; "they shall have their stockings, too."

"And we'll make the tree pretty enough," said Polly, enthusiastically; "we shan't want the presents to hang on; we've got so many things. And then we'll have hickory nuts to eat; and perhaps mammy'll let us make some molasses candy the day before," she said, with a sly look at her mother.

"You may," said Mrs. Pepper, smiling.

"Oh, goody!" they both cried, hugging each other ecstatically.

"And we'll have a frolic in the Provision Room afterwards," finished Polly; "oh! ooh!"

And so the weeks flew by--one, two, three, four, five, six, seven, eight! till only the three days remained, and to think the fun that Polly and Ben had had already!

"It's better'n a Christmas," they told their mother, "to get ready for it!"

"It's too bad you can't hang up your stockings," said Mrs. Pepper, looking keenly at their flushed faces and bright eyes; "you've never hung 'em up."

"That isn't any matter, mamsie," they both said, cheerily; "it's a great deal better to have the children have a nice time--oh, won't it be elegant! p'r'aps we'll have ours next year!"

For two days before, the house was turned upside down for Joel to find the biggest stocking he could; but on Polly telling him it must be his own, he stopped his search, and bringing down his well- worn one, hung it by the corner of the chimney to be ready.

"You put yours up the other side, Dave," he advised.

"There isn't any nail," cried David, investigating.

"I'll drive one," said Joel, so he ran out to the tool-house, as one corner of the wood-shed was called, and brought in the hammer and one or two nails.

"Phronsie's a-goin' in the middle," he said, with a nail in his mouth.

"Yes, I'm a-goin' to hang up my stockin'," cried the child, hopping from one toe to the other.

"Run get it, Phronsie," said Joel, "and I'll hang it up for you.

"Why, it's two days before Christmas yet," said Polly, laughing; "how they'll look hanging there so long."

"I don't care," said Joel, giving a last thump to the nail; "we're a-goin' to be ready. Oh, dear! I wish 'twas to-night!"

"Can't Seraphina hang up her stocking?" asked Phronsie, coming up to Polly's side; "and Baby, too?"

"Oh, let her have part of yours," said Polly, "that'll be best-- Seraphina and Baby, and you have one stocking together."

"Oh, yes," cried Phronsie, easily pleased; "that'll be best." So for the next two days, they were almost distracted; the youngest ones asking countless questions about Santa Claus, and how he possibly could get down the chimney, Joel running his head up as far as he dared, to see if it was big enough.

"I guess he can," he said, coming back in a sooty state, looking very much excited and delighted.

"Will he be black like Joey?" asked Phronsie, pointing to his grimy face.

"No," said Polly; "he don't ever get black."

"Why?" they all asked; and then, over and over, they wanted the delightful mystery explained.

"We never'll get through this day," said Polly in despair, as the last one arrived. "I wish 'twas to-night, for we're all ready,"

"Santy's coming! Santy's coming!" sang Phronsie, as the bright afternoon sunlight went down over the fresh, crisp snow, "for it's night now."

"Yes, Santa is coming!" sang Polly; and "Santa Claus is acoming," rang back and forth through the old kitchen, till it seemed as if the three little old stockings would hop down and join in the dance going on so merrily.

"I'm glad mine is red," said Phronsie, at last, stopping in the wild jig, and going up to see if it was all safe, "cause then Santy'll know it's mine, won't he, Polly?"

"Yes, dear," cried Polly, catching her up. "Oh, Phronsie! you are going to have a Christmas!"

"Well, I wish," said Joel, "I had my name on mine! I know Dave'll get some of my things."

"Oh, no, Joe," said Mrs. Pepper, "Santa Claus is smart; he'll know yours is in the left-hand corner."

"Will he?" asked Joel, still a little fearful.

"Oh, yes, indeed," said Mrs. Pepper, confidently. "I never knew him to make a mistake."

"Now," said Ben, when they had all made a pretence of eating supper, for there was such an excitement prevailing that no one sat still long enough to eat much, "you must every one fly off to bed as quick as ever can be."

"Will Santa Claus come faster then?" asked Joel.

"Yes," said Ben, "just twice as fast."

"I'm going, then," said Joel; "but I ain't going to sleep, 'cause I mean to hear him come over the roof; then I'm going to get up, for I do so want a squint at the reindeer!"

"I am, too," cried Davie, excitedly. "Oh, do come, Joe!" and he began to mount the stairs.

"Good night," said Phronsie, going up to the centre of the chimney-piece, where the little red stocking dangled limply, "lift me up, Polly, do."

"What you want to do?" asked Polly, running and giving her a jump. "What you goin' to do, Phronsie?"

"I want to kiss it good night," said the child, with eyes big with anticipation and happiness, hugging the well worn toe of the little old stocking affectionately. "I wish I had something to give Santa, Polly, I do!" she cried, as she held her fast in her arms.

"Never mind, Pet," said Polly, nearly smothering her with kisses; "if you're a good girl, Phronsie, that pleases Santa the most of anything."

"Does it?" cried Phronsie, delighted beyond measure, as Polly carried her into the bedroom, "then I'll be good always,

I will!"

Day 142

1. Read the first part of chapter 17.
2. Tell someone about what is happening in the book.

Chapter 17 Christmas Bells!

In the middle of the night Polly woke up with a start.

"What in the world!" said she, and she bobbed up her head and looked over at her mother, who was still peacefully sleeping, and was just going to lie down again, when a second noise out in the kitchen made her pause and lean on her elbow to listen. At this moment she thought she heard a faint whisper, and springing out of bed she ran to Phronsie's crib-- it was empty! As quick as a flash she sped out into the kitchen. There, in front of the chimney, were two figures. One was Joel, and the other, unmistakably, was Phronsie!

"What are you doing?" gasped Polly, holding on to a chair.

The two little night-gowns turned around at this.

"Why, I thought it was morning," said Joel, "and I wanted my stocking. Oh!" as he felt the toe, which was generously stuffed, "give it to me, Polly Pepper, and I'll run right back to bed again!"

"Dear me!" said Polly; "and you, too, Phronsie! Why, it's the middle of the night! Did I ever!" and she had to pinch her mouth together tight to keep from bursting out into a loud laugh. "Oh, dear, I shall laugh! don't look so scared, Phronsie, there won't anything hurt you." For Phronsie who, on hearing Joel fumbling around the precious stockings, had been quite willing to hop out of bed and join him, had now, on Polly's saying the dire words "in the middle of the night," scuttled over to her protecting side like a frightened rabbit.

"It never'll be morning," said Joel taking up first one cold toe and then the other; "you might let us have 'em now, Polly,

"No," said Polly sobering down; "you can't have yours till Davie wakes up, too. Scamper off to bed, Joey, dear, and forget all about 'em--and it'll be morning before you know it."

"Oh, I'd rather go to bed," said Phronsie, trying to tuck up her feet in the little flannel night-gown, which was rather short, "but I don't know the way back, Polly. Take me, Polly, do," and she put up her arms to be carried.

"Oh, I ain't a-goin' back alone, either," whimpered Joel, coming up to Polly, too.

"Why, you came down alone, didn't you?" whispered Polly, with a little laugh.

376

"Yes, but I thought 'twas morning," said Joel, his teeth chattering with something beside the cold.

"Well, you must think of the morning that's coming," said Polly, cheerily. "I'll tell you--you wait till I put Phronsie into the crib, and then I'll come back and go half-way up the stairs with you."

"I won't never come down till it's mornin' again," said Joel, bouncing along the stairs, when Polly was ready to go with him, at a great rate.

"Better not," laughed Polly, softly. "Be careful and not wake Davie nor Ben."

"I'm in," announced Joel, in a loud whisper; and Polly could hear him snuggle down among the warm bedclothes. "Call us when 'tis mornin', Polly."

"Yes," said Polly, "I will; go to sleep."

Phronsie had forgotten stockings and everything else on Polly's return, and was fast asleep in the old crib. The result of it was that the children slept over, when morning did really come; and Polly had to keep her promise, and go to the foot of the stairs and call-- *Merry Christmas*! oh, Ben! and Joel! and Davie!"

"Oh!--oh!--oo-h!" and then the sounds that answered her, as with smothered whoops of expectation they one and all flew into their clothes!

Quick as a flash Joel and Davie were down and dancing around the chimney.

"Mammy! mammy!" screamed Phronsie, hugging her stocking, which Ben lifted her up to unhook from the big nail, "Santy did come, he did!" and then she spun around in the middle of the floor, not stopping to look in it.

"Well, open it, Phronsie," called Davie, deep in the exploring of his own; "oh! isn't that a splendid wind-mill, Joe?"

"Yes," said that individual, who, having found a big piece of molasses candy, was so engaged in enjoying a huge bite that, regardless alike of his other gifts or of the smearing his face was getting, he gave himself wholly up to its delights.

"Oh, Joey," cried Polly, laughingly, "molasses candy for breakfast!"

"That's prime!" cried Joel, swallowing the last morsel. "Now I'm going to see what's this--oh, Dave, see here! see here!" he cried in intense excitement, pulling out a nice little parcel which, unrolled, proved to be a bright pair of stout mittens. "See if you've got some--look quick!"

"Yes, I have," said David, picking up a parcel about as big. "No, that's molasses candy."

"Just the same as I had," said Joel; "do look for the mittens. P'r'aps Santa Claus thought you had some--oh, dear!"

"Here they are!" screamed Davie. "I have got some, Joe, just exactly like yours! See, Joe!"

"Goody!" said Joel, immensely relieved; for now he could quite enjoy his to see a pair on Davie's hands, also. "Look at Phron," he cried, "she hasn't got only half of her things out!"

To tell the truth, Phronsie was so bewildered by her riches that she sat on the floor with the little red stocking in her lap, laughing and cooing to herself amid the few things she had drawn out. When she came to Seraphina's bonnet she was quite overcome. She turned it over and over, and smoothed out the little white feather that had once adorned one of Grandma Bascom's chickens, until the two boys~ with their stockings, and the others sitting around in a group on the floor watching them, laughed in glee to see her enjoyment.

"Oh, dear," said Joel, at last, shaking his stocking; "I've got all there is. I wish there were forty Christmases coming!"

"I haven't!" screamed Davie; "there's some thing in the toe."

"It's an apple, I guess," said Joel; "turn it up, Dave."

"'Tisn't an apple," exclaimed Davie, "tisn't round--it's long and thin; here 'tis." And he pulled out a splendid long whistle on which he blew a blast long and terrible, and Joel immediately following, all quiet was broken up, and the wildest hilarity reigned.

"I don't know as you'll want any breakfast," at last said

Mrs. Pepper, when she had got Phronsie a little sobered down.

"I do, I do!" cried Joel.

"Dear me! after your candy?" said Polly.

"That's all gone," said Joel, tooting around the table on his whistle. "What are we going to have for breakfast?"

"Same as ever," said his mother; "it can't be Christmas all the time."

"I wish 'twas," said little Davie; "forever and ever!"

"Forever an' ever," echoed little Phronsie, flying up, her cheeks like two pinks, and Seraphina in her arms with her bonnet on upside down.

"Dear, dear," said Polly, pinching Ben to keep still as they tumbled down the little rickety steps to the Provision Room, after breakfast. The children, content in their treasures, were holding high carnival in the kitchen. "Suppose they should find it out now--I declare I should feel most awfully. Isn't it elegant?" she asked, in a subdued whisper, going all around and around the tree, magnificent in its dress of bright red and yellow balls, white festoons, and little candle-ends all ready for lighting. "Oh, Ben, did you lock the door?"

"Yes," he said. "That's a mouse," he added, as a little rustling noise made Polly stop where she stood back of the tree and prick up her ears in great distress of mind. "'Tis elegant," he said, turning around in admiration, and taking in the tree which, as Polly said, was quite "gorgeous," and the evergreen branches twisted up on the beams and rafters, and all the other festive arrangements. "Even Jappy's isn't better, I don't believe!"

"I wish Jappy was here," said Polly with a small sigh.

"Well, he isn't," said Ben; "come, we must go back into the kitchen, or all the children will be out here. Look your last, Polly; 'twon't do to come again till it's time to light up."

"Mammy says she'd rather do the lighting up," said Polly. "Had she?" said Ben, in surprise; "oh, I suppose she's afraid we'll set somethin' a-fire. Well, then, we shan't come in till we have it."

"I can't bear to go," said Polly, turning reluctantly away; "it's most beautiful--oh, Ben," and she faced him for the five-hundredth time with the question, "is your Santa Claus dress all safe?"

"Yes," said Ben, "I'll warrant they won't find that in one hurry! Such a time as we've had to make it!"

"I know it," laughed Polly; "don't that cotton wool look just like bits of fur, Ben?"

"Yes," said Ben, "and when the flour's shaken over me it'll be Santa himself"

"We've got to put back the hair into mamsie's cushion the first thing to-morrow," whispered Polly anxiously, "and we mustn't forget it, Bensie."

"I want to keep the wig awfully," said Ben. "You did make that just magnificent, Polly!"

Day 143

1. Finish reading chapter 17.
2. Tell someone about the chapter. What do you think will happen next?

Chapter 17 continued

"I want to keep the wig awfully," said Ben. "You did make that just magnificent, Polly!"

"If you could see yourself," giggled Polly; "did you put it in the straw bed? and are you sure you pulled the ticking over it smooth?"

"Yes, sir," replied Ben, "sure's my name's Ben Pepper! if you'll only keep them from seeing me when I'm in it till we're ready--that's all I ask."

"Well," said Polly a little relieved, "but I hope Joe won't look."

"Come on! they're a-comin'!" whispered Ben; "quick!"

"Polly!" rang a voice dangerously near; so near that Polly, speeding over the stairs to intercept it, nearly fell on her nose.

"Where you been?" asked one.

"Let's have a concert," put in Ben; Polly was so out of breath that she couldn't speak. "Come, now, each take a whistle, and we'll march round and round and see which can make the biggest noise."

In the rattle and laughter which this procession made all mystery was forgotten, and the two conspirators began to breathe freer.

Five o'clock! The small ones of the Pepper flock, being pretty well tired out with noise and excitement, all gathered around Polly and Ben, and clamored for a story.

"Do, Polly, do," begged Joel. "It's Christmas, and 'twon't come again for a year."

"I can't," said Polly, in such a twitter that she could hardly stand still, and for the first time in her life refusing, "I can't think of a thing."

"I will then," said Ben; "we must do something," he whispered to Polly.

"Tell it good," said Joel, settling himself.

So for an hour the small tyrants kept their entertainers well employed.

"Isn't it growing awful dark?" said Davie, rousing himself at last, as Ben paused to take breath.

Polly pinched Ben.

"Mammy's a-goin' to let us know," he whispered in reply. "We must keep on a little longer."

"Don't stop," said Joel, lifting his head where he sat on the floor. "What you whisperin' for, Polly?"

"I'm not," said Polly, glad to think she hadn't spoken.

"Well, do go on, Ben," said Joel, lying down again.

"Polly'll have to finish it," said Ben; "I've got to go upstairs now."

So Polly launched out into such an extravagant story that they all, perforce, had to listen.

All this time Mrs. Pepper had been pretty busy in her way. And now she came into the kitchen and set down her candle on the table. "Children," she said. Everybody turned and looked at her-- her tone was so strange; and when they saw her dark eyes shining with such a new light, little Davie skipped right out into the middle of the room. "What's the matter, mammy?"

"You may all come into the Provision Room," said she.

"What for?" shouted Joel, in amazement; while the others jumped to their feet, and stood staring.

Polly flew around like a general, arranging her forces. "Let's march there," said she; "Phronsie, you take hold of Davie's hand, and go first."

"I'm goin' first," announced Joel, squeezing up past Polly. "No, you mustn't, Joe," said Polly decidedly; "Phronsie and David are the youngest."

"They're always the youngest," said Joel, falling back with Polly to the rear.

"Forward! *March*!" sang Polly. "Follow mamsie!"

Down the stairs they went with military step, and into the Provision Room. And then, with one wild look, the little battalion broke ranks, and tumbling one over the other in decidedly unmilitary style, presented a very queer appearance!

And Captain Polly was the queerest of all; for she just gave one gaze at the tree, and then sat right down on the floor, and said, "Oh! *Oh*!"

Mrs. Pepper was flying around delightedly, and saying, "Please to come right in," and "How do you do?"

And before anybody knew it, there were the laughing faces of Mrs. Henderson and the Parson himself, Doctor Fisher and old Grandma Bascom; while the two Henderson boys, unwilling to be defrauded of any of the fun, were squeezing themselves in between everybody else, and coming up to Polly every third minute, and saying, "There--aren't you surprised?"

"It's Fairyland!" cried little Davie, out of his wits with joy; "Oh! aren't we in Fairyland, ma?"

The whole room was in one buzz of chatter and fun; and everybody beamed on everybody else; and nobody knew what they said, till Mrs. Pepper called, "Hush! Santa Claus is coming!"

A rattle at the little old window made everybody look there, just as a great snow-white head popped up over the sill.

"Oh!" screamed Joel, "'tis Santy!"

"He's a-comin' in!" cried Davie in chorus, which sent Phronsie flying to Polly. In jumped a little old man, quite spry for his years; with a jolly, red face and a pack on his back, and flew into their midst, prepared to do his duty; but what should he do, instead of making his speech, "this jolly Old Saint"--but first fly up to Mrs. Pepper, and say--"Oh, mammy how did you do it?"

"It's Ben!" screamed Phronsie; but the little Old Saint didn't hear, for he and Polly took hold of hands, and pranced around that tree while everybody laughed till they cried to see them go!

And then it all came out!

"Order!" said Parson Henderson in his deepest tones; and then he put into Santa Claus' hands a letter, which he requested him to read. And the jolly Old Saint, although he was very old, didn't need any spectacles, but piped out in Ben's loudest tones:

"Dear Friends--A Merry Christmas to you all! And that you'll have a good time, and enjoy it all as much as I've enjoyed my good times at your house, is the wish of your friend,
Jasper Elyot King"

"Hurrah for Jappy!" cried Santa Claus, pulling his beard; and "Hurrah for Jasper!" went all around the room; and this ended in three good cheers--Phronsie coming in too late with her little crow-- which was just as well, however!

"Do your duty now, Santa Claus!" commanded Dr. Fisher as master of ceremonies; and everything was as still as a mouse!

And the first thing she knew, a lovely brass cage, with a dear little bird with two astonished black eyes dropped down into Polly's hands. The card on it said: "For Miss Polly Pepper, to give her music everyday in the year."

"Mammy," said Polly; and then she did the queerest thing of the whole! she just burst into tears! "I never thought I should have a bird for my very own!"

"Hullo!" said Santa Claus, "I've got something myself!"

"Santa Claus' clothes are too old," laughed Dr. Fisher, holding up a stout, warm suit that a boy about as big as Ben would delight in.

And then that wonderful tree just rained down all manner of lovely fruit. Gifts came flying thick and fast, till the air seemed full, and each one was greeted with a shout of glee, as it was put into the hands of its owner. A shawl flew down on Mrs. Pepper's shoulders; and a work-basket tumbled on Polly's head; and tops and balls and fishing poles, sent Joel and David into a corner with howls of delight!

But the climax was reached when a large wax doll in a very gay pink silk dress, was put into Phronsie's hands, and Dr. Fisher, stooping down, read in loud tones: "*For Phronsie, from one who enjoyed her gingerbread boy.*"

After that, nobody had anything to say! Books jumped down unnoticed, and gay boxes of candy. Only Polly peeped into one of her books, and saw in Jappy's plain hand--"I hope we'll both read this next summer." And turning over to the title-page, she saw "A Complete Manual of Cookery."

"The best is to come," said Mrs. Henderson in her gentle way. When there was a lull in the gale, she took Polly's hand, and led her to a little stand of flowers in the corner concealed by a sheet-- pinks and geraniums, heliotropes and roses, blooming away, and nodding their pretty heads at the happy sight--Polly had her flowers.

"Why didn't we know?" cried the children at last, when everybody was tying on their hoods, and getting their hats to leave the festive scene, "how could you keep it secret, mammy?"

"They all went to Mrs. Henderson's," said Mrs. Pepper; "Jasper wrote me, and asked where to send 'em, and Mrs. Henderson was so kind as to say that they might come there. And we brought 'em over last evening, when you were all abed. I couldn't have done it," she said, bowing to the Parson and his wife, "if 'twasn't for their kindness--never, in all this world!"

"And I'm sure," said the minister, looking around on the bright group, "if we can help along a bit of happiness like this, it is a blessed thing!"

And here Joel had the last word. "You said 'twan't goin' to be Christmas always, mammy. I say," looking around on the overflow of treasures and the happy faces--"it'll be just forever!"

Day 144

1. Read the first part of chapter 18.
2. Tell someone what is happening in the book.

Chapter 18 Education Ahead

After that they couldn't thank Jasper enough! They tried to, lovingly, and an elaborate letter of thanks, headed by Mrs. Pepper, was drawn up and sent with a box of the results of Polly's diligent study of Jasper's book. Polly stripped off recklessly her choicest buds and blossoms from the gay little stand of flowers in the corner, that had already begun to blossom, and tucked them into every little nook in the box that could possibly hold a posy. But as for thanking him enough!

"We can't do it, mammy," said Polly, looking around on all the happy faces, and then up at Cherry, who was singing in the window, and who immediately swelled up his little throat and poured out such a merry burst of song that she had to wait for him to finish. "No, not if we tried a thousand years!"

"I'm a-goin'," said Joel, who was busy as a bee with his new tools that the tree had shaken down for him, "to make Jappy the splendidest box you ever saw, Polly! I guess that'll thank him!"

"Do," cried Polly; "he'd be so pleased, Joey."

"And I," said Phronsie, over in the corner with her children, "I'm goin' to see my poor sick man sometime, Polly, I am!"

"Oh, dear!" cried Polly, whirling around, and looking at her mother in dismay. "She'll be goin' to-morrow! Oh, no, Phronsie, you can't; he lives miles and miles away--oh, ever so far!"

"Does he live as far as the moon?" asked little Phronsie, carefully laying Seraphina down, and looking up at Polly, anxiously.

"Oh, I don't know," said Polly, giving Cherry a piece of bread, and laughing to see how cunning he looked. "Oh, no, of course not, but it's an awful long ways, Phronsie."

"I don't care," said Phronsie, determinedly, giving the new doll a loving little pat, "I'm goin' sometime, Polly, to thank my poor sick man, yes, I am!"

"You'll see him next summer, Phronsie," sang Polly skipping around the kitchen, "and Jappy's sister Marian, the lovely lady, and all the boys. Won't that be nice?" and Polly stopped to pat the yellow head bending in motherly attentions over her array of dolls.

"Ye-es," said Phronsie, slowly; "the whole of 'em, Polly?"

"Yes, indeed!" said Polly, gayly; "the whole of 'em, Phronsie!

"Hooray!" shouted the two boys, while Phronsie only gave a long sigh, and clasped her hands.

"Better not be looking for summer," said Mrs. Pepper, "until you do your duty by the winter; then you can enjoy it," and she took a fresh needleful of thread.

"Mamsie's right," said Ben, smiling over at her. And he threw down his book and jumped for his cap. "Now for a good chop!" he cried, and snatching a kiss from Phronsie, he rushed out of the door to his work, whistling as he went.

"Warn't Mr. Henderson good, ma," asked Polly, watching his retreating figure, "to give Ben learning?"

"Yes, he was," replied Mrs. Pepper, enthusiastically. "We've got a parson, if anybody has in this world!"

"And Ben's learning," said Polly, swelling with pride, as she sat down by her mother, and began to sew rapidly, "so that he'll be a big man right off! Oh, dear," as a thought made her needle pause a minute in its quick flying in and out.

"What is it, Polly?" Mrs. Pepper looked keenly at the troubled face and downcast eyes.

"Why--" began Polly, and then she finished very slowly, "I shan't know anything, and Ben'll be ashamed of me.

"Yes, you will!" cried Mrs. Pepper, energetically, "you keep on trying, and the Lord'll send some way; don't you go to bothering your head about it now, Polly--it'll come when it's time."

"Will it?" asked Polly, doubtfully, taking up her needle again.

"Yes, indeed!" cried Mrs. Pepper, briskly; "come fly at your sewing; that's your learning now."

"So 'tis," said Polly, with a little laugh. "Now let's see which'll get their seam done first, mamsie?"

And now letters flew thick and fast from the city to the little brown house, and back again, warming Jasper's heart, and filling the tedious months of that winter with more of jollity and fun than the lad ever enjoyed before; and never was fun and jollity more needed than now; for Mr. King, having nothing to do, and each year finding himself less inclined to exercise any thoughtful energy for others, began to look at life something in the light of a serious bore, and accordingly made it decidedly disagreeable for all around him, and particularly for Jasper who was his constant companion. But the boy was looking forward to summer, and so held on bravely.

"I do verily believe, Polly," he wrote, "that Badgertown'll see the gayest times it ever knew! Sister Marian wants to go, so that's all right. Now, hurrah for a good time--it's surely coming!"

But alas! for Jasper! as spring advanced, his father took a decided aversion to Hingham, Badgertown, and all other places that could be mentioned in that vicinity.

"It's a wretched climate," he asserted, over and over; "and the foundation of all my ill feelings this winter was laid, I'm convinced, in Hingham last summer."

385

No use to urge the contrary; and all Jasper's pleadings were equally vain. At last, sister Marian, who was kind-hearted to a fault, sorry to see her brother's dismay and disappointment said, one day, "Why not have one of the children come here? I should like it very much--do invite Ben."

"I don't want Ben," said Jasper gloomily, "I want Polly." He added this in much the same tone as Phronsie's when she had rushed up to him the day she was lost, declaring, "I want Polly!"

"Very well, then," said sister Marian, laughing, "I'm sure I didn't mean to dictate which one; let it be Polly then; yes, I should prefer Polly myself, I think, as we've enough boys now," smiling to think of her own brood of wide awake youngsters.

"If you only will, father, I'll try to be ever so good!" said Jasper, turning suddenly to his father.

"Jasper needs some change," said sister Marian kindly, "he really has grown very pale and thin."

"Hey!" said Mr. King, sharply, looking at him over his eyeglasses. "The boy's well enough; well enough!" But he twisted uneasily in his chair, all the same. At last he flung down his paper, twitched his fingers through his hair two or three times, and then burst out-- "Well, why don't you send for her? I'm sure I don't care-- I'll write myself, and I had better do it now. Tell Thomas to be ready to take it right down; it must get into this mail."

When Mr. King had made up his mind to do anything, everybody else must immediately give up their individual plans, and stand out of the way for him to execute his at just that particular moment! Accordingly Thomas was dragged from his work to post the letter, while the old gentleman occupied the time in pulling out his watch every third second until the slightly-out-of-breath Thomas reported on his return that the letter did get in. Then Mr. King settled down satisfied, and everything went on smoothly as before.

But Polly didn't come! A grateful, appreciative letter, expressed in Mrs. Pepper's own stiff way, plainly showed the determination of that good woman not to accept what was such a favor to her child.

In vain Mr. King stormed, and fretted, and begged, offering every advantage possible--Polly should have the best foundation for a musical education that the city could afford; also lessons in the schoolroom under the boys' private tutor-- it was all of no avail. In vain sister Marian sent a gentle appeal, fully showing her heart was in it; nothing broke down Mrs. Pepper's resolve, until, at last, the old gentleman wrote one day that Jasper, being in such failing health, really depended on Polly to cheer him up. That removed the last straw that made it "putting one's self under an obligation," which to Mrs. Pepper's independent soul, had seemed insurmountable.

And now, it was decided that Polly was really to go! and pretty soon all Badgertown knew that Polly Pepper was going to the big city. And there wasn't a man, woman, or child but what greatly rejoiced that a sunny time was coming to one of the chicks in the little brown house. With many warm words, and some substantial gifts, kind friends helped forward the "outing." Only one person doubted that this delightful chance should be grasped at once--and that one was Polly herself!

Day 145

1. Read the next part of chapter 18.
2. Tell someone about what you read.

Vocabulary

1. What do these prefixes mean? **tri, mono, oct, bi**
2. Here are words to help you out. What do they have in common? You can use a dictionary if you need to.
   - tricycle, triangle, tripod
   - monosyllabic, monocle
   - octopus, octagon
   - bicycle, biannual, bifocals
   - Did you figure them out? They all mean certain numbers: three, one, eight, and two.
   - What does pent mean? How many sides does the Pentagon building have?

Chapter 18 continued

And now, it was decided that Polly was really to go! and pretty soon all Badgertown knew that Polly Pepper was going to the big city. And there wasn't a man, woman, or child but what greatly rejoiced that a sunny time was coming to one of the chicks in the little brown house. With many warm words, and some substantial gifts, kind friends helped forward the "outing." Only one person doubted that this delightful chance should be grasped at once--and that one was Polly herself!

"I can't," she said, and stood quite pale and still, when the Hendersons advised her mother's approval, and even Grandma Bascom said, "Go." "I can't go and leave mammy to do all the work."

"But don't you see, Polly," said Mrs. Henderson, drawing her to her side, "that you will help your mother twice as much as you possibly could here, by getting a good education? Think what your music will be; only think, Polly!"

Polly drew a long breath at this and turned away.

"Oh, Polly!" cried Ben, though his voice choked, "if you give this up, there never'll be another chance," and the boy put his arm around her, and whispered something in her ear.

"I know," said Polly quietly--and then she burst out, "oh, but I can't! 'tisn't right."

"Polly," said Mrs. Pepper--and never in all their lives had the children seen such a look in mamsie's eyes as met them then; "it does seem as if my heart would be broken if you didn't go!" And then she burst out crying, right before them all!

"Oh mammy," cried Polly, breaking away from everybody, and flinging herself into her arms. "I'll go--if you think I ought to. But it's too good! don't cry--don't, mammy dear," and Polly stroked the careworn face lovingly, and patted the smooth hair that was still so black.

"And, Polly," said Mrs. Pepper, smiling through her tears, "just think what a comfort you'll be to me, and us all," she added, taking in the children who were crowding around Polly as the centre of attraction. "Why, you'll be the making of us," she added hopefully.

"I'll do something," said Polly, her brown eyes kindling, "or I shan't be worthy of you, mammy."

"O, you'll do it," said Mrs. Pepper, confidently, "now that you're going."

But when Polly stepped into the stage, with her little hair trunk strapped on behind, containing her one brown merino that Mrs. Henderson had made over for her out of one of her own, and her two new ginghams, her courage failed again, and she astonished everybody, and nearly upset a mild-faced old lady who was in the corner placidly eating doughnuts, by springing out and rushing up through the little brown gate, past all the family, drawn up to see her off. She flew over the old flat door-stone, and into the bedroom, where she flung herself down between the old bed and Phronsie's crib, in a sudden torrent of tears. "I can't go!" she sobbed--"oh I can't!"

"Why, Polly!" cried Mrs. Pepper, hurrying in, followed by Joel and the rest of the troops at his heels. "What are you thinking of!"

"Think of by-and-by, Polly," put in Ben, patting her on the back with an unsteady hand, while Joel varied the proceedings by running back and forth, screaming at the top of his lungs, "The stage's going! your trunk'll be taken!"

"Dear me!" ejaculated Mrs. Pepper, "do stop it somebody! there, Polly, come now! Do as mother says!"

"I'll try again," said poor Polly, choking back her sobs, and getting on her feet.

Then Polly's tears were wiped away, her hat straightened, after which she was kissed all round again by the whole family, Phronsie waiting for the last two, and then was helped again into the stage, the bags and parcels, and a box for Jappy, which, as it wouldn't go into the trunk, Joel had insisted Polly should carry in her hand, were again piled around her, and Mr. Tisbett mounted to his seat, and with a crack of the whip, bore her safely off this time.

The doughnut lady, viewing poor Polly with extreme sympathy, immediately forced upon her acceptance three of the largest and sugariest.

"Twill do you good," she said, falling to, herself, on another with good zeal. "I always eat 'em, and then there ain't any room for homesickness!"

And away, and away, and away they rumbled and jumbled to the cars.

Here Mr. Tisbett put Polly and her numerous bundles under the care of the conductor, with manifold charges and explicit directions, to see her safely into Mr. King's own hands. He left her sitting straight up among her parcels, her sturdy little figure drawn up to its full height, and the clear brown eyes regaining a little of their dancing light; for although a dreadful feeling tugged at her heart, as she thought of the little brown house she was fast flying away from, there was something else; our Polly had begun to realize that now she was going to "help mother."

And now they neared the big city, and everybody began to bustle around, and get ready to jump out, and the minute the train stopped, the crowd poured out from the cars, making way for the crowd pouring in, for this was a through train.

"All aboard!" sang the conductor. "Oh my senses!" springing to Polly; "I forgot you--here!"

But as quick as a flash he was pushed aside, and a bright, boyish figure dashed up.

"Oh, Polly!" he said in such a ringing voice! and in another second, Polly and her bag, and the bundle of cakes and apples that Grandma Bascom had put up for her, and Joel's box, were one and all bundled out upon the platform, and the train whizzed on, and there Mr. King was fuming up and down, berating the departing conductor, and speaking his mind in regard to all the railroad officials he could think of. He pulled himself up long enough to give Polly a hearty welcome; and then away again he flew in righteous indignation, while Jasper rushed off into the baggage room with Polly's check.

However, every now and then, turning to look down into the little rosy face beside him, the old gentleman would burst forth, "Bless me, child! I'm glad you're here, Polly!--how could the fellow forget when"-- "Oh well, you know," said Polly, with a happy little wriggle under her brown coat, "I'm here now."

"So you are! so you are!" laughed the old gentleman suddenly; "where can Jasper be so long."

"They're all in the carriage," answered the boy skipping back. "Now, father! now Polly!"

He was fairly bubbling over with joy and Mr. King forgot his dudgeon and joined in the general glee, which soon became so great that travellers gave many a glance at the merry trio who bundled away to Thomas and the waiting grays.

"You're sure you've got the right check?" asked Mr. King, nervously, getting into a handsome coach lined with dark green satin, and settling down among its ample cushions with a sigh of relief.

389

"Oh yes," laughed Jasper; "Polly didn't have any one else's check, I guess."

Over through the heart of the city, down narrow, noisy business streets, out into wide avenues, with handsome stately mansions on either side--they flew along.

"Oh," said Polly; and then she stopped, and blushed very hard.

"What is it, my dear?" asked Mr. King, kindly.

Polly couldn't speak at first, but when Jasper stopped his merry chat and begged to know what it was, she turned on him, and burst out, "You live here?"

"Why, yes," laughed the boy; "why not?"

"Oh!" said Polly again, her cheeks as red as two roses, "it's so lovely!"

And then the carriage turned in at a brown stone gateway, and winding up among some fine old trees, stopped before a large, stately residence that in Polly's eyes seemed like one of the castles of Ben's famous stories. And then Mr. King got out, and gallantly escorted Polly out, and up the steps, while Jasper followed with Polly's bag which he couldn't be persuaded to resign to Thomas. A stiff waiter held the door open--and then, the rest was only a pleasant, confused jumble of kind welcoming words, smiling faces, with a background of high spacious walls, bright pictures, and soft elegant hangings, everything and all inextricably mixed--till Polly herself seemed floating--away--away, fast to the Fairyland of her dreams; now, Mr. King was handing her around, like a precious parcel, from one to the other--now Jasper was bobbing in and out everywhere, introducing her on all sides, and then Prince was jumping up and trying to lick her face every minute--but best of all was, when a lovely face looked down into hers, and Jasper's sister bent to kiss her.

Day 146

1. Finish reading chapter 18. Write or tell a summary of the chapter. If your summary is one sentence, get a high five and/or hug.

Chapter 18 continued

And then the carriage turned in at a brown stone gateway, and winding up among some fine old trees, stopped before a large, stately residence that in Polly's eyes seemed like one of the castles of Ben's famous stories. And then Mr. King got out, and gallantly escorted Polly out, and up the steps, while Jasper followed with Polly's bag which he couldn't be persuaded to resign to Thomas. A stiff waiter held the door open--and then, the rest was only a pleasant, confused jumble of kind welcoming words, smiling faces, with a background of high spacious walls, bright pictures, and soft elegant hangings, everything and all inextricably mixed--till Polly herself seemed floating--away--away, fast to the Fairyland of her dreams; now, Mr. King was handing her around, like a precious parcel, from one to the other--now Jasper was bobbing in and out everywhere, introducing her on all sides, and then Prince was jumping up and trying to lick her face every minute--but best of all was, when a lovely face looked down into hers, and Jasper's sister bent to kiss her.

"I am very glad to have you here, little Polly." The words were simple, but Polly, lifting up her clear brown eyes, looked straight into the heart of the speaker, and from that moment never ceased to love her.

"It was a good inspiration," thought Mrs. Whitney to herself; "this little girl is going to be a comfort, I know." And then she set herself to conduct successfully her three boys into friendliness and good fellowship with Polly, for each of them was following his own sweet will in the capacity of host, and besides staring at her with all his might, was determined to do the whole of the entertaining, a state of things which might become unpleasant. However, Polly stood it like a veteran.

"This little girl must be very tired," said Mrs. Whitney, at last with a bright smile. "Besides I am going to have her to myself now."

"Oh, no, no," cried little Dick in alarm; "why, she's just come; we want to see her."

"For shame, Dick!" said Percy, the eldest, a boy of ten years, who took every opportunity to reprove Dick in public; "she's come a great ways, so she ought to rest, you know."

"You wanted her to come out to the greenhouse yourself, you know you did," put in Van, the next to Percy, who never would be reproved or patronized, "only she wouldn't go."

"You'll come down to dinner," said Percy, politely, ignoring Van. "Then you won't be tired, perhaps."

"Oh, I'm not very tired now," said Polly, brightly, with a merry little laugh, "only I've never been in the cars before, and"-- "Never been in the cars before!" exclaimed Van, crowding up, while Percy made a big round O with his mouth, and little Dick's eyes stretched to their widest extent.

"No," said Polly simply, "never in all my life."

"Come, dear," said sister Marian, rising quickly, and taking Polly's hand; while Jasper, showing unmistakable symptoms of pitching into all the three boys, followed with the bag.

Up the broad oak staircase they went, Polly holding by Mrs. Whitney's soft hand, as if for dear life, and Jasper tripping up two steps at a time, in front of them. They turned after reaching the top, down a hall soft to the foot and brightly lighted.

"Now, Polly," said sister Marian, "I'm going to have you here, right next to my dressing room; this is your nest, little bird, and I hope you'll be very happy in it."

And here Mrs. Whitney turned up the gas, and then, just because she couldn't help it, gathered Polly up in her arms without another word. Jasper set down the bag on a chair, and came and stood by his sister's side, looking down at her as she stroked the brown wavy hair on her bosom.

"It's so nice to have Polly here, sister," he said, and he put his hand on Mrs. Whitney's neck; and then with the other hand took hold of both of Polly's chubby ones, who looked up and smiled; and in that smile the little brown house seemed to hop right out, and bring back in a flash all the nice times those eight happy weeks had brought him.

"Oh, 'twas so perfectly splendid, sister Marian," he cried, flinging himself down on the floor by her chair. "You don't know what good times we had--does she, Polly?" and then he launched out into a perfect shower of "Don't you remember this?" or "Oh, Polly! you surely haven't forgotten that!" Mrs. Whitney good naturedly entering into it and enjoying it all with them, until, warned by the lateness of the hour, she laughingly reminded Jasper of dinner, and dismissed him to prepare for it.

When the three boys saw Polly coming in again, they welcomed her with a cordial shout, for one and all, after careful measurement of her, had succumbed entirely to Polly; and each was unwilling that the others should get ahead of him in her regard.

"This is your seat, Polly," said sister Marian, touching the chair next to her own.

Thereupon a small fight ensued between the little Whitneys, while Jasper looked decidedly discomfited.

"Let Polly sit next to me," said Van, as if a seat next to him was of all things most to be desired.

"Oh, no, I want her," said little Dick.

"Pshaw, Dick! you're too young," put in Percy. "You'd spill the bread and butter all over her."

"I wouldn't either," said little Dick, indignantly, and beginning to crawl into his seat; "I don't spill bread and butter, now Percy, you know."

"See here," said Jasper, decidedly, "she's coming up here by father and me; that is, sister Marian," he finished more politely, "if you're willing."

All this while Polly had stood quietly watching the group, the big, handsome table, the bright lights, and the well-trained servants with a curious feeling at her heart--what were the little-brown- house-people doing?

"Polly shall decide it," said sister Marian, laughing. "Now, where will you sit, dear?" she added, looking down on the little quiet figure beside her.

"Oh, by Jappy, please," said Polly, quickly, as if there could be no doubt; "and kind Mr. King," she added, smiling at him.

"That's right; that's right, my dear," cried the old gentleman, pleased beyond measure at her honest choice. And he pulled out her chair, and waited upon her into it so handsomely that Polly was happy at once; while Jasper, with a proud toss of his dark, wavy hair, marched up delightedly, and took the chair on her other side.

And now, in two or three minutes it seemed as if Polly had always been there; it was the most natural thing in the world that sister Marian should smile down the table at the bright-faced narrator, who answered all their numerous questions, and entertained them all with accounts of Ben's skill, of Phronsie's cunning ways, of the boys who made fun for all, and above everything else of the dear mother whom they all longed to help, and of all the sayings and doings in the little brown house. No wonder that the little boys forgot to eat; and for once never thought of the attractions of the table. And when, as they left the table at last, little Dick rushed impulsively up to Polly, and flinging himself into her arms, declared-- "I love you!--and you're my sister!" Nothing more was needed to make Polly feel at home.

"Yes," said Mrs. Whitney, and nodded to herself in the saying, "it was a good thing; and a comfort, I believe, has come to this house this day!"

Day 147

1. Read chapter 19.
2. Tell someone about the chapter.

Chapter 19 Brave Work and the Reward

And on the very first morrow came Polly's music teacher!

The big drawing-room, with its shaded light and draped furniture, with its thick soft carpet, on which no foot-fall could be heard, with all its beauty and loveliness on every side was nothing to Polly's eyes, only the room that contained the piano!

That was all she saw! And when the teacher came he was simply the Fairy (an ugly little one, it is true, but still a most powerful being) who was to unlock its mysteries, and conduct her into Fairyland itself. He was a homely little Frenchman, with a long, curved nose, and an enormous black moustache, magnificently waxed, who bowed elaborately, and called her "Mademoiselle Pep-paire;" but he had music in his soul, and Polly couldn't reverence him too much.

And now the big piano gave out new sounds; sounds that told of a strong purpose and steady patience. Every note was struck for mother and the home brood. Monsieur Tourtelotte, after watching her keenly out of his little black eyes, would nod to himself like a mandarin, and the nod would be followed by showers of extra politeness, as his appreciation of her patient energy and attention.

Every chance she could get, Polly would steal away into the drawing-room from Jappy and the three boys and all the attractions they could offer, and laboriously work away over and over at the tedious scales and exercises that were to be stepping-stones to so much that was glorious beyond. Never had she sat still for so long a time in her active little life; and now, with her arms at just such an angle, with the stiff, chubby fingers kept under training and restraint--well, Polly realized, years after, that only her love of the little brown house could ever have kept her from flying up and spinning around in perfect despair.

"She likes it!" said Percy, in absolute astonishment, one day, when Polly had refused to go out driving with all the other children in the park, and had gone resolutely, instead, into the drawing-room and shut the door. "She likes those hateful old exercises and she don't like anything else."

"Much you know about it," said Jappy; "she's perfectly aching to go, now Percy Whitney!"

"Well, why don't she then?" said Percy, opening his eyes to their widest extent.

"Cause," said Jasper, stopping on his way to the door to look him full in the face, "she's commenced to learn to play, and there won't anything stop her."

"I'm going to try," said Percy, gleefully. "I know lots of ways I can do to try, anyway."

"See here, now," said Jasper, turning back, "you let her alone! Do you hear?" he added, and there must have been something in his eye to command attention, for Percy instantly signified his intention not to tease this young music student in the least.

"Come on then, old fellow," and Jasper swung his cap on his head, "Thomas will be like forty bears if we keep him waiting much longer."

And Polly kept at it steadily day after day; getting through with the lessons in the schoolroom as quickly as possible to rush to her music, until presently the little Frenchman waxed enthusiastic to that degree that, as day after day progressed and swelled into weeks, and each lesson came to an end, he would skip away on the tips of his toes, his nose in the air, and the waxed ends of his moustache, fairly trembling with delight-- "Ah, such patience as Mademoiselle Pep-paire has! I know no other such little Americane!"

"I think," said Jasper one evening after dinner, when all the children were assembled as usual in their favorite place on the big rug in front of the fire in the library, Prince in the middle of the group, his head on his paws, watching everything in infinite satisfaction, "that Polly's getting on in music as I never saw anyone do; and that's a fact!"

"I mean to begin," said Van, ambitiously, sitting up straight and staring at the glowing coals. "I guess I will to-morrow," which announcement was received with a perfect shout--Van's taste being anything rather than of a musical nature.

"If you do," said Jappy, when the merriment had a little subsided, "I shall go out of the house at every lesson; there won't anyone stay in it, Van."

"I can bang all I want to, then," said Van, in no way disturbed by the reflection, and pulling one of Prince's long ears, "you think you're so big, Jappy, just because you're thirteen."

"He's only three ahead of me, Van," bristled Percy, who never could forgive Jappy for being his uncle, much less the still greater sin of having been born three years earlier than himself.

"Three's just as bad as four," said Van.

"Let's tell stories," began Polly, who never could remember such goings on in the little brown house; "we must each tell one," she added with the greatest enthusiasm, "and see which will be the biggest and the best."

"Oh, no," said Van, who perfectly reveled in Polly's stories, und who now forgot his trials in the prospect of one, "You tell, Polly--you tell alone."

"Yes, do, Polly," said Jasper; "we'd rather."

So Polly launched out into one of her gayest and finest; and soon they were in such a peal of laughter, and had reached such heights of enjoyment, that Mr. King popped his head in at the door, and then came in, and took a seat in a big rocking-chair in the corner to hear the fun go on.

"Oh, dear," said Van, leaning back with a long sigh, and wiping his flushed face as Polly wound up with a triumphant flourish, 'how ever do you think of such things, Polly Pepper?

"That isn't anything," said Jappy, bringing his handsome face out into the strong light; "why, it's just nothing to what she has told time and again in the little brown house in Badgertown;" and then he caught sight of Polly's face, which turned a little pale in the firelight as he spoke; and the brown eyes had such a pathetic droop in them that it went to the boy's very heart.

Was Polly homesick? and so soon!

Day 148

1. Read chapter 20.
2. Tell someone about this chapter.

Chapter 20 Polly is Comforted

Yes, it must be confessed. Polly was homesick. All her imaginations of her mother's hard work, increased by her absence, loomed up before her, till she was almost ready to fly home without a minute's warning. At night, when no one knew it, the tears would come racing over the poor, forlorn little face, and would not be squeezed back. It got to be noticed finally; and one and all redoubled their exertions to make everything twice as pleasant as ever!

The only place, except in front of the grand piano, where Polly approached a state of comparative happiness, was in the greenhouse.

Here she would stay, comforted and soothed among the lovely plants and rich exotics, rejoicing the heart of Old Turner the gardener, who since Polly's first rapturous entrance, had taken her into his good graces for all time.

Every chance she could steal after practice hours were over, and after the clamorous demands of the boys upon her time were fully satisfied, was seized to fly on the wings of the wind, to the flowers.

But even with the music and flowers the dancing light in the eyes went down a little; and Polly, growing more silent and pale, moved around with a little droop to the small figure that had only been wont to fly through the wide halls and spacious rooms with gay and springing step.

"Polly don't like us," at last said Van one day in despair. "Then, dear," said Mrs. Whitney, "you must be kinder to her than ever; think what it would be for one of you to be away from home even among friends."

"I'd like it first rate to be away from Percy," said Van, reflectively; "I wouldn't come back in three, no, six weeks."

"My son," said his mamma, "just stop and think how badly you would feel, if you really couldn't see Percy."

"Well," said Van, and he showed signs of relenting a little at that; "but Percy is perfectly awful, mamma, you don't know; and he feels so smart too," he said vindictively.

"Well," said Mrs. Whitney, softly, "let's think what we can do for Polly; it makes me feel very badly to see her sad little face."

"I don't know," said Van, running over in his mind all the possible ways he could think of for entertaining anybody, "unless she'd like my new book of travels--or my velocipede," he added.

"I'm afraid those wouldn't quite answer the purpose," said his mamma, smiling--"especially the last; yet we must think of something."

But just here Mr. King thought it about time to take matters into his hands. So, with a great many chucklings and shruggings when no one was by, he had departed after breakfast one day, simply saying he shouldn't be back to lunch.

Polly sat in the drawing-room, near the edge of the twilight, practicing away bravely. Somehow, of all the days when the home feeling was the strongest, this day it seemed as if she could bear it no longer. If she could only see Phronsie for just one moment! "I shall have to give up!" she moaned. "I can't bear it!" and over went her head on the music rack.

"Where is she?" said a voice over in front of the piano, in the gathering dusk--unmistakably Mr. King's.

"Oh, she's always at the piano," said Van. "She must be there now, somewhere," and then somebody laughed. Then came in the loudest of whispers from little Dick, "Oh, Jappy, what'll she say?"

"Hush!" said one of the other boys; "do be still, Dick!"

Polly sat up very straight, and whisked off the tears quickly. Up came Mr. King with an enormous bundle in his arms; and he marched up to the piano, pulling with his exertions.

"Here, Polly, hold your arms," he had only strength to gasp. And then he broke out into a loud burst of merriment, in which all the troop joined, until the big room echoed with the sound.

At this, the bundle opened suddenly, and--out popped Phronsie!

"Here I am! I'm here, Polly!"

But Polly couldn't speak; and if Jasper hadn't caught her just in time, she would have tumbled over backward from the stool, Phronsie and all!

"Aren't you glad I've come, Polly?" asked Phronsie, with her little face close to Polly's own.

That brought Polly to. "Oh, Phronsie!" she cried, and strained her to her heart; while the boys crowded around, and plied her with sudden questions.

"Now you'll stay," cried Van; "say, Polly, won't you."

"Weren't you awfully surprised?" cried Percy; "say, Polly, awfully?"

"Is her name Phronsie," put in Dick, unwilling to be left out, and not thinking of anything else to ask.

"Boys," whispered their mother, warningly, "she can't answer you; just look at her face."

And to be sure, our Polly's face was a study to behold. All its old sunniness was as nothing to the joy that now transfigured it.

"Oh!" she cried, coming out of her rapture a little, and springing over to Mr. King with Phronsie still in her arms. "Oh, you are the dearest and best Mr. King I ever saw! but how did you make mammy let her come?"

"Isn't he splendid!" cried Jasper in intense pride, swelling up. "Father knew how to do it."

But Polly's arms were around the old gentleman's neck, so she didn't hear. "There, there," he said soothingly, patting her brown, fuzzy head. Something was going down the old gentleman's neck, that wet his collar, and made him whisper very tenderly in her ear, "don't give way now, Polly; Phronsie'll see you."

"I know," gasped Polly, controlling her sobs; "I won't--only--I can't thank you!"

"Phronsie," said Jasper quickly, "what do you suppose Prince said the other day?"

"What?" asked Phronsie in intense interest slipping down out of Polly's arms, and crowding up close to Jasper's side. "What did he, Japser?"

"Oh-ho, how funny!" laughed Van, while little Dick burst right out, "Japser!"

"Be still," said Jappy warningly, while Phronsie stood surveying them all with grave eyes.

"Well, I asked him, 'Don't you want to see Phronsie Pepper, Prince?' And do you know, he just stood right upon his hind legs, Phronsie, and said: 'Bark! yes, Bark! Bark!"

"Did he really, Japser?" cried Phronsie, delighted beyond measure; and clasping her hands in rapture, "all alone by himself?"

"Yes, all alone by himself," asserted Jasper, vehemently,

and winking furiously to the others to stop their laughing; "he did now, truly, Phronsie."

"Then mustn't I go and see him now, Japser? yes, pretty soon now?"

"So you must," cried Jasper, enchanted at his success in amusing; "and I'll go with you."

"Oh, no," cried Phronsie, shaking her yellow head. "Oh no, Japser; I must go by my very own self."

"There Jap, you've caught it," laughed Percy; while the others screamed at the sight of Jasper's face.

"Oh Phronsie!" cried Polly, turning around at the last words; "how could you!"

"Don't mind it, Polly," whispered Jasper; "twasn't her fault."

"Phronsie," said Mrs. Whitney, smilingly, stooping over the child, "would you like to see a little pussy I have for you?"

But the chubby face didn't look up brightly, as usual: and the next moment, without a bit of warning, Phronsie sprang past them all, even Polly, and flung herself into Mr. King's arms, in a perfect torrent of sobs. "Oh! let's go back!" was all they heard!

"Dear me!" ejaculated the old gentleman, in the utmost amazement; "and such a time as I've had to get her here too!" he added, staring around on the astonished group, none of whom had a word to say.

But Polly stood like a statue! All Jasper's frantic efforts at comfort, utterly failed. To think that Phronsie had left her for any one!-- even good Mr. King! The room seemed to buzz, and everything to turn upside down--and just then, she heard another cry--"Oh, I want Polly, I do!"

With a bound, Polly was at Mr. King's side, with her face on his coat, close to the little tear-stained one. The fat, little arms unclasped their hold, and transferred themselves willingly to Polly's neck; and Phronsie hugged up comfortably to Polly's heart, who poured into her ear all the loving words she had so longed to say.

Just then there was a great rush and a scuffling noise; and something rushed up to Phronsie "Oh!" And then the next minute, she had her arms around Prince's neck, too, who was jumping all over her and trying as hard as he could, to express his overwhelming delight.

"She's the funningest little thing I ever saw," said Mrs. Whitney, enthusiastically, afterward, aside to Mr. King. "Such lovely yellow hair, and such exquisite brown eyes--the combination is very striking. How did her mother ever let her go?" she asked impulsively, "I didn't believe you could persuade her, father."

"I didn't have any fears, if I worked it rightly," said the old gentleman complacently. "I wasn't coming without her, Marian, if it could possibly be managed. The truth is, that Phronsie had been pining for Polly to such an extent, that there was no other way but for her to have Polly; and her mother was just on the point, although it almost killed her, of sending for Polly--as if we should have let her go!" he cried in high dudgeon; just as if he owned the whole of the Peppers, and could dispose of them all to suit his fancy! "So you see, I was just in time; in the very nick of time, in fact!"

"So her mother was willing?" asked his daughter, curiously. "Oh, she couldn't help it," cried Mr. King, beginning to walk up and down the floor, and beaming as he recalled his successful strategy; "there wasn't the smallest use in thinking of anything else. I told her 'twould just stop Polly from ever being a musician if she broke off now--and so 'twould, you know yourself, Marian, for we should never get the child here again, if we let her go now; and I talked--well, I had to talk some; but, well--the upshot is I did get her, and I did bring her--and here she is!" And the old gentleman was so delighted with his success, that he had to burst out into a series of short, happy bits of laughter, that occupied quite a space of time. At last he came out of them, and wiped his face vigorously.

"And to think how fond the little girl is of you, father!" said Mrs. Whitney, who hadn't yet gotten over her extreme surprise at the old gentleman's complete subjection to the little Peppers: he, whom all children had by instinct always approached so carefully, and whom every one found it necessary to conciliate!

"Well, she's a nice child," he said, "a very nice child; and," straightening himself up to his fullest height, and looking so very handsome, that his daughter could not conceal her admiration, "I shall always take care of Phronsie Pepper, Marian!"

"So I hope," said Mrs. Whitney; "and father, I do believe they'll repay you; for I do think there's good blood there; these children have a look about them that shows them worthy to be trusted."

"So they have: so they have," assented Mr. King, and then the conversation dropped.

Day 149

1. Read the beginning of chapter 21.
2. Tell someone about what you read.

Chapter 21 Phronsie

Phronsie was toiling up and down the long, oak staircase the next morning; slowly going from one step to the other, drawing each little fat foot into place laboriously, but with a pleased expression on her face that only gave some small idea of the rapture within. Up and down she had been going for a long time, perfectly fascinated; seeming to care for nothing else in the world but to work her way up to the top of the long flight, only to turn and come down again. She had been going on so for some time, till at last, Polly, who was afraid she would tire herself all out, sat down at the foot and begged and implored the little girl, who had nearly reached the top, to stop and rest.

"You'll be tired to death, Phronsie!" she said, looking up at the small figure on its toilsome journey. "Why you must have gone up a million times! Do sit down, pet; we're all going out riding, Phronsie, this afternoon; and you can't go if you're all tired out."

"I won't be tired, Polly," said Phronsie, turning around and looking at her, "do let me go just once more!"

"Well," said Polly, who never could refuse her anything, "just once, Phronsie, and then you must stop."

So Phronsie kept on her way rejoicing, while Polly still sat on the lowest stair, and drummed impatiently on the stair above her, waiting for her to get through.

Jappy came through the hail and found them thus. "Hallo, Polly!" he said, stopping suddenly; "what's the matter?"

"Oh, Phronsie's been going so," said Polly, looking up at the little figure above them, which had nearly reached the top in delight, "that I can't stop her. She has really, Jappy, almost all the morning; you can't think how crazy she is over it."

"Is that so?" said Jasper, with a little laugh. "Hullo, Phronsie, is it nice?" and he tossed a kiss to the little girl, and then sat down by Polly.

"Oh," said Phronsie, turning to come down, "it's the beyew-tifiest place I ever saw, Japser! the very be-yew-tiflest!"

"I wish she could have her picture painted," whispered Jasper, enthusiastically. "Look at her now, Polly, quick!"

"Yes," said Polly, "isn't she sweet!"

"Sweeter," said Jasper. "I should think she was!"

The sunlight through an oriel window fell on the childish face and figure, glinting the yellow hair, and lighting up the radiant face, that yet had a tender, loving glance for the two who waited for her below. One little foot was poised, just in the act of stepping down to the next lower stair, and the fat hand grasped the polished railing, expressive of just enough caution to make it truly childish. In after years Jasper never thought of Phronsie without bringing up this picture on that April morning, when Polly and he sat at the foot of the stairs, and looked up and saw it.

"Where's Jap?" called one of the boys; and then there was a clatter out into the hall.

"What are you doing?" and Van came to a full stop of amazement and stared at them.

"Resting," said Jappy, concisely, "what do you want, Van?"

"I want you," said Van, "we can't do anything without you, Jappy; you know that."

"Very well," said Jasper, getting up. "Come on, Polly, we must go."

"And Phronsie," said Van, anxiously, looking up to Phronsie, who had nearly reached them by this time, "we want her, too."

"Of course," said Polly, running up and meeting her to give her a hug; "I don't go unless she does."

"Where are we going, Polly?" asked Phronsie, looking back longingly to her beloved stairs as she was borne off.

"To the greenhouse, chick!" said Jasper, "to help Turner; and it'll be good fun, won't it, Polly?"

"What is a greenhouse?" asked the child, wonderingly. "All green, Japser?"

"Oh, dear me," said Van, doubling up, "do you suppose she thinks it's painted green?"

"It's green inside, Phronsie, dear," said Jasper, kindly, "and that's the best of all."

When Phronsie was really let loose in the greenhouse she thought it decidedly best of all; and she went into nearly as much of a rapture as Polly did on her first visit to it.

In a few moments she was cooing and jumping among the plants, while old Turner, staid and particular as he was, laughed to see her go.

"She's your sister, Miss Mary, ain't she?" at last he asked, as Phronsie bent lovingly over a little pot of heath, and just touched one little leaf carefully with her finger.

"Yes," said Polly, "but she don't look like me."

"She is like you," said Turner, respectfully, "if she don't look like you; and the flowers know it, too," he added, "and they'll love to see her coming, just as they do you."

For Polly had won the old gardener's heart completely by her passionate love for flowers, and nearly every morning a little nosegay, fresh and beautiful, came up to the house for "Miss Mary."

And now nobody liked to think of the time, or to look back to it, when Phronsie hadn't been in the house. When the little feet went pattering through halls and over stairs, it seemed to bring sunshine and happiness into every one's heart just to hear the sounds. Polly and the boys in the schoolroom would look up from their books and nod away brightly to each other, and then fall to faster than ever on their lessons, to get through the quicker to be with her again.

One thing Phronsie always insisted on, and kept to it pertinaciously--and that was to go into the drawing-room with Polly when she went to practice, and there, with one of her numerous family of dolls, to sit down quietly in some corner and wait till she got through.

Day after day she did it, until Polly, who was worried to think how tedious it must be for her, would look around and say-- "Oh, childie, do run out and play."

"I want to stay," Phronsie would beg in an injured tone; "please let me, Polly."

So Polly would jump and give her a kiss, and then, delighted to know that she was there, would go at her practicing with twice the vigor and enthusiasm.

But Phronsie's chief occupation, at least when she wasn't with Polly, was the entertainment and amusement of Mr. King. And never was she very long absent from his side, which so pleased the old gentleman that he could scarcely contain himself, as with a gravity befitting the importance of her office, she would follow him around in a happy contented way, that took with him immensely. And now-a-days, no one ever saw the old gentleman going out of a morning, when Jasper was busy with his lessons, without Phronsie by his side, and many people turned to see the portly figure with the handsome head bent to catch the prattle of a little sunny-haired child, who trotted along, clasping his hand confidingly. And nearly all of them stopped to gaze the second time before they could convince themselves that it was really that queer, stiff old Mr. King of whom they had heard so much.

And now the accumulation of dolls in the house became something alarming, for Mr. King, observing Phronsie's devotion to her family, thought there couldn't possibly be too many of them; so he scarcely ever went out without bringing home one at least to add to them, until Phronsie had such a remarkable collection as would have driven almost any other child nearly crazy with delight. She, however, regarded them something in the light of a grave responsibility, to be taken care of tenderly, to be watched over carefully as to just the right kind of bringing up; and to have small morals and manners taught in just the right way.

Phronsie was playing in the corner of Mrs. Whitney's little boudoir, engaged in sending out invitations for an elaborate tea-party to be given by one of the dolls, when Polly rushed in with consternation in her tones, and dismay written all over her face.

Day 150

1. Finish reading chapter 21.
2. Write or tell a summary of the chapter. If you can do it in one sentence, get a high five and/or hug.

Vocabulary

1. Can you figure out what these word parts mean? Each list of words has something in common. Use the clue words to make a good guess about what that word part means. If you don't know the clue words, you can use a dictionary. (Answers)
   - **chron**: chronicle, chronological, chronic
   - **cred**: credit, credible, credential
   - **dem**: democracy, epidemic

Chapter 21 continued

Phronsie was playing in the corner of Mrs. Whitney's little boudoir, engaged in sending out invitations for an elaborate tea-party to be given by one of the dolls, when Polly rushed in with consternation in her tones, and dismay written all over her face.

"What is it, dear?" asked Mrs. Whitney, looking up from her embroidery.

"Why," said Polly, "how could I! I don't see--but I've forgotten to write to mamsie to-day; it's Wednesday, you know, and there's Monsieur coming." And poor Polly looked out in despair to see the lively little music teacher advancing towards the house at an alarming rate of speed.

"That is because you were helping Van so long last evening over his lessons," said Mrs. Whitney; "I am so sorry."

"Oh, no," cried Polly honestly, "I had plenty of time--but I forgot 'twas mamsie's day. What will she do!"

"You will have to let it go now till the afternoon, dear; there's no other way; it can go in the early morning mail."

"Oh, dear," sighed Polly, "I suppose I must." And she went down to meet Monsieur with a very distressed little heart.

Phronsie laid down the note of invitation she was scribbling, and stopped to think; and a moment or two after, at a summons from a caller, Mrs. Whitney left the room.

"I know I ought to," said Phronsie to herself and the dolls, "yes, I know I had; mamsie will feel, oh! so bad, when she don't get Polly's letter; and I know the way, I do, truly."

She got up and went to the window, where she thought a minute; and then, coming back, she took up her little stubby pencil, and bending over a small bit of paper, she commenced to trace with laborious efforts and much hard breathing, some very queer hieroglyphics that to her seemed to be admirable, as at last she held them up with great satisfaction.

"Good-bye," she said then, getting up and bowing to the dolls who sat among the interrupted invitations, "I won't be gone but a little bit of one minute," and she went out determinedly and shut the door.

Nobody saw the little figure going down the carriage drive, so of course nobody could stop her. When Phronsie got to the gateway she looked up and down the street carefully, either way.

"Yes," she said, at last, "it was down here, I'm very sure, I went with grandpa," and immediately turned down the wrong way, and went on and on, grasping carefully her small, and by this time rather soiled bit of paper.

At last she reached the business streets; and although she didn't come to the Post Office, she comforted herself by the thought--"it must be coming soon. I guess it's round this corner."

She kept turning corner after corner, until, at last, a little anxious feeling began to tug at her heart; and she began to think--"I wish I could see Polly"---- And now, she had all she could do to get out of the way of the crowds of people who were pouring up and down the thoroughfare. Everybody jostled against her, and gave her a push. "Oh dear!" thought Phronsie, "there's such a many big people!" and then there was no time for anything else but to stumble in and out, to keep from being crushed completely beneath their feet. At last, an old huckster woman, in passing along, knocked off her bonnet with the end of her big basket, which flew around and struck Phronsie's head. Not stopping to look into the piteous brown eyes, she strode on without a word. Phronsie turned in perfect despair to go down a street that looked as if there might be room enough for her in it. Thoroughly frightened, she plunged over the crossing, to reach it!

"Look out!" cried a ringing voice. "Stop!"

"The little girl'll be killed!" said others with bated breath, as a powerful pair of horses whose driver could not pull them up in time, dashed along just in front of her! With one cry, Phronsie sprang between their feet, and reached the opposite curbstone in safety!

The plunge brought her up against a knot of gentlemen who were standing talking on the corner.

"What's this!" asked one, whose back being next to the street, hadn't seen the commotion, as the small object dashed into their midst, and fell up against him.

"Didn't you see that narrow escape?" asked a second, whose face had paled in witnessing it. "This little girl was nearly killed a moment ago--careless driving enough!" And he put out his hand to catch the child.

"Bless me!" cried a third, whirling around suddenly, "Bless me! you don't say so! why"---- With a small cry, but gladsome and distinct in its utterance, Phronsie gave one look--"Oh, grandpa!" was all she could say.

"Oh! where"--Mr. King couldn't possibly have uttered another word, for then his breath gave out entirely, as he caught the small figure.

"I went to the Post Office," said the child, clinging to him in delight, her tangled hair waving over the little white face, into which a faint pink color was quickly coming back. "Only it wouldn't come; and I walked and walked--where is it, grandpa?" And Phronsie gazed up anxiously into the old gentleman's face.

"Why, my child, what were you going to do?"

"Mamsie's letter," said Phronsie, holding up for inspection the precious bit, which by this time, was decidedly forlorn-- "Polly couldn't write; and Mamsie'd feel so bad not to get one--she would really" said the child, shaking her head very soberly, "for Polly said so."

"And you've been--oh! I can't think of it," said Mr. King, tenderly taking her up on his shoulder, "well, we must get home now, or I don't know what Polly will do!" And without stopping to say a word to his friends, he hailed a passing carriage, and putting Phronsie in, he commanded the driver to get them as quickly as possible to their destination.

In a few moments they were home. Mr. King pushed into the house with his burden. "Don't anybody know," he burst out, puffing up the stairs, and scolding furiously at every step, "enough to take better care of this child, than to have such goings on!"

"What is the matter, father?" asked Mrs. Whitney, coming up the stairs, after him. "What has happened out of the way?"

"Out of the way!" roared the old gentleman, irascibly, "well, if you want Phronsie racing off to the Post Office by herself, and nearly getting killed, poor child! yes, Marian, I say nearly killed!" he continued.

"What do you mean?" gasped Mrs. Whitney.

"Why, where have you been?" asked the old gentleman, who wouldn't let Phronsie get down out of his arms, under any circumstances; so there she lay, poking up her head like a little bird, and trying to say she wasn't in the least hurt, "where's everybody been not to know she'd gone?" he exclaimed, "where's Polly--and Jasper--and all of 'em?"

"Polly's taking her music lesson," said Mrs. Whitney. "Oh, Phronsie darling!" and she bent over the child in her father's arms, and nearly smothered her with kisses.

"Twas a naughty horse," said Phronsie, sitting up straight and looking at her, "or I should have found the Post Office; and I lost off my bonnet, too," she added, for the first time realizing her loss, putting her hand to her head; "a bad old woman knocked it off with a basket--and now mamsie won't get her letter!" and she waved the bit, which she still grasped firmly between her thumb and finger, sadly towards Mrs. Whitney.

"Oh, dear," groaned that lady, "how could we talk before her! But who would have thought it! Darling," and she took the little girl from her father's arms, who at last let her go, "don't think of your mamma's letter; we'll tell her how it was," and she sat down in the first chair that she could reach; while Phronsie put her tumbled little head down on the kind shoulder and gave a weary little sigh.

"It was so long," she said, "and my shoes hurt," and she thrust out the dusty little boots, that spoke pathetically of the long and unaccustomed tramp.

"Poor little lamb!" said Mr. King, getting down to unbutton them. "What a shame!" he mumbled pulling off half of the buttons in his frantic endeavors to get them off quickly.

But Phronsie never heard the last of his objurgations, for in a minute she was fast asleep. The tangled hair fell off from the tired little face; the breathing came peaceful and regular, and with her little hand fast clasped in Mrs. Whitney's she slept on and on.

Polly came flying up-stairs, two or three at a time, and humming a scrap of her last piece that she had just conquered.

"Phronsie," she called, with a merry little laugh, "where"-- "Hush!" said Mr. King, warningly, and then just because he couldn't explain there without waking Phronsie up, he took hold of Polly's two shoulders and marched her into the next room, where he carefully closed the door, and told her the whole thing, using his own discretion about the very narrow escape she had passed through. He told enough, however, for Polly to see what had been so near them; and she stood there so quietly, alternately paling and flushing as he proceeded, till at last, when he finished, Mr. King was frightened almost to death at the sight of her face.

"Oh, goodness me, Polly!" he said, striding up to her, and then fumbling around on the table to find a glass of water, "you are not going to faint, are you? Phronsie's all well now, she isn't hurt in the least, I assure you; I assure you--where is a glass of water! Marian ought to see that there's some here--that stupid Jane!" and in utter bewilderment he was fussing here and there, knocking down so many things in general, that the noise soon brought Polly to, with a little gasp.

"Oh, don't mind me, dear Mr. King--I'm---all well."

"So you are," said the old gentleman, setting up a toilet bottle that he had knocked over, "so you are; I didn't think you'd go and tumble over, Polly, I really didn't," and he beamed admiringly down on her.

And then Polly crept away to Mrs. Whitney's side where she threw herself down on the floor, to watch the little sleeping figure. Her hand was gathered up, into the kind one that held Phronsie's; and there they watched and watched and waited.

"Oh, dear," said Phronsie, suddenly, turning over with a little sigh, and bobbing up her head to look at Polly; "I'm so hungry! I haven't had anything to eat in over an' ever so long, Polly!" and she gazed at her with a very injured countenance.

"So you must be," said Mrs. Whitney, kissing the flushed little face. "Polly must ring the bell for Jane to bring this little bird some crumbs.

"Can I have a great many?" asked Phronsie, lifting her eyes, with the dewy look of sleep hill lingering in them, "as many as two birdies?"

"Yes, dear," said Mrs. Whitney, laughing; "I think as many as three little birdies could eat, Phronsie."

"Oh," said Phronsie, and leaned back satisfied, while Polly gave the order, which was presently followed by Jane with a well-filled tray.

"Now," said Jappy, when he heard the account of the adventure, "I say that letter ought to go to your mother, Polly."

"Oh," said Polly, "it would scare mamsie most to death, Jappy!"

"Don't tell her the whole," said Jasper, quickly, "I didn't mean that--about the horses and all that--but only enough to let her see how Phronsie tried to get it to her."

"And I'm going to write to your brother Joel," said Van, drawing up to the library table; "I'll scare him, Polly, I guess; he won't tell your mother."

"Your crow-tracks'll scare him enough without anything else," said Percy, pleasantly, who really could write very nicely, while Polly broke out in an agony:

"Oh, no, Van, you mustn't! you mustn't!"

"If Van does," said Jasper, decidedly, "it'll be the last time he'll write to the 'brown house,' I can tell him; and besides, he'll go to Coventry." This had the desired effect.

"Let's all write," said Polly.

So a space on the table was cleared, and the children gathered around it, when there was great scratching of pens, and clearing of ideas; which presently resulted in a respectable budget of letters, into which Phronsie's was lovingly tucked in the centre; and then they all filed out to put it into the letterbox in the hall, for Thomas to mail with the rest in the morning.

Day 151

1. Read the beginning of chapter 22.
2. Tell someone about what you read.

Chapter 22 Getting Ready for Mamsie and the Boys

"And I'll tell you, Marian, what I am going to do."

Mr. King's voice was pitched on a higher key than usual; and extreme determination was expressed in every line of his face. He had met Mrs. Whitney at the foot of the staircase, dressed for paying visits. "Oh, are you going out?" he said, glancing impatiently at her attire. "And I'd just started to speak to you on a matter of great importance! Of the greatest importance indeed!" he repeated irritably, as he stood with one gloved hand resting on the balustrade.

"Oh, it's no matter, father," she replied pleasantly; "if it's really important, I can postpone going for another day, and--"

"Really important!" repeated the old gentleman irascibly. "Haven't I just told you it's of the greatest importance? There's no time to be lost; and with my state of health too, it's of the utmost consequence that I shouldn't be troubled. It's very bad for me; I should think you would realize that, Marian."

"I'll tell Thomas to take the carriage directly back," said Mrs. Whitney stepping to the door. "Or stay, father; I'll just run up and send the children out for a little drive. The horses ought to be used too, you know," she said lightly, preparing to run up to carry out the changed plan.

"Never mind that now," said Mr. King abruptly. "I want you to give me your attention directly." And walking towards the library door, getting a fresh accession of impatience with every step, he beckoned her to follow.

But his progress was somewhat impeded by little Dick--or rather, little Dick and Prince, who were standing at the top of the stairs to see Mrs. Whitney off. When he saw his mother retrace her steps, supposing her yielding to the urgent entreaties that he was sending after her to stay at home, the child suddenly changed his "Good-byes" to vociferous howls of delight, and speedily began to plunge down the stairs to welcome her.

But the staircase was long, and little Dick was in a hurry, and besides, Prince was in the way. The consequence was, nobody knew just how, that a bumping noise struck into the conversation that made the two below in the hall look up quickly, to see the child and dog come rolling over the stairs at a rapid rate.

"Zounds!" cried the old gentleman. "Here, Thomas, Thomas!" But as that individual was waiting patiently outside the door on the carriage box, there was small hope of his being in time to catch the boy, who was already in his mother's arms, not quite clear by the suddenness of the whole thing, as to how he came there.

"Oh! oh! Dicky's hurt!" cried somebody up above--followed by every one within hearing distance, and all came rushing to the spot to ask a thousand questions all in the same minute.

There sat Mrs. Whitney in one of the big carved chairs, with little Dick in her lap, and Prince walking gravely around and around him with the greatest expression of concern on his noble face. Mr. King was storming up and down, and calling on everybody to bring a "bowl of water, and some brown paper; and be quick!" interpolated with showers of blame on Prince for sitting on the stairs, and tripping people up! while Dick meanwhile was laughing and chatting, and enjoying the distinction of making so many people run, and of otherwise being the object of so much attention!

"I don't think he was sitting on the stairs, father," said Jasper, who, when he saw that Dicky was really unhurt, began to vindicate his dog. "He never does that; do you Sir?" he said patting the head that was lifted up to him, as if to be defended.

"And I expect we shall all be killed some day, Jasper," said Mr. King, warming with his subject; and forgetting all about the brown paper and water which he had ordered, and which was now waiting for him at his elbow, "just by that creature."

"He's the noblest"--began Jasper, throwing his arms around his neck; an example which was immediately followed by the Whitney boys, and the two little Peppers. When Dick saw this, he began to struggle to get down to add himself to the number.

"Where's the brown paper?" began Mr. King, seeing this and whirling around suddenly. "Hasn't any body brought it yet?"

"Here 'tis sir," said Jane, handing him a generous supply. "Oh, I don't want to," cried little Dick in dismay, seeing his grandfather advance with an enormous piece of paper, which previously wet in the bowl of water, was now unpleasantly clammy and wet--"oh, no, I don't want to be all stuck up with old horrid wet paper!"

"Hush, dear!" said his mamma, soothingly. "Grandpapa wants to put it on--there"--as Mr. King dropped it scientifically on his head, and then proceeded to paste another one over his left eye.

"And I hope they'll all drop off," cried Dick, savagely, shaking his head to facilitate matters. "Yes, I do, every single one of 'em!" he added, with an expression that seen under the brown bits was anything but benign.

"Was Prince on the stairs, Dick?" asked Jasper, coming up and peering under his several adornments. "Tell us how you fell!"

"No," said little Dick, crossly, and giving his head another shake. "He was up in the hall--oh, dear, I want to get down," and he began to stretch his legs and to struggle with so much energy, that two or three pieces fell off, and landed on the floor to his intense delight.

"And how did you fall then?" said Jasper, perseveringly. "Can't you remember, Dicky, boy?"

"I pushed Princey," said Dick, feeling, with freedom from some of his encumbrances, more disposed for conversation, "and made him go ahead--and then I fell on top of him-- that's all."

"I guess Prince has saved him, father," cried Jasper, turning around with eyes full of pride and love on the dog, who was trying as hard as he could to tell all the children how much he enjoyed their caresses.

And so it all came about that the consultation so summarily interrupted was never held. For, as Mrs. Whitney was about retiring that evening, Mr. King rapped at her door, on his way to bed.

"Oh," he said popping in his head, in response to her invitation to come in, "it's nothing--only I thought I'd just tell you a word or two about what I've decided to do."

"Do you mean what you wanted to see me about this afternoon?" asked Mrs. Whitney, who hadn't thought of it since. "Do come in, father."

"It's no consequence," said the old gentleman; "no consequence at all," he repeated, waving his hand emphatically, "because I've made up my mind and arranged all my plans-- it's only about the Peppers--"

"The Peppers?" repeated Mrs. Whitney.

"Yes. Well, the fact of it is, I'm going to have them here for a visit--the whole of them, you understand; that's all there is to it. And I shall go down to see about all the arrangements-- Jasper and I--day after to-morrow," said the old gentleman, as if he owned the whole Pepper family inclusive, and was the only responsible person to be consulted about their movements.

"Will they come?" asked Mrs. Whitney, doubtfully.

"Come? of course," said Mr. King, sharply, "there isn't any other way; or else Mrs. Pepper will be sending for her children--and of course you know, Marian, we couldn't allow that----well, that's all; so good night," and the door closed on his retreating footsteps.

And so Polly and Phronsie soon knew that mamsie and the boys were to be invited! And then the grand house, big as it was, didn't seem large enough to contain them.

"I declare," said Jasper, next day, when they had been laughing and planning till they were all as merry as grigs, "if this old dungeon don't begin to seem a little like 'the little brown house,' Polly."

"Twon't," answered Polly, hopping around on one toe, followed by Phronsie, "till mamsie and the boys get here, Jasper King!"

"Well, they'll be here soon," said Jappy, pleased at Polly's exultation over it, "for we're going to-morrow to do the inviting."

"And Polly's to write a note to slip into Marian's," said Mr. King, putting his head in at the door. "And if you want your mother to come, child, why, you'd better mention it as strong as you can."

"I'm going to write," said Phronsie, pulling up after a prolonged skip, all out of breath. "I'm going to write, and beg mamsie dear. Then she'll come, I guess."

"I guess she will," said Mr. King, looking at her. "You go on, Phronsie, and write; and that letter shall go straight in my coat pocket alone by itself."

"Shall it?" asked Phronsie, coming up to him, "and nobody will take it out till you give it to mamsie?"

"No, nobody shall touch it," said the old gentleman, stooping to kiss the upturned face, "till I put it into her own hand."

"Then," said Phronsie, in the greatest satisfaction, "I'm going to write this very one minute!" and she marched away to carry her resolve into immediate execution.

Day 152

1. Read the next part of chapter 22.
2. Tell someone about what you read.

Chapter 22 continued

Before they got through they had quite a bundle of invitations and pleadings; for each of the three boys insisted on doing his part, so that when they were finally done up in an enormous envelope and put into Mr. King's hands, he told them with a laugh that there was no use for Jappy and himself to go, as those were strong enough to win almost anybody's consent.

However, the next morning they set off, happy in their hopes, and bearing the countless messages, which the children would come up every now and then to entrust to them, declaring that they had forgotten to put them in the letters.

"You'd had to have had an express wagon to carry the letters if you had put them all in," at last cried Jasper. "You've given us a bushel of things to remember."

"And oh! don't forget to ask Ben to bring Cherry," cried Polly, the last minute as they were driving off although she had put it in her letter at least a dozen times; "and oh, dear! of course the flowers can't come."

"We've got plenty here," said Jasper. "You would not know what to do with them, Polly."

"Well, I do wish mamsie would give some to kind Mrs. Henderson, then," said Polly, on the steps, clasping her hands anxiously, while Jasper told Thomas to wait till he heard the rest of the message, "and to grandma--you know Grandma Bascom; she was so good to us," she said impulsively. "And, oh! don't let her forget to carry some to dear, dear Dr. Fisher; and don't forget to give him our love, Jappy; don't forget that!" and Polly ran down the steps to the carriage door, where she gazed up imploringly to the boy's face.

"I guess I won't," cried Jasper, "when I think how he saved your eyes, Polly! He's the best fellow I know!" he finished in an impulsive burst.

"And don't let mamsie forget to carry some in to good old Mr. and Mrs. Beebe in town--where Phronsie got her shoes, you know; that is, if mamsie can," she added, remembering how very busy her mother would be.

"I'll carry them myself," said Jasper; "we're going to stay over till the next day, you know."

"O!" cried Polly, radiant as a rose, "will you, really, Jappy? you're so good!"

"Yes, I will," said Jasper, "everything you want done, Polly; anything else?" he asked, quickly, as Mr. King, impatient to be off, showed unmistakable symptoms of hurrying up Thomas.

"Oh, no," said Polly, "only do look at the little brown house, Jasper, as much as you can," and Polly left the rest unfinished. Jasper seemed to understand, however, for he smiled brightly as he said, looking into the brown eyes, "I'll do it all, Polly; every single thing." And then they were off.

Mamsie and the boys! could Polly ever wait till the next afternoon that would bring the decision?

Long before it was possibly time for the carriage to come back from the depot, Polly, with Phronsie and the three boys, who, improving Jasper's absence, had waited upon her with the grace and persistence of cavaliers of the olden time, were drawn up at the old stone gateway.

"Oh, dear," said Van with an impatient fling; "they never will come!"

"Won't they, Polly?" asked Phronsie, anxiously, and standing quite still.

"Dear me, yes," said Polly, with a little laugh, "Van only means they'll be a good while, Phronsie. They're sure to come some time."

"Oh!" said Phronsie, quite relieved; and she commenced her capering again in extreme enjoyment.

"I'm going," said little Dick, "to run down and meet them." Accordingly off he went, and was immediately followed by Percy, who started with the laudable desire of bringing him back; but finding it so very enjoyable, he stayed himself and frolicked with Dick, till the others, hearing the fun, all took hold of hands and flew off to join them.

"Now," said Polly, when they recovered their breath a little, "let's all turn our backs to the road; and the minute we hear the carriage we must whirl round; and the one who sees 'em first can ask first, 'Is mamsie coming?'"

"All right," cried the boys.

"Turn round, Dick," said Percy, with a little shove, for Dick was staring with all his might right down the road. And so they all flew around till they looked like five statues set up to grace the sidewalk.

"Suppose a big dog should come," suggested Van, pleasantly, "and snap at our backs!"

At this little Dick gave a small howl, and turned around in a fright.

"There isn't any dog coming," said Polly. "What does make you say such awful things, Van?"

"I hear a noise," said Phronsie; and so they all whirled around in expectation. But it proved to be only a market wagon coming at a furious pace down the road, with somebody's belated dinner.

So they all had to whirl back again as before. The consequence was that when the carriage did come, nobody heard it.

Jasper, looking out, was considerably astonished to see, drawn up in solemn array with their backs to the road, five children, who stood as if completely petrified.

"What in the world!" he began, and called to Thomas to stop, whose energetic "Whoa!" reaching the ears of the frozen line, caused it to break ranks, and spring into life at an alarming rate.

"Oh, is she coming Jappy? Is she? Is she?" they all screamed together, swarming up to the carriage door, and over the wheels.

"Yes," said Jasper looking at Polly.

At that, Phronsie made a little cheese and sat right down on the pavement in an ecstasy.

"Get in here, all of you;" said Jasper merrily; "help Polly in first. For shame Dick! don't scramble so."

"Dick always shoves," said Percy, escorting Polly up with quite an air.

"I don't either," said Dick; "you pushed me awful, just a little while ago," he added indignantly.

"Do say awfully," corrected Van, crowding up to get in. "You leave off your lys so," he finished critically.

"I don't know anything about any lees," said little Dick, who, usually so good natured, was now thoroughly out of temper; "I want to get in and go home," and he showed evident symptoms of breaking into a perfect roar.

"There," said Polly, lilting him up, "there he goes! now-- one, two, three!" arid little Dick was spun in so merrily that the tears changed into a happy laugh.

"Now then, bundle in, all the rest of you," put in Mr. King, who seemed to be in the best of spirits. "That's it; go on, Thomas!"

"When are they coming?" Polly found time to ask in the general jumble.

"In three weeks from tomorrow," said Jasper. "And everything's all right, Polly! and the whole of them, Cherry and all, will be here then!"

"Oh!" said Polly.

"Here we are!" cried Van, jumping out almost before the carriage door was open. "Mamma; mamma," he shouted to Mrs. Whitney in the doorway, "the Peppers are coming, and the little brown house too!--everything and everybody!"

"They are!" said Percy, as wild as his brother; "and everything's just splendid! Jappy said so."

"Everything's coming," said little Dick, tumbling up the steps--"and the bird--and--and--"

"And mamsie!" finished Phronsie, impatient to add her part --while Polly didn't say anything-- only looked.

Three weeks! "I can't wait!" thought Polly at first, in counting over the many hours before the happy day would come. But on Jasper's suggesting that they should all do something to get ready for the visitors, and have a general trimming up with vines and flowers beside--the time passed away much more rapidly than was feared.

Polly chose a new and more difficult piece of music to learn to surprise mamsie. Phronsie had aspired to an elaborate pin cushion, that was nearly done, made of bits of worsted and canvas, over whose surface she had wandered according to her own sweet will, in a way charming to behold.

"I don't know what to do," said Van in despair, "cause I don't know what she'd like."

"Can't you draw her a little picture?" asked Polly. "She'd like that."

"Does she like pictures?" asked Van with the greatest interest.

"Yes indeed!" said Polly, "I guess you'd think so if you could see her!"

"I know what I shall do," with a dignified air said Percy, who couldn't draw, and therefore looked down on all Van's attempts with the greatest scorn. "And it won't be any old pictures either," he added.

"What is it, old fellow?" asked Jasper, "tell on, now, your grand plan."

"No, I'm not going to tell," said Percy, with the greatest secrecy, "until the very day."

"What will you do, sir?" asked Jasper, pulling one of Dick's ears, who stood waiting to speak, as if his mind was made up, and wouldn't be changed for anyone!

Day 153

1. Finish chapter 22.

2. Write or tell a summary of the chapter. If you can do it in one sentence, get a high five and/or hug.

Chapter 22 continued

"I shall give Ben one of my kitties--the littlest and the best!" he said, with heroic self-sacrifice.

A perfect shout greeted this announcement.

"Fancy Ben going round with one of those awful little things," whispered Jappy to Polly, who shook at the very thought.

"Don't laugh! oh, it's dreadful to laugh at him, Jappy," she said, when she could get voice enough.

"No, I sha'n't tell," said Percy, when the fun had subsided; who, finding that no one teased him to divulge his wonderful plan, kept trying to harrow up their feelings by parading it.

"You needn't then," screamed Van, who was nearly dying to know. "I don't believe it's so very dreadful much, anyway."

"What's yours, Jappy?" asked Polly, "I know yours will be just splendid."

"Oh, no, it isn't," said Jasper, smiling brightly, "but as I didn't know what better I could do, I'm going to get a little stand, and then beg some flowers of Turner to fill it, and--"

"Why, that's mine!" screamed Percy, in the greatest disappointment. "That's just what I was going to do!"

"Hoh, hoh!" shouted Van; "I thought you wouldn't tell, Mr. Percy! hoh, hoh!"

"Hoh, hoh!" echoed Dick.

"Hush," said Jappy. "Why, Percy, I didn't know as you had thought of that," he said kindly. "Well, then, you do it, and I'll take something else. I don't care as long as Mrs. Pepper gets 'em."

"I didn't exactly mean that," began Percy; "mine was roots and little flowers growing."

"He means what he gets in the woods," said Polly, explaining; "don't you, Percy?"

"Yes," said the boy. "And then I was going to put stones and things in among them to make them look pretty."

"And they will," cried Jasper. "Go ahead, Percy, they'll look real pretty, and then Turner will give you some flowers for the stand, I know; I'll ask him to-morrow."

"Will you?" cried Percy, "that'll be fine!"

"Mine is the best," said Van, just at this juncture; but it was said a little anxiously, as he saw how things were prospering with Percy; "for my flowers in the picture will always be there, and your old roots and things will die."

"What will yours be, then, Jappy?" asked Polly very soberly. "The stand of flowers would have been just lovely! and you do fix them so nice," she added sorrowfully.

"Oh, I'll find something else," said Jappy, cheerfully, who had quite set his heart on giving the flowers. "Let me see--I might carve her a bracket."

"Do," cried Polly, clapping her hands enthusiastically. "And do carve a little bird, like the one you did on your father's."

"I will," said Jasper, "just exactly like it. Now, we've got something to do, before we welcome the 'little brown house' people--so let's fly at it, and the time won't seem so long."

And at last the day came when they could all say--To-morrow they'll be here!

Well, the vines were all up; and pots of lovely climbing ferns, and all manner of pretty green things had been arranged and re-arranged a dozen times till everything was pronounced perfect; and a big green "Welcome" over the library door, made of laurel leaves, by the patient fingers of all the children, stared down into their admiring eyes as much as to say, "I'll do my part!"

"Oh, dear," said Phronsie, when evening came, and the children were, as usual, assembled on the rug before the fire, their tongues running wild with anticipation and excitement, "I don't mean to go to bed at all, Polly; I don't truly."

"Oh, yes, you do," said Polly laughing; "then you'll be all fresh and rested to see mammy when she does come."

"Oh, no," said Phronsie, shaking her head soberly, and speaking in an injured tone. "I'm not one bit tired, Polly; not one bit."

"You needn't go yet, Phronsie," said Polly. "You can sit up half an hour yet, if you want to."

"But I don't want to go to bed at all," said the child anxiously, "for then I may be asleep when mamsie comes, Polly."

"She's afraid she won't wake up," said Percy, laughing. "Oh, there'll be oceans of time before they come, Phronsie."

"What is oceans," asked Phronsie, coming up and looking at him, doubtfully.

"He means mamsie won't get here till afternoon," said Polly, catching her up and kissing her; "then I guess you'll be awake, Phronsie, pet."

So Phronsie allowed herself to be persuaded, at the proper time, to be carried off and inducted into her little nightgown. And when Polly went up to bed, she found the little pin-cushion, with its hieroglyphics, that she had insisted on taking to bed with her, still tightly grasped in the little fat hand.

"She'll roll over and muss it," thought Polly; "and then she'll feel bad in the morning. I guess I'd better lay it on the bureau."

So she drew it carefully away, without awaking the little sleeper, and placed it where she knew Phronsie's eyes would rest on it the first thing in the morning.

It was going on towards the middle of the night when Phronsie, whose exciting dreams of mamsie and the boys wouldn't let her rest quietly, woke up; and in the very first flash she thought of her cushion.

"Why, where--" she said, in the softest little tones, only half awake, "why, Polly, where is it?" and she began to feel all around her pillow to see if it had fallen down there.

But Polly's brown head with its crowd of anticipations and busy plans was away off in dreamland, and she breathed on and on perfectly motionless.

"I guess I better," said Phronsie to herself, now thoroughly awake, and sitting up in bed, "not wake her up. Poor Polly's tired; I can find it myself, I know I can."

So she slipped out of bed, and prowling around on the floor, felt all about for the little cushion.

"'Tisn't here, oh, no, it isn't," she sighed at last, and getting up, she stood still a moment, lost in thought. "Maybe Jane's put it out in the hall," she said, as a bright thought struck her. "I can get it there," and out she pattered over the soft carpet to the table at the end of the long hail, where Jane often placed the children's playthings over night. As she was coming back after her fruitless search, she stopped to peep over the balustrade down the fascinating flight of stairs, now so long and dark. Just then a little faint ray of light shot up from below, and met her eyes.

"Why!" she said in gentle surprise, "they're all downstairs! I guess they're making something for mamsie--I'm going to see."

So, carefully picking her way over the stairs with her little bare feet, and holding on to the balustrade at every step, she went slowly down, guided by the light, which, as she neared the bottom of the flight, she saw came from the library door.

"Oh, isn't it funny!" and she gave a little happy laugh. "They won't know I'm comin'!" and now the soft little feet went pattering over the thick carpet, until she stood just within the door. There she stopped perfectly still.

Two dark figures, big and powerful, were bending over something that Phronsie couldn't see, between the two big windows. A lantern on the floor flung its rays over them as they were busily occupied; and the firelight from the dying coals made the whole stand out distinctly to the gaze of the motionless little figure.

"Why! what are you doing with my grandpa's things?"

The soft, clear notes fell like a thunderbolt upon the men. With a start they brought themselves up, and stared--only to see a little white-robed figure, with its astonished eyes uplifted with childlike, earnest gaze, as she waited for her answer.

For an instant they were powerless to move; and stood as if frozen to the spot, till Phronsie, moving one step forward, piped forth:

"Naughty men, to touch my dear grandpa's things!"

With a smothered cry one of them started forward with arm uplifted; but the other sprang like a cat and intercepted the blow.

"Stop!" was all he said. A noise above the stairs--a rushing sound through the hail! Something will save Phronsie, for the household is aroused! The two men sprang through the window, having no time to catch the lantern or their tools, as Polly, followed by one and another, rushed in and surrounded the child.

"What!" gasped Polly, and got no further.

"*Stop, thief*!" roared Mr. King, hurrying over the stairs. The children, frightened at the strange noises, began to cry and scream, as they came running through the halls to the spot. Jasper rushed for the men-servants.

And there stood Phronsie, surrounded by the pale group. "Twas two naughty men," she said, lifting her little face with the grieved, astonished look still in the big brown eyes, "and they were touching my grandpa's things, Polly!"

"I should think they were," said Jasper, running over amongst the few scattered tools and the lantern, to the windows, where, on the floor, was a large table cover hastily caught up by the corners, into which a vast variety of silver, jewelry, and quantities of costly articles were gathered ready for flight. "They've broken open your safe, father!" he cried in excitement, "see!"

"And they put up their hand--one man did," went on Phronsie. "And the other said 'Stop!'--oh, Polly, you hurt me!" she cried, as Polly, unable to bear the strain any longer, held her so tightly she could hardly breathe.

"Go on," said Jasper, "how did they look?"

"All black," said the child, pushing back her wavy hair and looking at him, "very all black, Japser."

"And their faces, Phronsie?" said Mr. King, getting down on his old knees on the floor beside her. "Bless me! somebody else ask her, I can't talk!"

"How did their faces look, Phronsie, dear?" asked Jasper, taking one of the cold hands in his. "Can't you think?"

"Oh!" said Phronsie--and then she gave a funny little laugh, "two big holes, Japser, that's all they had!"

"She means they were masked," whispered Jasper.

"What did you get up for?" Mrs. Whitney asked. "Dear child, what made you get out of bed?"

"Why, my cushion-pin," said Phronsie looking worried at once. "I couldn't find it, and--"

But just at this, without a bit of warning, Polly tumbled over in a dead faint.

And then it was all confusion again.

And so, on the following afternoon, it turned out that the Peppers, about whose coming there had been so many plans and expectations, just walked in as if they had always lived there. The greater excitement completely swallowed up the less!

Day 154

1. Read the first part of chapter 23.
2. Tell someone about what you read.

Vocabulary

1. Review your vocabulary from Aesop's fables by going to Day 25 or to the review game page on the Easy Peasy website.

Chapter 23 Which Treats of a Good Many Matters

"Phooh!" said Joel a few mornings after the emptying of the little brown house into the big one, when he and Van were rehearsing for the fiftieth time all the points of the eventful night, "phooh! if I'd been here they wouldn't got away, I guess!"

"What would you have done?" asked Van, bristling up at this reflection on their courage, and squaring up to him. "What would you have done, Joel Pepper?"

"I'd a-pitched right into 'em--like--everything!" said Joel valiantly; "and a-caught 'em! Yes, every single one of the Bunglers!"

"The what?" said Van, bursting into a loud laugh.

"The Bunglers," said Joel with a red face. "That's what you said they were, anyway," he added positively.

"I said Burglars," said Van, doubling up with amusement, while Joel stood, a little sturdy figure, regarding him with anything but a sweet countenance.

"Well anyway, I'd a-caught 'em, so there!" he said, as Van at last showed signs of coming out of his fit of laughter, and got up and wiped his eyes.

"How'd you caught 'em?" asked Van, scornfully surveying the square little country figure before him. "You can't hit any.

"Can't?" said Joel, the black eyes flashing volumes, and coming up in front of Van. "You better believe I can, Van Whitney!"

"Come out in the back yard and try then," said Van hospitably, perfectly delighted at the prospect, and flying alone towards the door. "Come right out and try."

"All right!" said Joel, following sturdily, equally delighted to show his skill.

"There," said Van, taking off his jacket, and flinging it on the grass, while Joel immediately followed suit with his little homespun one. "Now we can begin perfectly splendid! I won't hit hard," he added patronizingly, as both boys stood ready.

"Hit as hard as you've a-mind to," said Joel, "I'm a-going to."

"Oh, you may," said Van politely, "because you're company. All right--now!"

So at it they went. Before very many minutes were over, Van relinquished all ideas of treating his company with extra consideration, and was only thinking how he could possibly hold his own with the valiant little country lad. Oh, if he could only be called to his lessons--anything that would summon him into the house! Just then a window above their heads was suddenly thrown up, and his mamma's voice in natural surprise and distress called quickly: "Children what are you doing? Oh, Van, how could you!"

Both contestants turned around suddenly. Joel looked up steadily. "We're a-hitting, ma'am; he said I couldn't, and so we came out and--"

"Oh, Vanny," said Mrs. Whitney reproachfully, "to treat a little guest in this way!"

"I wanted to," said Joel cheerfully; "twas great fun. Let's begin again, Van!"

"We mustn't," said Van, readily giving up the charming prospect, and beginning to edge quickly towards the house. "Mamma wouldn't like it you know. He hits splendidly, mamma," he added generously, looking up. "He does really."

"And so does Van," cried Joel, his face glowing at the praise. "We'll come out every day," he added slipping into his jacket, and turning enthusiastically back to Van.

"And perhaps he could have pitched into the Burglars," finished Van, ignoring the invitation, and tumbling into his jacket with alarming speed.

"I know I could!" cried Joel, scampering after him into the house. "If I'd only a-been here!"

"Where's Ben?" said Van, bounding into the hail, and flinging himself down on one of the chairs. "Oh dear, I'm so hot! Say, Joe, where do you s'pose Ben is?"

"I don't know," replied Joel, who didn't even puff.

"I saw him a little while ago with master Percy," said Jane, who was going through the hall.

"There now! and they've gone off somewhere," cried Van in extreme irritation, and starting up quickly. "I know they have. Which way did they go, Jane? And how long ago?"

"Oh, I don't know," replied Jane carelessly, "half an hour maybe; and they didn't go no where as I see, at least they were talking at the door, and I was going up-stairs."

"Right here?" cried Van, and stamping with his foot to point out the exact place; "at this door, Jane?"

"Yes, yes," said Jane; "at that very door," and then she went into the dining-room to her work.

"Oh dear me!" cried Van, and flying out on the veranda, he began to peer wildly up and down the drive. "And they've gone to some splendid place, I know, and wouldn't tell us. That's just like Percy!" he added vindictively, "he's always stealing away! don't you see 'em, Joel? oh, do come out and look!"

"'Tisn't any use," said Joel coolly, sitting down on the chair Van had just vacated, and swinging his feet comfortably; "they're miles away if they've been gone half an hour. I'm goin' up-stairs," and he sprang up, and energetically pranced to the stairs.

"They aren't up-stairs!" screamed Van, in scorn, bounding into the hall. "Don't go; I know that they've gone down to the museum!"

"The what?" exclaimed Joel, nearly at the top, peering over the railing. "What's that you said-- what is it?"

"A museum," shouted Van, "and it's a perfectly elegant place, Joel Pepper, and Percy knows I like to go; and now he's taken Ben off; and he'll show him all the things! and they'll all be old when I take him--and--and--oh! I hope the snakes will bite him!" he added, trying to think of something bad enough.

"Do they have snakes there?" asked Joel, staring.

"Yes, they do," snapped out Van. "They have everything!"

"Well, they shan't bite Ben!" cried Joel in terror. "Oh! do you suppose they will?" and he turned right straight around on the stairs, and looked at Van.

"No," said Van, "they won't bite--what's the matter, Joe?"

"Oh, they may," said Joel, his face working, and screwing both fists into his eyes; at last he burst right out into a torrent of sobs. "Oh, don't let 'em Van--don't!"

"Why, they can't," said Van in an emphatic voice, running up the stairs to Joel's side, frightened to death at his tears.

Then he began to shake his jacket sleeve violently to bring him back to reason, "Wait Joe! oh, do stop! oh, dear, what shall I do! I tell you, they can't bite," he screamed as loud as he could into his ear.

"You said--you--hoped--they--would," said Joel's voice in smothered tones.

"Well, they won't anyway," said Van decidedly. "Cause they're all stuffed--so there now!"

"Ain't they alive--nor anythin'?" asked Joel, bringing one black eye into sight from behind his chubby hands.

"No," said Van, "they're just as dead as anything, Joel Pepper--been dead years! and there's old crabs there too, old dead crabs--and they're just lovely! Oh, such a lots of eggs as they've got! And there are shells and bugs and stones--and an awful old crocodile, and"---- "Oh, dear!" sighed

Joel, perfectly overcome at such a vision, and sitting down on the stairs to think. "Well, mamsie'll know where Ben is," he said, springing up. "And then I tell you Van, we'll just tag 'em!"

"So she will," cried Van. "Why didn't we think of that before? I wanted to think."

"I did," said Joel. "That was where I was goin'."

Without any more ado they rushed into Mrs. Pepper's big, sunny room, there to see, seated at the square table between the two large windows, the two lost ones bending over what seemed to be an object of the greatest importance, for Polly was hanging over Ben's shoulder with intense pride and delight, which she couldn't possibly conceal, and Davie was crowded as near as he could get to Percy's elbow.

Phronsie and little Dick were perched comfortably on the corner of the table, surveying the whole scene in quiet rapture; and Mrs. Pepper with her big mending basket, was ensconced over by the deep window seat just on the other side of the room, underneath Cherry's cage, and looking up between quick energetic stitches, over at the busy group, with the most placid expression on her face.

Day 155

1. Read the next part of chapter 23.
2. Learn the parts of a story.
   - o characters: who the story is about
     1. There is a main character, or sometimes main characters, and there are supporting characters.
     2. The big question of the story revolves around the main character.
   - o setting: when and where a story takes place
     1. There is a main setting, such as America in 1776.
     2. There are also lots of minor settings, like Independence Hall, or inside a kitchen.
   - o plot: what happens in the story, what is the problem and how it is solved
     1. The plot is the story, what happens.
     2. A story has to have conflict, something has to happen that needs resolving. It could be simple like I can't find my shoes to go outside! The problem would be solved when I find my shoes. The story is all that I do to try to find my shoes.

Chapter 23 continued

Phronsie and little Dick were perched comfortably on the corner of the table, surveying the whole scene in quiet rapture; and Mrs. Pepper with her big mending basket, was ensconced over by the deep window seat just on the other side of the room, underneath Cherry's cage, and looking up between quick energetic stitches, over at the busy group, with the most placid expression on her face.

"Oh!--what you doin'?" cried Joel, flying up to them. "Let us see, do Ben!"

"What is it?" exclaimed Van, squeezing in between Percy and Ben.

"Don't"----began Percy. "There, see, you've knocked his elbow and spoilt it!"

"Oh no, he hasn't," said Ben, putting down his pencil, and taking up a piece of rubber. "There, see it all comes out--as good as ever."

"Isn't it just elegant?" said Percy in the most pleased tone, and wriggling his toes under the table to express his satisfaction,

"Yes," said Van, craning his neck to get a better view of the picture, now nearly completed, "It's perfectly splendid. How'd you do it, Ben?"

"I don't know," replied Ben with a smile, carefully shading in a few last touches. "It just drew itself."

"Tisn't anything to what he can do," said Polly, standing up as tall as she could, and beaming at Ben, "He used to draw most beautiful at home."

"Better than this?" asked Van, with great respect and taking up the picture, after some demur on Percy's part, and examining it critically. "I don't believe it, Polly."

"Phooh; he did!" exclaimed Joel, looking over his shoulder at a wonderful view of a dog in an extremely excited state of mind running down an interminable hill to bark at a locomotive and train of cars whizzing along a curve in the foreground. Lots better'n that! Ben can do anything!" he added, in an utterly convincing way.

"Now give it back," cried Percy, holding out his hand in alarm. "I'm going to ask mamma to have it framed; and then I'm going to hang it right over my bed," he finished, as Van reluctantly gave up the treasure.

"Did you draw all the time in the little brown house?" asked Van, lost in thought. "How I wish I'd been there!"

"Dear, no!" cried Polly with a little skip, turning away to laugh. "He didn't have hardly any time, and"----"Why not?" asked Percy.

"Cause there was. things to do," said Polly. "But sometimes when it rained, and he couldn't go out and work, and there wasn't anything to do in the house--then we'd have----oh!" and she drew a long breath at the memory, "such a time, you can't think!"

"Didn't you wish it would always rain?" asked Van, still gazing at the picture.

"Dear, no!" began Polly.

"I didn't," broke in Joel, in horror. "I wouldn't a-had it rain for anything!--only once in a while," he added, as he thought of the good times that Polly had spoken of.

"Twas nice outdoors," said little Davie, reflectively; "and nice inside, too." And then he glanced over to his mother, who gave him a smile in return. "And 'twas nice always."

"Well," said Van, returning to the picture, "I do wish you'd tell me how to draw, Ben. I can't do anything but flowers," he said in a discouraged way.

"Flowers aren't anything," said Percy, pleasantly. "That's girls' work; but dogs and horses and cars--those are just good!"

"Will you, Ben?" asked Van, looking down into the big blue eyes, so kindly turned up to his.

"Yes, indeed I will," cried Ben, "that is, all I know; 'tisn't much, but everything I can, I'll tell you."

"Then I can learn, can't I?" cried Van joyfully.

"Oh, tell me too, Ben," cried Percy, "will you? I want to learn too."

"And me!" cried Dick, bending forward, nearly upsetting Phronsie as he did so. "Yes, say I may, Ben, do!"

"You're too little," began Percy. But Ben nodded his head at Dick, which caused him to clap his hands and return to his original position, satisfied.

"Well, I guess we're going to, too," said Joel. "Dave an' me; there isn't anybody goin' to learn without us."

"Of course not," said Polly, "Ben wouldn't leave you out, Joey."

Phronsie sat quite still all this time, on the corner of the table, her feet tucked up under her, and her hands clasped in her lap, and never said a word. But Ben looking up, saw the most grieved expression settling on her face, as the large eyes were fixed in wonder on the faces before her.

"And there's my pet," he cried in enthusiasm, and reaching over the table, he caught hold of one of the little fat hands. "Why we couldn't think of getting along without her! She shall learn to draw--she shall!"

"Really, Bensie?" said Phronsie, the sunlight breaking all over the gloomy little visage, and setting the brown eyes to dancing. "Real, true, splendid pictures?"

"Yes, the splendidest," said Ben, "the very splendidest pictures, Phronsie Pepper, you ever saw!"

"Oh!" cried Phronsie; and before any one knew what she was about, she tripped right into the middle of the table, over the papers and everything, and gave a happy little whirl!

"Dear me, Phronsie!" cried Polly catching her up and hugging her; "you mustn't dance on the table."

"I'm going to learn," said Phronsie, coming out of Polly's embrace, "to draw whole pictures, all alone by myself--Ben said so!"

"I know it," said Polly, "and then you shall draw one for mamsie-- you shall!"

"I will," said Phronsie, dreadfully excited; "I'll draw her a cow, and two chickens, Polly, just like Grandma Bascom's!"

"Yes," whispered Polly, "but don't you tell her yet till you get it done, Phronsie."

"I won't," said Phronsie in the loudest of tones--but putting her mouth close to Polly's ear. "And then she'll be so s'prised, Polly! won't she?"

Just then came Jasper's voice at the door. "Can I come in?"

"Oh, do, Jappy," cried Polly, rushing along with Phronsie in her arms to open the door. "We're so glad you've got home!"

"So am I," said Jasper, coming in, his face flushed and his eyes sparkling; "I thought father never would be through downtown, Polly!"

"We're going to learn to draw," said Percy, over by the table, who wouldn't on any account leave his seat by Ben, though he was awfully tired of sitting still so long, for fear somebody else would hop into it. "Ben's going to teach us."

"Yes, he is," put in Van, bounding up to Jasper and pulling at all the buttons on his jacket he could reach, to command attention.

"And us," said Joel, coming up too. "You forgot us, Van."

"The whole of us--every single one in this room," said Van decidedly, "all except Mrs. Pepper."

"Hullo!" said Jasper, "that is a class! Well, Professor Ben, you've got to teach me then, for I'm coming too."

"You?" said Ben, turning around his chair, and looking at him; "I can't teach you anything, Jappy. You know everything already"-.-

"Let him come, anyway," said Polly, hopping up and down.

"Oh, I'm coming, Professor," laughed Jasper. "Never you fear, Polly; I'll be on hand when the rest of the class comes in!"

"And Van," said Mrs. Pepper, pausing a minute in her work, and smiling over at him in a lull in the chatter--"I think flowers are most beautiful!" and she pointed to a little framed picture on the mantel, of the bunch of buttercups and one huge rose that Van had with infinite patience drawn, and then colored to suit his fancy.

"Do you?" cried Van, perfectly delighted; and leaving the group he rushed up to her side. "Do you really think they're nice, Mrs. Pepper?"

"Of course I do," said Mrs. Pepper briskly, and beaming on him; "I think everything of them, and I shall keep them as long as I live, Van!"

"Well, then," said Van, very much pleased, "I shall paint you ever so many more--just as many as you want!"

"Do!" said Mrs. Pepper, taking up her work again. "And I'll hang them every one up."

"Yes, I will," said Van; "and I'll go right to work on one to-morrow. What you mending our jackets for?" he asked abruptly as a familiar hole caught his attention.

"Because they're torn," said Mrs. Pepper cheerfully, "an' they won't mend themselves."

"Why don't you let Jane?" he persisted. "She always does them."

"Jane's got enough to do," replied Mrs. Pepper, smiling away as hard as she could, "and I haven't, so I'm going to look around and pick up something to keep my hands out of mischief as much as Jane, while I'm here."

"Do you ever get into mischief?" asked little Dick, coming up and looking into Mrs. Pepper's face wonderingly. "Why, you're a big woman!"

"Dear me, yes!" said Mrs. Pepper. "The bigger you are, the more mischief you can get into. You'll find that out, Dickey."

"And then do you have to stand in a corner?" asked Dick, determined to find out just what were the consequences, and reverting to his most dreaded punishment.

"No," said Mrs. Pepper laughing. "Corners are for little folks; but when people who know better, do wrong, there aren't any corners they can creep into, or they'd get into them pretty quick!"

"I wish," said little Dick, "you'd let me get into your lap. That would be a nice corner!"

"Do, mamsie," said Polly, coming up, "that's just the way I used to feel; and I'll finish the mending."

So Mrs. Pepper put down her work, and moved the big basket for little Dick to clamber up, when he laid his head contentedly back in her motherly arms with a sigh of happiness. Phronsie regarded him with a very grave expression. At last she drew near: "I'm tired; do, mamsie, take me!"

Day 156

1. Finish reading chapter 23
2. Write a summary of the chapter. If you write your summary in one sentence, get a high five and/or hug.

Chapter 23 continued

So Mrs. Pepper put down her work, and moved the big basket for little Dick to clamber up, when he laid his head contentedly back in her motherly arms with a sigh of happiness. Phronsie regarded him with a very grave expression. At last she drew near: "I'm tired; do, mamsie, take me!"

"So mamsie will," said Mrs. Pepper, opening her arms, when Phronsie immediately crawled up into their protecting shelter, with a happy little crow.

"Oh, now, tell us a story, Mrs. Pepper," cried Van; "please, please do!"

"No, no;" exclaimed Percy, scuttling out of his chair, and coming up, "let's talk of the little brown house. Do tell us what you used to do there--that's best."

"So 'tis!" cried Van; "*All* the nice times you used to have in it! Wait just a minute, do." And he ran back for a cricket which he placed at Mrs. Pepper's feet; and then sitting down on it, he leaned on her comfortable lap, in order to hear better.

"Wait for me too, till I get a chair," called Percy, starting. "Don't begin till I get there."

"Here, let me, Percy," said Ben; and he drew forward a big easy-chair that the boy was tugging at with all his might.

"Now I'm ready, too," said Polly, setting small finishing stitches quickly with a merry little flourish, and drawing her chair nearer her mother's as she spoke.

"Now begin, please," said Van, "all the nice times you know."

"She couldn't tell all the nice times if she had ten years to tell them in, could she, Polly?" said Jasper.

"Well, in the first place then," said Mrs. Pepper, clearing her throat, "the little brown house had got to be, you know, so we made up our minds to make it just the nicest brown house that ever was!"

"And it was!" declared Jasper, with an emphatic ring to his voice. "The very nicest place in the whole world!"

"Oh dear," broke in Van enviously; "Jappy's always said so. I wish we'd been there, too!"

"We didn't want anybody but Jappy," said Joel not very politely.

"Oh Joey, for shame!" cried Polly.

"Jappy used to bake," cried little Davie; "an' we all made pies; an' then we sat round an' ate 'em, an' then told stories."

"Oh what fun!" cried Percy. "Do tell us!"

So the five little Peppers and Jasper flew off into reminiscences and accounts of the funny doings, and Mrs. Pepper joined in heartily till the room got very merry with the glee and enthusiasm called forth; so much so, that nobody heard Mrs. Whitney knock gently at the door, and nobody answering, she was obliged to come in by herself.

"Well, well," she cried, merrily, looking at the swarm of little ones around Mrs. Pepper and the big chair. "You are having a nice time! May I come and listen?"

"Oh, if you will, sister," cried Jasper, springing off from his arm of the chair, while Ben flew from the other side, to hurry and get her a chair.

Percy and Van rushed too, knocking over so many things that they didn't help much; and little Dick poked his head out from Mrs. Pepper's arms when he saw his mamma sitting down to stay and began to scramble down to get into her lap.

"There now," said Mrs. Whitney, smiling over at Mrs. Pepper, who was smiling at her. "You have your baby, and I have mine! Now children, what's it all about? What has Mrs. Pepper been telling you?"

"Oh, the little brown house," cried Dicky, his cheeks all a-flame. "The dearest little house mamma! I wish I could live in one!

"Twouldn't be the same without the Peppers in it," said Jasper. "Not a bit of it!"

"And they had such perfectly elegant times," cried Percy, enviously, drawing up to her side. "Oh, you can't think, mamma!"

"Well now," said his mamma, "do go on, and let me hear some of the nice times."

So away they launched again, and Mrs. Whitney was soon enjoying it as hugely as the children, when a heavy step sounded in the middle of the room, and a voice spoke in such a tone that everybody skipped.

"Well, I should like to know what all this means! I've been all over the house, and not a trace of anybody could I find."

"Oh father!" cried Mrs. Whitney. "Van, dear, get up and get grandpapa a chair."

"No, no!" said the old gentleman, waving him off impatiently. "I'm not going to stay; I must go and lie down. My head is in a bad condition to-day; very bad indeed," he added.

"Oh!" said Phronsie, popping up her head and looking at him. "I must get right down."

"What's the matter, Phronsie?" asked Mrs. Pepper, trying to hold her back.

"Oh, but I must," said Phronsie, energetically wriggling. "My poor sick man wants me, he does." And flying out of her mother's arms, she ran up to Mr. King, and standing on tiptoe, said softly, "I'll rub your head, grandpa dear, poor sick man; yes I will!"

"And you're the best child," cried the old gentleman, catching her up and marching over to the other side of the room where there was a lounging chair. "There now, you and I, Phronsie, will stay by ourselves. Then my head will feel better."

And he sat down and drew her into his arms.

"Does it ache very bad?" said Phronsie, in a soft little voice. Then reaching up she began to pat and smooth it gently with one little hand, "Very bad, dear grandpa?"

"It won't," said the old gentleman, "if you only keep on taking care of it, little Phronsie."

"Then," said the child, perfectly delighted, "I'm going to take all care of you, grandpa, always!"

"So you shall, so you shall!" cried Mr. King, no less delighted than she was. "Mrs. Pepper!"

"Sir?" said Mrs. Pepper, trying to answer, which she couldn't do very well surrounded as she was by the crowd of little chatterers. "Yes, Sir; excuse me what is it, sir?"

"We've got to come to an understanding about this thing," said the old gentleman, "and I can't talk much to-day, because my headache won't allow it.

Here the worried look came into Phronsie's face again, and she began to try to smooth his head with both little hands.

"And so I must say it all in as few words as possible," he continued.

"What is it, sir?" again asked Mrs. Pepper, wonderingly. "Well, the fact is, I've got to have somebody who will keep this house. Now Marian, not a word!" as he saw symptoms of Mrs. Whitney's joining in the conversation. "You've been good; just as good as can be under the circumstances; but Mason will be home in the fall, and then I suppose you'll have to go with him. "Now I," said the old gentleman, forgetting all about his head, and straightening himself up suddenly in the chair, "am going to get things into shape, so that the house will be kept for all of us; so that we can come or go. And how can I do it better than to have the Peppers--you, Mrs. Pepper, and all your children--come here and live, and"-- "Oh, father!" cried Jasper, rushing up to him; and flinging his arms around his neck, he gave him such a hug as he hadn't received for many a day.

"Goodness, Jasper!" cried his father, feeling of his throat. "How can you express your feelings so violently! And, besides, you interrupt."

"Beg pardon, sir," said Jasper, swallowing his excitement, and trying to control his eagerness.

"Do you say yes, Mrs. Pepper?" queried the old gentleman impatiently. "I must get this thing fixed up today. I'm really too ill to be worried, ma'am."

"Why sir," stammered Mrs. Pepper, "I don't know what to say. I couldn't think of imposing all my children on you, and"—

"Imposing! Who's talking of imposing!" said Mr. King in a loud key. "I want my house kept; will you live here and keep it? That is the question."

"But sir," began Mrs. Pepper again, "you don't think"—

"I do think; I tell you, ma'am, I do think," snapped the old gentleman. "It's just because I have thought that I've made up my mind. Will you do it Mrs. Pepper?"

"What you goin' to do, mamsie?" asked Joel quickly.

"I don't know as I'm going to do anything yet," said poor Mrs. Pepper, who was almost stunned.

"To come here and live!" cried Jasper, unable to keep still any longer--and springing to the children. "Don't you want to, Joe?"

"To live!" screamed Joel. "Oh whickety, yes! Do ma, do come here and live--do!"

"To live?" echoed Phronsie, over in the old gentleman's lap. "In this be-yew-ti-ful place? Oh, oh!"

"Oh, mamsie!" that was all Polly could say.

And even Ben had his arms around his mother's neck, whispering "Do" into her ear, while little Davie got into her lap and teased her with all his might.

What shall I do! cried the poor woman. Did ever anybody see the like?"

"It's the very best thing you could possibly do," cried the

old gentleman. "Don't you see it's for the children's advantage? They'll get such educations, Mrs. Pepper, as you want for them. And it accommodates me immensely. What obstacle can there be to it?"

"If I was only sure 'twas best?" said Mrs. Pepper doubtfully.

"Oh, dear Mrs. Pepper," said Mrs. Whitney, laying her hand on hers. "Can you doubt it?"

"Then," said Mr. King, getting up, but still holding on to Phronsie, "we'll consider it settled. This is your home, children," he said, waving his hand at the five little Peppers in a bunch. And having thus summarily disposed of the whole business, he marched out with Phronsie on his shoulder.

Day 157

1. Read chapter 24.
2. Why do you think the chapter is called, "Polly's Dismal Morning?"

Chapter 24 Polly's Dismal Morning

Everything had gone wrong with Polly that day. It began with her boots.

Of all things in the world that tried Polly's patience most were the troublesome little black buttons that originally adorned those useful parts of her clothing, and that were fondly supposed to be

434

there when needed. But they never were. The little black things seemed to be invested with a special spite, for one by one they would hop off on the slightest provocation, and go rolling over the floor, just when she was in her most terrible hurry, compelling her to fly for needle and thread on the instant. For one thing Mrs. Pepper was very strict about--and that was, Polly should do nothing else till the buttons were all on again, and the boots buttoned up firm and snug.

"Oh dear!" said Polly, sitting down on the floor, and pulling on her stockings. "There now, see that hateful old shoe, mamsie!" And she thrust out one foot in dismay.

"What's the matter with it?" said Mrs. Pepper straightening the things on the bureau. "You haven't worn it out already, Polly?"

"Oh no," said Polly, with a little laugh. "I hope not yet, but it's these dreadful hateful old buttons!" And she twitched the boot off from her foot with such an impatient little pull, that three or four more went flying under the bed. "There now--there's a lot more. I don't care! I wish they'd all go; they might as well!" she cried, tossing that boot on the floor in intense scorn, while she investigated the state of the other one.

"Are they all off?" asked Phronsie, pulling herself up out of a little heap in the middle of the bed, and leaning over the side, where she viewed Polly sorrowfully. "Every one, Polly?"

"No," said Polly, "but I wish they were, mean old things; when I was going down to play a duet with Jasper! We should have had a good long time before breakfast. Oh, mayn't I go just once, mamsie? Nobody'll see me if I tuck my foot under the piano; and I can sew 'em on afterwards-- there'll be plenty of time. Do, just once, mamsie!"

"No," said Mrs. Pepper firmly, "there isn't any time but now. And piano playing isn't very nice when you've got to stick your toes under it to keep your shoes on."

"Well then," grumbled Polly, hopping around in her stocking-feet, "where is the work-basket, mamsie? Oh--here it is on the window-seat." A rattle of spools, scissors and necessary utensils showed plainly that Polly had found it, followed by a jumble of words and despairing ejaculations as she groped hurriedly under chairs and tables to collect the scattered contents.

When she got back with a very red face, she found Phronsie, who had crawled out of bed, sitting down on the floor in her little nightgown and examining the boot with profound interest.

"I can sew 'em, Polly," she said, holding up her hand for the big needle that Polly was trying to thread--"I can now truly; let me, Polly, do!"

"Dear no!" said Polly with a little laugh, beginning to be very much ashamed. "What could you do with your little mites of hands pulling this big thread through that old leather? There, scamper into bed again; you'll catch cold out here.

"Tisn't very cold," said Phronsie, tucking up her toes under the night-gown, but Polly hurried her into bed, where she curled herself up under the clothes, watching her make a big knot. But the knot didn't stay; for when Polly drew up the long thread triumphantly to the end--out it flew, and away the button hopped again as if glad to be released. And then the thread kinked horribly, and got all twisted up in disagreeable little snarls that took all Polly's patience to unravel.

"It's because you're in such a hurry," said Mrs. Pepper, who was getting Phionsie's clothes. And coming over across the room she got down on one knee, and looked over Polly's shoulder. "There now, let mother see what's the matter."

"Oh dear," said Polly, resigning the needle with a big sigh, and leaning back to take a good stretch, followed by Phronsie's sympathizing eyes; "they never'll be on! And there goes the first bell!" as the loud sounds under Jane's vigorous ringing pealed up over the stairs. "There won't be time anyway, now! I wish there wasn't such a thing as shoes in the world!" And she gave a flounce and sat up straight in front of her mother.

"Polly!" said Mrs. Pepper sternly, deftly fastening the little buttons tightly into place with quick, firm stitches, "better be glad you've got them to sew at all. There now, here they are. Those won't come off in a hurry!"

"Oh, mamsie!" cried Polly, ignoring for a moment the delights of the finished shoe to fling her arms around her mother's neck and give her a good hug. "You're just the splendidest, goodest mamsie in all the world. And I'm a hateful, cross old bear, so I am!" she cried remorsefully, buttoning herself into her boots. Which done, she flew at the rest of her preparations and tried to make up for lost time.

But 'twas all of no use. The day seemed to be always just racing ahead of her, and turning a corner, before she could catch up to it, and Ben and the other boys only caught dissolving views of her as she flitted through halls or over stairs.

"Where's Polly?" said Percy at last, coming with great dissatisfaction in his voice to the library door. "We've called her, I guess a million times, and she won't hurry."

"What do you want to have her do?" asked Jasper, looking up from the sofa where he had flung himself with a book.

"Why, she said she'd make Van and me our sails you know," said Percy, holding up a rather forlorn looking specimen of a boat, but which the boys had carved with the greatest enthusiasm, "and we want her now."

"Can't you let her alone till she's ready to come?" said Jasper quickly. "You're always teasing her to do something," he added.

"I didn't tease," said Percy indignantly, coming up to the sofa, boat in hand, to enforce his words. "She said she'd love to do 'em, so there, Jasper King!"

"Coming! coming!" sang Polly over the stairs, and bobbing into the library, "Oh--here you are, Percy! I couldn't come before; mamsie wanted me. Now, says I, for the sails." And she began to flap out a long white piece of cotton cloth on the table to trim into just the desired shape.

"That isn't the way," said Percy, crowding up, the brightness that had flashed over his face at Polly's appearance beginning to fade. "Hoh! those won't be good for anything-- those ain't sails."

"I haven't finished," said Polly, snipping away vigorously, and longing to get back to mamsie. "Wait till they're done; then they'll be good--as good as can be!"

"And it's bad enough to have to make them," put in Jasper, flinging aside his book and rolling over to watch them, "without having to be found fault with every second, Percy."

"They're too big," said Percy, surveying them critically, and then looking at his boat.

"Oh, that corner's coming off," cried Polly cheerfully, giving it a sharp cut that sent it flying on the floor. "And they won't be too big when they're done, Percy, all hemmed and everything. There," as she held one up for inspection, "that's just the way I used to make Ben's and mine, when we sailed boats."

"Is it?" asked Percy, looking with more respect at the piece of cloth Polly was waving alluringly before him. "Just exactly like it, Polly?"

"Yes," said Polly, laying it down again for a pattern--"oh, how does this go--oh--that's it, there-- yes, this is just exactly like Bensie's and mine--that was when I was ever so little; and then I used to make Joel's and Davie's afterwards and"-- "And were theirs just like this?" asked Percy, laying his hand on the sail she had finished cutting out.

"Pre-cisely," said Polly, with a pin in her mouth. "Just as like as two peas, Percy Whitney."

"Then I like them," cried Percy, veering round and regarding them with great satisfaction--as Van bounded in with a torrent of complaints, and great disappointment in every line of his face.

"Oh now, that's too bad!" he cried, seeing Polly fold up the remaining bits of cloth, and pick up the scraps on the floor. "And you've gone and let her cut out every one of 'em, and never told me a word! You're a mean, old hateful thing, Percy Whitney!"

"Oh don't!" said Polly, on her knees on the floor.

"I forgot--" began Percy, "and she cut 'em so quick--and--"

"And I've been waiting," said Van, in a loud wrathful key, "and waiting--and waiting!"

"Never mind, Van," said Jasper consolingly, getting off from the sofa and coming up to the table.

"They're done and done beautifully, aren't they?" be said, holding up one.

But this only proved fresh fuel for the fire of Van's indignation.

"And you shan't have 'em, so I" he cried, making a lunge at the one on the table, "for I made most of the boat, there!"

"Oh no, you didn't!" cried Percy in the greatest alarm, hanging on to the boat in his hand. "I cut-- all the keel--and the bow--and--"

"Oh dear!" said Polly, in extreme dismay, looking at Jasper. "Come, I'll tell you what I'll do, boys."

"What?" said Van, cooling off a little, and allowing Percy to edge into a corner with the beloved boat and one sail. "What will you, Polly?"

"I'll make you another pair of sails," said Polly groaning within herself as she thought of the wasted minutes, "and then you can see me cut 'em, Van."

"Will you really," he said, delight coming all over his flushed face.

"Yes, I will," cried Polly, "wait a minute till I get some more cloth." And she started for the door.

"Oh now, that's too bad!" said Jasper. "To have to cut more of those tiresome old things! Van, let her off!"

"Oh no, I won't! I won't!" he cried in the greatest alarm, running up to her as she stood by the door. "You did say so, Polly! You know you did!"

"Of course I did, Vanny," said Polly, smiling down into his eager face, "and we'll have a splendid pair in just--one----minute!" she sang.

And so the sails were cut out, and the hems turned down and basted, and tucked away into Polly's little work-basket ready for the sewing on the morrow. And then Mr. King came in and took Jasper off with him; and the two Whitney boys went up to mamma for a story; and Polly sat down in mamsie's room to tackle her French exercise.

Day 158

1. Read the beginning of chapter 26. There is no chapter 25.
2. This is the last chapter of the book. How would you end the book? What would you have happen?

Chapter 26 Polly's Big Bundle

The room was very quiet; but presently Phronsie strayed in, and seeing Polly studying, climbed up in a chair by the window to watch the birds hop over the veranda and pick up worms in the grass beside the carriage drive. And then came Mrs. Pepper with the big mending basket, and ensconced herself opposite by the table; and nothing was to be heard but the "tick, tick" of the clock, and an occasional dropping of a spool of thread, or scissors, from the busy hands flying in and out among the stockings.

All of a sudden there was a great rustling in Cherry's cage that swung in the big window on the other side of the room. And then he set up a loud and angry chirping, flying up and down, and opening his mouth as if he wanted to express his mind, but couldn't, and otherwise acting in a very strange and unaccountable manner.

"Dear me!" said Mrs. Pepper, "what's that?"

"It's Cherry," said Polly, lifting up her head from "Fasquelle," "and--oh, dear me!" and flinging down the pile of books in her lap on a chair, she rushed across the room and flew up to the cage and began to wildly gesticulate and explain and shower down on him every endearing name she could think of.

"What is the matter?" asked her mother, turning around in her chair in perfect astonishment. "What upon earths Polly!" "How could I!" cried Polly, in accents of despair, not heeding her mother's question. "Oh, mamsie, will he die, do you think?"

"I guess not," said Mrs. Pepper, laying down her work and coming up to the cage, while Phronsie scrambled off from her chair and hurried to the scene. "Why, he does act queer, don't he? P'raps he's been eating too much?"

"Eating!" said Polly, "oh mamsie, he hasn't had anything." And she pointed with shame and remorse to the seed-cup with only a few dried husks in the very bottom.

"Oh, Polly," began Mrs. Pepper; but seeing the look on her face, she changed her tone for one more cheerful. "Well, hurry and get him some now; he'll be all right, poor little thing, in a minute. There, there," she said, nodding persuasively at the cage, "you pretty creature you! so you sha'n't be starved."

At the word "starved," Polly winced as though a pin had been pointed at her.

"There isn't any, mamsie, in the house," she stammered; "he had the last yesterday."

"And you forgot him to-day?" asked Mrs. Pepper, with a look in her black eyes Polly didn't like.

"Yes'm," said poor Polly in a low voice.

"Well, he must have something right away," said Mrs. Pepper, decidedly. "That's certain."

"I'll run right down to Fletcher's and get it," cried Polly.

"Twon't take me but a minute, mamsie; Jasper's gone, and Thomas, too, so I've got to go," she added, as she saw her mother hesitate.

"If you could wait till Ben gets home," said Mrs. Pepper, slowly. "I'm most afraid it will rain, Polly."

"Oh, no, mamsie," cried Polly, feeling as if she could fly to the ends of the earth to atone, and longing beside for the brisk walk down town. Going up to the window she pointed triumphantly to the little bit of blue sky still visible. "There, now, see, it can't rain yet awhile."

"Well," said Mrs. Pepper, while Phronsie, standing in a chair with her face pressed close to the cage, was telling Cherry through the bars "not to be hungry, please don't!" which he didn't seem to mind in the least, but went on screaming harder than ever! "And besides, 'tisn't much use to wait for Ben. Nobody knows where he'll get shoes to fit himself and Joe and Davie, in one afternoon! But be sure, Polly, to hurry, for it's getting late, and I shall be worried about you.

"Oh, mamsie," said Polly, turning back just a minute, "I know the way to Fletcher's just as easy as anything. I couldn't get lost."

"I know you do," said Mrs. Pepper, "but it'll be dark early on account of the shower. Well," she said, pulling out her well-worn purse from her pocket, "if it does sprinkle, you get into a car, Polly, remember."

"Oh, yes, I will," she cried, taking the purse.

"And there's ten cents for your bird seed in that pocket," said Mrs. Pepper, pointing to a coin racing away into a corner by itself.

"Yes'm," said Polly, wild to be off.

"And there's a five-cent piece in that one for you to ride up with," said her mother, tying up the purse carefully. "Remember, for you to ride up with. Well, I guess you better ride up anyway, Polly, come to think, and then you'll get home all the quicker."

"Where you going?" asked Phronsie, who on seeing the purse knew there was some expedition on foot, and beginning to clamber down out of the chair. "Oh, I want to go too, I do. Take me, Polly!"

"Oh, no, Pet, I can't," cried Polly, "I've got to hurry like everything!"

"I can hurry too," cried Phronsie, drawing her small figure to its utmost height, "oh, so fast, Polly!"

"And it's ever so far," cried Polly, in despair, as she saw the small under lip of the child begin to quiver. "Oh, dear me, mamsie, what shall I do!"

"Run right along," said Mrs. Pepper, briskly. "Now, Phronsie, you and I ought to take care of Cherry, poor thing."

At this Phronsie turned and wiped away two big tears, while she gazed up at the cage in extreme commiseration.

"I guess I'll give him a piece of bread," said Mrs. Pepper to herself. At this word "bread," Polly, who was half way down the hall, came running back.

"Oh, mamsie, don't," she said. "It made him sick before, don't you know it did--so fat and stuffy."

"Well, hurry along then," said Mrs. Pepper, and Polly was off.

Over the ground she sped, only intent on reaching the bird store, her speed heightened by the dark and rolling bank of cloud that seemed to shut right down suddenly over her and envelop her warningly.

"It's good I've got the money to ride up with," she thought to herself, hurrying along through the busy streets, filled now with anxious crowds homeward rushing to avoid the threatening shower. "Well, here I am," she said with a sigh of relief, as she at last reached Mr. Fletcher's big bird store.

Here she steadily resisted all temptations to stop and look at the new arrivals of birds, and to feed the carrier-pigeons who seemed to be expecting her, and who turned their soft eyes up at her reproachfully when she failed to pay her respects to them. Even the cunning blandishments of a very attractive monkey that always had entertained the children on their numerous visits, failed to interest her now. Mamsie would be worrying, she knew; and besides, the sight of so many birds eating their suppers out of generously full seed-cups, only filled her heart with remorse as she thought of poor Cherry and his empty one.

So she put down her ten cents silently on the counter, and took up the little package of seed, and went out.

But what a change! The cloud that had seemed but a cloud when she went in, was now fast descending in big ominous sprinkles that told of a heavy shower to follow. Quick and fast they came, making everybody fly to the nearest shelter.

"I don't care," said Polly to herself, holding fast her little package. "I'll run and get in the car-- then I'll be all right."

So she went on with nimble footsteps, dodging the crowd, and soon came to the corner. A car was just in sight--that was fine! Polly put her hand in her pocket for her purse, to have it all ready-- but as quickly drew it out again and stared wildly at the car, which she allowed to pass by. Her pocket was empty!

"Oh, dear," she said to herself, as a sudden gust of wind blew around the corner, and warned her to move on, "now what shall I do! Well, I must hurry. Nothing for it but to run now!"

And secretly glad at the chance for a good hearty run along the hard pavements, a thing she had been longing to do ever since she came to the city, Polly gathered her bundle of seed up under her arm, and set out for a jolly race. She was enjoying it hugely, when--a sudden turn of the corner brought her up against a gentleman, who, having his umbrella down to protect his face, hadn't seen her till it was too late.

Polly never could tell how it was done; but the first thing she knew she was being helped up from the wet, slippery pavement by a kind hand; and a gentleman's voice said in the deepest concern:

"I beg your pardon; it was extremely careless in me."

"It's no matter," said Polly, hopping up with a little laugh, and straightening her hat. "Only--" and she began to look for her parcel that had been sent spinning.

"What is it?" said the gentleman, bending down and beginning to explore, too, in the darkness.

"My bundle," began Polly. "Oh, dear!"

No need to ask for it now! There lay the paper wet and torn, down at their feet. The seed lay all over the pavement, scattered far and wide even out to the puddles in the street. And not a cent of money to get any more with! The rain that was falling around them as they stood there sent with the sound of every drop such a flood of misery into Polly's heart!

"What was it, child?" asked the gentleman, peering sharply to find out what the little shiny things were.

"Bird-seed," gasped Polly.

"Is that all?" said the gentleman with a happy laugh. "I'm very glad."

442

"All!" Polly's heart stood still as she thought of Cherry, stark and stiff in the bottom of his cage, if he didn't get it soon. "Now," said the kind tones, briskly, "come, little girl, we'll make this all right speedily. Let's see--here's a bird store. Now, then."

"But, sir--" began Polly, holding back.

Day 159

    1.   Read the next part of chapter 26.

Chapter 26 continued

"But, sir--" began Polly, holding back.

Even Cherry had better die than to do anything her mother wouldn't like. But the gentleman already had her in the shop, and was delighting the heart of the shop-keeper by ordering him to do up a big package of all kinds of seed. And then he added a cunning arrangement for birds to swing in, and two or three other things that didn't have anything to do with birds at all. And then they came out on the wet, slippery street again.

"Now, then, little girl," said the gentleman, tucking the bundle under his arm, and opening the umbrella; then he took hold of Polly's hand, who by this time was glad of a protector. "Where do you live? For I'm going to take you safely home this time where umbrellas can't run into you."

"Oh!" said Polly, with a little skip. "Thank you sir! It's up to Mr. King's; and--"

"What!" said the gentleman, stopping short in the midst of an immense puddle, and staring at her, "Mr. Jasper King's?"

"I don't know sir," said Polly, "what his other name is. Yes it must be Jasper; that's what Jappy's is, anyway," she added with a little laugh, wishing very much that she could see Jappy at that identical moment.

"Jappy!" said the stranger, still standing as if petrified. "And are there little Whitney children in the same house!"

"Oh, yes," said Polly, raising her clear, brown eyes up at him. The gas lighter was just beginning his rounds, and the light from a neighboring lamp flashed full on Polly's face as she spoke, showing just how clear and brown the eyes were. "There's Percy, and Van, and little Dick--oh, he's so cunning!" she cried, impulsively.

The gentleman's face looked very queer just then; but he merely said:

"Why, you must be Polly?"

"Yes, sir, I am," said Polly, pleased to think he knew her. And then she told him how she'd forgotten Cherry's seed, and all about it. "And oh, sir," she said, and her voice began to tremble, "Mamsie'll be so frightened if I don't get there soon!"

"I'm going up there myself, so that it all happens very nicely," said the gentleman, commencing to start off briskly, and grasping her hand tighter. "Now, then, Polly."

So off they went at a very fast pace; she, skipping through the puddles that his long, even strides carried him safely over, chattered away by his side under the umbrella, and answered his many questions, and altogether got so very well acquainted that by the time they turned in at the old stone gateway, she felt as if she had known him for years.

And there, the first thing they either of them saw, down in a little corner back of the tall evergreens, was a small heap that rose as they splashed up the carriage-drive, and resolved itself into a very red dress and a very white apron, as it rushed impulsively up and flung itself into Polly's wet arms:

"And I was so tired waiting, Polly!"

"Oh dear me, Phronsie!" cried Polly, huddling her up from the dark, wet ground. "You'll catch your death! What will mamsie say!"

The stranger, amazed at this new stage of the proceedings, was vainly trying to hold the umbrella over both, till the procession could move on again.

"Oh!" cried Phronsie, shaking her yellow head decidedly, "they're all looking for you, Polly." She pointed one finger solemnly up to the big carved door as she spoke. At that Polly gathered her up close and began to walk with rapid footsteps up the path.

"Do let me carry you, little girl," said Polly's kind friend persuasively, bending down to the little face on Polly's neck.

"Oh, no, no, no!" said Phronsie, at each syllable grasping Polly around the throat in perfect terror, and waving him off with a very crumpled, mangy bit of paper, that had already done duty to wipe off the copious tears during her anxious watch. "Don't let him, Polly, don't!"

"There sha'n't anything hurt you," said Polly, kissing her reassuringly, and stepping briskly off with her burden, just as the door burst open, and Joel flew out on the veranda steps, followed by the rest of the troop in the greatest state of excitement.

"Oh, whickety! she's come!" he shouted, springing up to her over the puddles, and crowding under the umbrella. "Where'd you get Phronsie?" he asked, standing quite still at sight of the little feet tucked up to get out of the rain. And without waiting for an answer he turned and shot back into the house proclaiming in stentorian tones, "Ma, Polly's come--an' she's got Phronsie--an' an awful big man--and they're out by the gate!"

"Phronsie!" said Mrs. Pepper, springing to her feet, "why, I thought she was up-stairs with Jane."

"Now, somebody," exclaimed old Mr. King, who sat by the library table vainly trying to read a newspaper, which he now threw down in extreme irritation as he rose quickly and went to the door to welcome the wanderers, "somebody ought to watch that poor child, whose business it is to know where she is! She's caught her death-cold, no doubt, no doubt!"

Outside, in the rain, the children revolved around and around Polly and Phronsie, hugging and kissing them, until nobody could do much more than breathe, not seeming to notice the stranger, who stood quietly waiting till such time as he could be heard.

At last, in a lull in the scramble, as they were dragging Polly and her burden up the steps, each wild for the honor of escorting her into the house, he cried out in laughing tones:

"Isn't anybody going to kiss me, I wonder!"

The two little Whitneys, who were eagerly clutching Polly's arms, turned around; and Percy rubbed his eyes in a puzzled way, as Joel said, stopping a minute to look up at the tall figure:

"We don't ever kiss strangers--mamsie's told us not to."

"For shame, Joey!" cried Polly, feeling her face grow dreadfully red in the darkness, "the gentleman's been so kind to me!"

"You're right, my boy," said the stranger, laughing and bending down to Joel's upturned, sturdy countenance, at the same instant that Mrs. Pepper flung open the big door, and a bright, warm light fell straight across his handsome face. And then-- Well, then Percy gave a violent bound, and upsetting Joel as he did so, wriggled his way down the steps--at the same time that Van, on Polly's other side, rushed up to the gentleman:

"Papa--oh, papa!"

Polly, half way up the steps, turned around, and then, at the rush of feeling that gathered at her heart, sat right down on the wet slippery step.

"Why, Polly Pepper!" exclaimed Joel, not minding his own upset. "You're right in all the slush--mother won't like it, I tell you!"

"Hush!" cried Polly, catching his arm, "he's come--oh, Joel --he's come!"

"Who?" cried Joel, staring around blindly, "who, Polly?" Polly had just opened her lips to explain, when Mr. King's portly, handsome figure appeared in the doorway. "Do come in, children--why--good gracious, Mason!"

"Yes," cried the stranger, lightly, dropping his big bundle and umbrella as he passed in the door, with his little sons clinging to him. "Where is Marian?"

"Why didn't you write?" asked the old gentleman, testily. "These surprises aren't the right sort of things," and he began to feel vigorously of his heart. "Here, Mrs. Pepper, be so good as to call Mrs. Whitney."

"Pepper! Pepper!" repeated Mr. Whitney, perplexedly.

"She's coming--I hear her up-stairs," cried Van Whitney. "Oh, let me tell her!" He struggled to get down from his father's arms as he said this.

"No, I shall--I heard her first!" cried Percy. "Oh, dear me! Grandpapa's going to!"

Mr. King advanced to the foot of the staircase as his daughter, all unconscious, ran down with a light step, and a smile on her face.

"Has Polly come?" she asked, seeing only her father. "Yes," replied the old gentleman, shortly, "and she's brought a big bundle, Marian!"

"A big bundle?" she repeated wonderingly, and gazing at him.

"A very big bundle," he said, and taking hold of her shoulders he turned her around on--her husband.

So Polly and Phronsie crept in unnoticed after all.

"I wish Ben was here," said little Davie, capering around the Whitney group, "an' Jappy, I do!"

"Where are they!" asked Polly.

"Don't know," said Joel, tugging at his shoe-string. "See-- aren't these prime!" He held up a shining black shoe, fairly bristling with newness, for Polly to admire.

"Splendid," she cried heartily; "but where are the boys?"

"They went after you," said Davie, "after we came home with our shoes."

"No, they didn't," contradicted Joel, flatly; and sitting down on the floor he began to tie and untie his new possessions. "When we came home Ben drew us pictures--lots of 'em--don't you know?"

"Oh, yes," said Davie, nodding his head, "so he did; that was when we all cried 'cause you weren't home, Polly."

"He drawed me a be-yew-tiful one," cried Phronsie, holding up her mangy bit; "see, Polly, see!"

"That's the little brown house," said Davie, looking over her shoulder as Phronsie put it carefully into Polly's hand.

"It's all washed out," said Polly, smoothing it out, "when you stayed out in the rain."

Phronsie's face grew very grave at that.

"Bad, naughty old rain," she said, and then she began to cry as hard as she could.

"Oh dear, don't!" cried Polly in dismay, trying her best to stop her, "oh, Phronsie, do stop!" she implored, pointing into the next room whence the sound of happy voices issued, "they'll all hear you!"

But Phronsie in her grief didn't care, but wailed on steadily.

"Who is it anyway?" cried Joel, tired of admiring his precious shoes, and getting up to hear them squeak, "that great big man, you know, Polly, that came in with you?"

"Why, I thought I told you," said Polly, at her wit's end over Phronsie. "It's Percy and Van's father, Joey!"

"Whockey!" cried Joel, completely stunned, "really and truly, Polly Pepper?"

"Really and truly," cried Polly, bundling Phronsie up in her arms to lay the little wet cheek against hers.

Day 160

1. Finish reading the book!

Chapter 26 continued

"Then I'm going to peek," cried Joel, squeaking across the floor to carry his threat into execution.

"Oh, you mustn't, Joe!" cried Polly, frightened lest he should. "Come right back, or I'll tell mamsie!"

"They're all comin' in, anyway," cried little Davie, delightedly, and scuttling over to Polly's side.

"And here are the little friends I've heard so much about!" cried Mr. Whitney coming in amongst them. "Oh, you needn't introduce me to Polly--she brought me home!"

"They're all Pepperses," said Percy, waving his hand, and doing the business up at one stroke.

"Only the best of 'em isn't here," observed Van, rather ungallantly, "he draws perfectly elegant, papa!"

"1 like Polly best, I do!" cried little Dick, tumbling after. "Peppers!" again repeated Mr. Whitney in a puzzled way. "And here is Mrs. Pepper," said old Mr. King, pompously drawing her forward, "the children's mother, and--"

But here Mrs. Pepper began to act in a very queer way, rubbing her eyes and twisting one corner of her black apron in a decidedly nervous manner that, as the old gentleman looked up, he saw with astonishment presently communicated itself to the gentleman opposite.

"Is it," said Mr. Whitney, putting out his hand and grasping the hard, toil-worn one in the folds of the apron, "is it cousin Mary?"

"And aren't you cousin John?" she asked, the tears in her bright black eyes.

"Of all things in this world!" cried the old gentleman, waving his head helplessly from one to the other. "Will somebody have the extreme goodness to tell us what all this means?"

At this the little Peppers crowded around their mother, and into all the vacant places they could find, to get near the fascinating scene.

"Well," said Mr. Whitney, sitting down and drawing his wife to his side, "it's a long story. You see, when I was a little youngster, and--"

"You were John Whitney then," put in Mrs. Pepper, slyly. "That's the reason I never knew when they were all talking of Mason Whitney."

"John Whitney I was," said Mr. Whitney, laughing, "or rather, Johnny and Jack. But Grandmother Mason, when I grew older, wanted me called by my middle name to please grandfather. But to go back--when I was a little shaver, about as big as Percy here--"

"Oh, papa!" began Percy, deprecatingly. To be called "a little shaver" before all the others!

"He means, dearie," said his mamma, reassuringly, "when he was a boy like you. Now hear what papa is going to say."

"Well, I was sent up into Vermont to stay at the old place. There was a little girl there; a bright, black-eyed little girl. She was my cousin, and her name was Mary Bartlett."

"Who's Mary Bartlett?" asked Joel, interrupting.

"There she is, sir," said Mr. Whitney, pointing to Mrs. Pepper, who was laughing and crying together.

"Where?" said Joel, utterly bewildered. "I don't see any Mary Bartlett. What does he mean, Polly?"

"I don't know," said Polly. "Wait, Joey," she whispered, "he's going to tell us all about it."

"Well, this little cousin and I went to the district school, and had many good times together. And then my parents sent for me, and I went to Germany to school; and when I came back I lost sight of her. All I could find out was that she had married an Englishman by the name of Pepper."

"Oh!" cried all the children together.

"And I always supposed she had gone to England for despite all my exertions, I could find no trace of her. Ah, Mary," he said reproachfully, "why didn't you let me know where you were?"

"I heard," said Mrs. Pepper, "that you'd grown awfully rich, and I couldn't."

"You always were a proud little thing," he said laughing. "Well, but," broke in Mr. King, unable to keep silence any longer, "I'd like to inquire, Mason, why you didn't find all this out before, in Marian's letters, when she mentioned Mrs. Pepper?"

"She didn't ever mention her," said Mr. Whitney, turning around to face his questioner, "not as Mrs. Pepper--never once by name. It was always either 'Polly's mother,' or 'Phronsie's mother.' Just like a woman," he added, with a mischievous glance at his wife, "not to be explicit."

"And just like a man," she retorted, with a happy little laugh, "not to ask for explanations."

"I hear Jappy," cried Polly, in a glad voice, "and Ben--oh, good!" as a sound of rushing footsteps was heard over the veranda steps, and down the long hall.

The door was thrown suddenly open, and Jasper plunged in, his face flushed with excitement, and after him Ben, looking a little as he did when Phronsie was lost, while Prince squeezed panting in between the two boys.

"Has Polly got"--began Jasper.

"Oh, yes, I'm here," cried Polly, springing up to them; "oh, Ben!"

"She has," cried Joel, disentangling himself from the group, "don't you see, Jappy?"

"She's all home," echoed Pbronsie, flying up. "Oh, Ben, do draw me another little house!"

"And see--see!" cried the little Whitneys, pointing with jubilant fingers to their papa, "see what she brought!"

Jasper turned around at that--and then rushed forward.

"Oh, brother Mason!"

"Well, Jasper," said Mr. Whitney, a whole wealth of affection beaming on the boy, "how you have stretched up in six months!"

"Haven't I?" said Jasper, laughing, and drawing himself up to his fullest height.

"He's a-standin' on tip-toe," said Joel critically, who was hovering near. "I most know he is!" and he bent down to examine the position of Jasper's heels.

"Not a bit of it, Joe!" cried Jasper, with a merry laugh, and setting both feet with a convincing thud on the floor.

"Well, anyway, I'll be just as big," cried Joel, "when I'm thirteen, so!"

Just then a loud and quick rap on the table made all the children skip, and stopped everybody's tongue. It came from Mr. King.

"Phronsie," said he, "come here, child. I can't do anything without you," and held out his hand. Phronsie immediately left Ben, who was hanging over Polly as if he never meant to let her go out of his sight again, and went directly over to the old gentleman's side.

"Now, then!" He swung her upon his shoulder, where she perched like a little bird, gravely surveying the whole group. One little hand stole around the old gentleman's neck, and patted his cheek softly, which so pleased him that for a minute or two he stood perfectly still so that everybody might see it.

"Now, Phronsie, you must tell all these children so that they'll understand--say everything just as I tell you, mind!"

"I will," said Phronsie, shaking her small head wisely, "every single thing."

"Well, then, now begin--"

"Well, then, now begin," said Phronsie, looking down on the faces with an air as much like Mr. King's as was possible, and finishing up with two or three little nods.

"Oh, no, dear, that isn't it," cried the old gentleman, "I'll tell you. Say, Phronsie, 'you are all cousins--every one.'"

"You are all cousins--every one," repeated little Phronsie, simply, shaking her yellow head into the very middle of the group.

"Does she mean it, grandpapa? Does she mean it?" cried Percy, in the greatest excitement.

"As true as everything?" demanded Joel, crowding in between them.

"As true as--truth!" said the old gentleman solemnly, patting the child's little fat hand. "So make the most of it."

"Oh!" said Polly, with a long sigh. And then Jasper and she took hold of hands and had a good spin!

Joel turned around with two big eyes on Percy.

"We're cousins!" he said.

"I know it," said Percy, "and so's Van!"

"Yes," said Van, flying up, "and I'm cousin to Polly, too-- that's best!"

"Can't I be a Cousin?" cried little Dick, crowding up, with two red cheeks. "Isn't anybody going to be a cousin to me, too?"

"Everybody but Jasper," said the old gentleman, laughing heartily at them. "You and I, my boy," he turned to his son, "are left out in the cold."

At this a scream, loud and terrible to hear, struck upon them all, as Joel flung himself flat on the floor.

"Isn't Jappy--our---cousin? I--want --Jappy!"

"Goodness!" exclaimed the old gentleman, in the greatest alarm, "what is the matter with the boy! Do somebody stop him!"

"Joel," said Jasper, leaning over him, and trying to help Polly lift him up. "I'll tell you how we'll fix it! I'll be your brother . That's best of all--brother to Polly, and Ben and the whole of you--then we'll see!"

Joel bolted up at that, and began to smile through the tears running down the rosy face.

"Will you, really?" he said, "just like Ben--and everything?"

"I can't be as good as Ben," said Jappy, laughing, "but I'll be a real brother like him."

"Phoo--phoo! Then I don't care!" cried Joel wiping off the last tear on the back of his chubby hand. "Now I guess we're better'n you," he exclaimed with a triumphant glance over at the little Whitneys, as he began to make the new shoes skip at a lively pace up and down the long room.

"Oh, dear!" they both cried in great distress.

"Now, papa, Jappy's going to be Joey's brother--and he isn't anything but our old uncle! Make him be ours more, papa, do!"

And then Polly sprang up.

"Oh! oh--deary me!" And she rushed out into the hall and began to tug violently at the big bundle, tossed down in a corner. "Cherry'll die--Cherry'll die!" she cried, "do somebody help me off with the string!"

But Polly already had it off by the time Jasper's knife was half out of his pocket, and was kneeling down on the floor scooping out a big handful of the seed.

"Don't hurry so, Polly," said Jasper, as she jumped up to fly up-stairs. "He's had some a perfect age--he's all right."

"What!" said Polly, stopping so suddenly that two or three little seeds flew out of the outstretched hand and went dancing away to the foot of the stairs by themselves.

"Oh, I heard him scolding away there when I first came home," said Jasper, "so I just ran down a block or two, and got him some."

"Is that all there is in that big bundle?" said Joel in a disappointed tone, who had followed with extreme curiosity to see its contents. "Phoo!--that's no fun--old bird-seed!"

"I know," said Polly with a gay little laugh, pointing with the handful of seed into the library, "but I shouldn't have met the other big bundle if it hadn't have been for this, Joe!"

Day 161

1. Write a book report. Write a summary of the book including the title and author's name, Margaret Sydney. Tell whether or not you would recommend this book to a friend or if you would read more of Sydney's books and tell why. Write what you thought of the author's style.

2. The author's writing style is the way he or she writes: funny, interesting descriptions…
3. Save this for your portfolio.

Day 162

1. List the characters, setting and plot of the book.
2. For plot, what was the conflict, the problem, and how was it solved? Think about the first and last chapters for this.

Day 163

Vocabulary
1. Review your Heidi vocabulary by going to Day 35 or by going to the review game page on the Easy Peasy website and using the first Heidi vocabulary link under level 3.

Day 164

Vocabulary
1. Review your Heidi vocabulary by going to Day 40 or by going to the review game page on the Easy Peasy website and using the Heidi chapter 3 vocabulary link under level 3.

Day 165

Vocabulary
1. Review your Heidi vocabulary by going to Day 45 or by going to the review game page on the Easy Peasy website and using the last Heidi vocabulary link under level 3.

Day 166

1. You are going to be reading a play. A play is written in a different format than a novel. There's a list of characters. What that character says is written next to its name. What the actors do is written separately in parenthesis. There are stage directions telling where the different actors should be. The narrator is not part of the action. He or she is watching the action with the audience.

An Adaptation of the story of five Chinese brothers, by Renee Erickson

Cast:
Emperor
4 Court Attendants: Han, Chin, Lu, Shou
2 Court Guards: Sha, Huang
6 Imperial Guards: Peng, Bo, Wong, Min, Sung, Ming
5 Children: Deng, Chou, Jiang, Li, Yan
2 Parents: Zian, Mah
Narrators / Water bearers (the Sea & the Fleet)

Scene I:

Emperor: behind the screen

4 Court Attendants / 2 Court Guards: stage right "frozen" at chores

6 Imperial Guards: Upstage center, clustered near the benches, "frozen"

5 Children: Stage left, "frozen" in front of the dungeon wall

2 Parents/Narrators: Downstage center – reading from a scroll

Narrator 1: Sometimes it's not easy to know where a piece of the puzzle fits. It can turnout to be quite a surprise, as in our version of an old, old folk tale.

Narrator 2: Once upon a time and long ago in a far, far kingdom by the sea lived a people who knew what was important.

Narrators: (move downstage left)

Guards: (unfreeze but remain in position of disinterest and boredom)

Children: (move downstage and sit on the steps, observing the scene)

Court Persons & Court Guards: (stand as they speak, dramatically emphasizing their attributes – stay standing)

Huang: It's important to be handsome. I'm glad I'm handsome.

Chin: It's important to be smart. I'm glad I'm smart.

Han: It's important to be fast. I'm glad I'm fast.

Emperor: (comes from behind the screen and listens a moment)

Shou: It's important to be strong. I'm glad I'm strong.

Sha: It's important to be tall. I'm glad I'm tall.

Lu: It's important to be graceful. I'm glad I'm graceful.

Day 167

1. Read the next part of the play.
2. Are you able to picture the play in your mind? Remember, this was written to be performed on a stage. How is it different from what you are used to reading?

Emperor: (moves downstage to the throne) It's important to obey the emperor. I'm glad I'm the Emperor. (moves to the throne and sits)

Guards: (snap to attention)

All Court Persons: (bow and kneel to Emperor)

Han, Chin: (exit behind screen)

Lu & Shou: (move downstage to stairs and sit)

Court Guards: (stand beside the throne)

Narrator #1: But, she isn't (motions "tall")

Narrator #2: It doesn't matter. She is the <u>emperor</u>.

Emperor: (moves to the throne) (Clap Clap) Servants of the kitchen!

Han & Chin: (hurry in from the screen – bowing – move to center stage facing the emperor) Yes, emperor. Yes, emperor.

Emperor: My breakfast is late. Why is that?

Han: We're sorry, O imperial one, but the stove could not be lit.

Chin: Yes, o exalted one, someone left the cover off the woodpile last night and all the wood got wet from the rain.

Emperor: And who was that someone?

Han: Not me!

Chin: Not me!

Emperor: Well, who was it?

Han: It was that short, clumsy cook's helper.

Chin: It was all his fault.

Emperor: (considering a moment) Off with his head! (Clap, clap) Guards, see to it!

Peng & Bo: (moving from Up stage center to Center facing Stage right) (bowing to the emperor) Yes, your imperialness.

Peng & Bo: (Bowing, back away from the throne, exit behind the screen)

Offstage (sound of a loud whack.)

Court Guards and all on stage: (shudder)

Day 168

1. Read the next part of the play.

    Emperor: (claps hands) Servants of the bed chamber!

    Lu & Shou: (stand up with bowed heads, come to Center stage facing Stage right – the emperor)

Lu: Yes, O most magnificent emperor.

Shou: Yes, o royal one?

Emperor: (with a flourish!) Where is the red robe that I wanted to wear this morning?

Lu: (apologetically and fearfully) Oh, your royalness. It is ruined.

Shou: (apologetically and fearfully) A most unfortunate accident, your majesty.

Emperor: What sort of accident?

Lu: The not very pretty chambermaid mistakenly thought that she could wash it in hot water and (shrugs) all the color came out.

Shou: Alas, it is now a streaky pink and very wrinkled. It was all her fault.

Emperor: (thinks a moment) Off with her head. (clap, clap) Guards, see to it.

Sung & Ming: (moving from Upstage center to center facing Stage right) (bowing to the emperor) (move to exit behind the screen)

Off stage sound of a whack. All shudder.

Han & Chin: (enter bowing, but happy) Please excuse us, Your majesty.

Emperor: What now?

Chin: O, your royalness, we have finally lit the fire. Would you like to come into the breakfast room for your royal breakfast?

Emperor: Indeed. Guards, come with me. (exits behind screen)

Sha & Huang: (move throne to the wall stage right and exit behind the screen with the emperor)

All: exit behind screen

Day 169

1. Read the next part of the play, Scene II.

Lights come on to seaside garden wall home of "poor" family.

Children: (come up from the stairs and are seated, mending a fish net, etc.)

Zian and Mah: (stand and move to center stage) They look at their children and consider their attributes and their future.

Narrator 3: (standing down stage center) In the far away kingdom by the sea people also knew who was not important. (pauses then exits behind screen)

Mah: Zian, how could we have been so unfortunate?

Zian: What do you mean, Mah? We have five fine children. We are very fortunate.

Mah: We have five children. I don't know where you got the idea of fine. Are they tall?

Zian: (pauses) No

Mah: Are they handsome?

Zian: (pauses) No

Mah: Are they smart?

Zian: (pauses) Not especially.

Mah: Are they rich?

Zian: (pauses) By no means.

Mah: Are they fast?

Zian: (pauses) Are you kidding?

Mah: Well, are they graceful?

Zian: (annoyed) Well, you should know. But, Mah, they are kind and loving children.

Mah: You are right, Zian, but they just don't have any qualities that anyone thinks are important.

Day 170

1. Read the next part of the play.

Zian: Mah, have you forgotten that each one has a very special ability?

Mah: (now she's annoyed) Remind me.

Yan: (standing) Don't you remember, mother. Deng can swallow the sea.

Deng: (standing) And Chou has an iron neck.

Chou: (standing) And Jiang can stretch and stretch and stretch.

Jiang: (standing) Li cannot be burned.

Li: (standing) And Yan can hold his breath forever if need be.

Mah: Children, I know you have all these qualities, but what good are they? Have you EVER needed them?

Chou: Not so far, but you never know. They might come in handy sometime.

Mah: I'll tell you what would come in handy - some extra money.

Zian: Your mother speaks the truth, children. Go out and see if you can make yourselves useful. Perhaps you can earn a few coins for your efforts.

Mah: (shrugs and smiles at the children and pats them as they leave) You may not be strong, but you <u>are</u> willing.

Parents: (exit behind the wall)

Children: (sit back to their work)

Pause (Count 15 seconds)

Yan: (standing) I'm <u>not</u> very willing! It's too hot to work.

Deng: (standing) I agree.

Chou: (standing) Let's walk by the sea a bit before we try to be useful.

Children: (walk to center stage and look to Upstage left - seaside)

Jiang: (pointing) Li, isn't that the emperor's new fleet of ships?

Li: (shading his eyes) You're right. Don't they look beautiful out there on the horizon?

Yan: Deng, we could get a better look at them if you would swallow the sea and pull them closer to shore.

Li: (getting very excited) Maybe we could even climb aboard and look around.

Deng: I'm not so sure I should. The emperor might not like it.

Jiang: How would he ever know? He's probably up at the palace giving orders. You know how he likes to be obeyed.

"OFF WITH HER HEAD!" drifts in from off stage left.

Jiang: (nods his head) See what I mean?

Day 171

1. Read the next part of the play.

   Chou: Hurry up, Deng. Let us take a look at those ships.

   Deng: All right. All right. Here goes. (begins to "swallow" the sea)

   Sea holder: ("hands the sea" to Deng and slips behind the "water" and takes the ships from the other sea holder and moves them closer to Deng on the top of the water.

Ships: (come closer to Deng, almost close enough for the brothers to touch them)

Deng: (begins to "sneeze")

Jiang: (looking at Deng and pointing) Watch out! I think Deng is going to sneeze.

Yan: Quick, Li, Put your finger under his nose. (Li puts his finger under Deng's nose)

Deng: (shaking all over, but seems to gain control)

Li: (takes his finger away) Wow, that was close!!

Deng: (sneezes violently)

Ships: (are dropped to the ground)

Water: (billows up then falls to the ground as water bearer slides behind the wall)

Children: (Stunned, they point and gape at the destruction.) Oh No! Oh No!

Deng:(becomes distraught, pulls his hair and stamps his feet)

Deng: Oh, we're in so much trouble! What are we going to do?!

Li: What are WE going to do? You're the one who swallowed the sea!

Deng: You told me to. You told me to.

Chou: Oh no, here come the emperor's guards.

Guards: (rush up from stairs toward the "sea"– ready to battle the "enemy")

Peng: Where are they?

Bo: What enemy has destroyed our royal navy?

Wong: (noticing the children) Who are you?

Guards: (turn and face children at center stage – amazed and annoyed)

Deng: (bowing apologetically) I didn't mean to do it. (bows again and again) We only wanted to look more closely at the emperor's beautiful ships.

Jiang: Deng can't help it that he sneezed.

Min: What ARE you talking about? None of this makes any sense.

Peng: Hold on a minute!! You are not handsome or tall or strong or fast or graceful or smart. How could you have done anything of importance?

Li: Can it be important, even if it's bad?

Chou: Sirs, our brother Deng has a rather unusual ability. He can swallow the sea.

All Guards: (staring without believing) What?

Yan: (nodding) Yes, it is true. He can swallow the sea.

Jiang: That's what he was doing when he sneezed and accidentally destroyed the entire royal navy.

Bo: The emperor is not going to believe this.

Wong: And he's not going to like it either.

Min: Come along with us. We'd better get this over with.

Guards: (grab Deng roughly and drag him noisily downstage center and off)

Children: We're right behind you, Deng!! (follow a step or two, but then sneak back to their position at the wall and sit)

Guards and Deng: (go down the steps stage right and then back stage behind the screen)

Day 172

1. Read the next part of the play, Scene III.

    Lights come to the Emperor's throne room (stage right)

    Sha & Huang: (bring throne to mark and stand at attention)

    Court Persons: (come up from stairs and mill around discussing the situation in whispers. Wondering what will happen. Frightened!! As Emp. Enters, bow and cower)

    Emperor: (enters from the screen pacing back and forth in front of the throne)

    Emperor: (shouting, very angry) My royal fleet is destroyed! My royal fleet is destroyed! My royal fleet! But how can this be? Where is the enemy? Who is responsible for this outrage!! He will be punished. (shaking fists)

    Guards: (noisily approach from behind the screen with Deng)

    Sha: (points toward the Guards and Deng) Here come the guards, your majesty.

    Huang: (points toward the Guards and Deng) They have captured someone, but he doesn't look very important.

    Peng & Bo: (dragging Deng roughly to center stage – facing the emperor)

    All Imperial Guards: (come from screen and stand with guard group)

    Emperor: Yes? (glaring threateningly at the guards) What's the meaning of this outrage? Why aren't you out trying to solve this crime?

    Peng: (proudly facing the emperor) But we have solved it, your majesty.

    Bo: (indicating Deng) This man alone has destroyed your fleet.

    Emperor: Preposterous!!

Deng: (bowing) I'm so sorry, your majesty. My brothers and I, (pausing, looking for the right words) we just wanted to see your beautiful ships more closely, (haltingly, apologetically) so I swallowed the sea, but then I had to sneeze . . .

Emperor: Enough! (hands on hips) Are you trying to tell me that this, ah, "person" smashed my royal fleet all by himself? Well, are you?

Wong: (nodding) It seems so your majesty.

Min: He says he did it, and we don't see any enemy ships in the harbor.

Emperor: Well then, off with his head! (Clap! Clap!)

Deng: (pleading and bowing) But your majesty, I'm very sorry.

Emperor: Sorry?! Sorry?! I said, "Off with his head," IMMEDIATELY!

Guards: (backing away from the emperor, bowing and dragging Deng with them. They turn and go to Upstage right and exit through screen. Then re-enter from the stairs and drag Deng to the dungeon and throw Deng in, all sit)

Children: (are outside the wall, just out of sight of the guards)

Emperor: (speaking to the rest of the court) I need a nap. Maybe this will turn out to be just a bad dream. (exits behind the screen)

Sha & Huang : (move throne against the wall and exit behind screen with Emperor)

Court Attendants: (move downstage to the stairs and sit)

Day 173

1. Read the next part of the play, Scene IV.

    Lights come to stage left at the wall.

    Children: (sitting in front of wall –worried and whispering)

    Guards: (sitting on the bench outside the dungeon – "asleep")

    Li: (standing and moving to center stage, very excited) So, what are we going to do?

    Jiang: (standing and going to join Li, very excited) The Emperor, who is to be obeyed, just said that Deng should lose his head!

    Chou: (runs to join them, upset) Mother and Father are going to be very angry.

    Yan: (rushes to center stage) What? How can you worry about getting in trouble with our parents? Deng is about to become history.

Chou: Too bad they didn't take me. (holds his neck) They'd never be able to chop off my head.

Li: Why in the world not? Oh, that's right. You have a very strong neck.

Chou: (jumping up and down) Come with me. I'm going to see what I can do to help Deng.

Children: (move to the wall.)

Chou: (moves "through" the wall while the others watch for the guards)

Deng: (comes out to join the others)

Wong & Min: (get up and go into the dungeon, they drag out Chou downstage to the right and off, struggling and mumbling)

Yan: Do you think it will work?

Jiang: I hope so. Nothing more we can do now, but wait.

Off Stage: Whack – Whack – Whack – Whack

Wong & Min : (bring Chou upstage center, struggling and mumbling)

Sung: (to each other) How can this be happening? The Emperor says off with his head! But his head won't come off.

Ming: The Emperor always must be obeyed. He will be having our heads instead.

Guards: (push Chou into the dungeon space dejectedly)

Peng: (stops pacing, throws up his hands) It probably doesn't matter how we get rid of this unfortunate citizen as long as we get rid of him. Let's think.

Guards: (huddle for seven seconds)

Sung: (excited! Jumping up and down) I know. Let's bury him in a pit. I'll get the shovels!! (exits downstage center and down the steps to get the shovels)

Peng: (excited also) Excellent idea!

Guards: (sit down to wait outside the wall/dungeon – they sleep)

Children: (standing and moving to center stage)

Jiang: Too bad he isn't trying to bury me.

Li: Why is that?

Jiang: Don't you remember? (holds his neck) I have a very long neck.

Yan, Li, Chou, Deng: Oh, yes. (nodding to each other)

Jiang: I'll see what I can do.

Children: (move back to their wall.)

Jiang: (moves "through" the wall while the others watch for the guards)

Day 174

1. Read the next part of the play.

    Chou: (comes out to join the others) Wow! These guards are serious! They really tried to whack off my head!!

    Sung: (comes back with a shovel.)

    Peng & Sung: (reach into dungeon and drag out Jiang)

    Sung: (roughly take Jiang with them down stage and down the steps) Come with us!

    Chou: Do you think we can fool them again?

    Yan: If we don't, our fate is sealed.

    Bo & Ming: (stay outside the dungeon)

    Off stage - Peng: Dig that hole deeper!!

    Off stage - Sung: I'm digging as hard as I can

    Peng, Sung, Ming: (rush in, dragging Jiang back up steps to center stage)

    All guards jump up in surprise and amazed with fear!

    Min: You're not going to believe this.

    Wong: Don't tell us. Your plan didn't work. He's still alive.

    Sung: We buried him as deep as we could, but his head was always above the ground. You can see he is very much still alive.

    Guards: (throw Jiang back in the dungeon)

    Bo: The Emperor who is not very understanding will not understand why you have not followed his orders.

    Ming: I'm not going to be the one to tell him.

    Peng: Wait a minute. You haven't tried everything yet. Let's think.

    Guards: (huddle)

Day 175

1. Read the next part of the play.

Bo: Maybe you could burn him.

Peng: Excellent idea, I'll go for some burning coals. (runs downstage and off steps)

All guards sit and wait - loitering

Yan: Too bad he isn't trying to burn <u>you</u>, brother. You've been unburnable from the first day I knew you.

Li: A talent no one saw much use for until this very day. I'll see what I can do.

Li: (moves "through" the wall while the others watch for the guards)

Jiang: (comes out to join the others) They never noticed anything different!

Peng: (runs back to center stage with "coals")

Guards: (reach into dungeon and drag out Li)

Wong & Min: Come with us! (roughly take Li with them down stage and down the steps)

Deng: This is starting to be fun.

Jiang: As long as the guards don't get suspicious.

Yan: I hope we can do this for as long as they can come up with crazy ideas.

Off Stage - Wong: Get more wood!

Off Stage - Min: Hurry up! (pause) This isn't working!

Guards: (rush up from the steps, push Li into the dungeon)

Bo: (watching in disbelief!!) No, no. It can't be true.

Sung: We might as well try to leave the country right now.

Ming: I don't think we should take time to go to our homes. We must leave immediately.

Min: How can we go anywhere? The boats are all destroyed. The mountains surround us.

Bo: You're right. The emperor would find us before we had a chance to hide.

Wong: Oh woe, oh woe. We are ruined.

Peng: Wait a minute. We haven't tried everything. Let's think.

Guards: (huddle together outside the dungeon)

Day 176

1. Read the next part of the play. Can you guess what they will try next?

Min: I have an idea. Just because we can't chop of his head, or bury him, or burn him, doesn't mean we can't drown him.

Peng: Excellent idea. We'll lock him in a trunk and throw him into the deepest part of the sea. I'll go get a lock for the trunk! (runs down the steps to off stage right)

Wong: (Calls after him) Hurry. The Emperor will be expecting a report.

Guards: (sit down while they wait)

Yan: Now it's my chance to be important. You DO remember that I can hold my breath forever if I have to.

Jiang: Excellent idea.

Yan: (switches with Li)

Chou: I hope those guards run out of ideas soon because we're running out of specialness.

Deng: Perhaps something will happen to distract them.

Peng: (runs back up to center stage with a lock) I have it!!

Peng & Ming: (reach in the dungeon and roughly take Yan with them down stage and down the steps)

Ad Lib mumbling about the lock and trunk

Ming & Peng: (rush on stage, dragging Yan and push him into the dungeon ahead of him. He motions to the others to follow him in)

Guards all go in the dungeon door (mumbling) and come out the hidden opening.

Guards stumble over the children

Children hear the commotion and stumble aside to get out of the way

Wong: Just as I suspected! Here they are! (motioning to the children huddled near the wall)

Sung: Maybe we can hide you all somewhere and the Emperor will never find out that we didn't follow his orders.

Ming: Hurry, come with us.

All Children and Guards: (run down the steps to downstage right)

Day 177

1. Read the next part of the play.

    Court Attendants & Court Guards: (move up from the steps to their places and position the throne)

    Emperor: (bustles in from the hedge and moves to the throne)

    Emperor: Where's my breakfast? Did anyone write the poem for the day? I cannot find my slippers.

    Court Attendants: (scurry, maybe even bump into each other in their haste to obey.) mumbling all the while in fear.

    Court Guards: (rush in saluting / bowing -move to center stage facing emperor)

    Sha: O Emperor, your majesticness, a terrible thing has happened!

    Huang: Our enemies must have learned of the destruction of the royal navy, your excellency.

    Emperor: What? What?

    Sha: Yes, your importantness, several warships are approaching our harbor as we speak.

    Huang: We think they will be here within the hour, O Emperor.

    Sha: What would you like us to do?

    Emperor: Do? Do? I would like you to turn back time so that my royal fleet would still be in existence.

    Huang: I'm afraid we can't do that.

    Emperor: No, no, of course not. We must think. Call for all my guards. (clap, clap)

    Guards: (rush in from the screen, looking very uncomfortable and frightened)

    Emperor: We need an idea to restore our fleet and turn back the enemy!

    Emperor, Guards and Court Attendants: (pacing in a circle around center stage – following the Emperor)

    Emperor Stops and those following "bump" into each other – domino style

    Emperor: I have it!

Day 178

1. Read the next part of the play.

All Guards and CP: (stop and stare at the emperor – separate so no one has his back to the audience and the emperor is seen)

Emperor: Bring me that careless citizen who destroyed my fleet in the first place. He can just swallow the sea again and obliterate our enemies. Yes! Yes! Excellent idea!

Peng: (bowing) But, Emperor. Don't you remember? You ordered us to chop off his head.

Bo: And you always expect to be obeyed, oh imperial one.

Emperor: Quite right. Quite right. (pause) No, quite wrong. Why couldn't you have predicted that this man would turn out to be important?

Peng: Well, your highness, he wasn't handsome, or tall, or graceful, or fast, or strong. How were we to know?

Emperor: I know he wasn't all those things, but he could swallow the sea! That is turning out to be very important! If only I could turn back time before I gave that order.

Guards: (cowering and wondering what to do)

Min: (aside to the audience) Should we tell the emperor the man is still alive?

Ming: (aside to the audience) Then he would know the orders hadn't been obeyed.

Wong: (aside to the audience) But perhaps he would be happy to find out that the kingdom can be saved after all.

Min: (motions to the children back stage to come in)

Guards: (back up Upstage to allow for the children entering the stage)

Deng: (comes with brothers to the throne, bowing respectfully to the emperor)

Children: (follow Deng in and bow behind him)

Deng: There's no need to turn back time, your majesty. Your guards tried their very best to obey your orders, but with the help of my family my life has been spared. (motions for Children to come forward)

Chou: (moves to center stage) You see, oh wise and patient one, we were each born with a very unusual ability.

Jiang: (moves to center stage) Yes, Chou has an iron neck. And I can stretch and stretch. And Li can't be burned. And Yan can hold his breath forever if need be.

Day 179

1. Read the next part of the play.

Li: (moves to center stage) All our lives these abilities have been of little use, but this day they became very important.

Yan: (moves to center stage) Yes, we were able to save our brother's life and now he can save the kingdom. Go for it, Deng.

Emperor: (totally bewildered) I don't understand any of this, but somehow I was not obeyed and it has turned out to be a good thing. (shakes his head) Quickly, young man. (clap clap) To the harbor. Our enemies will be arriving very soon.

Deng, Children, Guards: (rush off stage behind screen and re-enter up stage from the steps to the sea)

Emperor: (waits - looking "out the window" toward the sea)

Court Attendants: (trying to see) (mumbling) Wow! Will you look at that!

"Water and ships" hand off to Deng

Emperor: Yippee! It's working!! (Suddenly, he jumps up and down and begins a wild dance)

Court Attendants: Yeah! They are saving the Empire!! (Wild cheering)

Deng: (swallows the sea)

Boats: (get closer to Deng)

Guards: Ahah! We got you now!! (seize the boats and dash them to the ground)

Water: (drops to the floor and the Water bearers move back)

Children, Guards: (run downstage center off the steps and return from the screen to center stage, showing elation)

Emperor: (joins in the celebration and then remembers his dignity)

Emperor: (on throne) Thank you, young man. Your name will be remembered by our royal storytellers for all time. How can I reward you? And your family?

Day 180

1. Finish the play.

Deng: Well, oh Emperor. We are very poor. Our family could use a bigger home.

469

Emperor: A home? Done! (clap, clap)

Chin: (hands Deng a scroll)

Chou: And a larger property to farm.

Emperor: More land? Done! (clap, clap)

Lu: (hands Chou a scroll)

Li: And more money.

Emperor: Gold and wealth? Done! (clap, clap)

Han: (hands Li a scroll)

Jiang: And we would like to be able to go to school and perhaps train for the imperial guards.

Emperor: Education and position? Done! (clap, clap)

Chin: (hands Jiang a scroll)

Yan: And oh generous and spontaneous emperor, would you mind telling our parents that we have done something important?

Emperor: You would like to be recognized as important? Of course, my son. Maybe we have all learned a few things about what is important. Send for the parents immediately. (clap, clap)

Ming & Zian: (rush behind the screen down and up steps over to the wall)

Parents are sitting near the wall at their home.

Min: (to the parents) Come with us quickly! The Emperor requests your presence!

Ming: Your children have done something important!

Zian: I told you they were fine children!

Mah: I'll believe it when I see it.

Parents and Min & Zian exit downstage right and come back up to behind the screen.

Chin: (excited but then sad and afraid) Oh, Emperor, who insists on being obeyed. I wrote the royal poem for the day, but the short, weak scribe who was copying it spilled the ink in a very clumsy way and smeared the paper beyond repair. The poem is lost.

Emperor: What? What? No Poem? Well then, Off with . . . ah . . .(pause hands ready to clap the order)

ALL: (turn and stare at the emperor, amazed!)

Emperor: (catches himself in a habit) Oh, well. Ha, ha. Even an emperor can make a mistake once in awhile. It's important to have a second chance. I order everyone to take a holiday to celebrate our victory – and (looking at them all severely) - and I expect to be obeyed! (laughs)

Chin &Han: Ha Ha, (timidly they laugh a little, then smile and nod)

Min & Zian: (return with parents from screen)

Parents: Bow to the Emperor and embrace children.

All continue to celebrate. -   Curtain !!

Congratulations on finishing the EP Third Reader!

ANSWERS

Day 2

1. musical instrument; He loves the music and it fills him with joy.
2. He thinks shepherds have a great job. He calls it a "sweet lot."
3. birds; There is a group of young people playing and a group of old people watching.
4. Jesus

Day 3

2. laugh
3. sweet
4. a lullaby, a song to sing to a baby while you rock it to sleep

Day 4

2. New Year's celebration
4. It's time to come inside and go to bed.
5. They are saying it's still light out and they want to play more.
6. Joy

Day 5

2. itself
3. itself
4. Love is supposed to be selfless, focused on others not ourselves.
5. "It does not look out for its own interests."

Day 7

2. play, away (there are many more)
4. sleep sleep, secret smiles

Day 8

7. 3, 4, 4, 4

Day 9

2. to go to sleep while it is still light out

Day 10

2. They built a pretend ship on the stairs, but the one boy gets hurt and then the other is left alone to play.
3. cats, mice, bats (It also mentions dogs and thieves.)

Day 11

3. a cat
4. no
5. In every stanza the second and fourth lines rhyme. The first and third lines all have 8 syllables and the second and fourth lines have 6 syllables. Kitty-cat and blue balloon are examples of alliteration.

Day 12

2. someone's faults, what is wrong with that person
3. snow
4. end of the year (year is old), leaves are dying, wind is cold

Day 14

    2. his love

    3. She thought it was something to see and hold.

    4. cough drops

    5. The second and fourth lines rhyme; each line has 8 syllables.

Day 15

    2. It followed her home. Wherever she went, the moon went too. The moon seems to stay with you.

Day 16

    2. rain, wind, still brown and bare

    3. She doesn't think it looks like spring yet.

    4. It's probably an evergreen tree.

Day 17

    2. happy, joyful

    3. joy, sweet, sing, shimmering

Day 18

    2. a cloud

    3. It goes between the earth and the sun and blocks the sun.

Day 19

    2. Mary, Joseph and Jesus when Jesus was an adult

    3. Mary is thinking about when Jesus was born and the wise men came and the angels sang.

Day 20

    2. She finds it soothing. It puts her to sleep.

Day 21

    2. The Cat and the Mice

Day 22

    3. someone who wastes money, spends freely without thinking

    4. It doesn't have to be one specific answer. It could be that you should be nice to people because maybe they will turn into your friend some day. Or, don't underestimate how helpful someone little can be. It doesn't have to be either of these, but they have to think of an answer. It's okay to be wrong, but it's never okay to not think.

Day 23

    2. Some suggestions: Don't assume that you will get something. Don't get ahead of yourself; first accomplish what's in front of you.

    3. When you really need something, you'll figure out a way to get it.

Day 24

    3. The Bear and The Travellers

Day 25

    Vocabulary 1.E 2.A 3.D 4.B 5.C

Day 26

    2. Help them! Help first. Don't rebuke them for getting into trouble until they are okay.

    3. Two Bags — They are both about seeing faults in others and not in your self.

Day 28

1. The soup was made from carrots and potatoes and beef and flavored with salt and pepper, etc. not with stones.

Day 29

2. The land of nod is his dreams.

Day 32

3. five

4. Alm

5. Deta

6. no; grandfather

7. Deta; She lived with Deta and Deta's mother.

8. She thinks it's an awful idea and will never work. She thinks he won't even listen to Deta for a second.

9. never talks to anyone; everyone is afraid of him, only comes down the mountain once a year

10. She wants to know what happened to turn everyone against him. She wants to know if he always hated everyone.

Day 33

5. Peter

6. So she wouldn't have to carry up a set of clothes, Deta made Heidi wear her play clothes and her good church clothes on top of each other.

Day 34

4. He doesn't want her. He asks what he's supposed to do when she cries.

Day 35

3. He is being nice. At first he acts like he doesn't care much, but then he helps her make her bed and gives her his own blanket.

Vocabulary 1.D 2.C 3.B 4.E 5.A 6.F

Day 36

2. She sets the table.

3. She is very happy. She's very interested and excited about everything her grandfather does.

4. He is impressed with her.

Day 37

4. Peter, the goatherd

5. It's probably an eagle. He says earlier that they might see and hear one.

Day 38

3. It was the biggest meal he ever had.

4. Turk, Thislefinch, Snowhopper

5. She wouldn't let him hurt one of the goats when he wanted to punish one of them.

Day 39

3. The flowers she picked all turned droopy and unappealing. Her grandfather said they were meant to bloom in the sun and not be kept in her apron.

4. No, she was describing the setting sun's light on the mountain side.

Day 40

    3. one that was really, really satisfying

    4. She's blind.

    5. It's in poor shape, falling apart.

    Vocabulary: b, c, c, d, a, c, d, a, c, d

Day 41

    3. She talks to her. She visits whenever the weather is nice enough.

    4. He fixes her hut.

Day 42

    3. the pastor of the village church, Deta

    4. She has found work for Heidi being a companion to an invalid.

Day 43

    2. obstinate — stubborn; infirm — weak, sickly, frail

    3. It seems like the town could try and force him to put the child in school and then he would have to live in the town. Deta threatened him that they could take him to court. There is something about the past that he doesn't want revealed it seems.

    4. No, she isn't being honest with Heidi so that Heidi won't fight going with her.

Day 44

    3. the invalid child

    4. the butler, servant in the house

    5. the woman in charge of Clara

Day 45

    3. I think she's going to try and get in the church tower.

    4. She heard trees rustling but can't see any.

    Vocabulary: 1.E 2.C 3.F 4.H 5.I 6.A 7.B 8.D 9.J 10.G

Day 46

    3. She doesn't want to give up the picture of a flower that Clara had just given her.

    4. She sees chimneys.

    5. two kittens

Day 47

    2. She's homesick. She wants to go home.

    3. her old straw hat

Day 48

    2. Mr. Sesemann, Clara's father

    3. Mr. Sesemann's mother, Clara's grandmother

Day 49

    2. She learns to read.

Day 51

    2. The door is always open in the morning and they see a figure in white.

Day 52

    3. Heidi

    4. She was sleep walking.

Day 54

    2. He has not changed and others' opinions of him have not changed.

    3. She had to go to school.

Day 55

    2. the prodigal son

Day 56

    2. church

    3. They will spend winter in the village so that Heidi can attend school.

    4. He has "made peace with God."

    5. He confessed that he was a sinner and asked God for forgiveness.

Day 57

    2. the doctor

    3. His wife and only daughter have died.

Day 58

    2. She thanks him for letting her come home.

    3. She had expected Clara and grandmama to come, but they didn't.

Day 59

    2. the doctor's visit

    3. the shawl

    4. the sausage

Day 60

    5. He is taking all of Heidi's attention.

    6. He doesn't want to leave.

    7. It means that the sun was at its highest point in the sky.

Day 61

    2. It is completely run down. There are vines growing in it. It is falling down in many places.

Day 62

    2. He doesn't want to get in trouble with Heidi's grandfather, "uncle."

    3. hearing the songs that Heidi reads to her

    4. I think that she is going to want to teach Peter to read.

Day 63

    2. Heidi teaches Peter to read.

Day 64

    2. a letter from Clara

    3. Grandmother is worried that Clara will take Heidi back with her.

Day 65

    2. Peter doesn't like sharing Heidi. He's jealous that others are getting her attention.

Day 66

    3. He is making her stand a little every day for a longer time each day. He is helping her gain strength in her legs.

Day 67

3. She is "content." She is feeling very happy and wants the happiness to last forever. She wishes she could help others instead of being helped by others.

Day 68

2. They thank God that Clara walked.

3. God has something better planned. She says we are to wait in hope that He will answer with something better.

Day 70

3. God, You can never hide from God what you have done.

Day 74

Vocabulary: 1.E 2.D 3.F 4.B 5.C 6.H 7.A 8.G

Day 76

3. Indiana

4. President Monroe

5. Balser

Day 77

2. He was going to calmly wait for it to come within a few yards and then shoot it straight in the heart.

3. He forgot all about shooting the bear and was sure the bear was going to eat him.

4. He swung his fish at him and the bear grabbed at the fish and fell into the water.

5. Balser shot the bear and killed it.

Day 78

3. His father was 21 when he was given a gun, and they are too expensive. They cost as much as his father makes in half a year.

4. He helps a man and woman run away so that they can be married. The man buys him a gun in return for the favor.

Day 79

2. He is scared and runs away.

3. His dogs attack the bear and allow him to escape and get his gun.

4. two bear cubs

Day 80

2. Tom and Jerry

3. They jumped down on top of the boys.

4. You don't have to be right, but you have to think.

Day 81

4. His ears were trained by hunting to follow a sound. He heard her scream and could tell just where to head to find her.

5. They were lost in the woods. A bear was chasing Liney and Balser was chasing the bear.

6. He lit the fire to alert the neighbors that there was a problem. They saw it and came right away.

Day 82

2. She was kidnapped by an Indian, Native American.

3. He vows to kill the one-eared bear that chased after Liney.

Day 83

2. Jim

3. They said that he was invincible, that no one could kill him. Someone said they shot him 20 times and he wasn't even wounded. Some say that he must have a demon because he has supernatural strength.

Day 84

2. He didn't want to follow the bear.

3. They were scared. It seemed as if the bear really wasn't natural because he seemed to appear and disappear right before their eyes.

4. The bear showed up again. They fell and the bear attacked them.

Day 85

3. The bear was squeezing Balser in order to kill him. Tom swung his hatchet at the bear's back like he was cutting down a tree.

Day 86

4. hot and quiet ("Sabbath hush")

5. how he went to Cincinnati with his father and saw a live elephant

Day 88

3. coffee, They thought it was bitter.

4. They had gotten into the bee hives and were being attacked by bees.

Day 89

2. They train the bears to pull a load.

Day 91

3. Liney had a lit torch and put the fire in the bear's face and then pushed him into the river.

Day 92

2. the fire bear; the bear that Liney had lit on fire; He said that it had been on fire when it started to chase him.

Day 93

6. Polly is the coward. He's scared of the area they are in and going to hunt there for the fire bear. He's scared he's going to die because of a superstition about seeing the fire bear. They say you will die within three months if you see the fire bear unless he's killed. So he's afraid to kill the bear and he's afraid to not kill the bear. That's his fear and counter-fear.

Day 94

2. wounding a bear

3. The bear bit down on a piece of wood that Balser had been swinging at him and his teeth sunk into the wood and stuck there.

Day 95

3. Father

4. He was attacked by wolves. His horse had come home and showed signs of the attack.

Day 96

2. He was just dreaming.

Day 97

2. an orange

3. a hollowed out sycamore tree

Day 98

2. Being satisfied means that they were happy with it. They weren't picky, especially about it being all cleaned and swept out like the boys did with their area.

3. Something is coming…

Day 99

2. Tom walked up within three yards of the bear. Jim went running at him with a hatchet. Balser shot the bear when it was risky to do so but more risky to not.

Day 100

2. They spend more than a week capturing lots of animals in their traps and collecting their skins.

Day 102

2. *The Lesson*

3. Benny

4. school, home, car

5. He pushes everyone aside to be first.

6. His teacher called his parents. He wasn't allowed to go to the basketball game.

7. He saw his dad disregard others to be first and it made him think. He decided not to act that way.

8. The main idea is that being first isn't more important than caring about others.

Day 103

2. Each little moment has a role in all of eternity.

Day 105

2. Children don't want to go to bed until they're very sleepy then it's nice to go to bed.

Day 106

5. A solar system is made up of a star and the rocks that orbit it.

6. The sun is the star in the center of our solar system. The rocks are eight planets that orbit the sun. Earth is one of them; Jupiter is the biggest. In our solar system there are also many moons which orbit individual planets.

Day 107

1. c, b

Day 108

1. Macedonia is a small country in the Balkans.

Turkey is a country that spans two continents.

Day 109

1. Homeschooling is the best way to learn.

Airplanes are a fast way to travel but not always so convenient.

Day 110

2. A little kid is going to bed and the mother is telling him stories. They are pretending his bed is the boat sailing off with him in it.

Day 112

3. The poet wants to be like the flower and be humble, content to enjoy life even if no one else sees and notices.

Day 114

2. because he has no brain

Day 115

2. No, he finds his supper "elsewhere."

Day 116

5. Ben, Polly, Joel, Davie, Phronsie

6. It says that Polly is ten and Ben is a year older, so he is 11.

Day 117

4. No, she is not their grandmother. She lives in the village and everyone calls her grandmother.

5. a cake recipe

Day 118

2. Her toe got hurt accidentally when Joel was hammering.

Day 120

3. all of the foods they would eat

4. She fell into a tub of water while trying to show how big she was.

Vocabulary: 1.F 2.G 3.E 4.H 5.A 6.B 7.C 8.D

Day 121

3. Phronsie and Ben — At the end of the chapter it mentions Ben's red face and how he took some of Phronsie's medicine.

Day 123

2. Something like: Phronsie and Ben are in bed sick with the measles. Polly is helping to take care of them. She gets sick too at the end of the chapter. **OR** Phronsie and Ben are in bed sick with the measles and Polly is helping to take care of them, but she gets sick too at the end of the chapter.

Day 150

Vocabulary The first has to do with time, the next belief, the last with people.

PLEASE consider passing this book along to a family in need. Just contact us at allinonehomeschool@gmail.com when your family is finished with it.

ABOUT THE EASY PEASY ALL-IN-ONE HOMESCHOOL

The Easy Peasy All-in-One Homeschool is a free, complete online homeschool. There are 180 days of ready-to-go assignments for every level and every subject. It's created for your children to work as independently as you want them to. Preschool through high school is available and courses ranging from English, math, science and history to art, music, computer, thinking, physical education and health. A daily Bible lesson is offered as well. The mission of Easy Peasy is to enable those to homeschool who otherwise thought they couldn't.

Look for other books in the EP Reader Series
and for our offline math and language arts courses.

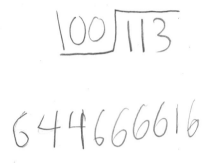

644666616

385462R00267

Made in the USA
Middletown, DE
30 August 2018